W9-ASQ-616

Amer. Psychological Assn   10/31/74   #12.00

Thesaurus of Psychological Index Terms

1974 Edition

Robert G. Kinkade, Editor

· KENRICK · SEMINARY · LIBRARY ·

WITHDRAWN

R
150
K55t

743543

American Psychological Association
Washington, D.C.

© 1974 by the American Psychological Association.

Library of Congress Catalog Card Number 74-131-90
Printed in the United States of America

Table of Contents

Acknowledgement

Many people contributed to the production of this thesaurus. In the early stages, William Learmouth helped conceptualize the approach and Kee Chang performed the initial term-sort from a computer listing of over 265,000 words that were used in *Psychological Abstracts (PA)* over a five year period. Subsequent word sorting was accomplished by Carol Lewis, Marion Simas, and Pat Zell. The Essex Corporation conducted a study that provided a basis for establishing term relationships and hierarchical structuring.

Eugene Wall provided invaluable advice about the mechanics of thesaurus construction and Carol Lewis managed the group responsible for the first relationship listing. Pat Zell developed the hierarchical listings with the assistance of Reneé Johnson. A special word of appreciation is due to Pat Zell for her dedication and the knowledge of psychological literature that she brought to the development of the thesaurus.

George Thomson provided computer programing expertise throughout the development, sometimes performing miracles with impossible schedules. Howard Flank served as a computer programing consultant.

In the final stages of development, Marjorie Wilson pulled together the experiences of the *PA* indexing staff and made the final modifications and corrections in the publication. Lois Granick established the photocomposition requirements and Sunday Lewis participated in the development of promotional material.

Financial assistance from the National Science Foundation in the early stages of development and continued support by the management of the American Psychological Association made this publication possible. However, a special debt of gratitude is owed to the many people who have contributed a part of themselves in this publication.

R. G. Kinkade
Editor

Overview of the Thesaurus and its Development

Introduction

About 100 years ago, psychology as a discipline was established as an outgrowth and extension of the older disciplines of philosophy, medicine, education, and physics. Since its inception there has been a tendency for psychologists to create various language constructs to express concepts and to communicate their ideas. Each generation of psychologists has added to the vocabulary in an attempt to describe and delineate their perceptions of behavioral processes. The uncontrolled evolution of a vocabulary in psychology has contributed to almost insurmountable search and retrieval problems, a diffusion and scattering of subject matter content in psychological journals, and difficulties in defining the boundaries of the discipline.

Responding to this problem, the American Psychological Association has developed this thesaurus. It is intended to be a recognized, unambiguous, and hierarchically structured set of terms related to psychological concepts. The terms serve as an authoritative list which allows for precise content representation of psychological literature and adds to the quality and precision of recall capabilities in search and retrieval operations. The thesaurus provides the means for structuring the subject matter content of psychology with the eventual goal of permitting the content of publications to be focused in accordance with interest patterns of psychologists.

Divisions of the Thesaurus

To assist the thesaurus user in selecting appropriate terms for different uses, the vocabulary has been displayed in three sections: The Relationship Section, the Alphabetic Section, and the Hierarchical Section. Each section is briefly described below. A more detailed explanation of display features appears at the beginning of each section.

Relationship Section. The relationship of each thesaurus term with other terms conceptually associated with it have been defined. The major relationships denoted are: synonymous, broader, narrower, and related. Synonymous relationships refer to different terms, or variations in the spelling of a term, used to represent a single concept. In this listing, the preferred term for representing the concept is denoted along with nonpreferred synonymous terms. Terms representing broader and narrower concepts, in the sense of genus-species relationships, are also denoted. Finally, terms representing concepts that are frequently associated with the concept represented by

the listed term are displayed. Secondarily, two additional relationships are noted: extremely broad conceptual areas are displayed as array terms; and extremely specific descriptors, name of a person, place, test, and document type are displayed as identifiers. Array terms are identified by a slash (/) following the term. Thesaurus users may use this section to find terms representing concepts at varying levels of specificity, to locate preferred synonymous terms, or to stimulate search activities by referring to terms representing concepts that are related to a listed term.

Alphabetic Section. Each thesaurus term used for indexing is listed in alphabetical order to facilitate rapid selection of search terms. This section includes all of the terms listed in the Relationship Section with the exception of nonpreferred synonymous terms.

Hierarchical Section. Terms representing different levels of related concepts are displayed in this section. The concepts represented by the 17 major classification categories used in *Psychological Abstracts (PA)* are placed at the highest level; all other terms representing concepts associated with these very broad areas are listed in descending order of breadth of concept represented. Associations of some concepts were defined empirically on the basis of patterns of competence within the psychological community. The listing was created by computer, based on broader and narrower term assignments. The thesaurus user who wishes to see how a particular term or concept is hierarchically related to all other concepts in a specific area or to examine the content of a broad area of psychology should refer to this section.

Development of the Thesaurus

The approach used to develop the thesaurus drew upon, (a) the terminology used in psychological literature, (b) word form conventions, (c) term relationship conventions, (d) empirical data concerning reported subject matter areas of competence within the psychological community, and (e) the expertise of subject matter specialists in psychology.

Terminology. The initial step in developing the thesaurus was the selection of candidate terms. Sources of possible terms included the 800 index terms used by *PA* prior to 1973 and a list showing the frequency with which single words were used in titles and abstracts appearing in *PA* over a 5-year period. In addition, phrases and precoordinated terms were obtained from key words in context (KWIC) lists produced from 10,000 titles of journal articles, books, separates, and dissertations.

Word Form Conventions. Once the terminology used within the field of psychology had been defined, inclusion/exclusion rules based on principles of thesaurus construction drawn from guidelines for thesaurus development were applied. Conventions dealing with word forms, singular and plural forms, direct and indirect word entries, abbreviations, acronyms, homographs, and punctuation were used to insure standardization of the vocabulary. For example, noun forms are preferred entries and plural forms are used when the term is a noun that can be counted (e.g., subjects, devices, and tests), whereas the singular form appears for processes, properties, and conditions (e.g., *learning, reliability,* and *heat*). Direct entries or natural word order is used when a concept is represented by two or more words, such as *mental health* rather than health/mental. In cases where ambiguity might occur and to clarify the meaning of homographs, qualifying expressions are included in parentheses, e.g., *culture (anthropological), recall (learning),* and *recall (dreams).* After inclusion/ exclusion rules had been applied, a list of about 3,000 potential terms was reviewed by subject matter specialists to determine whether these terms represented concepts relevant and specific to the field of psychology and whether they represented a desirable degree of specificity to discriminate among the content of the psychological literature.

Term Relationship Conventions. Once the relevancy and specificity of the candidate terms had been determined, thesaurus conventions dealing with term interrelationships were applied. The reference language used to express the interrelationships includes: **use, used for, broader, narrower,** and **related.** The function of each of these references is described below.

The **Use** reference is applied to indicate preferred forms of synonyms, abbreviations, near synonyms, quasi-synonyms, spelling, and word sequence, as in these examples:

Innovativeness	**Use**	*Creativity*
Marijuana	**Use**	*Marihuana*
LSD	**Use**	*Lysergic Acid Diethylmide*
Emotional Maladjustment	**Use**	*Emotional Adjustment*
Information Storage (Human)	**Use**	*Human Information Storage*

The **Use** designator is also used to refer from a specific term not used in indexing or searching to a more generic descriptor as with:

Inner City	**Use**	*Urban Environment*

The **Used For** reference is the reciprocal reference for the **Use** reference, as in the example:

Creativity	**Used For**	*Innovativeness*

The formal hierarchical relationships are indicated by the **Broader–Narrower** term designators. The **Broader–Narrower** relationships are reciprocals of one another and are applied in a strict genus-species relationship, i.e., the scope of the broad terms must always encompass the subject matter represented by its narrower term reciprocals, for example:

Psychosexual Behavior		
	Narrower	*Lesbianism*
		Homosexuality
		Sexual Deviations
		Transvestism
Psychomotor Development		
	Broader	*Motor Development*
		Physical Development
		Psychogenesis

A **Related** term designator is used to show relationships which are semantic or conceptual but not hierarchical. For example, researchers wanting information concerning *Mother-Child Relations* might use that term, but they would also be directed by a related term entry to the terms *Childrearing Practices* and *Parental Role.* **Related** terms serve to broaden the perspective of searchers or indexers by directing them to terms they might not have considered but which might have a bearing on their subject matter interest.

Those terms which represent a very broad area of subject matter are designated as **Array** terms. These terms may be used for indexing and searching when more specific terms cannot be used to represent the subject matter. Terms such as *mental disorders, communication,* and *behavior*, for example, are designated as array terms and are displayed in the thesaurus with only their related terms.

Names of people, geographic areas, and words used to describe specific forms or types of literature, e.g., book, case report, and conference proceedings, are designated as **identifiers** and are included in the thesaurus as legitimate indexing and searching terms.

Subject Matter Areas. In addition to being analyzed for relevancy and specificity, the potential terms were analyzed to determine the major classification categories of psychology represented by this vocabulary. About 1,000 editors, consulting editors, and volunteer abstractors of diverse psychological journals were asked to indicate those terms that represented subject matter content corresponding to their areas of competence within the field of psychology. The terms judged related or relevant to each field of psychology by about 400 respondents were cluster-analyzed, using a *k* means cluster program specifically developed for this project. After preliminary testing using a different number of cluster "seed" terms, 27 seed concepts were selected as being sufficiently comprehensive to accommodate the wide diversity of terms in the original list. After 10 iterations, the centroid movement was judged to be negligible, but convergence was not obtained. Intercorrelations between clusters showed that some clusters should be merged with other related clusters. The terms within each cluster were analyzed on the basis of their frequency in the literature and their representation of the major areas of study within psychology. This analysis produced 17 groups of terms representing major subject matter content areas within psychology that correspond to broad interest patterns of psychologists.

Based on the **Broader–Narrower** term designations shown in the Relationship Section, a hierarchical display of terms for each classification category was created with the intent of providing a guide to the structure of the major subject content areas of psychology. Each major classification category is defined by a display of relevant generic terms and their associated hierarchies.

Subject Matter Specialists. The development of this thesaurus drew upon subject matter expertise represented by the indexing staff of *PA* and upon members of boards and committees working for the American Psychological Association. In establishing term relationships, judgments frequently had to be made. Existing thesauri and dictionaries were consulted wherever possible in making these judgments. In addition, the thesaurus was used by the *PA* indexing staff for almost two years, who applied the terms to represent concepts described in the psychological literature and evaluated the appropriateness of word conventions and term relationships.

Consideration has been given to the natural growth of the vocabulary. Because of the flexibility inherent in the structure of the thesaurus, new candidate terms derived from indexing and searching operations can be introduced for a trial period during which their frequency, relevancy, and manner of use can be evaluated. At the end of this period, the terms will be reviewed for legitimacy and included in the structure of the thesaurus using computer updating procedures. It is expected that psychologists will also suggest terms over the course of the next several years.

Users Guide to the Relationship Section

Each thesaurus term is listed alphabetically, cross-referenced, and displayed with its broader, narrower and related terms. An **Array** term, one that represents an extremely broad conceptual area, is denoted by a slash (/). The relationships noted are:

Use

Used For

Broader

Narrower

Related

Identifier

The **Use** reference directs the user from a term that cannot be used in indexing or searching to a term that can be used. It is used to indicate preferred forms of synonyms, abbreviations, spelling, and word sequence, as in the examples:

Scholastic Aptitude

Use *Academic Aptitude*

Conditioning (Avoidance)

Use *Avoidance Conditioning*

LSD

Use *Lysergic Acid Diethylmide*

Marijuana

Use *Marihuana*

Emotional Maladjustment

Use *Emotional Adjustment*

The **Used For** reference is the reciprocal reference for the **Use** reference, as seen with:

Academic Aptitude

Used for Scholastic Aptitude

Avoidance Conditioning

Used for Conditioning (Avoidance)

The **Broader–Narrower** term designators are reciprocals and are used to indicate the genus-species hierarchical relationships, as in these examples:

Interpersonal Interaction

Narrower *Bargaining*

Conflict

Conversation

Cooperation

Psychomotor Development

Broader   *Motor Development*

                      Physical Development

                      Psychogenesis

A **Related** term designator is used to show relationships which are semantic or conceptual but not hierarchical. **Related** term references serve to broaden the perspective of searchers or indexers by directing them to terms they may not have considered but which may have a bearing on their subject matter interest, as in these examples:

Stress

Related   *Anxiety*
                      Disasters
                      Endurance

Very specific terms that appear frequently in the literature and represent a person, place, name, or a specific form or type of literature (e.g., book, case report, or conference proceedings) are designated as **identifiers**. An **identifier** is always a preferred term, facilitating retrieval of content on a very specific basis. Broader terms that are associated with identifiers are referenced by a (see) notation.

Those terms that represent an array of conceptually broad subject matter are designated as **array** terms and identified by a slash (/) following the term. These terms may be used for indexing and searching when a more specific term cannot be used to represent the subject matter. Terms such as *mental disorders, communication* and *measurement,* for example, are designated as **array** terms and are displayed in the thesaurus with only selected related terms.

Abdomen
Related   Anatomy

Abdominal Wall
Broader   Muscles
           Musculoskeletal System

Abducens Nerve
Used For   Nerve (Abducens)
Broader   Cranial Nerves
           Nervous System
           Peripheral Nerves

Ability Grouping
Related   Ability/
           Academic Aptitude
           Education/
           Special Education

Ability Level
Use   Ability/

Ability Tests
Use   Aptitude Measures

Ability/
Used For   Ability Level
           Aptitude
           Skills
           Talent
Related   Ability Grouping
           Academic Aptitude
           Achievement Potential
           Artistic Ability
           Cognitive Ability
           Communication Skills
           Creativity
           Employee Skills
           Gifted
           Idiot Savants
           Intelligence
           Learning Ability
           Mathematical Ability
           Mechanical Aptitude
           Motor Skills
           Reading Ability
           Verbal Ability

Ablation
Use   Lesions

Abortion (Induced)
Use   Induced Abortion

Abortion (Spontaneous)
Use   Spontaneous Abortion

Abortion Laws
Broader   Government Policy Making
           Laws
Related   Induced Abortion

Abreaction
Use   Catharsis

Absenteeism (Employee)
Use   Employee Absenteeism

Absorption (Physiological)
Related   Cells (Biology)
           Intestines
           Skin (Anatomy)

Abstinence (Sexual)
Use   Sexual Abstinence

Abstraction
Broader   Cognitive Processes
           Thinking
Narrower   Imagery
Related   Divergent Thinking

Abuse (Child)
Use   Child Abuse

Abuse (Drugs)
Use   Drug Abuse

Academic Achievement
Used For   Achievement (Academic)
           Gradepoint Average
           Scholastic Achievement
           School Achievement
Broader   Achievement
Narrower   Academic Overachievement
           Academic Underachievement
           College Academic Achievement
           Mathematics Achievement
           Reading Achievement
Related   Academic Achievement Motiva-
           tion
           Academic Achievement Predic-
           tion
           Academic Aptitude
           Education/
           School Learning

Academic Achievement Motivation
Broader   Achievement Motivation
           Motivation
Related   Academic Achievement

Academic Achievement Prediction
Related   Academic Achievement

Academic Aptitude
Used For   Aptitude (Academic)
           Scholastic Aptitude
Related   Ability Grouping
           Ability/
           Academic Achievement
           Education/
           Reading Ability
           Student Admission Criteria
           Verbal Ability

Academic Environment
Used For   Environment (Academic)
Broader   Environment
           Social Environments

Academic Environment — (Continued)
- Narrower　Classroom Environment
- 　　　　　College Environment
- 　　　　　School Environment

Academic Overachievement
- Used For　Overachievement (Academic)
- Broader　Academic Achievement
- 　　　　　Achievement

Academic Specialization
- Used For　College Major
- 　　　　　Specialization (Academic)

Academic Underachievement
- Used For　Underachievement (Academic)
- Broader　Academic Achievement
- 　　　　　Achievement
- Related　Failure

Acalculia
- Broader　Aphasia
- 　　　　　Brain Disorders
- 　　　　　Central Nervous System Disorders
- 　　　　　Nervous System Disorders
- Related　Learning Disabilities

Accelerated Speech
- Use　Speech Rate

Acceleration Effects
- Related　Aviation
- 　　　　　Decompression Effects
- 　　　　　Flight Simulation
- 　　　　　Gravitational Effects
- 　　　　　Physiological Stress
- 　　　　　Spaceflight

Accelerometers
- Broader　Apparatus

Acceptance (Social)
- Use　Social Acceptance

Accessory Nerve
- Use　Cranial Nerves

Accident Prevention
- Related　Accidents
- 　　　　　Prevention/
- 　　　　　Safety
- 　　　　　Transportation Accidents

Accident Proneness
- Related　Accidents
- 　　　　　Mental Disorders/
- 　　　　　Psychosomatic Disorders
- 　　　　　Safety

Accidents
- Narrower　Air Traffic Accidents
- 　　　　　Highway Hypnosis Accidents
- 　　　　　Home Accidents
- 　　　　　Industrial Accidents
- 　　　　　Motor Traffic Accidents

Accidents — (Continued)
- Narrower
- 　　　　　Pedestrian Accidents
- 　　　　　Transportation Accidents
- Related　Accident Prevention
- 　　　　　Accident Proneness
- 　　　　　Hazards
- 　　　　　Injuries
- 　　　　　Safety

Accidents (Cerebrovascular)
- Use　Cerebrovascular Accidents

Acclimatization (Thermal)
- Use　Thermal Acclimatization

Accomplishment
- Use　Achievement

Accountants
- Used For　Certified Public Accountants
- Broader　Business And Industrial Personnel
- 　　　　　White Collar Workers
- Related　Personnel/

Accreditation (Education Personnel)
- Used For　Teacher Accreditation
- Related　Education/

Acculturation
- Broader　Sociocultural Factors
- Related　Cultural Assimilation

Acetazolamide
- Broader　Diuretics
- Related　Antiepileptic Drugs
- 　　　　　Carbonic Anhydrase

Acetylcholine
- Broader　Cholinomimetic Drugs
- Related　Acetylcholinesterase
- 　　　　　Choline
- 　　　　　Cholinergic Nerves

Acetylcholinesterase
- Broader　Enzymes
- 　　　　　Esterases
- Related　Acetylcholine
- 　　　　　Cholinesterase

Acetylsalicylic Acid
- Use　Aspirin

Aches
- Use　Pain

Achievement
- Used For　Accomplishment
- 　　　　　Attainment (Achievement)
- 　　　　　Success
- Narrower　Academic Achievement
- 　　　　　Academic Overachievement
- 　　　　　Academic Underachievement
- 　　　　　College Academic Achievement

Achievement — (Continued)
Narrower
    Mathematics Achievement
    Reading Achievement
Related   Achievement Measures
    Failure

Achievement (Academic)
Use   Academic Achievement

Achievement Measures
Used For   Test (Achievement)
Related   Achievement
    Measurement/
Identifier   Iowa Tests of Basic Skills
    Stanford Achievement Test
    Wide Range Achievement Test

Achievement Motivation
Used For   NAch
    Need Achievement
Broader   Motivation
Narrower   Academic Achievement Motiva-
    tion
Related   Achievement Potential
    Needs

Achievement Potential
Used For   Potential (Achievement)
Related   Ability/
    Achievement Motivation

Achilles Tendon Reflex
Broader   Reflexes

Achromatic Color
Broader   Color

Acid Phosphatases
Broader   Enzymes
    Phosphatases

Acids
Narrower   Adenosine
    Alanines
    Amino Acids
    Ascorbic Acid
    Aspartic Acid
    Aspirin
    Deoxyribonucleic Acid
    Dopa
    Fatty Acids
    Folic Acid
    Glutamic Acid
    Glutamine
    Glycine
    Heparin
    Histidine
    Leucine
    Lysergic Acid Diethylamide
    Methionine
    Nicotinic Acid
    Nucleic Acids
    Phenylalanine

Acids — (Continued)
Narrower
    Phosphatides
    Ribonucleic Acid
    Tryptophan
    Tyrosine
    Uric Acid

Acne
Broader   Skin Disorders
Related   Puberty

Acoustic Nerve
Used For   Nerve (Acoustic)
Broader   Cranial Nerves
    Nervous System
    Peripheral Nerves

Acoustic Reflex
Broader   Reflexes

Acoustic Stimuli
Use   Auditory Stimulation

Acrophobia
Broader   Phobias

ACTH (Hormone)
Use   Corticotropin

Acting Out
Broader   Symptoms
Related   Behavior Disorders
    Emotionally Disturbed

Active Avoidance
Use   Avoidance Conditioning

Activism (Student)
Use   Student Activism

Activist Movements
Used For   Movements (Activist)
Broader   Social Movements
Narrower   Student Activism
Related   Black Power Movement
    Civil Rights Movement
    Homosexual Liberation Move-
    ment
    Racial Integration
    School Integration (Racial)
    Womens Liberation Movement

Actualization (Self)
Use   Self Actualization

Acuity
Use   Perceptual Discrimination

Acupuncture
Broader   Physical Treatment Methods

Acute Alcoholic Intoxication
Broader   Alcohol Intoxication
    Brain Disorders
    Toxic Disorders
    Toxic Encephalopathies

Acute Psychosis
Broader   Psychosis
Narrower   Acute Psychotic Episode
           Acute Schizophrenia

Acute Psychotic Episode
Used For   Psychotic Episode (Acute)
Broader   Acute Psychosis
           Psychosis
Related   Acute Schizophrenia

Acute Schizophrenia
Broader   Acute Psychosis
           Psychosis
           Schizophrenia
Related   Acute Psychotic Episode

Adaptability (Personality)
Used For   Flexibility (Personality)
Broader   Personality Traits
Related   Coping Behavior

Adaptation
Used For   Readaptation
Narrower   Dark Adaptation
           Sensory Adaptation

Adaptation (Dark)
Use   Dark Adaptation

Adaptation (Environmental)
Use   Environmental Adaptation

Adaptation (Sensory)
Use   Sensory Adaptation

Adaptation (Social)
Use   Social Adjustment

Addiction
Broader   Behavior Disorders
Narrower   Alcoholism
           Drug Addiction
           Heroin Addiction
Related   Drug Abuse
           Drug Dependency
           Drug Usage

Addisons Disease
Broader   Adrenal Gland Disorders
           Endocrine Disorders
           Syndromes
Related   Tuberculosis

Adenosine
Broader   Acids
           Nucleic Acids

Adjectives
Broader   Form Classes (Language)
           Grammar
           Language
           Linguistics
           Verbal Communication

Adjudication
Used For   Courts
           Jury
           Juvenile Court
Broader   Legal Processes

Adjustment/
Related   Emotional Adjustment
           Occupational Adjustment
           School Adjustment
           Social Adjustment

Adler (Alfred)

Administration (Test)
Use   Test Administration

Administrators
Use   Management Personnel

Admission (Hospital)
Use   Hospital Admission

Admission (Psychiatric Hospital)
Use   Psychiatric Hospital Admission

Admission Criteria (Student)
Use   Student Admission Criteria

Adolescence
Use   Adolescents

Adolescent Development
Related   Adolescents
           Childhood Development
           Development/
           Developmental Age Groups
           Developmental Differences
           Developmental Stages
           Human Development/
           Physical Development
           Psychogenesis
           Sex Linked Developmental Dif-
             ferences
           Sexual Development

Adolescent Psychology
Broader   Developmental Psychology
           Psychology
           Sciences
           Social Sciences

Adolescents
Used For   Adolescence
           Teenagers
           Youth (Adolescents)
Broader   Developmental Age Groups
Related   Adolescent Development
           Young Adults

Adopted Children
Broader   Family Members
Related   Adoption (Child)
           Children

Adoption (Child)
Broader	Legal Processes
Related	Adopted Children

Adoptive Parents
Broader	Family Members
	Parents

Adrenal Cortex Hormones
Broader	Hormones
Narrower	Aldosterone
	Corticosterone
	Cortisone
	Deoxycorticosterone
	Hydrocortisone
	Prednisolone
Related	Adrenal Glands
	Adrenal Medulla Hormones
	Corticosteroids
	Stress

Adrenal Cortex Steroids
Use	Corticosteroids

Adrenal Gland Disorders
Broader	Endocrine Disorders
Narrower	Addisons Disease
	Cushings Syndrome
Related	Endocrine Sexual Disorders
	Pituitary Disorders

Adrenal Gland Secretion
Broader	Endocrine Gland Secretion
	Secretion (Gland)

Adrenal Glands
Broader	Endocrine Glands
	Endocrine System
	Glands
Related	Adrenal Cortex Hormones

Adrenal Medulla Hormones
Broader	Hormones
Narrower	Norepinephrine
Related	Adrenal Cortex Hormones

Adrenalectomy
Broader	Endocrine Gland Surgery
	Physical Treatment Methods
	Surgery

Adrenaline
Use	Epinephrine

Adrenergic Blocking Drugs
Narrower	Dihydroergotamine
	Phenoxybenzamine
	Propranolol
Related	Adrenolytic Drugs
	Antihypertensive Drugs
	Drugs/
	Ergot Derivatives
	Sympathetic Nervous System
	Sympatholytic Drugs

Adrenergic Drugs
Narrower	Amphetamine
	Dextroamphetamine
	Ephedrine
	Methoxamine
	Tyramine
Related	Catecholamines
	Drugs/
	Serotonin
	Sympathetic Nervous System
	Sympathomimetic Drugs

Adrenergic Nerves
Used For	Nerves (Adrenergic)
Broader	Autonomic Nervous System
	Nervous System

Adrenochrome
Broader	Hallucinogenic Drugs
Related	Epinephrine
	Experimental Psychosis

Adrenocorticotropin
Use	Corticotropin

Adrenolytic Drugs
Narrower	Carphenazine
	Chlorpromazine
	Chlorprothixene
Related	Adrenergic Blocking Drugs
	Drugs/
	Epinephrine
	Sympathetic Nervous System
	Sympatholytic Drugs

Adult Education
Related	Education/

Adultery
Use	Extramarital Intercourse

Adulthood
Use	Adults

Adults
Used For	Adulthood
Broader	Developmental Age Groups
Narrower	Aged
	Middle Aged
	Young Adults

Adventitiously Handicapped
Broader	Handicapped
Related	Congenitally Handicapped

Adverbs
Broader	Form Classes (Language)
	Grammar
	Language
	Linguistics
	Verbal Communication

Advertising
Narrower	Television Advertising

Advertising — (Continued)
    Related   Marketing
                  Mass Media
                  Public Relations

Aerospace Personnel
    Narrower   Aircraft Pilots
                 Astronauts
    Related   Business And Industrial Personnel
                 Engineers
                 Personnel/
                 Physicists
                 Scientists/

Aesthetic Preferences
    Used For   Preferences (Aesthetic)
    Broader   Preferences
    Related   Aesthetics

Aesthetics
    Related   Aesthetic Preferences
                 Arts

Aetiology
    Use   Etiology

Affection
    Used For   Liking
    Related   Emotions/
                 Interpersonal Interaction
                 Love

Affective Disturbances
    Narrower   Anaclitic Depression
                 Depression (Emotion)
                 Involutional Depression
                 Neurotic Depressive Reaction
                 Psychotic Depressive Reaction
                 Reactive Depression
    Related   Anxiety
                 Mental Disorders/

Affective Psychosis
    Broader   Psychosis
    Narrower   Involutional Depression
                 Manic Depressive Psychosis
                 Psychotic Depressive Reaction
    Related   Cyclothymic Personality

Afferent Stimulation
    Used For   Afferentiation
    Broader   Stimulation
    Related   Nervous System
                 Stereotaxic Techniques
                 Surgery

Afferentiation
    Use   Afferent Stimulation

Affiliation Motivation
    Used For   Need For Affiliation
    Broader   Motivation
    Related   Needs

Africa

Aftercare
    Related   Outpatient Treatment
                 Posttreatment Followup
                 Treatment/

Aftereffect (Perceptual)
    Use   Perceptual Aftereffect

Afterimage
    Broader   Illusions (Perception)
                 Perceptual Aftereffect

Age
    Use   Developmental Age Groups

Age Differences
    Broader   Developmental Differences
    Related   Developmental Age Groups
                 Generation Gap
                 Physical Development
                 Psychogenesis

Aged
    Used For   Longevity
                 Old Age
                 Senescence
                 Senior Citizens
    Broader   Adults
                 Developmental Age Groups
    Related   Physiological Aging
                 Senile Dementia

Agencies (Groups)
    Use   Organizations

Aggressive Behavior
    Used For   Agonistic Behavior
                 Fighting
    Broader   Social Behavior
    Narrower   Animal Aggressive Behavior
                 Arguments
                 Attack Behavior
                 Conflict
                 Riots
                 Threat Postures
                 Violence
                 War
    Related   Behavior Disorders
                 Social Interaction

Aggressiveness
    Broader   Personality Traits

Agility (Physical)
    Use   Physical Agility

Aging (Physiological)
    Use   Physiological Aging

Agitated Depression
    Use   Depression (Emotion)

Agnosia
    Broader   Perceptual Disturbances

Agnosia — (Continued)
Related   Aphasia

Agnosticism
Broader   Religious Beliefs
Related   Atheism

Agonistic Behavior
Use   Aggressive Behavior

Agoraphobia
Broader   Phobias

Agraphia
Broader   Aphasia
    Brain Disorders
    Central Nervous System Disorders
    Nervous System Disorders
Related   Learning Disabilities

Agricultural Extension Workers
Used For   County Agricultural Agents
    Extension Workers (Agricultural)
    Workers (Agricultural Extension)
Broader   Government Personnel
Related   Agricultural Workers

Agricultural Workers
Used For   Farmers
    Laborers (Farm)
Narrower   Migrant Farm Workers
Related   Agricultural Extension Workers
    Business And Industrial Personnel
    Personnel/

Air Encephalography
Use   Pneumoencephalography

Air Force Personnel
Broader   Government Personnel
    Military Personnel
Related   National Guardsmen

Air Traffic Accidents
Used For   Traffic Accidents (Air)
Broader   Accidents
    Transportation Accidents
Related   Air Traffic Control
    Air Transportation
    Aviation Safety

Air Traffic Control
Used For   Control (Air Traffic)
    Traffic Control (Air)
Broader   Aviation Safety
    Safety
Related   Air Traffic Accidents
    Air Transportation
    Transportation Accidents

Air Transportation
Broader   Transportation

Air Transportation — (Continued)
Related   Air Traffic Accidents
    Air Traffic Control
    Aircraft
    Public Transportation
    Spacecraft

Aircraft
Used For   Airplane
Narrower   Helicopters
Related   Air Transportation
    Aircraft Pilots

Aircraft Pilots
Used For   Aviators
    Pilots (Aircraft)
Broader   Aerospace Personnel
Related   Aircraft
    Astronauts
    Aviation Safety

Airplane
Use   Aircraft

Akinesia
Use   Apraxia

Alanines
Broader   Acids
    Amino Acids
Narrower   Phenylalanine

Alarm Responses
Related   Animal Distress Calls
    Animal Escape Behavior
    Animal Ethology
    Animal Innate Behavior
    Animal Instinctive Behavior
    Fear
    Startle Reflex

Alaska

Albinism
Broader   Genetic Disorders
Related   Eye Disorders
    Skin Disorders

Albino Rats
Use   Rats

Albumins
Broader   Proteins
Narrower   Serum Albumin

Alcohol Dehydrogenases
Broader   Dehydrogenases
    Enzymes
Related   Alcohols

Alcohol Drinking Attitudes
Used For   Drinking Attitudes
Related   Attitudes/

Alcohol Drinking Patterns
Used For   Drinking (Alcohol)

Alcohol Drinking Patterns — (Continued)
Narrower	Problem Drinking
	Social Drinking
Related	Alcohol Intoxication
	Alcoholism

Alcohol Intoxication
Used For	Drunkenness
	Intoxication (Alcohol)
Broader	Brain Disorders
	Toxic Disorders
	Toxic Encephalopathies
Narrower	Acute Alcoholic Intoxication
	Chronic Alcoholic Intoxication
Related	Alcohol Drinking Patterns
	Alcoholism
	Problem Drinking
	Toxic Psychoses

Alcoholic Beverages
Used For	Beverages (Alcohol)
Narrower	Beer
	Liquor
	Wine

Alcoholic Hallucinosis
Broader	Alcoholic Psychosis
	Brain Disorders
	Central Nervous System Disorders
	Hallucinosis
	Nervous System Disorders
	Organic Brain Syndromes
	Psychosis
	Syndromes
Narrower	Delirium Tremens
	Korsakoffs Psychosis

Alcoholic Psychosis
Broader	Brain Disorders
	Central Nervous System Disorders
	Nervous System Disorders
	Organic Brain Syndromes
	Psychosis
	Syndromes
Narrower	Alcoholic Hallucinosis
	Delirium Tremens
	Korsakoffs Psychosis
Related	Nutritional Deficiencies
	Toxic Psychoses

Alcoholics Anonymous
Broader	Organizations
Related	Community Services

Alcoholism
Broader	Addiction
	Behavior Disorders
Narrower	Korsakoffs Psychosis
	Wernickes Syndrome

Alcoholism — (Continued)
Related	Alcohol Drinking Patterns
	Alcohol Intoxication
	Alcohols
	Nutritional Deficiencies
	Problem Drinking
	Toxic Disorders

Alcohols
Narrower	Denatured Alcohol
	Ephedrine
	Ethanol
	Isoproterenol
	Mephenesin
	Methanol
	Methoxamine
	Propranolol
	Tetrahydrocannabinol
	Trihexyphenidyl
Related	Alcohol Dehydrogenases
	Alcoholism
	Drugs/

Aldolases
Broader	Enzymes

Aldosterone
Broader	Adrenal Cortex Hormones
	Corticosteroids
	Hormones
	Steroids

Alexia
Use	Aphasia

Algebra
Use	Mathematics Education

Algorithms
Broader	Mathematics (Concepts)

Alienation
Used For	Anomie
Broader	Emotional States
Related	Depersonalization

Alkaloids
Used For	Opium Alkaloids
Narrower	Apomorphine
	Atropine
	Caffeine
	Cocaine
	Codeine
	Ephedrine
	Heroin
	Homatropine
	Hyoscyamine (L-)
	Mescaline
	Morphine
	Nicotine
	Papaverine
	Peyote
	Physostigmine
	Pilocarpine

Alkaloids — (Continued)
Narrower	Quinidine
	Quinine
	Reserpine
	Scopolamine
	Strychnine
	Theophylline
	Tubocurarine
Related	Curare
	Drugs/
	Ergot Derivatives

Allergic Disorders
Used For	Allergies
Broader	Immunologic Disorders
Narrower	Allergic Skin Disorders
	Drug Allergies
	Food Allergies
	Hay Fever
Related	Anaphylactic Shock

Allergic Skin Disorders
Broader	Allergic Disorders
	Immunologic Disorders
	Skin Disorders
Related	Dermatitis
	Eczema
	Neurodermatitis

Allergies
Use	Allergic Disorders

Alligators
Use	Crocodilians

Allport Vernon Lindzey Study Values
(See)	Attitude Measures

Alopecia
Used For	Hair Loss
Broader	Skin Disorders
Related	Genetic Disorders
	Hair

Alpha Rhythm
Broader	Electrical Activity
	Electrophysiology
Related	Electroencephalography

Alphabets
Broader	Language
	Linguistics
	Verbal Communication
	Written Language
Narrower	Initial Teaching Alphabet
	Letters (Alphabet)

Altitude Effects
Broader	Environmental Effects
Related	Aviation
	Gravitational Effects

Altruism
Broader	Social Behavior

Altruism — (Continued)
Related	Charitable Behavior

Alveoli (Lung)
Use	Pulmonary Alveoli

Alzheimers Disease
Broader	Brain Disorders
	Central Nervous System Disorders
	Nervous System Disorders
	Organic Brain Syndromes
	Presenile Dementia
	Syndromes
Related	Picks Disease

Amaurotic Familial Idiocy
Used For	Familial Idiocy (Amaurotic)
	Idiocy (Amaurotic Familial)
	Tay Sachs Disease
Broader	Genetic Disorders
	Lipid Metabolism Disorders
	Mental Retardation
	Metabolism Disorders
	Neonatal Disorders
	Neonatal Genetic Disorders

Ambiguity (Stimulus)
Use	Stimulus Ambiguity

Ambiguity (Tolerance)
Use	Tolerance For Ambiguity

Ambition
Use	Aspirations

Ambivalence
Broader	Emotional States

Amblyopia
Broader	Eye Disorders
	Sense Organ Disorders
Related	Refraction Errors
	Strabismus

Amenorrhea
Broader	Genital Disorders
	Gynecological Disorders
	Menstrual Disorders
	Urogenital Disorders
Narrower	Pseudocyesis
	Stein Leventhal Syndrome

Amentia
Use	Mental Retardation

American Indians
Used For	Apache Indians
	Arapaho Indians
	Cheyenne Indians
	Hopi Indians
	Indians (American)
	Mohave Indians
	Navaho Indians
	Ojibwa Indians

American Indians — (Continued)
Used For
     Shoshone Indians
     Spokane Indians
Broader   Ethnic Groups

Amine Oxidase Inhibitors
Narrower   Iproniazid
     Isocarboxazid
     Lysergic Acid Diethylamide
     Nialamide
Related   Amine Oxidases
     Drugs/
     Monoamine Oxidase Inhibitors

Amine Oxidases
Broader   Enzymes
     Oxidases
Narrower   Monoamine Oxidases
Related   Amine Oxidase Inhibitors

Amines
Narrower   Amitriptyline
     Amphetamine
     Atropine
     Bufotenine
     Catecholamines
     Chlordiazepoxide
     Chlorimipramine
     Chlorisondamine
     Chlorpromazine
     Chlorprothixene
     Cocaine
     Dextroamphetamine
     Diphenhydramine
     Dopamine
     Ephedrine
     Epinephrine
     Galanthamine
     Guanethidine
     Histamine
     Homatropine
     Hydroxylamine
     Hyoscyamine (L-)
     Imipramine
     Mecamylamine
     Meperidine
     Methamphetamine
     Methoxamine
     Methylphenidate
     Norepinephrine
     Orphenadrine
     Phenmetrazine
     Phenoxybenzamine
     Physostigmine
     Puromycin
     Scopolamine
     Serotonin
     Sympathomimetic Amines
     Thalidomide
     Trihexyphenidyl

Amines — (Continued)
Narrower
     Tryptamine
     Tyramine
Related   Amino Acids
     Drugs/

Amino Acids
Broader   Acids
Narrower   Alanines
     Aspartic Acid
     Cysteine
     Dopa
     Folic Acid
     Glutamic Acid
     Glutamine
     Glycine
     Histidine
     Leucine
     Methionine
     Phenylalanine
     Tryptophan
     Tyrosine
Related   Amines
     Drugs/
     Proteins

Aminotransferases
Use   Transaminases

Amitriptyline
Used For   Elavil
Broader   Amines
     Antidepressant Drugs
     Tranquilizing Drugs

Ammonium Bromide
Broader   Bromides
     Sedatives

Ammons Full Range Picture Vocab Test
(See)   Intelligence Measures

Amnesia
Broader   Dissociative Patterns
     Memory Disorders
     Thought Disturbances
Narrower   Fugue Reaction
Related   Forgetting

Amniotic Fluid
Broader   Body Fluids

Amobarbital
Used For   Amobarbital Sodium
     Amytal
Broader   Barbiturates
     CNS Affecting Drugs
     CNS Depressant Drugs
     Hypnotic Drugs
     Narcoanalytic Drugs
     Sedatives

Amobarbital Sodium
    Use   Amobarbital

Amphetamine
    Used For   Amphetamine (Dl-)
                Amphetamine Sulfate
                Benzedrine
    Broader   Adrenergic Drugs
                Amines
                Appetite Depressing Drugs
                CNS Affecting Drugs
                CNS Stimulating Drugs
                Sympathomimetic Amines
                Sympathomimetic Drugs
                Vasoconstrictor Drugs
    Related   Dextroamphetamine
                Drug Dependency

Amphetamine (D-)
    Use   Dextroamphetamine

Amphetamine (Dl-)
    Use   Amphetamine

Amphetamine Sulfate
    Use   Amphetamine

Amphibia
    Broader   Vertebrates
    Narrower   Frogs
                Salamanders
                Toads

Amplifiers (Apparatus)
    Broader   Apparatus

Amplitude (Response)
    Use   Response Amplitude

Amputation
    Broader   Physical Treatment Methods
                Surgery
    Narrower   Mastectomy
    Related   Phantom Limbs
                Prostheses
                Traumatic Amputations

Amputees
    Broader   Handicapped
                Physically Handicapped

Amygdaloid Body
    Broader   Basal Ganglia
                Brain
                Central Nervous System
                Cerebral Cortex
                Hippocampus
                Limbic System
                Nervous System
                Telencephalon

Amylases
    Broader   Enzymes

Amytal
    Use   Amobarbital

Anabolism
    Broader   Metabolism

Anaclitic Depression
    Broader   Affective Disturbances
                Depression (Emotion)
                Emotional States
    Related   Mother Child Relations

Anagram Problem Solving
    Broader   Cognitive Processes
                Problem Solving
    Related   Anagrams

Anagrams
    Broader   Language
                Verbal Communication
                Vocabulary
    Related   Anagram Problem Solving

Analeptic Drugs
    Used For   Antagonists (CNS Depressant
                Drugs)
                CNS Depressant Drug Antago-
                nists
    Broader   CNS Affecting Drugs
                CNS Stimulating Drugs
    Narrower   Bemegride
                Picrotoxin
                Strychnine
    Related   Barbiturate Poisoning
                Caffeine
                Cholinomimetic Drugs
                Drugs/
                Heart Rate Affecting Drugs
                Methylphenidate
                Pentylenetetrazol
                Theophylline

Analgesic Drugs
    Used For   Anodynes
                Pain Relieving Drugs
    Narrower   Aspirin
                Atropine
                Codeine
                Dihydroergotamine
                Eugenol
                Heroin
                Hyoscyamine (L-)
                Meperidine
                Methadone
                Morphine
                Novocaine
                Papaverine
                Phenacetin
                Potassium Bromide
                Quinine
                Scopolamine
    Related   Anesthetic Drugs
                CNS Depressant Drugs
                Drugs/
                Hypnotic Drugs

Analgesic Drugs — (Continued)
Related
      Narcotic Drugs
      Pain
      Sedatives

Analog Computers
Broader   Computers

Analysis of Covariance
Broader   Statistical Analysis
      Statistical Measurement
      Variability Measurement
Related   Analysis of Variance
      Analysis/

Analysis of Variance
Used For ANOVA (Statistics)
      Regression Analysis
Broader   Statistical Analysis
      Statistical Measurement
      Variability Measurement
Related   Analysis of Covariance
      Analysis/

Analysis/
Related   Analysis of Covariance
      Analysis of Variance
      Cluster Analysis
      Dream Analysis
      Factor Analysis
      Interaction Analysis (Statistics)
      Item Analysis (Statistical)
      Item Analysis (Test)
      Job Analysis
      Psychoanalysis
      Statistical Analysis
      Systems Analysis
      Task Analysis

Analysts
Use   Psychoanalysts

Analytical Psychotherapy
Broader   Psychotherapy

Anaphylactic Shock
Used For Protein Sensitization
      Sensitization (Protein)
Broader   Immunologic Disorders
Related   Allergic Disorders
      Shock

Anatomical Systems/
Related   Anatomy/
      Cardiovascular System
      Digestive System
      Endocrine System
      Lymphatic System
      Musculoskeletal System
      Nervous System
      Respiratory System
      Systems/
      Urogenital System

Anatomy/
Related   Abdomen
      Anatomical Systems/
      Back (Anatomy)
      Body Fluids
      Breast
      Cells (Biology)
      Face (Anatomy)
      Hair
      Head (Anatomy)
      Morphology
      Nails (Anatomy)
      Neck (Anatomy)
      Palm (Anatomy)
      Pelvis
      Physiology/
      Scalp (Anatomy)
      Sense Organs
      Thigh
      Tissues (Body)

Ancestors
Used For Great Grandparents
Broader   Family Members
Narrower Grandparents
      Parents

Androgens
Broader   Hormones
      Sex Hormones
Narrower Testosterone

Anemia
Broader   Blood and Lymphatic Disorders
Related   Genetic Disorders

Anencephaly
Broader   Brain Disorders
      Central Nervous System Disorders
      Mental Retardation
      Neonatal Disorders
      Nervous System Disorders

Anesthesia (Feeling)
Narrower Hysterical Anesthesia
Related   Disorders/
      Sense Organ Disorders
      Tactual Perception

Anesthesiology
Broader   Medical Sciences
      Sciences

Anesthetic Drugs
Narrower Chloroform
      Cocaine
      Ether (Anesthetic)
      Eugenol
      General Anesthetics
      Hexobarbital
      Lidocaine
      Local Anesthetics

Anesthetic Drugs — (Continued)

Narrower
: Methohexital
: Novocaine
: Pentobarbital
: Quinine
: Tetracaine
: Thiopental

Related
: Analgesic Drugs
: Anticonvulsive Drugs
: Barbiturates
: CNS Depressant Drugs
: Drugs/
: Hypnotic Drugs
: Muscle Relaxing Drugs
: Narcotic Drugs
: Sedatives

Aneurysms

Broader
: Cardiovascular Disorders

Anger

Used For
: Rage

Narrower
: Hostility

Related
: Emotions/
: Jealousy

Angina Pectoris

Broader
: Cardiovascular Disorders
: Heart Disorders

Related
: Myocardial Infarctions

Angiography

Broader
: Diagnosis
: Medical Diagnosis
: Roentgenography

Angiotensin

Broader
: Vasoconstrictor Drugs

Angst

Use
: Anxiety

Anguish

Use
: Distress

Animal Aggressive Behavior

Broader
: Aggressive Behavior
: Animal Ethology
: Animal Social Behavior
: Social Behavior

Narrower
: Attack Behavior
: Threat Postures

Related
: Animal Dominance
: Territoriality

Animal Behavior

Use
: Animal Ethology

Animal Biological Rhythms

Used For
: Biological Clocks (Animal)
: Biological Rhythms (Animal)

Broader
: Animal Ethology
: Biological Rhythms

Narrower
: Animal Circadian Rhythms

Animal Biological Rhythms — (Continued)

Related
: Animal Innate Behavior
: Animal Instinctive Behavior
: Animal Sexual Receptivity
: Estrus
: Hibernation

Animal Breeding

Used For
: Animal Strain Differences
: Breeding (Animal)
: Strain Differences (Animal)

Narrower
: Selective Breeding

Related
: Animal Mating Behavior
: Animals/
: Eugenics

Animal Circadian Rhythms

Used For
: Circadian Rhythms (Animal)
: Daily Biological Rhythms (Animal)

Broader
: Animal Biological Rhythms
: Animal Ethology
: Biological Rhythms

Related
: Animal Nocturnal Behavior

Animal Communication

Broader
: Animal Ethology
: Animal Social Behavior
: Social Behavior

Narrower
: Animal Distress Calls

Related
: Animal Vocalizations
: Communication/
: Vocalization

Animal Courtship Behavior

Used For
: Courtship (Animal)

Broader
: Animal Ethology
: Animal Social Behavior
: Social Behavior

Narrower
: Animal Courtship Displays

Related
: Animal Mating Behavior

Animal Courtship Displays

Used For
: Courtship Displays (Animal)

Broader
: Animal Courtship Behavior
: Animal Ethology
: Animal Social Behavior
: Displays
: Social Behavior

Related
: Animal Mating Behavior
: Territoriality

Animal Distress Calls

Used For
: Distress Calls (Animal)

Broader
: Animal Communication
: Animal Ethology
: Animal Social Behavior
: Animal Vocalizations
: Social Behavior
: Animal Vocalizations

Related
: Alarm Responses

Animal Division of Labor
Used For	Division of Labor (Animal)
Broader	Animal Ethology
	Animal Social Behavior
	Social Behavior
Related	Animal Dominance

Animal Dominance
Used For	Dominance (Animal)
	Pecking Order
Broader	Animal Ethology
	Animal Social Behavior
	Social Behavior
Related	Animal Aggressive Behavior
	Animal Division of Labor
	Dominance Hierarchy
	Dominance/
	Territoriality

Animal Drinking Behavior
Used For	Drinking Behavior (Animal)
Broader	Animal Ethology
Related	Animal Innate Behavior
	Animal Instinctive Behavior
	Thirst
	Water Intake

Animal Environments
Broader	Environment
	Social Environments
Related	Animals/

Animal Escape Behavior
Used For	Escape Behavior (Animal)
Broader	Animal Ethology
Related	Alarm Responses

Animal Ethology
Used For	Animal Behavior
	Ethology (Animal)
Narrower	Animal Aggressive Behavior
	Animal Biological Rhythms
	Animal Circadian Rhythms
	Animal Communication
	Animal Courtship Behavior
	Animal Courtship Displays
	Animal Distress Calls
	Animal Division of Labor
	Animal Dominance
	Animal Drinking Behavior
	Animal Escape Behavior
	Animal Exploratory Behavior
	Animal Feeding Behavior
	Animal Hoarding Behavior
	Animal Innate Behavior
	Animal Instinctive Behavior
	Animal Maternal Behavior
	Animal Mating Behavior
	Animal Nocturnal Behavior
	Animal Open Field Behavior
	Animal Play
	Animal Sex Differences

Animal Ethology — (Continued)
Narrower	Animal Sexual Receptivity
	Animal Social Behavior
	Animal Vocalizations
	Attack Behavior
	Hibernation
	Imprinting
	Migratory Behavior (Animal)
	Nest Building
	Territoriality
	Threat Postures
Related	Alarm Responses
	Animals/
	Echolocation
	Stereotyped Behavior

Animal Exploratory Behavior
Broader	Animal Ethology
	Exploratory Behavior
Related	Animal Innate Behavior
	Animal Instinctive Behavior

Animal Feeding Behavior
Used For	Feeding Behavior (Animal)
Broader	Animal Ethology
Related	Animal Innate Behavior
	Animal Instinctive Behavior
	Animal Maternal Behavior
	Food Intake
	Hunger

Animal Hoarding Behavior
Used For	Hoarding Behavior (Animal)
Broader	Animal Ethology
Related	Animal Innate Behavior
	Animal Instinctive Behavior

Animal Innate Behavior
Used For	Innate Behavior (Animal)
Broader	Animal Ethology
Related	Alarm Responses
	Animal Biological Rhythms
	Animal Drinking Behavior
	Animal Exploratory Behavior
	Animal Feeding Behavior
	Animal Hoarding Behavior
	Animal Instinctive Behavior
	Animal Nocturnal Behavior
	Animal Play
	Animal Vocalizations
	Hibernation
	Imprinting
	Migratory Behavior (Animal)
	Nest Building
	Territoriality

Animal Instinctive Behavior
Used For	Instinctive Behavior (Animal)
Broader	Animal Ethology
Related	Alarm Responses
	Animal Biological Rhythms

Animal Instinctive Behavior — (Continued)

Related	Animal Drinking Behavior
	Animal Exploratory Behavior
	Animal Feeding Behavior
	Animal Hoarding Behavior
	Animal Innate Behavior
	Animal Nocturnal Behavior
	Animal Play
	Animal Vocalizations
	Hibernation
	Imprinting
	Migratory Behavior (Animal)
	Nest Building
	Territoriality

Animal Maternal Behavior

Used For	Maternal Behavior (Animal)
	Maternal Deprivation
	Nurturance
Broader	Animal Ethology
	Animal Social Behavior
	Social Behavior
Related	Animal Feeding Behavior

Animal Mating Behavior

Used For	Coitus (Animal)
	Copulation (Animal)
	Mating Behavior (Animal)
Broader	Animal Ethology
	Animal Social Behavior
	Social Behavior
Narrower	Animal Sexual Receptivity
Related	Animal Breeding
	Animal Courtship Behavior
	Animal Courtship Displays
	Nest Building
	Pheromones
	Sexual Reproduction

Animal Motivation

Broader	Motivation
Related	Animals/
	Needs

Animal Navigation

Use	Migratory Behavior (Animal)

Animal Nocturnal Behavior

Used For	Nocturnal Behavior (Animal)
Broader	Animal Ethology
Related	Animal Circadian Rhythms
	Animal Innate Behavior
	Animal Instinctive Behavior

Animal Open Field Behavior

Used For	Field Behavior (Animal)
	Open Field Behavior (Animal)
Broader	Animal Ethology

Animal Play

Used For	Play (Animal)
Broader	Animal Ethology

Animal Play — (Continued)

Related	Animal Innate Behavior
	Animal Instinctive Behavior
	Animal Social Behavior

Animal Sex Differences

Used For	Sex Differences (Animal)
Broader	Animal Ethology

Animal Sexual Receptivity

Used For	Sexual Receptivity (Animal)
Broader	Animal Ethology
	Animal Mating Behavior
	Animal Social Behavior
	Social Behavior
Related	Animal Biological Rhythms
	Estrus

Animal Social Behavior

Broader	Animal Ethology
	Social Behavior
Narrower	Animal Aggressive Behavior
	Animal Communication
	Animal Courtship Behavior
	Animal Courtship Displays
	Animal Distress Calls
	Animal Division of Labor
	Animal Dominance
	Animal Maternal Behavior
	Animal Mating Behavior
	Animal Sexual Receptivity
	Attack Behavior
	Threat Postures
Related	Animal Play

Animal Strain Differences

Use	Animal Breeding
	Genetics/

Animal Vocalizations

Used For	Vocalizations (Animal)
Broader	Animal Ethology
	Vocalization
Narrower	Animal Distress Calls
Related	Animal Communication
	Animal Innate Behavior
	Animal Instinctive Behavior
	Echolocation

Animals/

Related	Animal Breeding
	Animal Environments
	Animal Ethology
	Animal Motivation
	Biological Symbiosis
	Female Animals
	Invertebrates
	Male Animals
	Vertebrates

Animism

Broader	Philosophies

17

Animism — (Continued)
   Related   Ethnology/
                 Myths
                 Taboos

Ankle
   Broader   Musculoskeletal System
   Related   Feet (Anatomy)
                 Leg (Anatomy)

Annual Leave
   Use   Employee Leave Benefits

Annual Report

Anodynes
   Use   Analgesic Drugs

Anomie
   Use   Alienation

Anonymity

Anorexia Nervosa
   Broader   Appetite Disorders
                 Psychosomatic Disorders
                 Symptoms
                 Underweight
   Related   Mental Disorders/
                 Nutritional Deficiencies

Anorexigenic Drugs
   Use   Appetite Depressing Drugs

Anosmia
   Broader   Sense Organ Disorders
   Related   Olfactory Perception

ANOVA (Statistics)
   Use   Analysis of Variance

Anoxia
   Used For   Asphyxia
                 Hypoxia
   Broader   Symptoms
   Narrower   Cerebral Anoxia
   Related   Ischemia
                 Respiratory Distress

Antagonism
   Use   Hostility

Antagonists (CNS Depressant Drugs)
   Use   Analeptic Drugs

Antarctica

Anthropologists
   Related   Personnel/
                 Scientists/
                 Sociologists

Anthropology
   Broader   Sciences
                 Social Sciences

Antibiotics
   Narrower   Cycloheximide
                 Penicillins
                 Puromycin
                 Tetracycline
   Related   Drugs/

Antibodies
   Broader   Globulins
                 Proteins
   Related   Blood Serum
                 Drugs/
                 Gamma Globulin
                 Immunization
                 Immunoglobulins

Anticholinergic Drugs
   Use   Cholinergic Blocking Drugs

Anticholinesterase Drugs
   Use   Cholinesterase Inhibitors

Anticipation (Serial Learning)
   Use   Serial Anticipation (Learning)

Anticoagulant Drugs
   Narrower   Heparin
   Related   Blood Coagulation Disorders
                 Drugs/

Anticonvulsive Drugs
   Narrower   Calcium Bromide
                 Chloral Hydrate
                 Diphenylhydantoin
                 Pentobarbital
                 Phenobarbital
                 Primidone
                 Sodium Bromide
   Related   Anesthetic Drugs
                 Antiepileptic Drugs
                 Antispasmodic Drugs
                 Barbiturates
                 CNS Depressant Drugs
                 Convulsions
                 Drugs/
                 Hypnotic Drugs
                 Muscle Relaxing Drugs
                 Narcotic Drugs
                 Sedatives
                 Spasms
                 Tranquilizing Drugs

Antidepressant Drugs
   Narrower   Amitriptyline
                 Desipramine
                 Imipramine
                 Iproniazid
                 Isocarboxazid
                 Lithium Carbonate
                 Methylphenidate
                 Nialamide
                 Phenelzine
                 Pheniprazine

Antidepressant Drugs — (Continued)
Narrower
- Pipradrol
- Tranylcypromine

Related
- Antipsychotic Drugs
- CNS Stimulating Drugs
- Depression (Emotion)
- Drugs/
- Monoamine Oxidase Inhibitors
- Psychic Energizers

Antidiabetic Agents
Use Hypoglycemic Agents

Antiemetic Drugs
Used For Antinauseant Drugs
Narrower
- Carphenazine
- Chlorpromazine
- Chlorprothixene
- Fluphenazine
- Perphenazine
- Prochlorperazine
- Promethazine
- Sulpiride

Related
- Cholinergic Blocking Drugs
- Drugs/
- Hypnotic Drugs
- Nausea
- Sedatives
- Tranquilizing Drugs
- Vomiting

Antiepileptic Drugs
Narrower
- Diphenylhydantoin
- Potassium Bromide
- Primidone
- Sodium Bromide
- Strontium Bromide

Related
- Acetazolamide
- Anticonvulsive Drugs
- CNS Depressant Drugs
- Drugs/
- Epilepsy

Antihistaminic Drugs
Narrower
- Chlorpheniramine
- Chlorprothixene
- Diphenhydramine
- Orphenadrine
- Promethazine

Related
- Drugs/
- Histamine
- Hydroxyzine
- Hypnotic Drugs
- Sedatives

Antihypertensive Drugs
Narrower
- Chlorisondamine
- Chlorpromazine
- Guanethidine
- Hexamethonium
- Hydralazine

Antihypertensive Drugs — (Continued)
Narrower
- Iproniazid
- Mecamylamine
- Methyldopa
- Pargyline
- Phenoxybenzamine
- Rauwolfia
- Reserpine

Related
- Adrenergic Blocking Drugs
- Diuretics
- Drugs/
- Ganglion Blocking Drugs
- Heart Rate Affecting Drugs
- Hypertension
- Hypnotic Drugs
- Muscle Relaxing Drugs
- Sedatives
- Tranquilizing Drugs
- Vasodilator Drugs

Antinauseant Drugs
Use Antiemetic Drugs

Antiparkinsonian Drugs
Use Antitremor Drugs

Antipathy
Use Aversion

Antipsychotic Drugs
Narrower
- Antischizophrenic Drugs
- Butyrylperazine
- Carphenazine
- Chlorpromazine
- Chlorprothixene
- Fluphenazine
- Nialamide
- Perphenazine
- Prochlorperazine
- Promazine
- Reserpine
- Tetrabenazine
- Trifluoperazine
- Triflupromazine

Related
- Antidepressant Drugs
- Drugs/
- Neuroleptic Drugs
- Psychosis

Antischizophrenic Drugs
Broader Antipsychotic Drugs
Narrower
- Butyrylperazine
- Carphenazine
- Chlorpromazine
- Chlorprothixene
- Fluphenazine
- Perphenazine
- Prochlorperazine
- Promazine
- Trifluoperazine
- Triflupromazine

Antischizophrenic Drugs — (Continued)
Related	Phenothiazine Derivatives
	Schizophrenia

Antisemitism
Broader	Race Attitudes
Related	Prejudice
	Racism

Antisocial Behavior
Used For	Deviant Behavior
	Sociopathology
Broader	Behavior Disorders
Narrower	Battered Child Syndrome
	Child Abuse
	Crime
	Homicide
	Juvenile Delinquency
	Rape
	Recidivism
	Runaway Behavior
	Shoplifting
	Theft
Related	Antisocial Personality

Antisocial Personality
Used For	Psychopath
	Sociopath
Broader	Personality Disorders
Related	Antisocial Behavior

Antispasmodic Drugs
Narrower	Atropine
	Chlorprothixene
	Hyoscyamine (L-)
	Meperidine
	Nitroglycerin
	Orphenadrine
	Papaverine
	Trihexyphenidyl
Related	Anticonvulsive Drugs
	Muscle Relaxing Drugs
	Spasms

Antitremor Drugs
Used For	Antiparkinsonian Drugs
Narrower	Diphenhydramine
	Orphenadrine
	Trihexyphenidyl
Related	Drugs/
	Parkinsons Disease
	Tremor

Antitubercular Drugs
Narrower	Iproniazid
	Isoniazid
Related	Drugs/
	Tuberculosis

Antitubocurarine Drugs
Narrower	Neostigmine

Antitubocurarine Drugs — (Continued)
Related	Curare
	Drugs/
	Tubocurarine

Antonyms
Broader	Language
	Linguistics
	Verbal Communication
	Vocabulary

Ants
Broader	Arthropoda
	Insects
	Invertebrates
Related	Larvae

Anxiety
Used For	Angst
	Anxiousness
	Apprehension
Narrower	Anxiety Neurosis
	Castration Anxiety
	Separation Anxiety
Related	Affective Disturbances
	Emotional States
	Emotions/
	Frustration
	Guilt
	Hypochondriasis
	Jealousy
	Stress
	Test Anxiety

Anxiety Neurosis
Broader	Anxiety
	Neurosis

Anxiety Reducing Drugs
Use	Tranquilizing Drugs

Anxiety Scale Questionnaire
Identifier	Self Analysis Form

Anxiousness
Use	Anxiety

Aorta
Broader	Arteries (Anatomy)
	Blood Vessels
	Cardiovascular System

Apache Indians
Use	American Indians

Apathy
Used For	Indifference
Related	Emotions/

Apes
Use	Primates (Nonhuman)

Aphagia
Broader	Pain
	Symptoms
Related	Appetite Disorders

Aphasia
Used For	Alexia
	Word Blindness (Aphasia)
	Word Deafness
Broader	Brain Disorders
	Central Nervous System Disorders
	Nervous System Disorders
Narrower	Acalculia
	Agraphia
Related	Agnosia
	Learning Disabilities
	Mental Disorders/
	Minimal Brain Disorders
	Minimally Brain Damaged
	Perceptual Disturbances
	Speech Disorders
	Speech Handicapped

Aphrodisiacs
Related	Cannabis

Apnea
Broader	Respiratory Distress
	Respiratory Tract Disorders
	Symptoms
Related	Neonatal Disorders

Apomorphine
Used For	Apomorphine Hydrochloride
Broader	Alkaloids
	Emetic Drugs
	Hypnotic Drugs
	Narcotic Drugs
	Opiates

Apomorphine Hydrochloride
Use	Apomorphine

Apoplexy
Use	Cerebrovascular Accidents

Appalachia

Apparatus
Used For	Devices (Experimental)
	Equipment
	Experimental Apparatus
Narrower	Accelerometers
	Amplifiers (Apparatus)
	Audiometers
	Cage Apparatus
	Cameras
	Computers
	Electrodes
	Generators (Apparatus)
	Incubators (Apparatus)
	Maze Pathways
	Mazes
	Memory Drums
	Metronomes
	Microscopes

Apparatus — (Continued)
Narrower	Oscilloscopes
	Polygraphs
	Shock Units
	Shuttle Box Grids
	Shuttle Box Hurdles
	Shuttle Boxes
	Skinner Boxes
	Sonar
	Stimulators (Apparatus)
	T Mazes
	Tachistoscopes
	Tape Recorders
	Timers (Apparatus)
	Transducers
	Transformers (Apparatus)
	Transistors (Apparatus)
	Vibrators (Apparatus)
	Videotape Recorders
	Volt Meters
	X Ray Equipment
	Yerkes Boxes
Related	Television

Apparent Distance
Broader	Distance Perception
	Spatial Perception

Apparent Movement
Used For	Stroboscopic Movement
Broader	Motion Perception
	Spatial Perception
Narrower	Autokinetic Illusion

Apparent Size
Used For	Size (Apparent)
Broader	Size Discrimination
	Spatial Perception

Apperception
Related	Attention
	Perception/

Appetite
Used For	Craving
Narrower	Hunger
Related	Appetite Depressing Drugs
	Appetite Disorders
	Eating
	Physiology/
	Satiation

Appetite Depressing Drugs
Used For	Anorexigenic Drugs
Narrower	Amphetamine
	Dextroamphetamine
	Phenmetrazine
Related	Appetite
	Drugs/

Appetite Disorders
Broader	Symptoms

Appetite Disorders — (Continued)

Narrower	Anorexia Nervosa
	Hyperphagia
	Obesity
Related	Aphagia
	Appetite
	Nausea
	Nutritional Deficiencies
	Underweight

Applied Psychology

Broader	Psychology
	Sciences
	Social Sciences
Narrower	Clinical Psychology
	Community Psychology
	Consumer Psychology
	Counseling Psychology
	Educational Psychology
	Engineering Psychology
	Industrial Psychology
	Medical Psychology
	Military Psychology
	School Psychology
	Social Psychology

Apprehension

Use	Anxiety

Apprenticeship

Broader	Personnel Training

Approval (Social)

Use	Social Approval

Apraxia

Used For	Akinesia
Broader	Symptoms

Aptitude

Use	Ability/

Aptitude (Academic)

Use	Academic Aptitude

Aptitude Measures

Used For	Ability Tests
	Test (Aptitude)
Related	Measurement/
Identifier	Army General Classification Test
	Coll Ent Exam Bd Scholastic Apt Test
	Differential Aptitude Tests
	General Aptitude Test Battery
	Graduate Record Examination
	Modern Language Aptitude Test
	School And College Ability Test
	SRA Primary Mental Abilities Test

Arachnida

Used For	Spiders

Arachnida — (Continued)

Broader	Arthropoda
	Invertebrates

Arachnoiditis

Broader	Central Nervous System Disorders
	Meningitis
	Nervous System Disorders

Arapaho Indians

Use	American Indians

Architects

Broader	Business And Industrial Personnel
Related	Personnel/

Architecture

Broader	Arts
Related	Environment
	Religious Buildings
	Urban Planning

Arecoline

Used For	Arecoline Hydrobromide
Broader	Cholinomimetic Drugs
Related	Bromides

Arecoline Hydrobromide

Use	Arecoline

Arguments

Broader	Aggressive Behavior
	Conflict
	Interpersonal Communication
	Interpersonal Interaction
	Social Behavior
	Social Interaction

Arithmetic

Use	Mathematics Education

Arm (Anatomy)

Broader	Musculoskeletal System
Related	Elbow (Anatomy)
	Hand (Anatomy)
	Shoulder (Anatomy)
	Wrist

Army General Classification Test

(See)	Aptitude Measures

Army Personnel

Broader	Government Personnel
	Military Personnel
Related	Draftees
	National Guardsmen

Arousal (Physiological)

Use	Physiological Arousal

Arousal (Sexual)

Use	Psychosexual Behavior

Arrest (Law)

Use	Legal Arrest

Arrhythmias (Heart)
Broader	Cardiovascular Disorders
	Heart Disorders
Narrower	Bradycardia
	Fibrillation (Heart)
	Tachycardia

Art
Used For	Artwork
Broader	Arts
Narrower	Crafts
	Drawing
	Painting (Art)
	Photographic Art
	Sculpturing

Art Education
Broader	Curriculum

Art Therapy
Broader	Recreation Therapy

Arterial Pulse
Used For	Pulse (Arterial)
Related	Blood Circulation

Arteries (Anatomy)
Used For	Coronary Vessels
	Retinal Vessels
Broader	Blood Vessels
	Cardiovascular System
Narrower	Aorta
	Carotid Arteries

Arteriosclerosis
Broader	Cardiovascular Disorders
Narrower	Atherosclerosis
	Cerebral Arteriosclerosis
Related	Blood Pressure Disorders

Arthritis
Used For	Rheumatism
Broader	Joint Disorders
	Musculoskeletal Disorders
Narrower	Rheumatoid Arthritis
Related	Infectious Disorders
	Psychosomatic Disorders

Arthropoda
Broader	Invertebrates
Narrower	Ants
	Arachnida
	Bees
	Beetles
	Butterflies
	Cockroaches
	Crabs
	Crayfish
	Crustacea
	Diptera
	Drosophila
	Grasshoppers
	Insects
	Larvae

Arthropoda — (Continued)
Narrower	
	Mantis
	Moths

Articulation (Speech)
Broader	Speech Characteristics
	Verbal Communication
Related	Pronunciation

Articulation Disorders
Broader	Speech Disorders
Narrower	Dysarthria
	Stammering
	Stuttering
Related	Speech Handicapped

Artificial Limbs
Use	Prostheses

Artificial Pacemakers
Used For	Pacemakers (Artificial)
Broader	Medical Therapeutic Devices

Artificial Respiration
Used For	Life Saving
	Respiration (Artificial)
Broader	Physical Treatment Methods
Related	Respiration
	Respiratory System
	Respiratory Tract Disorders

Artistic Ability
Narrower	Musical Ability
Related	Ability/

Artists
Related	Personnel/

Arts
Narrower	Architecture
	Art
	Autobiography
	Biography
	Crafts
	Dance
	Drama
	Drawing
	Literature
	Motion Pictures (Entertainment)
	Music
	Musical Instruments
	Painting (Art)
	Photographic Art
	Poetry
	Prose
	Sculpturing
	Theatre
Related	Aesthetics

Artwork
Use	Art

Asceticism
Broader	Philosophies
	Religious Practices
Related	Religious Beliefs

Ascorbic Acid
Used For	Vitamin C
Broader	Acids
	Vitamins

Ashkenazim
Use	Judaism

Asia

Aspartic Acid
Broader	Acids
	Amino Acids

Asphyxia
Use	Anoxia

Aspiration Level
Related	Aspirations

Aspirations
Used For	Ambition
	Objectives
Narrower	Educational Aspirations
	Occupational Aspirations
Related	Aspiration Level
	Goals

Aspirin
Used For	Acetylsalicylic Acid
Broader	Acids
	Analgesic Drugs

Assassination (Political)
Use	Political Assassination

Assertiveness
Broader	Personality Traits

Assessment
Use	Measurement/

Assimilation (Cultural)
Use	Cultural Assimilation

Assistance (Social Behavior)
Broader	Interpersonal Interaction
	Social Behavior
	Social Interaction
Related	Charitable Behavior

Association Learning (Paired)
Use	Paired Associate Learning

Associationism
Broader	History of Psychology

Associations (Contextual)
Use	Contextual Associations

Associations (Groups)
Use	Organizations

Associations (Word)
Use	Word Associations

Associative Processes
Used For	Processes (Associative)
Broader	Cognitive Processes
Narrower	Cognitive Contiguity
	Connotations
	Contextual Associations
Related	Cognitive Generalization
	Cues
	Word Associations

Asthenia
Broader	Symptoms
Narrower	Myasthenia
Related	Asthenic Personality
	Neurasthenic Neurosis

Asthenic Personality
Broader	Personality Disorders
Related	Asthenia
	Neurasthenic Neurosis

Asthma
Broader	Dyspnea
	Respiratory Tract Disorders
Related	Immunologic Disorders
	Psychosomatic Disorders

Astrology

Astronauts
Broader	Aerospace Personnel
Related	Aircraft Pilots
	Military Personnel
	Spacecraft

Asylums
Use	Psychiatric Hospitals

Ataractic Drugs
Use	Tranquilizing Drugs

Ataraxic Drugs
Use	Tranquilizing Drugs

Ataxia
Used For	Dysmetria
Broader	Central Nervous System Disorders
	Nervous System Disorders
	Symptoms
Related	Hyperkinesis

Atheism
Broader	Religious Beliefs
Related	Agnosticism

Atherosclerosis
Broader	Arteriosclerosis
	Cardiovascular Disorders

Athetosis
Broader	Brain Disorders

Athetosis — (Continued)
Broader	Central Nervous System Disorders
	Nervous System Disorders
Related	Cerebral Palsy

Athletes
Related	Athletic Participation
	Sports

Athletic Participation
Broader	Recreation
Related	Athletes
	Extracurricular Activities
	Sports

Atlas (Stereotaxic)
Use	Stereotaxic Atlas

Atmospheric Conditions
Used For	Barometric Pressure
	Pressure (Barometric)
Broader	Environmental Effects
Related	Pollution
	Temperature Effects
	Thermal Acclimatization

Atomism
Use	Reductionism

Atria (Heart)
Use	Heart Auricles

Atrophy (Muscular)
Use	Muscular Atrophy

Atropine
Used For	Hyoscyamine (Dl-)
	Methylatropine
Broader	Alkaloids
	Amines
	Analgesic Drugs
	Antispasmodic Drugs
	Cholinergic Blocking Drugs
	Mydriatic Drugs
	Narcotic Drugs
	Sedatives
Related	Hyoscyamine (L-)

Attack Behavior
Broader	Aggressive Behavior
	Animal Aggressive Behavior
	Animal Ethology
	Animal Social Behavior
	Social Behavior

Attainment (Achievement)
Use	Achievement

Attempted Suicide
Used For	Suicide (Attempted)
Broader	Behavior Disorders
Related	Suicide
	Suicide Prevention

Attendance (School)
Use	School Attendance

Attendants (Institutions)
Used For	Hospital Attendants
	Residential Care Attendants
Broader	Medical Personnel
	Paramedical Personnel
	Paraprofessional Personnel
Related	Prison Personnel
	Psychiatric Hospital Staff

Attention
Broader	Awareness
	Consciousness States
Narrower	Divided Attention
	Monitoring
	Selective Attention
	Vigilance
Related	Apperception
	Attention Span
	Human Channel Capacity
	Perception/
	Rotary Pursuit
	Signal Detection (Perception)
	Tracking

Attention Span
Related	Attention
	Vigilance

Attenuation (Stimulus)
Use	Stimulus Attenuation

Attitude Change
Used For	Opinion Change
Related	Attitudes/

Attitude Formation
Related	Attitudes/

Attitude Inventories
Use	Attitude Measures

Attitude Measurement
Related	Attitude Measures
	Attitudes/
	Measurement/

Attitude Measures
Used For	Attitude Inventories
	Attitude Tests
	Inventories (Attitude)
	Opinion Questionnaires
	Opinion Surveys
	Questionnaires (Attitude)
	Questionnaires (Opinion)
	Scales (Attitude)
	Surveys (Opinion)
Related	Attitude Measurement
	Measurement/
Identifier	Allport Vernon Lindzey Study Values

Attitude Measures — (Continued)
Identifier
> Minnesota Teacher Attitude Inventory
> Opinion Attitude And Interest Survey
> Parent Attitude Research Instrument
> Rehab Counselor Judgement Scale
> Situational Attitude Scale
> Wilson Patterson Conservatism Scale
> Work Attitude Scale

Attitude Similarity
Related   Attitudes/

Attitude Tests
Use   Attitude Measures

Attitudes/
Used For   Opinions
Related   Alcohol Drinking Attitudes
> Attitude Change
> Attitude Formation
> Attitude Measurement
> Attitude Similarity
> Attribution
> Childrearing Attitudes
> Community Attitudes
> Consumer Attitudes
> Counselor Attitudes
> Death Attitudes
> Drug Usage Attitudes
> Employee Attitudes
> Employer Attitudes
> Family Planning Attitudes
> Handicapped (Attitudes Toward)
> Hedonism
> Job Applicant Attitudes
> Marriage Attitudes
> Occupational Attitudes
> Parental Attitudes
> Political Attitudes
> Prejudice
> Psychotherapist Attitudes
> Public Opinion
> Race Attitudes
> Religious Beliefs
> Sexual Attitudes
> Socioeconomic Class Attitudes
> Stereotyped Attitudes
> Student Attitudes
> Teacher Attitudes
> Work (Attitudes Toward)

Attorneys
Used For   Lawyers
Related   Law Enforcement Personnel
> Personnel/

Attraction (Interpersonal)
Use   Interpersonal Attraction

Attribution
Broader   Social Behavior
> Social Perception
Related   Attitudes/

Audiences
Related   Observers

Audiology
Broader   Paramedical Sciences

Audiometers
Broader   Apparatus

Audiometry
Used For   Auditory Measurement
> Bekesy Audiometry
Narrower   Bone Conduction Audiometry
Related   Auditory Stimulation
> Perceptual Measures

Audiotapes
Broader   Audiovisual Communications Media
> Communications Media

Audiovisual Aids (Educational)
Use   Educational Audiovisual Aids

Audiovisual Communications Media
Broader   Communications Media
Narrower   Audiotapes
> Closed Circuit Television
> Educational Audiovisual Aids
> Educational Television
> Film Strips
> Motion Pictures
> Motion Pictures (Educational)
> Motion Pictures (Entertainment)
> Photographs
> Radio
> Television
> Television Advertising
> Videotapes

Audiovisual Instruction
Broader   Teaching
> Teaching Methods
Narrower   Televised Instruction
> Videotape Instruction
Related   Educational Audiovisual Aids

Audition
Use   Auditory Perception

Auditory Cortex
Used For   Cortex (Auditory)
Broader   Brain
> Central Nervous System
> Cerebral Cortex
> Nervous System

Auditory Cortex — (Continued)
Broader
        Telencephalon
        Temporal Lobe

Auditory Discrimination
Broader   Auditory Perception
Narrower Loudness Discrimination
        Pitch Discrimination

Auditory Displays
Broader   Displays

Auditory Evoked Potentials
Broader   Electrical Activity
        Electrophysiology
        Evoked Potentials
Related   Cortical Evoked Potentials

Auditory Feedback
Broader   Auditory Stimulation
        Feedback
        Perceptual Stimulation
        Sensory Feedback
Narrower Delayed Auditory Feedback

Auditory Hallucinations
Broader   Hallucinations
        Perceptual Disturbances

Auditory Localization
Used For Localization (Sound)
        Sound Localization
Broader   Auditory Perception
        Perceptual Localization

Auditory Masking
Broader   Masking
Related   Auditory Stimulation

Auditory Measurement
Use   Audiometry

Auditory Neurons
Broader   Cells (Biology)
        Nervous System
        Neurons
        Sensory Neurons

Auditory Perception
Used For Audition
        Listening
Narrower Auditory Discrimination
        Auditory Localization
        Loudness Discrimination
        Loudness Perception
        Pitch Discrimination
        Pitch Perception
        Speech Perception
Related   Auditory Thresholds
        Ear Disorders
        Perception/

Auditory Stimulation
Used For Acoustic Stimuli
        Noise (Sound)
        Sound
Broader   Perceptual Stimulation
        Stimulation
Narrower Auditory Feedback
        Delayed Auditory Feedback
        Filtered Noise
        Loudness
        Noise Levels (Work Areas)
        Pitch (Frequency)
        Speech Pitch
        Ultrasound
        White Noise
Related   Audiometry
        Auditory Masking
        Bone Conduction Audiometry
        Echoes
        Speech Processing (Mechanical)

Auditory Thresholds
Used For Loudness Threshold
Broader   Thresholds
Related   Auditory Perception
        Perceptual Measures

Aunts
Broader   Family Members

Aura
Broader   Symptoms
Related   Epilepsy

Aurally Handicapped
Used For Special Education (Aurally
          Handicap)
Broader   Handicapped
Narrower Deaf
        Partially Hearing Impaired
Related   Ear Disorders

Auricles (Heart)
Use   Heart Auricles

Auricular Fibrillation
Use   Fibrillation (Heart)

Australia

Austria

Authoritarianism
Used For Dogmatism
        Domination
Broader   Personality Traits

Authoritarianism (Parental)
Use   Parental Permissiveness

Authoritarianism Rebellion Scale
   (See)   Nonprojective Personality Measures
                Personality Measures

Authority

Autism
   Narrower   Early Infantile Autism
   Related   Autistic Children
              Autistic Thinking
              Mental Disorders/

Autistic Children
   Broader   Emotionally Disturbed
              Handicapped
   Related   Autism
              Childhood Psychosis
              Early Infantile Autism

Autistic Thinking
   Broader   Thinking
              Thought Disturbances
   Related   Autism

Autobiography
   Broader   Arts
              Biography
              Literature
              Prose

Autoeroticism
   Use   Masturbation

Autogenic Training
   Used For   Training (Autogenic)
   Broader   Psychotherapeutic Techniques

Autohypnosis
   Broader   Consciousness Disturbances
              Hypnosis
   Related   Catalepsy

Autoimmune Disorders
   Use   Immunologic Disorders

Autokinetic Illusion
   Used For   Illusion (Autokinetic)
   Broader   Apparent Movement
              Motion Perception
              Spatial Perception
              Vision
              Visual Perception

Automated Information Coding
   Broader   Automated Information Processing

Automated Information Processing
   Used For   Information Processing (Automated)
   Narrower   Automated Information Coding
              Automated Information Retrieval
              Automated Information Storage

Automated Information Processing — (Continued)
   Related   Communication Systems
              Information/

Automated Information Retrieval
   Used For   Information Retrieval (Automated)
   Broader   Automated Information Processing
   Related   Automated Information Storage
              Information/

Automated Information Storage
   Broader   Automated Information Processing
   Related   Automated Information Retrieval
              Information/

Automation
   Related   Computers

Automatism
   Broader   Symptoms

Automobile Accidents
   Use   Motor Traffic Accidents

Automobile Safety
   Use   Highway Safety

Automobiles
   Used For   Cars
              Motor Vehicles
   Broader   Ground Transportation
              Transportation
   Related   Drivers

Autonomic Fibers (Postganglionic)
   Use   Autonomic Ganglia

Autonomic Fibers (Preganglionic)
   Use   Autonomic Ganglia

Autonomic Ganglia
   Used For   Autonomic Fibers (Postganglionic)
              Autonomic Fibers (Preganglionic)
              Celiac Plexus
              Hypogastric Plexus
              Myenteric Plexus
              Postganglionic Autonomic Fibers
              Preganglionic Autonomic Fibers
              Stellate Ganglion
              Submucous Plexus
   Broader   Autonomic Nervous System
              Ganglia
              Nervous System

Autonomic Nervous System
   Broader   Nervous System
   Narrower   Adrenergic Nerves
              Autonomic Ganglia
              Carotid Body

Autonomic Nervous System — (Continued)
Narrower
        Cholinergic Nerves
        Nonchromaffin Paraganglia
        Parasympathetic Nervous System
        Sympathetic Nervous System
        Vagus Nerve
Related   Autonomic Nervous System Disorders

Autonomic Nervous System Disorders
Broader   Nervous System Disorders
Narrower Dysautonomia
Related   Autonomic Nervous System

Autonomy (Government)
Related   Government

Autopsy
Broader   Physical Treatment Methods
           Surgery
Related   Medical Diagnosis

Autoregulation
Use   Homeostasis

Autosome Disorders
Broader   Chromosome Disorders
           Genetic Disorders
Narrower Crying Cat Syndrome
           Downs Syndrome
           Neonatal Autosome Disorders
           Trisomy 18
           Trisomy 21
Related   Autosomes

Autosomes
Broader   Chromosomes
Related   Autosome Disorders

Aversion
Used For Antipathy
           Dislike
Narrower Hate
Related   Emotions/

Aversion Therapy
Broader   Behavior Modification
           Behavior Therapy
Related   Counterconditioning
           Shock Therapy

Aversive Stimulation
Broader   Stimulation

Aviation
Narrower Flight Instrumentation
           Spaceflight
Related   Acceleration Effects
           Altitude Effects
           Aviation Safety
           Gravitational Effects
           Monitoring

Aviation Safety
Broader   Safety
Narrower Air Traffic Control
Related   Air Traffic Accidents
           Aircraft Pilots
           Aviation
           Transportation Accidents

Aviators
Use   Aircraft Pilots

Avoidance
Used For Escape
Related   Avoidance Conditioning

Avoidance Conditioning
Used For Active Avoidance
           Conditioning (Avoidance)
           Passive Avoidance
Broader   Conditioning
           Operant Conditioning
Related   Avoidance

Awareness
Broader   Consciousness States
Narrower Attention
           Divided Attention
           Monitoring
           Selective Attention
           Vigilance

Axons
Broader   Cells (Biology)
           Nervous System
           Neurons

Babbling
Use   Infant Vocalization

Babies
Use   Infants

Babinski Reflex
Broader   Reflexes

Baboons
Broader   Mammals
           Primates (Nonhuman)
           Vertebrates

Back (Anatomy)
Narrower Lumbosacral Region
Related   Anatomy/

Background (Family)
Use   Family Background

Backward Masking
Use   Masking

Bacterial Disorders
Broader   Infectious Disorders
Narrower Bacterial Meningitis
           Gonorrhea
           Pulmonary Tuberculosis
           Syphilis

Bacterial Disorders — (Continued)
Narrower
    Tetanus (Disease)
    Tuberculosis
Related Disorders/
    Pneumonia
    Rheumatic Fever

Bacterial Meningitis
Broader Bacterial Disorders
    Central Nervous System Disorders
    Infectious Disorders
    Infectious Meningitis
    Meningitis
    Nervous System Disorders

Badminton
Broader Recreation
    Sports

Bahama Islands

Balance
Use Equilibrium

Ballet
Use Dance

Bannister Repertory Grid
(See) Nonprojective Personality Measures
    Personality Measures

Barbados

Barbital
Broader Barbiturates
    CNS Affecting Drugs
    CNS Depressant Drugs
    Hypnotic Drugs
    Sedatives

Barbiturate Poisoning
Broader Toxic Disorders
Related Analeptic Drugs
    Barbiturates

Barbiturates
Narrower Amobarbital
    Barbital
    Hexobarbital
    Methohexital
    Pentobarbital
    Phenobarbital
    Secobarbital
    Thiopental
Related Anesthetic Drugs
    Anticonvulsive Drugs
    Barbiturate Poisoning
    CNS Depressant Drugs
    Drug Dependency
    Drugs/

Barbiturates — (Continued)
Related
    Hypnotic Drugs
    Primidone
    Sedatives

Bargaining
Broader Interpersonal Communication
    Interpersonal Interaction
    Negotiation
    Social Behavior
    Social Interaction

Barium
Broader Chemical Elements
    Metallic Elements

Barometric Pressure
Use Atmospheric Conditions

Baroreceptors
Used For Pressoreceptors
Broader Nerve Endings
    Nervous System
    Neural Receptors

Barrett Lennard Relationship Invent
(See) Nonprojective Personality Measures
    Personality Measures

Barron Welsh Art Scale
(See) Nonprojective Personality Measures
    Personality Measures

Basal Ganglia
Broader Brain
    Central Nervous System
    Cerebral Cortex
    Ganglia
    Nervous System
    Telencephalon
Narrower Amygdaloid Body
    Caudate Nucleus
    Globus Pallidus

Basal Metabolism
Broader Metabolism

Basal Readers
Use Reading Materials

Basal Skin Resistance
Broader Electrophysiology
    Skin Electrical Properties
    Skin Resistance

Baseball
Broader Recreation
    Sports

Basketball
Broader Recreation
    Sports

Bass (Fish)
Broader   Fishes
            Vertebrates

Bass Famous Sayings Test
(See)   Nonprojective Personality Measures
            Personality Measures

Bats
Broader   Mammals
            Vertebrates

Battered Child Syndrome
Broader   Antisocial Behavior
            Behavior Disorders
            Child Abuse
            Syndromes

Bayes Theorem
Use   Statistical Probability

Beavers
Broader   Mammals
            Rodents
            Vertebrates

Beer
Broader   Alcoholic Beverages

Bees
Broader   Arthropoda
            Insects
            Invertebrates
Related   Larvae

Beetles
Broader   Arthropoda
            Insects
            Invertebrates
Related   Larvae

Behavior Change
Related   Behavior Modification

Behavior Disorders
Narrower   Addiction
            Alcoholism
            Antisocial Behavior
            Attempted Suicide
            Battered Child Syndrome
            Cheating
            Child Abuse
            Confabulation
            Crime
            Deception
            Drug Abuse
            Drug Addiction
            Head Banging
            Heroin Addiction
            Homicide
            Juvenile Delinquency
            Korsakoffs Psychosis
            Malingering
            Nail Biting

Behavior Disorders — (Continued)
Narrower
            Pathological Lying
            Rape
            Recidivism
            Self Mutilation
            Shoplifting
            Suicide
            Tantrums
            Theft
            Truancy
            Wernickes Syndrome
Related   Acting Out
            Aggressive Behavior
            Behavior Problems
            Body Rocking
            Disorders/
            Drug Usage
            Faking
            Fecal Incontinence
            Hair Pulling
            Mental Disorders/
            Symptoms
            Thumbsucking
            Urinary Incontinence

Behavior Modification
Narrower   Aversion Therapy
            Behavior Therapy
            Classroom Behavior Modification
            Contingency Management
            Implosive Therapy
            Reciprocal Inhibition Therapy
            Systematic Desensitization Therapy
            Token Economy Programs
Related   Behavior Change
            Counterconditioning
            Treatment/

Behavior Problems
Used For   Disruptive Behavior
            Misbehavior
            Misconduct
Related   Behavior Disorders

Behavior Therapy
Broader   Behavior Modification
Narrower   Aversion Therapy
            Implosive Therapy
            Reciprocal Inhibition Therapy
            Systematic Desensitization Therapy
Related   Counterconditioning
            Psychotherapy

Behavior/

Behavioral Sciences
Use   Social Sciences

Behaviorism
    Broader   History of Psychology

Bekesy Audiometry
    Use   Audiometry

Belgium

Beliefs (Religion)
    Use   Religious Beliefs

Bemegride
    Broader   Analeptic Drugs
                 CNS Affecting Drugs
                 CNS Stimulating Drugs

Benactyzine
    Used For   Benactyzine Hydrochloride
    Broader   Cholinergic Blocking Drugs
                 Tranquilizing Drugs

Benactyzine Hydrochloride
    Use   Benactyzine

Benadryl
    Use   Diphenhydramine

Bender Gestalt Test
    (See)   Personality Measures
                 Projective Personality Measures
                 Projective Techniques

Bene Anthony Family Relations Test
    (See)   Nonprojective Personality Measures
                 Personality Measures

Benign Neoplasms
    Broader   Neoplasms

Benton Revised Visual Retention Test
    (See)   Intelligence Measures

Benzedrine
    Use   Amphetamine

Beverages (Alcohol)
    Use   Alcoholic Beverages

Bias (Experimenter)
    Use   Experimenter Bias

Bias (Response)
    Use   Response Bias

Biased Sampling
    Broader   Sampling (Experimental)
    Related   Experiment Volunteers
                 Experimentation/

Bible
    Broader   Religious Literature
    Related   Christianity
                 Judaism
                 Religious Beliefs

Bibliography

Bibliotherapy
    Related   Treatment/

Bile
    Broader   Body Fluids

Bilingualism
    Broader   Language
                 Multilingualism
                 Verbal Communication

Binocular Vision
    Broader   Vision
                 Visual Perception

Binomial Distribution
    Broader   Chance (Fortune)
                 Probability
                 Statistical Analysis
                 Statistical Measurement
                 Statistical Probability

Biochemistry
    Broader   Chemistry
                 Sciences
    Narrower   Neurochemistry

Biofeedback
    Broader   Feedback
    Related   Conditioning
                 Reinforcement
                 Stimulation

Biographical Inventories
    Broader   Inventories

Biography
    Broader   Arts
                 Literature
                 Prose
    Narrower   Autobiography

Biological Clocks (Animal)
    Use   Animal Biological Rhythms

Biological Rhythms
    Narrower   Animal Biological Rhythms
                 Animal Circadian Rhythms
                 Human Biological Rhythms
    Related   Seasonal Variations

Biological Rhythms (Animal)
    Use   Animal Biological Rhythms

Biological Symbiosis
    Used For   Symbiosis (Biological)
    Related   Animals/
                 Biology

Biology
    Broader   Sciences
    Narrower   Botany
                 Neurobiology
                 Zoology
    Related   Biological Symbiosis
                 Biosynthesis
                 Phylogenesis

Biopsy
Broader	Diagnosis
	Medical Diagnosis
Related	Surgery

Biosynthesis
Related	Biology
	Physiology/

Birds
Used For	Fowl
Broader	Vertebrates
Narrower	Blackbirds
	Budgerigars
	Canaries
	Chickens
	Doves
	Ducks
	Geese
	Penguins
	Pigeons
	Quails
	Robins
	Sea Gulls

Birth
Used For	Childbirth
	Parturition
Narrower	Premature Birth
Related	Birth Injuries
	Birth Rites
	Birth Trauma
	Labor (Childbirth)
	Pregnancy
	Sexual Reproduction

Birth Control
Used For	Contraception
	Contraceptive Methods
	Population Control
Broader	Family Planning
Narrower	Coitus Interruptus
	Contraceptive Devices
	Diaphragms (Birth Control)
	Intrauterine Devices
	Oral Contraceptives
	Tubal Ligation
	Vasectomy
Related	Induced Abortion
	Overpopulation
	Rhythm Method
	Sexual Abstinence
	Sterilization (Sex)

Birth Injuries
Used For	Injuries (Birth)
Broader	Injuries
Related	Birth
	Birth Trauma
	Neonatal Disorders

Birth Order
Broader	Family Structure

Birth Rites
Used For	Circumcision
Broader	Rites of Passage
	Sociocultural Factors
Related	Birth

Birth Trauma
Related	Birth
	Birth Injuries

Bisexuality
Broader	Homosexuality
	Psychosexual Behavior
Related	Lesbianism
	Male Homosexuality
	Pedophilia
	Transsexualism
	Transvestism

Bitterness
Use	Taste Stimulation

Black Power Movement
Used For	Negro Militancy
Broader	Social Movements
Related	Activist Movements

Blackbirds
Broader	Birds
	Vertebrates

Blacks
Use	Negroes

Blacky Pictures Test
(See)	Personality Measures
	Projective Personality Measures
	Projective Techniques

Bladder
Broader	Urinary Tract
	Urogenital System

Blind
Broader	Handicapped
	Visually Handicapped

Blindness (Color)
Use	Color Blindness

Blood
Broader	Body Fluids
Narrower	Blood Plasma
	Blood Serum
Related	Blood and Lymphatic Disorders
	Heart

Blood and Lymphatic Disorders
Used For	Blood Disorders
	Hematologic Disorders
	Lymphatic Disorders
Narrower	Anemia
	Blood Coagulation Disorders
	Blood Group Incompatibility

Blood and Lymphatic Disorders — (Continued)
Narrower
        Hemophilia
        Leukemias
        Malaria
        Porphyria
        Rh Incompatibility
        Toxoplasmosis
Related   Blood
        Disorders/
        Lymphatic System

Blood Cells
Broader   Cells (Biology)
Narrower Erythrocytes
        Leucocytes
        Lymphocytes

Blood Circulation
Used For Circulation (Blood)
Related   Arterial Pulse

Blood Coagulation
Used For Coagulation (Blood)
Related   Blood Coagulation Disorders

Blood Coagulation Disorders
Used For Coagulation Disorders (Blood)
Broader   Blood and Lymphatic Disorders
Narrower Hemophilia
Related   Anticoagulant Drugs
        Blood Coagulation
        Immunoglobulins
        Rh Incompatibility

Blood Disorders
Use   Blood and Lymphatic Disorders

Blood Flow

Blood Glucose
Use   Blood Sugar

Blood Group Incompatibility
Used For Incompatibility (Blood Group)
Broader   Blood and Lymphatic Disorders
        Immunologic Disorders
Narrower Rh Incompatibility
Related   Blood Groups

Blood Groups
Used For Groups (Blood)
Related   Blood Group Incompatibility

Blood Plasma
Used For Plasma (Blood)
Broader   Blood
        Body Fluids
Narrower Blood Serum

Blood Platelets
Used For Platelets (Blood)

Blood Pressure
Used For Pressure (Blood)

Blood Pressure — (Continued)
Narrower Diastolic Pressure
        Systolic Pressure
Related   Blood Pressure Disorders
        Vasoconstrictor Drugs
        Vasodilator Drugs

Blood Pressure Disorders
Broader   Cardiovascular Disorders
Narrower Essential Hypertension
        Hypertension
        Hypotension
        Syncope
Related   Arteriosclerosis
        Blood Pressure
        Disorders/
        Vasoconstriction
        Vasodilation

Blood Proteins
Used For Proteins (Blood)
Broader   Proteins
Narrower Gamma Globulin
        Hemoglobin
        Immunoglobulins
        Serum Albumin
        Taraxein

Blood Serum
Used For Serum (Blood)
Broader   Blood
        Blood Plasma
        Body Fluids
Related   Antibodies

Blood Sugar
Used For Blood Glucose
Broader   Carbohydrates
        Glucose
        Sugars

Blood Transfusion
Used For Transfusion (Blood)
Broader   Physical Treatment Methods
Related   Hemodialysis

Blood Vessels
Used For Vessels (Blood)
Broader   Cardiovascular System
Narrower Aorta
        Arteries (Anatomy)
        Capillaries (Anatomy)
        Carotid Arteries
        Veins (Anatomy)
Related   Lymph Vessels

Blood Volume
Used For Volume (Blood)

Blue Collar Workers
Used For Laborers (Construct And Indust)
Broader   Business And Industrial Personnel

Blue Collar Workers — (Continued)
Narrower	Industrial Foremen
	Skilled Industrial Workers
	Unskilled Industrial Workers
Related	Technical Service Personnel

Body (Pineal)
Use	Pineal Body

Body Fluids
Narrower	Amniotic Fluid
	Bile
	Blood
	Blood Plasma
	Blood Serum
	Cerebrospinal Fluid
	Lymph
	Mucus
	Saliva
	Sweat
	Urine
Related	Anatomy/
	Physiology/

Body Height
Used For	Height (Body)
Broader	Physique

Body Image
Used For	Image (Body)
Narrower	Body Image Disturbances
	Phantom Limbs

Body Image Disturbances
Broader	Body Image
Narrower	Phantom Limbs
Related	Castration Anxiety
	Mental Disorders/
	Surgery

Body Language
Broader	Interpersonal Communication
	Nonverbal Communication

Body Rocking
Used For	Rocking (Body)
Broader	Symptoms
Related	Behavior Disorders

Body Sway Testing
Related	Measurement/

Body Temperature
Used For	Temperature (Body)
Narrower	Skin Temperature
	Thermoregulation (Body)
Related	Physiology/

Body Types
Use	Somatotypes

Body Weight
Used For	Weight (Body)
Broader	Physique

Body Weight — (Continued)
Narrower	Obesity
	Underweight

Bone Conduction Audiometry
Broader	Audiometry
Related	Auditory Stimulation
	Perceptual Measures

Bone Disorders
Broader	Musculoskeletal Disorders
Narrower	Osteochondritis

Bone Marrow
Broader	Tissues (Body)
Related	Bone Marrow Cells
	Bones

Bone Marrow Cells
Broader	Cells (Biology)
Related	Bone Marrow

Bones
Broader	Connective Tissues
	Musculoskeletal System
	Tissues (Body)
Related	Bone Marrow
	Jaw
	Ribs
	Spinal Column

Bonuses
Broader	Employee Benefits
Related	Salaries
	Stock Options

Book

Books
Broader	Communications Media
	Printed Communications Media
Related	Mass Media

Borderline Mental Retardation
Broader	Mental Retardation
Related	Mental Disorders/
	Psychosocial Mental Retardation

Borderline Mentally Retarded
Use	Slow Learners

Boredom
Broader	Emotional States

Botany
Broader	Biology
	Sciences
Related	Phylogenesis

Bottle Feeding
Broader	Feeding Practices

Botulism
Broader	Toxic Disorders

Bourgeois
Use	Middle Class

Bowel Disorders
Use   Colon Disorders

Boxes (Shuttle)
Use   Shuttle Boxes

Boxes (Skinner)
Use   Skinner Boxes

Boxes (Yerkes)
Use   Yerkes Boxes

Brachial Plexus
Use   Spinal Nerves

Bradycardia
Broader   Arrhythmias (Heart)
            Cardiovascular Disorders
            Heart Disorders

Braille Instruction
Broader   Curriculum
Related   Visually Handicapped

Brain
Broader   Central Nervous System
            Nervous System
Narrower   Amygdaloid Body
            Auditory Cortex
            Basal Ganglia
            Brain Stem
            Caudate Nucleus
            Cerebellum
            Cerebral Cortex
            Cerebral Ventricles
            Corpora Quadrigemina
            Corpus Callosum
            Diencephalon
            Frontal Lobe
            Geniculate Bodies (Thalamus)
            Globus Pallidus
            Gyrus Cinguli
            Hippocampus
            Hypothalamo Hypophyseal System
            Hypothalamus
            Inferior Colliculus
            Limbic System
            Medulla Oblongata
            Mesencephalon
            Motor Cortex
            Occipital Lobe
            Optic Chiasm
            Optic Lobe
            Parietal Lobe
            Pons
            Reticular Formation
            Somatosensory Cortex
            Superior Colliculus
            Telencephalon
            Temporal Lobe
            Thalamic Nuclei

Brain — (Continued)
Narrower
            Thalamus
            Visual Cortex
Related   Brain Disorders
            Brain Size
            Brain Weight
            Cerebral Dominance
            Lateral Dominance
            Ocular Dominance

Brain Ablation
Use   Brain Lesions

Brain Concussion
Used For   Concussion (Brain)
Broader   Brain Damage
            Brain Disorders
            Central Nervous System Disorders
            Head Injuries
            Injuries
            Nervous System Disorders

Brain Damage
Used For   Brain Injuries
Broader   Brain Disorders
            Central Nervous System Disorders
            Nervous System Disorders
Narrower   Brain Concussion
            Brain Lesions
            Hypothalamus Lesions
Related   Brain Damaged
            Epilepsy
            Head Injuries
            Mental Retardation

Brain Damaged
Broader   Handicapped
Narrower   Minimally Brain Damaged
Related   Brain Damage
            Congenitally Handicapped

Brain Disorders
Used For   Brain Dysfunction
Broader   Central Nervous System Disorders
            Nervous System Disorders
Narrower   Acalculia
            Acute Alcoholic Intoxication
            Agraphia
            Alcohol Intoxication
            Alcoholic Hallucinosis
            Alcoholic Psychosis
            Alzheimers Disease
            Anencephaly
            Aphasia
            Athetosis
            Brain Concussion
            Brain Damage
            Brain Lesions

Brain Disorders — (Continued)
Narrower
    Brain Neoplasms
    Cerebral Palsy
    Cerebrovascular Accidents
    Chronic Alcoholic Intoxication
    Delirium Tremens
    Encephalitis
    Epilepsy
    Epileptic Seizures
    Grand Mal Epilepsy
    Hydrocephaly
    Hypothalamus Lesions
    Korsakoffs Psychosis
    Microcephaly
    Minimal Brain Disorders
    Organic Brain Syndromes
    Parkinsons Disease
    Petit Mal Epilepsy
    Picks Disease
    Presenile Dementia
    Senile Dementia
    Senile Psychosis
    Toxic Encephalopathies
    Toxic Psychoses
Related   Brain
    Convulsions

Brain Dysfunction
Use   Brain Disorders

Brain Injuries
Use   Brain Damage

Brain Lesions
Used For   Brain Ablation
    Cerebral Lesions
    Septum (Brain) Lesions
    Subcortical Lesions
Broader   Brain Damage
    Brain Disorders
    Central Nervous System Disorders
    Lesions
    Nervous System Disorders
Narrower   Hypothalamus Lesions
Related   Hemispherectomy
    Neurosurgery

Brain Mapping
Use   Stereotaxic Atlas

Brain Maps
Use   Stereotaxic Atlas

Brain Metabolism
Use   Neurochemistry

Brain Neoplasms
Broader   Brain Disorders
    Central Nervous System Disorders
    Neoplasms

Brain Neoplasms — (Continued)
Broader
    Nervous System Disorders
    Nervous System Neoplasms

Brain Size
Related   Brain
    Brain Weight

Brain Stem
Broader   Brain
    Central Nervous System
    Nervous System
Narrower   Medulla Oblongata
    Pons
    Reticular Formation

Brain Stimulation
Broader   Stereotaxic Techniques
    Stimulation
Narrower   Chemical Brain Stimulation
    Electrical Brain Stimulation
    Spreading Depression
Related   Physiological Arousal

Brain Weight
Related   Brain
    Brain Size

Bravery
Use   Courage

Brazil

Breakthrough (Psychotherapeutic)
Use   Psychotherapeutic Breakthrough

Breast
Related   Anatomy/

Breast Feeding
Broader   Feeding Practices
Related   Weaning

Breast Neoplasms
Used For   Mammary Neoplasms
Broader   Neoplasms
Related   Mastectomy

Breathing
Use   Respiration

Breeding (Animal)
Use   Animal Breeding

Brief Psychotherapy
Used For   Short Term Psychotherapy
Broader   Psychotherapy

Brightness Perception
Used For   Luminance Threshold
    Successive Contrast
Broader   Vision
    Visual Perception
Related   Illumination

Bromides
Narrower	Ammonium Bromide
	Calcium Bromide
	Lithium Bromide
	Potassium Bromide
	Sodium Bromide
	Strontium Bromide
Related	Arecoline
	Drugs/
	Homatropine
	Hyoscyamine (L-)
	Neostigmine
	Scopolamine

Bronchi
Broader	Respiratory System

Bronchial Disorders
Broader	Respiratory Tract Disorders
Related	Common Colds

Brothers
Broader	Family Members
	Siblings

Bruises
Use	Contusions

Buddhism
Broader	Religious Affiliation
	Religious Beliefs
Narrower	Zen Buddhism

Budgerigars
Broader	Birds
	Vertebrates

Budgets
Use	Costs And Cost Analysis

Bufotenine
Broader	Amines
	Hallucinogenic Drugs
	Vasoconstrictor Drugs

Buildings (Religious)
Use	Religious Buildings

Bulls
Use	Cattle

Burns
Broader	Injuries
Related	Electrical Injuries
	Wounds

Bush Babies
Use	Lemurs

Business
Used For	Commerce
	Industry
	Manufacturing
Related	Business Management
	Business Organizations
	Business Students

Business And Industrial Personnel
Used For	Businessmen
	Industrial Personnel
Narrower	Accountants
	Architects
	Blue Collar Workers
	Clerical Personnel
	Industrial Foremen
	Industrial Psychologists
	Management Personnel
	Middle Level Managers
	Sales Personnel
	Secretarial Personnel
	Skilled Industrial Workers
	Top Level Managers
	Unskilled Industrial Workers
	White Collar Workers
Related	Aerospace Personnel
	Agricultural Workers
	Engineers
	Government Personnel
	Personnel/
	Scientists/
	Technical Service Personnel

Business Education
Broader	Curriculum
Related	Business Management
	Education/
	Management Training
	Personnel Management
	Personnel Training

Business Management
Related	Business
	Business Education
	Management Methods
	Management/
	Personnel Management

Business Organizations
Used For	Companies
	Corporations
Broader	Organizations
Related	Business

Business Students
Broader	Students
Related	Business

Businessmen
Use	Business And Industrial Person- nel

Butterflies
Broader	Arthropoda
	Insects
	Invertebrates
Related	Larvae

Butyrylperazine
Broader	Antipsychotic Drugs
	Antischizophrenic Drugs

38

Butyrylperazine — (Continued)
Broader
     Neuroleptic Drugs
     Phenothiazine Derivatives
     Tranquilizing Drugs

Buying
Use   Consumer Behavior

Cadres
Use   Social Groups

Caffeine
Used For   Coffee (Drug)
     Tea (Drug)
Broader   Alkaloids
     CNS Affecting Drugs
     CNS Stimulating Drugs
     Diuretics
     Heart Rate Affecting Drugs
     Respiration Stimulating Drugs
Related   Analeptic Drugs

Cage Apparatus
Broader   Apparatus

Calcification
Related   Physiology/

Calcium
Broader   Chemical Elements
     Metallic Elements
Narrower   Calcium Ions

Calcium Bromide
Broader   Anticonvulsive Drugs
     Bromides
     CNS Affecting Drugs
     CNS Depressant Drugs
     Hypnotic Drugs
     Sedatives

Calcium Ions
Broader   Calcium
     Chemical Elements
     Electrolytes
     Metallic Elements

Calcium Metabolism Disorders
Broader   Metabolism Disorders

Calculus
Use   Mathematics Education

California F Scale
(See)   Nonprojective Personality Measures
     Personality Measures

California Psychological Inventory
Used For   CPI (Test)
(See)   Nonprojective Personality Measures
     Personality Measures

California Test of Mental Maturity
(See)   Intelligence Measures

California Test of Personality
(See)   Nonprojective Personality Measures
     Personality Measures

Calories
Related   Energy Expenditure

Cambodia

Cameras
Broader   Apparatus

Campaigns (Political)
Use   Political Campaigns

Camping
Broader   Recreation
Related   Summer Camps (Recreation)
     Vacationing

Camps (Concentration)
Use   Concentration Camps

Campuses
Broader   School Facilities

Canada

Canaries
Broader   Birds
     Vertebrates

Cancers
Use   Neoplasms

Candidates (Political)
Use   Political Candidates

Cannabis
Used For   Hemp (Cannabis)
Narrower   Hashish
     Marihuana
Related   Aphrodisiacs
     Hallucinogenic Drugs
     Narcotic Drugs
     Tetrahydrocannabinol

Capillaries (Anatomy)
Broader   Blood Vessels
     Cardiovascular System

Capital Punishment
Used For   Death Penalty
     Punishment (Capital)

Capitalism
Broader   Political Economic Systems

Carbachol
Broader   Cholinomimetic Drugs

Carbohydrate Metabolism
Used For   Metabolism (Carbohydrate)
Broader   Metabolism
Related   Carbohydrate Metabolism Disorders

Carbohydrate Metabolism Disorders
  Broader   Metabolism Disorders
  Narrower   Cushings Syndrome
             Diabetes
             Diabetes Insipidus
             Diabetes Mellitus
  Related   Carbohydrate Metabolism

Carbohydrates
  Narrower   Blood Sugar
             Glucose
             Sugars

Carbon
  Broader   Chemical Elements
             Nonmetallic Elements

Carbon Dioxide
  Related   Respiration

Carbon Monoxide
  Related   Respiration

Carbon Monoxide Poisoning
  Used For   Carboxyhemoglobinemia
  Broader   Toxic Disorders

Carbonic Anhydrase
  Broader   Enzymes
  Related   Acetazolamide

Carboxyhemoglobinemia
  Use   Carbon Monoxide Poisoning

Carcinogens
  Related   Drugs/
             Pollution
             Tobacco Smoking

Carcinomas
  Use   Neoplasms

Cardiac Disorders
  Use   Heart Disorders

Cardiac Rate
  Use   Heart Rate

Cardiography
  Broader   Diagnosis
             Medical Diagnosis
  Narrower   Electrocardiography

Cardiology
  Broader   Medical Sciences
             Sciences
  Related   Cardiovascular System

Cardiovascular Disorders
  Used For   Circulatory Disorders
             Coronary Disorders
             Vascular Disorders
  Narrower   Aneurysms
             Angina Pectoris
             Arrhythmias (Heart)
             Arteriosclerosis
             Atherosclerosis

Cardiovascular Disorders — (Continued)
  Narrower
             Blood Pressure Disorders
             Bradycardia
             Cerebral Anoxia
             Cerebral Arteriosclerosis
             Cerebral Embolisms
             Cerebral Hemorrhage
             Cerebral Ischemia
             Cerebral Thromboses
             Cerebrovascular Accidents
             Cerebrovascular Disorders
             Coronary Thromboses
             Embolisms
             Essential Hypertension
             Fibrillation (Heart)
             Heart Disorders
             Hemorrhage
             Hypertension
             Hypotension
             Ischemia
             Myocardial Infarctions
             Syncope
             Tachycardia
             Thrombophlebitis
             Thromboses
  Related   Cardiovascular System
             Disorders/
             Dyspnea
             Heart Rate Affecting Drugs
             Psychosomatic Disorders

Cardiovascular System
  Narrower   Aorta
             Arteries (Anatomy)
             Blood Vessels
             Capillaries (Anatomy)
             Carotid Arteries
             Heart
             Heart Auricles
             Heart Valves
             Heart Ventricles
             Lymph Vessels
             Myocardium
             Pericardium
             Veins (Anatomy)
  Related   Anatomical Systems/
             Cardiology
             Cardiovascular Disorders
             Spleen

Career Aspirations
  Use   Occupational Aspirations

Career Choice
  Use   Occupational Choice

Career Goals
  Use   Occupational Aspirations

Career Guidance
  Use   Occupational Guidance

Career Preference
Use   Occupational Preference

Careers
Use   Occupations/

Carotid Arteries
Broader   Arteries (Anatomy)
      Blood Vessels
      Cardiovascular System

Carotid Body
Broader   Autonomic Nervous System
      Chemoreceptors
      Nerve Endings
      Nervous System
      Neural Receptors
      Nonchromaffin Paraganglia

Carp
Broader   Fishes
      Vertebrates
Narrower   Goldfish

Carphenazine
Broader   Adrenolytic Drugs
      Antiemetic Drugs
      Antipsychotic Drugs
      Antischizophrenic Drugs
      Cholinergic Blocking Drugs
      Neuroleptic Drugs
      Phenothiazine Derivatives
      Tranquilizing Drugs

Cars
Use   Automobiles

Cartilage
Broader   Connective Tissues
      Tissues (Body)

Cartoons (Humor)
Broader   Humor

Case History
Use   Patient History

Case Report

Caseworkers
Use   Social Workers

Caste System
Broader   Social Structure
Related   Systems/

Castration
Broader   Endocrine Gland Surgery
      Physical Treatment Methods
      Sterilization (Sex)
      Surgery
Narrower   Male Castration
      Ovariectomy

Castration Anxiety
Broader   Anxiety

Castration Anxiety — (Continued)
Related   Body Image Disturbances

Cat Learning
Related   Cats
      Learning/

Catabolism
Broader   Metabolism

Catalepsy
Broader   Symptoms
Related   Autohypnosis
      Hysteria
      Schizophrenia
      Suggestibility

Catamnesis
Use   Posttreatment Followup

Cataplexy
Broader   Muscular Disorders
      Musculoskeletal Disorders
      Nervous System Disorders
      Neuromuscular Disorders
Related   Narcolepsy

Cataracts
Broader   Eye Disorders
      Sense Organ Disorders

Catatonia
Broader   Symptoms
Related   Catatonic Schizophrenia

Catatonic Schizophrenia
Broader   Psychosis
      Schizophrenia
Related   Catatonia

Catecholamines
Broader   Amines
      Sympathomimetic Amines
      Sympathomimetic Drugs
Narrower   Dopamine
      Epinephrine
      Norepinephrine
Related   Adrenergic Drugs
      Drugs/
      Methyldopa

Categorizing
Use   Classification (Cognitive Process)

Catharsis
Used For   Abreaction
Related   Personality Processes/

Catheterization
Broader   Physical Treatment Methods

Cathexis
Related   Personality Processes/

Catholicism (Roman)
Use   Roman Catholicism

Cats
Used For Kittens
Broader Mammals
Vertebrates
Related Cat Learning

Cattell Culture Fair Intell Test
Identifier Culture Fair Intelligence Test

Cattell Infant Intelligence Scale
Identifier Infant Intelligence Scale

Cattle
Used For Bulls
Cows
Broader Mammals
Vertebrates

Caucasians
Used For Whites
Broader Race (Anthropological)

Cauda Equina
Use Spinal Nerves

Caudate Nucleus
Broader Basal Ganglia
Brain
Central Nervous System
Cerebral Cortex
Nervous System
Telencephalon

Celiac Plexus
Use Autonomic Ganglia

Celibacy
Use Sexual Abstinence

Cell Nucleus
Related Cells (Biology)

Cells (Biology)
Narrower Auditory Neurons
Axons
Blood Cells
Bone Marrow Cells
Chromosomes
Cones (Eye)
Connective Tissue Cells
Dendrites
Epithelial Cells
Erythrocytes
Germ Cells
Leucocytes
Lymphocytes
Motor Neurons
Neurons
Ovum
Rods (Eye)
Sensory Neurons
Sperm
Related Absorption (Physiological)
Anatomy/
Cell Nucleus

Cells (Biology) — (Continued)
Related
Cytology
Cytoplasm
Physiology/

Central America

Central Nervous System
Used For CNS (Nervous System)
Broader Nervous System
Narrower Amygdaloid Body
Auditory Cortex
Basal Ganglia
Brain
Brain Stem
Caudate Nucleus
Cerebellum
Cerebral Cortex
Cerebral Ventricles
Corpora Quadrigemina
Corpus Callosum
Cranial Spinal Cord
Diencephalon
Dorsal Roots
Extrapyramidal Tracts
Frontal Lobe
Geniculate Bodies (Thalamus)
Globus Pallidus
Gyrus Cinguli
Hippocampus
Hypothalamo Hypophyseal System
Hypothalamus
Inferior Colliculus
Limbic System
Lumbar Spinal Cord
Medulla Oblongata
Meninges
Mesencephalon
Motor Cortex
Neural Analyzers
Occipital Lobe
Optic Chiasm
Optic Lobe
Parietal Lobe
Pons
Pyramidal Tracts
Reticular Formation
Sacral Spinal Cord
Somatosensory Cortex
Spinal Cord
Spinothalamic Tracts
Superior Colliculus
Telencephalon
Temporal Lobe
Thalamic Nuclei
Thalamus
Thoracic Spinal Cord

Central Nervous System — (Continued)

Narrower
- Ventral Roots
- Visual Cortex

Related   Central Nervous System Disorders

Central Nervous System Disorders

Broader   Nervous System Disorders

Narrower
- Acalculia
- Agraphia
- Alcoholic Hallucinosis
- Alcoholic Psychosis
- Alzheimers Disease
- Anencephaly
- Aphasia
- Arachnoiditis
- Ataxia
- Athetosis
- Bacterial Meningitis
- Brain Concussion
- Brain Damage
- Brain Disorders
- Brain Lesions
- Brain Neoplasms
- Cerebral Palsy
- Cerebrovascular Accidents
- Chorea
- Delirium Tremens
- Dysautonomia
- Encephalitis
- Encephalomyelitis
- Epilepsy
- Epileptic Seizures
- Grand Mal Epilepsy
- Huntingtons Chorea
- Hydrocephaly
- Hypothalamus Lesions
- Infectious Meningitis
- Korsakoffs Psychosis
- Meningitis
- Microcephaly
- Minimal Brain Disorders
- Myelitis
- Neurosyphilis
- Organic Brain Syndromes
- Parkinsons Disease
- Petit Mal Epilepsy
- Picks Disease
- Poliomyelitis
- Presenile Dementia
- Senile Dementia
- Senile Psychosis
- Toxic Psychoses
- Viral Meningitis

Related
- Central Nervous System
- Hypothermia
- Paralysis
- Spinal Cord Injuries

Central Nervous System Drugs

Use   CNS Affecting Drugs

Central Tendency Measures

Used For   Tendency Measures (Central)

Broader
- Statistical Analysis
- Statistical Measurement

Narrower
- Mean
- Median
- Mode

Related
- Population (Statistics)
- T Test
- Variability Measurement

CER (Conditioning)

Use   Conditioned Emotional Responses

Cerebellar Cortex

Use   Cerebellum

Cerebellar Nuclei

Use   Cerebellum

Cerebellopontie Angle

Use   Cerebellum

Cerebellum

Used For
- Cerebellar Cortex
- Cerebellar Nuclei
- Cerebellopontie Angle

Broader
- Brain
- Central Nervous System
- Nervous System

Cerebral Anoxia

Broader
- Anoxia
- Cardiovascular Disorders
- Cerebrovascular Disorders

Related
- Cerebral Ischemia
- Cerebrovascular Accidents

Cerebral Aqueduct

Use   Cerebral Ventricles

Cerebral Arteriosclerosis

Broader
- Arteriosclerosis
- Cardiovascular Disorders
- Cerebrovascular Disorders

Related
- Cerebrovascular Accidents
- Senile Dementia

Cerebral Cortex

Used For   Cortex (Cerebral)

Broader
- Brain
- Central Nervous System
- Nervous System
- Telencephalon

Narrower
- Amygdaloid Body
- Auditory Cortex
- Basal Ganglia
- Caudate Nucleus
- Cerebral Ventricles
- Corpus Callosum
- Frontal Lobe

Cerebral Cortex — (Continued)
Narrower
        Globus Pallidus
        Gyrus Cinguli
        Hippocampus
        Limbic System
        Motor Cortex
        Occipital Lobe
        Parietal Lobe
        Somatosensory Cortex
        Temporal Lobe
        Visual Cortex

Cerebral Dominance
Narrower   Lateral Dominance
Related   Brain
        Dominance/
        Learning Disabilities
        Minimally Brain Damaged

Cerebral Embolisms
Broader   Cardiovascular Disorders
        Cerebrovascular Disorders
        Embolisms
Related   Cerebral Thromboses
        Cerebrovascular Accidents

Cerebral Hemorrhage
Broader   Cardiovascular Disorders
        Cerebrovascular Disorders
        Hemorrhage
Related   Cerebrovascular Accidents

Cerebral Ischemia
Broader   Cardiovascular Disorders
        Cerebrovascular Disorders
        Ischemia
Related   Cerebral Anoxia
        Cerebrovascular Accidents

Cerebral Lesions
Use   Brain Lesions

Cerebral Palsy
Broader   Brain Disorders
        Central Nervous System Disorders
        Nervous System Disorders
        Neuromuscular Disorders
        Paralysis
Related   Athetosis

Cerebral Thromboses
Broader   Cardiovascular Disorders
        Cerebrovascular Disorders
        Thromboses
Related   Cerebral Embolisms
        Cerebrovascular Accidents

Cerebral Vascular Disorders
Use   Cerebrovascular Disorders

Cerebral Ventricles
Used For   Cerebral Aqueduct
        Choroid Plexus
        Ependyma
        Ventricles (Cerebral)
Broader   Brain
        Central Nervous System
        Cerebral Cortex
        Nervous System
        Telencephalon

Cerebrospinal Fluid
Used For   Spinal Fluid
Broader   Body Fluids

Cerebrovascular Accidents
Used For   Accidents (Cerebrovascular)
        Apoplexy
        Stroke (Cerebrum)
Broader   Brain Disorders
        Cardiovascular Disorders
        Central Nervous System Disorders
        Cerebrovascular Disorders
        Nervous System Disorders
Related   Cerebral Anoxia
        Cerebral Arteriosclerosis
        Cerebral Embolisms
        Cerebral Hemorrhage
        Cerebral Ischemia
        Cerebral Thromboses
        Coma

Cerebrovascular Disorders
Used For   Cerebral Vascular Disorders
Broader   Cardiovascular Disorders
Narrower   Cerebral Anoxia
        Cerebral Arteriosclerosis
        Cerebral Embolisms
        Cerebral Hemorrhage
        Cerebral Ischemia
        Cerebral Thromboses
        Cerebrovascular Accidents
Related   Coma
        Hypertension
        Nervous System Disorders

Cerebrum Affecting Drugs
Broader   CNS Affecting Drugs
Narrower   Chlorpromazine

Certification (Professional)
Use   Professional Certification

Certified Public Accountants
Use   Accountants

Cervical Plexus
Use   Spinal Nerves

Cervix
Broader   Female Genitalia
        Urogenital System
        Uterus

CFF (Vision)
Use   Critical Flicker Fusion Threshold

Chains (Markov)
Use   Markov Chains

Chance (Fortune)
Narrower   Binomial Distribution
         Probability
         Response Probability
         Statistical Probability

Change (Organizational)
Use   Organizational Change

Change (Social)
Use   Social Change

Change (Stimulus)
Use   Stimulus Change

Chaplains
Broader   Clergy
         Religious Personnel
Related   Lay Religious Personnel
         Military Personnel
         Ministers (Religion)
         Priests
         Rabbis

Character
Use   Personality/

Character Development
Use   Personality Development

Character Disorders
Use   Personality Disorders

Character Formation
Use   Personality Development

Character Traits
Use   Personality Traits

Charitable Behavior
Used For   Donors
Broader   Interpersonal Interaction
         Social Behavior
         Social Interaction
Related   Altruism
         Assistance (Social Behavior)

Cheating
Broader   Behavior Disorders
         Deception

Chemical Brain Stimulation
Broader   Brain Stimulation
         Stereotaxic Techniques
         Stimulation

Chemical Elements
Narrower   Barium
         Calcium
         Calcium Ions
         Carbon

Chemical Elements — (Continued)
Narrower
         Chloride Ions
         Cobalt
         Copper
         Helium
         Hydrogen
         Iron
         Lead (Metal)
         Lithium
         Magnesium
         Magnesium Ions
         Mercury (Metal)
         Metallic Elements
         Nitrogen
         Nonmetallic Elements
         Oxygen
         Phosphorus
         Potassium
         Potassium Ions
         Sodium
         Sodium Ions
         Strontium
Related   Electrolytes

Chemistry
Broader   Sciences
Narrower   Biochemistry
         Neurochemistry

Chemoreceptors
Broader   Nerve Endings
         Nervous System
         Neural Receptors
Narrower   Carotid Body
Related   Olfactory Mucosa
         Taste Buds

Chemotherapy
Use   Drug Therapy

Chess
Broader   Games

Chest
Use   Thorax

Cheyenne Indians
Use   American Indians

Chi Square Test
Broader   Nonparametric Statistical Tests
         Statistical Analysis
         Statistical Tests
Related   Statistical Significance

Chickens
Used For   Chicks
Broader   Birds
         Vertebrates

Chicks
Use   Chickens

Child Abuse
Used For	Abuse (Child)
Broader	Antisocial Behavior
	Behavior Disorders
Narrower	Battered Child Syndrome

Child Behavior Diagnostic Inventory
(See)	Nonprojective Personality Measures
	Personality Measures

Child Day Care
Used For	Day Care (Child)
Related	Day Care Centers

Child Discipline
Used For	Discipline (Child)
Broader	Childrearing Practices
	Family Relations
Narrower	Parental Permissiveness
Related	Parent Child Relations
	Parental Role

Child Guidance Clinics
Used For	Child Psychiatric Clinics
Broader	Clinics
	Treatment Facilities
Related	Community Facilities
	Community Mental Health Centers
	Mental Health Programs
	Psychiatric Clinics

Child Psychiatric Clinics
Use	Child Guidance Clinics

Child Psychiatry
Broader	Medical Sciences
	Psychiatry
	Sciences

Child Psychology
Broader	Developmental Psychology
	Psychology
	Sciences
	Social Sciences

Child Psychotherapy
Broader	Psychotherapy
Narrower	Play Therapy
Related	Reality Therapy

Childbirth
Use	Birth

Childhood
Use	Children

Childhood Development
Narrower	Early Childhood Development
	Infant Development
	Neonatal Development
Related	Adolescent Development
	Children
	Development/

Childhood Development — (Continued)
Related	Developmental Age Groups
	Developmental Differences
	Developmental Stages
	Human Development/
	Motor Development
	Perceptual Development
	Physical Development
	Preschool Age Children
	Psychogenesis
	Psychomotor Development
	School Age Children

Childhood Neurosis
Used For	Infantile Neurosis
	Neurosis (Childhood)
Broader	Neurosis

Childhood Play Development
Used For	Play Development (Childhood)
Broader	Psychogenesis
	Psychosocial Development
Related	Childrens Recreational Games
	Emotional Development

Childhood Psychosis
Used For	Infantile Psychosis
Broader	Psychosis
Narrower	Childhood Schizophrenia
	Early Infantile Autism
	Symbiotic Infantile Psychosis
Related	Autistic Children
	Emotionally Disturbed

Childhood Schizophrenia
Broader	Childhood Psychosis
	Psychosis
	Schizophrenia
Related	Early Infantile Autism
	Symbiotic Infantile Psychosis

Childrearing Attitudes
Related	Attitudes/
	Family Relations
	Parental Attitudes

Childrearing Practices
Broader	Family Relations
Narrower	Child Discipline
	Parental Permissiveness
	Toilet Training
	Weaning
Related	Father Child Relations
	Feeding Practices
	Mother Child Relations
	Parent Child Relations
	Parental Attitudes
	Parental Role
	Sociocultural Factors

Children
Used For	Childhood
	Youth (Children)
Broader	Developmental Age Groups
Narrower	Infants
	Neonates
	Preschool Age Children
	School Age Children
Related	Adopted Children
	Childhood Development
	Developmental Differences
	Stepchildren

Childrens Apperception Test
(See)	Personality Measures
	Projective Personality Measures
	Projective Techniques

Childrens Manifest Anxiety Scale
Used For	CMA Scale
(See)	Nonprojective Personality Measures
	Personality Measures

Childrens Personality Questionnaire
(See)	Nonprojective Personality Measures
	Personality Measures

Childrens Recreational Games
Broader	Games
	Recreation
Related	Childhood Play Development
	Toys

Chimpanzees
Broader	Mammals
	Primates (Nonhuman)
	Vertebrates

Chinchillas
Broader	Mammals
	Rodents
	Vertebrates

Chloral Hydrate
Broader	Anticonvulsive Drugs
	Hypnotic Drugs
	Sedatives

Chloralose
Broader	Hypnotic Drugs

Chlordiazepoxide
Used For	Librium
Broader	Amines
	Minor Tranquilizers
	Tranquilizing Drugs

Chloride Ions
Broader	Chemical Elements
	Electrolytes
	Nonmetallic Elements

Chlorimipramine
Broader	Amines

Chlorisondamine
Broader	Amines
	Antihypertensive Drugs
	Ganglion Blocking Drugs

Chloroform
Broader	Anesthetic Drugs
	General Anesthetics

Chlorpheniramine
Broader	Antihistaminic Drugs

Chlorpromazine
Used For	Thorazine
Broader	Adrenolytic Drugs
	Amines
	Antiemetic Drugs
	Antihypertensive Drugs
	Antipsychotic Drugs
	Antischizophrenic Drugs
	Cerebrum Affecting Drugs
	CNS Affecting Drugs
	CNS Depressant Drugs
	Neuroleptic Drugs
	Phenothiazine Derivatives
	Sedatives
	Tranquilizing Drugs
Related	Drug Potentiation

Chlorprothixene
Broader	Adrenolytic Drugs
	Amines
	Antiemetic Drugs
	Antihistaminic Drugs
	Antipsychotic Drugs
	Antischizophrenic Drugs
	Antispasmodic Drugs
	Minor Tranquilizers
	Phenothiazine Derivatives
	Tranquilizing Drugs

Choice Behavior
Broader	Cognitive Processes
	Decision Making
Related	Classification (Cognitive Process)

Cholesterol
Broader	Steroids

Choline
Used For	Choline Chloride
Broader	Vitamins
Related	Acetylcholine
	Cholinesterase
	Succinylcholine

Choline Chloride
Use	Choline

Cholinergic Blocking Drugs
Used For	Anticholinergic Drugs
	Parasympatholytic Drugs

Cholinergic Blocking Drugs — (Continued)
Narrower	Atropine
	Benactyzine
	Carphenazine
	Homatropine
	Hyoscyamine (L-)
	Nicotine
	Orphenadrine
	Scopolamine
	Trihexyphenidyl
Related	Antiemetic Drugs
	Cholinergic Nerves
	Cholinesterase
	Cholinomimetic Drugs
	Drugs/
	Hallucinogenic Drugs
	Parasympathetic Nervous System
	Phenothiazine Derivatives

Cholinergic Drugs
Narrower	Physostigmine
	Pilocarpine
Related	Cholinomimetic Drugs
	Drugs/

Cholinergic Nerves
Used For	Nerves (Cholinergic)
Broader	Autonomic Nervous System
	Nervous System
Related	Acetylcholine
	Cholinergic Blocking Drugs
	Cholinomimetic Drugs

Cholinesterase
Broader	Enzymes
	Esterases
Related	Acetylcholinesterase
	Choline
	Cholinergic Blocking Drugs
	Cholinesterase Inhibitors

Cholinesterase Inhibitors
Used For	Anticholinesterase Drugs
Narrower	Galanthamine
	Neostigmine
	Physostigmine
Related	Cholinesterase
	Cholinomimetic Drugs
	Drugs/

Cholinomimetic Drugs
Used For	Parasympathomimetic Drugs
Narrower	Acetylcholine
	Arecoline
	Carbachol
	Neostigmine
	Physostigmine
	Pilocarpine
Related	Analeptic Drugs
	Cholinergic Blocking Drugs
	Cholinergic Drugs
	Cholinergic Nerves

Cholinomimetic Drugs — (Continued)
Related	Cholinesterase Inhibitors
	Drugs/
	Parasympathetic Nervous System

Chorazepate Dipotassium
Broader	Tranquilizing Drugs

Chorea
Broader	Central Nervous System Disorders
	Nervous System Disorders
Narrower	Huntingtons Chorea
Related	Infectious Disorders

Choroid
Use	Eye (Anatomy)

Choroid Plexus
Use	Cerebral Ventricles

Christianity
Broader	Religious Affiliation
	Religious Beliefs
Narrower	Fundamentalism
	Protestantism
	Roman Catholicism
Related	Bible

Chromosome Disorders
Used For	Karyotype Disorders
Broader	Genetic Disorders
Narrower	Autosome Disorders
	Crying Cat Syndrome
	Deletion (Chromosome)
	Downs Syndrome
	Klinefelters Syndrome
	Neonatal Autosome Disorders
	Neonatal Chromosome Disorders
	Neonatal Sex Chromosome Disorders
	Nondisjunction (Chromosome)
	Sex Chromosome Disorders
	Translocation (Chromosome)
	Trisomy
	Trisomy 18
	Trisomy 21
	Turners Syndrome
Related	Chromosomes

Chromosomes
Broader	Cells (Biology)
Narrower	Autosomes
	Sex Chromosomes
Related	Chromosome Disorders
	Genes
	Genetics/
	Mutations

Chronic Alcoholic Intoxication
Broader	Alcohol Intoxication
	Brain Disorders

Chronic Alcoholic Intoxication — (Continued)
Broader
    Toxic Disorders
    Toxic Encephalopathies

Chronic Psychosis
Broader   Psychosis
Narrower Chronic Schizophrenia

Chronic Schizophrenia
Broader   Chronic Psychosis
    Psychosis
    Schizophrenia

Cichlids
Broader   Fishes
    Vertebrates

Cigarette Smoking
Use   Tobacco Smoking

Circadian Rhythms (Animal)
Use   Animal Circadian Rhythms

Circulation (Blood)
Use   Blood Circulation

Circulatory Disorders
Use   Cardiovascular Disorders

Circumcision
Use   Birth Rites
    Surgery

Cirrhosis (Liver)
Broader   Digestive System Disorders
    Liver Disorders
Related   Jaundice

Cities
Use   Urban Environments

Citizenship

Civil Rights Movement
Broader   Social Movements
Related   Activist Movements

Civil Servants
Use   Government Personnel

Clairvoyance
Broader   Extrasensory Perception
    Parapsychological Phenomena
    Parapsychology
Narrower Precognition

Class Attitudes
Use   Socioeconomic Class Attitudes

Classical Conditioning
Used For Conditioning (Classical)
    Pavlovian Conditioning
    Respondent Conditioning
Broader   Conditioning
Narrower Conditioned Emotional Responses

Classical Conditioning — (Continued)
Narrower
    Conditioned Responses
    Conditioned Stimulus
    Conditioned Suppression
    Unconditioned Responses
    Unconditioned Stimulus
Related   Learning/

Classificat (Psychiatric Taxonomies)
Use   Psychodiagnostic Typologies

Classificat (Psychodiagnost Taxono)
Use   Psychodiagnostic Typologies

Classificat (Psychodiagnostic Proc)
Use   Psychodiagnosis

Classification (Cognitive Process)
Used For Categorizing
    Sorting (Cognition)
Broader   Cognitive Processes
Related   Choice Behavior

Classification (Psychiatric Process)
Use   Psychodiagnosis

Classification Systems
Use   Taxonomies

Classmates
Broader   Students

Classroom Behavior
Related   Classroom Behavior Modification
    Classroom Discipline
    Classroom Environment

Classroom Behavior Modification
Broader   Behavior Modification
Related   Classroom Behavior
    Classroom Discipline
    Education/

Classroom Discipline
Used For Discipline (Classroom)
Related   Classroom Behavior
    Classroom Behavior Modification
    Education/
    Teacher Student Interaction

Classroom Environment
Broader   Academic Environment
    Environment
    Social Environments
Related   Classroom Behavior
    Classrooms
    School Environment

Classroom Instruction
Use   Teaching

Classroom Teachers
Use   Teachers

Classrooms
  Broader   School Facilities
  Related   Classroom Environment

Claustrophobia
  Broader   Phobias

Cleft Palate
  Broader   Congenital Disorders
         Neonatal Disorders
  Related   Speech Disorders
         Speech Handicapped

Clergy
  Broader   Religious Personnel
  Narrower   Chaplains
         Ministers (Religion)
         Monks
         Nuns
         Priests
         Rabbis
  Related   Evangelists
         Lay Religious Personnel
         Missionaries

Clerical Personnel
  Used For   Clerks
         Keypunch Operators
         Typists
  Broader   Business And Industrial Personnel
         White Collar Workers
  Related   Secretarial Personnel

Clerical Secretarial Skills
  Used For   Secretarial Skills
         Typing
  Broader   Employee Skills

Clerks
  Use   Clerical Personnel

Client Centered Therapy
  Used For   Nondirective Therapy
  Broader   Psychotherapy
  Related   Psychotherapeutic Techniques

Client Characteristics
  Used For   Patient Characteristics
  Related   Clients
         Patient History

Client Counselor Interaction
  Use   Psychotherapeutic Processes

Clients
  Used For   Counselees
  Related   Client Characteristics

Climacteric Depression
  Use   Involutional Depression

Climacteric Paranoia
  Use   Involutional Paranoid Psychosis

Climate (Organizational)
  Use   Organizational Climate

Climax (Sexual)
  Use   Orgasm

Clinical Judgment (Med Diagnosis)
  Use   Medical Diagnosis

Clinical Judgment (Not Diagnosis)
  Related   Psychodiagnostic Typologies

Clinical Judgment (Psychodiagnosis)
  Use   Psychodiagnosis

Clinical Methods Training
  Used For   Training (Clinical Methods)
  Narrower   Clinical Psychology Grad Training
         Clinical Psychology Internship
         Community Mental Health Training
         Counselor Education
         Mental Health Inservice Training
         Psychiatric Training
         Psychoanalytic Training
         Psychotherapy Training
  Related   Education/

Clinical Psychologists
  Broader   Mental Health Personnel
         Psychologists
  Related   Clinicians
         Hypnotherapists
         Psychotherapists

Clinical Psychology
  Broader   Applied Psychology
         Psychology
         Sciences
         Social Sciences

Clinical Psychology Grad Training
  Used For   Training (Clinical Psychology Grad)
  Broader   Clinical Methods Training
         Graduate Education
         Graduate Psychology Education
         Higher Education
         Postgraduate Training
  Related   Clinical Psychology Internship

Clinical Psychology Internship
  Broader   Clinical Methods Training
         Higher Education
         Postgraduate Training
  Related   Clinical Psychology Grad Training

Clinicians
  Related   Clinical Psychologists
         Medical Personnel
         Personnel/
         Physicians
         Psychiatrists

Clinics
Broader	Treatment Facilities
Narrower	Child Guidance Clinics
	Psychiatric Clinics
	Walk In Clinics
Related	Community Mental Health Centers
	Crisis Intervention Services
	Hospitals

Clipped Speech (Mechanical)
Broader	Speech Processing (Mechanical)
	Verbal Communication

Cliques
Use	Social Groups

Clitoris
Broader	Female Genitalia
	Urogenital System

Clonidine
Broader	CNS Affecting Drugs
	CNS Stimulating Drugs

Closed Circuit Television
Broader	Audiovisual Communications Media
	Communications Media
	Mass Media
	Telecommunications Media
	Television

Closure (Perceptual)
Use	Perceptual Closure

Clothing Fashions
Broader	Fads And Fashions

Cloze Testing
Related	Measurement/

Clubs (Social Organizations)
Broader	Recreation

Cluster Analysis
Used For	Clustering
Broader	Factor Analysis
	Statistical Analysis
	Statistical Measurement
Related	Analysis/

Clustering
Use	Cluster Analysis

CMA Scale
Identifier	Childrens Manifest Anxiety Scale

CNS (Nervous System)
Use	Central Nervous System

CNS Affecting Drugs
Used For	Central Nervous System Drugs
Narrower	Amobarbital
	Amphetamine
	Analeptic Drugs

CNS Affecting Drugs — (Continued)
Narrower	Barbital
	Bemegride
	Caffeine
	Calcium Bromide
	Cerebrum Affecting Drugs
	Chlorpromazine
	Clonidine
	CNS Depressant Drugs
	CNS Stimulating Drugs
	Dextroamphetamine
	Ephedrine
	Glutethimide
	Haloperidol
	Hydantoins
	Lithium Bromide
	Methamphetamine
	Methylphenidate
	Pentylenetetrazol
	Pipradrol
	Scopolamine
	Strychnine
Related	Drugs/
	Heart Rate Affecting Drugs

CNS Depressant Drug Antagonists
Use	Analeptic Drugs

CNS Depressant Drugs
Broader	CNS Affecting Drugs
Narrower	Amobarbital
	Barbital
	Calcium Bromide
	Chlorpromazine
	Glutethimide
	Haloperidol
	Lithium Bromide
	Scopolamine
Related	Analgesic Drugs
	Anesthetic Drugs
	Anticonvulsive Drugs
	Antiepileptic Drugs
	Barbiturates
	Hypnotic Drugs
	Muscle Relaxing Drugs
	Narcotic Drugs
	Sedatives

CNS Stimulating Drugs
Broader	CNS Affecting Drugs
Narrower	Amphetamine
	Analeptic Drugs
	Bemegride
	Caffeine
	Clonidine
	Dextroamphetamine
	Ephedrine
	Methamphetamine
	Methylphenidate
	Pentylenetetrazol

CNS Stimulating Drugs — (Continued)

Narrower	Picrotoxin
	Pipradrol
	Strychnine
Related	Antidepressant Drugs
	Emetic Drugs
	Heart Rate Affecting Drugs

Coaches
Use Teachers

Coagulation (Blood)
Use Blood Coagulation

Coagulation Disorders (Blood)
Use Blood Coagulation Disorders

Coalition Formation
Broader Social Processes

Cobalt
Broader	Chemical Elements
	Metallic Elements

Cocaine
Broader	Alkaloids
	Amines
	Anesthetic Drugs
	Local Anesthetics
	Mydriatic Drugs

Cochlea
Used For	Organ of Corti
Broader	Ear (Anatomy)
	Labyrinth (Anatomy)
	Sense Organs

Cochran Q Test
Used For	Q Test
Broader	Nonparametric Statistical Tests
	Statistical Analysis
	Statistical Tests

Cockroaches
Broader	Arthropoda
	Insects
	Invertebrates
Related	Larvae

Codeine
Used For	Codeine Sulfate
	Methylmorphine
Broader	Alkaloids
	Analgesic Drugs
	Hypnotic Drugs
	Narcotic Drugs
	Opiates
Related	Drug Dependency

Codeine Sulfate
Use Codeine

Coeds
Use College Students

Coeducation
Related Education/

Coefficient (Phi)
Use Phi Coefficient

Coenzymes
Related	Drugs/
	Enzymes

Coffee (Drug)
Use Caffeine

Cognition
Related	Cognitive Development
	Cognitive Processes

Cognitive Ability
Related Ability/

Cognitive Complexity
Used For	Complexity (Cognitive)
Broader	Cognitive Style

Cognitive Contiguity
Used For	Contiguity (Cognitive)
Broader	Associative Processes
	Cognitive Processes

Cognitive Development
Broader	Psychogenesis
Narrower	Intellectual Development
	Language Development
	Perceptual Development
Related	Cognition
	Speech Development

Cognitive Discrimination
Used For	Discrimination (Cognitive)
Broader	Cognitive Processes
Related	Discrimination/

Cognitive Dissonance
Used For	Dissonance (Cognitive)
Related	Cognitive Processes

Cognitive Generalization
Used For	Generalization (Cognitive)
Broader	Cognitive Processes
Related	Associative Processes
	Semantic Generalization

Cognitive Mediation
Used For	Mediation (Cognitive)
Broader	Cognitive Processes

Cognitive Processes
Used For	Human Information Processes
	Information Processes (Human)
	Processes (Cognitive)
Narrower	Abstraction
	Anagram Problem Solving
	Associative Processes
	Choice Behavior
	Classification (Cognitive Process)
	Cognitive Contiguity
	Cognitive Discrimination

Cognitive Processes — (Continued)

Narrower	Cognitive Generalization
	Cognitive Mediation
	Concept Formation
	Connotations
	Contextual Associations
	Decision Making
	Divergent Thinking
	Group Problem Solving
	Ideation
	Imagination
	Inductive Deductive Reasoning
	Inference
	Logical Thinking
	Management Decision Making
	Problem Solving
	Reasoning
	Semantic Generalization
	Thinking
	Transposition (Cognition)
Related	Cognition
	Cognitive Dissonance
	Memory
	Word Associations

Cognitive Style

Narrower	Cognitive Complexity
Related	Field Dependence
	Perceptual Style
	Personality Traits

Cohabitation

Related	Common Law Marriage
	Family/

Cohesion (Group)

Use	Group Cohesion

Coitus

Use	Sexual Intercourse (Human)

Coitus (Animal)

Use	Animal Mating Behavior

Coitus Interruptus

Used For	Withdrawal (Coitus Interruptus)
Broader	Birth Control
	Family Planning

Cold Effects

Broader	Environmental Effects
	Temperature Effects

Colds (Common)

Use	Common Colds

Colitis

Broader	Colon Disorders
	Digestive System Disorders
	Gastrointestinal Disorders
Narrower	Ulcerative Colitis
Related	Gastrointestinal Ulcers

Coll Ent Exam Bd Scholastic Apt Test

Used For	Preliminary Scholastic Aptitude Test
(See)	Aptitude Measures

Collaboration

Use	Cooperation

Collective Behavior

Used For	Group Behavior
Broader	Interpersonal Interaction
	Social Behavior
	Social Interaction
Narrower	Riots
Related	Entrapment Games
	Group Participation
	Mass Hysteria
	Social Demonstrations

College Academic Achievement

Broader	Academic Achievement
	Achievement

College Degrees

Use	Educational Degrees

College Dropouts

Broader	Dropouts

College Environment

Broader	Academic Environment
	Environment
	Social Environments
Related	Colleges

College Major

Use	Academic Specialization

College Students

Used For	Coeds
	Undergraduates
Broader	Students
Narrower	Community College Students
	Dental Students
	Graduate Students
	Junior College Students
	Medical Students
	Postgraduate Students
	ROTC Students

College Teachers

Used For	Professors
Broader	Educational Personnel
	Teachers

Colleges

Used For	Community Colleges
	Junior Colleges
	Universities
Broader	Schools
Related	College Environment
	Military Schools

Colon
Broader	Digestive System
	Gastrointestinal System
	Intestines
Related	Colon Disorders

Colon Disorders
Used For	Bowel Disorders
Broader	Digestive System Disorders
	Gastrointestinal Disorders
Narrower	Colitis
	Constipation
	Diarrhea
	Fecal Incontinence
	Ulcerative Colitis
Related	Colon

Color
Narrower	Achromatic Color
	Hue
Related	Visual Stimulation

Color Blindness
Used For	Blindness (Color)
	Hysterical Color Blindness
Broader	Eye Disorders
	Sense Organ Disorders
Related	Color Perception
	Genetic Disorders

Color Perception
Used For	Color Vision
	Spectral Sensitivity
Broader	Vision
	Visual Perception
Related	Color Blindness
	Prismatic Stimulation

Color Pyramid Test
(See)	Personality Measures
	Projective Personality Measures
	Projective Techniques

Color Vision
Use	Color Perception

Colostomy
Broader	Physical Treatment Methods
	Surgery

Columbia Mental Maturity Scale
(See)	Intelligence Measures

Coma
Broader	Symptoms
Related	Cerebrovascular Accidents
	Cerebrovascular Disorders
	Epileptic Seizures
	Injuries
	Insulin Shock Therapy

Commerce
Use	Business

Commissioned Officers
Used For	Military Officers
	Officers (Commissioned)
Broader	Government Personnel
	Military Personnel
Related	Management Personnel

Commitment (Psychiatric)
Broader	Hospitalization
	Institutionalization
	Legal Processes
	Psychiatric Hospitalization

Common Colds
Used For	Colds (Common)
Broader	Infectious Disorders
	Respiratory Tract Disorders
	Viral Disorders
Related	Bronchial Disorders
	Pharyngeal Disorders

Common Law Marriage
Broader	Marriage
Related	Cohabitation
	Family Structure

Communes
Broader	Communities
	Environment
	Social Environments
Narrower	Kibbutz

Communication (Privileged)
Use	Privileged Communication

Communication (Professional)
Use	Scientific Communication

Communication Skills
Related	Ability/
	Communication/

Communication Systems
Related	Automated Information Processing
	Communication/
	Systems/

Communication Theory
Related	Communication/
	Cybernetics
	Theories/

Communication/
Related	Animal Communication
	Communication Skills
	Communication Systems
	Communication Theory
	Communications Media
	Information/
	Interpersonal Communication
	Messages
	Nonverbal Communication
	Persuasive Communication
	Scientific Communication

Communication/ — (Continued)
Related
    Symbolism
    Verbal Communication
    Vocalization
    Voice

Communications Media
Used For   Media (Communications)
Narrower   Audiotapes
    Audiovisual Communications
      Media
    Books
    Closed Circuit Television
    Educational Audiovisual Aids
    Educational Television
    Film Strips
    Magazines
    Mass Media
    Motion Pictures
    Motion Pictures (Educational)
    Motion Pictures (Entertainment)
    Newspapers
    Photographs
    Printed Communications Media
    Radio
    Telecommunications Media
    Telephone Systems
    Television
    Television Advertising
    Videotapes
Related   Communication/

Communism
Used For   Marxism
Broader   Political Economic Systems

Communities
Broader   Environment
    Social Environments
Narrower   Communes
    Kibbutz
    Neighborhoods

Community Attitudes
Related   Attitudes/

Community College Students
Broader   College Students
    Students

Community Colleges
Use   Colleges

Community Facilities
Narrower   Community Mental Health Centers
    Housing
    Public Transportation
    Shopping Centers
    Suicide Prevention Centers
Related   Child Guidance Clinics
    Community Services

Community Facilities — (Continued)
Related
    Day Care Centers
    Halfway Houses
    Recreation Areas
    Rehabilitation Centers
    Religious Buildings
    Schools
    Sheltered Workshops
    Urban Planning

Community Mental Health
Broader   Health
    Mental Health
Related   Community Mental Health Centers
    Community Mental Health Training
    Community Psychiatry
    Community Psychology
    Mental Health Programs

Community Mental Health Centers
Used For   Mental Health Centers (Community)
Broader   Community Facilities
    Treatment Facilities
Related   Child Guidance Clinics
    Clinics
    Community Mental Health
    Crisis Intervention Services
    Day Care Centers
    Hot Line Services
    Mental Health Programs
    Psychiatric Clinics
    Suicide Prevention Centers

Community Mental Health Training
Used For   Mental Health Training (Community)
    Training (Community Mental Health)
Broader   Clinical Methods Training
Narrower   Mental Health Inservice Training
Related   Community Mental Health
    Mental Health Programs

Community Psychiatry
Broader   Medical Sciences
    Psychiatry
    Sciences
Related   Community Mental Health
    Community Psychology
    Mental Health
    Mental Health Programs

Community Psychology
Broader   Applied Psychology
    Psychology
    Sciences
    Social Sciences

Community Psychology — (Continued)
Related   Community Mental Health
            Community Psychiatry
            Mental Health
            Mental Health Programs

Community Services
Narrower   Community Welfare Services
            Crisis Intervention Services
            Home Visiting Programs
            Hot Line Services
            Public Health Services
Related   Alcoholics Anonymous
            Community Facilities
            Mental Health Programs

Community Welfare Services
Used For   Public Welfare Services
Broader   Community Services
Related   Welfare Services (Government)

Companies
Use   Business Organizations

Comparative Psychology
Broader   Psychology
            Sciences
            Social Sciences

Compatibility (Interpersonal)
Use   Interpersonal Compatibility

Compensation (Defense Mechanism)
Broader   Defense Mechanisms

Compensatory Education
Broader   Curriculum
Related   Education/
            Educational Programs

Competition
Broader   Social Behavior

Complex (Electra)
Use   Electra Complex

Complex (Oedipal)
Use   Oedipal Complex

Complexity (Cognitive)
Use   Cognitive Complexity

Complexity (Stimulus)
Use   Stimulus Complexity

Complexity (Task)
Use   Task Complexity

Compliance
Broader   Social Behavior

Comprehension
Used For   Understanding
Narrower   Listening Comprehension
            Number Comprehension
            Reading Comprehension
            Sentence Comprehension

Comprehension — (Continued)
Related   Meaning
            Meaningfulness

Comprehension Tests
Related   Measurement/

Compressed Speech
Broader   Speech Processing (Mechanical)
            Verbal Communication

Compulsions
Narrower   Compulsive Orderliness
            Compulsive Repetition
            Serial Compulsions
Related   Mental Disorders/
            Obsessions
            Obsessive Compulsive Neurosis
            Obsessive Compulsive Personality

Compulsions (Serial)
Use   Serial Compulsions

Compulsive Neurosis
Use   Obsessive Compulsive Neurosis

Compulsive Orderliness
Used For   Orderliness (Compulsive)
Broader   Compulsions

Compulsive Repetition
Used For   Repetition (Compulsive)
Broader   Compulsions

Computer Applications
Narrower   Computer Assisted Diagnosis
            Computer Assisted Instruction
            Computer Simulation
Related   Computers

Computer Assisted Diagnosis
Broader   Computer Applications
            Diagnosis
Related   Medical Diagnosis
            Psychodiagnosis

Computer Assisted Instruction
Used For   Instruction (Computer Assisted)
Broader   Computer Applications
            Teaching
            Teaching Methods
Related   Individualized Instruction
            Programed Instruction
            Teaching Machines

Computer Programing Languages
Used For   FORTRAN
            Programing Languages (Computer)
Related   Computers
            Data Processing

Computer Programs
Use   Computer Software

Computer Simulation
Broader	Computer Applications
	Simulation
Related	Simulation Games

Computer Software
Used For	Computer Programs
	Programing (Computer)
Related	Computers
	Data Processing
	Systems/

Computers
Broader	Apparatus
Narrower	Analog Computers
	Digital Computers
Related	Automation
	Computer Applications
	Computer Programing Languages
	Computer Software
	Cybernetics
	Data Processing
	Systems/

Concentration Camps
Used For	Camps (Concentration)
Related	Correctional Institutions

Concept (Self)
Use	Self Concept

Concept Formation
Used For	Conceptualization
Broader	Cognitive Processes
Related	Concepts
	Conservation (Concept)

Concept Learning
Narrower	Nonreversal Shift Learning
	Reversal Shift Learning
Related	Concepts
	Learning/

Concept Mastery Test
(See)	Intelligence Measures

Concepts
Used For	Information (Concepts)
Related	Concept Formation
	Concept Learning
	Information/

Conceptual Imagery
Used For	Imagery (Conceptual)
Broader	Imagery
Related	Imagination

Conceptualization
Use	Concept Formation

Concussion (Brain)
Use	Brain Concussion

Conditioned Emotional Responses
Used For	CER (Conditioning)

Conditioned Emotional Responses — (Continued)
Broader	Classical Conditioning
	Conditioned Responses
	Conditioning
	Emotional Responses
	Operant Conditioning
	Responses

Conditioned Reflex
Use	Conditioned Responses

Conditioned Responses
Used For	Conditioned Reflex
	CR (Conditioning)
	Reflex (Conditioned)
Broader	Classical Conditioning
	Conditioning
	Responses
Narrower	Conditioned Emotional Responses
	Conditioned Suppression

Conditioned Stimulus
Used For	CS (Conditioning)
	Stimulus (Conditioned)
Broader	Classical Conditioning
	Conditioning
Related	Stimulation

Conditioned Suppression
Used For	Suppression (Conditioned)
Broader	Classical Conditioning
	Conditioned Responses
	Conditioning
	Responses

Conditioning
Narrower	Avoidance Conditioning
	Classical Conditioning
	Conditioned Emotional Responses
	Conditioned Responses
	Conditioned Stimulus
	Conditioned Suppression
	Counterconditioning
	Escape Conditioning
	Eyelid Conditioning
	Operant Conditioning
	Unconditioned Responses
	Unconditioned Stimulus
Related	Biofeedback
	Learning/
	Reinforcement
	Spontaneous Recovery (Learning)
	Stimulation

Conditioning (Avoidance)
Use	Avoidance Conditioning

Conditioning (Classical)
Use	Classical Conditioning

Conditioning (Escape)
  Use   Escape Conditioning

Conditioning (Eyelid)
  Use   Eyelid Conditioning

Conditioning (Operant)
  Use   Operant Conditioning

Conditioning (Verbal)
  Use   Verbal Learning

Cones (Eye)
  Broader   Cells (Biology)
             Eye (Anatomy)
             Nervous System
             Neurons
             Photoreceptors
             Retina
             Sense Organs
             Sensory Neurons

Confabulation
  Broader   Behavior Disorders
             Deception
             Thought Disturbances
  Related   Korsakoffs Psychosis
             Pathological Lying

Conference Proceedings

Confession (Religion)
  Broader   Religious Practices

Confidence Limits (Statistics)
  Broader   Statistical Analysis
  Related   Hypothesis Testing
             Predictability (Measurement)
             Statistical Measurement
             Statistical Significance
             Statistical Tests

Confidentiality of Information
  Use   Privileged Communication

Conflict
  Broader   Aggressive Behavior
             Interpersonal Interaction
             Social Behavior
             Social Interaction
  Narrower   Arguments
             Riots
             Violence
             War

Conflicts (Role)
  Use   Role Conflicts

Conformity (Personality)
  Broader   Personality Traits
             Social Behavior
  Related   Nonconformity (Personality)

Confusion (Mental)
  Use   Mental Confusion

Congenital Disorders
  Narrower   Cleft Palate
             Drug Induced Congenital Disor-
               ders
             Hermaphroditism
  Related   Congenitally Handicapped
             Disorders/
             Dysautonomia
             Genetic Disorders
             Hydrocephaly
             Microcephaly
             Myotonia
             Neonatal Disorders
             Syphilis

Congenitally Handicapped
  Broader   Handicapped
  Related   Adventitiously Handicapped
             Brain Damaged
             Congenital Disorders

Conjoint Therapy
  Used For   Multiple Therapists
  Broader   Psychotherapeutic Counseling
             Psychotherapy

Connective Tissue Cells
  Broader   Cells (Biology)
  Related   Connective Tissues

Connective Tissues
  Broader   Tissues (Body)
  Narrower   Bones
             Cartilage
  Related   Connective Tissue Cells

Connotations
  Broader   Associative Processes
             Cognitive Processes
  Related   Semantic Generalization

Consanguineous Marriage
  Broader   Endogamous Marriage
             Marriage

Conscience
  Broader   Psychoanalytic Personality Fac-
               tors
             Superego

Conscious (Personality Factors)
  Broader   Psychoanalytic Personality Fac-
               tors

Consciousness Disturbances
  Narrower   Autohypnosis
             Delirium
             Hypnosis
             Insomnia
             Narcolepsy
             Place Disorientation
             Sleep Disorders
             Sleep Talking
             Sleepwalking

Consciousness Disturbances — (Continued)

Narrower
    Somnambulism
    Suggestibility
    Time Disorientation

Related   Consciousness States
    Mental Disorders/
    Sleep

Consciousness States

Narrower   Attention
    Awareness
    Divided Attention
    Monitoring
    Selective Attention
    Vigilance
    Wakefulness

Related   Consciousness Disturbances
    Physiological Arousal
    Sleep

Conservation (Concept)

Related   Concept Formation
    Perceptual Development

Conservatism

Broader   Personality Traits
Related   Political Conservatism

Conservatism (Political)

Use   Political Conservatism

Consistency (Measurement)

Broader   Statistical Analysis
    Statistical Measurement
Related   Prediction Errors
    Statistical Reliability
    Statistical Validity

Consonants

Broader   Language
    Linguistics
    Phonemes
    Phonetics
    Verbal Communication

Constipation

Broader   Colon Disorders
    Digestive System Disorders
    Gastrointestinal Disorders

Construction (Test)

Use   Test Construction

Consultation (Professional)

Use   Professional Consultation

Consumer Attitudes

Related   Attitudes/

Consumer Behavior

Used For   Buying
    Shopping
Related   Shopping Centers

Consumer Protection

Consumer Psychology

Broader   Applied Psychology
    Psychology
    Sciences
    Social Sciences

Consumer Research

Narrower   Consumer Surveys
Related   Experimentation/

Consumer Surveys

Broader   Consumer Research
    Surveys

Contact (Eye)

Use   Eye Contact

Contact Lenses

Broader   Medical Therapeutic Devices
    Optical Aids

Content (Emotional)

Use   Emotional Content

Content Analysis (Test)

Broader   Test Construction
    Testing
Related   Measurement/

Contextual Associations

Used For   Associations (Contextual)
Broader   Associative Processes
    Cognitive Processes
Related   Word Frequency
    Word Meaning

Contiguity (Cognitive)

Use   Cognitive Contiguity

Contingency Management

Broader   Behavior Modification
Narrower   Token Economy Programs
Related   Management/

Continuing Education

Use   Higher Education

Continuous Reinforcement

Use   Reinforcement Schedules

Contour

Use   Form And Shape Perception

Contraception

Use   Birth Control

Contraceptive Devices

Broader   Birth Control
    Family Planning
Narrower   Diaphragms (Birth Control)
    Intrauterine Devices
    Oral Contraceptives

Contraceptive Methods

Use   Birth Control

Contribution (Professional)
Identifier   Professional Contribution

Control (Air Traffic)
Use   Air Traffic Control

Control (Locus of)
Use   Internal External Locus of
            Control

Control (Stimulus)
Use   Stimulus Control

Contusions
Used For   Bruises
Broader   Injuries

Convergent Thinking
Use   Inductive Deductive Reasoning

Conversation
Broader   Interpersonal Communication
            Interpersonal Interaction
            Language
            Social Behavior
            Social Interaction
            Verbal Communication

Conversion Hysteria
Use   Conversion Neurosis

Conversion Neurosis
Used For   Conversion Hysteria
            Hysterical Neurosis (Conversion)
Broader   Neurosis
Narrower   Hysterical Anesthesia
            Hysterical Paralysis
            Hysterical Vision Disturbances
Related   Hysteria
            Hysterical Personality

Conviction (Criminal)
Use   Criminal Conviction

Convulsions
Used For   Seizures
Broader   Nervous System Disorders
            Symptoms
Related   Anticonvulsive Drugs
            Brain Disorders
            Epileptic Seizures
            Hydrocephaly
            Spasms

Cooperation
Used For   Collaboration
Broader   Interpersonal Interaction
            Social Behavior
            Social Interaction

Coordination (Motor)
Use   Motor Coordination

Coordination (Perceptual Motor)
Use   Perceptual Motor Coordination

Coping Behavior
Broader   Emotional Adjustment
            Emotional Control
Related   Adaptability (Personality)

Copper
Broader   Chemical Elements
            Metallic Elements

Copulation
Use   Sexual Intercourse (Human)

Copulation (Animal)
Use   Animal Mating Behavior

Cornea
Broader   Eye (Anatomy)
            Sense Organs

Coronary Disorders
Use   Cardiovascular Disorders

Coronary Thromboses
Broader   Cardiovascular Disorders
            Heart Disorders
            Thromboses
Related   Myocardial Infarctions

Coronary Vessels
Use   Arteries (Anatomy)

Corpora Quadrigemina
Used For   Quadrigemina (Corpora)
Broader   Brain
            Central Nervous System
            Mesencephalon
            Nervous System
Narrower   Inferior Colliculus
            Optic Lobe
            Superior Colliculus

Corporations
Use   Business Organizations

Corpus Callosum
Broader   Brain
            Central Nervous System
            Cerebral Cortex
            Nervous System
            Telencephalon

Correctional Institutions
Used For   Institutions (Correctional)
Narrower   Prisons
            Reformatories
Related   Concentration Camps
            Halfway Houses
            Incarceration
            Institution Visitation
            Token Economy Programs

Correlation (Statistical)
Use   Statistical Correlation

Cortex (Auditory)
Use   Auditory Cortex

60

Cortex (Cerebral)
  Use   Cerebral Cortex

Cortex (Motor)
  Use   Motor Cortex

Cortex (Somatosensory)
  Use   Somatosensory Cortex

Cortex (Visual)
  Use   Visual Cortex

Cortical Evoked Potentials
  Broader   Electrical Activity
           Electrophysiology
           Evoked Potentials
  Related   Auditory Evoked Potentials
           Olfactory Evoked Potentials
           Somatosensory Evoked Potentials
           Visual Evoked Potentials

Corticoids
  Use   Corticosteroids

Corticosteroids
  Used For Adrenal Cortex Steroids
           Corticoids
  Broader   Steroids
  Narrower   Aldosterone
           Corticosterone
           Cortisone
           Deoxycorticosterone
           Hydrocortisone
           Prednisolone
  Related   Adrenal Cortex Hormones

Corticosterone
  Broader   Adrenal Cortex Hormones
           Corticosteroids
           Hormones
           Steroids

Corticotropin
  Used For ACTH (Hormone)
           Adrenocorticotropin
  Broader   Hormones
           Pituitary Hormones

Cortisol
  Use   Hydrocortisone

Cortisone
  Broader   Adrenal Cortex Hormones
           Corticosteroids
           Hormones
           Steroids

Costs And Cost Analysis
  Used For Budgets
  Related   Economy
           Money

Counselees
  Use   Clients

Counseling (Group)
  Use   Group Counseling

Counseling Psychology
  Broader   Applied Psychology
           Psychology
           Sciences
           Social Sciences
  Related   Counseling/

Counseling/
  Related   Counseling Psychology
           Counselors
           Educational Counseling
           Family Therapy
           Group Counseling
           Marriage Counseling
           Occupational Guidance
           Pastoral Counseling
           Premarital Counseling
           Psychotherapeutic Counseling

Counselor Attitudes
  Related   Attitudes/
           Counselor Characteristics
           Counselor Role
           Counselors

Counselor Characteristics
  Used For Counselor Effectiveness
           Counselor Personality
  Related   Counselor Attitudes
           Counselors

Counselor Client Interaction
  Use   Psychotherapeutic Processes

Counselor Education
  Broader   Clinical Methods Training
  Related   Education/

Counselor Effectiveness
  Use   Counselor Characteristics

Counselor Personality
  Use   Counselor Characteristics

Counselor Role
  Used For Role (Counselor)
  Related   Counselor Attitudes
           Counselors

Counselor Trainees
  Related   Counselors

Counselors
  Narrower   School Counselors
           Vocational Counselors
  Related   Counseling/
           Counselor Attitudes
           Counselor Characteristics
           Counselor Role
           Counselor Trainees
           Mental Health Personnel
           Personnel/

Counselors — (Continued)
Related
    Psychologists
    Social Workers
    Sociologists

Counterconditioning
Broader   Conditioning
Related   Aversion Therapy
    Behavior Modification
    Behavior Therapy
    Reciprocal Inhibition Therapy

Countertransference
Broader   Psychotherapeutic Processes

Countries

Related   Geography

County Agricultural Agents
Use   Agricultural Extension Workers

Courage
Used For   Bravery
Broader   Personality Traits

Courts
Use   Adjudication

Courtship (Animal)
Use   Animal Courtship Behavior

Courtship (Human)
Use   Human Courtship

Courtship Displays (Animal)
Use   Animal Courtship Displays

Cousins
Broader   Family Members

Cows
Use   Cattle

CPI (Test)
Identifier   California Psychological Inventory

CR (Conditioning)
Use   Conditioned Responses

Crabs
Broader   Arthropoda
    Crustacea
    Invertebrates

Crafts
Used For   Handicrafts
Broader   Art
    Arts

Cramps (Muscle)
Use   Muscular Disorders

Cranial Nerves
Used For   Accessory Nerve
    Glossopharyngeal Nerve
    Hypoglossal Nerve

Cranial Nerves — (Continued)
Used For
    Nerve (Accessory)
    Nerves (Cranial)
    Oculomotor Nerve
    Trochlear Nerve
Broader   Nervous System
    Peripheral Nerves
Narrower   Abducens Nerve
    Acoustic Nerve
    Facial Nerve
    Olfactory Nerve
    Optic Nerve
    Trigeminal Nerve
    Vagus Nerve

Cranial Spinal Cord
Broader   Central Nervous System
    Nervous System
    Spinal Cord

Craving
Use   Appetite

Crayfish
Broader   Arthropoda
    Crustacea
    Invertebrates

Creative Writing
Use   Literature

Creativity
Used For   Innovativeness
    Originality
Broader   Personality Traits
Related   Ability/
    Gifted
    Intelligence

Creativity Measurement
Related   Measurement/

Credibility
Related   Interpersonal Communication

Cretinism
Broader   Endocrine Disorders
    Hypothyroidism
    Mental Retardation
    Thyroid Disorders
Related   Genetic Disorders
    Mental Disorders/

Cri Du Chat Syndrome
Use   Crying Cat Syndrome

Crime
Used For   Felonies
    Misdemeanors
Broader   Antisocial Behavior
    Behavior Disorders
Narrower   Homicide
    Rape

Crime — (Continued)
Narrower
    Shoplifting
    Theft
Related   Criminals

Criminal Conviction
Used For   Conviction (Criminal)
Related   Criminals

Criminal Law
Broader   Law (Government)

Criminals
Used For   Offenders (Adult)
Narrower   Female Criminals
    Male Criminals
Related   Crime
    Criminal Conviction
    Juvenile Delinquents
    Recidivism

Criminology
Related   Penology

Crippled
Use   Physically Handicapped

Crises
Narrower   Family Crises
    Identity Crisis
    Organizational Crises
Related   Crisis Intervention
    Crisis Intervention Services
    Disasters
    Stress

Crisis (Reactions to)
Use   Stress Reactions

Crisis Intervention
Used For   Psychotherapeutic Intervention Tech
Narrower   Suicide Prevention
Related   Crises
    Treatment/

Crisis Intervention Services
Broader   Community Services
    Mental Health Programs
Narrower   Hot Line Services
    Suicide Prevention Centers
Related   Clinics
    Community Mental Health Centers
    Crises
    Emergency Services
    Treatment Facilities
    Walk In Clinics

Critical Flicker Fusion Threshold
Used For   CFF (Vision)
Broader   Thresholds
    Vision

Critical Flicker Fusion Threshold — (Continued)
Broader
    Visual Perception
    Visual Thresholds
Related   Perceptual Measures

Criticism
Broader   Social Behavior
    Social Influences
Related   Social Approval

Criticism (Professional)
Identifier   Professional Criticism

Crocodiles
Use   Crocodilians

Crocodilians
Used For   Alligators
    Crocodiles
Broader   Reptiles
    Vertebrates

Cromwells Adult Locus of Cont Scale
(See)   Nonprojective Personality Measures
    Personality Measures

Cross Cultural Differences
Used For   Differences (Cross Cultural)
Broader   Sociocultural Factors

Crossed Eyes
Use   Strabismus

Crowding
Use   Overpopulation

Cruelty
Broader   Personality Traits

Crustacea
Broader   Arthropoda
    Invertebrates
Narrower   Crabs
    Crayfish

Crying
Broader   Vocalization
    Voice
Related   Infant Vocalization

Crying Cat Syndrome
Used For   Cri Du Chat Syndrome
Broader   Autosome Disorders
    Chromosome Disorders
    Genetic Disorders
    Mental Retardation
    Neonatal Autosome Disorders
    Neonatal Chromosome Disorders
    Neonatal Disorders
    Neonatal Genetic Disorders
    Syndromes
Related   Mental Disorders/

CS (Conditioning)
Use	Conditioned Stimulus

Cuba

Cues
Related	Associative Processes
	Memory
	Mnemonic Learning

Cultism
Related	Ethnology/
	Myths
	Religious Beliefs
	Shamanism
	Sociocultural Factors

Cultural Assimilation
Used For	Assimilation (Cultural)
Broader	Sociocultural Factors
Related	Acculturation

Cultural Deprivation
Used For	Culturally Disadvantaged
Broader	Deprivation
	Sociocultural Factors
Related	Poverty Areas
	Social Environments

Cultural Familial Mental Retardation
Use	Psychosocial Mental Retardation

Cultural Test Bias
Used For	Test Bias (Cultural)
Broader	Test Construction
	Testing
Related	Measurement/
	Response Bias

Culturally Disadvantaged
Use	Cultural Deprivation

Culture (Anthropological)
Narrower	Subculture (Anthropological)
Related	Ethnic Groups
	Ethnology/
	Family Structure
	Sociocultural Factors

Culture Change
Broader	Sociocultural Factors

Culture Fair Intelligence Test
Used For	Cattell Culture Fair Intell Test
(See)	Intelligence Measures

Culture Shock
Related	Ethnology/
	Shock

Curare
Broader	Muscle Relaxing Drugs
Related	Alkaloids
	Antitubocurarine Drugs
	Tubocurarine

Curiosity
Used For	Inquisitiveness
Broader	Personality Traits

Curriculum
Narrower	Art Education
	Braille Instruction
	Business Education
	Compensatory Education
	Driver Education
	Drug Education
	Foreign Language Education
	Health Education
	Language Arts Education
	Mathematics Education
	Music Education
	Phonics
	Physical Education
	Reading Education
	Science Education
	Sex Education
	Spelling
	Vocational Education
Related	Curriculum Development
	Education/

Curriculum Development
Related	Curriculum

Cursive Writing
Used For	Writing (Cursive)
Broader	Handwriting
	Language
	Verbal Communication
	Written Language

Cushings Syndrome
Broader	Adrenal Gland Disorders
	Carbohydrate Metabolism Disorders
	Endocrine Disorders
	Metabolism Disorders
	Syndromes

Cutaneous Sense
Used For	Haptic Perception
Broader	Somesthetic Perception
Narrower	Tactual Perception
	Vibrotactile Thresholds

Cybernetics
Related	Communication Theory
	Computers
	Man Machine Systems

Cycles (Work Rest)
Use	Work Rest Cycles

Cycloheximide
Broader	Antibiotics

Cyclothymic Personality
Broader	Personality Disorders

Cyclothymic Personality — (Continued)
   Related   Affective Psychosis
               Manic Depressive Psychosis

Cynicism
   Broader   Personality Traits
   Related   Negativism

Cysteine
   Broader   Amino Acids

Cytochrome Oxidase
   Broader   Enzymes
               Oxidases

Cytology
   Related   Cells (Biology)

Cytoplasm
   Related   Cells (Biology)

Czechoslovakia

Daily Biological Rhythms (Animal)
   Use   Animal Circadian Rhythms

Dance
   Used For   Ballet
               Performing Arts
   Broader   Arts
               Recreation
   Related   Dance Therapy

Dance Therapy
   Broader   Recreation Therapy
   Related   Dance

Dark Adaptation
   Used For   Adaptation (Dark)
   Broader   Adaptation
               Sensory Adaptation
               Thresholds
               Vision
               Visual Perception
               Visual Thresholds
   Related   Perceptual Measures

Darwinism
   Related   Theories/
               Theory of Evolution

DAT (Test)
   Identifier   Differential Aptitude Tests

Data Processing
   Related   Computer Programing Languages
               Computer Software
               Computers

Dating (Social)
   Use   Social Dating

Daughters
   Broader   Family Members

Day Camps (Recreation)
   Use   Summer Camps (Recreation)

Day Care (Child)
   Use   Child Day Care

Day Care Centers
   Related   Child Day Care
               Community Facilities
               Community Mental Health Centers

Daydreaming
   Related   Fantasy (Defense Mechanism)

DDT (Insecticide)
   Broader   Insecticides

Deaf
   Broader   Aurally Handicapped
               Handicapped
   Related   Lipreading
               Partially Hearing Impaired

Death And Dying
   Used For   Dying
               Mortality
   Narrower   Euthanasia
   Related   Death Attitudes
               Death Rites
               Mortality Rate
               Terminal Cancer
               Terminally Ill Patients

Death Attitudes
   Related   Attitudes/
               Death And Dying
               Euthanasia
               Religious Beliefs

Death Penalty
   Use   Capital Punishment

Death Rate
   Use   Mortality Rate

Death Rites
   Broader   Rites of Passage
               Sociocultural Factors
   Related   Death And Dying

Decarboxylases
   Broader   Enzymes

Deception
   Used For   Lying
   Broader   Behavior Disorders
   Narrower   Cheating
               Confabulation
               Faking
               Malingering
               Pathological Lying
   Related   Dishonesty

Decerebration
- Broader   Neurosurgery
-      Physical Treatment Methods
-      Surgery

Decision Making
- Broader   Cognitive Processes
- Narrower   Choice Behavior
-      Management Decision Making

Decompression Effects
- Related   Acceleration Effects
-      Gravitational Effects
-      Physiological Stress
-      Spaceflight
-      Underwater Effects

Decortication (Brain)
- Broader   Neurosurgery
-      Physical Treatment Methods
-      Surgery

Deductive Reasoning
- Use   Inductive Deductive Reasoning

Deer
- Broader   Mammals
-      Vertebrates

Defecation
- Broader   Excretion

Defense Mechanisms
- Narrower   Compensation (Defense Mechanism)
-      Denial
-      Displacement (Defense Mechanism)
-      Fantasy (Defense Mechanism)
-      Identification (Defense Mechanism)
-      Intellectualization
-      Introjection
-      Isolation (Defense Mechanism)
-      Projection (Defense Mechanism)
-      Rationalization
-      Reaction Formation
-      Regression (Defense Mechanism)
-      Repression (Defense Mechanism)
-      Sublimation
-      Suppression (Defense Mechanism)
-      Withdrawal (Defense Mechanism)
- Related   Mental Disorders/
-      Personality Disorders
-      Personality Processes/

Defensiveness
- Broader   Personality Traits

Deficiency Disorders (Nutritional)
- Use   Nutritional Deficiencies

Degrees (Educational)
- Use   Educational Degrees

Dehydrogenases
- Broader   Enzymes
- Narrower   Alcohol Dehydrogenases
-      Lactate Dehydrogenase

Delayed Auditory Feedback
- Broader   Auditory Feedback
-      Auditory Stimulation
-      Delayed Feedback
-      Feedback
-      Perceptual Stimulation
-      Sensory Feedback

Delayed Development
- Broader   Developmental Differences
- Related   Developmental Age Groups
-      Physical Development
-      Psychogenesis

Delayed Feedback
- Broader   Feedback
-      Perceptual Stimulation
- Narrower   Delayed Auditory Feedback

Delayed Reinforcement
- Use   Reinforcement Schedules

Deletion (Chromosome)
- Broader   Chromosome Disorders
-      Genetic Disorders

Delinquency (Juvenile)
- Use   Juvenile Delinquency

Delirium
- Broader   Consciousness Disturbances
-      Symptoms
- Related   Hyperthermia

Delirium Tremens
- Broader   Alcoholic Hallucinosis
-      Alcoholic Psychosis
-      Brain Disorders
-      Central Nervous System Disorders
-      Hallucinosis
-      Nervous System Disorders
-      Organic Brain Syndromes
-      Psychosis
-      Syndromes

Delta Rhythm
- Broader   Electrical Activity
-      Electrophysiology
- Related   Electroencephalography

Delusions
- Broader   Thought Disturbances
- Narrower   Megalomania

Dementia (Presenile)
- Use   Presenile Dementia

Dementia (Senile)
  Use   Senile Dementia

Dementia Paralytica
  Use   General Paresis

Dementia Praecox
  Use   Schizophrenia

Democracy
  Broader   Political Economic Systems

Democratic Party
  Use   Political Parties

Demographic Characteristics
  Used For   Population Characteristics
  Related   Population

Demonstrations (Social)
  Use   Social Demonstrations

Denatured Alcohol
  Broader   Alcohols
  Related   Ethanol
             Methanol

Dendrites
  Broader   Cells (Biology)
             Nervous System
             Neurons

Denial
  Broader   Defense Mechanisms

Denmark

Dental Education
  Used For   Education (Dental)
  Broader   Graduate Education
             Higher Education

Dental Students
  Broader   College Students
             Students

Dental Surgery
  Broader   Dental Treatment
             Physical Treatment Methods
             Surgery

Dental Treatment
  Broader   Physical Treatment Methods
  Narrower   Dental Surgery

Dentistry
  Broader   Medical Sciences
             Sciences

Dentists
  Broader   Medical Personnel

Deoxycorticosterone
  Broader   Adrenal Cortex Hormones
             Corticosteroids
             Hormones
             Steroids

Deoxyribonucleic Acid
  Used For   DNA (Deoxyribonucleic Acid)
  Broader   Acids
             Nucleic Acids

Departmentalized Teaching Method
  Broader   Teaching
             Teaching Methods

Dependency (Drug)
  Use   Drug Dependency

Dependency (Personality)
  Broader   Personality Traits
  Related   Field Dependence

Dependent Variables
  Broader   Statistical Variables

Depersonalization
  Broader   Symptoms
  Related   Alienation

Depression (Emotion)
  Used For   Agitated Depression
             Dysthymia
             Melancholia
  Broader   Affective Disturbances
             Emotional States
  Narrower   Anaclitic Depression
             Involutional Depression
             Manic Depression
             Neurotic Depressive Reaction
             Postpartum Depression
             Psychotic Depressive Reaction
             Reactive Depression
  Related   Antidepressant Drugs
             Manic Depressive Psychosis
             Sadness

Depression (Spreading)
  Use   Spreading Depression

Depressive Reaction (Neurotic)
  Use   Neurotic Depressive Reaction

Deprivation
  Narrower   Cultural Deprivation
             Food Deprivation
             REM Dream Deprivation
             Sensory Deprivation
             Sleep Deprivation
             Social Deprivation
             Social Isolation
             Stimulus Deprivation
             Water Deprivation
  Related   Environmental Stress
             Isolation Effect
             Motivation
             Physiological Stress
             Psychological Stress
             Stress
             Stress Reactions

Depth Perception
Broader	Spatial Perception
Narrower	Stereoscopic Vision

Depth Psychology
Broader	Psychology

Dermatitis
Broader	Skin Disorders
Narrower	Eczema
	Neurodermatitis
Related	Allergic Skin Disorders
	Infectious Disorders
	Toxic Disorders

Describing Personality Test
(See)	Nonprojective Personality Measures
	Personality Measures

Desensitization (Systematic)
Use	Systematic Desensitization Therapy

Design (Experimental)
Use	Experimental Design

Design (Man Machine Systems)
Use	Man Machine Systems Design

Desipramine
Broader	Antidepressant Drugs

Desirability (Social)
Use	Social Desirability

Desires
Use	Motivation

Detached Retina
Use	Retinal Detachment

Detection (Signal)
Use	Signal Detection (Perception)

Detention (Legal)
Use	Legal Detention

Detoxification
Related	Drug Therapy
	Drug Withdrawal
	Treatment/

Development/
Used For	Growth
	Ontogeny
Related	Adolescent Development
	Childhood Development
	Developmental Age Groups
	Developmental Differences
	Developmental Stages
	Human Development/
	Organizational Development
	Physical Development
	Psychogenesis
	Sexual Development

Developmental Age Groups
Used For	Age
Narrower	Adolescents
	Adults
	Aged
	Children
	Infants
	Middle Aged
	Neonates
	Preschool Age Children
	School Age Children
	Young Adults
Related	Adolescent Development
	Age Differences
	Childhood Development
	Delayed Development
	Development/
	Developmental Differences
	Developmental Stages
	Emotional Development
	Human Development/
	Motor Development
	Physical Development
	Precocious Development
	Psychogenesis

Developmental Differences
Narrower	Age Differences
	Delayed Development
	Precocious Development
	Sex Linked Developmental Differences
Related	Adolescent Development
	Childhood Development
	Children
	Development/
	Developmental Age Groups
	Developmental Stages
	Early Childhood Development
	Human Development/
	Infant Development
	Motor Development
	Neonatal Development
	Physical Development
	Psychogenesis
	School Age Children

Developmental Psychology
Broader	Psychology
	Sciences
	Social Sciences
Narrower	Adolescent Psychology
	Child Psychology
	Gerontology

Developmental Stages
Narrower	Embryo
	Fetus
	Menopause
	Prenatal Developmental Stages

Developmental Stages — (Continued)

Narrower
       Puberty
       Zygote

Related
       Adolescent Development
       Childhood Development
       Development/
       Developmental Age Groups
       Developmental Differences
       Human Development/
       Perceptual Development
       Physical Development
       Psychogenesis

Deviant Behavior
Use   Antisocial Behavior

Deviations (Sexual)
Use   Sexual Deviations

Devices (Experimental)
Use   Apparatus

Devices (Safety)
Use   Safety Devices

Dexamphetamine
Use   Dextroamphetamine

Dexedrine
Use   Dextroamphetamine

Dexterity (Physical)
Use   Physical Dexterity

Dextroamphetamine
Used For   Amphetamine (D-)
       Dexamphetamine
       Dexedrine
Broader   Adrenergic Drugs
       Amines
       Appetite Depressing Drugs
       CNS Affecting Drugs
       CNS Stimulating Drugs
       Sympathomimetic Amines
       Sympathomimetic Drugs
Related   Amphetamine

Diabetes
Broader   Carbohydrate Metabolism Disorders
       Endocrine Disorders
       Metabolism Disorders
Narrower   Diabetes Insipidus
       Diabetes Mellitus
Related   Hypoglycemic Agents

Diabetes Insipidus
Broader   Carbohydrate Metabolism Disorders
       Diabetes
       Endocrine Disorders
       Metabolism Disorders
Related   Genetic Disorders

Diabetes Mellitus
Broader   Carbohydrate Metabolism Disorders
       Diabetes
       Endocrine Disorders
       Metabolism Disorders

Diacetylmorphine
Use   Heroin

Diagnosis
Narrower   Angiography
       Biopsy
       Cardiography
       Computer Assisted Diagnosis
       Differential Diagnosis
       Echoencephalography
       Electro Oculography
       Electrocardiography
       Electroencephalography
       Electromyography
       Electronystagmography
       Electroplethysmography
       Electroretinography
       Encephalography
       Galvanic Skin Response
       Medical Diagnosis
       Ophthalmologic Examination
       Plethysmography
       Pneumoencephalography
       Psychodiagnosis
       Psychodiagnostic Interview
       Rheoencephalography
       Roentgenography
       Urinalysis
Related   Patient History
       Prognosis

Dialect
Broader   Language
       Verbal Communication
Narrower   Nonstandard English

Dialectics
Related   Reasoning

Dialysis
Broader   Physical Treatment Methods
Narrower   Hemodialysis

Diaphragm (Anatomy)
Broader   Muscles
       Musculoskeletal System
       Respiratory System
Related   Thorax

Diaphragms (Birth Control)
Broader   Birth Control
       Contraceptive Devices
       Family Planning

Diarrhea
Broader   Colon Disorders
        Digestive System Disorders
        Gastrointestinal Disorders
Related   Fecal Incontinence

Diastolic Pressure
Used For   Pressure (Diastolic)
Broader   Blood Pressure

Diazepam
Used For   Valium
Broader   Muscle Relaxing Drugs
        Tranquilizing Drugs

Dicaine
Use   Tetracaine

Dictionary

Dieldrin
Broader   Insecticides

Diencephalon
Broader   Brain
        Central Nervous System
        Nervous System
Narrower   Geniculate Bodies (Thalamus)
        Hypothalamo Hypophyseal System
        Hypothalamus
        Optic Chiasm
        Thalamic Nuclei
        Thalamus

Differences (Cross Cultural)
Use   Cross Cultural Differences

Differences (Individual)
Use   Individual Differences

Differences (Racial)
Use   Racial Differences

Differential Aptitude Tests
Used For   DAT (Test)
(See)   Aptitude Measures

Differential Diagnosis
Broader   Diagnosis
Related   Medical Diagnosis
        Psychodiagnosis

Differential Limen
Use   Thresholds

Differential Personality Inventory
(See)   Nonprojective Personality Measures
        Personality Measures

Differential Reinforcement
Broader   Reinforcement

Difficulty Level (Test)
Broader   Test Construction
        Testing

Difficulty Level (Test) — (Continued)
Related   Measurement/

Digestion
Related   Digestive System Physiology/
        Salivation

Digestive System
Narrower   Colon
        Esophagus
        Gall Bladder
        Gastrointestinal System
        Intestines
        Lips (Face)
        Liver
        Mouth (Anatomy)
        Peritoneum
        Pharynx
        Stomach
        Taste Buds
        Teeth (Anatomy)
        Tongue
Related   Anatomical Systems/
        Digestion
        Digestive System Disorders
        Salivary Glands

Digestive System Disorders
Narrower   Cirrhosis (Liver)
        Colitis
        Colon Disorders
        Constipation
        Diarrhea
        Fecal Incontinence
        Gastrointestinal Disorders
        Gastrointestinal Ulcers
        Hepatitis
        Jaundice
        Liver Disorders
        Toxic Hepatitis
        Ulcerative Colitis
        Vomiting
Related   Digestive System Disorders/
        Infectious Disorders
        Neoplasms
        Symptoms
        Toxic Disorders

Digit Span Testing
Related   Measurement/

Digital Computers
Broader   Computers

Digits (Mathematics)
Use   Numbers (Numerals)

Dihydroergotamine
Broader   Adrenergic Blocking Drugs
        Analgesic Drugs

Dihydroergotamine — (Continued)
Broader
      Ergot Derivatives
      Vasoconstrictor Drugs

Dilantin
Use   Diphenylhydantoin

Dilation (Pupil)
Use   Pupil Dilation

Dilation (Pupil) Drugs
Use   Mydriatic Drugs

Diphenhydramine
Used For   Benadryl
Broader   Amines
      Antihistaminic Drugs
      Antitremor Drugs

Diphenylhydantoin
Used For   Dilantin
      Diphenylhydantoin Sodium
Broader   Anticonvulsive Drugs
      Antiepileptic Drugs

Diphenylhydantoin Sodium
Use   Diphenylhydantoin

Diplomacy (Foreign Policy)
Broader   Foreign Policy Making
      Government Policy Making
Related   Government
      International Relations

Diptera
Used For   Flies
Broader   Arthropoda
      Insects
      Invertebrates
Narrower   Drosophila
Related   Larvae

Directed Discussion Method
Broader   Teaching
      Teaching Methods
Related   Lecture Method

Disadvantaged
Used For   Economically Disadvantaged
      Socially Disadvantaged
      Underprivileged
Related   Poverty
      Social Class
      Socioeconomic Status

Disappointment
Related   Dissatisfaction
      Emotions/

Disasters
Narrower   Natural Disasters
Related   Crises
      Stress

Discipline (Child)
Use   Child Discipline

Discipline (Classroom)
Use   Classroom Discipline

Discovery Teaching Method
Broader   Teaching
      Teaching Methods
Related   Montessori Method
      Nondirected Discussion Method
      Open Classroom Method

Discrimination (Cognitive)
Use   Cognitive Discrimination

Discrimination/
Related   Cognitive Discrimination
      Odor Discrimination
      Perception/
      Perceptual Discrimination
      Racial Discrimination
      Spatial Perception
      Stimulus Discrimination
      Tactual Perception
      Taste Perception

Discussion (Group)
Use   Group Discussion

Diseases
Use   Disorders/

Diseases (Venereal)
Use   Venereal Diseases

Dishonesty
Broader   Personality Traits
Related   Deception

Dislike
Use   Aversion

Disorders/
Used For   Diseases
      Illness (Physical)
Related   Anesthesia (Feeling)
      Bacterial Disorders
      Behavior Disorders
      Blood and Lymphatic Disorders
      Blood Pressure Disorders
      Cardiovascular Disorders
      Congenital Disorders
      Digestive System Disorders
      Endocrine Disorders
      Etiology
      Genetic Disorders
      Immunologic Disorders
      Infectious Disorders
      Injuries
      Mental Disorders/
      Metabolism Disorders
      Musculoskeletal Disorders
      Neonatal Disorders
      Neoplasms
      Nervous System Disorders
      Nutritional Deficiencies

Disorders/ — (Continued)
Related
         Onset (Disorders)
         Predisposition
         Prognosis
         Psychosomatic Disorders
         Recovery (Disorders)
         Relapse (Disorders)
         Remission (Disorders)
         Respiratory Tract Disorders
         Sense Organ Disorders
         Skin Disorders
         Speech Disorders
         Susceptibility (Disorders)
         Symptoms
         Syndromes
         Toxic Disorders
         Urogenital Disorders

Disorientation (Place)
Use   Place Disorientation

Disorientation (Time)
Use   Time Disorientation

Displacement (Defense Mechanism)
Broader   Defense Mechanisms

Displays
Narrower   Animal Courtship Displays
         Auditory Displays
         Tactual Displays
         Visual Displays

Disposition
Use   Personality/

Disruptive Behavior
Use   Behavior Problems

Dissatisfaction
Related   Disappointment
         Emotions/
         Frustration

Dissociative Neurosis
Used For   Hysterical Neurosis (Dissocia-tion)
Broader   Neurosis
Related   Hysteria
         Hysterical Personality

Dissociative Patterns
Narrower   Amnesia
         Fugue Reaction
         Multiple Personality
         Somnambulism
Related   Hysteria
         Hysterical Personality
         Mental Disorders/
         Personality Disorders

Dissonance (Cognitive)
Use   Cognitive Dissonance

Distance Discrimination
Use   Distance Perception

Distance Perception
Used For   Distance Discrimination
Broader   Spatial Perception
Narrower   Apparent Distance

Distortion (Perceptual)
Use   Illusions (Perception)

Distractibility
Broader   Symptoms

Distress
Used For   Anguish
Broader   Emotional States
Related   Suffering

Distress Calls (Animal)
Use   Animal Distress Calls

Distributed Practice
Broader   Learning Schedules
         Practice

Distribution (Frequency)
Use   Frequency Distribution

Distrust
Use   Suspicion

Disturbed (Emotionally)
Use   Emotionally Disturbed

Diuresis
Broader   Medical Treatment (General)
         Physical Treatment Methods

Diuretics
Narrower   Acetazolamide
         Caffeine
Related   Antihypertensive Drugs
         Drugs/
         Urination

Diurnal Variations
Use   Human Biological Rhythms

Divergent Thinking
Broader   Cognitive Processes
         Thinking
Related   Abstraction

Divided Attention
Broader   Attention
         Awareness
         Consciousness States
Related   Selective Attention

Division of Labor (Animal)
Use   Animal Division of Labor

Divorce
Broader   Marital Separation
Related   Divorced Persons

Divorced Persons
Related   Divorce
           Family/
           Marital Separation
           Marital Status
           Parental Absence

Dizziness
Use   Vertigo

DNA (Deoxyribonucleic Acid)
Use   Deoxyribonucleic Acid

Doctors
Use   Physicians

Dogmatism
Use   Authoritarianism

Dogs
Used For   Puppies
Broader   Mammals
           Vertebrates

Doll Play
Broader   Recreation

Dolphins
Broader   Mammals
           Vertebrates
Related   Porpoises

Domestic Service Personnel
Used For   Maids
Related   Personnel/

Dominance (Animal)
Use   Animal Dominance

Dominance Hierarchy
Related   Animal Dominance
           Dominance/
           Social Behavior
           Social Structure

Dominance/
Related   Animal Dominance
           Cerebral Dominance
           Dominance Hierarchy
           Genetic Dominance
           Ocular Dominance

Domination
Use   Authoritarianism

Dominican Republic

Donors
Use   Charitable Behavior

Dopa
Broader   Acids
           Amino Acids
Related   Dopamine
           Levodopa
           Methyldopa

Dopamine
Broader   Amines
           Catecholamines
           Sympathomimetic Amines
           Sympathomimetic Drugs
Related   Dopa
           Heart Rate Affecting Drugs
           Hypotension
           Levodopa
           Methyldopa

Dormitories
Used For   Residence Halls
Broader   School Facilities

Dorsal Roots
Broader   Central Nervous System
           Nervous System
           Spinal Cord

Dosage (Drug)
Use   Drug Dosages

Double Bind Interaction
Used For   Interaction (Double Bind)
Broader   Interpersonal Communication
           Interpersonal Interaction
           Social Behavior
           Social Interaction
Related   Schizophrenogenic Family
           Schizophrenogenic Mothers

Doubt
Broader   Emotional States
           Mental Confusion
Related   Suspicion

Doves
Broader   Birds
           Vertebrates

Downs Syndrome
Used For   Mongolism
Broader   Autosome Disorders
           Chromosome Disorders
           Genetic Disorders
           Mental Retardation
           Neonatal Autosome Disorders
           Neonatal Chromosome Disor-
             ders
           Neonatal Disorders
           Neonatal Genetic Disorders
           Syndromes
Related   Mental Disorders/
           Trainable Mentally Retarded
           Trisomy 21

Draftees
Broader   Enlisted Military Personnel
           Military Personnel
Related   Army Personnel
           Navy Personnel

Drama
 Used For Performing Arts
 Broader Arts
   Theatre
 Related Motion Pictures (Entertainment)

Drawing
 Broader Art
   Arts

Dream Analysis
 Used For Dream Interpretation
 Broader Psychoanalysis
   Psychotherapeutic Techniques
   Psychotherapy
 Related Analysis/
   Parapsychology

Dream Content
 Related Dreaming
   Nightmares
   Sleep

Dream Interpretation
 Use Dream Analysis

Dream Recall
 Used For Recall (Dreams)
 Related Dreaming

Dreaming
 Narrower Nightmares
   REM Dreams
 Related Dream Content
   Dream Recall
   Sleep

Drinking (Alcohol)
 Use Alcohol Drinking Patterns

Drinking Attitudes
 Use Alcohol Drinking Attitudes

Drinking Behavior (Animal)
 Use Animal Drinking Behavior

Drive
 Use Motivation

Driver Education
 Used For Education (Driver)
 Broader Curriculum
 Related Drivers

Driver Safety
 Use Highway Safety

Drivers
 Related Automobiles
   Driver Education
   Driving Behavior
   Highway Safety
   Motor Traffic Accidents

Driving Behavior
 Related Drivers
   Highway Hypnosis Accidents

Driving Behavior — (Continued)
 Related
   Highway Safety
   Motor Traffic Accidents
   Pedestrian Accidents
   Safety Belts

Dropouts
 Narrower College Dropouts
   Potential Dropouts
   School Dropouts
 Related Education/
   School Enrollment

Drosophila
 Used For Fruit Fly
 Broader Arthropoda
   Diptera
   Insects
   Invertebrates
 Related Larvae

Drowsiness
 Use Sleep Onset

Drug Abuse
 Used For Abuse (Drugs)
 Broader Behavior Disorders
   Drug Usage
 Narrower Drug Addiction
   Heroin Addiction
 Related Addiction
   Drug Dependency

Drug Addiction
 Broader Addiction
   Behavior Disorders
   Drug Abuse
   Drug Dependency
   Drug Effects
   Drug Usage
   Side Effects (Drug)
 Narrower Heroin Addiction
 Related Drug Withdrawal
   Drug Withdrawal Effects

Drug Administration Methods
 Related Drugs/
   Injections

Drug Adverse Reactions
 Used For Reaction (Drugs)
 Broader Drug Effects
   Side Effects (Drug)
 Related Drug Allergies
   Drug Sensitivity

Drug Allergies
 Broader Allergic Disorders
   Drug Effects
   Immunologic Disorders
   Side Effects (Drug)
 Related Drug Adverse Reactions
   Drug Sensitivity

Drug Dependency
Used For	Dependency (Drug)
Broader	Drug Effects
	Drug Usage
	Side Effects (Drug)
Narrower	Drug Addiction
	Heroin Addiction
Related	Addiction
	Amphetamine
	Barbiturates
	Codeine
	Drug Abuse
	Drug Withdrawal Effects
	Glue Sniffing
	Glutethimide
	Marihuana Usage
	Mental Disorders/
	Meperidine
	Methadone
	Methamphetamine
	Morphine
	Narcotic Drugs
	Nicotine

Drug Dosages
Used For	Dosage (Drug)
Related	Drugs/

Drug Education
Used For	Education (Drug)
Broader	Curriculum
	Health Education

Drug Effects
Narrower	Drug Addiction
	Drug Adverse Reactions
	Drug Allergies
	Drug Dependency
	Drug Sensitivity
	Heroin Addiction
	Side Effects (Drug)
Related	Drug Withdrawal Effects
	Drugs/
	Psychedelic Experiences

Drug Induced Congenital Disorders
Broader	Congenital Disorders
	Toxic Disorders
Related	Thalidomide

Drug Induced Hallucinations
Broader	Hallucinations
	Perceptual Disturbances

Drug Laws
Broader	Government Policy Making
	Laws
Narrower	Marihuana Laws
	Marihuana Legalization
Related	Drugs/

Drug Potentiation
Used For	Enhancement (Drugs)
	Potentiation (Drugs)
Related	Chlorpromazine
	Drug Synergism
	Drugs/

Drug Rehabilitation
Used For	Methadone Maintenance
	Rehabilitation (Drug)
Broader	Rehabilitation
Related	Psychosocial Rehabilitation
	Treatment/

Drug Sensitivity
Used For	Sensitivity (Drugs)
Broader	Drug Effects
	Side Effects (Drug)
Related	Drug Adverse Reactions
	Drug Allergies

Drug Synergism
Used For	Synergism (Drugs)
Related	Drug Potentiation
	Drugs/

Drug Therapy
Used For	Chemotherapy
	Medication
	Pharmacotherapy
	Therapy (Drug)
Broader	Organic Therapies
Narrower	Narcoanalysis
	Sleep Treatment
Related	Detoxification
	Outpatient Treatment

Drug Tolerance
Used For	Tolerance (Drug)
Related	Drugs/
	Side Effects (Drug)

Drug Usage
Narrower	Drug Abuse
	Drug Addiction
	Drug Dependency
	Glue Sniffing
	Heroin Addiction
	Marihuana Usage
Related	Addiction
	Behavior Disorders
	Drugs/
	Habituation

Drug Usage Attitudes
Related	Attitudes/
	Marihuana Legalization

Drug Withdrawal
Used For	Withdrawal (Drug)
Related	Detoxification
	Drug Addiction
	Drug Withdrawal Effects

Drug Withdrawal Effects
Used For   Withdrawal Effects (Drug)
Related   Drug Addiction
          Drug Dependency
          Drug Effects
          Drug Withdrawal
          Drugs/

Drugs/
Related   Adrenergic Blocking Drugs
          Adrenergic Drugs
          Adrenolytic Drugs
          Alcohols
          Alkaloids
          Amine Oxidase Inhibitors
          Amines
          Amino Acids
          Analeptic Drugs
          Analgesic Drugs
          Anesthetic Drugs
          Antibiotics
          Antibodies
          Anticoagulant Drugs
          Anticonvulsive Drugs
          Antidepressant Drugs
          Antiemetic Drugs
          Antiepileptic Drugs
          Antihistaminic Drugs
          Antihypertensive Drugs
          Antipsychotic Drugs
          Antitremor Drugs
          Antitubercular Drugs
          Antitubocurarine Drugs
          Appetite Depressing Drugs
          Barbiturates
          Bromides
          Carcinogens
          Catecholamines
          Cholinergic Blocking Drugs
          Cholinergic Drugs
          Cholinesterase Inhibitors
          Cholinomimetic Drugs
          CNS Affecting Drugs
          Coenzymes
          Diuretics
          Drug Administration Methods
          Drug Dosages
          Drug Effects
          Drug Laws
          Drug Potentiation
          Drug Synergism
          Drug Tolerance
          Drug Usage
          Drug Withdrawal Effects
          Enzymes
          Ergot Derivatives
          Ganglion Blocking Drugs
          Hallucinogenic Drugs
          Hashish

Drugs/ — (Continued)
Related
          Heart Rate Affecting Drugs
          Heparin
          Hormones
          Hypnotic Drugs
          Hypoglycemic Agents
          Insecticides
          Lipoproteins
          Marihuana
          Monoamine Oxidase Inhibitors
          Muscle Relaxing Drugs
          Mydriatic Drugs
          Narcoanalytic Drugs
          Narcotic Antagonists
          Nucleic Acids
          Opiates
          Oxytocic Drugs
          Pepsinogen
          Peptides
          Placebo
          Proteins
          Psychedelic Drugs
          Psychic Energizers
          Psychotomimetic Drugs
          Respiration Stimulating Drugs
          Sedatives
          Serotonin Antagonists
          Steroids
          Sympatholytic Drugs
          Sympathomimetic Drugs
          Thyroid Extract
          Toxicity
          Tranquilizing Drugs
          Vasoconstrictor Drugs
          Vasodilator Drugs
          Vitamins

Drunkenness
Use   Alcohol Intoxication

Dualism
Broader   Philosophies

Ducklings
Use   Ducks

Ducks
Used For   Ducklings
Broader   Birds
          Vertebrates

Duct (Thoracic)
Use   Thoracic Duct

Duodenum
Use   Intestines

Duration (Response)
Use   Response Duration

Duration (Stimulus)
Use   Stimulus Duration

Dwarfism (Pituitary)
Use   Hypopituitarism

Dyads
Broader   Social Groups

Dying
Use   Death And Dying

Dying Patients
Use   Terminally Ill Patients

Dynamics (Group)
Use   Group Dynamics

Dysarthria
Broader   Articulation Disorders
              Speech Disorders
Narrower   Stammering
              Stuttering
Related   Dysphonia
              Muscular Dystrophy
              Paralysis

Dysautonomia
Used For   Riley Day Syndrome
Broader   Autonomic Nervous System Disorders
              Central Nervous System Disorders
              Nervous System Disorders
Related   Congenital Disorders

Dyskinesia
Broader   Nervous System Disorders
              Symptoms
Related   Neuromuscular Disorders

Dyslexia
Used For   Word Blindness (Dyslexia)
Broader   Learning Disabilities
              Learning Disorders
              Reading Disabilities
Related   Reading

Dysmenorrhea
Broader   Genital Disorders
              Gynecological Disorders
              Menstrual Disorders
              Urogenital Disorders

Dysmetria
Use   Ataxia

Dysmorphophobia
Broader   Phobias

Dyspareunia
Broader   Psychosexual Behavior
              Sexual Function Disturbances
              Sexual Intercourse (Human)
Related   Frigidity
              Vaginismus

Dysphonia
Broader   Speech Disorders

Dysphonia — (Continued)
Related   Dysarthria
              Speech Handicapped

Dysphoria
Use   Restlessness

Dyspnea
Broader   Respiratory Distress
              Respiratory Tract Disorders
              Symptoms
Narrower   Asthma
Related   Cardiovascular Disorders
              Lung Disorders
              Psychosomatic Disorders

Dysthymia
Use   Depression (Emotion)

Dystonia
Use   Muscular Disorders

Dystrophy (Muscular)
Use   Muscular Dystrophy

Eagerness
Use   Enthusiasm

Ear (Anatomy)
Broader   Sense Organs
Narrower   Cochlea
              External Ear
              Labyrinth (Anatomy)
              Middle Ear
              Semicircular Canals
              Vestibular Apparatus
Related   Ear Disorders

Ear Canal
Use   External Ear

Ear Disorders
Broader   Sense Organ Disorders
Narrower   Labyrinth Disorders
              Menieres Disease
              Motion Sickness
              Otosclerosis
              Tinnitus
Related   Auditory Perception
              Aurally Handicapped
              Ear (Anatomy)

Ear Ossicles
Use   Middle Ear

Early Childhood
Use   Preschool Age Children

Early Childhood Development
Broader   Childhood Development
Related   Developmental Differences
              Early Experience
              Physical Development
              Psychogenesis

Early Experience
Broader   Experiences (Events)

Early Experience — (Continued)
Related	Early Childhood Development

Early Infantile Autism
Broader	Autism
	Childhood Psychosis
	Psychosis
Related	Autistic Children
	Childhood Schizophrenia
	Symbiotic Infantile Psychosis

Earthworms
Broader	Invertebrates
	Worms

East German Democratic Republic

Eating
Broader	Food Intake
Related	Appetite
	Eating Patterns

Eating Patterns
Related	Eating

Echinodermata
Used For	Starfish
Broader	Invertebrates

Echoencephalography
Broader	Diagnosis
	Encephalography
	Medical Diagnosis

Echoes
Related	Auditory Stimulation

Echolalia
Broader	Speech Disorders
Related	Gilles De La Tourette Disorder
	Speech Handicapped

Echolocation
Related	Animal Ethology
	Animal Vocalizations

Ecological Factors
Narrower	Pollution
	Topography
Related	Ecology

Ecology
Related	Ecological Factors
	Environment
	Pollution

Economically Disadvantaged
Use	Disadvantaged

Economy
Related	Costs And Cost Analysis
	Money
	Political Economic Systems

ECS Therapy
Use	Electroconvulsive Shock Therapy

ECT (Therapy)
Use	Electroconvulsive Shock Therapy

Eczema
Broader	Dermatitis
	Skin Disorders
Related	Allergic Skin Disorders

Educable Mentally Retarded
Used For	Mildly Mentally Retarded
	Morons
Broader	Handicapped
	Mentally Retarded
Related	Slow Learners

Education (Dental)
Use	Dental Education

Education (Driver)
Use	Driver Education

Education (Drug)
Use	Drug Education

Education/
Used For	Educational Process
	Training
Related	Ability Grouping
	Academic Achievement
	Academic Aptitude
	Accreditation (Education Personnel)
	Adult Education
	Business Education
	Classroom Behavior Modification
	Classroom Discipline
	Clinical Methods Training
	Coeducation
	Compensatory Education
	Counselor Education
	Curriculum
	Dropouts
	Educational Administration
	Educational Aspirations
	Educational Background
	Educational Counseling
	Educational Degrees
	Educational Financial Assistance
	Educational Incentives
	Educational Measurement
	Educational Personnel
	Educational Programs
	Elementary Education
	Extracurricular Activities
	Higher Education
	Nursing Education
	Paraprofessional Education
	Personnel Training
	Preschool Education
	Private School Education
	Public School Education

LIBRARY
KENRICK SEMINARY
7800 KENRICK ROAD
ST. LOUIS, MISSOURI 63119

Education/ — (Continued)

Related
    Religious Education
    School Adjustment
    School Enrollment
    School Facilities
    School Integration (Racial)
    School Learning
    School Readiness
    Schools
    Secondary Education
    Social Work Education
    Special Education
    Student Admission Criteria
    Student Attitudes
    Students
    Study Habits
    Teacher Attitudes
    Teacher Education
    Teacher Personality
    Teacher Student Interaction
    Teacher Tenure
    Teaching
    Theories of Education
    Vocational Education

Educational Administration
Used For   School Administration
    School Organization
Related   Education/

Educational Aspirations
Broader   Aspirations
Related   Education/

Educational Audiovisual Aids
Used For   Audiovisual Aids (Educational)
Broader   Audiovisual Communications
    Media
    Communications Media
    Instructional Media
    Teaching
Narrower   Motion Pictures (Educational)
Related   Audiovisual Instruction
    Educational Television
    Film Strips
    Televised Instruction
    Videotape Instruction

Educational Background
Narrower   Parent Educational Background
Related   Education/

Educational Background (Parents)
Use   Parent Educational Background

Educational Counseling
Used For   Educational Guidance
    Guidance (Educational)
Related   Counseling/
    Education/
    Occupational Guidance

Educational Degrees
Used For   College Degrees
    Degrees (Educational)
    Graduate Degrees
    High School Diplomas
    Undergraduate Degrees
Related   Education/
    Higher Education

Educational Field Trips
Used For   Field Trips (Educational)
Broader   Teaching
    Teaching Methods

Educational Financial Assistance
Used For   Educational Financial Need
    Financial Assistance (Education-
      al)
    Scholarships
    School Federal Aid
    School Financial Assistance
    Stipends
Related   Education/

Educational Financial Need
Use   Educational Financial Assistance

Educational Guidance
Use   Educational Counseling

Educational Incentives
Broader   Incentives
    Motivation
Related   Education/

Educational Laboratories
Used For   Laboratories (Educational)
Broader   School Facilities
Narrower   Language Laboratories

Educational Measurement
Narrower   Entrance Examinations
    Grading (Educational)
Related   Education/
    Measurement/

Educational Personnel
Used For   Faculty
Narrower   College Teachers
    Elementary School Teachers
    High School Teachers
    Junior High School Teachers
    Resource Teachers
    School Administrators
    School Counselors
    School Nurses
    School Principals
    School Psychologists
    School Superintendents
    Special Education Teachers
    Student Teachers
    Teacher Aides
    Teachers

Educational Personnel — (Continued)
Related	Education/
	Educational Psychologists
	Mental Health Personnel
	Missionaries
	Personnel/
	Speech Therapists
	Volunteer Personnel

Educational Process
Use	Education/

Educational Program Evaluation
Used For	Evaluation (Educational Program)
	Program Evaluation (Educational)
Broader	Evaluation
Related	Educational Programs

Educational Program Planning
Used For	Program Planning (Educational)
Related	Educational Programs

Educational Programs
Used For	Work Study Programs
Narrower	Foreign Study
	Project Follow Through
	Project Head Start
	Title V Projects
	Upward Bound
Related	Compensatory Education
	Education/
	Educational Program Evaluation
	Educational Program Planning

Educational Psychologists
Broader	Psychologists
Narrower	School Psychologists
Related	Educational Personnel

Educational Psychology
Broader	Applied Psychology
	Psychology
	Sciences
	Social Sciences
Narrower	School Psychology

Educational Television
Broader	Audiovisual Communications Media
	Communications Media
	Mass Media
	Telecommunications Media
	Television
Related	Educational Audiovisual Aids
	Televised Instruction

Educational Toys
Broader	Toys

Edwards Personal Preference Schedule
Used For	EPPS (Test)

Edwards Personal Preference Schedule — (Continued)
(See)	Nonprojective Personality Measures
	Personality Measures

Edwards Personality Inventory
(See)	Nonprojective Personality Measures
	Personality Measures

Edwards Social Desirability Scale
(See)	Nonprojective Personality Measures
	Personality Measures

EEG (Electrophysiology)
Use	Electroencephalography

Efficiency (Employee)
Use	Employee Efficiency

Effort
Use	Energy Expenditure

Ego
Broader	Psychoanalytic Personality Factors

Egocentrism
Use	Egotism

Egotism
Used For	Egocentrism
Broader	Personality Traits

Eidetic Imagery
Broader	Memory

Ejaculation
Use	Male Orgasm

EKG (Electrophysiology)
Use	Electrocardiography

Elavil
Use	Amitriptyline

Elbow (Anatomy)
Broader	Musculoskeletal System
Related	Arm (Anatomy)

Elections (Political)
Use	Political Elections

Elective Abortion
Use	Induced Abortion

Elective Mutism
Broader	Mutism
	Speech Disorders
Related	Mental Disorders/

Electra Complex
Used For	Complex (Electra)
Broader	Psychoanalytic Personality Factors

Electric Fishes
Broader	Fishes
	Vertebrates

Electrical Activity
Broader Electrophysiology
Narrower Alpha Rhythm
Auditory Evoked Potentials
Cortical Evoked Potentials
Delta Rhythm
Evoked Potentials
Olfactory Evoked Potentials
Somatosensory Evoked Potentials
Theta Rhythm
Visual Evoked Potentials
Related Electrocardiography
Electroencephalography

Electrical Brain Stimulation
Broader Brain Stimulation
Electrical Stimulation
Electrophysiology
Stereotaxic Techniques
Stimulation
Related Evoked Potentials
Self Stimulation

Electrical Injuries
Broader Injuries
Related Burns
Shock
Wounds

Electrical Properties (Skin)
Use Skin Electrical Properties

Electrical Stimulation
Narrower Electrical Brain Stimulation
Electroconvulsive Shock
Related Shock

Electro Oculography
Used For EOG (Electrophysiology)
Broader Diagnosis
Electrophysiology
Medical Diagnosis
Ophthalmologic Examination
Related Electroretinography

Electrocardiography
Used For EKG (Electrophysiology)
Broader Cardiography
Diagnosis
Electrophysiology
Medical Diagnosis
Related Electrical Activity

Electroconvulsive Shock
Broader Electrical Stimulation
Narrower Electroconvulsive Shock Therapy
Related Shock

Electroconvulsive Shock Therapy
Used For ECS Therapy
ECT (Therapy)
Electroshock Therapy

Electroconvulsive Shock Therapy — (Continued)
Broader Electroconvulsive Shock
Organic Therapies
Shock Therapy

Electrodermal Response
Use Galvanic Skin Response

Electrodes
Broader Apparatus
Related Stimulators (Apparatus)

Electroencephalography
Used For EEG (Electrophysiology)
Broader Diagnosis
Electrophysiology
Encephalography
Medical Diagnosis
Related Alpha Rhythm
Delta Rhythm
Electrical Activity
Rheoencephalography
Theta Rhythm

Electrolytes
Used For Ions
Narrower Calcium Ions
Chloride Ions
Magnesium Ions
Potassium Ions
Sodium Ions
Related Chemical Elements

Electromyography
Used For EMG (Electrophysiology)
Broader Diagnosis
Electrophysiology
Medical Diagnosis

Electronystagmography
Broader Diagnosis
Electrophysiology
Medical Diagnosis

Electrophysiology
Narrower Alpha Rhythm
Auditory Evoked Potentials
Basal Skin Resistance
Cortical Evoked Potentials
Delta Rhythm
Electrical Activity
Electrical Brain Stimulation
Electro Oculography
Electrocardiography
Electroencephalography
Electromyography
Electronystagmography
Electroplethysmography
Electroretinography
Evoked Potentials
Galvanic Skin Response
Olfactory Evoked Potentials
Rheoencephalography

Electrophysiology — (Continued)
Narrower
      Skin Electrical Properties
      Skin Potential
      Skin Resistance
      Somatosensory Evoked Potentials
      Theta Rhythm
      Visual Evoked Potentials
Related   Medical Diagnosis
      Physiology/

Electroplethysmography
Broader   Diagnosis
      Electrophysiology
      Medical Diagnosis
      Plethysmography

Electroretinography
Broader   Diagnosis
      Electrophysiology
      Medical Diagnosis
      Ophthalmologic Examination
Related   Electro Oculography

Electroshock Therapy
Use   Electroconvulsive Shock Therapy

Elementarism
Use   Reductionism

Elementary Education
Related   Education/

Elementary School Students
Broader   Students
Narrower   Intermediate School Students
      Primary School Students

Elementary School Teachers
Broader   Educational Personnel
      Teachers

Elementary Schools
Used For   Grammar Schools
      Primary Schools
Broader   Schools

Elephants
Broader   Mammals
      Vertebrates

Elimination (Excretion)
Use   Excretion

Elopement (Marriage)
Broader   Marriage

Embarrassment
Narrower   Humiliation
Related   Emotions/

Embedded Figures Testing
Broader   Nonprojective Personality Measures
      Personality Measures

Embolisms
Broader   Cardiovascular Disorders
Narrower   Cerebral Embolisms
Related   Thromboses

Embryo
Broader   Developmental Stages
      Prenatal Development
      Prenatal Developmental Stages

Emergency Services
Related   Crisis Intervention Services
      Natural Disasters

Emetic Drugs
Used For   Vomit Inducing Drugs
Narrower   Apomorphine
Related   CNS Stimulating Drugs
      Narcotic Drugs

EMG (Electrophysiology)
Use   Electromyography

Emotional Adjustment
Used For   Emotional Maladjustment
      Maladjustment (Emotional)
      Personal Adjustment
Narrower   Coping Behavior
      Emotional Control
      Identity Crisis
Related   Adjustment/
      Emotionally Disturbed
      Emotions/
      Personality/

Emotional Content
Used For   Content (Emotional)

Emotional Control
Used For   Emotional Restraint
Broader   Emotional Adjustment
Narrower   Coping Behavior

Emotional Development
Broader   Psychogenesis
Related   Childhood Play Development
      Developmental Age Groups
      Emotions/
      Personality Development
      Physical Development
      Psychosocial Development

Emotional Disorders
Use   Mental Disorders/

Emotional Immaturity
Used For   Immaturity (Emotional)
Broader   Personality Traits
Related   Emotional Maturity

Emotional Inferiority
Used For   Inferiority (Emotional)
Broader   Personality Traits

Emotional Insecurity
Use   Emotional Security

Emotional Instability
Used For	Instability (Emotional)
Broader	Personality Traits
Related	Emotional Stability

Emotional Maladjustment
Use	Emotional Adjustment

Emotional Maturity
Used For	Maturity (Emotional)
Broader	Personality Traits
Related	Emotional Immaturity

Emotional Responses
Broader	Responses
Narrower	Conditioned Emotional Responses
Related	Emotions/

Emotional Restraint
Use	Emotional Control

Emotional Security
Used For	Emotional Insecurity
	Insecurity (Emotional)
	Security (Emotional)
Broader	Personality Traits

Emotional Stability
Used For	Stability (Emotional)
Broader	Personality Traits
Related	Emotional Instability

Emotional States
Used For	Moods
Narrower	Alienation
	Ambivalence
	Anaclitic Depression
	Boredom
	Depression (Emotion)
	Distress
	Doubt
	Emotional Trauma
	Euphoria
	Fear
	Involutional Depression
	Loneliness
	Mental Confusion
	Neurotic Depressive Reaction
	Optimism
	Panic
	Pessimism
	Pleasure
	Psychotic Depressive Reaction
	Reactive Depression
	Restlessness
	Suffering
Related	Anxiety
	Emotionally Disturbed
	Emotions/

Emotional Superiority
Used For	Superiority (Emotional)
Broader	Personality Traits

Emotional Trauma
Used For	Trauma (Emotional)
Broader	Emotional States

Emotionality (Personality)
Broader	Personality Traits
Related	Emotions/

Emotionally Disturbed
Used For	Disturbed (Emotionally)
	Special Education (Emot Disturbed)
Broader	Handicapped
Narrower	Autistic Children
Related	Acting Out
	Childhood Psychosis
	Emotional Adjustment
	Emotional States
	Emotions/

Emotions/
Used For	Feelings
Related	Affection
	Anger
	Anxiety
	Apathy
	Aversion
	Disappointment
	Dissatisfaction
	Embarrassment
	Emotional Adjustment
	Emotional Development
	Emotional Responses
	Emotional States
	Emotionality (Personality)
	Emotionally Disturbed
	Enthusiasm
	Frustration
	Grief
	Guilt
	Happiness
	Jealousy
	Love
	Pride
	Sadness
	Suspicion
	Sympathy

Empathy
Broader	Personality Traits

Emphysema (Pulmonary)
Use	Pulmonary Emphysema

Empirical Methods
Narrower	Observation Methods
Related	Experimental Methods
	Experimentation/
	Methodology/

Employability
Related	Employee Skills
	Personnel/

Employee Absenteeism
Used For	Absenteeism (Employee)
Related	Personnel/

Employee Attitudes
Narrower	Job Satisfaction
Related	Attitudes/
	Employee Motivation
	Job Performance
	Personnel/
	Work (Attitudes Toward)

Employee Benefits
Narrower	Bonuses
	Employee Health Insurance
	Employee Leave Benefits
	Employee Life Insurance
	Employee Pension Plans
	Salaries
	Stock Options
	Workmens Compensation Insurance
Related	Personnel/

Employee Efficiency
Used For	Efficiency (Employee)
Broader	Job Performance

Employee Health Insurance
Broader	Employee Benefits
	Health Insurance
	Insurance
Narrower	Workmens Compensation Insurance

Employee Leave Benefits
Used For	Annual Leave
	Sick Leave
	Vacation Benefits
Broader	Employee Benefits

Employee Life Insurance
Broader	Employee Benefits
	Insurance
	Life Insurance

Employee Motivation
Broader	Motivation
Related	Employee Attitudes
	Personnel/

Employee Pension Plans
Used For	Pension Plans (Employee)
Broader	Employee Benefits

Employee Performance Appraisal
Use	Job Performance
	Personnel Evaluation

Employee Productivity
Used For	Productivity (Employee)
Broader	Job Performance

Employee Selection
Use	Personnel Selection

Employee Skills
Narrower	Clerical Secretarial Skills
Related	Ability/
	Employability
	Personnel/

Employee Turnover
Used For	Turnover
Related	Personnel/

Employees
Use	Personnel/

Employer Attitudes
Related	Attitudes/
	Personnel/
	Work (Attitudes Toward)

Employment
Use	Occupations/

Employment Interviews
Use	Job Applicant Interviews

Employment Processes
Use	Personnel Recruitment

Employment Tests
Related	Measurement/

Encephalitis
Broader	Brain Disorders
	Central Nervous System Disorders
	Nervous System Disorders
	Viral Disorders
Related	Encephalomyelitis
	Infectious Disorders

Encephalography
Broader	Diagnosis
	Medical Diagnosis
Narrower	Echoencephalography
	Electroencephalography
	Pneumoencephalography
	Rheoencephalography
Related	Roentgenography

Encephalography (Air)
Use	Pneumoencephalography

Encephalomyelitis
Broader	Central Nervous System Disorders
	Myelitis
	Nervous System Disorders
Related	Encephalitis
	Infectious Disorders

Encephalopathies (Toxic)
Use	Toxic Encephalopathies

Encopresis
Use	Fecal Incontinence

Encounter Group Therapy
Used For	Therapy (Encounter Group)

Encounter Group Therapy — (Continued)
Broader	Group Psychotherapy
	Psychotherapy
Narrower	Marathon Group Therapy
Related	Sensitivity Training

Encounter Groups
Use	Sensitivity Training

Encouragement
Broader	Social Behavior
	Social Interaction
Related	Social Reinforcement

Endocrine Disorders
Narrower	Addisons Disease
	Adrenal Gland Disorders
	Cretinism
	Cushings Syndrome
	Diabetes
	Diabetes Insipidus
	Diabetes Mellitus
	Endocrine Neoplasms
	Endocrine Sexual Disorders
	Goiters
	Hyperthyroidism
	Hypogonadism
	Hypopituitarism
	Hypothyroidism
	Klinefelters Syndrome
	Parathyroid Disorders
	Pituitary Disorders
	Premenstrual Tension
	Stein Leventhal Syndrome
	Testicular Feminization Syndrome
	Thyroid Disorders
	Thyrotoxicosis
	Turners Syndrome
Related	Disorders/
	Endocrine System
	Hypothermia
	Migraine Headache
	Psychosomatic Disorders
	Secretion (Gland)

Endocrine Gland Secretion
Broader	Secretion (Gland)
Narrower	Adrenal Gland Secretion
Related	Endocrine Glands

Endocrine Gland Surgery
Broader	Physical Treatment Methods
	Surgery
Narrower	Adrenalectomy
	Castration
	Hypophysectomy
	Male Castration
	Ovariectomy
	Pancreatectomy
	Pinealectomy

Endocrine Gland Surgery — (Continued)
Narrower	
	Thymectomy
	Thyroidectomy

Endocrine Glands
Broader	Endocrine System
	Glands
Narrower	Adrenal Glands
	Gonads
	Hypothalamo Hypophyseal System
	Ovaries
	Parathyroid Glands
	Pineal Body
	Pituitary Gland
	Testes
	Thyroid Gland
Related	Endocrine Gland Secretion
	Hormones
	Pancreas

Endocrine Neoplasms
Broader	Endocrine Disorders
	Neoplasms
Related	Stein Leventhal Syndrome

Endocrine Sexual Disorders
Used For	Ovary Disorders
	Testes Disorders
Broader	Endocrine Disorders
	Genital Disorders
	Urogenital Disorders
Narrower	Hypogonadism
	Klinefelters Syndrome
	Premenstrual Tension
	Stein Leventhal Syndrome
	Testicular Feminization Syndrome
	Turners Syndrome
Related	Adrenal Gland Disorders
	Gynecological Disorders
	Hermaphroditism
	Infertility
	Male Genital Disorders
	Pituitary Disorders
	Thyroid Disorders

Endocrine System
Narrower	Adrenal Glands
	Endocrine Glands
	Gonads
	Hypothalamo Hypophyseal System
	Ovaries
	Parathyroid Glands
	Pineal Body
	Pituitary Gland
	Testes
	Thyroid Gland

Endocrine System — (Continued)
   Related   Anatomical Systems/
               Endocrine Disorders
               Pancreas

Endocrinology
   Broader   Medical Sciences
               Sciences

Endogamous Marriage
   Broader   Marriage
   Narrower   Consanguineous Marriage

Endurance
   Narrower   Physical Endurance
               Psychological Endurance
   Related   Stress

Energy Expenditure
   Used For   Effort
   Related   Calories
               Physiology/

Engineering Psychology
   Broader   Applied Psychology
               Psychology
               Sciences
               Social Sciences
   Related   Human Factors Engineering

Engineers
   Related   Aerospace Personnel
               Business And Industrial Person-
               nel
               Personnel/
               Scientists/

England

English (Nonstandard)
   Use   Nonstandard English

English Language
   Use   Language

Enhancement (Drugs)
   Use   Drug Potentiation

Enjoyment
   Use   Pleasure

Enlisted Military Personnel
   Broader   Government Personnel
               Military Personnel
   Narrower   Draftees

Enlistees
   Use   Volunteer Military Personnel

Enlistment (Military)
   Use   Military Enlistment

Enrichment (Jobs)
   Use   Job Enrichment

Enrollment (School)
   Use   School Enrollment

Enthusiasm
   Used For   Eagerness
   Related   Emotions/

Entrance Examinations
   Broader   Educational Measurement
   Related   Student Admission Criteria

Entrapment Games
   Broader   Games
   Related   Collective Behavior
               Game Theory
               Non Zero Sum Games
               Panic
               Prisoners Dilemma Game

Enuresis
   Use   Urinary Incontinence

Environment
   Narrower   Academic Environment
               Animal Environments
               Classroom Environment
               College Environment
               Communes
               Communities
               Ghettoes
               Home Environment
               Kibbutz
               Neighborhoods
               Poverty Areas
               Rural Environments
               School Environment
               Social Environments
               Suburban Environments
               Towns
               Urban Environments
               Working Conditions
   Related   Architecture
               Ecology
               Environmental Adaptation
               Environmental Stress
               Geography
               Urban Planning

Environment (Academic)
   Use   Academic Environment

Environmental Adaptation
   Used For   Adaptation (Environmental)
   Broader   Social Environments
   Related   Environment

Environmental Effects
   Narrower   Altitude Effects
               Atmospheric Conditions
               Cold Effects
               Gravitational Effects
               Heat Effects
               Noise Effects
               Seasonal Variations
               Temperature Effects

Environmental Effects — (Continued)
Narrower
    Underwater Effects
    Weightlessness
Related   Environmental Stress
    Physiological Stress

Environmental Stress
Broader   Stress
Related   Deprivation
    Environment
    Environmental Effects
    Overpopulation
    Physiological Stress
    Thermal Acclimatization

Envy
Use   Jealousy

Enzymes
Narrower   Acetylcholinesterase
    Acid Phosphatases
    Alcohol Dehydrogenases
    Aldolases
    Amine Oxidases
    Amylases
    Carbonic Anhydrase
    Cholinesterase
    Cytochrome Oxidase
    Decarboxylases
    Dehydrogenases
    Esterases
    Glutathione
    Hydroxylases
    Isozymes
    Lactate Dehydrogenase
    Monoamine Oxidases
    Oxidases
    Pepsin
    Phosphatases
    Phosphorylases
    Proteases
    Proteinases
    Ribonuclease
    Transaminases
    Transferases
Related   Coenzymes
    Drugs/
    Proteins

EOG (Electrophysiology)
Use   Electro Oculography

Ependyma
Use   Cerebral Ventricles

Ephedrine
Broader   Adrenergic Drugs
    Alcohols
    Alkaloids
    Amines
    CNS Affecting Drugs

Ephedrine — (Continued)
Broader
    CNS Stimulating Drugs
    Mydriatic Drugs
    Sympathomimetic Amines
    Sympathomimetic Drugs
    Vasoconstrictor Drugs
Related   Local Anesthetics

Epidemiology
Broader   Medical Sciences
    Sciences

Epilepsy
Broader   Brain Disorders
    Central Nervous System Disorders
    Nervous System Disorders
Narrower   Epileptic Seizures
    Grand Mal Epilepsy
    Petit Mal Epilepsy
Related   Antiepileptic Drugs
    Aura
    Brain Damage
    Fugue Reaction

Epileptic Seizures
Broader   Brain Disorders
    Central Nervous System Disorders
    Epilepsy
    Nervous System Disorders
Related   Coma
    Convulsions

Epinephrine
Used For   Adrenaline
Broader   Amines
    Catecholamines
    Heart Rate Affecting Drugs
    Hormones
    Sympathomimetic Amines
    Sympathomimetic Drugs
Related   Adrenochrome
    Adrenolytic Drugs
    Vasoconstriction
    Vasodilation

Epistemology
Broader   Philosophies

Epithelial Cells
Broader   Cells (Biology)
Related   Skin (Anatomy)

Epithelium
Use   Skin (Anatomy)

EPPS (Test)
Identifier   Edwards Personal Preference Schedule

Equality (Social)
Use   Social Equality

Equilibrium
Used For   Balance
Related   Physiology/

Equimax Rotation
Broader   Factor Analysis
            Orthogonal Rotation
            Statistical Analysis
            Statistical Measurement
            Statistical Rotation

Equipment
Use   Apparatus

Erection (Penis)
Broader   Psychosexual Behavior
Related   Impotence

Ergonomics
Use   Human Factors Engineering

Ergot Derivatives
Narrower   Dihydroergotamine
Related   Adrenergic Blocking Drugs
            Alkaloids
            Drugs/
            Lysergic Acid Diethylamide
            Oxytocic Drugs
            Tyramine

Eroticism
Broader   Psychosexual Behavior

Error Analysis
Related   Errors
            Man Machine Systems

Errors
Used For   Mistakes
Narrower   Prediction Errors
            Refraction Errors
Related   Error Analysis

Erythroblastis Fetalis
Use   Rh Incompatibility

Erythrocytes
Broader   Blood Cells
            Cells (Biology)

Escape
Use   Avoidance

Escape Behavior (Animal)
Use   Animal Escape Behavior

Escape Conditioning
Used For   Conditioning (Escape)
Broader   Conditioning
            Operant Conditioning

Eserine
Use   Physostigmine

Eskimos
Broader   Ethnic Groups

Esophagus
Broader   Digestive System

ESP (Parapsychology)
Use   Extrasensory Perception

Essay Testing
Related   Measurement/

Essential Hypertension
Broader   Blood Pressure Disorders
            Cardiovascular Disorders
            Hypertension

Esteem (Self)
Use   Self Esteem

Esterases
Broader   Enzymes
Narrower   Acetylcholinesterase
            Cholinesterase
            Ribonuclease
Related   Hydroxylases
            Phosphatases

Estimation
Narrower   Time Estimation

Estimation (Time)
Use   Time Estimation

Estradiol
Broader   Estrogens
            Hormones
            Sex Hormones

Estrogens
Broader   Hormones
            Sex Hormones
Narrower   Estradiol
            Estrone

Estrone
Broader   Estrogens
            Hormones
            Sex Hormones

Estrus
Related   Animal Biological Rhythms
            Animal Sexual Receptivity
            Menstrual Cycle
            Menstruation

Ethanol
Used For   Ethyl Alcohol
Broader   Alcohols
Related   Denatured Alcohol

Ether (Anesthetic)
Used For   Ethyl Ether (Anesthetic)
Broader   Anesthetic Drugs
            General Anesthetics

Ethics
Narrower   Personal Values
            Professional Ethics

88

Ethics — (Continued)

Narrower	Social Values
	Values
Related	Euthanasia
	Morality
	Religious Beliefs
	Social Influences

Ethnic Disorders

Use	Ethnospecific Disorders

Ethnic Groups

Used For	Groups (Ethnic)
Narrower	American Indians
	Eskimos
	Gypsies
	Mexican Americans
	Tribes
Related	Culture (Anthropological)
	Ethnic Values
	Ethnolinguistics
	Ethnology/
	Ethnospecific Disorders
	Race (Anthropological)
	Rites of Passage
	Shamanism
	Sociocultural Factors
	Taboos

Ethnic Identity

Used For	Identity (Ethnic)
Broader	Sociocultural Factors

Ethnic Values

Broader	Social Influences
	Sociocultural Factors
	Values
Related	Ethnic Groups

Ethnocentrism

Broader	Race Attitudes

Ethnography

Related	Ethnology/
	Kinship Structure
	Race (Anthropological)
	Rites of Passage
	Sociocultural Factors

Ethnolinguistics

Broader	Language
	Linguistics
	Verbal Communication
Related	Ethnic Groups
	Ethnology/
	Psycholinguistics
	Sociocultural Factors

Ethnology/

Related	Animism
	Cultism
	Culture (Anthropological)
	Culture Shock

Ethnology/ — (Continued)

Related	Ethnic Groups
	Ethnography
	Ethnolinguistics
	Ethnospecific Disorders
	Folk Medicine
	Kinship Structure
	Myths
	Race (Anthropological)
	Shamanism
	Sociocultural Factors
	Taboos
	Transcultural Psychiatry
	Witchcraft

Ethnospecific Disorders

Used For	Ethnic Disorders
Related	Ethnic Groups
	Ethnology/
	Mental Disorders/
	Personality Disorders
	Transcultural Psychiatry

Ethology (Animal)

Use	Animal Ethology

Ethyl Alcohol

Use	Ethanol

Ethyl Ether (Anesthetic)

Use	Ether (Anesthetic)

Etiology

Used For	Aetiology
	Pathogenesis
Related	Disorders/
	Patient History

Etymology

Used For	Linguistic Analysis
	Words (Origin)
Broader	Language
	Linguistics
	Verbal Communication

Eugenics

Related	Animal Breeding
	Genetics/
	Selective Breeding

Eugenol

Broader	Analgesic Drugs
	Anesthetic Drugs
	Local Anesthetics

Euphoria

Broader	Emotional States
Related	Happiness
	Pleasure

Europe

Eustachian Tube
Use   Middle Ear

Euthanasia
Used For   Mercy Killing
Broader   Death And Dying
Related   Death Attitudes
             Ethics
             Professional Ethics

Evaluation
Narrower   Educational Program Evaluation
             Mental Health Program Evalua-
             tion
             Personnel Evaluation
             Self Evaluation

Evaluation (Educational Program)
Use   Educational Program Evaluation

Evaluation (Mental Health Program)
Use   Mental Health Program Evalua-
             tion

Evaluation (Personnel)
Use   Personnel Evaluation

Evaluation (Self)
Use   Self Evaluation

Evaluation (Treatment Effectiveness)
Use   Treatment Effectiveness Evalua-
             tion

Evangelists
Broader   Religious Personnel
Related   Clergy
             Lay Religious Personnel
             Missionaries

Evoked Potentials
Used For   Potentials (Evoked)
Broader   Electrical Activity
             Electrophysiology
Narrower   Auditory Evoked Potentials
             Cortical Evoked Potentials
             Olfactory Evoked Potentials
             Somatosensory Evoked Poten-
             tials
             Visual Evoked Potentials
Related   Electrical Brain Stimulation

Evolution (Theory of)
Use   Theory of Evolution

Exceptional Children (Gifted)
Use   Gifted

Exceptional Children (Handicapped)
Use   Handicapped

Excretion
Used For   Elimination (Excretion)
Narrower   Defecation
             Urination
Related   Physiology/

Executives
Use   Top Level Managers

Exercise
Used For   Physical Exercise
Broader   Motor Processes
Related   Physical Fitness

Exhalation
Use   Respiration

Exhaustion
Use   Fatigue

Exhibitionism
Broader   Psychosexual Behavior
             Sexual Deviations
Related   Voyeurism

Existential Therapy
Broader   Psychotherapy

Existentialism
Broader   Philosophies
Related   Religious Beliefs

Exogamous Marriage
Used For   Intermarriage
Broader   Marriage
Narrower   Interfaith Marriage
             Interracial Marriage

Expectations

Narrower   Experimenter Expectations

Expectations (Experimenter)
Use   Experimenter Expectations

Expectations (Role)
Use   Role Expectations

Experience (Practice)
Use   Practice

Experience Level (Job)
Use   Job Experience Level

Experiences (Events)
Narrower   Early Experience
             Life Experiences
             Vicarious Experiences
Related   Familiarity
             Practice

Experiences (Life)
Use   Life Experiences

Experiential Psychotherapy
Broader   Psychotherapy

Experiment Controls
Related   Experimental Design
             Experimentation/

Experiment Volunteers
Used For   Volunteers (Experiment)
Related   Biased Sampling
             Experimental Design

Experiment Volunteers — (Continued)
Related	Experimentation/
	Measurement/
	Random Sampling

Experimental Apparatus
Use	Apparatus

Experimental Design
Used For	Design (Experimental)
	Research Design
Narrower	Followup Studies
	Hypothesis Testing
	Longitudinal Studies
	Null Hypothesis Testing
Related	Experiment Controls
	Experiment Volunteers
	Experimental Methods
	Experimentation/
	Population (Statistics)
	Psychometrics
	Sampling (Experimental)
	Statistical Analysis
	Statistical Variables
	Test Construction

Experimental Instructions
Used For	Instructions (Experimental)
Related	Experimentation/

Experimental Laboratories
Used For	Laboratories (Experimental)
Related	Experimentation/

Experimental Methods
Used For	Scientific Methods
Related	Empirical Methods
	Experimental Design
	Experimentation/
	Methodology/

Experimental Neurosis
Broader	Neurosis
Related	Experimental Psychosis

Experimental Psychologists
Broader	Psychologists

Experimental Psychology
Broader	Psychology
	Sciences
	Social Sciences

Experimental Psychosis
Broader	Psychosis
Related	Adrenochrome
	Experimental Neurosis
	Hallucinogenic Drugs
	Psychotomimetic Drugs

Experimental Replication

Experimentation/
Used For	Investigation
	Research
Related	Biased Sampling
	Consumer Research
	Empirical Methods
	Experiment Controls
	Experiment Volunteers
	Experimental Design
	Experimental Instructions
	Experimental Laboratories
	Experimental Methods
	Experimenters
	Followup Studies
	Hypothesis Testing
	Longitudinal Studies
	Measurement/
	Methodology/
	Null Hypothesis Testing
	Population (Statistics)
	Psychometrics
	Psychophysics
	Random Sampling
	Sampling (Experimental)
	Statistical Analysis
	Statistical Correlation
	Statistical Reliability
	Statistical Significance
	Statistical Validity
	Statistical Variables

Experimenter Bias
Used For	Bias (Experimenter)
Related	Experimenters

Experimenter Expectations
Used For	Expectations (Experimenter)
Broader	Expectations
Related	Experimenters

Experimenters
Related	Experimentation/
	Experimenter Bias
	Experimenter Expectations

Expert Testimony
Used For	Testimony (Expert)
Broader	Legal Processes

Exploratory Behavior
Narrower	Animal Exploratory Behavior
Related	Motivation

Explosive Personality
Broader	Personality Disorders

Exposure Time (Stimulus)
Use	Stimulus Duration

Expressions (Facial)
Use	Facial Expressions

Expressive Psychotherapy
Broader	Psychotherapy

Expulsion (School)
Use　　　　School Expulsion

Extended Family
Broader　　Family Structure

Extension Workers (Agricultural)
Use　　　　Agricultural Extension Workers

External Ear
Used For　　Ear Canal
Broader　　Ear (Anatomy)
　　　　　　Sense Organs

External Rewards
Used For　　Extrinsic Rewards
Broader　　Reinforcement
　　　　　　Rewards
Related　　Extrinsic Motivation
　　　　　　Internal External Locus of
　　　　　　　　Control

Externalization
Related　　Personality Processes/

Extinction (Learning)
Related　　Learning/
　　　　　　Reinforcement

Extracurricular Activities
Narrower　　Fraternity Membership
　　　　　　School Club Membership
　　　　　　Sorority Membership
Related　　Athletic Participation
　　　　　　Education/

Extramarital Intercourse
Used For　　Adultery
　　　　　　Mate Swapping
Broader　　Psychosexual Behavior
　　　　　　Sexual Intercourse (Human)
Related　　Promiscuity

Extrapyramidal Tracts
Broader　　Central Nervous System
　　　　　　Nervous System
　　　　　　Spinal Cord

Extrasensory Perception
Used For　　ESP (Parapsychology)
Broader　　Parapsychological Phenomena
　　　　　　Parapsychology
Narrower　　Clairvoyance
　　　　　　Precognition
　　　　　　Psychokinesis
Related　　Perception/
　　　　　　Telepathy

Extraversion
Broader　　Personality Traits

Extrinsic Motivation
Broader　　Motivation
Related　　External Rewards
　　　　　　Goals

Extrinsic Motivation — (Continued)
Related
　　　　　　Internal External Locus of
　　　　　　　　Control
　　　　　　Needs

Extrinsic Rewards
Use　　　　External Rewards

Eye (Anatomy)
Used For　　Choroid
　　　　　　Sclera
Broader　　Sense Organs
Narrower　　Cones (Eye)
　　　　　　Cornea
　　　　　　Iris (Eye)
　　　　　　Lens (Eye)
　　　　　　Pupil (Eye)
　　　　　　Retina
　　　　　　Rods (Eye)
Related　　Eye Disorders
　　　　　　Eye Movements
　　　　　　Ocular Dominance
　　　　　　Pupil Dilation
　　　　　　Retinal Image
　　　　　　Visual Perception

Eye Contact
Used For　　Contact (Eye)
Broader　　Interpersonal Communication
　　　　　　Interpersonal Interaction
　　　　　　Nonverbal Communication
　　　　　　Social Behavior
　　　　　　Social Interaction
Related　　Social Reinforcement

Eye Disorders
Broader　　Sense Organ Disorders
Narrower　　Amblyopia
　　　　　　Cataracts
　　　　　　Color Blindness
　　　　　　Glaucoma
　　　　　　Hay Fever
　　　　　　Hemianopia
　　　　　　Hyperopia
　　　　　　Hypotonia (Eye)
　　　　　　Myopia
　　　　　　Nystagmus
　　　　　　Refraction Errors
　　　　　　Retinal Detachment
　　　　　　Scotoma
　　　　　　Strabismus
　　　　　　Tunnel Vision
Related　　Albinism
　　　　　　Eye (Anatomy)
　　　　　　Hysterical Vision Disturbances
　　　　　　Ocular Dominance
　　　　　　Visual Perception
　　　　　　Visually Handicapped

Eye Examination
Use　　　　Ophthalmologic Examination

92

Eye Movements
Used For	Movements (Eye)
	Oculomotor Response
Narrower	Rapid Eye Movement
Related	Eye (Anatomy)
	REM Dreams
	REM Sleep

Eyeblink Reflex
Broader	Reflexes

Eyelid Conditioning
Used For	Conditioning (Eyelid)
Broader	Conditioning
	Operant Conditioning

Eysenck Personality Inventory
(See)	Nonprojective Personality Measures
	Personality Measures

F Test
Broader	Parametric Statistical Tests
	Statistical Analysis
	Statistical Tests
Related	Variability Measurement

Face (Anatomy)
Related	Anatomy/
	Facial Features
	Head (Anatomy)

Facial Expressions
Used For	Expressions (Facial)
Broader	Nonverbal Communication
Narrower	Grimaces
	Smiles
Related	Facial Features

Facial Features
Related	Face (Anatomy)
	Facial Expressions
	Physical Attractiveness

Facial Muscles
Broader	Muscles
	Musculoskeletal System

Facial Nerve
Used For	Nerve (Facial)
Broader	Cranial Nerves
	Nervous System
	Peripheral Nerves

Facilitation (Social)
Use	Social Facilitation

Facism
Broader	Political Economic Systems

Factor Analysis
Broader	Statistical Analysis
	Statistical Measurement
Narrower	Cluster Analysis
	Equimax Rotation
	Interaction Analysis (Statistics)

Factor Analysis — (Continued)
Narrower	Item Analysis (Statistical)
	Oblique Rotation
	Orthogonal Rotation
	Quartimax Rotation
	Statistical Rotation
	Varimax Rotation
Related	Analysis/
	Statistical Correlation
	Statistical Significance

Factorial Validity
Broader	Statistical Validity

Factors (Sociocultural)
Use	Sociocultural Factors

Factory Environments
Use	Working Conditions

Faculty
Use	Educational Personnel

Fads And Fashions
Narrower	Clothing Fashions
Related	Social Change

Failure
Related	Academic Underachievement
	Achievement

Fainting
Use	Syncope

Faith Healing
Broader	Religious Practices
Related	Folk Medicine
	Shamanism
	Witchcraft

Faking
Broader	Deception
Narrower	Malingering
Related	Behavior Disorders

False Pregnancy
Use	Pseudocyesis

Familial Idiocy (Amaurotic)
Use	Amaurotic Familial Idiocy

Familiarity
Related	Experiences (Events)
	Practice

Family Background
Used For	Background (Family)
Narrower	Family Socioeconomic Level
	Parent Educational Background
	Parental Occupation
Related	Family/
	Marital Status

Family Counseling
Use	Family Therapy

Family Crises
Broader   Crises
Related   Family/
Stress

Family Life
Use   Family Relations

Family Members
Narrower   Adopted Children
Adoptive Parents
Ancestors
Aunts
Brothers
Cousins
Daughters
Fathers
Foster Children
Foster Parents
Grandchildren
Grandparents
Heterozygotic Twins
Housewives
Husbands
Illegitimate Children
Monozygotic Twins
Mothers
Multiple Births
Orphans
Parents
Quadruplets
Schizophrenogenic Mothers
Siblings
Sisters
Sons
Spouses
Stepchildren
Stepparents
Surrogate Parents (Humans)
Triplets
Twins
Uncles
Unwed Mothers
Wives
Related   Family/

Family Physicians
Broader   General Practitioners
Medical Personnel
Physicians

Family Planning
Narrower   Birth Control
Coitus Interruptus
Contraceptive Devices
Diaphragms (Birth Control)
Intrauterine Devices
Oral Contraceptives
Rhythm Method
Tubal Ligation
Vasectomy

Family Planning — (Continued)
Related   Fertility Enhancement
Induced Abortion
Sterilization (Sex)

Family Planning Attitudes
Related   Attitudes/
Family Relations
Religious Beliefs

Family Relations
Used For   Family Life
Narrower   Child Discipline
Childrearing Practices
Father Child Relations
Marital Conflict
Marital Relations
Mother Child Relations
Parent Child Relations
Parental Attitudes
Parental Permissiveness
Parental Role
Sibling Relations
Related   Childrearing Attitudes
Family Planning Attitudes
Family/
Marriage Attitudes

Family Size
Broader   Family Structure

Family Socioeconomic Level
Broader   Family Background
Socioeconomic Status
Related   Parent Educational Background
Parental Occupation

Family Structure
Narrower   Birth Order
Extended Family
Family Size
Father Absence
Matriarchy
Mother Absence
Nuclear Family
Parental Absence
Patriarchy
Polygamy
Schizophrenogenic Family
Related   Common Law Marriage
Culture (Anthropological)
Family/
Kinship Structure
Sociocultural Factors

Family Therapy
Used For   Family Counseling
Broader   Psychotherapeutic Counseling
Psychotherapy
Related   Counseling/
Social Casework

Family/
Related	Cohabitation
	Divorced Persons
	Family Background
	Family Crises
	Family Members
	Family Relations
	Family Structure
	Marital Separation
	Marital Status
	Marriage
	Widowers
	Widows

Fantasies (Thought Disturbances)
Broader	Thought Disturbances
Related	Magical Thinking

Fantasy (Defense Mechanism)
Broader	Defense Mechanisms
Related	Daydreaming

Farmers
Use	Agricultural Workers

Fascia
Broader	Musculoskeletal System

Fat Metabolism
Use	Lipid Metabolism

Fatalism
Broader	Philosophies

Father Absence
Broader	Family Structure
	Parental Absence
Related	Matriarchy

Father Child Relations
Broader	Family Relations
	Parent Child Relations
Related	Childrearing Practices
	Parental Attitudes
	Parental Permissiveness
	Parental Role

Fathers
Broader	Family Members
	Parents

Fatigue
Used For	Exhaustion
	Tiredness
Broader	Symptoms

Fatty Acids
Broader	Acids
	Lipids
Narrower	Phosphatides

Fear
Broader	Emotional States
Narrower	Panic
Related	Alarm Responses
	Phobias

Fear Survey Schedule
(See)	Nonprojective Personality Measures
	Personality Measures

Fecal Incontinence
Used For	Encopresis
	Incontinence (Fecal)
Broader	Colon Disorders
	Digestive System Disorders
	Gastrointestinal Disorders
Related	Behavior Disorders
	Diarrhea
	Symptoms

Feeblemindedness
Use	Mental Retardation

Feedback
Narrower	Auditory Feedback
	Biofeedback
	Delayed Auditory Feedback
	Delayed Feedback
	Knowledge of Results
	Sensory Feedback
	Visual Feedback
Related	Learning/
	Reinforcement
	Stimulation

Feeding Behavior (Animal)
Use	Animal Feeding Behavior

Feeding Practices
Used For	Mealtimes
Narrower	Bottle Feeding
	Breast Feeding
	Weaning
Related	Childrearing Practices

Feelings
Use	Emotions/

Feet (Anatomy)
Used For	Heels (Anatomy)
	Toes (Anatomy)
Broader	Musculoskeletal System
Related	Ankle
	Leg (Anatomy)
	Nails (Anatomy)

Felonies
Use	Crime

Female Animals
Related	Animals/

Female Criminals
Broader	Criminals

Female Delinquents
Broader	Juvenile Delinquents

Female Genitalia
Used For	Genitalia (Female)
Broader	Urogenital System

Female Genitalia — (Continued)
- Narrower Cervix
  - Clitoris
  - Ovaries
  - Uterus
  - Vagina

Female Orgasm
- Broader Orgasm
  - Psychosexual Behavior
- Related Frigidity
  - Masturbation
  - Sexual Intercourse (Human)

Females (Human)
- Use Human Females

Femininity
- Broader Personality Traits
- Related Masculinity

Feminization Syndrome (Testicular)
- Use Testicular Feminization Syndrome

Femoral Nerve
- Use Spinal Nerves

Fenfluramine
- Broader Sympathomimetic Drugs

Fertility Enhancement
- Related Family Planning
  - Hormones
  - Oral Contraceptives

Fertilization
- Related Pregnancy
  - Sexual Reproduction

Fetishism
- Used For Sexual Fetishism
- Broader Psychosexual Behavior
  - Sexual Deviations
- Related Sexual Masochism
  - Sexual Sadism
  - Sexual Sadomasochism
  - Transvestism

Fetus
- Broader Developmental Stages
  - Prenatal Development
  - Prenatal Developmental Stages

Fever
- Use Hyperthermia

Fever (Hay)
- Use Hay Fever

Fibrillation (Heart)
- Used For Auricular Fibrillation
  - Ventricular Fibrillation
- Broader Arrhythmias (Heart)
  - Cardiovascular Disorders
  - Heart Disorders

Fiction
- Use Literature

Field (Visual)
- Use Visual Field

Field Behavior (Animal)
- Use Animal Open Field Behavior

Field Dependence
- Related Cognitive Style
  - Dependency (Personality)
  - Personality Traits

Field Trips (Educational)
- Use Educational Field Trips

Fighting
- Use Aggressive Behavior

Figure Ground Discrimination
- Used For Noise (Visual)
- Broader Perceptual Discrimination
- Related Form And Shape Perception
  - Pattern Discrimination
  - Spatial Perception

Film Strips
- Broader Audiovisual Communications Media
  - Communications Media
- Related Educational Audiovisual Aids

Filtered Noise
- Broader Auditory Stimulation
  - Perceptual Stimulation

Filtered Speech
- Broader Speech Processing (Mechanical)
  - Verbal Communication

Financial Assistance (Educational)
- Use Educational Financial Assistance

Fine Motor Skill Learning
- Broader Perceptual Motor Learning
  - Skill Learning

Finger Tapping
- Broader Motor Performance
  - Motor Processes

Fingernails
- Use Nails (Anatomy)

Fingers (Anatomy)
- Broader Musculoskeletal System
- Narrower Thumb
- Related Hand (Anatomy)
  - Nails (Anatomy)

Fingerspelling
- Broader Verbal Communication
- Related Sign Language

Finland

Fire Prevention
Related   Prevention/
            Safety

FIRO B
Identifier Fund Interper Rela Orientat
            Beh Ques

Fishes
Broader   Vertebrates
Narrower   Bass (Fish)
            Carp
            Cichlids
            Electric Fishes
            Goldfish
            Salmon
            Sticklebacks

Fixed Interval Reinforcement
Used For   Interval Reinforcement
Broader   Reinforcement
            Reinforcement Schedules

Fixed Ratio Reinforcement
Used For   Ratio Reinforcement
Broader   Reinforcement
            Reinforcement Schedules

Flexibility (Personality)
Use   Adaptability (Personality)

Flexion Reflex
Broader   Reflexes

Flies
Use   Diptera

Flight Instrumentation
Used For   Instrumentation (Flight)
Broader   Aviation
Related   Monitoring

Flight Simulation
Broader   Simulation
Related   Acceleration Effects
            Gravitational Effects

Flooding Therapy
Use   Implosive Therapy

Fluency
Use   Verbal Fluency

Fluphenazine
Used For   Prolixin
Broader   Antiemetic Drugs
            Antipsychotic Drugs
            Antischizophrenic Drugs
            Neuroleptic Drugs
            Phenothiazine Derivatives
            Tranquilizing Drugs

Folic Acid
Broader   Acids
            Amino Acids

Folie A Deux
Broader   Psychosis
Related   Involutional Paranoid Psychosis
            Paranoia (Psychosis)
            Paranoid Schizophrenia

Folk Medicine
Related   Ethnology/
            Faith Healing
            Medical Sciences
            Shamanism
            Transcultural Psychiatry

Folklore
Use   Myths

Folktales
Use   Myths

Followup (Posttreatment)
Use   Posttreatment Followup

Followup Studies
Used For   Studies (Followup)
Broader   Experimental Design
Related   Experimentation/

Food Allergies
Broader   Allergic Disorders
            Immunologic Disorders

Food Deprivation
Broader   Deprivation
            Stimulus Deprivation
Related   Hunger
            Nutritional Deficiencies
            Starvation

Food Intake
Narrower   Eating
Related   Animal Feeding Behavior

Food Preferences
Used For   Preferences (Food)
Broader   Preferences

Football
Broader   Recreation
            Sports

Forced Choice (Testing Method)
Broader   Testing Methods
Related   Measurement/

Foreign Language Education
Broader   Curriculum

Foreign Language Learning
Related   Foreign Languages
            Language Development
            Learning/

Foreign Language Translation
Related   Foreign Languages

Foreign Languages
Broader   Language
            Verbal Communication

Foreign Languages — (Continued)
- Related   Foreign Language Learning
            Foreign Language Translation

Foreign Organizations
- Broader   Organizations
- Related   International Organizations

Foreign Policy Making
- Used For   Policy Making (Foreign)
- Broader   Government Policy Making
- Narrower   Diplomacy (Foreign Policy)
- Related   Government
            International Relations
            War

Foreign Students
- Broader   Students
- Related   Foreign Study

Foreign Study
- Broader   Educational Programs
- Related   Foreign Students

Foremen (Industrial)
- Use   Industrial Foremen

Forensic Psychiatry
- Broader   Medical Sciences
            Psychiatry
            Sciences

Forgetting
- Related   Amnesia
            Fugue Reaction
            Interference (Learning)
            Learning/
            Memory
            Retention
            Suppression (Defense Mechanism)

Form And Shape Perception
- Used For   Contour
            Form Perception
            Shape Perception
- Related   Figure Ground Discrimination
            Pattern Discrimination
            Perception/

Form Classes (Language)
- Used For   Words (Form Classes)
- Broader   Grammar
            Language
            Linguistics
            Verbal Communication
- Narrower   Adjectives
            Adverbs
            Nouns
            Pronouns
            Verbs

Form Perception
- Use   Form And Shape Perception

FORTRAN
- Use   Computer Programing Languages

Foster Children
- Broader   Family Members

Foster Parents
- Broader   Family Members
            Parents

Fowl
- Use   Birds

Foxes
- Broader   Mammals
            Vertebrates

Fragmentation (Schizophrenia)
- Broader   Thought Disturbances
- Related   Schizophrenia

France

Franck Drawing Completion Test
- (See)   Personality Measures
            Projective Personality Measures
            Projective Techniques

Frankness
- Use   Honesty

Fraternity Membership
- Broader   Extracurricular Activities

Free Recall
- Broader   Recall (Learning)
            Retention Measures
- Related   Retention

Frequency (Response)
- Use   Response Frequency

Frequency (Stimulus)
- Use   Stimulus Frequency

Frequency Distribution
- Used For   Distribution (Frequency)
- Broader   Statistical Analysis
            Statistical Measurement
- Narrower   Normal Distribution
            Skewed Distribution
- Related   Standard Deviation

Freud (Sigmund)

Freudian Psychoanalytic School
- Used For   Psychoanalytic School (Freudian)
- Broader   History of Psychology
- Related   Psychoanalytic Interpretation
            Psychoanalytic Theory

Friendship
Broader	Interpersonal Interaction
	Social Behavior
	Social Interaction
Related	Interpersonal Compatibility
	Social Dating

Frigidity
Broader	Psychosexual Behavior
	Sexual Function Disturbances
Related	Dyspareunia
	Female Orgasm
	Impotence
	Orgasm
	Symptoms
	Vaginismus

Frogs
Broader	Amphibia
	Vertebrates

Frontal Lobe
Broader	Brain
	Central Nervous System
	Cerebral Cortex
	Nervous System
	Telencephalon
Narrower	Gyrus Cinguli
	Motor Cortex

Frostig Development Test Vis Percept
(See)	Intelligence Measures

Fruit Fly
Use	Drosophila

Frustration
Related	Anxiety
	Dissatisfaction
	Emotions/
	Mental Confusion

Fugue Reaction
Used For	Reaction (Fugue)
Broader	Amnesia
	Dissociative Patterns
	Memory Disorders
	Thought Disturbances
Related	Epilepsy
	Forgetting

Fulfillment
Use	Satisfaction

Functionalism
Broader	History of Psychology

Fund Interper Rela Orientat Beh Ques
Used For	FIRO B
(See)	Nonprojective Personality Measures
	Personality Measures

Fundamentalism
Broader	Christianity
	Protestantism
	Religious Affiliation
	Religious Beliefs

Galanthamine
Broader	Amines
	Cholinesterase Inhibitors

Gall Bladder
Broader	Digestive System
	Gastrointestinal System

Galvanic Skin Response
Used For	Electrodermal Response
	GSR (Electrophysiology)
Broader	Diagnosis
	Electrophysiology
	Medical Diagnosis
Related	Skin Potential
	Skin Resistance

Gambling
Broader	Recreation
	Risk Taking
	Social Behavior
Related	Games

Game Theory
Related	Entrapment Games
	Games
	Non Zero Sum Games
	Prisoners Dilemma Game
	Simulation

Games
Narrower	Chess
	Childrens Recreational Games
	Entrapment Games
	Non Zero Sum Games
	Prisoners Dilemma Game
	Simulation Games
Related	Gambling
	Game Theory
	Recreation
	Toys

Gamma Globulin
Broader	Blood Proteins
	Globulins
	Immunoglobulins
	Proteins
Related	Antibodies

Ganglia
Broader	Nervous System
Narrower	Autonomic Ganglia
	Basal Ganglia
	Spinal Ganglia

Ganglion Blocking Drugs
Narrower	Chlorisondamine
	Hexamethonium

99

Ganglion Blocking Drugs — (Continued)
Narrower
    Mecamylamine
    Nicotine
Related   Antihypertensive Drugs
    Drugs/

Gangs (Juvenile)
Use   Juvenile Gangs

Gastrointestinal Disorders
Broader   Digestive System Disorders
Narrower Colitis
    Colon Disorders
    Constipation
    Diarrhea
    Fecal Incontinence
    Gastrointestinal Ulcers
    Ulcerative Colitis
    Vomiting
Related   Influenza
    Neoplasms
    Psychosomatic Disorders
    Toxic Disorders

Gastrointestinal System
Broader   Digestive System
Narrower Colon
    Gall Bladder
    Intestines
    Liver
    Stomach
Related   Pancreas

Gastrointestinal Ulcers
Used For Peptic Ulcers
    Ulcers (Gastrointestinal)
Broader   Digestive System Disorders
    Gastrointestinal Disorders
Related   Colitis

Gastropods
Use   Mollusca

Gates MacGinitie Reading Test
Used For Gates Reading Readiness Test
    Gates Reading Test
(See)   Reading Measures

Gates Reading Readiness Test
Identifier Gates MacGinitie Reading Test

Gates Reading Test
Identifier Gates MacGinitie Reading Test

Gay Liberation Movement
Use   Homosexual Liberation Movement

Geese
Used For Goose
Broader   Birds
    Vertebrates

General Anesthetics
Broader   Anesthetic Drugs
Narrower Chloroform
    Ether (Anesthetic)
    Methohexital
    Thiopental

General Aptitude Test Battery
(See)   Aptitude Measures

General Hospital Psychiatric Units
Use   Psychiatric Hospitals

General Paresis
Used For Dementia Paralytica
    Paresis (General)
Broader   Nervous System Disorders
    Neuromuscular Disorders
    Paralysis
Related   Neurosyphilis
    Syphilis

General Practitioners
Broader   Medical Personnel
    Physicians
Narrower Family Physicians

Generalization (Cognitive)
Use   Cognitive Generalization

Generalization (Response)
Use   Response Generalization

Generalization (Semantic)
Use   Semantic Generalization

Generalization (Stimulus)
Use   Stimulus Generalization

Generation Gap
Related   Age Differences
    Parent Child Relations

Generators (Apparatus)
Broader   Apparatus

Genes
Related   Chromosomes
    Genetics/

Genetic Disorders
Used For Hereditary Disorders
Narrower Albinism
    Amaurotic Familial Idiocy
    Autosome Disorders
    Chromosome Disorders
    Crying Cat Syndrome
    Deletion (Chromosome)
    Downs Syndrome
    Hemophilia
    Klinefelters Syndrome
    Maple Syrup Urine Disease
    Neonatal Autosome Disorders
    Neonatal Chromosome Disorders
    Neonatal Genetic Disorders

Genetic Disorders — (Continued)

Narrower
Neonatal Sex Chromosome Disorders
Nondisjunction (Chromosome)
Phenylketonuria
Porphyria
Rh Incompatibility
Sex Chromosome Disorders
Sex Linked Hereditary Disorders
Testicular Feminization Syndrome
Translocation (Chromosome)
Trisomy
Trisomy 18
Trisomy 21
Turners Syndrome

Related
Alopecia
Anemia
Color Blindness
Congenital Disorders
Cretinism
Diabetes Insipidus
Disorders/
Genetics/
Hypopituitarism
Mutations
Picks Disease
Refraction Errors

Genetic Dominance

Related
Dominance/
Genetic Recessiveness
Genetics/

Genetic Recessiveness

Used For Recessiveness (Genetic)
Related Genetic Dominance
Genetics/

Genetics/

Used For
Animal Strain Differences
Heredity
Strain Differences (Animal)

Related
Chromosomes
Eugenics
Genes
Genetic Disorders
Genetic Dominance
Genetic Recessiveness
Genotypes
Hybrids (Biology)
Mutations
Nucleic Acids
Phenotypes
Physiology/
Population Genetics
Predisposition
Sexual Reproduction
Twins

Geniculate Bodies (Thalamus)

Broader
Brain
Central Nervous System
Diencephalon
Nervous System
Thalamus

Genital Disorders

Used For
Sex Differentiation Disorders
Sexual Disorders (Physiological)
Broader Urogenital Disorders
Narrower
Amenorrhea
Dysmenorrhea
Endocrine Sexual Disorders
Gynecological Disorders
Hermaphroditism
Hypogonadism
Infertility
Klinefelters Syndrome
Male Genital Disorders
Menstrual Disorders
Premenstrual Tension
Pseudocyesis
Stein Leventhal Syndrome
Sterility
Testicular Feminization Syndrome
Turners Syndrome
Related Sex/

Genitalia (Female)

Use Female Genitalia

Genitalia (Male)

Use Male Genitalia

Geniuses

Use Gifted

Genotypes

Related Genetics/
Phenotypes

Geographic Regions

Use Geography

Geography

Used For
Geographic Regions
Physical Divisions (Geographic)
Physical Geography
Political Divisions (GeogRaphic)
Broader Sciences
Related Countries
Environment

Geometry

Use Mathematics Education

Gerbils

Broader
Mammals
Rodents
Vertebrates

Geriatric Patients

Broader Patients

Geriatric Psychotherapy
Broader	Psychotherapy
Related	Geriatrics
	Physiological Aging

Geriatrics
Broader	Medical Sciences
	Sciences
Related	Geriatric Psychotherapy
	Gerontology
	Physiological Aging

Germ Cells
Broader	Cells (Biology)
Narrower	Ovum
	Sperm

German Measles
Use	Rubella

Gerontology
Broader	Developmental Psychology
	Psychology
	Sciences
	Social Sciences
Related	Geriatrics

Gestalt Psychology
Broader	History of Psychology

Gestalt Therapy
Broader	Psychotherapy

Gestation
Use	Pregnancy

Gestures
Broader	Nonverbal Communication

Ghettoes
Used For	Urban Ghettoes
Broader	Environment
	Social Environments
	Urban Environments
Related	Poverty Areas

Gifted
Used For	Exceptional Children (Gifted)
	Geniuses
	Intellectually Gifted
	Special Education (Gifted)
	Talented
Related	Ability/
	Creativity
	Intelligence

Gilles De La Tourette Disorder
Broader	Nervous System Disorders
	Neuromuscular Disorders
Related	Echolalia

Glands
Narrower	Adrenal Glands
	Endocrine Glands
	Gonads

Glands — (Continued)
Narrower	Hypothalamo Hypophyseal System
	Mammary Glands
	Ovaries
	Pancreas
	Parathyroid Glands
	Pineal Body
	Pituitary Gland
	Salivary Glands
	Testes
	Thyroid Gland
Related	Pheromones

Glaucoma
Broader	Eye Disorders
	Sense Organ Disorders

Globulins
Broader	Proteins
Narrower	Antibodies
	Gamma Globulin
	Immunoglobulins

Globus Pallidus
Broader	Basal Ganglia
	Brain
	Central Nervous System
	Cerebral Cortex
	Nervous System
	Telencephalon

Glossary

Glossolalia
Broader	Religious Practices

Glossopharyngeal Nerve
Use	Cranial Nerves

Glucagon
Broader	Hormones

Glucose
Broader	Carbohydrates
	Sugars
Narrower	Blood Sugar
Related	Glycogen

Glue Sniffing
Used For	Sniffing (Glue)
Broader	Drug Usage
Related	Drug Dependency

Glutamic Acid
Broader	Acids
	Amino Acids

Glutamine
Broader	Acids
	Amino Acids

Glutathione
Broader	Enzymes
	Peptides

Glutethimide
Broader	CNS Affecting Drugs
	CNS Depressant Drugs
	Hypnotic Drugs
	Sedatives
Related	Drug Dependency

Glycine
| Broader | Acids |
| | Amino Acids |

Glycogen
| Related | Glucose |

Goals
Related	Aspirations
	Extrinsic Motivation
	Incentives
	Intrinsic Motivation
	Motivation
	Needs

Goats
| Broader | Mammals |
| | Vertebrates |

God Concepts
| Broader | Religious Beliefs |

Goiters
Broader	Endocrine Disorders
	Thyroid Disorders
Related	Hyperthyroidism
	Hypothyroidism

Goldfish
Broader	Carp
	Fishes
	Vertebrates

Goldstein Scheerer Object Sort Test
| (See) | Nonprojective Personality Measures |
| | Personality Measures |

Gonadotropic Hormones
Used For	Gonadotropin
Broader	Hormones
Narrower	Prolactin
Related	Pituitary Hormones
	Placental Hormones
	Sex Hormones

Gonadotropin
| Use | Gonadotropic Hormones |

Gonads
Broader	Endocrine Glands
	Endocrine System
	Glands
	Urogenital System
Narrower	Ovaries
	Testes

Gonorrhea
Broader	Bacterial Disorders
	Infectious Disorders
	Venereal Diseases

Goodenough Harris Draw A Person Test
| (See) | Intelligence Measures |

Goose
| Use | Geese |

Gorillas
Broader	Mammals
	Primates (Nonhuman)
	Vertebrates

Gough Adjective Check List
| (See) | Nonprojective Personality Measures |
| | Personality Measures |

Government
Used For	Government Bureaucracy
Related	Autonomy (Government)
	Diplomacy (Foreign Policy)
	Foreign Policy Making
	Government Agencies
	Government Personnel
	Government Policy Making
	Government Programs
	Gun Control Laws
	Job Corps
	Law (Government)
	Laws
	Legal Processes
	Legislative Processes
	Marihuana Laws
	Marihuana Legalization
	Peace Corps
	Political Economic Systems
	Politics
	Project Follow Through
	Project Head Start
	Title V Projects
	Upward Bound
	Volunteers In Service To America
	War
	Welfare Services (Government)

Government Agencies
| Broader | Organizations |
| Related | Government |

Government Bureaucracy
| Use | Government |

Government Personnel
Used For	Civil Servants
Narrower	Agricultural Extension Workers
	Air Force Personnel
	Army Personnel
	Commissioned Officers
	Enlisted Military Personnel

Government Personnel — (Continued)
Narrower
　　　　　Law Enforcement Personnel
　　　　　Marine Personnel
　　　　　Military Medical Personnel
　　　　　Military Personnel
　　　　　National Guardsmen
　　　　　Navy Personnel
　　　　　Noncommissioned Officers
　　　　　Parole Officers
　　　　　Police Personnel
　　　　　Prison Personnel
　　　　　Probation Officers
　　　　　Public Health Service Nurses
　　　　　ROTC Students
　　　　　Volunteer Military Personnel
Related　Business And Industrial Person-
　　　　　　nel
　　　　　Government
　　　　　Personnel/

Government Policy Making
Used For　Policy Making (Government)
Narrower　Abortion Laws
　　　　　Diplomacy (Foreign Policy)
　　　　　Drug Laws
　　　　　Foreign Policy Making
　　　　　Gun Control Laws
　　　　　Laws
　　　　　Legislative Processes
　　　　　Marihuana Laws
　　　　　Marihuana Legalization
Related　Government
　　　　　Legal Processes
　　　　　War

Government Programs
Used For　Programs (Government)
Narrower　Job Corps
　　　　　Peace Corps
　　　　　Project Follow Through
　　　　　Project Head Start
　　　　　Title V Projects
　　　　　Upward Bound
　　　　　Volunteers In Service To Amer-
　　　　　　ica
　　　　　Welfare Services (Government)
Related　Government

Gradepoint Average
Use　　Academic Achievement

Grading (Educational)
Broader　Educational Measurement

Graduate Degrees
Use　　Educational Degrees

Graduate Education
Broader　Higher Education
Narrower　Clinical Psychology Grad Train-
　　　　　ing

Graduate Education — (Continued)
Narrower
　　　　　Dental Education
　　　　　Graduate Psychology Education
　　　　　Medical Education
　　　　　Psychiatric Training

Graduate Psychology Education
Used For　Training (Graduate Psychology)
Broader　Graduate Education
　　　　　Higher Education
Narrower　Clinical Psychology Grad Train-
　　　　　ing

Graduate Record Examination
Used For　GRE (Test)
(See)　　Aptitude Measures

Graduate Schools
Broader　Schools

Graduate Students
Broader　College Students
　　　　　Students
Related　Postgraduate Students

Grammar
Broader　Language
　　　　　Linguistics
　　　　　Verbal Communication
Narrower　Adjectives
　　　　　Adverbs
　　　　　Form Classes (Language)
　　　　　Inflection
　　　　　Morphology (Language)
　　　　　Nouns
　　　　　Orthography
　　　　　Phonology
　　　　　Pronouns
　　　　　Sentence Structure
　　　　　Syntax
　　　　　Transformational Generative
　　　　　　Grammar
　　　　　Verbs

Grammar Schools
Use　　Elementary Schools

Grand Mal Epilepsy
Broader　Brain Disorders
　　　　　Central Nervous System Disor-
　　　　　　ders
　　　　　Epilepsy
　　　　　Nervous System Disorders

Grandchildren
Broader　Family Members

Grandparents
Broader　Ancestors
　　　　　Family Members

Graphology
Use　　Handwriting

Grasshoppers
Broader	Arthropoda
	Insects
	Invertebrates
Related	Larvae

Gravitational Effects
Broader	Environmental Effects
Narrower	Weightlessness
Related	Acceleration Effects
	Altitude Effects
	Aviation
	Decompression Effects
	Flight Simulation
	Spaceflight
	Underwater Effects

GRE (Test)
Identifier	Graduate Record Examination

Great Britain

Great Grandparents
Use	Ancestors

Greater Antilles

Greece

Gregariousness
Broader	Personality Traits
Related	Sociability

Grid (Shuttle Box)
Use	Shuttle Box Grids

Grief
Used For	Mourning
Related	Emotions/
	Suffering

Grimaces
Broader	Facial Expressions
	Nonverbal Communication

Gross Motor Skill Learning
Broader	Perceptual Motor Learning
	Skill Learning

Ground Transportation
Broader	Transportation
Narrower	Automobiles
	Railroad Trains
Related	Highway Safety

Group Behavior
Use	Collective Behavior

Group Cohesion
Used For	Cohesion (Group)
Broader	Group Dynamics

Group Counseling
Used For	Counseling (Group)
Related	Counseling/

Group Discussion
Used For	Discussion (Group)
Broader	Group Dynamics
	Interpersonal Communication
	Interpersonal Interaction
	Social Behavior
	Social Interaction

Group Dynamics
Used For	Dynamics (Group)
Narrower	Group Cohesion
	Group Discussion
	Group Participation
	Group Performance
	Group Size
	Group Structure
	Intergroup Dynamics
Related	Group Instruction
	Group Psychotherapy
	Sensitivity Training

Group Instruction
Broader	Teaching
	Teaching Methods
Related	Group Dynamics

Group Participation
Broader	Group Dynamics
	Interpersonal Interaction
	Participation
	Social Behavior
	Social Interaction
Related	Collective Behavior

Group Performance
Broader	Group Dynamics
	Interpersonal Interaction
	Social Behavior
	Social Interaction

Group Problem Solving
Broader	Cognitive Processes
	Problem Solving

Group Psychotherapy
Used For	Group Therapy
Broader	Psychotherapy
Narrower	Encounter Group Therapy
	Marathon Group Therapy
	Therapeutic Community
Related	Group Dynamics
	Psychodrama

Group Size
Used For	Size (Group)
Broader	Group Dynamics

Group Structure
Broader	Group Dynamics

Group Testing
Related	Measurement/
	Test Administration

Group Therapy
Use   Group Psychotherapy

Groups (Blood)
Use   Blood Groups

Groups (Ethnic)
Use   Ethnic Groups

Groups (Organizations)
Use   Organizations

Groups (Social)
Use   Social Groups

Groups (Statistics)
Use   Population (Statistics)

Growth
Use   Development/

GSR (Electrophysiology)
Use   Galvanic Skin Response

Guanethidine
Broader   Amines
          Antihypertensive Drugs
Related   Norepinephrine

Guessing

Guidance (Educational)
Use   Educational Counseling

Guidance (Occupational)
Use   Occupational Guidance

Guilford Zimmerman Temperament Surv
(See)   Nonprojective Personality Measures
          Personality Measures

Guilt
Used For   Shame
Related   Anxiety
          Emotions/

Guinea Pigs
Broader   Mammals
          Rodents
          Vertebrates

Gulls
Use   Sea Gulls

Gun Control Laws
Broader   Government Policy Making
          Laws
Related   Government

Gustatory Perception
Use   Taste Perception

Gymnasiums
Broader   School Facilities
Related   Sports

Gymnastic Therapy
Use   Recreation Therapy

Gynecological Disorders
Broader   Genital Disorders
          Urogenital Disorders
Narrower   Amenorrhea
          Dysmenorrhea
          Menstrual Disorders
          Premenstrual Tension
          Pseudocyesis
          Stein Leventhal Syndrome
Related   Endocrine Sexual Disorders
          Hermaphroditism
          Hypogonadism
          Infertility
          Sterility

Gynecologists
Used For   Obstetricians
Broader   Medical Personnel
          Physicians
Related   Surgeons

Gypsies
Broader   Ethnic Groups
Related   Human Migration

Gyrus Cinguli
Broader   Brain
          Central Nervous System
          Cerebral Cortex
          Frontal Lobe
          Limbic System
          Nervous System
          Telencephalon

Habitat Selection
Use   Territoriality

Habits
Used For   Mannerisms
Narrower   Hair Pulling
          Nail Biting
          Thumbsucking
          Tobacco Smoking
Related   Learning/

Habituation
Related   Drug Usage

Hair
Related   Alopecia
          Anatomy/
          Scalp (Anatomy)
          Skin (Anatomy)

Hair Loss
Use   Alopecia

Hair Pulling
Broader   Habits
Related   Behavior Disorders

Haiti

Halfway Houses

Broader	Residential Care Institutions
	Treatment Facilities
Related	Community Facilities
	Correctional Institutions
	Psychiatric Hospital Programs
	Psychiatric Hospitals

Hallucinations

Broader	Perceptual Disturbances
Narrower	Auditory Hallucinations
	Drug Induced Hallucinations
	Hypnagogic Hallucinations
	Visual Hallucinations
Related	Hallucinogenic Drugs
	Hallucinosis

Hallucinogenic Drugs

Narrower	Adrenochrome
	Bufotenine
	Lysergic Acid Diethylamide
	Mescaline
	Peyote
	Psilocybin
Related	Cannabis
	Cholinergic Blocking Drugs
	Drugs/
	Experimental Psychosis
	Hallucinations
	Psychedelic Drugs
	Psychotomimetic Drugs
	Tetrahydrocannabinol

Hallucinosis

Broader	Psychosis
Narrower	Alcoholic Hallucinosis
	Delirium Tremens
	Korsakoffs Psychosis
Related	Hallucinations

Haloperidol

Broader	CNS Affecting Drugs
	CNS Depressant Drugs
	Sedatives
	Tranquilizing Drugs

Hamsters

Broader	Mammals
	Rodents
	Vertebrates

Hand (Anatomy)

Broader	Musculoskeletal System
Related	Arm (Anatomy)
	Fingers (Anatomy)
	Palm (Anatomy)
	Wrist

Handedness

Use	Lateral Dominance

Handicapped

Used For	Exceptional Children (Handicapped)

Handicapped — (Continued)

Narrower	Adventitiously Handicapped
	Amputees
	Aurally Handicapped
	Autistic Children
	Blind
	Brain Damaged
	Congenitally Handicapped
	Deaf
	Educable Mentally Retarded
	Emotionally Disturbed
	Health Impaired
	Home Reared Mentally Retarded
	Idiot Savants
	Institutionalized Mentally Retarded
	Mentally Retarded
	Minimally Brain Damaged
	Multiply Handicapped
	Partially Hearing Impaired
	Partially Sighted
	Physically Handicapped
	Profoundly Mentally Retarded
	Severely Mentally Retarded
	Slow Learners
	Speech Handicapped
	Trainable Mentally Retarded
	Visually Handicapped
Related	Handicapped (Attitudes Toward)
	Learning Disabilities

Handicapped (Attitudes Toward)

Narrower	Mental Illness (Attitudes Toward)
	Mental Retardation (Attit Toward)
	Physical Handicaps (Attit Toward)
	Sensory Handicaps (Attit Toward)
Related	Attitudes/
	Handicapped

Handicrafts

Use	Crafts

Handwriting

Used For	Graphology
	Writing (Handwriting)
Broader	Language
	Verbal Communication
	Written Language
Narrower	Cursive Writing
	Handwriting Legibility
	Printing (Handwriting)

Handwriting Legibility

Used For	Legibility (Handwriting)
Broader	Handwriting
	Language

Handwriting Legibility — (Continued)
Broader
Verbal Communication
Written Language

Happiness
Used For   Joy
Related   Emotions/
Euphoria
Pleasure

Haptic Perception
Use   Cutaneous Sense

Hashish
Broader   Cannabis
Related   Drugs/
Marihuana
Tetrahydrocannabinol

Hate
Broader   Aversion
Related   Hostility

Hawaii

Hay Fever
Used For   Fever (Hay)
Broader   Allergic Disorders
Eye Disorders
Immunologic Disorders
Respiratory Tract Disorders
Related   Psychosomatic Disorders

Hazards
Related   Accidents
Safety
Safety Devices

Head (Anatomy)
Related   Anatomy/
Face (Anatomy)
Scalp (Anatomy)
Skin (Anatomy)

Head Banging
Broader   Behavior Disorders
Self Mutilation

Head Injuries
Broader   Injuries
Narrower   Brain Concussion
Related   Brain Damage
Wounds

Head Start
Use   Project Head Start

Headache
Broader   Pain
Symptoms
Narrower   Migraine Headache
Muscle Contraction Headache
Related   Psychosomatic Disorders

Health
Used For   Hygiene
Narrower   Community Mental Health
Mental Health
Related   Preventive Medicine
Public Health Services

Health Education
Broader   Curriculum
Narrower   Drug Education
Sex Education

Health Impaired
Broader   Handicapped
Physically Handicapped

Health Insurance
Broader   Insurance
Narrower   Employee Health Insurance
Workmens Compensation Insurance
Related   Hospitalization

Hearing Aids
Broader   Medical Therapeutic Devices

Hearing Impaired (Partially)
Use   Partially Hearing Impaired

Hearing Measures
Use   Speech And Hearing Measures

Heart
Broader   Cardiovascular System
Narrower   Heart Auricles
Heart Valves
Heart Ventricles
Myocardium
Pericardium
Related   Blood
Vagus Nerve

Heart Auricles
Used For   Atria (Heart)
Auricles (Heart)
Broader   Cardiovascular System
Heart

Heart Disorders
Used For   Cardiac Disorders
Broader   Cardiovascular Disorders
Narrower   Angina Pectoris
Arrhythmias (Heart)
Bradycardia
Coronary Thromboses
Fibrillation (Heart)
Myocardial Infarctions
Tachycardia
Related   Rheumatic Fever

Heart Rate
Used For   Cardiac Rate
Heartbeat
Rate (Heart)

Heart Rate Affecting Drugs
Narrower	Caffeine
	Epinephrine
	Quinidine
	Theophylline
Related	Analeptic Drugs
	Antihypertensive Drugs
	Cardiovascular Disorders
	CNS Affecting Drugs
	CNS Stimulating Drugs
	Dopamine
	Drugs/
	Muscle Relaxing Drugs
	Oxytocic Drugs
	Vasoconstrictor Drugs
	Vasodilator Drugs

Heart Surgery
Broader	Physical Treatment Methods
	Surgery
Related	Organ Transplantation

Heart Transplants
Use	Organ Transplantation

Heart Valves
Used For	Valves (Heart)
Broader	Cardiovascular System
	Heart

Heart Ventricles
Used For	Ventricles (Heart)
Broader	Cardiovascular System
	Heart

Heartbeat
Use	Heart Rate

Heat Effects
Broader	Environmental Effects
	Temperature Effects

Hebephrenic Schizophrenia
Broader	Psychosis
	Schizophrenia

Hedonism
Related	Attitudes/
	Philosophies

Heels (Anatomy)
Use	Feet (Anatomy)

Height (Body)
Use	Body Height

Helicopters
Broader	Aircraft

Helium
Broader	Chemical Elements
	Nonmetallic Elements

Hematologic Disorders
Use	Blood and Lymphatic Disorders

Hematoma
Broader	Hemorrhage
	Symptoms
Related	Injuries

Hemianopia
Used For	Hemiopia
Broader	Eye Disorders
	Sense Organ Disorders
Related	Nervous System Disorders

Hemiopia
Use	Hemianopia

Hemispherectomy
Broader	Neurosurgery
	Physical Treatment Methods
	Surgery
Related	Brain Lesions

Hemodialysis
Broader	Dialysis
	Physical Treatment Methods
Related	Blood Transfusion

Hemoglobin
Broader	Blood Proteins
	Pigments
	Proteins

Hemophilia
Broader	Blood and Lymphatic Disorders
	Blood Coagulation Disorders
	Genetic Disorders
	Sex Linked Hereditary Disorders

Hemorrhage
Broader	Cardiovascular Disorders
	Symptoms
Narrower	Cerebral Hemorrhage
	Hematoma

Hemp (Cannabis)
Use	Cannabis

Henman Nelson Tests Mental Ability
(See)	Intelligence Measures

Heparin
Broader	Acids
	Anticoagulant Drugs
Related	Drugs/

Hepatic Disorders
Use	Liver Disorders

Hepatitis
Broader	Digestive System Disorders
	Liver Disorders
Narrower	Toxic Hepatitis
Related	Infectious Disorders
	Jaundice

Hereditary Disorders
Use	Genetic Disorders

Heredity
Use   Genetics/

Hermaphroditism
Broader   Congenital Disorders
            Genital Disorders
            Urogenital Disorders
Related   Endocrine Sexual Disorders
            Gynecological Disorders
            Male Genital Disorders
            Sterility
            Testicular Feminization Syn-
            drome

Heroin
Used For   Diacetylmorphine
Broader   Alkaloids
            Analgesic Drugs
            Narcotic Drugs
            Opiates
            Sedatives
Related   Heroin Addiction

Heroin Addiction
Broader   Addiction
            Behavior Disorders
            Drug Abuse
            Drug Addiction
            Drug Dependency
            Drug Effects
            Drug Usage
            Side Effects (Drug)
Related   Heroin

Herpes Simplex
Broader   Infectious Disorders
            Skin Disorders
            Viral Disorders

Heterosexuality
Broader   Psychosexual Behavior
Related   Sex Linked Developmental Dif-
            ferences
            Sex Roles
            Sexual Development

Heterozygotic Twins
Broader   Family Members
            Multiple Births
            Siblings
            Twins

Heuristic Modeling
Broader   Simulation
Related   Mathematical Modeling

Hexamethonium
Broader   Antihypertensive Drugs
            Ganglion Blocking Drugs

Hexobarbital
Broader   Anesthetic Drugs
            Barbiturates

Hexobarbital — (Continued)
Broader
            Hypnotic Drugs
            Sedatives

Hibernation
Broader   Animal Ethology
Related   Animal Biological Rhythms
            Animal Innate Behavior
            Animal Instinctive Behavior

Hidden Figures Test
(See)   Intelligence Measures

High Sch Personality Questionnaire
(See)   Nonprojective Personality Meas-
            ures
            Personality Measures

High School Diplomas
Use   Educational Degrees

High School Students
Broader   Students

High School Teachers
Broader   Educational Personnel
            Teachers

High Schools
Broader   Schools
Related   Military Schools

Higher Education
Used For   Continuing Education
Narrower   Clinical Psychology Grad Train-
            ing
            Clinical Psychology Internship
            Dental Education
            Graduate Education
            Graduate Psychology Education
            Medical Education
            Medical Internship
            Medical Residency
            Postgraduate Training
            Psychiatric Training
Related   Education/
            Educational Degrees

Highway Hypnosis Accidents
Broader   Accidents
            Motor Traffic Accidents
            Transportation Accidents
Related   Driving Behavior
            Highway Safety

Highway Safety
Used For   Automobile Safety
            Driver Safety
Broader   Safety
Related   Drivers
            Driving Behavior
            Ground Transportation
            Highway Hypnosis Accidents

Highway Safety — (Continued)
Related
    Motor Traffic Accidents
    Transportation Accidents

Hinduism
Broader   Religious Affiliation
    Religious Beliefs

Hippies
Use   Subculture (Anthropological)

Hippocampus
Broader   Brain
    Central Nervous System
    Cerebral Cortex
    Limbic System
    Nervous System
    Telencephalon
Narrower   Amygdaloid Body

Hips
Broader   Musculoskeletal System

Hiring
Use   Personnel Selection

Hispaniola

Histamine
Broader   Amines
Related   Antihistaminic Drugs
    Histidine

Histidine
Broader   Acids
    Amino Acids
Related   Histamine

Histology
Related   Morphology
    Physiology/
    Tissues (Body)

History

History of Psychology
Narrower   Associationism
    Behaviorism
    Freudian Psychoanalytic School
    Functionalism
    Gestalt Psychology
    Individual Psychology
    Jungian Psychology
    Neopsychoanalytic School
    Structuralism
Related   Phenomenology
    Psychology
    Theories/

Hoarding Behavior (Animal)
Use   Animal Hoarding Behavior

Hobbies
Use   Recreation

Hoffmanns Reflex
Broader   Reflexes

Holtzman Inkblot Technique
(See)   Personality Measures
    Projective Personality Measures
    Projective Techniques

Homatropine
Broader   Alkaloids
    Amines
    Cholinergic Blocking Drugs
    Mydriatic Drugs
Related   Bromides

Home Accidents
Broader   Accidents

Home Environment
Broader   Environment
    Social Environments

Home Reared Mentally Retarded
Broader   Handicapped
    Mentally Retarded
Related   Institutionalized Mentally Retarded

Home Visiting Programs
Broader   Community Services
    Mental Health Programs

Homeostasis
Used For   Autoregulation
Related   Physiology/

Homicide
Used For   Murder
Broader   Antisocial Behavior
    Behavior Disorders
    Crime

Homographs
Broader   Language
    Linguistics
    Verbal Communication
    Vocabulary
Related   Homonyms

Homonyms
Broader   Language
    Verbal Communication
    Vocabulary
Related   Homographs

Homosexual Liberation Movement
Used For   Gay Liberation Movement
Broader   Social Movements
Related   Activist Movements

Homosexuality
Broader   Psychosexual Behavior
Narrower   Bisexuality
    Lesbianism
    Male Homosexuality

Homosexuality — (Continued)
Related   Sex Roles
              Transsexualism
              Transvestism

Honesty
Used For   Frankness
Broader   Personality Traits

Hopi Indians
Use   American Indians

Hormones
Narrower   Adrenal Cortex Hormones
              Adrenal Medulla Hormones
              Aldosterone
              Androgens
              Corticosterone
              Corticotropin
              Cortisone
              Deoxycorticosterone
              Epinephrine
              Estradiol
              Estrogens
              Estrone
              Glucagon
              Gonadotropic Hormones
              Hydrocortisone
              Insulin
              Melatonin
              Norepinephrine
              Oxytocin
              Parathyroid Hormone
              Pituitary Hormones
              Placental Hormones
              Posterior Pituitary Hormones
              Prednisolone
              Progesterone
              Prolactin
              Sex Hormones
              Somatotropin
              Testosterone
              Thyroid Hormones
              Thyrotropin
              Thyroxine
              Triiodothyronine
              Vasopressin
Related   Drugs/
              Endocrine Glands
              Fertility Enhancement
              Oxytocic Drugs
              Pheromones
              Steroids

Horses
Broader   Mammals
              Vertebrates

Hospital Accreditation
Related   Hospitals

Hospital Admission
Used For   Admission (Hospital)
              Readmission (Hospital)
Broader   Hospitalization
              Institutionalization
Narrower   Psychiatric Hospital Admission
              Psychiatric Hospital Readmission
Related   Hospital Discharge
              Psychiatric Hospitalization

Hospital Attendants
Use   Attendants (Institutions)

Hospital Discharge
Broader   Hospitalization
              Institutionalization
Related   Hospital Admission
              Psychiatric Hospital Admission
              Psychiatric Hospital Readmission
              Psychiatric Hospitalization

Hospital Staff
Use   Medical Personnel

Hospitalization
Broader   Institutionalization
Narrower   Commitment (Psychiatric)
              Hospital Admission
              Hospital Discharge
              Psychiatric Hospital Admission
              Psychiatric Hospital Readmission
              Psychiatric Hospitalization
Related   Health Insurance

Hospitalized Patients
Broader   Patients

Hospitals
Used For   Infirmaries
Broader   Residential Care Institutions
              Treatment Facilities
Narrower   Psychiatric Hospitals
              Sanatoriums
Related   Clinics
              Hospital Accreditation
              Nursing Homes
              Psychiatric Clinics

Hostility
Used For   Antagonism
              Resentment
Broader   Anger
Related   Hate

Hot Line Services
Used For   Telephone Hot Lines
Broader   Community Services
              Crisis Intervention Services
              Mental Health Programs

Hot Line Services — (Continued)
Related Community Mental Health Centers
Suicide Prevention Centers

Housewives
Broader Family Members
Spouses
Wives

Housing
Broader Community Facilities
Related Social Programs

Hue
Broader Color

Human Biological Rhythms
Used For Diurnal Variations
Broader Biological Rhythms

Human Channel Capacity
Related Attention
Human Information Storage

Human Courtship
Used For Courtship (Human)
Broader Psychosexual Behavior
Narrower Social Dating

Human Development/
Used For Maturation
Related Adolescent Development
Childhood Development
Development/
Developmental Age Groups
Developmental Differences
Developmental Stages
Physical Development
Psychogenesis

Human Factors Engineering
Used For Ergonomics
Related Engineering Psychology
Man Machine Systems
Working Conditions

Human Females
Used For Females (Human)

Human Figures Drawing
Broader Personality Measures
Projective Personality Measures
Projective Techniques

Human Information Processes
Use Cognitive Processes

Human Information Storage
Used For Information Storage (Human)
Related Human Channel Capacity
Memory

Human Males
Used For Males (Human)

Human Migration
Used For Migration (Human)
Broader Social Processes
Related Gypsies

Human Relations Training
Use Sensitivity Training

Human Sex Differences
Used For Sex Differences (Human)
Narrower Sex Linked Developmental Differences
Related Sex/

Humanism
Broader Philosophies

Humiliation
Broader Embarrassment

Humor
Narrower Cartoons (Humor)
Jokes

Hungary

Hunger
Broader Appetite
Motivation
Related Animal Feeding Behavior
Food Deprivation
Starvation

Huntingtons Chorea
Broader Central Nervous System Disorders
Chorea
Nervous System Disorders

Hurdle (Shuttle Box)
Use Shuttle Box Hurdles

Husbands
Broader Family Members
Spouses

Hybrids (Biology)
Related Genetics/

Hydantoins
Broader CNS Affecting Drugs

Hydralazine
Broader Antihypertensive Drugs
Sympatholytic Drugs

Hydrocephaly
Broader Brain Disorders
Central Nervous System Disorders
Nervous System Disorders
Related Congenital Disorders
Convulsions
Infectious Disorders
Mental Retardation
Neonatal Disorders

Hydrocortisone
Used For	Cortisol
Broader	Adrenal Cortex Hormones
	Corticosteroids
	Hormones
	Steroids

Hydrogen
Broader	Chemical Elements
	Nonmetallic Elements

Hydroxylamine
Broader	Amines

Hydroxylases
Broader	Enzymes
Related	Esterases
	Phosphatases

Hydroxytryptamine (5-)
Use	Serotonin

Hydroxyzine
Broader	Tranquilizing Drugs
Related	Antihistaminic Drugs

Hygiene
Use	Health

Hyoscine
Use	Scopolamine

Hyoscyamine (Dl-)
Use	Atropine

Hyoscyamine (L-)
Broader	Alkaloids
	Amines
	Analgesic Drugs
	Antispasmodic Drugs
	Cholinergic Blocking Drugs
	Sedatives
Related	Atropine
	Bromides

Hyperactivity
Use	Hyperkinesis

Hyperglycemia
Broader	Symptoms
Related	Metabolism Disorders

Hyperkinesis
Used For	Hyperactivity
Broader	Nervous System Disorders
	Symptoms
Related	Ataxia
	Minimal Brain Disorders
	Neuromuscular Disorders
	Restlessness

Hypermania
Broader	Mania

Hyperopia
Broader	Eye Disorders
	Refraction Errors
	Sense Organ Disorders
Related	Myopia

Hyperparathyroidism
Use	Parathyroid Disorders

Hyperphagia
Broader	Appetite Disorders
	Symptoms
Related	Obesity
	Psychosomatic Disorders

Hypersensitivity (Immunologic)
Use	Immunologic Disorders

Hypersexuality
Used For	Nymphomania
Broader	Psychosexual Behavior
Related	Promiscuity

Hypertension
Broader	Blood Pressure Disorders
	Cardiovascular Disorders
Narrower	Essential Hypertension
Related	Antihypertensive Drugs
	Cerebrovascular Disorders

Hyperthermia
Used For	Fever
Broader	Symptoms
Related	Delirium

Hyperthyroidism
Broader	Endocrine Disorders
	Thyroid Disorders
Related	Goiters
	Tachycardia
	Thyrotoxicosis
	Underweight

Hyperventilation
Broader	Respiratory Distress
	Respiratory Tract Disorders
	Symptoms
Related	Psychosomatic Disorders

Hypnagogic Hallucinations
Broader	Hallucinations
	Perceptual Disturbances
Related	Sleep Disorders

Hypnoanalysis
Use	Hypnotherapy

Hypnosis
Broader	Consciousness Disturbances
Narrower	Autohypnosis
Related	Hypnotherapy

Hypnotherapists
Broader	Hypnotists
	Mental Health Personnel
	Psychotherapists

Hypnotherapists — (Continued)
Related	Clinical Psychologists
	Psychiatrists
	Psychoanalysts

Hypnotherapy
Used For	Hypnoanalysis
Broader	Psychotherapy
Related	Hypnosis
	Psychoanalysis

Hypnotic Drugs
Used For	Sleep Inducing Drugs
Narrower	Amobarbital
	Apomorphine
	Barbital
	Calcium Bromide
	Chloral Hydrate
	Chloralose
	Codeine
	Glutethimide
	Hexobarbital
	Lithium Bromide
	Meprobamate
	Methaqualone
	Paralydehyde
	Pentobarbital
	Phenobarbital
	Potassium Bromide
	Secobarbital
	Sodium Bromide
	Thalidomide
	Thiopental
Related	Analgesic Drugs
	Anesthetic Drugs
	Anticonvulsive Drugs
	Antiemetic Drugs
	Antihistaminic Drugs
	Antihypertensive Drugs
	Barbiturates
	CNS Depressant Drugs
	Drugs/
	Narcotic Drugs
	Sedatives

Hypnotic Susceptibility
Used For	Susceptibility (Hypnotic)
Broader	Personality Traits

Hypnotists
Narrower	Hypnotherapists
Related	Personnel/

Hypochondriasis
Broader	Psychosomatic Disorders
	Symptoms
Related	Anxiety

Hypogastric Plexus
Use	Autonomic Ganglia

Hypoglossal Nerve
Use	Cranial Nerves

Hypoglycemia
Broader	Symptoms
Related	Metabolism Disorders

Hypoglycemic Agents
Used For	Antidiabetic Agents
Narrower	Insulin
	Tolbutamide
Related	Diabetes
	Drugs/

Hypogonadism
Broader	Endocrine Disorders
	Endocrine Sexual Disorders
	Genital Disorders
	Urogenital Disorders
Narrower	Klinefelters Syndrome
	Turners Syndrome
Related	Gynecological Disorders
	Hypopituitarism
	Male Genital Disorders
	Sterility

Hypomania
Broader	Mania

Hypoparathyroidism
Use	Parathyroid Disorders

Hypophysectomy
Used For	Pituitary Gland Surgery
Broader	Endocrine Gland Surgery
	Physical Treatment Methods
	Surgery

Hypophysis Disorders
Use	Pituitary Disorders

Hypopituitarism
Used For	Dwarfism (Pituitary)
	Pituitary Dwarfism
Broader	Endocrine Disorders
	Pituitary Disorders
Related	Genetic Disorders
	Hypogonadism

Hypotension
Broader	Blood Pressure Disorders
	Cardiovascular Disorders
Related	Dopamine

Hypothalamo Hypophyseal System
Broader	Brain
	Central Nervous System
	Diencephalon
	Endocrine Glands
	Endocrine System
	Glands
	Hypothalamus
	Nervous System
	Pituitary Gland

Hypothalamus
Used For	Mammilary Bodies (Hypothalamic)

Hypothalamus — (Continued)
- **Broader** Brain
  Central Nervous System
  Diencephalon
  Nervous System
- **Narrower** Hypothalamo Hypophyseal System
  Optic Chiasm

Hypothalamus Lesions
- **Broader** Brain Damage
  Brain Disorders
  Brain Lesions
  Central Nervous System Disorders
  Lesions
  Nervous System Disorders

Hypothermia
- **Broader** Symptoms
- **Related** Central Nervous System Disorders
  Endocrine Disorders

Hypothesis Testing
- **Used For** Testing (Hypothesis)
- **Broader** Experimental Design
- **Narrower** Null Hypothesis Testing
- **Related** Confidence Limits (Statistics)
  Experimentation/
  Kolmogarov Smirnov Test
  Predictability (Measurement)
  Prediction Errors
  Probability
  Statistical Analysis
  Statistical Significance

Hypothyroidism
- **Used For** Myxedema
- **Broader** Endocrine Disorders
  Thyroid Disorders
- **Narrower** Cretinism
- **Related** Goiters
  Infertility
  Metabolism Disorders
  Thyroid Extract
  Thyrotropin
  Thyroxine

Hypotonia (Eye)
- **Broader** Eye Disorders
  Sense Organ Disorders

Hypoxia
- **Use** Anoxia

Hysterectomy
- **Broader** Physical Treatment Methods
  Sterilization (Sex)
  Surgery
- **Related** Ovariectomy

Hysteria
- **Narrower** Mass Hysteria

Hysteria — (Continued)
- **Related** Catalepsy
  Conversion Neurosis
  Dissociative Neurosis
  Dissociative Patterns
  Hysterical Personality
  Mental Disorders/
  Suggestibility

Hysterical Anesthesia
- **Broader** Anesthesia (Feeling)
  Conversion Neurosis
  Neurosis

Hysterical Blindness
- **Use** Hysterical Vision Disturbances

Hysterical Color Blindness
- **Use** Color Blindness
  Hysterical Vision Disturbances

Hysterical Neurosis (Conversion)
- **Use** Conversion Neurosis

Hysterical Neurosis (Dissociation)
- **Use** Dissociative Neurosis

Hysterical Paralysis
- **Used For** Paralysis (Hysterical)
- **Broader** Conversion Neurosis
  Neurosis

Hysterical Personality
- **Broader** Personality Disorders
- **Related** Conversion Neurosis
  Dissociative Neurosis
  Dissociative Patterns
  Hysteria

Hysterical Vision Disturbances
- **Used For** Hysterical Blindness
  Hysterical Color Blindness
  Vision Disturbances (Hysterical)
- **Broader** Conversion Neurosis
  Neurosis
- **Related** Eye Disorders

Id
- **Broader** Psychoanalytic Personality Factors
- **Related** Unconscious (Personality Factor)

Idealism
- **Broader** Personality Traits
  Philosophies

Ideation
- **Broader** Cognitive Processes
- **Narrower** Imagination

Identical Twins
- **Use** Monozygotic Twins

Identification (Defense Mechanism)
- **Broader** Defense Mechanisms
- **Related** Introjection

116

Identity (Ethnic)
Use   Ethnic Identity

Identity (Personal)
Use   Self Concept

Identity Crisis
Broader   Crises
              Emotional Adjustment
Related   Stress

Idiocy
Use   Mental Retardation

Idiocy (Amaurotic Familial)
Use   Amaurotic Familial Idiocy

Idiot Savants
Broader   Handicapped
              Mentally Retarded
Related   Ability/

Idiots
Use   Profoundly Mentally Retarded

Ileum
Use   Intestines

Illegitimate Children
Broader   Family Members

Illinois Test Psycholinguist Abil
Used For   ITPA (Test)
(See)   Intelligence Measures

Illiteracy
Use   Literacy

Illness (Physical)
Use   Disorders/

Illumination
Used For   Light
              Luminance
              Photic Threshold
Broader   Perceptual Stimulation
              Visual Stimulation
Narrower   Photopic Stimulation
              Scotopic Stimulation
Related   Brightness Perception

Illusion (Autokinetic)
Use   Autokinetic Illusion

Illusions (Perception)
Used For   Distortion (Perceptual)
              Optical Illusions
              Perceptual Distortion
Narrower   Afterimage
              Perceptual Aftereffect
              Spatial Distortion
Related   Perception/
              Perceptual Disturbances

Image (Body)
Use   Body Image

Image (Retinal)
Use   Retinal Image

Imagery
Broader   Abstraction
Narrower   Conceptual Imagery
Related   Imagination

Imagery (Conceptual)
Use   Conceptual Imagery

Imagination

Broader   Cognitive Processes
              Ideation
Related   Conceptual Imagery
              Imagery
              Magical Thinking
              Vicarious Experiences

Imbeciles
Use   Severely Mentally Retarded
              Trainable Mentally Retarded

Imbecility
Use   Mental Retardation

Imipramine
Used For   Tofranil
Broader   Amines
              Antidepressant Drugs
              Psychic Energizers

Imitation (Learning)
Used For   Modeling Behavior
Broader   Social Learning

Immaturity (Emotional)
Use   Emotional Immaturity

Immigrants
Use   Immigration

Immigration
Used For   Immigrants
Broader   Social Processes

Immunization
Used For   Vaccination
Broader   Physical Treatment Methods
Related   Antibodies

Immunoglobulins
Broader   Blood Proteins
              Globulins
              Proteins
Narrower   Gamma Globulin
Related   Antibodies
              Blood Coagulation Disorders
              Immunologic Disorders

Immunologic Disorders
Used For   Autoimmune Disorders
              Hypersensitivity (Immunologic)
Narrower   Allergic Disorders
              Allergic Skin Disorders
              Anaphylactic Shock

117

Immunologic Disorders — (Continued)
Narrower
　　　Blood Group Incompatibility
　　　Drug Allergies
　　　Food Allergies
　　　Hay Fever
　　　Rh Incompatibility
Related　Asthma
　　　Disorders/
　　　Immunoglobulins

Immunology
Used For　Immunopathology
Broader　Medical Sciences
　　　Sciences

Immunopathology
Use　Immunology

Implosive Therapy
Used For　Flooding Therapy
Broader　Behavior Modification
　　　Behavior Therapy

Impotence
Broader　Psychosexual Behavior
　　　Sexual Function Disturbances
Related　Erection (Penis)
　　　Frigidity
　　　Male Orgasm
　　　Orgasm
　　　Premature Ejaculation

Imprinting
Broader　Animal Ethology
　　　Social Learning
Related　Animal Innate Behavior
　　　Animal Instinctive Behavior

Impulsiveness
Broader　Personality Traits

Inadequate Personality
Broader　Personality Disorders

Incarceration
Broader　Institutionalization
　　　Legal Processes
Related　Correctional Institutions
　　　Institution Visitation

Incentives
Broader　Motivation
Narrower　Educational Incentives
　　　Monetary Incentives
Related　Goals
　　　Needs
　　　Rewards
　　　Temptation

Incest
Broader　Psychosexual Behavior
　　　Sexual Deviations
　　　Sexual Intercourse (Human)
Related　Pedophilia

Incidental Learning
Narrower　Latent Learning
Related　Learning/

Income (Economic)
Related　Income Level
　　　Poverty
　　　Socioeconomic Status

Income Level
Broader　Socioeconomic Status
Narrower　Lower Income Level
　　　Middle Income Level
　　　Upper Income Level
Related　Income (Economic)
　　　Social Class

Incompatibility (Blood Group)
Use　Blood Group Incompatibility

Incompatibility (Rh)
Use　Rh Incompatibility

Incomplete Man Test
(See)　Projective Techniques

Incontinence (Fecal)
Use　Fecal Incontinence

Incontinence (Urinary)
Use　Urinary Incontinence

Incubators (Apparatus)
Broader　Apparatus

Independence (Personality)
Broader　Personality Traits

Independent Party (Political)
Use　Political Parties

Independent Variables
Broader　Statistical Variables

India

Indians (American)
Use　American Indians

Indifference
Use　Apathy

Individual Counseling
Use　Individual Psychotherapy

Individual Differences
Used For　Differences (Individual)
Related　Personality/

Individual Problem Solving
Use　Problem Solving

Individual Psychology
Broader　History of Psychology
　　　Neopsychoanalytic School

Individual Psychotherapy
Used For	Individual Counseling
	Individual Therapy
	Therapy (Individual)
Broader	Psychotherapy

Individual Testing
Related	Measurement/
	Test Administration

Individual Therapy
Use	Individual Psychotherapy

Individualism
Use	Individuality

Individuality
Used For	Individualism
Broader	Personality Traits
Related	Nonconformity (Personality)

Individualized Instruction
Used For	Instruction (Individualized)
Broader	Teaching
	Teaching Methods
Related	Computer Assisted Instruction
	Open Classroom Method
	Programed Instruction
	Tutoring

Induced Abortion
Used For	Abortion (Induced)
	Elective Abortion
	Therapeutic Abortion
Broader	Physical Treatment Methods
	Surgery
Related	Abortion Laws
	Birth Control
	Family Planning
	Spontaneous Abortion

Inductive Deductive Reasoning
Used For	Convergent Thinking
	Deductive Reasoning
	Syllogistic Reasoning
Broader	Cognitive Processes
	Reasoning
	Thinking
Narrower	Inference

Industrial Accidents
Broader	Accidents
Related	Occupational Safety

Industrial Foremen
Used For	Foremen (Industrial)
Broader	Blue Collar Workers
	Business And Industrial Personnel
Related	Management Personnel

Industrial Personnel
Use	Business And Industrial Personnel

Industrial Psychologists
Broader	Business And Industrial Personnel
	Psychologists
Related	Social Psychologists

Industrial Psychology
Broader	Applied Psychology
	Psychology
	Sciences
	Social Sciences

Industrial Safety
Use	Occupational Safety

Industrialization
Broader	Social Processes
Related	Urbanization

Industry
Use	Business

Infancy
Use	Infants

Infant Development
Broader	Childhood Development
Narrower	Neonatal Development
Related	Developmental Differences
	Physical Development
	Psychogenesis

Infant Intelligence Scale
Used For	Cattell Infant Intelligence Scale
(See)	Intelligence Measures

Infant Vocalization
Used For	Babbling
	Vocalization (Infant)
Broader	Vocalization
	Voice
Related	Crying

Infantile Neurosis
Use	Childhood Neurosis

Infantile Paralysis
Use	Poliomyelitis

Infantile Psychosis
Use	Childhood Psychosis

Infantilism
Related	Mental Disorders/

Infants
Used For	Babies
	Infancy
Broader	Children
	Developmental Age Groups
Narrower	Neonates

Infarctions (Myocardial)
Use	Myocardial Infarctions

Infections
Use	Infectious Disorders

Infectious Disorders
Used For	Infections
	Neuroinfections
Narrower	Bacterial Disorders
	Bacterial Meningitis
	Common Colds
	Gonorrhea
	Herpes Simplex
	Infectious Meningitis
	Influenza
	Malaria
	Measles
	Neurosyphilis
	Parasitic Disorders
	Poliomyelitis
	Pulmonary Tuberculosis
	Rubella
	Syphilis
	Tetanus (Disease)
	Toxoplasmosis
	Tuberculosis
	Venereal Diseases
	Viral Disorders
	Viral Meningitis
Related	Arthritis
	Chorea
	Dermatitis
	Digestive System Disorders
	Disorders/
	Encephalitis
	Encephalomyelitis
	Hepatitis
	Hydrocephaly
	Jaundice
	Liver Disorders
	Myelitis

Infectious Meningitis
Broader	Central Nervous System Disorders
	Infectious Disorders
	Meningitis
	Nervous System Disorders
Narrower	Bacterial Meningitis
	Viral Meningitis

Inference
Broader	Cognitive Processes
	Inductive Deductive Reasoning
	Reasoning
	Thinking

Inferior Colliculus
Broader	Brain
	Central Nervous System
	Corpora Quadrigemina
	Mesencephalon
	Nervous System

Inferiority (Emotional)
Use	Emotional Inferiority

Infertility
Broader	Genital Disorders
	Urogenital Disorders
Narrower	Sterility
Related	Endocrine Sexual Disorders
	Gynecological Disorders
	Hypothyroidism
	Klinefelters Syndrome
	Male Genital Disorders
	Psychosomatic Disorders
	Venereal Diseases

Infirmaries
Use	Hospitals

Inflection
Broader	Grammar
	Language
	Linguistics
	Verbal Communication
Related	Speech Characteristics

Influence (Interpersonal)
Use	Interpersonal Influences

Influences (Social)
Use	Social Influences

Influenza
Broader	Infectious Disorders
	Viral Disorders
Related	Gastrointestinal Disorders
	Nervous System Disorders
	Respiratory Tract Disorders

Information (Concepts)
Use	Concepts

Information (Messages)
Use	Messages

Information Exchange
Related	Information/

Information Processes (Human)
Use	Cognitive Processes

Information Processing (Automated)
Use	Automated Information Processing

Information Retrieval (Automated)
Use	Automated Information Retrieval

Information Seeking
Related	Information/

Information Storage (Human)
Use	Human Information Storage

Information Theory
Related	Information/
	Stochastic Modeling
	Theories/

Information/
Related   Automated Information Processing
               Automated Information Retrieval
               Automated Information Storage
               Communication/
               Concepts
               Information Exchange
               Information Seeking
               Information Theory
               Messages

Inhalation
Use   Respiration

Inhibition (Personality)
Related   Personality Processes/

Inhibition (Proactive)
Use   Proactive Inhibition

Inhibition (Retroactive)
Use   Retroactive Inhibition

Initial Teaching Alphabet
Used For   ITA (Alphabet)
Broader   Alphabets
               Language
               Verbal Communication
               Written Language
Related   Language Arts Education
               Reading
               Reading Education
               Teaching Methods

Initiation Rites
Broader   Rites of Passage
               Sociocultural Factors

Initiative
Broader   Personality Traits

Injections
Narrower   Intramuscular Injections
               Intraperitoneal Injections
               Intravenous Injections
               Subcutaneous Injections
Related   Drug Administration Methods

Injuries
Used For   Physical Trauma
               Trauma (Physical)
Narrower   Birth Injuries
               Brain Concussion
               Burns
               Contusions
               Electrical Injuries
               Head Injuries
               Self Inflicted Wounds
               Spinal Cord Injuries
               Traumatic Amputations
               Wounds

Injuries — (Continued)
Related   Accidents
               Coma
               Disorders/
               Hematoma
               Safety
               Shock

Injuries (Birth)
Use   Birth Injuries

Inmates (Prison)
Use   Prisoners

Innate Behavior (Animal)
Use   Animal Innate Behavior

Inner City
Use   Urban Environments

Innovativeness
Use   Creativity

Inquisitiveness
Use   Curiosity

Insanity
Use   Mental Disorders/
               Psychosis

Insecticides
Narrower   DDT (Insecticide)
               Dieldrin
               Parathion
Related   Drugs/
               Insects
               Nicotine
               Poisons

Insects
Broader   Arthropoda
               Invertebrates
Narrower   Ants
               Bees
               Beetles
               Butterflies
               Cockroaches
               Diptera
               Drosophila
               Grasshoppers
               Larvae
               Mantis
               Moths
Related   Insecticides

Insecurity (Emotional)
Use   Emotional Security

Insensitivity (Personality)
Use   Sensitivity (Personality)

Inservice Teacher Education
Broader   Personnel Training
               Teacher Education
Related   On The Job Training

Inservice Training (Mental Health)
  Use   Mental Health Inservice Training

Insight
  Broader   Personality Traits
  Related   Perceptiveness (Personality)

Insight (Psychotherapeutic Process)
  Broader   Psychotherapeutic Processes

Insight Therapy
  Broader   Psychotherapy

Insomnia
  Broader   Consciousness Disturbances
            Sleep Disorders
            Symptoms

Instability (Emotional)
  Use   Emotional Instability

Instinctive Behavior (Animal)
  Use   Animal Instinctive Behavior

Institution Visitation
  Used For Visitation (Hospital)
            Visitation (Institution)
            Visitation (Psychiatric Hospital)
  Related   Correctional Institutions
            Incarceration
            Residential Care Institutions

Institutional Functioning Inventory
  (See)   Inventories

Institutionalization
  Narrower Commitment (Psychiatric)
            Hospital Admission
            Hospital Discharge
            Hospitalization
            Incarceration
            Psychiatric Hospital Admission
            Psychiatric Hospital Readmission
            Psychiatric Hospitalization
  Related   Orphanages

Institutionalized Mentally Retarded
  Broader   Handicapped
            Mentally Retarded
  Related   Home Reared Mentally Retarded
            Residential Care Institutions

Institutions (Correctional)
  Use   Correctional Institutions

Institutions (Residential Care)
  Use   Residential Care Institutions

Instruction
  Use   Teaching

Instruction (Computer Assisted)
  Use   Computer Assisted Instruction

Instruction (Individualized)
  Use   Individualized Instruction

Instruction (Programed)
  Use   Programed Instruction

Instructional Media
  Used For Media (Educational)
  Broader   Teaching
  Narrower Educational Audiovisual Aids
            Motion Pictures (Educational)
            Programed Textbooks
            Reading Materials
            Teaching Machines

Instructions (Experimental)
  Use   Experimental Instructions

Instructors
  Use   Teachers

Instrumental Conditioning
  Use   Operant Conditioning

Instrumental Learning
  Use   Operant Conditioning

Instrumentation (Flight)
  Use   Flight Instrumentation

Insulin
  Broader   Hormones
            Hypoglycemic Agents
  Related   Insulin Shock Therapy

Insulin Coma Therapy
  Use   Insulin Shock Therapy

Insulin Shock Therapy
  Used For Insulin Coma Therapy
            Therapy (Insulin Shock)
  Broader   Organic Therapies
            Shock Therapy
  Related   Coma
            Insulin

Insurance
  Narrower Employee Health Insurance
            Employee Life Insurance
            Health Insurance
            Life Insurance
            Workmens Compensation Insurance

Insurance Agents
  Use   Sales Personnel

Integration (Racial)
  Use   Racial Integration

Intellectual Development
  Broader   Cognitive Development
            Psychogenesis
  Narrower Language Development
  Related   Intelligence

Intellectualism
  Broader   Philosophies

Intellectualization
  Broader   Defense Mechanisms
  Related   Isolation (Defense Mechanism)

Intellectually Gifted
  Use   Gifted

Intelligence
  Related   Ability/
           Creativity
           Gifted
           Intellectual Development
           Intelligence Quotient

Intelligence Measures
  Used For   Intelligence Scales
           Scales (Intelligence)
           Test (Intelligence)
  Related   Measurement/
  Identifier   Ammons Full Range Picture
           Vocab Test
           Benton Revised Visual Reten-
           tion Test
           California Test of Mental Ma-
           turity
           Columbia Mental Maturity
           Scale
           Concept Mastery Test
           Culture Fair Intelligence Test
           Frostig Development Test Vis
           Percept
           Goodenough Harris Draw A
           Person Test
           Henman Nelson Tests Mental
           Ability
           Hidden Figures Test
           Illinois Test Psycholinguist Abil
           Infant Intelligence Scale
           Kohs Block Design Test
           Leiter Adult Intelligence Scale
           Lorge Thorndike Intelligence
           Test
           Lowenfeld Mosaic Test
           Miller Analogies Test
           Peabody Picture Vocabulary
           Test
           Porteus Maze Test
           Raven Coloured Progressive
           Matrices
           Ravens Progressive Matrices
           Remote Associates Test
           Slosson Intelligence Test For
           Child
           SRA Primary Mental Abilities
           Test
           Stanford Binet Intelligence Scale
           Temporal Spatial Concept Scale
           Vane Kindergarten Test
           Wechsler Adult Intelligence
           Scale

Intelligence Measures — (Continued)
  Identifier
           Wechsler Bellevue Intelligence
           Scale
           Wechsler Intelligence Scale
           Children

Intelligence Quotient
  Related   Intelligence

Intelligence Scales
  Use   Intelligence Measures

Intensity (Stimulus)
  Use   Stimulus Intensity

Intentional Learning
  Related   Learning/

Interaction (Double Bind)
  Use   Double Bind Interaction

Interaction (Interpersonal)
  Use   Interpersonal Interaction

Interaction (Social)
  Use   Social Interaction

Interaction Analysis (Statistics)
  Broader   Factor Analysis
           Statistical Analysis
           Statistical Measurement
  Related   Analysis/

Interaction Variance
  Broader   Statistical Analysis
           Statistical Measurement
           Variability Measurement

Intercostal Muscles
  Broader   Muscles
           Musculoskeletal System

Intercourse (Sexual)
  Use   Sexual Intercourse (Human)

Interdisciplinary Treatment Approach
  Related   Treatment/

Interest Inventories
  Used For   Interest Scales
           Interest Surveys
           Scales (Interest)
           Surveys (Interest)
  Broader   Inventories

Interest Patterns
  Related   Interests

Interest Scales
  Use   Interest Inventories

Interest Surveys
  Use   Interest Inventories

Interests
  Narrower   Occupational Interests
  Related   Interest Patterns

Interfaith Marriage
Broader   Exogamous Marriage
              Marriage

Interference (Learning)
Narrower   Proactive Inhibition
              Retroactive Inhibition
Related   Forgetting
              Learning/
              Retention

Intergroup Dynamics
Broader   Group Dynamics

Intermarriage
Use   Exogamous Marriage

Intermediate School Students
Broader   Elementary School Students
              Students

Intermittent Reinforcement
Use   Reinforcement Schedules

Internal External Locus of Control
Used For   Control (Locus of)
              Locus of Control
Broader   Personality Traits
Related   External Rewards
              Extrinsic Motivation
              Internal Rewards
              Intrinsic Motivation

Internal Rewards
Used For   Intrinsic Rewards
Broader   Reinforcement
              Rewards
Related   Internal External Locus of
              Control
              Intrinsic Motivation

International Organizations
Broader   Organizations
Related   Foreign Organizations

International Relations
Used For   Relations (International)
Related   Diplomacy (Foreign Policy)
              Foreign Policy Making

Internists
Broader   Medical Personnel
              Physicians

Internship (Medical)
Use   Medical Internship

Interpersonal Attraction
Used For   Attraction (Interpersonal)
              Rapport
Broader   Interpersonal Interaction
              Social Behavior
              Social Interaction
Related   Physical Attractiveness

Interpersonal Communication
Broader   Interpersonal Interaction
              Social Behavior
              Social Interaction
Narrower   Arguments
              Bargaining
              Body Language
              Conversation
              Double Bind Interaction
              Eye Contact
              Group Discussion
              Interviewing
              Interviews
              Job Applicant Interviews
              Negotiation
              Parent Child Communication
              Psychodiagnostic Interview
Related   Communication/
              Credibility
              Scientific Communication
              Self Disclosure

Interpersonal Compatibility
Used For   Compatibility (Interpersonal)
Broader   Interpersonal Interaction
              Social Behavior
              Social Interaction
Related   Friendship

Interpersonal Influences
Used For   Influence (Interpersonal)
Broader   Interpersonal Interaction
              Social Behavior
              Social Interaction
Related   Social Influences

Interpersonal Interaction
Used For   Interaction (Interpersonal)
Broader   Social Behavior
              Social Interaction
Narrower   Arguments
              Assistance (Social Behavior)
              Bargaining
              Charitable Behavior
              Collective Behavior
              Conflict
              Conversation
              Cooperation
              Double Bind Interaction
              Eye Contact
              Friendship
              Group Discussion
              Group Participation
              Group Performance
              Interpersonal Attraction
              Interpersonal Communication
              Interpersonal Compatibility
              Interpersonal Influences
              Interviewing
              Interviews
              Job Applicant Interviews

Interpersonal Interaction — (Continued)

Narrower	Negotiation
	Participation
	Peer Relations
	Persecution
	Psychodiagnostic Interview
	Riots
	Rivalry
	Social Dating
	Violence
	War
Related	Affection
	Intimacy

Interpersonal Perception

Use	Social Perception

Interpretation (Psychoanalytic)

Use	Psychoanalytic Interpretation

Interracial Marriage

Used For	Miscegenous Marriage
Broader	Exogamous Marriage
	Marriage

Interresponse Time

Used For	Time (Interresponse)
Broader	Response Parameters
	Time

Interstimulus Interval

Broader	Stimulus Intervals
	Stimulus Parameters

Intertrial Interval

Broader	Stimulus Intervals
	Stimulus Parameters

Interval Reinforcement

Use	Fixed Interval Reinforcement
	Variable Interval Reinforcement

Intervals (Stimulus)

Use	Stimulus Intervals

Interviewing

Broader	Interpersonal Communication
	Interpersonal Interaction
	Social Behavior
	Social Interaction
Related	Interviews

Interviews

Broader	Interpersonal Communication
	Interpersonal Interaction
	Social Behavior
	Social Interaction
Narrower	Job Applicant Interviews
	Psychodiagnostic Interview
Related	Interviewing

Intestines

Used For	Duodenum
	Ileum

Intestines — (Continued)

Broader	Digestive System
	Gastrointestinal System
Narrower	Colon
Related	Absorption (Physiological)

Intimacy

Related	Interpersonal Interaction

Intoxication

Use	Toxic Disorders

Intoxication (Alcohol)

Use	Alcohol Intoxication

Intramuscular Injections

Broader	Injections

Intraperitoneal Injections

Broader	Injections

Intrauterine Devices

Broader	Birth Control
	Contraceptive Devices
	Family Planning

Intravenous Injections

Broader	Injections

Intrinsic Motivation

Broader	Motivation
Related	Goals
	Internal External Locus of Control
	Internal Rewards
	Needs

Intrinsic Rewards

Use	Internal Rewards

Introjection

Broader	Defense Mechanisms
Related	Identification (Defense Mechanism)

Introspection

Related	Personality Processes/

Introversion

Broader	Personality Traits

Intuition

Inventories

Narrower	Biographical Inventories
	Interest Inventories
Related	Measurement/
Identifier	Institutional Functioning Inventory
	Inventory of College Activities

Inventories (Attitude)

Use	Attitude Measures

Inventories (Personality)

Use	Personality Measures

Inventories (Preference)
  Use   Preference Measures

Inventory of College Activities
  (See)   Inventories

Invertebrates
  Narrower   Ants
              Arachnida
              Arthropoda
              Bees
              Beetles
              Butterflies
              Cockroaches
              Crabs
              Crayfish
              Crustacea
              Diptera
              Drosophila
              Earthworms
              Echinodermata
              Grasshoppers
              Insects
              Larvae
              Mantis
              Mollusca
              Moths
              Octopus
              Planarians
              Protozoa
              Snails
              Worms
  Related   Animals/
              Vertebrates

Investigation
  Use   Experimentation/

Involutional Depression
  Used For   Climacteric Depression
  Broader   Affective Disturbances
              Affective Psychosis
              Depression (Emotion)
              Emotional States
              Psychosis

Involutional Paranoid Psychosis
  Used For   Climacteric Paranoia
  Broader   Psychosis
  Related   Folie A Deux
              Paranoia (Psychosis)
              Paranoid Schizophrenia

Involvement

  Broader   Social Behavior

Ions
  Use   Electrolytes

Iowa Tests of Basic Skills
  (See)   Achievement Measures

Iproniazid
  Broader   Amine Oxidase Inhibitors
              Antidepressant Drugs
              Antihypertensive Drugs
              Antitubercular Drugs
              Monoamine Oxidase Inhibitors
              Psychic Energizers

Iran

Ireland

Iris (Eye)
  Broader   Eye (Anatomy)
              Sense Organs

Iron
  Broader   Chemical Elements
              Metallic Elements

Irradiation
  Use   Radiation

Ischemia
  Broader   Cardiovascular Disorders
  Narrower   Cerebral Ischemia
  Related   Anoxia

Islam
  Used For   Moslems
              Muslims
  Broader   Religious Affiliation
              Religious Beliefs

Isocarboxazid
  Broader   Amine Oxidase Inhibitors
              Antidepressant Drugs
              Monoamine Oxidase Inhibitors
              Psychic Energizers

Isoenzymes
  Use   Isozymes

Isolation (Defense Mechanism)
  Broader   Defense Mechanisms
  Related   Intellectualization

Isolation (Social)
  Use   Social Isolation

Isolation Effect
  Related   Deprivation

Isoniazid
  Broader   Antitubercular Drugs

Isoproterenol
  Broader   Alcohols
              Sympathomimetic Drugs

Isozymes
  Used For   Isoenzymes
  Broader   Enzymes

Israel

ITA (Alphabet)
Use   Initial Teaching Alphabet

Italy

Itching
Use   Pruritus

Item Analysis (Statistical)
Broader   Factor Analysis
      Statistical Analysis
      Statistical Measurement
Related   Analysis/

Item Analysis (Test)
Broader   Test Construction
      Testing
Related   Analysis/
      Measurement/

Item Content (Test)
Broader   Test Construction
      Testing
Related   Measurement/

ITPA (Test)
Identifier   Illinois Test Psycholinguist Abil

Jails
Use   Prisons

Jamaica

Japan

Jaundice
Broader   Digestive System Disorders
      Liver Disorders
Related   Cirrhosis (Liver)
      Hepatitis
      Infectious Disorders

Jaw
Used For   Mandibula
      Maxilla
Broader   Musculoskeletal System
Related   Bones

Jealousy
Used For   Envy
Related   Anger
      Anxiety
      Emotions/

Jews
Use   Judaism

Job Analysis
Used For   Job Descriptions
      Job Requirements
Broader   Personnel Management
Related   Analysis/
      Task Analysis

Job Applicant Attitudes
Related   Attitudes/
      Occupational Attitudes
      Personnel/

Job Applicant Interviews
Used For   Employment Interviews
Broader   Interpersonal Communication
      Interpersonal Interaction
      Interviews
      Personnel Evaluation
      Personnel Management
      Social Behavior
      Social Interaction

Job Applicant Screening
Used For   Job Applicant Testing
      Screening (Job Applicants)
      Testing (Job Applicant)
Broader   Personnel Evaluation
      Personnel Management

Job Applicant Testing
Use   Job Applicant Screening

Job Corps
Broader   Government Programs
Related   Government

Job Descriptions
Use   Job Analysis

Job Enrichment
Used For   Enrichment (Jobs)
Broader   Working Conditions

Job Experience Level
Used For   Experience Level (Job)

Job Mobility
Use   Occupational Mobility

Job Performance
Used For   Employee Performance Apprais-
      al
      Job Performance Evaluation
Narrower   Employee Efficiency
      Employee Productivity
Related   Employee Attitudes
      Personnel Evaluation
      Personnel/

Job Performance Evaluation
Use   Job Performance
      Personnel Evaluation

Job Requirements
Use   Job Analysis

Job Satisfaction
Broader   Employee Attitudes
      Satisfaction

Job Selection
Use   Occupational Choice

Jobs
Use   Occupations/

Joint Disorders
Broader   Musculoskeletal Disorders
Narrower   Arthritis
           Rheumatoid Arthritis
Related   Joints (Anatomy)

Joints (Anatomy)
Broader   Musculoskeletal System
Related   Joint Disorders

Jokes
Broader   Humor

Journalists
Related   Personnel/

Joy
Use   Happiness

Jr Sr High School Personality Quest
(See)   Nonprojective Personality Measures
           Personality Measures

Judaism
Used For   Ashkenazim
           Jews
           Sephardim
Broader   Religious Affiliation
           Religious Beliefs
Related   Bible

Judgment
Related   Judgment Disturbances

Judgment Disturbances
Broader   Thought Disturbances
Related   Judgment

Judo
Broader   Recreation
           Sports

Jumping
Broader   Motor Performance
           Motor Processes

Jung (Carl)

Jungian Psychology
Broader   History of Psychology
           Neopsychoanalytic School

Junior College Students
Broader   College Students
           Students

Junior Colleges
Use   Colleges

Junior High School Students
Broader   Students

Junior High School Teachers
Broader   Educational Personnel
           Teachers

Junior High Schools
Broader   Schools

Jury
Use   Adjudication

Justice
Related   Law (Government)

Juvenile Court
Use   Adjudication

Juvenile Delinquency
Used For   Delinquency (Juvenile)
Broader   Antisocial Behavior
           Behavior Disorders
Related   Juvenile Delinquents

Juvenile Delinquents
Used For   Offenders (Juvenile)
Narrower   Female Delinquents
           Male Delinquents
Related   Criminals
           Juvenile Delinquency
           Juvenile Gangs

Juvenile Gangs
Used For   Gangs (Juvenile)
Related   Juvenile Delinquents

Kangaroos
Broader   Mammals
           Marsupials
           Vertebrates

Karyotype Disorders
Use   Chromosome Disorders

Keypunch Operators
Use   Clerical Personnel

Kibbutz
Broader   Communes
           Communities
           Environment
           Social Environments

Kidney Transplants
Use   Organ Transplantation

Kidneys
Broader   Urinary Tract
           Urogenital System

Kindergarten Students
Broader   Students

Kindergartens
Broader   Schools

Kinesthetic Perception
Broader   Somesthetic Perception

Kinship Structure
Related   Ethnography
             Ethnology/
             Family Structure
             Sociocultural Factors

Kittens
Use   Cats

Kleptomania
Broader   Mania

Klinefelters Syndrome
Broader   Chromosome Disorders
             Endocrine Disorders
             Endocrine Sexual Disorders
             Genetic Disorders
             Genital Disorders
             Hypogonadism
             Male Genital Disorders
             Neonatal Chromosome Disor-
                ders
             Neonatal Disorders
             Neonatal Genetic Disorders
             Neonatal Sex Chromosome Dis-
                orders
             Sex Chromosome Disorders
             Syndromes
             Urogenital Disorders
Related   Infertility
             Mental Retardation

Knee
Broader   Musculoskeletal System
Related   Leg (Anatomy)

Knowledge of Results
Broader   Feedback

Kohs Block Design Test
(See)   Intelligence Measures

Kolmogarov Smirnov Test
Broader   Nonparametric Statistical Tests
             Statistical Analysis
             Statistical Tests
Related   Hypothesis Testing

Korea

Korsakoffs Psychosis
Used For   Korsakoffs Syndrome
Broader   Alcoholic Hallucinosis
             Alcoholic Psychosis
             Alcoholism
             Behavior Disorders
             Brain Disorders
             Central Nervous System Disor-
                ders
             Hallucinosis
             Nervous System Disorders
             Organic Brain Syndromes

Korsakoffs Psychosis — (Continued)
Broader
             Psychosis
             Syndromes
Related   Confabulation
             Mental Disorders/

Korsakoffs Syndrome
Use   Korsakoffs Psychosis

Kuder Occupational Interest Survey
(See)   Occupational Interest Measures

Kuder Preference Record
(See)   Preference Measures

Kuder Richardson Test
Broader   Nonparametric Statistical Tests
             Statistical Analysis
             Statistical Tests
Related   Statistical Reliability

Kupfer Detre Self Rating Scale
(See)   Nonprojective Personality Meas-
                ures
             Personality Measures

Kwashiorkor
Broader   Nutritional Deficiencies
             Protein Deficiency Disorders

L Dopa
Use   Levodopa

Labor (Childbirth)
Related   Birth
             Oxytocic Drugs

Labor Management Relations
Used For   Labor Relations
Broader   Personnel Management
Related   Labor Unions
             Management/
             Strikes

Labor Relations
Use   Labor Management Relations

Labor Union Members
Related   Personnel/

Labor Unions
Broader   Organizations
Related   Labor Management Relations

Laboratories (Educational)
Use   Educational Laboratories

Laboratories (Experimental)
Use   Experimental Laboratories

Laborers (Construct And Indust)
Use   Blue Collar Workers

Laborers (Farm)
Use   Agricultural Workers

Labyrinth (Anatomy)
Broader   Ear (Anatomy)
          Sense Organs
Narrower   Cochlea
          Semicircular Canals
          Vestibular Apparatus

Labyrinth (Apparatus)
Use   Mazes

Labyrinth Disorders
Broader   Ear Disorders
          Sense Organ Disorders
Narrower   Menieres Disease
          Motion Sickness
Related   Somesthetic Perception
          Vertigo

Lactate Dehydrogenase
Broader   Dehydrogenases
          Enzymes

Lactation
Broader   Secretion (Gland)
Related   Postnatal Period

Lag (Response)
Use   Reaction Time

Lambs
Use   Sheep

Landscapes
Use   Topography

Language
Used For   English Language
Broader   Verbal Communication
Narrower   Adjectives
          Adverbs
          Alphabets
          Anagrams
          Antonyms
          Bilingualism
          Consonants
          Conversation
          Cursive Writing
          Dialect
          Ethnolinguistics
          Etymology
          Foreign Languages
          Form Classes (Language)
          Grammar
          Handwriting
          Handwriting Legibility
          Homographs
          Homonyms
          Inflection
          Initial Teaching Alphabet
          Language Development
          Letters (Alphabet)
          Linguistics
          Literacy
          Monolingualism

Language — (Continued)
Narrower
          Morphemes
          Morphology (Language)
          Multilingualism
          Neologisms
          Nonstandard English
          Nouns
          Numbers (Numerals)
          Orthography
          Paragraphs
          Phonemes
          Phonetics
          Phonology
          Phrases
          Printing (Handwriting)
          Pronouns
          Psycholinguistics
          Public Speaking
          Semantics
          Sentence Structure
          Sentences
          Sight Vocabulary
          Sign Language
          Slang
          Syllables
          Synonyms
          Syntax
          Transformational Generative
            Grammar
          Verbs
          Vocabulary
          Vowels
          Words (Phonetic Units)
          Written Language
Related   Symbolism

Language Arts Education
Broader   Curriculum
Narrower   Phonics
          Reading Education
          Spelling
Related   Initial Teaching Alphabet

Language Development
Broader   Cognitive Development
          Intellectual Development
          Language
          Psychogenesis
          Verbal Communication
Related   Foreign Language Learning
          Speech Development

Language Laboratories
Broader   Educational Laboratories
          School Facilities

Larvae
Broader   Arthropoda
          Insects
          Invertebrates

Larvae — (Continued)
Related	Ants
	Bees
	Beetles
	Butterflies
	Cockroaches
	Diptera
	Drosophila
	Grasshoppers
	Mantis
	Moths

Laryngeal Disorders
Broader	Respiratory Tract Disorders

Larynx
Broader	Respiratory System
Narrower	Vocal Cords

Laser Irradiation
Broader	Radiation

Latency (Response)
Use	Response Latency

Latent Learning
Broader	Incidental Learning

Lateral Dominance
Used For	Handedness
Broader	Cerebral Dominance
Related	Brain
	Learning Disabilities
	Minimally Brain Damaged

Latin Squares Test
Broader	Statistical Analysis
	Statistical Tests

Law (Government)
Narrower	Criminal Law
Related	Government
	Justice
	Laws

Law Enforcement Personnel
Broader	Government Personnel
Narrower	Parole Officers
	Police Personnel
	Prison Personnel
	Probation Officers
Related	Attorneys
	Social Workers

Laws
Broader	Government Policy Making
Narrower	Abortion Laws
	Drug Laws
	Gun Control Laws
	Marihuana Laws
	Marihuana Legalization
Related	Government
	Law (Government)
	Legal Processes
	Legislative Processes

Lawyers
Use	Attorneys

Lay Religious Personnel
Broader	Religious Personnel
Related	Chaplains
	Clergy
	Evangelists
	Missionaries

Lead (Metal)
Broader	Chemical Elements
	Metallic Elements

Lead Poisoning
Broader	Metal Poisoning
	Toxic Disorders
Related	Pica

Leadership
Broader	Social Behavior
Narrower	Leadership Style

Leadership Style
Used For	Style (Leadership)
Broader	Leadership
	Social Behavior

Learning (Programed)
Use	Programed Instruction

Learning Ability
Related	Ability/

Learning Centers (Educational)
Broader	School Facilities

Learning Disabilities
Used For	Special Education (Learning Disabil)
Broader	Learning Disorders
Narrower	Dyslexia
Related	Acalculia
	Agraphia
	Aphasia
	Cerebral Dominance
	Handicapped
	Lateral Dominance
	Minimally Brain Damaged
	Perceptual Disturbances

Learning Disorders
Narrower	Dyslexia
	Learning Disabilities
	Reading Disabilities
Related	Mental Disorders/

Learning Rate
Related	Learning/

Learning Schedules
Used For	Schedules (Learning)
Narrower	Distributed Practice
	Massed Practice
Related	Learning/

Learning Theory
   Related   Learning/
               Theories/

Learning/
   Related   Cat Learning
               Classical Conditioning
               Concept Learning
               Conditioning
               Extinction (Learning)
               Feedback
               Foreign Language Learning
               Forgetting
               Habits
               Incidental Learning
               Intentional Learning
               Interference (Learning)
               Learning Rate
               Learning Schedules
               Learning Theory
               Maze Learning
               Memory
               Mnemonic Learning
               Nonverbal Learning
               Observational Learning
               Operant Conditioning
               Overlearning
               Perceptual Motor Learning
               Primacy Effect
               Probability Learning
               Rat Learning
               Recency Effect
               Reinforcement
               Relearning
               Retention
               Rote Learning
               School Learning
               Sequential Learning
               Serial Anticipation (Learning)
               Serial Learning
               Skill Learning
               Social Learning
               Spontaneous Recovery (Learning)
               Transfer (Learning)
               Trial And Error Learning
               Verbal Learning

Leary Interpersonal Check List
   (See)   Nonprojective Personality Measures
               Personality Measures

Least Preferred Coworker Scale
   (See)   Preference Measures

Lecture Method
   Broader   Teaching
               Teaching Methods
   Related   Directed Discussion Method

Leeward Islands

Leg (Anatomy)
   Broader   Musculoskeletal System
   Related   Ankle
               Feet (Anatomy)
               Knee
               Thigh

Legal Arrest
   Used For   Arrest (Law)
   Broader   Legal Processes

Legal Detention
   Used For   Detention (Legal)
   Broader   Legal Processes

Legal Processes
   Narrower   Adjudication
               Adoption (Child)
               Commitment (Psychiatric)
               Expert Testimony
               Incarceration
               Legal Arrest
               Legal Detention
               Legislative Processes
               Parole
               Probation
   Related   Government
               Government Policy Making
               Laws

Legalization (Marihuana)
   Use   Marihuana Legalization

Legibility (Handwriting)
   Use   Handwriting Legibility

Legislative Processes
   Broader   Government Policy Making
               Legal Processes
   Related   Government
               Laws

Leisure Time
   Related   Recreation
               Relaxation

Leiter Adult Intelligence Scale
   (See)   Intelligence Measures

Lemurs
   Used For   Bush Babies
   Broader   Mammals
               Vertebrates

Lens (Eye)
   Broader   Eye (Anatomy)
               Sense Organs

Lesbianism
   Broader   Homosexuality
               Psychosexual Behavior

Lesbianism — (Continued)
- Related   Bisexuality
-           Transsexualism
-           Transvestism

Lesions
- Used For Ablation
-           Sectioning (Lesion)
- Narrower Brain Lesions
-           Hypothalamus Lesions
-           Neural Lesions
- Related   Surgery

Lesser Antilles

Lesson Plans
- Broader Teaching
-           Teaching Methods

Letters (Alphabet)
- Broader Alphabets
-           Language
-           Linguistics
-           Verbal Communication
-           Written Language

Leucine
- Broader Acids
-           Amino Acids

Leucocytes
- Used For Leukocytes
-           White Blood Cells
- Broader Blood Cells
-           Cells (Biology)
- Narrower Lymphocytes

Leukemias
- Broader Blood and Lymphatic Disorders
-           Neoplasms

Leukocytes
- Use   Leucocytes

Leukotomy
- Use   Psychosurgery

Levodopa
- Used For L Dopa
- Related   Dopa
-           Dopamine

Liberalism
- Broader Personality Traits
- Related   Political Liberalism

Liberalism (Political)
- Use   Political Liberalism

Libido
- Broader Psychoanalytic Personality Factors

Libraries (School)
- Use   School Libraries

Librium
- Use   Chlordiazepoxide

Licensing (Professional)
- Use   Professional Licensing

Lidocaine
- Used For Xylocaine
- Broader Anesthetic Drugs
-           Local Anesthetics

Life Experiences

- Used For Experiences (Life)
- Broader Experiences (Events)

Life Insurance
- Broader Insurance
- Narrower Employee Life Insurance

Life Saving
- Use   Artificial Respiration

Life Style
- Use   Personality Processes/

Ligaments
- Broader Musculoskeletal System

Light
- Use   Illumination

Liking
- Use   Affection

Limbic System
- Broader Brain
-           Central Nervous System
-           Cerebral Cortex
-           Nervous System
-           Telencephalon
- Narrower Amygdaloid Body
-           Gyrus Cinguli
-           Hippocampus
-           Olfactory Bulb

Limen
- Use   Thresholds

Linear Regression
- Broader Statistical Correlation

Linguistic Analysis
- Use   Etymology

Linguistics
- Broader Language
-           Verbal Communication
- Narrower Adjectives
-           Adverbs
-           Alphabets
-           Antonyms
-           Consonants
-           Ethnolinguistics
-           Etymology
-           Form Classes (Language)
-           Grammar

Linguistics — (Continued)
Narrower
- Homographs
- Inflection
- Letters (Alphabet)
- Morphemes
- Morphology (Language)
- Nouns
- Orthography
- Paragraphs
- Phonemes
- Phonetics
- Phonology
- Phrases
- Pronouns
- Psycholinguistics
- Semantics
- Sentence Structure
- Sentences
- Syllables
- Syntax
- Transformational Generative Grammar
- Verbs
- Vowels
- Words (Phonetic Units)

Lipid Metabolism
Used For Fat Metabolism
Broader Metabolism
Related Lipids

Lipid Metabolism Disorders
Broader Metabolism Disorders
Narrower Amaurotic Familial Idiocy

Lipids
Narrower Fatty Acids
     Phosphatides
Related Lipid Metabolism
     Steroids

Lipoproteins
Related Drugs/
     Proteins

Lipreading
Related Deaf
     Speech Perception
     Visual Perception

Lips (Face)
Broader Digestive System
Related Mouth (Anatomy)

Liquor
Broader Alcoholic Beverages

Listening
Use Auditory Perception

Listening Comprehension
Broader Comprehension

Literacy
Used For Illiteracy
Broader Language
     Verbal Communication
     Written Language
Related Reading

Literature
Used For Creative Writing
     Fiction
     Mythology
     Writing (Creative)
Broader Arts
Narrower Autobiography
     Biography
     Poetry
     Prose

Literature (Religion)
Use Religious Literature

Literature Review
Used For Review (of Literature)

Lithium
Broader Chemical Elements
     Metallic Elements

Lithium Bromide
Broader Bromides
     CNS Affecting Drugs
     CNS Depressant Drugs
     Hypnotic Drugs
     Sedatives

Lithium Carbonate
Broader Antidepressant Drugs

Liver
Broader Digestive System
     Gastrointestinal System

Liver Disorders
Used For Hepatic Disorders
Broader Digestive System Disorders
Narrower Cirrhosis (Liver)
     Hepatitis
     Jaundice
     Toxic Hepatitis
Related Infectious Disorders
     Neoplasms
     Toxic Disorders

Lizards
Broader Reptiles
     Vertebrates

Lobotomy
Use Psychosurgery

Local Anesthetics
Broader Anesthetic Drugs
Narrower Cocaine
     Eugenol
     Lidocaine

Local Anesthetics — (Continued)
Narrower　　Novocaine
　　　　　　Quinine
　　　　　　Tetracaine
Related　　　Ephedrine
　　　　　　Methoxamine

Localization (Perceptual)
Use　　　　　Perceptual Localization

Localization (Sound)
Use　　　　　Auditory Localization

Locus of Control
Use　　　　　Internal External Locus of
　　　　　　Control

Logic (Philosophy)
Broader　　　Philosophies

Logical Thinking
Used For　　Ratiocination
Broader　　　Cognitive Processes
　　　　　　Thinking

Logotherapy
Broader　　　Psychotherapy

Loneliness
Broader　　　Emotional States

Long Term Memory
Broader　　　Memory

Longevity
Use　　　　　Aged
　　　　　　Physiological Aging

Longitudinal Studies
Used For　　Studies (Longitudinal)
Broader　　　Experimental Design
Related　　　Experimentation/

Lorge Thorndike Intelligence Test
(See)　　　　Intelligence Measures

Loudness
Used For　　Sound Pressure Level
Broader　　　Auditory Stimulation
　　　　　　Perceptual Stimulation
Narrower　　Noise Levels (Work Areas)

Loudness Discrimination
Broader　　　Auditory Discrimination
　　　　　　Auditory Perception
　　　　　　Loudness Perception

Loudness Perception
Broader　　　Auditory Perception
Narrower　　Loudness Discrimination

Loudness Threshold
Use　　　　　Auditory Thresholds

Love
Related　　　Affection
　　　　　　Emotions/

Lowenfeld Mosaic Test
(See)　　　　Intelligence Measures

Lower Class
Broader　　　Social Class
　　　　　　Social Structure
　　　　　　Socioeconomic Status

Lower Class Attitudes
Broader　　　Socioeconomic Class Attitudes

Lower Income Level
Broader　　　Income Level
　　　　　　Socioeconomic Status
Related　　　Poverty

Loyalty
Broader　　　Personality Traits

LSD (Drug)
Use　　　　　Lysergic Acid Diethylamide

Lumbar Spinal Cord
Broader　　　Central Nervous System
　　　　　　Nervous System
　　　　　　Spinal Cord

Lumbosacral Region
Broader　　　Back (Anatomy)

Lumbrosacral Plexus
Use　　　　　Spinal Nerves

Luminance
Use　　　　　Illumination

Luminance Threshold
Use　　　　　Brightness Perception
　　　　　　Visual Thresholds

Lunar Synodic Cycle

Lung
Broader　　　Respiratory System
Narrower　　Pulmonary Alveoli

Lung Disorders
Broader　　　Respiratory Tract Disorders
Narrower　　Pneumonia
　　　　　　Pulmonary Emphysema
　　　　　　Pulmonary Tuberculosis
Related　　　Dyspnea

Lupus
Broader　　　Skin Disorders
Related　　　Tuberculosis

Lying
Use　　　　　Deception

Lying (Pathological)
Use　　　　　Pathological Lying

Lymph
Broader　　　Body Fluids
Related　　　Lymph Vessels
　　　　　　Lymphatic System

Lymph Nodes
  Used For   Nodes (Lymph)
  Broader   Lymphatic System
  Related   Lymph Vessels

Lymph Vessels
  Used For   Vessels (Lymph)
  Broader   Cardiovascular System
              Lymphatic System
  Related   Blood Vessels
              Lymph
              Lymph Nodes

Lymphatic Disorders
  Use   Blood and Lymphatic Disorders

Lymphatic System
  Narrower   Lymph Nodes
              Lymph Vessels
              Thoracic Duct
  Related   Anatomical Systems/
              Blood and Lymphatic Disorders
              Lymph

Lymphocytes
  Broader   Blood Cells
              Cells (Biology)
              Leucocytes

Lysergic Acid Diethylamide
  Used For   LSD (Drug)
  Broader   Acids
              Amine Oxidase Inhibitors
              Hallucinogenic Drugs
              Psychedelic Drugs
              Psychotomimetic Drugs
              Serotonin Antagonists
  Related   Ergot Derivatives

MA Scale (Test)
  Identifier Taylor Manifest Anxiety Scale

Machiavellianism
  Broader   Personality Traits

Magazines
  Broader   Communications Media
              Mass Media
              Printed Communications Media

Magical Thinking
  Broader   Thinking
              Thought Disturbances
  Related   Fantasies (Thought Disturb-
              ances)
              Imagination

Magnesium
  Broader   Chemical Elements
              Metallic Elements
  Narrower   Magnesium Ions

Magnesium Ions
  Broader   Chemical Elements
              Electrolytes

Magnesium Ions — (Continued)
  Broader
              Magnesium
              Metallic Elements

Magnetic Test
  (See)   Nonprojective Personality Meas-
              ures
              Personality Measures

Maids
  Use   Domestic Service Personnel

Major Tranquilizers
  Use   Neuroleptic Drugs

Maladjustment (Emotional)
  Use   Emotional Adjustment

Maladjustment (Social)
  Use   Social Adjustment

Malaria
  Broader   Blood and Lymphatic Disorders
              Infectious Disorders
              Parasitic Disorders
  Related   Nervous System Disorders

Male Animals
  Related   Animals/

Male Castration
  Broader   Castration
              Endocrine Gland Surgery
              Physical Treatment Methods
              Sterilization (Sex)
              Surgery

Male Criminals
  Broader   Criminals

Male Delinquents
  Broader   Juvenile Delinquents

Male Genital Disorders
  Broader   Genital Disorders
              Urogenital Disorders
  Narrower   Klinefelters Syndrome
              Testicular Feminization Syn-
              drome
  Related   Endocrine Sexual Disorders
              Hermaphroditism
              Hypogonadism
              Infertility
              Sterility

Male Genitalia
  Used For   Genitalia (Male)
  Broader   Urogenital System
  Narrower   Penis
              Prostate
              Testes

Male Homosexuality
  Broader   Homosexuality
              Psychosexual Behavior

Male Homosexuality — (Continued)
Related   Bisexuality
           Pedophilia
           Transsexualism
           Transvestism

Male Orgasm
Used For   Ejaculation
Broader   Orgasm
           Psychosexual Behavior
Narrower   Nocturnal Emission
           Premature Ejaculation
Related   Impotence
           Masturbation
           Sexual Intercourse (Human)

Males (Human)
Use   Human Males

Malignant Neoplasms
Use   Neoplasms

Malingering
Broader   Behavior Disorders
           Deception
           Faking
Related   Mental Disorders/
           Psychosomatic Disorders

Malnutrition
Use   Nutritional Deficiencies

Mammals
Broader   Vertebrates
Narrower   Baboons
           Bats
           Beavers
           Cats
           Cattle
           Chimpanzees
           Chinchillas
           Deer
           Dogs
           Dolphins
           Elephants
           Foxes
           Gerbils
           Goats
           Gorillas
           Guinea Pigs
           Hamsters
           Horses
           Kangaroos
           Lemurs
           Marsupials
           Mice
           Minks
           Monkeys
           Norway Rats
           Opossums
           Pigs
           Porpoises

Mammals — (Continued)
Narrower
           Primates (Nonhuman)
           Rabbits
           Rats
           Rodents
           Seals (Animal)
           Sheep
           Squirrels
           Wolves

Mammary Glands
Broader   Glands

Mammary Neoplasms
Use   Breast Neoplasms

Mammilary Bodies (Hypothalamic)
Use   Hypothalamus

Man Machine Systems
Related   Cybernetics
           Error Analysis
           Human Factors Engineering
           Man Machine Systems Design
           Systems Analysis
           Systems/

Man Machine Systems Design
Used For   Design (Man Machine Systems)
Related   Man Machine Systems
           Systems/

Management Decision Making
Broader   Cognitive Processes
           Decision Making
Related   Management Methods
           Management Planning
           Management/

Management Methods
Related   Business Management
           Management Decision Making
           Management Planning
           Management/
           Work Scheduling

Management Personnel
Used For   Administrators
           Managers
           Supervisors
Broader   Business And Industrial Person-
           nel
           White Collar Workers
Narrower   Middle Level Managers
           Top Level Managers
Related   Commissioned Officers
           Industrial Foremen
           Management/
           Personnel/
           School Administrators

Management Planning
Used For   Planning (Management)

Management Planning — (Continued)
Related	Management Decision Making
	Management Methods
	Management/
	Marketing

Management Training
Broader	Personnel Training
Related	Business Education
	Management/

Management/
Related	Business Management
	Contingency Management
	Labor Management Relations
	Management Decision Making
	Management Methods
	Management Personnel
	Management Planning
	Management Training
	Personnel Management

Managers
Use	Management Personnel

Mandibula
Use	Jaw

Mania
Narrower	Hypermania
	Hypomania
	Kleptomania
	Megalomania
	Pica
	Pyromania
	Toxicomania
Related	Manic Depression
	Mental Disorders/

Manic Depression
Broader	Depression (Emotion)
Related	Mania

Manic Depressive Psychosis
Broader	Affective Psychosis
	Psychosis
Related	Cyclothymic Personality
	Depression (Emotion)

Mann Whitney U Test
Broader	Nonparametric Statistical Tests
	Statistical Analysis
	Statistical Tests

Mannerisms
Use	Habits

Manpower
Use	Personnel/

Mantis
Used For	Praying Mantis
Broader	Arthropoda
	Insects
	Invertebrates

Mantis — (Continued)
Related	Larvae

Manufacturing
Use	Business

Maple Syrup Urine Disease
Broader	Genetic Disorders
	Metabolism Disorders
	Neonatal Disorders
	Neonatal Genetic Disorders
Related	Mental Retardation

Maps (Brain)
Use	Stereotaxic Atlas

Marathon Group Therapy
Broader	Encounter Group Therapy
	Group Psychotherapy
	Psychotherapy
Related	Sensitivity Training

Marihuana
Used For	Marijuana
Broader	Cannabis
Related	Drugs/
	Hashish
	Marihuana Laws
	Marihuana Usage
	Tetrahydrocannabinol

Marihuana Laws
Broader	Drug Laws
	Government Policy Making
	Laws
Narrower	Marihuana Legalization
Related	Government
	Marihuana
	Marihuana Usage

Marihuana Legalization
Used For	Legalization (Marihuana)
Broader	Drug Laws
	Government Policy Making
	Laws
	Marihuana Laws
Related	Drug Usage Attitudes
	Government

Marihuana Usage
Broader	Drug Usage
Related	Drug Dependency
	Marihuana
	Marihuana Laws

Marijuana
Use	Marihuana

Marine Personnel
Broader	Government Personnel
	Military Personnel

Marital Adjustment
Use	Marital Relations

Marital Conflict
Broader	Family Relations
	Marital Relations

Marital Problems
Use	Marital Relations

Marital Relations
Used For	Marital Adjustment
	Marital Problems
Broader	Family Relations
Narrower	Marital Conflict

Marital Separation
Used For	Separation (Marital)
Narrower	Divorce
Related	Divorced Persons
	Family/
	Marital Status
	Parental Absence

Marital Status
Related	Divorced Persons
	Family Background
	Family/
	Marital Separation
	Single Persons
	Widowers
	Widows

Marketing
Related	Advertising
	Management Planning

Markov Chains
Used For	Chains (Markov)
Broader	Simulation
	Stochastic Modeling

Marlowe Crowne Soc Desirabil Scale
(See)	Nonprojective Personality Measures
	Personality Measures

Marriage
Narrower	Common Law Marriage
	Consanguineous Marriage
	Elopement (Marriage)
	Endogamous Marriage
	Exogamous Marriage
	Interfaith Marriage
	Interracial Marriage
	Polygamy
Related	Family/
	Marriage Rites

Marriage Attitudes
Related	Attitudes/
	Family Relations
	Religious Beliefs

Marriage Counseling
Used For	Marriage Therapy

Marriage Counseling — (Continued)
Related	Counseling/
	Psychotherapeutic Counseling
	Psychotherapy

Marriage Rites
Broader	Rites of Passage
	Sociocultural Factors
Related	Marriage

Marriage Therapy
Use	Marriage Counseling

Married Couples
Use	Spouses

Marsupials
Broader	Mammals
	Vertebrates
Narrower	Kangaroos
	Opossums

Marxism
Use	Communism

Masculinity
Broader	Personality Traits
Related	Femininity

Masking
Used For	Backward Masking
Narrower	Auditory Masking
	Visual Masking
Related	Perceptual Stimulation

Masochism
Broader	Sadomasochism
Narrower	Sexual Masochism
Related	Masochistic Personality
	Sadism

Masochistic Personality
Broader	Personality Disorders
	Sadomasochistic Personality
Related	Masochism
	Sexual Masochism

Mass Hysteria
Broader	Hysteria
Related	Collective Behavior

Mass Media
Used For	Media (Mass)
Broader	Communications Media
Narrower	Closed Circuit Television
	Educational Television
	Magazines
	Newspapers
	Radio
	Telephone Systems
	Television
	Television Advertising
Related	Advertising
	Books

Massed Practice
Broader　　Learning Schedules
　　　　　Practice

Mastectomy
Broader　　Amputation
　　　　　Physical Treatment Methods
　　　　　Surgery
Related　　Breast Neoplasms

Masticatory Muscles
Broader　　Muscles
　　　　　Musculoskeletal System

Masturbation
Used For　Autoeroticism
Broader　　Psychosexual Behavior
Related　　Female Orgasm
　　　　　Male Orgasm

Mate Swapping
Use　　　Extramarital Intercourse

Materialism
Broader　　Philosophies

Maternal Behavior (Animal)
Use　　　Animal Maternal Behavior

Maternal Behavior (Human)
Use　　　Mother Child Relations

Maternal Deprivation
Use　　　Animal Maternal Behavior
　　　　　Mother Absence
　　　　　Mother Child Relations

Mates (Humans)
Use　　　Spouses

Mathematical Ability
Used For　Numerical Ability
Related　　Ability/
　　　　　Mathematics (Concepts)

Mathematical Modeling
Broader　　Simulation
Related　　Heuristic Modeling
　　　　　Stochastic Modeling

Mathematical Psychology
Broader　　Psychology
　　　　　Sciences
　　　　　Social Sciences

Mathematicians
Related　　Personnel/
　　　　　Physicists
　　　　　Scientists/

Mathematics (Concepts)
Narrower　Algorithms
　　　　　Number Systems
　　　　　Numbers (Numerals)
Related　　Mathematical Ability
　　　　　Mathematics Achievement

Mathematics (Concepts) — (Continued)
Related
　　　　　Mathematics Education
　　　　　Statistical Analysis

Mathematics Achievement
Broader　　Academic Achievement
　　　　　Achievement
Related　　Mathematics (Concepts)

Mathematics Education
Used For　Algebra
　　　　　Arithmetic
　　　　　Calculus
　　　　　Geometry
Broader　　Curriculum
Related　　Mathematics (Concepts)

Mating Behavior (Animal)
Use　　　Animal Mating Behavior

Matriarchy
Broader　　Family Structure
Related　　Father Absence

Matriculation
Use　　　School Enrollment

Maturation
Use　　　Human Development/

Maturity (Emotional)
Use　　　Emotional Maturity

Maturity (Physical)
Use　　　Physical Maturity

Maudsley Personality Inventory
Used For　MPI (Test)
(See)　　　Nonprojective Personality Meas-
　　　　　ures
　　　　　Personality Measures

Maxilla
Use　　　Jaw

Maze Learning
Related　　Learning/

Maze Pathways
Used For　Maze Runways
　　　　　Pathways (Maze)
　　　　　Runways (Maze)
Broader　　Apparatus
　　　　　Mazes

Maze Runways
Use　　　Maze Pathways

Mazes
Used For　Labyrinth (Apparatus)
Broader　　Apparatus
Narrower　Maze Pathways
　　　　　T Mazes

Mazes (T)
Use　　　T Mazes

MBTI (Test)
Identifier	Myers Briggs Type Indicator

McNemar Test
Broader	Nonparametric Statistical Tests
	Statistical Analysis
	Statistical Tests
Related	Statistical Significance

Mealtimes
Use	Feeding Practices

Mean
Broader	Central Tendency Measures
	Statistical Analysis
	Statistical Measurement

Meaning
Narrower	Nonverbal Meaning
	Verbal Meaning
	Word Meaning
Related	Comprehension
	Meaningfulness

Meaningfulness
Related	Comprehension
	Meaning

Measles
Broader	Infectious Disorders
	Viral Disorders
Related	Rubella

Measurement/
Used For	Assessment
	Tests
Related	Achievement Measures
	Aptitude Measures
	Attitude Measurement
	Attitude Measures
	Body Sway Testing
	Cloze Testing
	Comprehension Tests
	Content Analysis (Test)
	Creativity Measurement
	Cultural Test Bias
	Difficulty Level (Test)
	Digit Span Testing
	Educational Measurement
	Employment Tests
	Essay Testing
	Experiment Volunteers
	Experimentation/
	Forced Choice (Testing Method)
	Group Testing
	Individual Testing

Measurement/ — (Continued)
Related	Intelligence Measures
	Inventories
	Item Analysis (Test)
	Item Content (Test)
	Multiple Choice (Testing Method)
	Nonprojective Personality Measures
	Occupational Interest Measures
	Perceptual Measures
	Performance Tests
	Personality Measures
	Piagetian Tasks
	Population (Statistics)
	Posttesting
	Prediction Errors
	Preference Measures
	Pretesting
	Profiles (Measurement)
	Projective Testing Technique
	Psychometrics
	Q Sort Testing Technique
	Questionnaires
	Rating
	Rating Scales
	Reading Measures
	Response Bias
	Retention Measures
	Scaling (Testing)
	Scoring (Testing)
	Selection Tests
	Semantic Differential
	Sensorimotor Measures
	Sociograms
	Sociometric Tests
	Speech And Hearing Measures
	Statistical Analysis
	Statistical Correlation
	Statistical Measurement
	Statistical Reliability
	Statistical Significance
	Statistical Tests
	Statistical Validity
	Statistical Variables
	Subtests
	Surveys
	Test Administration
	Test Construction
	Test Items
	Test Norms
	Test Reliability
	Test Scores
	Test Standardization
	Test Validity
	Testing
	Testing Methods
	Verbal Tests

Measures (Retention)
  Use   Retention Measures

Mecamylamine
  Broader   Amines
             Antihypertensive Drugs
             Ganglion Blocking Drugs

Mechanical Aptitude
  Related   Ability/

Mechanoreceptors
  Broader   Nerve Endings
             Nervous System
             Neural Receptors

Media (Communications)
  Use   Communications Media

Media (Educational)
  Use   Instructional Media

Media (Mass)
  Use   Mass Media

Median
  Broader   Central Tendency Measures
             Statistical Analysis
             Statistical Measurement

Median Nerve
  Use   Spinal Nerves

Mediated Responses
  Broader   Responses

Mediation (Cognitive)
  Use   Cognitive Mediation

Medical Diagnosis
  Used For   Clinical Judgment (Med Diag-
             nosis)
  Broader   Diagnosis
  Narrower   Angiography
             Biopsy
             Cardiography
             Echoencephalography
             Electro Oculography
             Electrocardiography
             Electroencephalography
             Electromyography
             Electronystagmography
             Electroplethysmography
             Electroretinography
             Encephalography
             Galvanic Skin Response
             Ophthalmologic Examination
             Plethysmography
             Pneumoencephalography
             Rheoencephalography
             Roentgenography
             Urinalysis
  Related   Autopsy
             Computer Assisted Diagnosis
             Differential Diagnosis

Medical Diagnosis — (Continued)
  Related
             Electrophysiology
             Patient History
             Prognosis

Medical Education
  Broader   Graduate Education
             Higher Education
  Narrower   Psychiatric Training
  Related   Medical Internship
             Medical Residency
             Nursing Education

Medical History
  Use   Patient History

Medical Internship
  Used For   Internship (Medical)
  Broader   Higher Education
             Postgraduate Training
  Related   Medical Education

Medical Patients
  Broader   Patients

Medical Personnel
  Used For   Hospital Staff
  Narrower   Attendants (Institutions)
             Dentists
             Family Physicians
             General Practitioners
             Gynecologists
             Internists
             Medics
             Military Medical Personnel
             Neurologists
             Nurses
             Optometrists
             Paramedical Personnel
             Pathologists
             Pediatricians
             Physical Therapists
             Physicians
             Psychiatric Aides
             Psychiatric Hospital Staff
             Psychiatric Nurses
             Psychiatrists
             Public Health Service Nurses
             School Nurses
             Surgeons
  Related   Clinicians
             Medical Sciences
             Mental Health Personnel
             Personnel/
             Scientists/

Medical Personnel Supply
  Broader   Personnel Supply

Medical Psychology
  Broader   Applied Psychology
             Psychology

Medical Psychology — (Continued)

Broader	Sciences
	Social Sciences
Related	Medical Sciences

Medical Residency

Used For	Residency (Medical)
Broader	Higher Education
	Postgraduate Training
Related	Medical Education

Medical Sciences

Used For	Medicine (Science of)
Broader	Sciences
Narrower	Anesthesiology
	Cardiology
	Child Psychiatry
	Community Psychiatry
	Dentistry
	Endocrinology
	Epidemiology
	Forensic Psychiatry
	Geriatrics
	Immunology
	Neurology
	Neuropathology
	Neuropsychiatry
	Obstetrics Gynecology
	Ophthalmology
	Orthopsychiatry
	Pathology
	Pediatrics
	Psychiatry
	Psychopathology
	Radiology
	Social Psychiatry
	Surgery
	Transcultural Psychiatry
	Veterinary Medicine
Related	Folk Medicine
	Medical Personnel
	Medical Psychology
	Neurosciences
	Paramedical Sciences

Medical Students

Broader	College Students
	Students

Medical Therapeutic Devices

Used For	Therapeutic Devices (Medical)
Narrower	Artificial Pacemakers
	Contact Lenses
	Hearing Aids
	Optical Aids
	Prostheses

Medical Treatment (General)

Broader	Physical Treatment Methods
Narrower	Diuresis

Medication

Use	Drug Therapy

Medicine (Science of)

Use	Medical Sciences

Medics

Broader	Medical Personnel
	Paramedical Personnel
	Paraprofessional Personnel
Related	Military Medical Personnel

Meditation

Broader	Religious Practices
Related	Prayer

Medulla Oblongata

Broader	Brain
	Brain Stem
	Central Nervous System
	Nervous System

Megalomania

Broader	Delusions
	Mania
	Thought Disturbances

Melancholia

Use	Depression (Emotion)

Melancholy

Use	Sadness

Melanin

Broader	Pigments
Related	Melatonin
	Tyrosine

Melatonin

Broader	Hormones
Related	Melanin
	Pineal Body

Melleril

Use	Thioridazine

Membranes

Broader	Tissues (Body)
Narrower	Meninges
	Nasal Mucosa
	Nictitating Membrane
	Olfactory Mucosa

Memory

Narrower	Eidetic Imagery
	Long Term Memory
	Memory Decay
	Memory Trace
	Short Term Memory
	Spontaneous Recovery (Learning)
Related	Cognitive Processes
	Cues
	Forgetting
	Human Information Storage
	Learning/

Memory — (Continued)
Related
    Memory Disorders
    Memory Drums
    Relearning
    Retention
    Rote Learning

Memory Decay
  Broader   Memory

Memory Disorders
  Broader   Thought Disturbances
  Narrower Amnesia
            Fugue Reaction
  Related   Memory

Memory Drums
  Broader   Apparatus
  Related   Memory

Memory For Designs Test
  (See)   Nonprojective Personality Measures
            Personality Measures

Memory Trace
  Used For Trace (Memory)
  Broader   Memory

Menarche
  Broader   Menstrual Cycle
            Menstruation
  Related   Puberty

Menieres Disease
  Broader   Ear Disorders
            Labyrinth Disorders
            Sense Organ Disorders
            Syndromes
  Related   Vertigo

Meninges
  Broader   Central Nervous System
            Membranes
            Nervous System
            Tissues (Body)

Meningitis
  Broader   Central Nervous System Disorders
            Nervous System Disorders
  Narrower Arachnoiditis
            Bacterial Meningitis
            Infectious Meningitis
            Viral Meningitis

Menopause
  Broader   Developmental Stages
  Related   Menstrual Cycle

Menstrual Cycle
  Narrower Menarche
            Menstruation
            Ovulation

Menstrual Cycle — (Continued)
  Related   Estrus
            Menopause

Menstrual Disorders
  Broader   Genital Disorders
            Gynecological Disorders
            Urogenital Disorders
  Narrower Amenorrhea
            Dysmenorrhea
            Premenstrual Tension
            Pseudocyesis
            Stein Leventhal Syndrome

Menstruation
  Broader   Menstrual Cycle
  Narrower Menarche
  Related   Estrus

Mental Age

Mental Confusion
  Used For Confusion (Mental)
  Broader   Emotional States
  Narrower Doubt
  Related   Frustration
            Thought Disturbances

Mental Deficiency
  Use   Mental Retardation

Mental Disorders/
  Used For Emotional Disorders
            Insanity
            Mental Illness
            Nervous Breakdown
            Psychiatric Disorders
  Related   Accident Proneness
            Affective Disturbances
            Anorexia Nervosa
            Aphasia
            Autism
            Behavior Disorders
            Body Image Disturbances
            Borderline Mental Retardation
            Compulsions
            Consciousness Disturbances
            Cretinism
            Crying Cat Syndrome
            Defense Mechanisms
            Disorders/
            Dissociative Patterns
            Downs Syndrome
            Drug Dependency
            Elective Mutism
            Ethnospecific Disorders
            Hysteria
            Infantilism
            Korsakoffs Psychosis
            Learning Disorders
            Malingering

Mental Disorders/ — (Continued)
Related
      Mania
      Mental Retardation
      Microcephaly
      Narcissism
      Neurosis
      Onset (Disorders)
      Organic Brain Syndromes
      Penis Envy
      Perceptual Disturbances
      Personality Disorders
      Phobias
      Picks Disease
      Porphyria
      Predisposition
      Presenile Dementia
      Prognosis
      Psychopathology
      Psychopathy
      Psychosis
      Psychosocial Mental Retardation
      Psychosomatic Disorders
      Reality Testing
      Recovery (Disorders)
      Relapse (Disorders)
      Remission (Disorders)
      Sadomasochism
      Schizophrenogenic Family
      Senile Dementia
      Sexual Deviations
      Suicide
      Susceptibility (Disorders)
      Symptoms
      Thought Disturbances

Mental Health
Broader   Health
Narrower Community Mental Health
Related   Community Psychiatry
      Community Psychology
      Mental Health Personnel
      Mental Health Programs
      Primary Mental Health Prevention

Mental Health Centers (Community)
Use   Community Mental Health Centers

Mental Health Consultation
Broader   Professional Consultation

Mental Health Inservice Training
Used For   Inservice Training (Mental Health)
      Training (Mental Health Inservice)
Broader   Clinical Methods Training
      Community Mental Health Training

Mental Health Inservice Training — (Continued)
Related   Mental Health Programs

Mental Health Personnel
Narrower Clinical Psychologists
      Hypnotherapists
      Psychiatric Aides
      Psychiatric Hospital Staff
      Psychiatric Nurses
      Psychiatric Social Workers
      Psychiatrists
      Psychoanalysts
      Psychotherapists
      School Psychologists
Related   Counselors
      Educational Personnel
      Medical Personnel
      Mental Health
      Mental Health Personnel Supply
      Occupational Therapists
      Paraprofessional Personnel
      Personnel/
      Psychologists
      Social Workers

Mental Health Personnel Supply
Broader   Personnel Supply
Related   Mental Health Personnel

Mental Health Program Evaluation
Used For   Evaluation (Mental Health Program)
      Program Evaluation (Mental Health)
Broader   Evaluation
Related   Mental Health Programs
      Psychotherapeutic Outcomes
      Sociotherapy
      Treatment Effectiveness Evaluation
      Treatment/

Mental Health Programs
Used For   Programs (Mental Health)
Narrower Crisis Intervention Services
      Home Visiting Programs
      Hot Line Services
      Suicide Prevention Centers
Related   Child Guidance Clinics
      Community Mental Health
      Community Mental Health Centers
      Community Mental Health Training
      Community Psychiatry
      Community Psychology
      Community Services
      Mental Health
      Mental Health Inservice Training

Mental Health Programs — (Continued)
Related
  Mental Health Program Evaluation
  Primary Mental Health Prevention
  Psychiatric Clinics
  Public Health Services

Mental Health Training (Community)
Use Community Mental Health Training

Mental Hospitals
Use Psychiatric Hospitals

Mental Illness
Use Mental Disorders/

Mental Illness (Attitudes Toward)
Broader Handicapped (Attitudes Toward)

Mental Retardation
Used For Amentia
  Feeblemindedness
  Idiocy
  Imbecility
  Mental Deficiency
  Oligophrenia
  Retardation (Mental)
  Subnormality (Mental)
Narrower Amaurotic Familial Idiocy
  Anencephaly
  Borderline Mental Retardation
  Cretinism
  Crying Cat Syndrome
  Downs Syndrome
  Microcephaly
  Psychosocial Mental Retardation
Related Brain Damage
  Hydrocephaly
  Klinefelters Syndrome
  Maple Syrup Urine Disease
  Mental Disorders/
  Mental Retardation (Attit Toward)
  Mentally Retarded
  Phenylketonuria
  Trisomy 18

Mental Retardation (Attit Toward)
Broader Handicapped (Attitudes Toward)
Related Mental Retardation

Mentally Retarded
Used For Retarded (Mentally)
  Special Education (Mentally Retard)
Broader Handicapped
Narrower Educable Mentally Retarded
  Home Reared Mentally Retarded
  Idiot Savants

Mentally Retarded — (Continued)
Narrower
  Institutionalized Mentally Retarded
  Profoundly Mentally Retarded
  Severely Mentally Retarded
  Trainable Mentally Retarded
Related Mental Retardation
  Slow Learners

Meperidine
Broader Amines
  Analgesic Drugs
  Antispasmodic Drugs
  Narcotic Drugs
  Sedatives
Related Drug Dependency

Mephenesin
Broader Alcohols
  Muscle Relaxing Drugs

Meprobamate
Broader Hypnotic Drugs
  Muscle Relaxing Drugs
  Tranquilizing Drugs

Mercury (Metal)
Broader Chemical Elements
  Metallic Elements

Mercury Poisoning
Broader Metal Poisoning
  Toxic Disorders

Mercy Killing
Use Euthanasia

Mescaline
Broader Alkaloids
  Hallucinogenic Drugs
  Psychotomimetic Drugs
Related Peyote

Mesencephalon
Used For Red Nucleus
  Substantia Nigra
Broader Brain
  Central Nervous System
  Nervous System
Narrower Corpora Quadrigemina
  Inferior Colliculus
  Optic Lobe
  Superior Colliculus

Mesoridazine
Broader Neuroleptic Drugs
  Phenothiazine Derivatives
  Tranquilizing Drugs

Messages
Used For Information (Messages)
Related Communication/
  Information/

Metabolic Rates
Related	Metabolism
	Physiology/

Metabolism
Narrower	Anabolism
	Basal Metabolism
	Carbohydrate Metabolism
	Catabolism
	Lipid Metabolism
	Metabolites
	Protein Metabolism
Related	Metabolic Rates
	Metabolism Disorders
	Physiology/

Metabolism (Carbohydrate)
Use	Carbohydrate Metabolism

Metabolism Disorders
Narrower	Amaurotic Familial Idiocy
	Calcium Metabolism Disorders
	Carbohydrate Metabolism Disorders
	Cushings Syndrome
	Diabetes
	Diabetes Insipidus
	Diabetes Mellitus
	Lipid Metabolism Disorders
	Maple Syrup Urine Disease
	Phenylketonuria
	Porphyria
Related	Disorders/
	Hyperglycemia
	Hypoglycemia
	Hypothyroidism
	Metabolism
	Nutritional Deficiencies

Metabolites
Broader	Metabolism

Metal Poisoning
Broader	Toxic Disorders
Narrower	Lead Poisoning
	Mercury Poisoning
Related	Metallic Elements
	Toxic Psychoses

Metallic Elements
Broader	Chemical Elements
Narrower	Barium
	Calcium
	Calcium Ions
	Cobalt
	Copper
	Iron
	Lead (Metal)
	Lithium
	Magnesium
	Magnesium Ions
	Mercury (Metal)

Metallic Elements — (Continued)
Narrower	Potassium
	Potassium Ions
	Sodium
	Sodium Ions
	Strontium
Related	Metal Poisoning

Metaphysics
Broader	Philosophies

Meters (Volt)
Use	Volt Meters

Methadone
Used For	Methadone Maintenance
Broader	Analgesic Drugs
	Narcotic Drugs
Related	Drug Dependency

Methadone Maintenance
Use	Drug Rehabilitation
	Methadone

Methamphetamine
Used For	Methedrine
Broader	Amines
	CNS Affecting Drugs
	CNS Stimulating Drugs
	Sympathomimetic Amines
	Sympathomimetic Drugs
	Vasoconstrictor Drugs
Related	Drug Dependency

Methanol
Used For	Methyl Alcohol
Broader	Alcohols
Related	Denatured Alcohol

Methaqualone
Broader	Hypnotic Drugs
	Sedatives

Methedrine
Use	Methamphetamine

Methionine
Broader	Acids
	Amino Acids

Methodology/
Used For	Research Methods
Related	Empirical Methods
	Experimental Methods
	Experimentation/
	Theory Formulation

Methohexital
Broader	Anesthetic Drugs
	Barbiturates
	General Anesthetics

Methoxamine
Broader	Adrenergic Drugs
	Alcohols

Methoxamine — (Continued)
Broader
    Amines
    Sympathomimetic Amines
    Sympathomimetic Drugs
    Vasoconstrictor Drugs
 Related Local Anesthetics

Methyl Alcohol
 Use Methanol

Methylatropine
 Use Atropine

Methyldopa
 Broader Antihypertensive Drugs
 Related Catecholamines
    Dopa
    Dopamine

Methylmorphine
 Use Codeine

Methylphenidate
 Used For Ritalin
 Broader Amines
    Antidepressant Drugs
    CNS Affecting Drugs
    CNS Stimulating Drugs
 Related Analeptic Drugs

Metrazole
 Use Pentylenetetrazol

Metronomes
 Broader Apparatus

Metropolitan Reading Readiness Test
 (See) Reading Measures

Mexican Americans
 Broader Ethnic Groups

Mexico

Mice
 Broader Mammals
    Rodents
    Vertebrates

Microcephaly
 Broader Brain Disorders
    Central Nervous System Disorders
    Mental Retardation
    Nervous System Disorders
 Related Congenital Disorders
    Mental Disorders/
    Neonatal Disorders

Microscopes
 Broader Apparatus

Micturition
 Use Urination

Middle Aged
 Broader Adults
    Developmental Age Groups

Middle Class
 Used For Bourgeois
 Broader Social Class
    Social Structure
    Socioeconomic Status

Middle Class Attitudes
 Broader Socioeconomic Class Attitudes

Middle Ear
 Used For Ear Ossicles
    Eustachian Tube
    Tympanic Membrane
 Broader Ear (Anatomy)
    Sense Organs

Middle Income Level
 Broader Income Level
    Socioeconomic Status

Middle Level Managers
 Broader Business And Industrial Personnel
    Management Personnel
    White Collar Workers
 Related Top Level Managers

Migraine Headache
 Broader Headache
    Pain
    Symptoms
 Related Endocrine Disorders
    Nausea
    Psychosomatic Disorders

Migrant Farm Workers
 Broader Agricultural Workers

Migration (Human)
 Use Human Migration

Migratory Behavior (Animal)
 Used For Animal Navigation
 Broader Animal Ethology
 Related Animal Innate Behavior
    Animal Instinctive Behavior

Mildly Mentally Retarded
 Use Educable Mentally Retarded

Milieu Therapy
 Use Therapeutic Community

Militancy
 Broader Social Behavior

Military Enlistment
 Used For Enlistment (Military)
    Reenlistment (Military)
 Related Military Recruitment

Military Medical Personnel
Broader	Government Personnel
	Medical Personnel
	Military Personnel
Related	Medics

Military Officers
Use	Commissioned Officers

Military Personnel
Used For	Servicemen
Broader	Government Personnel
Narrower	Air Force Personnel
	Army Personnel
	Commissioned Officers
	Draftees
	Enlisted Military Personnel
	Marine Personnel
	Military Medical Personnel
	National Guardsmen
	Navy Personnel
	Noncommissioned Officers
	ROTC Students
	Volunteer Military Personnel
Related	Astronauts
	Chaplains
	Military Veterans

Military Psychology
Broader	Applied Psychology
	Psychology
	Sciences
	Social Sciences

Military Recruitment
Used For	Recruitment (Military)
Broader	Personnel Management
	Personnel Recruitment
Related	Military Enlistment

Military Schools
Broader	Schools
Related	Colleges
	High Schools

Military Training
Broader	Personnel Training

Military Veterans
Used For	Veterans (Military)
Related	Military Personnel
	Personnel/

Miller Analogies Test
(See)	Intelligence Measures

Mineral Deficiency Disorders
Broader	Nutritional Deficiencies

Minimal Brain Disorders
Used For	Minimal Brain Dysfunction
Broader	Brain Disorders
	Central Nervous System Disorders
	Nervous System Disorders

Minimal Brain Disorders — (Continued)
Related	Aphasia
	Hyperkinesis
	Minimally Brain Damaged

Minimal Brain Dysfunction
Use	Minimal Brain Disorders

Minimally Brain Damaged
Broader	Brain Damaged
	Handicapped
Related	Aphasia
	Cerebral Dominance
	Lateral Dominance
	Learning Disabilities
	Minimal Brain Disorders

Ministers (Religion)
Used For	Parsons
	Pastors
Broader	Clergy
	Religious Personnel
Related	Chaplains
	Missionaries

Minks
Broader	Mammals
	Rodents
	Vertebrates

Minn Multiphasic Personality Inven
Used For	MMPI (Test)
(See)	Nonprojective Personality Measures
	Personality Measures

Minnesota Teacher Attitude Inventory
(See)	Attitude Measures

Minor Tranquilizers
Broader	Tranquilizing Drugs
Narrower	Chlordiazepoxide
	Chlorprothixene
Related	Neurosis

Minority Groups
Broader	Social Groups

Misanthropy
Used For	Misogyny
Broader	Personality Traits

Misbehavior
Use	Behavior Problems

Miscarriage
Use	Spontaneous Abortion

Miscegenous Marriage
Use	Interracial Marriage

Misconduct
Use	Behavior Problems

Misdemeanors
Use	Crime

Misogyny
Use　　　　Misanthropy

Missionaries
Broader　　Religious Personnel
Related　　Clergy
　　　　　Educational Personnel
　　　　　Evangelists
　　　　　Lay Religious Personnel
　　　　　Ministers (Religion)
　　　　　Nuns
　　　　　Priests

Mistakes
Use　　　　Errors

MMPI (Test)
Identifier　Minn Multiphasic Personality
　　　　　Inven

Mnemonic Learning
Related　　Cues
　　　　　Learning/

Mobility (Occupational)
Use　　　　Occupational Mobility

Mobility (Social)
Use　　　　Social Mobility

Mode
Broader　　Central Tendency Measures
　　　　　Statistical Analysis
　　　　　Statistical Measurement

Modeling
Use　　　　Simulation

Modeling Behavior
Use　　　　Imitation (Learning)

Models

Moderately Mentally Retarded
Use　　　　Trainable Mentally Retarded

Modern Language Aptitude Test
(See)　　　Aptitude Measures

Mohave Indians
Use　　　　American Indians

Mollusca
Used For　Gastropods
Broader　　Invertebrates
Narrower　Octopus
　　　　　Snails

Monetary Incentives
Broader　　Incentives
　　　　　Motivation
Related　　Monetary Rewards
　　　　　Needs

Monetary Rewards
Broader　　Reinforcement
　　　　　Rewards

Monetary Rewards — (Continued)
Related　　Monetary Incentives

Money
Related　　Costs And Cost Analysis
　　　　　Economy

Mongolism
Use　　　　Downs Syndrome

Monitoring
Broader　　Attention
　　　　　Awareness
　　　　　Consciousness States
Narrower　Vigilance
Related　　Aviation
　　　　　Flight Instrumentation
　　　　　Perception/
　　　　　Selective Attention
　　　　　Tracking

Monkeys
Broader　　Mammals
　　　　　Primates (Nonhuman)
　　　　　Vertebrates

Monks
Broader　　Clergy
　　　　　Religious Personnel
Related　　Priests

Monoamine Oxidase Inhibitors
Narrower　Iproniazid
　　　　　Isocarboxazid
　　　　　Nialamide
　　　　　Pargyline
　　　　　Phenelzine
　　　　　Tranylcypromine
Related　　Amine Oxidase Inhibitors
　　　　　Antidepressant Drugs
　　　　　Drugs/
　　　　　Monoamine Oxidases

Monoamine Oxidases
Broader　　Amine Oxidases
　　　　　Enzymes
　　　　　Oxidases
Related　　Monoamine Oxidase Inhibitors

Monocular Vision
Broader　　Vision
　　　　　Visual Perception

Monolingualism
Broader　　Language
　　　　　Verbal Communication

Monozygotic Twins
Used For　Identical Twins
Broader　　Family Members
　　　　　Multiple Births
　　　　　Siblings
　　　　　Twins

Montessori Method
Broader	Teaching
	Teaching Methods
Related	Discovery Teaching Method
	Open Classroom Method

Moodiness
Broader	Personality Traits

Moods
Use	Emotional States

Mooney Problem Check List
(See)	Nonprojective Personality Measures
	Personality Measures

Moral Development
Broader	Psychogenesis
Related	Morality
	Morals
	Personality Development
	Psychosocial Development

Morality
Related	Ethics
	Moral Development
	Personal Values
	Religious Beliefs
	Social Values
	Values

Morals
Related	Moral Development

Mores
Use	Values

Morons
Use	Educable Mentally Retarded

Morphemes
Broader	Language
	Linguistics
	Phonetics
	Verbal Communication

Morphine
Broader	Alkaloids
	Analgesic Drugs
	Narcotic Drugs
	Opiates
Related	Drug Dependency

Morphology
Related	Anatomy/
	Histology

Morphology (Language)
Broader	Grammar
	Language
	Linguistics
	Verbal Communication
Related	Words (Phonetic Units)

Mortality
Use	Death And Dying

Mortality Rate
Used For	Death Rate
Related	Death And Dying

Moslems
Use	Islam

Mother Absence
Used For	Maternal Deprivation
Broader	Family Structure
	Parental Absence
Related	Patriarchy

Mother Child Relations
Used For	Maternal Behavior (Human)
	Maternal Deprivation
Broader	Family Relations
	Parent Child Relations
Related	Anaclitic Depression
	Childrearing Practices
	Parental Attitudes
	Parental Permissiveness
	Parental Role
	Schizophrenogenic Mothers
	Symbiotic Infantile Psychosis

Mothers
Broader	Family Members
	Parents
Narrower	Schizophrenogenic Mothers
	Unwed Mothers

Moths
Broader	Arthropoda
	Insects
	Invertebrates
Related	Larvae

Motion Perception
Used For	Movement Perception
Broader	Spatial Perception
Narrower	Apparent Movement
	Autokinetic Illusion

Motion Pictures
Broader	Audiovisual Communications Media
	Communications Media
Narrower	Motion Pictures (Educational)
	Motion Pictures (Entertainment)

Motion Pictures (Educational)
Broader	Audiovisual Communications Media
	Communications Media
	Educational Audiovisual Aids
	Instructional Media
	Motion Pictures
	Teaching

Motion Pictures (Entertainment)
Used For	Movies

Motion Pictures (Entertainment) — (Continued)

Broader	Arts
	Audiovisual Communications Media
	Communications Media
	Motion Pictures
Related	Drama
	Photographic Art

Motion Sickness

Used For	Sickness (Motion)
Broader	Ear Disorders
	Labyrinth Disorders
	Sense Organ Disorders

Motivation

Used For	Desires
	Drive
	Urges
	Wishes
Narrower	Academic Achievement Motivation
	Achievement Motivation
	Affiliation Motivation
	Animal Motivation
	Educational Incentives
	Employee Motivation
	Extrinsic Motivation
	Hunger
	Incentives
	Intrinsic Motivation
	Monetary Incentives
	Sex Drive
	Temptation
	Thirst
Related	Deprivation
	Exploratory Behavior
	Goals
	Motivation Training
	Needs
	Reinforcement
	Satiation

Motivation Training

Used For	Training (Motivation)
Related	Motivation

Motor Coordination

Used For	Coordination (Motor)
Broader	Motor Processes
Related	Motor Performance
	Motor Skills
	Perceptual Motor Coordination
	Physical Agility

Motor Cortex

Used For	Cortex (Motor)
Broader	Brain
	Central Nervous System
	Cerebral Cortex
	Frontal Lobe

Motor Cortex — (Continued)

Broader	Nervous System
	Telencephalon

Motor Development

Used For	Perceptual Motor Development
	Prehension
Broader	Physical Development
Narrower	Psychomotor Development
	Speech Development
Related	Childhood Development
	Developmental Age Groups
	Developmental Differences
	Motor Processes

Motor Disorders

Use	Nervous System Disorders

Motor End Plates

Broader	Nerve Endings
	Nervous System

Motor Evoked Potentials

Use	Somatosensory Evoked Potentials

Motor Neurons

Broader	Cells (Biology)
	Nervous System
	Neurons

Motor Performance

Broader	Motor Processes
Narrower	Finger Tapping
	Jumping
	Running
	Walking
Related	Motor Coordination

Motor Processes

Used For	Processes (Motor)
Narrower	Exercise
	Finger Tapping
	Jumping
	Motor Coordination
	Motor Performance
	Motor Skills
	Physical Agility
	Physical Dexterity
	Running
	Walking
Related	Motor Development
	Perceptual Motor Processes
	Posture

Motor Skill Learning

Use	Perceptual Motor Learning

Motor Skills

Broader	Motor Processes
Related	Ability/
	Motor Coordination
	Tracking

Motor Traffic Accidents
Used For   Automobile Accidents
            Traffic Accidents (Motor)
Broader   Accidents
            Transportation Accidents
Narrower   Highway Hypnosis Accidents
Related   Drivers
            Driving Behavior
            Highway Safety
            Pedestrian Accidents

Motor Vehicles
Use   Automobiles

Mourning
Use   Grief

Mouth (Anatomy)
Broader   Digestive System
Related   Lips (Face)
            Salivary Glands
            Teeth (Anatomy)
            Tongue

Movement Perception
Use   Motion Perception

Movements (Activist)
Use   Activist Movements

Movements (Eye)
Use   Eye Movements

Movements (Social)
Use   Social Movements

Movies
Use   Motion Pictures (Entertainment)

MPI (Test)
Identifier   Maudsley Personality Inventory

Mucus
Broader   Body Fluids

Multilingualism
Broader   Language
            Verbal Communication
Narrower   Bilingualism

Multiple Births
Broader   Family Members
            Siblings
Narrower   Heterozygotic Twins
            Monozygotic Twins
            Quadruplets
            Triplets
            Twins

Multiple Choice (Testing Method)
Broader   Testing Methods
Related   Measurement/

Multiple Personality
Used For   Split Personality
Broader   Dissociative Patterns

Multiple Sclerosis
Broader   Nervous System Disorders
            Sclerosis (Nervous System)
Related   Myelitis

Multiple Therapists
Use   Conjoint Therapy

Multiply Handicapped
Broader   Handicapped

Murder
Use   Homicide

Muscle Contraction Headache
Broader   Headache
            Muscular Disorders
            Musculoskeletal Disorders
            Pain
            Symptoms

Muscle Contractions
Used For   Rigidity (Muscles)
Related   Muscle Relaxation
            Muscles

Muscle Cramps
Use   Muscular Disorders

Muscle Relaxation
Related   Muscle Contractions
            Muscles
            Relaxation

Muscle Relaxation Therapy
Use   Systematic Densensitization
            Therapy

Muscle Relaxing Drugs
Used For   Neuromuscular Blocking Drugs
            Skeletal Muscle Relaxant Drugs
            Smooth Muscle Relaxant Drugs
Narrower   Curare
            Diazepam
            Mephenesin
            Meprobamate
            Papaverine
            Succinylcholine
            Theophylline
            Tubocurarine
Related   Anesthetic Drugs
            Anticonvulsive Drugs
            Antihypertensive Drugs
            Antispasmodic Drugs
            CNS Depressant Drugs
            Drugs/
            Heart Rate Affecting Drugs
            Tranquilizing Drugs
            Vasodilation

Muscle Spasms
Related   Muscles

Muscles
Broader   Musculoskeletal System

Muscles — (Continued)
Narrower	Abdominal Wall
	Diaphragm (Anatomy)
	Facial Muscles
	Intercostal Muscles
	Masticatory Muscles
	Oculomotor Muscles
	Pectoralis Muscles
Related	Muscle Contractions
	Muscle Relaxation
	Muscle Spasms
	Tissues (Body)

Muscular Atrophy
Used For	Atrophy (Muscular)
Broader	Muscular Disorders
	Musculoskeletal Disorders

Muscular Disorders
Used For	Cramps (Muscle)
	Dystonia
	Muscle Cramps
Broader	Musculoskeletal Disorders
Narrower	Cataplexy
	Muscle Contraction Headache
	Muscular Atrophy
	Muscular Dystrophy
	Myasthenia Gravis
	Myoclonia
	Myotonia
	Torticollis
Related	Neuromuscular Disorders

Muscular Dystrophy
Used For	Dystrophy (Muscular)
Broader	Muscular Disorders
	Musculoskeletal Disorders
	Nervous System Disorders
	Neuromuscular Disorders
Related	Dysarthria
	Peripheral Nerve Disorders

Musculocutaneous Nerve
Use	Spinal Nerves

Musculoskeletal Disorders
Used For	Skeletomuscular Disorders
Narrower	Arthritis
	Bone Disorders
	Cataplexy
	Joint Disorders
	Muscle Contraction Headache
	Muscular Atrophy
	Muscular Disorders
	Muscular Dystrophy
	Myasthenia Gravis
	Myoclonia
	Myotonia
	Osteochondritis
	Rheumatoid Arthritis
	Torticollis

Musculoskeletal Disorders — (Continued)
Related	Disorders/
	Musculoskeletal System
	Neuromuscular Disorders
	Paralysis
	Poliomyelitis
	Tuberculosis

Musculoskeletal System
Narrower	Abdominal Wall
	Ankle
	Arm (Anatomy)
	Bones
	Diaphragm (Anatomy)
	Elbow (Anatomy)
	Facial Muscles
	Fascia
	Feet (Anatomy)
	Fingers (Anatomy)
	Hand (Anatomy)
	Hips
	Intercostal Muscles
	Jaw
	Joints (Anatomy)
	Knee
	Leg (Anatomy)
	Ligaments
	Masticatory Muscles
	Muscles
	Oculomotor Muscles
	Pectoralis Muscles
	Ribs
	Shoulder (Anatomy)
	Skull
	Spinal Column
	Synovial Bursa
	Tendons
	Thorax
	Thumb
	Wrist
Related	Anatomical Systems/
	Musculoskeletal Disorders
	Nose

Music
Used For	Performing Arts
Broader	Arts
Narrower	Musical Instruments

Music Education
Broader	Curriculum

Music Therapy
Used For	Therapy (Music)
Broader	Recreation Therapy

Musical Ability
Broader	Artistic Ability

Musical Instruments
Used For	Piano

154

Musical Instruments — (Continued)
Broader	Arts
	Music

Muslims
Use	Islam

Mutations
Related	Chromosomes
	Genetic Disorders
	Genetics/

Mutilation (Self)
Use	Self Mutilation

Mutism
Broader	Speech Disorders
Narrower	Elective Mutism
Related	Speech Handicapped

Mutual Storytelling Technique
Used For	Storytelling Technique
Broader	Psychotherapeutic Techniques

Myasthenia
Broader	Asthenia
	Symptoms

Myasthenia Gravis
Broader	Muscular Disorders
	Musculoskeletal Disorders
	Nervous System Disorders
	Neuromuscular Disorders
	Peripheral Nerve Disorders

Mydriatic Drugs
Used For	Dilation (Pupil) Drugs
	Pupil Dilating Drugs
Narrower	Atropine
	Cocaine
	Ephedrine
	Homatropine
	Scopolamine
Related	Drugs/
	Ophthalmologic Examination

Myelin Sheath
Used For	Sheath (Myelin)
Broader	Nerve Tissues
	Nervous System
	Tissues (Body)

Myelitis
Broader	Central Nervous System Disorders
	Nervous System Disorders
Narrower	Encephalomyelitis
	Poliomyelitis
Related	Infectious Disorders
	Multiple Sclerosis

Myenteric Plexus
Use	Autonomic Ganglia

Myers Briggs Type Indicator
Used For	MBTI (Test)

Myers Briggs Type Indicator — (Continued)
(See)	Nonprojective Personality Measures
	Personality Measures

Myocardial Infarctions
Used For	Infarctions (Myocardial)
Broader	Cardiovascular Disorders
	Heart Disorders
Related	Angina Pectoris
	Coronary Thromboses

Myocardium
Broader	Cardiovascular System
	Heart

Myoclonia
Broader	Muscular Disorders
	Musculoskeletal Disorders

Myopia
Used For	Nearsightedness
Broader	Eye Disorders
	Refraction Errors
	Sense Organ Disorders
Related	Hyperopia

Myotonia
Broader	Muscular Disorders
	Musculoskeletal Disorders
Related	Congenital Disorders

Mysticism
Used For	Visions (Mysticism)
Broader	Philosophies
Related	Religious Beliefs
	Religious Practices

Mythology
Use	Literature

Myths
Used For	Folklore
	Folktales
Related	Animism
	Cultism
	Ethnology/
	Transcultural Psychiatry

Myxedema
Use	Hypothyroidism

NAch
Use	Achievement Motivation

Nail Biting
Broader	Behavior Disorders
	Habits

Nails (Anatomy)
Used For	Fingernails
	Toenails
Related	Anatomy/
	Feet (Anatomy)
	Fingers (Anatomy)

Nalorphine
   Broader   Narcotic Antagonists

Narcissism
   Related   Mental Disorders/
             Narcissistic Personality

Narcissistic Personality
   Broader   Personality Disorders
   Related   Narcissism

Narcoanalysis
   Broader   Drug Therapy
             Organic Therapies
   Narrower Sleep Treatment
   Related   Narcoanalytic Drugs

Narcoanalytic Drugs
   Narrower Amobarbital
             Thiopental
   Related   Drugs/
             Narcoanalysis

Narcolepsy
   Broader   Consciousness Disturbances
             Sleep Disorders
   Related   Cataplexy

Narcosis
   Broader   Toxic Disorders
   Related   Narcotic Drugs

Narcotic Antagonists
   Narrower Nalorphine
   Related   Drugs/
             Narcotic Drugs

Narcotic Drugs
   Narrower Apomorphine
             Atropine
             Codeine
             Heroin
             Meperidine
             Methadone
             Morphine
   Related   Analgesic Drugs
             Anesthetic Drugs
             Anticonvulsive Drugs
             Cannabis
             CNS Depressant Drugs
             Drug Dependency
             Emetic Drugs
             Hypnotic Drugs
             Narcosis
             Narcotic Antagonists
             Tranquilizing Drugs

Nasal Mucosa
   Broader   Membranes
             Nose
             Respiratory System
             Tissues (Body)
   Narrower Olfactory Mucosa

National Guardsmen
   Broader   Government Personnel
             Military Personnel
             Volunteer Military Personnel
             Volunteer Personnel
   Related   Air Force Personnel
             Army Personnel

Nationalism
   Broader   Political Attitudes

Natural Disasters
   Broader   Disasters
   Related   Emergency Services
             Stress

Natural Sleep
   Use   Sleep

Nausea
   Broader   Symptoms
   Related   Antiemetic Drugs
             Appetite Disorders
             Migraine Headache
             Vomiting

Navaho Indians
   Use   American Indians

Navy Personnel
   Broader   Government Personnel
             Military Personnel
   Related   Draftees

Nearsightedness
   Use   Myopia

Neck (Anatomy)
   Related   Anatomy/

Neck (Wry)
   Use   Torticollis

Need Achievement
   Use   Achievement Motivation

Need For Affiliation
   Use   Affiliation Motivation

Need Fulfillment
   Use   Need Satisfaction

Need Satisfaction
   Used For Need Fulfillment
   Broader   Satisfaction
   Related   Needs

Needs
   Related   Achievement Motivation
             Affiliation Motivation
             Animal Motivation
             Extrinsic Motivation
             Goals
             Incentives
             Intrinsic Motivation
             Monetary Incentives

Needs — (Continued)
Related
         Motivation
         Need Satisfaction

Negative Correlation
Broader   Statistical Correlation

Negative Reinforcement
Broader   Reinforcement

Negative Transfer
Broader   Transfer (Learning)

Negativism
Broader   Personality Traits
Related   Cynicism
         Pessimism

Negotiation
Broader   Interpersonal Communication
         Interpersonal Interaction
         Social Behavior
         Social Interaction
Narrower   Bargaining

Negro Militancy
Use   Black Power Movement

Negroes
Used For   Blacks
Broader   Race (Anthropological)

Neighborhoods
Broader   Communities
         Environment
         Social Environments

Nembutal
Use   Pentobarbital

NeoFreudian School
Use   Neopsychoanalytic School

Neologisms
Broader   Language
         Verbal Communication
         Vocabulary
Related   Word Salad

Neonatal Autosome Disorders
Broader   Autosome Disorders
         Chromosome Disorders
         Genetic Disorders
         Neonatal Chromosome Disorders
         Neonatal Disorders
         Neonatal Genetic Disorders
Narrower   Crying Cat Syndrome
         Downs Syndrome

Neonatal Chromosome Disorders
Broader   Chromosome Disorders
         Genetic Disorders
         Neonatal Disorders
         Neonatal Genetic Disorders

Neonatal Chromosome Disorders — (Continued)
Narrower   Crying Cat Syndrome
         Downs Syndrome
         Klinefelters Syndrome
         Neonatal Autosome Disorders
         Neonatal Sex Chromosome Disorders
         Turners Syndrome

Neonatal Development
Broader   Childhood Development
         Infant Development
Related   Developmental Differences
         Physical Development
         Psychogenesis

Neonatal Disorders
Narrower   Amaurotic Familial Idiocy
         Anencephaly
         Cleft Palate
         Crying Cat Syndrome
         Downs Syndrome
         Klinefelters Syndrome
         Maple Syrup Urine Disease
         Neonatal Autosome Disorders
         Neonatal Chromosome Disorders
         Neonatal Genetic Disorders
         Neonatal Sex Chromosome Disorders
         Phenylketonuria
         Turners Syndrome
Related   Apnea
         Birth Injuries
         Congenital Disorders
         Disorders/
         Hydrocephaly
         Microcephaly
         Rh Incompatibility

Neonatal Genetic Disorders
Broader   Genetic Disorders
         Neonatal Disorders
Narrower   Amaurotic Familial Idiocy
         Crying Cat Syndrome
         Downs Syndrome
         Klinefelters Syndrome
         Maple Syrup Urine Disease
         Neonatal Autosome Disorders
         Neonatal Chromosome Disorders
         Neonatal Sex Chromosome Disorders
         Phenylketonuria
         Turners Syndrome

Neonatal Sex Chromosome Disorders
Broader   Chromosome Disorders
         Genetic Disorders
         Neonatal Chromosome Disorders

Neonatal Sex Chromosome Disorders — (Continued)

Broader	Neonatal Disorders
	Neonatal Genetic Disorders
	Sex Chromosome Disorders
Narrower	Klinefelters Syndrome
	Turners Syndrome

Neonates

Used For	Newborn Infants
Broader	Children
	Developmental Age Groups
	Infants

Neoplasms

Used For	Cancers
	Carcinomas
	Malignant Neoplasms
	Sarcomas
	Tumors
Narrower	Benign Neoplasms
	Brain Neoplasms
	Breast Neoplasms
	Endocrine Neoplasms
	Leukemias
	Nervous System Neoplasms
	Terminal Cancer
Related	Digestive System Disorders
	Disorders/
	Gastrointestinal Disorders
	Liver Disorders

Neopsychoanalytic School

Used For	NeoFreudian School
Broader	History of Psychology
Narrower	Individual Psychology
	Jungian Psychology

Neostigmine

Used For	Proserine
Broader	Antitubocurarine Drugs
	Cholinesterase Inhibitors
	Cholinomimetic Drugs
Related	Bromides

Nerve (Abducens)

Use	Abducens Nerve

Nerve (Accessory)

Use	Cranial Nerves

Nerve (Acoustic)

Use	Acoustic Nerve

Nerve (Facial)

Use	Facial Nerve

Nerve Cells

Use	Neurons

Nerve Endings

Broader	Nervous System
Narrower	Baroreceptors
	Carotid Body
	Chemoreceptors

Nerve Endings — (Continued)

Narrower	Mechanoreceptors
	Motor End Plates
	Neural Receptors
	Photoreceptors
	Proprioceptors
	Synapses
	Thermoreceptors

Nerve Tissues

Broader	Nervous System
	Tissues (Body)
Narrower	Myelin Sheath
Related	Neurons

Nerves (Adrenergic)

Use	Adrenergic Nerves

Nerves (Cholinergic)

Use	Cholinergic Nerves

Nerves (Cranial)

Use	Cranial Nerves

Nerves (Peripheral)

Use	Peripheral Nerves

Nerves (Spinal)

Use	Spinal Nerves

Nervous Breakdown

Use	Mental Disorders/

Nervous System

Narrower	Abducens Nerve
	Acoustic Nerve
	Adrenergic Nerves
	Amygdaloid Body
	Auditory Cortex
	Auditory Neurons
	Autonomic Ganglia
	Autonomic Nervous System
	Axons
	Baroreceptors
	Basal Ganglia
	Brain
	Brain Stem
	Carotid Body
	Caudate Nucleus
	Central Nervous System
	Cerebellum
	Cerebral Cortex
	Cerebral Ventricles
	Chemoreceptors
	Cholinergic Nerves
	Cones (Eye)
	Corpora Quadrigemina
	Corpus Callosum
	Cranial Nerves
	Cranial Spinal Cord
	Dendrites
	Diencephalon
	Dorsal Roots

Nervous System — (Continued)
Narrower

    Extrapyramidal Tracts
    Facial Nerve
    Frontal Lobe
    Ganglia
    Geniculate Bodies (Thalamus)
    Globus Pallidus
    Gyrus Cinguli
    Hippocampus
    Hypothalamo Hypophyseal System
    Hypothalamus
    Inferior Colliculus
    Limbic System
    Lumbar Spinal Cord
    Mechanoreceptors
    Medulla Oblongata
    Meninges
    Mesencephalon
    Motor Cortex
    Motor End Plates
    Motor Neurons
    Myelin Sheath
    Nerve Endings
    Nerve Tissues
    Neural Analyzers
    Neural Receptors
    Neurons
    Nonchromaffin Paraganglia
    Occipital Lobe
    Olfactory Nerve
    Optic Chiasm
    Optic Lobe
    Optic Nerve
    Parasympathetic Nervous System
    Parietal Lobe
    Peripheral Nerves
    Photoreceptors
    Pons
    Proprioceptors
    Pyramidal Tracts
    Reticular Formation
    Rods (Eye)
    Sacral Spinal Cord
    Sensory Neurons
    Somatosensory Cortex
    Spinal Cord
    Spinal Ganglia
    Spinal Nerves
    Spinothalamic Tracts
    Superior Colliculus
    Sympathetic Nervous System
    Synapses
    Telencephalon
    Temporal Lobe
    Thalamic Nuclei
    Thalamus
    Thermoreceptors

Nervous System — (Continued)
Narrower

    Thoracic Spinal Cord
    Trigeminal Nerve
    Vagus Nerve
    Ventral Roots
    Visual Cortex
Related   Afferent Stimulation
    Anatomical Systems/
    Nervous System Disorders
    Stereotaxic Techniques

Nervous System Disorders
Used For   Motor Disorders
    Neuroinfections
    Neurological Disorders
    Neuropathy
Narrower   Acalculia
    Agraphia
    Alcoholic Hallucinosis
    Alcoholic Psychosis
    Alzheimers Disease
    Anencephaly
    Aphasia
    Arachnoiditis
    Ataxia
    Athetosis
    Autonomic Nervous System Disorders
    Bacterial Meningitis
    Brain Concussion
    Brain Damage
    Brain Disorders
    Brain Lesions
    Brain Neoplasms
    Cataplexy
    Central Nervous System Disorders
    Cerebral Palsy
    Cerebrovascular Accidents
    Chorea
    Convulsions
    Delirium Tremens
    Dysautonomia
    Dyskinesia
    Encephalitis
    Encephalomyelitis
    Epilepsy
    Epileptic Seizures
    General Paresis
    Gilles De La Tourette Disorder
    Grand Mal Epilepsy
    Huntingtons Chorea
    Hydrocephaly
    Hyperkinesis
    Hypothalamus Lesions
    Infectious Meningitis
    Korsakoffs Psychosis
    Meningitis

Nervous System Disorders — (Continued)

Narrower
- Microcephaly
- Minimal Brain Disorders
- Multiple Sclerosis
- Muscular Dystrophy
- Myasthenia Gravis
- Myelitis
- Nervous System Neoplasms
- Neuralgia
- Neuritis
- Neuromuscular Disorders
- Neurosyphilis
- Organic Brain Syndromes
- Paralysis
- Parkinsons Disease
- Peripheral Nerve Disorders
- Petit Mal Epilepsy
- Picks Disease
- Poliomyelitis
- Polyneuritis
- Presenile Dementia
- Radiculitis
- Sclerosis (Nervous System)
- Senile Dementia
- Senile Psychosis
- Toxic Psychoses
- Trigeminal Neuralgia
- Viral Meningitis

Related
- Cerebrovascular Disorders
- Disorders/
- Hemianopia
- Influenza
- Malaria
- Nervous System
- Nystagmus
- Symptoms
- Tetanus (Disease)
- Tuberculosis

Nervous System Neoplasms

Broader   Neoplasms
            Nervous System Disorders
Narrower   Brain Neoplasms

Nervousness

Broader   Personality Traits

Nest Building

Broader   Animal Ethology
Related   Animal Innate Behavior
            Animal Instinctive Behavior
            Animal Mating Behavior

Netherlands

Netherlands West Indies

Neural Analyzers

Broader   Central Nervous System
            Nervous System

Neural Lesions

Broader   Lesions

Neural Receptors

Used For   Receptors (Neural)
Broader   Nerve Endings
            Nervous System
Narrower   Baroreceptors
            Carotid Body
            Chemoreceptors
            Mechanoreceptors
            Photoreceptors
            Proprioceptors
            Thermoreceptors

Neuralgia

Broader   Nervous System Disorders
            Peripheral Nerve Disorders
Narrower   Trigeminal Neuralgia

Neurasthenic Neurosis

Broader   Neurosis
Related   Asthenia
            Asthenic Personality

Neuritis

Broader   Nervous System Disorders
            Peripheral Nerve Disorders
Narrower   Polyneuritis
            Radiculitis
Related   Paralysis

Neuroanatomy

Broader   Neurosciences
            Sciences

Neurobiology

Broader   Biology
            Neurosciences
            Sciences

Neurochemistry

Used For   Brain Metabolism
Broader   Biochemistry
            Chemistry
            Neurosciences
            Sciences

Neurodermatitis

Broader   Dermatitis
            Psychosomatic Disorders
            Skin Disorders
Related   Allergic Skin Disorders

Neuroinfections

Use   Infectious Disorders
            Nervous System Disorders

Neuroleptic Drugs

Used For   Major Tranquilizers
Broader   Tranquilizing Drugs

Neuroleptic Drugs — (Continued)
- Narrower   Butyrylperazine
-     Carphenazine
-     Chlorpromazine
-     Fluphenazine
-     Mesoridazine
-     Perphenazine
-     Phenothiazine Derivatives
-     Prochlorperazine
-     Promazine
-     Reserpine
-     Sulpiride
-     Tetrabenazine
-     Trifluoperazine
-     Triflupromazine
- Related   Antipsychotic Drugs

Neurological Disorders
- Use   Nervous System Disorders

Neurologists
- Used For   Neuropathologists
- Broader   Medical Personnel
-     Physicians
- Related   Surgeons

Neurology
- Broader   Medical Sciences
-     Neurosciences
-     Sciences
- Related   Neuropathology

Neuromuscular Blocking Drugs
- Use   Muscle Relaxing Drugs

Neuromuscular Disorders
- Broader   Nervous System Disorders
- Narrower   Cataplexy
-     Cerebral Palsy
-     General Paresis
-     Gilles De La Tourette Disorder
-     Muscular Dystrophy
-     Myasthenia Gravis
-     Paralysis
-     Parkinsons Disease
- Related   Dyskinesia
-     Hyperkinesis
-     Muscular Disorders
-     Musculoskeletal Disorders
-     Sclerosis (Nervous System)
-     Spinal Cord Injuries

Neurons
- Used For   Nerve Cells
- Broader   Cells (Biology)
-     Nervous System
- Narrower   Auditory Neurons
-     Axons
-     Cones (Eye)
-     Dendrites
-     Motor Neurons

Neurons — (Continued)
- Narrower
-     Rods (Eye)
-     Sensory Neurons
- Related   Nerve Tissues

Neuropathologists
- Use   Neurologists

Neuropathology
- Broader   Medical Sciences
-     Neurosciences
-     Pathology
-     Sciences
- Related   Neurology

Neuropathy
- Use   Nervous System Disorders

Neurophysiology
- Broader   Neurosciences
-     Sciences
- Related   Physiology/

Neuropsychiatrists
- Use   Psychiatrists

Neuropsychiatry
- Broader   Medical Sciences
-     Neurosciences
-     Psychiatry
-     Sciences

Neuropsychology
- Broader   Neurosciences
-     Physiological Psychology
-     Psychology
-     Sciences
-     Social Sciences

Neurosciences
- Broader   Sciences
- Narrower   Neuroanatomy
-     Neurobiology
-     Neurochemistry
-     Neurology
-     Neuropathology
-     Neurophysiology
-     Neuropsychiatry
-     Neuropsychology
- Related   Medical Sciences

Neurosis
- Used For   Psychoneurosis
- Narrower   Anxiety Neurosis
-     Childhood Neurosis
-     Conversion Neurosis
-     Dissociative Neurosis
-     Experimental Neurosis
-     Hysterical Anesthesia
-     Hysterical Paralysis
-     Hysterical Vision Disturbances
-     Neurasthenic Neurosis
-     Neurotic Depressive Reaction

Neurosis — (Continued)

Narrower
Obsessive Compulsive Neurosis
Occupational Neurosis
Phobic Neurosis
Traumatic Neurosis
Related Mental Disorders/
Minor Tranquilizers
Pseudoneurotic Schizophrenia

Neurosis (Childhood)
Use Childhood Neurosis

Neurosurgeons
Use Surgeons

Neurosurgery
Broader Physical Treatment Methods
Surgery
Narrower Decerebration
Decortication (Brain)
Hemispherectomy
Psychosurgery
Pyramidotomy
Sympathectomy
Thalamotomy
Tractotomy
Vagotomy
Related Brain Lesions

Neurosyphilis
Broader Central Nervous System Disorders
Infectious Disorders
Nervous System Disorders
Syphilis
Related General Paresis

Neurotic Depressive Reaction
Used For Depressive Reaction (Neurotic)
Broader Affective Disturbances
Depression (Emotion)
Emotional States
Neurosis
Related Reactive Depression

Neuroticism

Broader Personality Traits

Neuroticism Scale Questionnaire
(See) Nonprojective Personality Measures
Personality Measures

New Guinea

New Zealand

Newborn Infants
Use Neonates

Newsletters (Professional)
Use Scientific Communication

Newspapers
Broader Communications Media
Mass Media
Printed Communications Media

Niacin
Use Nicotinic Acid

Niacinamide
Use Nicotinamide

Nialamide
Broader Amine Oxidase Inhibitors
Antidepressant Drugs
Antipsychotic Drugs
Monoamine Oxidase Inhibitors

Nicotinamide
Used For Niacinamide
Nicotinic Acid Amide
Broader Vitamins
Related Nicotinic Acid
Pellagra

Nicotine
Used For Tobacco (Drug)
Broader Alkaloids
Cholinergic Blocking Drugs
Ganglion Blocking Drugs
Related Drug Dependency
Insecticides
Tobacco Smoking

Nicotinic Acid
Used For Niacin
Broader Acids
Vasodilator Drugs
Vitamins
Related Nicotinamide

Nicotinic Acid Amide
Use Nicotinamide

Nictitating Membrane
Broader Membranes
Tissues (Body)

Nightmares
Broader Dreaming
Related Dream Content

Nihilism
Broader Philosophies

Nitrogen
Broader Chemical Elements
Nonmetallic Elements

Nitroglycerin
Broader Antispasmodic Drugs
Vasodilator Drugs

Nocturnal Behavior (Animal)
Use Animal Nocturnal Behavior

Nocturnal Emission
Broader   Male Orgasm
               Orgasm
               Psychosexual Behavior

Nocturnal Teeth Grinding
Used For   Teeth Grinding (Nocturnal)
Related   Sleep

Nodes (Lymph)
Use   Lymph Nodes

Noise (Sound)
Use   Auditory Stimulation

Noise (Visual)
Use   Figure Ground Discrimination
               Visual Stimulation

Noise Effects
Broader   Environmental Effects
Related   Pollution

Noise Levels (Work Areas)
Broader   Auditory Stimulation
               Loudness
               Perceptual Stimulation
               Working Conditions

Nomenclature (Psychological)
Use   Psychological Terminology

Non Zero Sum Games
Broader   Games
Related   Entrapment Games
               Game Theory
               Prisoners Dilemma Game

Nonchromaffin Paraganglia
Used For   Paraganglia (Nonchromaffin)
Broader   Autonomic Nervous System
               Nervous System
Narrower   Carotid Body

Noncommissioned Officers
Used For   Officers (Noncommissioned)
Broader   Government Personnel
               Military Personnel

Nonconformity (Personality)
Broader   Personality Traits
Related   Conformity (Personality)
               Individuality

Nondirected Discussion Method
Broader   Teaching
               Teaching Methods
Related   Discovery Teaching Method

Nondirective Therapy
Use   Client Centered Therapy

Nondisjunction (Chromosome)
Broader   Chromosome Disorders
               Genetic Disorders
Related   Trisomy

Nongraded Schools
Broader   Schools

Nonlinear Regression
Broader   Statistical Correlation

Nonmetallic Elements
Broader   Chemical Elements
Narrower   Carbon
               Chloride Ions
               Helium
               Hydrogen
               Nitrogen
               Oxygen
               Phosphorus

Nonparametric Statistical Tests
Broader   Statistical Analysis
               Statistical Tests
Narrower   Chi Square Test
               Cochran Q Test
               Kolmogarov Smirnov Test
               Kuder Richardson Test
               Mann Whitney U Test
               McNemar Test
               Rulon Test
               Sign Test
               Walsh Test
               Wilcoxon Sign Rank Test
               Yates Test

Nonprofessional Personnel
Use   Paraprofessional Personnel

Nonprofit Organizations
Broader   Organizations

Nonprojective Personality Measures
Broader   Personality Measures
Narrower   Embedded Figures Testing
Related   Measurement/
Identifier   Authoritarianism Rebellion Scale
               Bannister Repertory Grid
               Barrett Lennard Relationship
                 Invent
               Barron Welsh Art Scale
               Bass Famous Sayings Test
               Bene Anthony Family Relations
                 Test
               California F Scale
               California Psychological Invento-
                 ry
               California Test of Personality
               Child Behavior Diagnostic In-
                 ventory
               Childrens Manifest Anxiety
                 Scale
               Childrens Personality Question-
                 naire
               Cromwells Adult Locus of Cont
                 Scale
               Describing Personality Test

163

Nonprojective Personality Measures — (Continued)
Identifier

Differential Personality Inventory
Edwards Personal Preference Schedule
Edwards Personality Inventory
Edwards Social Desirability Scale
Eysenck Personality Inventory
Fear Survey Schedule
Fund Interper Rela Orientat Beh Ques
Goldstein Scheerer Object Sort Test
Gough Adjective Check List
Guilford Zimmerman Temperament Surv
High Sch Personality Questionnaire
Jr Sr High School Personality Quest
Kupfer Detre Self Rating Scale
Leary Interpersonal Check List
Magnetic Test
Marlowe Crowne Soc Desirabil Scale
Maudsley Personality Inventory
Memory For Designs Test
Minn Multiphasic Personality Inven
Mooney Problem Check List
Myers Briggs Type Indicator
Neuroticism Scale Questionnaire
Omnibus Personality Inventory
Personal Orientation Inventory
Psychological Screening Inventory
Repression Sensitization Scale
Rod And Frame Test
Rokeach Dogmatism Scale
Rotter Intern Extern Locus Cont Scal
Self Analysis Form
Sensation Seeking Scale
Sixteen Personality Factors Question
State Trait Anxiety Inventory
Taylor Manifest Anxiety Scale
Tennessee Self Concept Scale
Vineland Social Maturity Scale
Wakefield Self Assessment Depression
Welsh Figure Preference Test
White Betz A B Scale
Zungs Self Rating Depression Scale

Nonrapid Eye Movement Sleep
Use   NREM Sleep

NonREM Sleep
Use   NREM Sleep

Nonreversal Shift Learning
Broader   Concept Learning

Nonsense Syllable Learning
Broader   Verbal Learning

Nonstandard English
Used For   English (Nonstandard)
Broader   Dialect
                Language
                Verbal Communication
Related   Slang

Nonverbal Communication
Narrower   Body Language
                Eye Contact
                Facial Expressions
                Gestures
                Grimaces
                Smiles
Related   Communication/

Nonverbal Learning
Broader   Social Learning
Related   Learning/

Nonverbal Meaning
Broader   Meaning

Nonverbal Reinforcement
Broader   Reinforcement
                Social Behavior
                Social Reinforcement

Noradrenaline
Use   Norepinephrine

Norepinephrine
Used For   Noradrenaline
Broader   Adrenal Medulla Hormones
                Amines
                Catecholamines
                Hormones
                Sympathomimetic Amines
                Sympathomimetic Drugs
                Vasoconstrictor Drugs
Related   Guanethidine

Normal Distribution
Broader   Frequency Distribution
                Statistical Analysis
                Statistical Measurement

Normalization (Test)
Use   Test Standardization

Norms (Statistical)
Use   Statistical Norms

Norms (Test)
Use   Test Norms

North America

North Vietnam

Northern Ireland

Norway

Norway Rats
Broader	Mammals
	Rats
	Rodents
	Vertebrates

Nose
Broader	Respiratory System
Narrower	Nasal Mucosa
	Olfactory Mucosa
Related	Musculoskeletal System

Nouns
Broader	Form Classes (Language)
	Grammar
	Language
	Linguistics
	Verbal Communication

Novel Stimuli
Use	Stimulus Novelty

Novocaine
Used For	Procaine
Broader	Analgesic Drugs
	Anesthetic Drugs
	Local Anesthetics

NREM Sleep
Used For	Nonrapid Eye Movement Sleep
	NonREM Sleep
	Slow Wave Sleep
Broader	Sleep

Nuclear Family
Broader	Family Structure

Nucleic Acids
Broader	Acids
Narrower	Adenosine
	Deoxyribonucleic Acid
	Ribonucleic Acid
Related	Drugs/
	Genetics/

Nudity

Null Hypothesis Testing
Broader	Experimental Design
	Hypothesis Testing
Related	Experimentation/

Number Comprehension
Broader	Comprehension

Number Systems
Broader	Mathematics (Concepts)
Related	Numbers (Numerals)

Numbers (Numerals)
Used For	Digits (Mathematics)
Broader	Language
	Mathematics (Concepts)
	Verbal Communication
	Written Language
Related	Number Systems

Numerical Ability
Use	Mathematical Ability

Numerosity Perception
Related	Perception/

Nuns
Broader	Clergy
	Religious Personnel
Related	Missionaries

Nursery School Students
Broader	Students

Nursery Schools
Broader	Schools

Nurses
Broader	Medical Personnel
Narrower	Psychiatric Nurses
	Public Health Service Nurses
	School Nurses

Nursing
Broader	Paramedical Sciences

Nursing Education
Related	Education/
	Medical Education

Nursing Homes
Broader	Residential Care Institutions
	Treatment Facilities
Related	Hospitals
	Sanatoriums

Nursing Students
Broader	Students

Nurturance
Use	Animal Maternal Behavior
	Parent Child Relations

Nutrition
Related	Nutritional Deficiencies
	Physiology/

Nutritional Deficiencies
Used For	Deficiency Disorders (Nutrition- al)
	Malnutrition
Narrower	Kwashiorkor
	Mineral Deficiency Disorders
	Pellagra
	Protein Deficiency Disorders

Nutritional Deficiencies — (Continued)
Narrower
Starvation
Vitamin Deficiency Disorders
Wernickes Syndrome
Related Alcoholic Psychosis
Alcoholism
Anorexia Nervosa
Appetite Disorders
Disorders/
Food Deprivation
Metabolism Disorders
Nutrition
Underweight

Nymphomania
Use Hypersexuality

Nystagmus
Broader Eye Disorders
Sense Organ Disorders
Related Nervous System Disorders

Obedience
Used For Submissiveness
Broader Personality Traits

Obesity
Used For Overweight
Broader Appetite Disorders
Body Weight
Physique
Symptoms
Related Hyperphagia
Psychosomatic Disorders

Obituary

Objectives
Use Aspirations

Objectives (Organizational)
Use Organizational Objectives

Objectivity
Used For Subjectivity
Broader Personality Traits

Oblique Rotation
Broader Factor Analysis
Statistical Analysis
Statistical Measurement
Statistical Rotation

Observation Methods
Broader Empirical Methods

Observational Learning
Related Learning/

Observers
Related Audiences

Obsessions
Broader Thought Disturbances

Obsessions — (Continued)
Related Compulsions
Obsessive Compulsive Neurosis
Obsessive Compulsive Personality

Obsessive Compulsive Neurosis
Used For Compulsive Neurosis
Obsessive Neurosis
Broader Neurosis
Related Compulsions
Obsessions
Obsessive Compulsive Personality

Obsessive Compulsive Personality
Broader Personality Disorders
Related Compulsions
Obsessions
Obsessive Compulsive Neurosis

Obsessive Neurosis
Use Obsessive Compulsive Neurosis

Obstetricians
Use Gynecologists

Obstetrics Gynecology
Broader Medical Sciences
Sciences

Obturator Nerve
Use Spinal Nerves

Occipital Lobe
Broader Brain
Central Nervous System
Cerebral Cortex
Nervous System
Telencephalon
Narrower Visual Cortex

Occupation (Parental)
Use Parental Occupation

Occupational Adjustment
Used For Vocational Adjustment
Related Adjustment/
Occupational Neurosis
Occupations/

Occupational Aspirations
Used For Career Aspirations
Career Goals
Vocational Aspirations
Broader Aspirations
Related Occupations/

Occupational Attitudes
Related Attitudes/
Job Applicant Attitudes
Work (Attitudes Toward)

Occupational Choice
Used For	Career Choice
	Job Selection
	Vocational Choice
Related	Occupational Preference
	Occupations/

Occupational Guidance
Used For	Career Guidance
	Guidance (Occupational)
	Vocational Counseling
	Vocational Guidance
Related	Counseling/
	Educational Counseling
	Occupational Success Prediction
	Occupations/

Occupational Interest Measures
Related	Measurement/
Identifier	Kuder Occupational Interest Survey
	Strong Vocational Interest Blank

Occupational Interests
Used For	Vocational Interests
Broader	Interests
Related	Occupations/

Occupational Mobility
Used For	Job Mobility
	Mobility (Occupational)
	Vocational Mobility
Related	Occupational Tenure
	Occupations/

Occupational Neurosis
Used For	Vocational Neurosis
Broader	Neurosis
Related	Occupational Adjustment

Occupational Preference
Used For	Career Preference
	Preferences (Occupational)
	Vocational Preference
Broader	Preferences
Related	Occupational Choice
	Occupations/

Occupational Safety
Used For	Industrial Safety
Broader	Safety
	Working Conditions
Related	Industrial Accidents

Occupational Stress
Broader	Stress
Related	Occupations/

Occupational Success Prediction
Broader	Personnel Evaluation
	Personnel Management
	Prediction
Related	Occupational Guidance

Occupational Tenure
Used For	Tenure (Occupational)
Narrower	Teacher Tenure
Related	Occupational Mobility
	Occupations/

Occupational Therapists
Related	Mental Health Personnel
	Paraprofessional Personnel
	Personnel/
	Psychiatric Hospital Staff
	Therapists/

Occupational Therapy
Related	Treatment/

Occupations/
Used For	Careers
	Employment
	Jobs
	Vocations
Related	Occupational Adjustment
	Occupational Aspirations
	Occupational Choice
	Occupational Guidance
	Occupational Interests
	Occupational Mobility
	Occupational Preference
	Occupational Stress
	Occupational Tenure
	Personnel/

Octopus
Broader	Invertebrates
	Mollusca

Ocular Dominance
Related	Brain
	Dominance/
	Eye (Anatomy)
	Eye Disorders

Oculomotor Muscles
Broader	Muscles
	Musculoskeletal System

Oculomotor Nerve
Use	Cranial Nerves

Oculomotor Response
Use	Eye Movements

Odor Discrimination
Broader	Olfactory Perception
	Perceptual Discrimination
Related	Discrimination/
	Olfactory Thresholds

Oedipal Complex
Used For	Complex (Oedipal)
Broader	Psychoanalytic Personality Factors

Offenders (Adult)
Use	Criminals

Offenders (Juvenile)
Use   Juvenile Delinquents

Officers (Commissioned)
Use   Commissioned Officers

Officers (Noncommissioned)
Use   Noncommissioned Officers

Ojibwa Indians
Use   American Indians

Old Age
Use   Aged

Olfactory Bulb
Broader   Limbic System

Olfactory Evoked Potentials
Broader   Electrical Activity
Electrophysiology
Evoked Potentials
Related   Cortical Evoked Potentials

Olfactory Mucosa
Broader   Membranes
Nasal Mucosa
Nose
Respiratory System
Sense Organs
Tissues (Body)
Related   Chemoreceptors

Olfactory Nerve
Broader   Cranial Nerves
Nervous System
Peripheral Nerves

Olfactory Perception
Used For   Smell Perception
Narrower   Odor Discrimination
Olfactory Thresholds
Related   Anosmia
Perception/
Taste Perception

Olfactory Thresholds
Broader   Olfactory Perception
Thresholds
Related   Odor Discrimination
Perceptual Measures

Oligophrenia
Use   Mental Retardation

Oligophrenia (Phenylpyruvic)
Use   Phenylketonuria

Omnibus Personality Inventory
(See)   Nonprojective Personality Measures
Personality Measures

On The Job Training
Broader   Personnel Training
Related   Inservice Teacher Education

Onomatopoeia And Images Test
(See)   Personality Measures
Projective Personality Measures
Projective Techniques

Onset (Disorders)
Related   Disorders/
Mental Disorders/

Ontogeny
Use   Development/

Open Classroom Method
Broader   Teaching
Teaching Methods
Related   Discovery Teaching Method
Individualized Instruction
Montessori Method
Team Teaching Method

Open Field Behavior (Animal)
Use   Animal Open Field Behavior

Operant Conditioning
Used For   Conditioning (Operant)
Instrumental Conditioning
Instrumental Learning
Broader   Conditioning
Narrower   Avoidance Conditioning
Conditioned Emotional Responses
Escape Conditioning
Eyelid Conditioning
Related   Learning/
Reinforcement
Self Stimulation

Operation (Surgery)
Use   Surgery

Ophidiophobia
Used For   Snake Phobia
Broader   Phobias

Ophthalmologic Examination
Used For   Eye Examination
Broader   Diagnosis
Medical Diagnosis
Narrower   Electro Oculography
Electroretinography
Related   Mydriatic Drugs

Ophthalmology
Broader   Medical Sciences
Sciences
Related   Optometry

Opiates
Used For   Opium Alkaloids
Opium Containing Drugs
Opium Derivatives
Narrower   Apomorphine
Codeine
Heroin

Opiates — (Continued)
Narrower
       Morphine
       Papaverine
   Related   Drugs/

Opinion (Public)
   Use   Public Opinion

Opinion Attitude And Interest Survey
   (See)   Attitude Measures

Opinion Change
   Use   Attitude Change

Opinion Questionnaires
   Use   Attitude Measures

Opinion Surveys
   Use   Attitude Measures

Opinions
   Use   Attitudes/

Opium Alkaloids
   Use   Alkaloids
       Opiates

Opium Containing Drugs
   Use   Opiates

Opium Derivatives
   Use   Opiates

Opossums
   Broader   Mammals
       Marsupials
       Vertebrates

Optic Chiasm
   Broader   Brain
       Central Nervous System
       Diencephalon
       Hypothalamus
       Nervous System
   Related   Optic Nerve

Optic Lobe
   Broader   Brain
       Central Nervous System
       Corpora Quadrigemina
       Mesencephalon
       Nervous System

Optic Nerve
   Broader   Cranial Nerves
       Nervous System
       Peripheral Nerves
   Related   Optic Chiasm

Optical Aids
   Broader   Medical Therapeutic Devices
   Narrower   Contact Lenses

Optical Illusions
   Use   Illusions (Perception)

Optimism
   Broader   Emotional States
       Personality Traits
   Related   Positivism

Optometrists
   Broader   Medical Personnel

Optometry
   Broader   Paramedical Sciences
   Related   Ophthalmology

Oral Communication
   Use   Verbal Communication

Oral Contraceptives
   Broader   Birth Control
       Contraceptive Devices
       Family Planning
   Related   Fertility Enhancement

Oral Reading
   Broader   Reading

Orderliness (Compulsive)
   Use   Compulsive Orderliness

Organ of Corti
   Use   Cochlea

Organ Transplantation
   Used For   Heart Transplants
       Kidney Transplants
       Transplants (Organ)
   Broader   Physical Treatment Methods
       Surgery
   Related   Heart Surgery

Organic Brain Syndromes
   Broader   Brain Disorders
       Central Nervous System Disorders
       Nervous System Disorders
       Syndromes
   Narrower   Alcoholic Hallucinosis
       Alcoholic Psychosis
       Alzheimers Disease
       Delirium Tremens
       Korsakoffs Psychosis
       Picks Disease
       Presenile Dementia
       Senile Dementia
       Senile Psychosis
       Toxic Psychoses
   Related   Mental Disorders/

Organic Therapies
   Narrower   Drug Therapy
       Electroconvulsive Shock Therapy
       Insulin Shock Therapy
       Narcoanalysis
       Psychosurgery
       Shock Therapy
       Sleep Treatment

Organic Therapies — (Continued)
- Related   Psychotherapy
Treatment/

Organization (Spatial)
- Use   Spatial Organization

Organizational Change
- Used For   Change (Organizational)
- Narrower   Organizational Merger
- Related   Organizational Climate
Organizational Crises
Organizational Development

Organizational Climate
- Used For   Climate (Organizational)
- Related   Organizational Change
Organizational Crises
Working Conditions

Organizational Crises
- Broader   Crises
- Related   Organizational Change
Organizational Climate
Stress

Organizational Development
- Related   Development/
Organizational Change
Organizational Objectives
Organizational Structure

Organizational Goals
- Use   Organizational Objectives

Organizational Merger
- Broader   Organizational Change
- Related   Organizational Structure

Organizational Objectives
- Used For   Objectives (Organizational)
Organizational Goals
- Related   Organizational Development

Organizational Structure
- Related   Organizational Development
Organizational Merger
Organizations

Organizations
- Used For   Agencies (Groups)
Associations (Groups)
Groups (Organizations)
- Narrower   Alcoholics Anonymous
Business Organizations
Foreign Organizations
Government Agencies
International Organizations
Labor Unions
Nonprofit Organizations
Professional Organizations
- Related   Organizational Structure

Orgasm
- Used For   Climax (Sexual)

Orgasm — (Continued)
- Broader   Psychosexual Behavior
- Narrower   Female Orgasm
Male Orgasm
Nocturnal Emission
Premature Ejaculation
- Related   Frigidity
Impotence

Orientation (Perceptual)
- Use   Perceptual Orientation

Orientation (Spatial)
- Use   Spatial Orientation (Perception)

Orienting Reflex
- Broader   Reflexes
Sensory Adaptation

Orienting Responses
- Broader   Responses
Sensory Adaptation

Originality
- Use   Creativity

Orphanages
- Broader   Residential Care Institutions
- Related   Institutionalization
Orphans

Orphans
- Broader   Family Members
- Related   Orphanages

Orphenadrine
- Broader   Amines
Antihistaminic Drugs
Antispasmodic Drugs
Antitremor Drugs
Cholinergic Blocking Drugs

Orthogonal Rotation
- Broader   Factor Analysis
Statistical Analysis
Statistical Measurement
Statistical Rotation
- Narrower   Equimax Rotation
Quartimax Rotation
Varimax Rotation

Orthography
- Broader   Grammar
Language
Linguistics
Verbal Communication
- Related   Spelling

Orthopedically Handicapped
- Use   Physically Handicapped

Orthopsychiatry
- Broader   Medical Sciences
Psychiatry
Sciences

Oscilloscopes
Broader   Apparatus

Osteochondritis
Broader   Bone Disorders
           Musculoskeletal Disorders

Otosclerosis
Broader   Ear Disorders
           Sense Organ Disorders

Outcomes (Psychotherapeutic)
Use   Psychotherapeutic Outcomes

Outpatient Psychiatric Clinics
Use   Psychiatric Clinics

Outpatient Treatment
Related   Aftercare
           Drug Therapy
           Outpatients
           Psychiatric Clinics
           Treatment/

Outpatients
Broader   Patients
Related   Outpatient Treatment

Ovariectomy
Broader   Castration
           Endocrine Gland Surgery
           Physical Treatment Methods
           Sterilization (Sex)
           Surgery
Related   Hysterectomy

Ovaries
Broader   Endocrine Glands
           Endocrine System
           Female Genitalia
           Glands
           Gonads
           Urogenital System

Ovary Disorders
Use   Endocrine Sexual Disorders

Overachievement (Academic)
Use   Academic Overachievement

Overlearning
Related   Learning/

Overpopulation
Used For   Crowding
Broader   Population
Related   Birth Control
           Environmental Stress

Overweight
Use   Obesity

Ovulation
Broader   Menstrual Cycle
Related   Ovum

Ovum
Broader   Cells (Biology)
           Germ Cells
Related   Ovulation
           Sexual Reproduction

Oxidases
Broader   Enzymes
Narrower   Amine Oxidases
           Cytochrome Oxidase
           Monoamine Oxidases

Oxygen
Broader   Chemical Elements
           Nonmetallic Elements

Oxygenation
Related   Physiology/

Oxytocic Drugs
Narrower   Oxytocin
           Quinine
           Tyramine
Related   Drugs/
           Ergot Derivatives
           Heart Rate Affecting Drugs
           Hormones
           Labor (Childbirth)

Oxytocin
Broader   Hormones
           Oxytocic Drugs
           Pituitary Hormones
           Posterior Pituitary Hormones

Pacemakers (Artificial)
Use   Artificial Pacemakers

Pacifism
Broader   Philosophies

Pain
Used For   Aches
Broader   Symptoms
Narrower   Aphagia
           Headache
           Migraine Headache
           Muscle Contraction Headache
           Psychogenic Pain
           Sympathetic Pain
Related   Analgesic Drugs
           Pain Perception
           Pain Thresholds
           Spasms
           Suffering

Pain (Psychogenic)
Use   Psychogenic Pain

Pain Perception
Broader   Somesthetic Perception
Narrower   Pain Thresholds
Related   Pain

Pain Relieving Drugs
Use   Analgesic Drugs

Pain Thresholds
Broader   Pain Perception
          Somesthetic Perception
          Thresholds
Related   Pain
          Perceptual Measures

Painting (Art)
Broader   Art
          Arts

Paired Associate Learning
Used For Association Learning (Paired)
Broader   Verbal Learning
Related   Word Associations

Palm (Anatomy)
Related   Anatomy/
          Hand (Anatomy)

Palsy
Use   Paralysis

Pancreas
Broader   Glands
Related   Endocrine Glands
          Endocrine System
          Gastrointestinal System

Pancreatectomy
Broader   Endocrine Gland Surgery
          Physical Treatment Methods
          Surgery

Panic
Broader   Emotional States
          Fear
Related   Entrapment Games

Papaverine
Broader   Alkaloids
          Analgesic Drugs
          Antispasmodic Drugs
          Muscle Relaxing Drugs
          Opiates

Paradoxical Sleep
Use   REM Sleep

Paraganglia (Nonchromaffin)
Use   Nonchromaffin Paraganglia

Paragraphs
Broader   Language
          Linguistics
          Verbal Communication
          Written Language

Paralydehyde
Broader   Hypnotic Drugs
          Sedatives

Paralysis
Used For Palsy

Paralysis — (Continued)
Broader   Nervous System Disorders
          Neuromuscular Disorders
Narrower Cerebral Palsy
          General Paresis
          Parkinsons Disease
Related   Central Nervous System Disorders
          Dysarthria
          Musculoskeletal Disorders
          Neuritis
          Peripheral Nerve Disorders
          Poliomyelitis
          Sclerosis (Nervous System)
          Spinal Cord Injuries

Paralysis (Hysterical)
Use   Hysterical Paralysis

Paralysis (Infantile)
Use   Poliomyelitis

Paralysis Agitans
Use   Parkinsons Disease

Paramedical Personnel
Broader   Medical Personnel
          Paraprofessional Personnel
Narrower Attendants (Institutions)
          Medics
          Physical Therapists
          Psychiatric Aides
Related   Paramedical Sciences
          Psychiatric Hospital Staff

Paramedical Sciences
Narrower Audiology
          Nursing
          Optometry
          Pharmacology
          Physical Therapy
          Psychopharmacology
Related   Medical Sciences
          Paramedical Personnel

Parameters (Response)
Use   Response Parameters

Parameters (Stimulus)
Use   Stimulus Parameters

Parametric Statistical Tests
Broader   Statistical Analysis
          Statistical Tests
Narrower F Test
          T Test

Paranasal Sinuses
Broader   Respiratory System

Paranoia (Psychosis)
Broader   Psychosis
Related   Folie A Deux
          Involutional Paranoid Psychosis

172

Paranoia (Psychosis) — (Continued)
Related   Paranoid Personality
Paranoid Schizophrenia

Paranoid Personality
Broader   Personality Disorders
Related   Paranoia (Psychosis)
Paranoid Schizophrenia

Paranoid Schizophrenia
Broader   Psychosis
Schizophrenia
Related   Folie A Deux
Involutional Paranoid Psychosis
Paranoia (Psychosis)
Paranoid Personality

Paraprofessional Education
Related   Education/

Paraprofessional Personnel
Used For   Nonprofessional Personnel
Subprofessional Personnel
Narrower   Attendants (Institutions)
Medics
Paramedical Personnel
Physical Therapists
Psychiatric Aides
Teacher Aides
Visiting Homemakers
Related   Mental Health Personnel
Occupational Therapists
Personnel/
Volunteer Civilian Personnel
Volunteer Personnel

Parapsychological Phenomena
Used For   Phenomena (Parapsychological)
Broader   Parapsychology
Narrower   Clairvoyance
Extrasensory Perception
Precognition
Psychokinesis
Telepathy

Parapsychology
Narrower   Clairvoyance
Extrasensory Perception
Parapsychological Phenomena
Precognition
Psychokinesis
Telepathy
Related   Dream Analysis
Witchcraft

Parasitic Disorders
Broader   Infectious Disorders
Narrower   Malaria
Toxoplasmosis

Parasympathetic Nervous System
Broader   Autonomic Nervous System
Nervous System

Parasympathetic Nervous System — (Continued)
Narrower   Vagus Nerve
Related   Cholinergic Blocking Drugs
Cholinomimetic Drugs

Parasympatholytic Drugs
Use   Cholinergic Blocking Drugs

Parasympathomimetic Drugs
Use   Cholinomimetic Drugs

Parathion
Broader   Insecticides

Parathyroid Disorders
Used For   Hyperparathyroidism
Hypoparathyroidism
Broader   Endocrine Disorders

Parathyroid Glands
Broader   Endocrine Glands
Endocrine System
Glands
Related   Parathyroid Hormone

Parathyroid Hormone
Broader   Hormones
Related   Parathyroid Glands

Parent Attitude Research Instrument
(See)   Attitude Measures

Parent Child Communication
Broader   Interpersonal Communication
Related   Parent Child Relations

Parent Child Relations
Used For   Nurturance
Parental Influence
Broader   Family Relations
Narrower   Father Child Relations
Mother Child Relations
Parental Attitudes
Parental Permissiveness
Related   Child Discipline
Childrearing Practices
Generation Gap
Parent Child Communication
Parental Role

Parent Educational Background
Used For   Educational Background (Parents)
Broader   Educational Background
Family Background
Related   Family Socioeconomic Level
Parental Occupation

Parental Absence
Broader   Family Structure
Narrower   Father Absence
Mother Absence
Related   Divorced Persons
Marital Separation

Parental Absence — (Continued)
Related	Widowers
	Widows

Parental Attitudes
Broader	Family Relations
	Parent Child Relations
Related	Attitudes/
	Childrearing Attitudes
	Childrearing Practices
	Father Child Relations
	Mother Child Relations
	Parental Permissiveness
	Parental Role

Parental Authoritarianism
Use	Parental Permissiveness

Parental Influence
Use	Parent Child Relations

Parental Occupation
Used For	Occupation (Parental)
Broader	Family Background
Related	Family Socioeconomic Level
	Parent Educational Background

Parental Permissiveness
Used For	Authoritarianism (Parental)
	Parental Authoritarianism
	Permissiveness (Parental)
Broader	Child Discipline
	Childrearing Practices
	Family Relations
	Parent Child Relations
Related	Father Child Relations
	Mother Child Relations
	Parental Attitudes
	Parental Role

Parental Role
Broader	Family Relations
	Roles
Related	Child Discipline
	Childrearing Practices
	Father Child Relations
	Mother Child Relations
	Parent Child Relations
	Parental Attitudes
	Parental Permissiveness

Parents
Broader	Ancestors
	Family Members
Narrower	Adoptive Parents
	Fathers
	Foster Parents
	Mothers
	Schizophrenogenic Mothers
	Stepparents
	Surrogate Parents (Humans)
	Unwed Mothers

Parents — (Continued)
Related	Spouses

Paresis (General)
Use	General Paresis

Pargyline
Broader	Antihypertensive Drugs
	Monoamine Oxidase Inhibitors

Parietal Lobe
Broader	Brain
	Central Nervous System
	Cerebral Cortex
	Nervous System
	Telencephalon
Narrower	Somatosensory Cortex

Parkinsons Disease
Used For	Paralysis Agitans
Broader	Brain Disorders
	Central Nervous System Disorders
	Nervous System Disorders
	Neuromuscular Disorders
	Paralysis
Related	Antitremor Drugs
	Tremor

Parks (Recreational)
Use	Recreation Areas

Parochial School Education
Use	Private School Education

Parole
Broader	Legal Processes
Related	Probation

Parole Officers
Broader	Government Personnel
	Law Enforcement Personnel
Related	Probation Officers

Parsons
Use	Ministers (Religion)

Partial Reinforcement
Use	Reinforcement Schedules

Partially Hearing Impaired
Used For	Hearing Impaired (Partially)
Broader	Aurally Handicapped
	Handicapped
Related	Deaf

Partially Sighted
Broader	Handicapped
	Visually Handicapped

Participation
Broader	Interpersonal Interaction
	Social Behavior
	Social Interaction
Narrower	Group Participation

Parties (Political)
Use   Political Parties

Parturition
Use   Birth

Passage (Rites of)
Use   Rites of Passage

Passive Aggressive Personality
Broader   Personality Disorders

Passive Avoidance
Use   Avoidance Conditioning

Passiveness
Broader   Personality Traits

Pastoral Counseling
Related   Counseling/
            Psychotherapy

Pastors
Use   Ministers (Religion)

Pathogenesis
Use   Etiology

Pathological Lying
Used For   Lying (Pathological)
Broader   Behavior Disorders
            Deception
Related   Confabulation

Pathologists
Broader   Medical Personnel
            Physicians
Related   Surgeons

Pathology
Broader   Medical Sciences
Narrower   Neuropathology
            Psychopathology

Pathways (Maze)
Use   Maze Pathways

Patient Characteristics
Use   Client Characteristics
            Patients
            Personality Traits

Patient History
Used For   Case History
            Medical History
            Psychiatric History
Related   Client Characteristics
            Diagnosis
            Etiology
            Medical Diagnosis
            Prognosis
            Psychodiagnosis
            Treatment/

Patient Therapist Interaction
Use   Psychotherapeutic Processes

Patients
Used For   Patient Characteristics
            Physically Ill Patients
Narrower   Geriatric Patients
            Hospitalized Patients
            Medical Patients
            Outpatients
            Psychiatric Patients
            Surgical Patients
            Terminally Ill Patients

Patriarchy
Broader   Family Structure
Related   Mother Absence

Pattern (Stimulus)
Use   Stimulus Variability

Pattern Discrimination
Broader   Perceptual Discrimination
Related   Figure Ground Discrimination
            Form And Shape Perception
            Perceptual Closure

Pavlovian Conditioning
Use   Classical Conditioning

Pay
Use   Salaries

Peabody Picture Vocabulary Test
(See)   Intelligence Measures

Peace Corps
Broader   Government Programs
Related   Government

Pearson Prod Moment Correl Coeff
Use   Statistical Correlation

Pecking Order
Use   Animal Dominance

Pectoralis Muscles
Broader   Muscles
            Musculoskeletal System

Pederasty
Use   Pedophilia

Pedestrian Accidents
Broader   Accidents
Related   Driving Behavior
            Motor Traffic Accidents
            Pedestrians

Pedestrians
Related   Pedestrian Accidents

Pediatricians
Broader   Medical Personnel
            Physicians

Pediatrics
Broader   Medical Sciences

Pedophilia
Used For   Pederasty

Pedophilia — (Continued)
Broader	Psychosexual Behavior
	Sexual Deviations
Related	Bisexuality
	Incest
	Male Homosexuality

Peer Relations
Used For	Relations (Peer)
Broader	Interpersonal Interaction
	Social Behavior
	Social Interaction

Peer Tutoring
Broader	Teaching
	Teaching Methods
	Tutoring

Pellagra
Broader	Nutritional Deficiencies
	Vitamin Deficiency Disorders
Related	Nicotinamide

Pelvis
Related	Anatomy/

Penguins
Broader	Birds
	Vertebrates

Penicillins
Broader	Antibiotics

Penis
Broader	Male Genitalia
	Urogenital System

Penis Envy
Related	Mental Disorders/

Penitentiaries
Use	Prisons

Penology
Related	Criminology

Pension Plans (Employee)
Use	Employee Pension Plans

Pentobarbital
Used For	Nembutal
	Sodium Pentobarbital
Broader	Anesthetic Drugs
	Anticonvulsive Drugs
	Barbiturates
	Hypnotic Drugs
	Sedatives

Pentothal
Use	Thiopental

Pentylenetetrazol
Used For	Metrazole
	Pentylenetetrazole
Broader	CNS Affecting Drugs
	CNS Stimulating Drugs
Related	Analeptic Drugs

Pentylenetetrazole
Use	Pentylenetetrazol

Peoples Republic of China

Pepsin
Broader	Enzymes
Related	Pepsinogen

Pepsinogen
Related	Drugs/
	Pepsin

Peptic Ulcers
Use	Gastrointestinal Ulcers

Peptides
Narrower	Glutathione
Related	Drugs/
	Proteins

Perception (Self)
Use	Self Perception

Perception/
Used For	Sensation
Related	Apperception
	Attention
	Auditory Perception
	Discrimination/
	Extrasensory Perception
	Form And Shape Perception
	Illusions (Perception)
	Monitoring
	Numerosity Perception
	Olfactory Perception
	Perceptual Closure
	Perceptual Discrimination
	Perceptual Disturbances
	Perceptual Localization
	Perceptual Measures
	Perceptual Motor Processes
	Perceptual Stimulation
	Perceptual Style
	Role Perception
	Signal Detection (Perception)
	Social Perception
	Somesthetic Perception
	Spatial Perception
	Subliminal Perception
	Tactual Perception
	Taste Perception
	Time Perception
	Visual Perception
	Weight Perception

Perceptiveness (Personality)
Broader	Personality Traits
Related	Insight

Perceptual Aftereffect
Used For	Aftereffect (Perceptual)
Broader	Illusions (Perception)

Perceptual Aftereffect — (Continued)
Narrower   Afterimage

Perceptual Closure
Used For   Closure (Perceptual)
          Perceptual Fill
Related   Pattern Discrimination
          Perception/

Perceptual Development
Used For   Perceptual Motor Development
Broader   Cognitive Development
          Psychogenesis
Related   Childhood Development
          Conservation (Concept)
          Developmental Stages
          Physical Development
          Psychomotor Development

Perceptual Discrimination
Used For   Acuity
Narrower   Figure Ground Discrimination
          Odor Discrimination
          Pattern Discrimination
Related   Discrimination/
          Perception/

Perceptual Distortion
Use   Illusions (Perception)

Perceptual Disturbances
Narrower   Agnosia
          Auditory Hallucinations
          Drug Induced Hallucinations
          Hallucinations
          Hypnagogic Hallucinations
          Visual Hallucinations
Related   Aphasia
          Illusions (Perception)
          Learning Disabilities
          Mental Disorders/
          Perception/

Perceptual Fill
Use   Perceptual Closure

Perceptual Localization
Used For   Localization (Perceptual)
Narrower   Auditory Localization
Related   Perception/

Perceptual Measures
Related   Audiometry
          Auditory Thresholds
          Bone Conduction Audiometry
          Critical Flicker Fusion Threshold
          Dark Adaptation
          Measurement/
          Olfactory Thresholds
          Pain Thresholds
          Perception/
          Psychophysical Measurement
          Thresholds

Perceptual Measures — (Continued)
Related
          Vibrotactile Thresholds
          Visual Thresholds
Identifier   Rod And Frame Test
          Stroop Color Word Test

Perceptual Motor Coordination
Used For   Coordination (Perceptual Motor)
Broader   Perceptual Motor Processes
Narrower   Physical Dexterity
Related   Motor Coordination

Perceptual Motor Development
Use   Motor Development
          Perceptual Development

Perceptual Motor Learning
Used For   Motor Skill Learning
Narrower   Fine Motor Skill Learning
          Gross Motor Skill Learning
Related   Learning/
          Skill Learning
          Tracking

Perceptual Motor Processes
Used For   Psychomotor Processes
          Sensory Motor Processes
Narrower   Perceptual Motor Coordination
          Physical Dexterity
          Rotary Pursuit
          Tracking
          Visual Tracking
Related   Motor Processes
          Perception/

Perceptual Orientation
Used For   Orientation (Perceptual)
Narrower   Spatial Orientation (Perception)

Perceptual Stimulation
Broader   Stimulation
Narrower   Auditory Feedback
          Auditory Stimulation
          Delayed Auditory Feedback
          Delayed Feedback
          Filtered Noise
          Illumination
          Loudness
          Noise Levels (Work Areas)
          Pitch (Frequency)
          Prismatic Stimulation
          Sensory Feedback
          Somesthetic Stimulation
          Speech Pitch
          Stereoscopic Presentation
          Tachistoscopic Presentation
          Tactual Stimulation
          Taste Stimulation
          Ultrasound
          Visual Feedback

Perceptual Stimulation — (Continued)
Narrower
    Visual Stimulation
    White Noise
Related Masking
    Perception/
    Roughness
    Size

Perceptual Style
Related Cognitive Style
    Perception/

Performance

Performance Tests
Related Measurement/

Performing Arts
Use Dance
    Drama
    Music

Pericardium
Broader Cardiovascular System
    Heart

Peripheral Nerve Disorders
Broader Nervous System Disorders
Narrower Myasthenia Gravis
    Neuralgia
    Neuritis
    Polyneuritis
    Radiculitis
    Trigeminal Neuralgia
Related Muscular Dystrophy
    Paralysis
    Peripheral Nerves

Peripheral Nerves
Used For Nerves (Peripheral)
Broader Nervous System
Narrower Abducens Nerve
    Acoustic Nerve
    Cranial Nerves
    Facial Nerve
    Olfactory Nerve
    Optic Nerve
    Spinal Nerves
    Trigeminal Nerve
    Vagus Nerve
Related Peripheral Nerve Disorders

Peritoneum
Broader Digestive System

Permissiveness (Parental)
Use Parental Permissiveness

Perphenazine
Broader Antiemetic Drugs
    Antipsychotic Drugs
    Antischizophrenic Drugs
    Neuroleptic Drugs

Perphenazine — (Continued)
Broader
    Phenothiazine Derivatives
    Tranquilizing Drugs

Persecution
Broader Interpersonal Interaction
    Social Behavior
    Social Interaction

Perseverance
Use Persistence

Perseveration
Broader Thought Disturbances

Persistence
Used For Perseverance
Broader Personality Traits

Personal Adjustment
Use Emotional Adjustment

Personal Construct Theory
Use Personality Theory

Personal Orientation Inventory
(See) Nonprojective Personality Measures
    Personality Measures

Personal Space
Used For Space (Personal)
Related Social Behavior

Personal Values
Broader Ethics
    Values
Related Morality

Personality Assessment
Use Personality Measures

Personality Change
Related Personality/

Personality Characteristics
Use Personality Traits

Personality Correlates
Related Personality/

Personality Development
Used For Character Development
    Character Formation
Broader Psychogenesis
    Psychosocial Development
Related Emotional Development
    Moral Development

Personality Disorders
Used For Character Disorders
Narrower Antisocial Personality
    Asthenic Personality
    Cyclothymic Personality
    Explosive Personality
    Hysterical Personality
    Inadequate Personality

Personality Disorders — (Continued)
Narrower

Masochistic Personality
Narcissistic Personality
Obsessive Compulsive Personality
Paranoid Personality
Passive Aggressive Personality
Sadistic Personality
Sadomasochistic Personality
Schizoid Personality

Related

Defense Mechanisms
Dissociative Patterns
Ethnospecific Disorders
Mental Disorders/
Personality Traits
Personality/

Personality Factors (Psychoanalytic)
Use   Psychoanalytic Personality Factors

Personality Inventories
Use   Personality Measures

Personality Measures
Used For   Inventories (Personality)
Personality Assessment
Personality Inventories
Personality Questionnaires
Personality Scales
Personality Surveys
Personality Tests
Questionnaires (Personality)
Scales (Personality)
Surveys (Personality)
Tests (Personality)

Narrower   Embedded Figures Testing
Human Figures Drawing
Nonprojective Personality Measures

(Identifier)   Authoritarianism Rebellion Scale
Bannister Repertory Grid
Barrett Lennard Relationship Invent
Barron Welsh Art Scale
Bass Famous Sayings Test
Bene Anthony Family Relations Test
California F Scale
California Psychological Inventory
California Test of Personality
Child Behavior Diagnostic Inventory
Childrens Manifest Anxiety Scale
Childrens Personality Questionnaire

Personality Measures — (Continued)
(Identifier)

Cromwells Adult Locus of Cont Scale
Describing Personality Test
Differential Personality Inventory
Edwards Personal Preference Schedule
Edwards Personality Inventory
Edwards Social Desirability Scale
Eysenck Personality Inventory
Fear Survey Schedule
Fund Interper Rela Orientat Beh Ques
Goldstein Scheerer Object Sort Test
Gough Adjective Check List
Guilford Zimmerman Temperament Surv
High Sch Personality Questionnaire
Jr Sr High School Personality Quest
Kupfer Detre Self Rating Scale
Leary Interpersonal Check List
Magnetic Test
Marlowe Crowne Soc Desirabil Scale
Maudsley Personality Inventory
Memory For Designs Test
Minn Multiphasic Personality Inven
Mooney Problem Check List
Myers Briggs Type Indicator
Neuroticism Scale Questionnaire
Omnibus Personality Inventory
Personal Orientation Inventory
Psychological Screening Inventory
Repression Sensitization Scale
Rod And Frame Test
Rokeach Dogmatism Scale
Rotter Intern Extern Locus Cont Scal
Self Analysis Form
Sensation Seeking Scale
Sixteen Personality Factors Question
State Trait Anxiety Inventory
Taylor Manifest Anxiety Scale
Tennessee Self Concept Scale

Personality Measures — (Continued)
(Identifier)

Vineland Social Maturity
Scale
Wakefield Self Assessment
Depression
Welsh Figure Preference Test
White Betz A B Scale
Zungs Self Rating Depression
Scale

Narrower
(Identifier)   Projective Personality Measures
Bender Gestalt Test
Blacky Pictures Test
Childrens Apperception Test
Color Pyramid Test
Franck Drawing Completion
Test
Holtzman Inkblot Technique
Onomatopoeia And Images
Test
Rorschach Test
Rosenzweig Picture Frustration
Stud
Rotter Incomplete Sentences
Blank
Szoudi Test
Thematic Apperception Test
Zulliger Z Test

Related   Measurement/

Personality Processes/
Used For   Life Style
Related   Catharsis
Cathexis
Defense Mechanisms
Externalization
Inhibition (Personality)
Introspection
Personality/
Reality Testing

Personality Questionnaires
Use   Personality Measures

Personality Scales
Use   Personality Measures

Personality Surveys
Use   Personality Measures

Personality Tests
Use   Personality Measures

Personality Theory
Used For   Personal Construct Theory
Related   Personality/
Theories/

Personality Traits
Used For   Character Traits
Patient Characteristics
Personality Characteristics
Narrower   Adaptability (Personality)
Aggressiveness
Assertiveness

Personality Traits — (Continued)
Narrower

Authoritarianism
Conformity (Personality)
Conservatism
Courage
Creativity
Cruelty
Curiosity
Cynicism
Defensiveness
Dependency (Personality)
Dishonesty
Egotism
Emotional Immaturity
Emotional Inferiority
Emotional Instability
Emotional Maturity
Emotional Security
Emotional Stability
Emotional Superiority
Emotionality (Personality)
Empathy
Extraversion
Femininity
Gregariousness
Honesty
Hypnotic Susceptibility
Idealism
Impulsiveness
Independence (Personality)
Individuality
Initiative
Insight
Internal External Locus of
Control
Introversion
Liberalism
Loyalty
Machiavellianism
Masculinity
Misanthropy
Moodiness
Negativism
Nervousness
Neuroticism
Nonconformity (Personality)
Obedience
Objectivity
Optimism
Passiveness
Perceptiveness (Personality)
Persistence
Pessimism
Positivism
Repression Sensitization
Rigidity (Personality)
Self Control
Selfishness

Personality Traits — (Continued)

Narrower	Sensitivity (Personality)
	Seriousness
	Sexuality
	Sincerity
	Sociability
	Suggestibility
	Timidity
	Tolerance
Related	Cognitive Style
	Field Dependence
	Personality Disorders
	Personality/

Personality/

Used For	Character
	Disposition
	Temperament
Related	Emotional Adjustment
	Individual Differences
	Personality Change
	Personality Correlates
	Personality Disorders
	Personality Processes/
	Personality Theory
	Personality Traits
	Predisposition
	Psychoanalytic Personality Factors
	Psychodynamics
	Self Actualization
	Self Concept
	Self Disclosure
	Self Evaluation
	Self Perception
	Somatotypes
	Teacher Personality
	Tolerance For Ambiguity

Personnel (Prison)

Use	Prison Personnel

Personnel Development

Use	Personnel Training

Personnel Evaluation

Used For	Employee Performance Appraisal
	Evaluation (Personnel)
	Job Performance Evaluation
	Teacher (Evaluation of)
Broader	Evaluation
	Personnel Management
Narrower	Job Applicant Interviews
	Job Applicant Screening
	Occupational Success Prediction
Related	Job Performance
	Personnel Selection

Personnel Management

Narrower	Job Analysis
	Job Applicant Interviews
	Job Applicant Screening
	Labor Management Relations
	Military Recruitment
	Occupational Success Prediction
	Personnel Evaluation
	Personnel Placement
	Personnel Recruitment
	Personnel Selection
	Personnel Termination
	Teacher Recruitment
Related	Business Education
	Business Management
	Management/
	Personnel/

Personnel Placement

Used For	Placement (Personnel)
Broader	Personnel Management

Personnel Recruitment

Used For	Employment Processes
	Recruitment (Personnel)
Broader	Personnel Management
Narrower	Military Recruitment
	Teacher Recruitment

Personnel Selection

Used For	Employee Selection
	Hiring
	Selection (Personnel)
Broader	Personnel Management
Related	Personnel Evaluation

Personnel Supply

Narrower	Medical Personnel Supply
	Mental Health Personnel Supply
	Teacher Supply
Related	Personnel/

Personnel Termination

Broader	Personnel Management
Related	Retirement
	Unemployment

Personnel Training

Used For	Personnel Development
	Training (Personnel)
Narrower	Apprenticeship
	Inservice Teacher Education
	Management Training
	Military Training
	On The Job Training
Related	Business Education
	Education/
	Personnel/
	Sensitivity Training

Personnel/
Used For	Employees
	Manpower
	Workers
Related	Accountants
	Aerospace Personnel
	Agricultural Workers
	Anthropologists
	Architects
	Artists
	Attorneys
	Business And Industrial Personnel
	Clinicians
	Counselors
	Domestic Service Personnel
	Educational Personnel
	Employability
	Employee Absenteeism
	Employee Attitudes
	Employee Benefits
	Employee Motivation
	Employee Skills
	Employee Turnover
	Employer Attitudes
	Engineers
	Government Personnel
	Hypnotists
	Job Applicant Attitudes
	Job Performance
	Journalists
	Labor Union Members
	Management Personnel
	Mathematicians
	Medical Personnel
	Mental Health Personnel
	Military Veterans
	Occupational Therapists
	Occupations/
	Paraprofessional Personnel
	Personnel Management
	Personnel Supply
	Personnel Training
	Physicists
	Psychologists
	Religious Personnel
	Retirement
	Scientists/
	Social Workers
	Sociologists
	Speech Therapists
	Technical Service Personnel
	Unemployment
	Volunteer Personnel
	Working Conditions

Perspiration
Use	Sweat

Persuasion Therapy
Broader	Psychotherapy

Persuasive Communication
Related	Communication/

Pessimism
Broader	Emotional States
	Personality Traits
Related	Negativism

Petit Mal Epilepsy
Broader	Brain Disorders
	Central Nervous System Disorders
	Epilepsy
	Nervous System Disorders

Petting
Broader	Psychosexual Behavior
Related	Sexual Intercourse (Human)
	Social Dating

Peyote
Broader	Alkaloids
	Hallucinogenic Drugs
	Psychotomimetic Drugs
Related	Mescaline

Phantom Limbs
Broader	Body Image
	Body Image Disturbances
Related	Amputation

Pharmacology
Broader	Paramedical Sciences
Narrower	Psychopharmacology

Pharmacotherapy
Use	Drug Therapy

Pharyngeal Disorders
Broader	Respiratory Tract Disorders
Related	Common Colds

Pharynx
Broader	Digestive System
	Respiratory System

Phenacetin
Broader	Analgesic Drugs

Phenaglycodol
Broader	Sedatives

Phenelzine
Broader	Antidepressant Drugs
	Monoamine Oxidase Inhibitors

Pheniprazine
Broader	Antidepressant Drugs

Phenmetrazine
Broader	Amines
	Appetite Depressing Drugs
	Sympathomimetic Amines
	Sympathomimetic Drugs

Phenobarbital
Broader	Anticonvulsive Drugs
	Barbiturates
	Hypnotic Drugs
	Sedatives

Phenomena (Parapsychological)
Use	Parapsychological Phenomena

Phenomenology
Related	History of Psychology

Phenothiazine Derivatives
Broader	Neuroleptic Drugs
	Tranquilizing Drugs
Narrower	Butyrylperazine
	Carphenazine
	Chlorpromazine
	Chlorprothixene
	Fluphenazine
	Mesoridazine
	Perphenazine
	Prochlorperazine
	Promazine
	Thioridazine
	Trifluoperazine
	Triflupromazine
Related	Antischizophrenic Drugs
	Cholinergic Blocking Drugs

Phenotypes
Related	Genetics/
	Genotypes

Phenoxybenzamine
Broader	Adrenergic Blocking Drugs
	Amines
	Antihypertensive Drugs

Phenylalanine
Broader	Acids
	Alanines
	Amino Acids

Phenylketonuria
Used For	Oligophrenia (Phenylpyruvic)
	PKU (Hereditary Disorder)
Broader	Genetic Disorders
	Metabolism Disorders
	Neonatal Disorders
	Neonatal Genetic Disorders
Related	Mental Retardation

Pheromones
Related	Animal Mating Behavior
	Glands
	Hormones

Phi Coefficient
Used For	Coefficient (Phi)
Broader	Statistical Correlation

Philippines

Philosophies
Narrower	Animism
	Asceticism
	Dualism
	Epistemology
	Existentialism
	Fatalism
	Humanism
	Idealism
	Intellectualism
	Logic (Philosophy)
	Materialism
	Metaphysics
	Mysticism
	Nihilism
	Pacifism
	Pragmatism
	Realism (Philosophy)
	Reductionism
	Skepticism
Related	Hedonism

Phobias
Narrower	Acrophobia
	Agoraphobia
	Claustrophobia
	Dysmorphophobia
	Ophidiophobia
	School Phobia
Related	Fear
	Mental Disorders/
	Phobic Neurosis

Phobic Neurosis
Broader	Neurosis
Related	Phobias

Phonemes
Broader	Language
	Linguistics
	Phonetics
	Verbal Communication
Narrower	Consonants
	Vowels
Related	Phonology

Phonetics
Broader	Language
	Linguistics
	Verbal Communication
Narrower	Consonants
	Morphemes
	Phonemes
	Syllables
	Vowels
	Words (Phonetic Units)

Phonics
Broader	Curriculum
	Language Arts Education
Related	Reading Education

Phonology
Broader	Grammar
	Language
	Linguistics
	Verbal Communication
Related	Phonemes

Phosphatases
Broader	Enzymes
Narrower	Acid Phosphatases
Related	Esterases
	Hydroxylases

Phosphatides
Used For	Phospholipids
Broader	Acids
	Fatty Acids
	Lipids

Phospholipids
Use	Phosphatides

Phosphorus
Broader	Chemical Elements
	Nonmetallic Elements

Phosphorylases
Broader	Enzymes

Photic Threshold
Use	Illumination
	Visual Thresholds

Photographic Art
Broader	Art
	Arts
Related	Motion Pictures (Entertainment)

Photographs
Broader	Audiovisual Communications Media
	Communications Media

Photopic Stimulation
Broader	Illumination
	Visual Stimulation
Related	Scotopic Stimulation

Photoreceptors
Broader	Nerve Endings
	Nervous System
	Neural Receptors
Narrower	Cones (Eye)
	Rods (Eye)

Phrases
Broader	Language
	Linguistics
	Verbal Communication

Phrenic Nerve
Use	Spinal Nerves

Phylogenesis
Related	Biology
	Botany

Physical Agility
Used For	Agility (Physical)
Broader	Motor Processes
Narrower	Physical Dexterity
Related	Motor Coordination

Physical Attractiveness
Related	Facial Features
	Interpersonal Attraction

Physical Development
Used For	Physical Growth
Narrower	Motor Development
	Prenatal Development
	Psychomotor Development
	Sexual Development
	Speech Development
Related	Adolescent Development
	Age Differences
	Childhood Development
	Delayed Development
	Development/
	Developmental Age Groups
	Developmental Differences
	Developmental Stages
	Early Childhood Development
	Emotional Development
	Human Development/
	Infant Development
	Neonatal Development
	Perceptual Development
	Physical Maturity
	Precocious Development
	Psychogenesis
	Sex Linked Developmental Differences

Physical Dexterity
Used For	Dexterity (Physical)
Broader	Motor Processes
	Perceptual Motor Coordination
	Perceptual Motor Processes
	Physical Agility

Physical Divisions (Geographic)
Use	Geography

Physical Education
Broader	Curriculum

Physical Endurance
Broader	Endurance
Related	Physical Fitness
	Physical Strength
	Physiological Stress

Physical Exercise
Use	Exercise

Physical Fitness
Related	Exercise
	Physical Endurance
	Physical Strength

Physical Geography
Use   Geography

Physical Growth
Use   Physical Development

Physical Handicaps (Attit Toward)
Broader   Handicapped (Attitudes Toward)

Physical Maturity
Used For   Maturity (Physical)
Related   Physical Development

Physical Strength
Used For   Strength (Physical)
Related   Physical Endurance
            Physical Fitness

Physical Therapists
Broader   Medical Personnel
            Paramedical Personnel
            Paraprofessional Personnel
Related   Therapists/

Physical Therapy
Used For   Physiotherapy
Broader   Paramedical Sciences
Related   Treatment/

Physical Trauma
Use   Injuries

Physical Treatment Methods
Used For   Treatment Methods (Physical)
Narrower   Acupuncture
            Adrenalectomy
            Amputation
            Artificial Respiration
            Autopsy
            Blood Transfusion
            Castration
            Catheterization
            Colostomy
            Decerebration
            Decortication (Brain)
            Dental Surgery
            Dental Treatment
            Dialysis
            Diuresis
            Endocrine Gland Surgery
            Heart Surgery
            Hemispherectomy
            Hemodialysis
            Hypophysectomy
            Hysterectomy
            Immunization
            Induced Abortion
            Male Castration
            Mastectomy
            Medical Treatment (General)
            Neurosurgery
            Organ Transplantation
            Ovariectomy

Physical Treatment Methods — (Continued)
Narrower
            Pancreatectomy
            Pinealectomy
            Plastic Surgery
            Psychosurgery
            Pyramidotomy
            Radiation Therapy
            Surgery
            Sympathectomy
            Thalamotomy
            Thymectomy
            Thyroidectomy
            Tractotomy
            Vagotomy
Related   Treatment/

Physically Handicapped
Used For   Crippled
            Orthopedically Handicapped
            Special Education (Phys Handicaps)
Broader   Handicapped
Narrower   Amputees
            Health Impaired

Physically Ill Patients
Use   Patients

Physicians
Used For   Doctors
Broader   Medical Personnel
Narrower   Family Physicians
            General Practitioners
            Gynecologists
            Internists
            Neurologists
            Pathologists
            Pediatricians
            Psychiatrists
            Surgeons
Related   Clinicians

Physicists
Related   Aerospace Personnel
            Mathematicians
            Personnel/
            Scientists/

Physics
Broader   Sciences

Physiological Aging
Used For   Aging (Physiological)
            Longevity
Related   Aged
            Geriatric Psychotherapy
            Geriatrics
            Senile Dementia

Physiological Arousal
Used For   Arousal (Physiological)

Physiological Arousal — (Continued)
- Related   Brain Stimulation
-       Consciousness States

Physiological Correlates
- Related   Physiological Stress
-       Symptoms

Physiological Psychology
- Broader   Psychology
-       Sciences
-       Social Sciences
- Narrower   Neuropsychology

Physiological Stress
- Broader   Stress
- Related   Acceleration Effects
-       Decompression Effects
-       Deprivation
-       Environmental Effects
-       Environmental Stress
-       Physical Endurance
-       Physiological Correlates
-       Pollution
-       Thermal Acclimatization

Physiology/
- Related   Anatomy/
-       Appetite
-       Biosynthesis
-       Body Fluids
-       Body Temperature
-       Calcification
-       Cells (Biology)
-       Digestion
-       Electrophysiology
-       Energy Expenditure
-       Equilibrium
-       Excretion
-       Genetics/
-       Histology
-       Homeostasis
-       Metabolic Rates
-       Metabolism
-       Neurophysiology
-       Nutrition
-       Oxygenation
-       Psychophysiology
-       Reflexes
-       Salivation
-       Secretion (Gland)
-       Sexual Reproduction
-       Tissues (Body)

Physiotherapy
- Use   Physical Therapy

Physique
- Narrower   Body Height
-       Body Weight
-       Obesity
-       Underweight

Physique — (Continued)
- Related   Posture
-       Somatotypes

Physostigmine
- Used For   Eserine
- Broader   Alkaloids
-       Amines
-       Cholinergic Drugs
-       Cholinesterase Inhibitors
-       Cholinomimetic Drugs

Piaget (Jean)

Piagetian Tasks
- Related   Measurement/

Piano
- Use   Musical Instruments

Pica
- Broader   Mania
- Related   Lead Poisoning
-       Toxicomania

Picketing
- Use   Social Demonstrations

Picks Disease
- Broader   Brain Disorders
-       Central Nervous System Disorders
-       Nervous System Disorders
-       Organic Brain Syndromes
-       Presenile Dementia
-       Syndromes
- Related   Alzheimers Disease
-       Genetic Disorders
-       Mental Disorders/

Picrotoxin
- Broader   Analeptic Drugs
-       CNS Stimulating Drugs

Pigeons
- Broader   Birds
-       Vertebrates

Pigments
- Narrower   Hemoglobin
-       Melanin

Pigs
- Broader   Mammals
-       Vertebrates

Pilocarpine
- Broader   Alkaloids
-       Cholinergic Drugs
-       Cholinomimetic Drugs

Pilots (Aircraft)
- Use   Aircraft Pilots

Pimozide
- Broader   Tranquilizing Drugs

Pineal Body
Used For	Body (Pineal)
Broader	Endocrine Glands
	Endocrine System
	Glands
Related	Melatonin

Pinealectomy
Broader	Endocrine Gland Surgery
	Physical Treatment Methods
	Surgery

Pipradrol
Broader	Antidepressant Drugs
	CNS Affecting Drugs
	CNS Stimulating Drugs

Pitch (Frequency)
Used For	Tone (Frequency)
Broader	Auditory Stimulation
	Perceptual Stimulation
Narrower	Speech Pitch
	Ultrasound

Pitch Discrimination
Broader	Auditory Discrimination
	Auditory Perception
	Pitch Perception

Pitch Perception
Broader	Auditory Perception
Narrower	Pitch Discrimination

Pituitary Disorders
Used For	Hypophysis Disorders
Broader	Endocrine Disorders
Narrower	Hypopituitarism
Related	Adrenal Gland Disorders
	Endocrine Sexual Disorders
	Thyroid Disorders

Pituitary Dwarfism
Use	Hypopituitarism

Pituitary Gland
Broader	Endocrine Glands
	Endocrine System
	Glands
Narrower	Hypothalamo Hypophyseal System

Pituitary Gland Surgery
Use	Hypophysectomy

Pituitary Hormones
Broader	Hormones
Narrower	Corticotropin
	Oxytocin
	Posterior Pituitary Hormones
	Somatotropin
	Thyrotropin
	Vasopressin
Related	Gonadotropic Hormones

PK (Parapsychology)
Use	Psychokinesis

PKU (Hereditary Disorder)
Use	Phenylketonuria

Place Disorientation
Used For	Disorientation (Place)
Broader	Consciousness Disturbances

Placebo
Related	Drugs/
	Psychosomatic Disorders

Placement (Personnel)
Use	Personnel Placement

Placenta
Related	Pregnancy
	Uterus

Placental Hormones
Broader	Hormones
Related	Gonadotropic Hormones

Planarians
Broader	Invertebrates
	Worms

Planning (Management)
Use	Management Planning

Plasma (Blood)
Use	Blood Plasma

Plastic Surgery
Broader	Physical Treatment Methods
	Surgery

Platelets (Blood)
Use	Blood Platelets

Play
Use	Recreation

Play (Animal)
Use	Animal Play

Play Development (Childhood)
Use	Childhood Play Development

Play Therapy
Broader	Child Psychotherapy
	Psychotherapy

Playgrounds
Broader	Recreation Areas
Related	School Facilities

Pleasure
Used For	Enjoyment
Broader	Emotional States
Related	Euphoria
	Happiness

Plethysmography
Broader	Diagnosis
	Medical Diagnosis
Narrower	Electroplethysmography

Pneumoencephalography
Used For	Air Encephalography
	Encephalography (Air)
Broader	Diagnosis
	Encephalography
	Medical Diagnosis
	Roentgenography

Pneumonia
Broader	Lung Disorders
	Respiratory Tract Disorders
Related	Bacterial Disorders
	Viral Disorders

Poetry
Broader	Arts
	Literature

Point Biserial Correlation
Broader	Statistical Correlation

Poisoning
Use	Toxic Disorders

Poisons
Used For	Toxins
Related	Insecticides

Poisson Distribution
Use	Skewed Distribution

Poland

Police Personnel
Broader	Government Personnel
	Law Enforcement Personnel

Policy Making (Foreign)
Use	Foreign Policy Making

Policy Making (Government)
Use	Government Policy Making

Poliomyelitis
Used For	Infantile Paralysis
	Paralysis (Infantile)
Broader	Central Nervous System Disorders
	Infectious Disorders
	Myelitis
	Nervous System Disorders
	Viral Disorders
Related	Musculoskeletal Disorders
	Paralysis
	Respiratory Tract Disorders

Political Anarchy
Broader	Radical Movements

Political Assassination
Used For	Assassination (Political)

Political Attitudes
Broader	Politics
Narrower	Nationalism
	Political Conservatism

Political Attitudes — (Continued)
Narrower	Political Liberalism
	Political Radicalism
Related	Attitudes/
	Voting Behavior

Political Campaigns
Used For	Campaigns (Political)
Broader	Political Processes
	Politics
Related	Political Candidates
	Political Elections
	Political Issues
	Political Parties

Political Candidates
Used For	Candidates (Political)
Broader	Politics
Related	Political Campaigns
	Political Elections

Political Conservatism
Used For	Conservatism (Political)
	Traditionalism
Broader	Political Attitudes
Related	Conservatism

Political Divisions (Geographic)
Use	Geography

Political Economic Systems
Narrower	Capitalism
	Communism
	Democracy
	Facism
	Socialism
	Totalitarianism
Related	Economy
	Government

Political Elections
Used For	Elections (Political)
Broader	Political Processes
	Politics
Related	Political Campaigns
	Political Candidates
	Political Parties
	Voting Behavior

Political Issues
Broader	Politics
Related	Political Campaigns
	Voting Behavior

Political Liberalism
Used For	Liberalism (Political)
Broader	Political Attitudes
Related	Liberalism

Political Parties
Used For	Democratic Party
	Independent Party (Political)

Political Parties — (Continued)
Used For
               Parties (Political)
               Republican Party
Broader   Politics
Related   Political Campaigns
               Political Elections

Political Processes
Used For   Processes (Political)
Broader   Politics
Narrower   Political Campaigns
               Political Elections
               Voting Behavior
Related   Political Revolution
               Social Processes

Political Radicalism
Used For   Radicalism (Political)
Broader   Political Attitudes

Political Revolution
Used For   Revolutions (Political)
Broader   Radical Movements
Related   Political Processes

Politics
Narrower   Political Attitudes
               Political Campaigns
               Political Candidates
               Political Elections
               Political Issues
               Political Parties
               Political Processes
               Voting Behavior
Related   Government

Pollution
Broader   Ecological Factors
Related   Atmospheric Conditions
               Carcinogens
               Ecology
               Noise Effects
               Physiological Stress
               Temperature Effects

Polygamy
Broader   Family Structure
               Marriage

Polygraphs
Broader   Apparatus

Polyneuritis
Broader   Nervous System Disorders
               Neuritis
               Peripheral Nerve Disorders

Polyradiculoneuritis
Use   Radiculitis

Pons
Broader   Brain
               Brain Stem

Pons — (Continued)
Broader
               Central Nervous System
               Nervous System

Popularity
Use   Social Approval

Population
Narrower   Overpopulation
               Population (Statistics)
Related   Demographic Characteristics

Population (Statistics)
Used For   Groups (Statistics)
Broader   Population
Narrower   Statistical Sample Parameters
               Statistical Samples
Related   Central Tendency Measures
               Experimental Design
               Experimentation/
               Measurement/
               Sampling (Experimental)
               Statistical Analysis
               Statistical Reliability
               Statistical Variables

Population Characteristics
Use   Demographic Characteristics

Population Control
Use   Birth Control

Population Genetics
Related   Genetics/

Pornography
Related   Psychosexual Behavior
               Sexual Deviations

Porphyria
Broader   Blood and Lymphatic Disorders
               Genetic Disorders
               Metabolism Disorders
Related   Mental Disorders/

Porpoises
Broader   Mammals
               Vertebrates
Related   Dolphins

Porteus Maze Test
(See)   Intelligence Measures

Positive Reinforcement
Broader   Reinforcement
Narrower   Praise

Positive Transfer
Broader   Transfer (Learning)

Positivism
Broader   Personality Traits
Related   Optimism

Posterior Pituitary Hormones
Broader   Hormones
        Pituitary Hormones
Narrower   Oxytocin
        Vasopressin

Postganglionic Autonomic Fibers
Use   Autonomic Ganglia

Postgraduate Students
Broader   College Students
        Students
Related   Graduate Students

Postgraduate Training
Broader   Higher Education
Narrower   Clinical Psychology Grad Train-
        ing
        Clinical Psychology Internship
        Medical Internship
        Medical Residency

Postnatal Period
Related   Lactation
        Pregnancy

Postpartum Depression
Broader   Depression (Emotion)

Postsurgical Complications (Physical
Used For   Surgical Complications
Related   Recovery (Disorders)
        Relapse (Disorders)
        Surgery

Posttesting
Related   Measurement/
        Testing Methods

Posttreatment Followup
Used For   Catamnesis
        Followup (Posttreatment)
Related   Aftercare
        Treatment/

Posture
Related   Motor Processes
        Physique

Potassium
Broader   Chemical Elements
        Metallic Elements
Narrower   Potassium Ions

Potassium Bromide
Broader   Analgesic Drugs
        Antiepileptic Drugs
        Bromides
        Hypnotic Drugs
        Sedatives

Potassium Ions
Broader   Chemical Elements
        Electrolytes
        Metallic Elements
        Potassium

Potential (Achievement)
Use   Achievement Potential

Potential Dropouts
Broader   Dropouts

Potentials (Evoked)
Use   Evoked Potentials

Potentiation (Drugs)
Use   Drug Potentiation

Poverty
Related   Disadvantaged
        Income (Economic)
        Lower Income Level
        Socioeconomic Status

Poverty Areas
Used For   Slums
Broader   Environment
        Social Environments
Related   Cultural Deprivation
        Ghettoes

Power

Broader   Social Influences

Practice
Used For   Experience (Practice)
Narrower   Distributed Practice
        Massed Practice
Related   Experiences (Events)
        Familiarity
        Practice Effects

Practice Effects
Related   Practice

Pragmatism
Broader   Philosophies

Praise
Broader   Positive Reinforcement
        Reinforcement
        Social Behavior
        Social Reinforcement
        Verbal Reinforcement

Prayer
Broader   Religious Practices
Related   Meditation

Praying Mantis
Use   Mantis

Precocious Development
Broader   Developmental Differences
Related   Developmental Age Groups
        Physical Development
        Psychogenesis

Precognition
Broader   Clairvoyance
        Extrasensory Perception

Precognition — (Continued)
Broader
        Parapsychological Phenomena
        Parapsychology

Predictability (Measurement)
Broader   Statistical Analysis
        Statistical Measurement
Related   Confidence Limits (Statistics)
        Hypothesis Testing
        Prediction
        Prediction Errors
        Probability

Prediction
Narrower Occupational Success Prediction
Related   Predictability (Measurement)
        Prediction Errors
        Predictive Validity
        Prognosis

Prediction Errors
Broader   Errors
Narrower Type I Errors
        Type II Errors
Related   Consistency (Measurement)
        Hypothesis Testing
        Measurement/
        Predictability (Measurement)
        Prediction
        Statistical Analysis
        Statistical Reliability
        Statistical Validity
        Statistical Variables

Predictive Validity
Broader   Statistical Validity
Related   Prediction

Predisposition
Related   Disorders/
        Genetics/
        Mental Disorders/
        Personality/
        Response Bias

Prednisolone
Broader   Adrenal Cortex Hormones
        Corticosteroids
        Hormones
        Steroids

Preference Measures
Used For Inventories (Preference)
        Scales (Preference)
        Surveys (Preference)
Related   Measurement/
        Preferences
Identifier Kuder Preference Record
        Least Preferred Coworker Scale

Preferences
Narrower Aesthetic Preferences
        Food Preferences
        Occupational Preference
Related   Preference Measures
        Preferred Rewards

Preferences (Aesthetic)
Use   Aesthetic Preferences

Preferences (Food)
Use   Food Preferences

Preferences (Occupational)
Use   Occupational Preference

Preferred Rewards
Broader   Reinforcement
        Rewards
Related   Preferences

Preganglionic Autonomic Fibers
Use   Autonomic Ganglia

Pregnancy
Used For Gestation
Related   Birth
        Fertilization
        Placenta
        Postnatal Period
        Sexual Reproduction

Pregnancy (False)
Use   Pseudocyesis

Prehension
Use   Motor Development

Prejudice
Broader   Social Influences
Narrower Religious Prejudices
Related   Antisemitism
        Attitudes/
        Race Attitudes
        Racism

Preliminary Scholastic Aptitude Test
Identifier Coll Ent Exam Bd Scholastic
        Apt Test

Premarital Counseling
Related   Counseling/
        Psychotherapeutic Counseling

Premarital Intercourse
Broader   Psychosexual Behavior
        Sexual Intercourse (Human)
Related   Promiscuity
        Social Dating
        Virginity

Premature Birth
Broader   Birth

Premature Ejaculation
Broader   Male Orgasm
        Orgasm

Premature Ejaculation — (Continued)
Broader
     Psychosexual Behavior
     Sexual Function Disturbances
   Related   Impotence

Premenstrual Tension
   Used For   Tension (Premenstrual)
   Broader   Endocrine Disorders
     Endocrine Sexual Disorders
     Genital Disorders
     Gynecological Disorders
     Menstrual Disorders
     Urogenital Disorders
   Related   Psychosomatic Disorders

Prenatal Development
   Broader   Physical Development
   Narrower   Embryo
     Fetus
     Prenatal Developmental Stages
     Zygote
   Related   Psychogenesis

Prenatal Developmental Stages
   Broader   Developmental Stages
     Prenatal Development
   Narrower   Embryo
     Fetus
     Zygote

Preschool Age Children
   Used For   Early Childhood
   Broader   Children
     Developmental Age Groups
   Related   Childhood Development

Preschool Education
   Related   Education/
     Project Head Start

Presenile Dementia
   Used For   Dementia (Presenile)
   Broader   Brain Disorders
     Central Nervous System Disorders
     Nervous System Disorders
     Organic Brain Syndromes
     Syndromes
   Narrower   Alzheimers Disease
     Picks Disease
   Related   Mental Disorders/
     Senile Dementia

Presentation Methods
   Use   Stimulus Presentation Methods

Presentation Modes
   Use   Stimulus Presentation Methods

Pressoreceptors
   Use   Baroreceptors

Pressors (Drugs)
   Use   Vasoconstrictor Drugs

Pressure (Barometric)
   Use   Atmospheric Conditions

Pressure (Blood)
   Use   Blood Pressure

Pressure (Diastolic)
   Use   Diastolic Pressure

Pressure (Systolic)
   Use   Systolic Pressure

Pressure Sensation
   Related   Somesthetic Perception

Pretesting
   Related   Measurement/
     Testing Methods

Prevention/
   Related   Accident Prevention
     Fire Prevention
     Preventive Medicine
     Primary Mental Health Prevention
     Safety
     Suicide Prevention

Preventive Medicine
   Related   Health
     Prevention/

Pride
   Related   Emotions/

Priests
   Broader   Clergy
     Religious Personnel
   Related   Chaplains
     Missionaries
     Monks

Primacy Effect
   Related   Learning/
     Recency Effect

Primary Mental Health Prevention
   Related   Mental Health
     Mental Health Programs
     Prevention/

Primary Reinforcement
   Broader   Reinforcement

Primary School Students
   Broader   Elementary School Students
     Students

Primary Schools
   Use   Elementary Schools

Primates (Nonhuman)
   Used For   Apes
   Broader   Mammals
     Vertebrates
   Narrower   Baboons
     Chimpanzees

Primates (Nonhuman) — (Continued)
Narrower	Gorillas
	Monkeys

Primidone
Broader	Anticonvulsive Drugs
	Antiepileptic Drugs
Related	Barbiturates

Printed Communications Media
Broader	Communications Media
Narrower	Books
	Magazines
	Newspapers

Printing (Handwriting)
Broader	Handwriting
	Language
	Verbal Communication
	Written Language

Prismatic Stimulation
Broader	Perceptual Stimulation
	Stimulation
	Visual Stimulation
Related	Color Perception

Prison Personnel
Used For	Personnel (Prison)
Broader	Government Personnel
	Law Enforcement Personnel
Related	Attendants (Institutions)

Prisoners
Used For	Inmates (Prison)
Narrower	Prisoners of War

Prisoners Dilemma Game
Broader	Games
Related	Entrapment Games
	Game Theory
	Non Zero Sum Games

Prisoners of War
Broader	Prisoners

Prisons
Used For	Jails
	Penitentiaries
Broader	Correctional Institutions
Related	Reformatories

Privacy
Related	Social Behavior

Private School Education
Used For	Parochial School Education
Related	Education/

Privileged Communication
Used For	Communication (Privileged)
	Confidentiality of Information

Proactive Inhibition
Used For	Inhibition (Proactive)
Broader	Interference (Learning)

Probability
Broader	Chance (Fortune)
Narrower	Binomial Distribution
	Response Probability
	Statistical Probability
Related	Hypothesis Testing
	Predictability (Measurement)
	Probability

Probability Learning
Related	Learning/
	Probability

Probation
Broader	Legal Processes
Related	Parole

Probation Officers
Broader	Government Personnel
	Law Enforcement Personnel
Related	Parole Officers

Problem Drinking
Broader	Alcohol Drinking Patterns
Related	Alcohol Intoxication
	Alcoholism

Problem Solving
Used For	Individual Problem Solving
Broader	Cognitive Processes
Narrower	Anagram Problem Solving
	Group Problem Solving
Related	Reasoning

Procaine
Use	Novocaine

Process Psychosis
Used For	Process Schizophrenia
Broader	Psychosis

Process Schizophrenia
Use	Process Psychosis
	Schizophrenia

Processes (Associative)
Use	Associative Processes

Processes (Cognitive)
Use	Cognitive Processes

Processes (Motor)
Use	Motor Processes

Processes (Political)
Use	Political Processes·

Processes (Social)
Use	Social Processes

Prochlorperazine
Broader	Antiemetic Drugs
	Antipsychotic Drugs
	Antischizophrenic Drugs
	Neuroleptic Drugs
	Phenothiazine Derivatives
	Tranquilizing Drugs

Productivity (Employee)
   Use   Employee Productivity

Professional Certification
   Used For   Certification (Professional)
   Related   Professional Licensing

Professional Communication
   Use   Scientific Communication

Professional Consultation
   Used For   Consultation (Professional)
   Narrower   Mental Health Consultation

Professional Contribution
   Used For   Contribution (Professional)
            Support (For Theories)

Professional Criticism
   Used For   Criticism (Professional)

Professional Criticism Reply
   Used For   Rebuttal
            Reply (To Professional Criticism)

Professional Ethics
   Broader   Ethics
   Related   Euthanasia

Professional Licensing
   Used For   Licensing (Professional)
   Related   Professional Certification

Professional Meetings And Symposia
   Used For   Symposia
   Broader   Scientific Communication

Professional Newsletters
   Use   Scientific Communication

Professional Organizations
   Broader   Organizations

Professional Referral
   Used For   Referral (Professional)

Professional Standards
   Used For   Standards (Professional)

Professors
   Use   College Teachers

Profiles (Measurement)
   Related   Measurement/

Profoundly Mentally Retarded
   Used For   Idiots
   Broader   Handicapped
            Mentally Retarded

Progesterone
   Broader   Hormones
            Sex Hormones

Prognosis
   Related   Diagnosis
            Disorders/
            Medical Diagnosis
            Mental Disorders/

Prognosis — (Continued)
   Related
            Patient History
            Prediction
            Psychodiagnosis

Program Evaluation (Educational)
   Use   Educational Program Evaluation

Program Evaluation (Mental Health)
   Use   Mental Health Program Evaluation

Program Planning (Educational)
   Use   Educational Program Planning

Programed Instruction
   Used For   Instruction (Programed)
            Learning (Programed)
            Programed Learning
            Programed Teaching
            Teaching (Programed)
   Broader   Teaching
            Teaching Methods
   Related   Computer Assisted Instruction
            Individualized Instruction
            Programed Textbooks
            Teaching Machines

Programed Learning
   Use   Programed Instruction

Programed Teaching
   Use   Programed Instruction

Programed Textbooks
   Used For   Textbooks (Programed)
   Broader   Instructional Media
            Teaching
   Related   Programed Instruction

Programing (Computer)
   Use   Computer Software

Programing Languages (Computer)
   Use   Computer Programing Languages

Programs (Government)
   Use   Government Programs

Programs (Mental Health)
   Use   Mental Health Programs

Project Follow Through
   Broader   Educational Programs
            Government Programs
   Related   Government

Project Head Start
   Used For   Head Start
   Broader   Educational Programs
            Government Programs
   Related   Government
            Preschool Education
            School Readiness

Projection (Defense Mechanism)
Broader	Defense Mechanisms

Projective Personality Measures
Broader	Personality Measures
	Projective Techniques
Narrower	Human Figures Drawing
Identifier	Bender Gestalt Test
	Blacky Pictures Test
	Childrens Apperception Test
	Color Pyramid Test
	Franck Drawing Completion Test
	Holtzman Inkblot Technique
	Onomatopoeia and Images Test
	Rorschach Test
	Rosenzweig Picture Frustration Study
	Rotter Incomplete Sentences Blank
	Szondi Test
	Thematic Apperception Test
	Zulliger Z Test

Projective Techniques
Used For	Projective Tests
Narrower	Human Figures Drawing
(Identifier)	Incomplete Man Test
Narrower	Projective Personality Measures
(Identifier)	Bender Gestalt Test
	Blacky Pictures Test
	Childrens Apperception Test
	Color Pyramid Test
	Franck Drawing Completion Test
	Holtzman Inkblot Technique
	Onomatopoeia And Images Test
	Rorschach Test
	Rosenzweig Picture Frustration Study
	Rotter Incomplete Sentences Blank
	Szondi Test
	Thematic Apperception Test
	Zulliger Z Test

Projective Testing Technique
Used For	Technique (Projective Testing)
Related	Measurement/

Projective Tests
Use	Projective Techniques

Prolactin
Broader	Gonadotropic Hormones
	Hormones

Prolixin
Use	Fluphenazine

Promazine
Broader	Antipsychotic Drugs
	Antischizophrenic Drugs
	Neuroleptic Drugs
	Phenothiazine Derivatives
	Tranquilizing Drugs

Promethazine
Broader	Antiemetic Drugs
	Antihistaminic Drugs
	Sedatives

Promiscuity
Used For	Sexual Delinquency
Broader	Psychosexual Behavior
Narrower	Prostitution
Related	Extramarital Intercourse
	Hypersexuality
	Premarital Intercourse

Pronouns
Broader	Form Classes (Language)
	Grammar
	Language
	Linguistics
	Verbal Communication

Pronunciation
Broader	Speech Characteristics
	Verbal Communication
Related	Articulation (Speech)

Propaganda
Broader	Social Influences

Propranolol
Broader	Adrenergic Blocking Drugs
	Alcohols

Proprioceptors
Broader	Nerve Endings
	Nervous System
	Neural Receptors

Prose
Broader	Arts
	Literature
Narrower	Autobiography
	Biography

Proserine
Use	Neostigmine

Prostate
Broader	Male Genitalia
	Urogenital System

Prostheses
Used For	Artificial Limbs
Broader	Medical Therapeutic Devices
Related	Amputation
	Silicones

Prostitution
Broader	Promiscuity
	Psychosexual Behavior

Proteases
Broader	Enzymes
Narrower	Proteinases

Protein Deficiency Disorders
Broader	Nutritional Deficiencies
Narrower	Kwashiorkor

Protein Metabolism
Broader	Metabolism

Protein Sensitization
Use	Anaphylactic Shock

Proteinases
Broader	Enzymes
	Proteases

Proteins
Narrower	Albumins
	Antibodies
	Blood Proteins
	Gamma Globulin
	Globulins
	Hemoglobin
	Immunoglobulins
	Serum Albumin
	Taraxein
Related	Amino Acids
	Drugs/
	Enzymes
	Lipoproteins
	Peptides

Proteins (Blood)
Use	Blood Proteins

Protest (Student)
Use	Student Activism

Protestantism
Broader	Christianity
	Religious Affiliation
	Religious Beliefs
Narrower	Fundamentalism

Protozoa
Broader	Invertebrates

Pruritus
Used For	Itching
Broader	Skin Disorders
	Symptoms
Related	Scratching

Pseudocyesis
Used For	False Pregnancy
	Pregnancy (False)
	Pseudopregnancy
Broader	Amenorrhea
	Genital Disorders
	Gynecological Disorders
	Menstrual Disorders
	Psychosomatic Disorders
	Urogenital Disorders

Pseudoneurotic Schizophrenia
Broader	Psychosis
	Schizophrenia
Related	Neurosis

Pseudopregnancy
Use	Pseudocyesis

Pseudopsychopathic Schizophrenia
Broader	Psychosis
	Schizophrenia
Related	Psychopathy

Psilocybin
Broader	Hallucinogenic Drugs

Psychedelic Drugs
Narrower	Lysergic Acid Diethylamide
Related	Drugs/
	Hallucinogenic Drugs
	Psychotomimetic Drugs

Psychedelic Experiences
Related	Drug Effects

Psychiatric Aides
Broader	Medical Personnel
	Mental Health Personnel
	Paramedical Personnel
	Paraprofessional Personnel
	Psychiatric Hospital Staff
Related	Psychiatric Social Workers

Psychiatric Classification (Process)
Use	Psychodiagnosis

Psychiatric Classifications (Taxon)
Use	Psychodiagnostic Typologies

Psychiatric Clinics
Used For	Outpatient Psychiatric Clinics
Broader	Clinics
	Treatment Facilities
Related	Child Guidance Clinics
	Community Mental Health Centers
	Hospitals
	Mental Health Programs
	Outpatient Treatment
	Walk In Clinics

Psychiatric Disorders
Use	Mental Disorders/

Psychiatric History
Use	Patient History

Psychiatric Hospital Admission
Used For	Admission (Psychiatric Hospital)
Broader	Hospital Admission
	Hospitalization
	Institutionalization
	Psychiatric Hospitalization
Narrower	Psychiatric Hospital Readmission
Related	Hospital Discharge

Psychiatric Hospital Programs
Narrower	Therapeutic Community
Related	Halfway Houses
	Token Economy Programs

Psychiatric Hospital Readmission
Used For	Readmission (Psychiatric Hospital)
Broader	Hospital Admission
	Hospitalization
	Institutionalization
	Psychiatric Hospital Admission
	Psychiatric Hospitalization
Related	Hospital Discharge

Psychiatric Hospital Staff
Broader	Medical Personnel
	Mental Health Personnel
Narrower	Psychiatric Aides
Related	Attendants (Institutions)
	Occupational Therapists
	Paramedical Personnel
	Psychiatric Nurses
	Psychiatrists

Psychiatric Hospitalization
Broader	Hospitalization
	Institutionalization
Narrower	Commitment (Psychiatric)
	Psychiatric Hospital Admission
	Psychiatric Hospital Readmission
Related	Hospital Admission
	Hospital Discharge

Psychiatric Hospitals
Used For	Asylums
	General Hospital Psychiatric Units
	Mental Hospitals
	State Hospitals
Broader	Hospitals
	Residential Care Institutions
	Treatment Facilities
Related	Halfway Houses
	Sanatoriums

Psychiatric Nurses
Broader	Medical Personnel
	Mental Health Personnel
	Nurses
Related	Psychiatric Hospital Staff

Psychiatric Patients
Broader	Patients

Psychiatric Social Workers
Broader	Mental Health Personnel
	Social Workers
Related	Psychiatric Aides

Psychiatric Training
Used For	Training (Psychiatric)

Psychiatric Training — (Continued)
Broader	Clinical Methods Training
	Graduate Education
	Higher Education
	Medical Education
Related	Psychoanalytic Training
	Psychotherapy Training

Psychiatrists
Used For	Neuropsychiatrists
Broader	Medical Personnel
	Mental Health Personnel
	Physicians
Related	Clinicians
	Hypnotherapists
	Psychiatric Hospital Staff
	Psychoanalysts
	Psychologists
	Psychotherapists

Psychiatry
Broader	Medical Sciences
	Sciences
Narrower	Child Psychiatry
	Community Psychiatry
	Forensic Psychiatry
	Neuropsychiatry
	Orthopsychiatry
	Social Psychiatry
	Transcultural Psychiatry

Psychic Energizers
Narrower	Imipramine
	Iproniazid
	Isocarboxazid
Related	Antidepressant Drugs
	Drugs/

Psychoanalysis
Used For	Psychoanalytic Therapy
Broader	Psychotherapy
Narrower	Dream Analysis
Related	Analysis/
	Hypnotherapy
	Psychotherapeutic Processes

Psychoanalysts
Used For	Analysts
Broader	Mental Health Personnel
	Psychotherapists
Related	Hypnotherapists
	Psychiatrists

Psychoanalytic Interpretation
Used For	Interpretation (Psychoanalytic)
Related	Freudian Psychoanalytic School
	Psychoanalytic Theory

Psychoanalytic Personality Factors
Used For	Personality Factors (Psychoanalytic)
Narrower	Conscience
	Conscious (Personality Factors)

Psychoanalytic Personality Factors — (Continued)
Narrower
        Ego
        Electra Complex
        Id
        Libido
        Oedipal Complex
        Subconscious
        Superego
        Unconscious (Personality Factor)
Related   Personality/

Psychoanalytic School (Freudian)
Use   Freudian Psychoanalytic School

Psychoanalytic Theory
Related   Freudian Psychoanalytic School
        Psychoanalytic Interpretation
        Theories/

Psychoanalytic Therapy
Use   Psychoanalysis

Psychoanalytic Training
Used For   Training (Psychoanalytic)
Broader   Clinical Methods Training
Related   Psychiatric Training

Psychodiagnosis
Used For   Classificat (Psychodiagnostic
        Proc)
        Classification (Psychiatric Proc-
        ess)
        Clinical Judgment (Psychodiag-
        nosis)
        Psychiatric Classification (Proc-
        ess)
        Psychodiagnostic Classificat
        (Proc)
Broader   Diagnosis
Narrower   Psychodiagnostic Interview
Related   Computer Assisted Diagnosis
        Differential Diagnosis
        Patient History
        Prognosis
        Psychodiagnostic Typologies

Psychodiagnostic Classificat (Proc)
Use   Psychodiagnosis

Psychodiagnostic Classificat (Taxon)
Use   Psychodiagnostic Typologies

Psychodiagnostic Interview
Broader   Diagnosis
        Interpersonal Communication
        Interpersonal Interaction
        Interviews
        Psychodiagnosis
        Social Behavior
        Social Interaction

Psychodiagnostic Typologies
Used For   Classificat (Psychiatric Taxono-
        mies)
        Classificat (Psychodiagnost Tax-
        ono)
        Psychiatric Classifications (Tax-
        on)
        Psychodiagnostic Classificat
        (Taxon)
        Typologies (Psychodiagnostic)
Related   Clinical Judgment (Not Diagno-
        sis)
        Psychodiagnosis

Psychodrama
Broader   Psychotherapeutic Techniques
        Psychotherapy
Related   Group Psychotherapy

Psychodynamics

Used For   Psychological Correlates
Related   Personality/
        Social Behavior
        Social Interaction

Psychogenesis
Narrower   Childhood Play Development
        Cognitive Development
        Emotional Development
        Intellectual Development
        Language Development
        Moral Development
        Perceptual Development
        Personality Development
        Psychomotor Development
        Psychosocial Development
        Speech Development
Related   Adolescent Development
        Age Differences
        Childhood Development
        Delayed Development
        Development/
        Developmental Age Groups
        Developmental Differences
        Developmental Stages
        Early Childhood Development
        Human Development/
        Infant Development
        Neonatal Development
        Physical Development
        Precocious Development
        Prenatal Development
        Sex Linked Developmental Dif-
        ferences
        Sexual Development

Psychogenic Pain
Used For   Pain (Psychogenic)

Psychogenic Pain — (Continued)
Broader	Pain
	Psychosomatic Disorders
	Symptoms

Psychokinesis
Used For	PK (Parapsychology)
	Telekinesis
Broader	Extrasensory Perception
	Parapsychological Phenomena
	Parapsychology

Psycholinguistics
Broader	Language
	Linguistics
	Verbal Communication
Related	Ethnolinguistics

Psychological Correlates
Use	Psychodynamics

Psychological Endurance
Broader	Endurance
Related	Psychological Stress
	Stress Reactions

Psychological Screening Inventory
(See)	Nonprojective Personality Measures
	Personality Measures
	Selection Tests

Psychological Stress
Broader	Stress
Related	Deprivation
	Psychological Endurance
	Stress Reactions

Psychological Terminology
Used For	Nomenclature (Psychological)
	Terminology (Psychological)
Broader	Scientific Communication

Psychologists
Narrower	Clinical Psychologists
	Educational Psychologists
	Experimental Psychologists
	Industrial Psychologists
	School Psychologists
	Social Psychologists
Related	Counselors
	Mental Health Personnel
	Personnel/
	Psychiatrists
	Psychotherapists
	Scientists/
	Social Workers

Psychology
Broader	Sciences
	Social Sciences
Narrower	Adolescent Psychology
	Applied Psychology
	Child Psychology

Psychology — (Continued)
Narrower	Clinical Psychology
	Community Psychology
	Comparative Psychology
	Consumer Psychology
	Counseling Psychology
	Depth Psychology
	Developmental Psychology
	Educational Psychology
	Engineering Psychology
	Experimental Psychology
	Gerontology
	Industrial Psychology
	Mathematical Psychology
	Medical Psychology
	Military Psychology
	Neuropsychology
	Physiological Psychology
	School Psychology
	Social Psychology
Related	History of Psychology
	Psychophysiology

Psychometrics
Related	Experimental Design
	Experimentation/
	Measurement/
	Testing

Psychomotor Development
Broader	Motor Development
	Physical Development
	Psychogenesis
Narrower	Speech Development
Related	Childhood Development
	Perceptual Development

Psychomotor Processes
Use	Perceptual Motor Processes

Psychoneurosis
Use	Neurosis

Psychopath
Use	Antisocial Personality

Psychopathology
Broader	Medical Sciences
	Pathology
	Sciences
Related	Mental Disorders/

Psychopathy
Related	Mental Disorders/
	Pseudopsychopathic Schizophrenia

Psychopharmacology
Broader	Paramedical Sciences
	Pharmacology

Psychophysical Measurement
Related	Perceptual Measures

Psychophysics
Related	Experimentation/

Psychophysiologic Disorders
Use	Psychosomatic Disorders

Psychophysiology
Related	Physiology/
	Psychology

Psychosexual Behavior
Used For	Arousal (Sexual)
	Sexual Arousal
	Sexual Behavior
Narrower	Bisexuality
	Dyspareunia
	Erection (Penis)
	Eroticism
	Exhibitionism
	Extramarital Intercourse
	Female Orgasm
	Fetishism
	Frigidity
	Heterosexuality
	Homosexuality
	Human Courtship
	Hypersexuality
	Impotence
	Incest
	Lesbianism
	Male Homosexuality
	Male Orgasm
	Masturbation
	Nocturnal Emission
	Orgasm
	Pedophilia
	Petting
	Premarital Intercourse
	Premature Ejaculation
	Promiscuity
	Prostitution
	Rape
	Sex Roles
	Sexual Abstinence
	Sexual Deviations
	Sexual Function Disturbances
	Sexual Intercourse (Human)
	Sexual Masochism
	Sexual Sadism
	Sexual Sadomasochism
	Transsexualism
	Transvestism
	Vaginismus
	Virginity
	Voyeurism
Related	Pornography
	Sex Linked Developmental Differences
	Sex/
	Sexual Attitudes
	Sexual Development

Psychosis
Used For	Insanity
Narrower	Acute Psychosis
	Acute Psychotic Episode
	Acute Schizophrenia
	Affective Psychosis
	Alcoholic Hallucinosis
	Alcoholic Psychosis
	Catatonic Schizophrenia
	Childhood Psychosis
	Childhood Schizophrenia
	Chronic Psychosis
	Chronic Schizophrenia
	Delirium Tremens
	Early Infantile Autism
	Experimental Psychosis
	Folie A Deux
	Hallucinosis
	Hebephrenic Schizophrenia
	Involutional Depression
	Involutional Paranoid Psychosis
	Korsakoffs Psychosis
	Manic Depressive Psychosis
	Paranoia (Psychosis)
	Paranoid Schizophrenia
	Process Psychosis
	Pseudoneurotic Schizophrenia
	Pseudopsychopathic Schizophrenia
	Psychotic Depressive Reaction
	Reactive Psychosis
	Schizophrenia
	Senile Psychosis
	Simple Schizophrenia
	Symbiotic Infantile Psychosis
	Toxic Psychoses
	Undifferentiated Schizophrenia
	Windigo Psychosis
Related	Antipsychotic Drugs
	Mental Disorders/

Psychosocial Development
Broader	Psychogenesis
Narrower	Childhood Play Development
	Personality Development
Related	Emotional Development
	Moral Development

Psychosocial Mental Retardation
Used For	Cultural Familial Mental Retardation
Broader	Mental Retardation
Related	Borderline Mental Retardation
	Mental Disorders/

Psychosocial Readjustment
Used For	Readjustment (Psychosocial)
Related	Psychosocial Rehabilitation
	Psychosocial Resocialization
	Treatment/

Psychosocial Rehabilitation
Used For	Rehabilitation (Psychosocial)
Broader	Rehabilitation
Narrower	Therapeutic Social Clubs
	Vocational Rehabilitation
Related	Drug Rehabilitation
	Psychosocial Readjustment
	Psychosocial Resocialization
	Treatment/

Psychosocial Resocialization
Used For	Resocialization (Psychosocial)
Related	Psychosocial Readjustment
	Psychosocial Rehabilitation
	Treatment/

Psychosomatic Disorders
Used For	Psychophysiologic Disorders
Narrower	Anorexia Nervosa
	Hypochondriasis
	Neurodermatitis
	Pseudocyesis
	Psychogenic Pain
	Sympathetic Pain
Related	Accident Proneness
	Arthritis
	Asthma
	Cardiovascular Disorders
	Disorders/
	Dyspnea
	Endocrine Disorders
	Gastrointestinal Disorders
	Hay Fever
	Headache
	Hyperphagia
	Hyperventilation
	Infertility
	Malingering
	Mental Disorders/
	Migraine Headache
	Obesity
	Placebo
	Premenstrual Tension
	Pulmonary Tuberculosis
	Sexual Function Disturbances
	Skin Disorders
	Symptoms
	Urinary Function Disorders
	Urogenital Disorders

Psychosurgery
Used For	Leukotomy
	Lobotomy
Broader	Neurosurgery
	Organic Therapies
	Physical Treatment Methods
	Surgery
Narrower	Thalamotomy
Related	Sympathectomy
	Tractotomy

Psychotherapeutic Breakthrough
Used For	Breakthrough (Psychotherapeutic)
Broader	Psychotherapeutic Processes

Psychotherapeutic Counseling
Broader	Psychotherapy
Narrower	Conjoint Therapy
	Family Therapy
Related	Counseling/
	Marriage Counseling
	Premarital Counseling

Psychotherapeutic Intervention Tech
Use	Crisis Intervention

Psychotherapeutic Methods
Use	Psychotherapeutic Techniques

Psychotherapeutic Outcomes
Used For	Outcomes (Psychotherapeutic)
Related	Mental Health Program Evaluation
	Treatment Effectiveness Evaluation
	Treatment/

Psychotherapeutic Processes
Used For	Client Counselor Interaction
	Counselor Client Interaction
	Patient Therapist Interaction
	Therapist Patient Interaction
Narrower	Countertransference
	Insight (Psychotherapeutic Process)
	Psychotherapeutic Breakthrough
	Psychotherapeutic Resistance
	Psychotherapeutic Transference
Related	Psychoanalysis
	Psychotherapy
	Treatment/

Psychotherapeutic Resistance
Used For	Resistance (Psychotherapeutic)
Broader	Psychotherapeutic Processes

Psychotherapeutic Techniques
Used For	Psychotherapeutic Methods
	Therapeutic Techniques (Psychother)
Narrower	Autogenic Training
	Dream Analysis
	Mutual Storytelling Technique
	Psychodrama
Related	Client Centered Therapy
	Psychotherapy
	Reality Therapy
	Role Playing
	Treatment/

Psychotherapeutic Transference
Used For	Transference (Psychotherapeutic)
Broader	Psychotherapeutic Processes

Psychotherapist Attitudes
Related   Attitudes/

Psychotherapist Trainees
Use   Therapist Trainees

Psychotherapists
Broader   Mental Health Personnel
Narrower   Hypnotherapists
           Psychoanalysts
Related   Clinical Psychologists
           Psychiatrists
           Psychologists
           Therapists/

Psychotherapy
Used For   Reconstructive Psychotherapy
           Supportive Psychotherapy
Narrower   Analytical Psychotherapy
           Brief Psychotherapy
           Child Psychotherapy
           Client Centered Therapy
           Conjoint Therapy
           Dream Analysis
           Encounter Group Therapy
           Existential Therapy
           Experiential Psychotherapy
           Expressive Psychotherapy
           Family Therapy
           Geriatric Psychotherapy
           Gestalt Therapy
           Group Psychotherapy
           Hypnotherapy
           Individual Psychotherapy
           Insight Therapy
           Logotherapy
           Marathon Group Therapy
           Persuasion Therapy
           Play Therapy
           Psychoanalysis
           Psychodrama
           Psychotherapeutic Counseling
           Reality Therapy
           Relationship Therapy
           Therapeutic Community
           Transactional Analysis
Related   Behavior Therapy
           Marriage Counseling
           Organic Therapies
           Pastoral Counseling
           Psychotherapeutic Processes
           Psychotherapeutic Techniques
           Spontaneous Remission
           Treatment/

Psychotherapy Training
Used For   Training (Psychotherapy)
Broader   Clinical Methods Training
Related   Psychiatric Training

Psychotic Depressive Reaction
Broader   Affective Disturbances
           Affective Psychosis
           Depression (Emotion)
           Emotional States
           Psychosis
Related   Reactive Depression

Psychotic Episode (Acute)
Use   Acute Psychotic Episode

Psychotomimetic Drugs
Narrower   Lysergic Acid Diethylamide
           Mescaline
           Peyote
           Taraxein
Related   Drugs/
           Experimental Psychosis
           Hallucinogenic Drugs
           Psychedelic Drugs

Puberty
Broader   Developmental Stages
Related   Acne
           Menarche

Pubescence
Use   Sexual Development

Public Attitudes
Use   Public Opinion

Public Health Service Nurses
Broader   Government Personnel
           Medical Personnel
           Nurses
Related   Public Health Services

Public Health Services
Broader   Community Services
Related   Health
           Mental Health Programs
           Public Health Service Nurses

Public Opinion
Used For   Opinion (Public)
           Public Attitudes
Related   Attitudes/

Public Relations
Related   Advertising

Public School Education
Related   Education/

Public Speaking
Broader   Language
           Verbal Communication

Public Transportation
Broader   Community Facilities
           Transportation
Related   Air Transportation
           Railroad Trains

Public Welfare Services
Use   Community Welfare Services

Puerto Rico

Pulmonary Alveoli
Used For	Alveoli (Lung)
Broader	Lung
	Respiratory System

Pulmonary Emphysema
Used For	Emphysema (Pulmonary)
Broader	Lung Disorders
	Respiratory Tract Disorders

Pulmonary Tuberculosis
Broader	Bacterial Disorders
	Infectious Disorders
	Lung Disorders
	Respiratory Tract Disorders
	Tuberculosis
Related	Psychosomatic Disorders

Pulse (Arterial)
Use	Arterial Pulse

Punishment
Broader	Reinforcement
Related	Threat

Punishment (Capital)
Use	Capital Punishment

Pupil (Eye)
Broader	Eye (Anatomy)
	Sense Organs

Pupil Dilating Drugs
Use	Mydriatic Drugs

Pupil Dilation
Used For	Dilation (Pupil)
Related	Eye (Anatomy)

Puppies
Use	Dogs

Purdue Perceptual Motor Survey
(See)	Sensorimotor Measures

Puromycin
Broader	Amines
	Antibiotics

Pursuit (Rotary)
Use	Rotary Pursuit

Pyramidal Tracts
Broader	Central Nervous System
	Nervous System
	Spinal Cord

Pyramidotomy
Broader	Neurosurgery
	Physical Treatment Methods
	Surgery
Related	Tractotomy

Pyromania
Broader	Mania

Q Sort Testing Technique
Used For	Technique (Q Sort Testing)
Broader	Testing Methods
Related	Measurement/

Q Test
Use	Cochran Q Test

Quadrigemina (Corpora)
Use	Corpora Quadrigemina

Quadruplets
Broader	Family Members
	Multiple Births
	Siblings

Quails
Broader	Birds
	Vertebrates

Quartimax Rotation
Broader	Factor Analysis
	Orthogonal Rotation
	Statistical Analysis
	Statistical Measurement
	Statistical Rotation

Questionnaires
Related	Measurement/

Questionnaires (Attitude)
Use	Attitude Measures

Questionnaires (Opinion)
Use	Attitude Measures

Questionnaires (Personality)
Use	Personality Measures

Quinidine
Used For	Quinidine Sulfate
Broader	Alkaloids
	Heart Rate Affecting Drugs
Related	Quinine

Quinidine Sulfate
Use	Quinidine

Quinine
Used For	Quinine Sulfate
Broader	Alkaloids
	Analgesic Drugs
	Anesthetic Drugs
	Local Anesthetics
	Oxytocic Drugs
Related	Quinidine

Quinine Sulfate
Use	Quinine

Rabbis
Broader	Clergy
	Religious Personnel
Related	Chaplains

Rabbits
Broader	Mammals
	Vertebrates

Race (Anthropological)
Narrower	Caucasians
	Negroes
Related	Ethnic Groups
	Ethnography
	Ethnology/
	Race Attitudes
	Racial Differences
	Sociocultural Factors

Race Attitudes
Narrower	Antisemitism
	Ethnocentrism
	Racism
Related	Attitudes/
	Prejudice
	Race (Anthropological)
	Stereotyped Attitudes

Racial Differences
Used For	Differences (Racial)
Related	Race (Anthropological)

Racial Discrimination
Related	Discrimination/
	Racial Integration

Racial Integration
Used For	Integration (Racial)
	Segregation (Racial)
Broader	Social Processes
Narrower	School Integration (Racial)
Related	Activist Movements
	Racial Discrimination
	Social Equality

Racial Segregation (Schools)
Use	School Integration (Racial)

Racism
Broader	Race Attitudes
Related	Antisemitism
	Prejudice

Radial Nerve
Use	Spinal Nerves

Radiation
Used For	Irradiation
Narrower	Laser Irradiation
Related	Radiation Therapy
	Roentgenography

Radiation Therapy
Used For	X Ray Therapy
Broader	Physical Treatment Methods
Related	Radiation

Radical Movements
Narrower	Political Anarchy
	Political Revolution
Related	Social Movements

Radicalism (Political)
Use	Political Radicalism

Radiculitis
Used For	Polyradiculoneuritis
Broader	Nervous System Disorders
	Neuritis
	Peripheral Nerve Disorders

Radio
Broader	Audiovisual Communications Media
	Communications Media
	Mass Media
	Telecommunications Media

Radiology
Broader	Medical Sciences
	Sciences

Rage
Use	Anger

Railroad Trains
Used For	Trains (Railroad)
Broader	Ground Transportation
	Transportation
Related	Public Transportation

Rams
Use	Sheep

Random Sampling
Broader	Sampling (Experimental)
Related	Experiment Volunteers
	Experimentation/

Rank Difference Correlation
Used For	Spearman Rho
Broader	Statistical Correlation

Rank Order Correlation
Broader	Statistical Correlation

Rape
Broader	Antisocial Behavior
	Behavior Disorders
	Crime
	Psychosexual Behavior
	Sexual Intercourse (Human)

Rapid Eye Movement
Used For	REM
Broader	Eye Movements
Related	REM Dream Deprivation
	REM Dreams
	REM Sleep

Rapid Eye Movement Dreams
Use	REM Dreams

Rapid Eye Movement Sleep
Use	REM Sleep

Rapport
Use	Interpersonal Attraction

Rat Learning
Related	Learning/

Rate (Heart)
Use   Heart Rate

Rating
Broader   Testing
Related   Measurement/

Rating Scales
Used For   Scales (Rating)
Related   Measurement/

Ratio Reinforcement
Use   Fixed Ratio Reinforcement
             Variable Ratio Reinforcement

Ratiocination
Use   Logical Thinking

Rationalization
Broader   Defense Mechanisms

Rats
Used For   Albino Rats
             White Rats
Broader   Mammals
             Rodents
             Vertebrates
Narrower   Norway Rats

Rauwolfia
Broader   Antihypertensive Drugs
             Sedatives
Related   Reserpine

Raven Coloured Progressive Matrices
(See)   Intelligence Measures

Ravens Progressive Matrices
(See)   Intelligence Measures

Reaction (Drugs)
Use   Drug Adverse Reactions

Reaction (Fugue)
Use   Fugue Reaction

Reaction Formation
Broader   Defense Mechanisms

Reaction Time
Used For   Lag (Response)
             Response Lag
             Response Speed
             Response Time
             RT (Response)
             Speed (Response)
Broader   Response Parameters

Reactions To Crisis
Use   Stress Reactions

Reactive Depression
Broader   Affective Disturbances
             Depression (Emotion)
             Emotional States
Related   Neurotic Depressive Reaction
             Psychotic Depressive Reaction

Reactive Psychosis
Used For   Reactive Schizophrenia
             Traumatic Psychosis
Broader   Psychosis

Reactive Schizophrenia
Use   Reactive Psychosis
             Schizophrenia

Readaptation
Use   Adaptation

Readiness (Reading)
Use   Reading Readiness

Readiness (School)
Use   School Readiness

Reading
Narrower   Oral Reading
             Remedial Reading
             Silent Reading
Related   Dyslexia
             Initial Teaching Alphabet
             Literacy
             Reading Ability
             Reading Achievement
             Reading Comprehension
             Reading Disabilities
             Reading Education
             Reading Materials
             Reading Readiness
             Reading Skills
             Reading Speed
             Sight Vocabulary

Reading Ability
Related   Ability/
             Academic Aptitude
             Reading
             Reading Skills

Reading Achievement
Broader   Academic Achievement
             Achievement
Related   Reading

Reading Comprehension
Broader   Comprehension
Related   Reading

Reading Disabilities
Broader   Learning Disorders
Narrower   Dyslexia
Related   Reading

Reading Education
Broader   Curriculum
             Language Arts Education
Related   Initial Teaching Alphabet
             Phonics
             Reading
             Remedial Reading

Reading Materials
Used For	Basal Readers
Broader	Instructional Media
	Teaching
Related	Reading

Reading Measures
Related	Measurement/
Identifier	Gates MacGinitie Reading Test
	Metropolitan Reading Readiness Test
	UNESCO Silent Reading Test

Reading Readiness
Used For	Readiness (Reading)
Related	Reading

Reading Skills
Related	Reading
	Reading Ability

Reading Speed
Related	Reading

Readjustment (Psychosocial)
Use	Psychosocial Readjustment

Readmission (Hospital)
Use	Hospital Admission

Readmission (Psychiatric Hospital)
Use	Psychiatric Hospital Readmission

Realism (Philosophy)
Broader	Philosophies

Reality
Related	Reality Testing
	Reality Therapy

Reality Testing
Used For	Testing (Reality)
Related	Mental Disorders/
	Personality Processes/
	Reality

Reality Therapy
Broader	Psychotherapy
Related	Child Psychotherapy
	Psychotherapeutic Techniques
	Reality

Reasoning
Broader	Cognitive Processes
	Thinking
Narrower	Inductive Deductive Reasoning
	Inference
Related	Dialectics
	Problem Solving

Rebuttal
Identifier	Professional Criticism Reply

Recall (Dreams)
Use	Dream Recall

Recall (Learning)
Broader	Retention
	Retention Measures
Narrower	Free Recall

Recency Effect
Related	Learning/
	Primacy Effect

Receptors (Neural)
Use	Neural Receptors

Recessiveness (Genetic)
Use	Genetic Recessiveness

Recidivism
Broader	Antisocial Behavior
	Behavior Disorders
Related	Criminals

Reciprocal Inhibition Therapy
Broader	Behavior Modification
	Behavior Therapy
Related	Counterconditioning
	Systematic Desensitization Therapy

Reciprocity
Used For	Retaliation
Broader	Social Behavior

Recognition (Learning)
Broader	Retention
	Retention Measures

Reconstruction (Learning)
Broader	Retention
	Retention Measures

Reconstructive Psychotherapy
Use	Psychotherapy

Recorders (Tape)
Use	Tape Recorders

Recovery (Disorders)
Related	Disorders/
	Mental Disorders/
	Postsurgical Complications (Physical
	Remission (Disorders)

Recreation
Used For	Hobbies
	Play
Narrower	Athletic Participation
	Badminton
	Baseball
	Basketball
	Camping
	Childrens Recreational Games
	Clubs (Social Organizations)
	Dance
	Doll Play
	Football
	Gambling

Recreation — (Continued)
Narrower
        Judo
        Sports
        Summer Camps (Recreation)
        Swimming
        Television Viewing
        Tennis
        Traveling
        Vacationing
Related   Games
        Leisure Time
        Relaxation
        Toys

Recreation Areas
Used For   Parks (Recreational)
Narrower   Playgrounds
Related   Community Facilities
        Urban Planning

Recreation Therapy
Used For   Gymnastic Therapy
Narrower   Art Therapy
        Dance Therapy
        Music Therapy
Related   Treatment/

Recreational Day Camps
Use   Summer Camps (Recreation)

Recruitment (Military)
Use   Military Recruitment

Recruitment (Personnel)
Use   Personnel Recruitment

Recruitment (Teachers)
Use   Teacher Recruitment

Red Nucleus
Use   Mesencephalon

Reductionism
Used For   Atomism
        Elementarism
Broader   Philosophies

Reenlistment (Military)
Use   Military Enlistment

Referral (Professional)
Identifier   Professional Referral

Reflex (Conditioned)
Use   Conditioned Responses

Reflex (Unconditioned)
Use   Unconditioned Responses

Reflexes
Narrower   Achilles Tendon Reflex
        Acoustic Reflex
        Babinski Reflex
        Eyeblink Reflex
        Flexion Reflex
        Hoffmans Reflex

Reflexes — (Continued)
Narrower
        Orienting Reflex
        Startle Reflex
Related   Physiology/

Reformatories
Broader   Correctional Institutions
Related   Prisons

Refraction Errors
Broader   Errors
        Eye Disorders
        Sense Organ Disorders
Narrower   Hyperopia
        Myopia
Related   Amblyopia
        Genetic Disorders

Regression (Defense Mechanism)
Broader   Defense Mechanisms

Regression Analysis
Use   Analysis of Variance

Rehab Counselor Judgement Scale
(See)   Attitude Measures

Rehabilitation
Narrower   Drug Rehabilitation
        Psychosocial Rehabilitation
        Vocational Rehabilitation
Related   Rehabilitation Centers

Rehabilitation (Drug)
Use   Drug Rehabilitation

Rehabilitation (Psychosocial)
Use   Psychosocial Rehabilitation

Rehabilitation (Vocational)
Use   Vocational Rehabilitation

Rehabilitation Centers
Narrower   Sheltered Workshops
Related   Community Facilities
        Rehabilitation

Reinforcement
Narrower   Differential Reinforcement
        External Rewards
        Fixed Interval Reinforcement
        Fixed Ratio Reinforcement
        Internal Rewards
        Monetary Rewards
        Negative Reinforcement
        Nonverbal Reinforcement
        Positive Reinforcement
        Praise
        Preferred Rewards
        Primary Reinforcement
        Punishment
        Reinforcement Amounts
        Reinforcement Schedules
        Rewards

Reinforcement — (Continued)
Narrower
    Secondary Reinforcement
    Self Reinforcement
    Social Reinforcement
    Variable Interval Reinforcement
    Variable Ratio Reinforcement
    Verbal Reinforcement
Related   Biofeedback
    Conditioning
    Extinction (Learning)
    Feedback
    Learning/
    Motivation
    Operant Conditioning
    Self Stimulation
    Vicarious Experiences

Reinforcement (Vicarious)
Use   Vicarious Experiences

Reinforcement Amounts
Broader   Reinforcement

Reinforcement Schedules
Used For   Continuous Reinforcement
    Delayed Reinforcement
    Intermittent Reinforcement
    Partial Reinforcement
    Schedules (Reinforcement)
Broader   Reinforcement
Narrower   Fixed Interval Reinforcement
    Fixed Ratio Reinforcement
    Variable Interval Reinforcement
    Variable Ratio Reinforcement

Relapse (Disorders)
Related   Disorders/
    Mental Disorders/
    Postsurgical Complications
    (Physical

Relations (International)
Use   International Relations

Relations (Peer)
Use   Peer Relations

Relationship Therapy
Broader   Psychotherapy

Relaxation
Related   Leisure Time
    Muscle Relaxation
    Recreation

Relaxation Therapy
Use   Systematic Desensitization Therapy

Relearning
Related   Learning/
    Memory

Reliability (Statistical)
Use   Statistical Reliability

Reliability (Test)
Use   Test Reliability

Religion/
Used For   Theology
Related   Religious Beliefs
    Religious Buildings
    Religious Education
    Religious Literature
    Religious Personnel
    Religious Practices
    Religious Prejudices

Religiosity
Broader   Religious Beliefs

Religious Affiliation
Broader   Religious Beliefs
Narrower   Buddhism
    Christianity
    Fundamentalism
    Hinduism
    Islam
    Judaism
    Protestantism
    Roman Catholicism
    Shamanism
    Zen Buddhism
Related   Religious Practices

Religious Beliefs
Used For   Beliefs (Religion)
Narrower   Agnosticism
    Atheism
    Buddhism
    Christianity
    Fundamentalism
    God Concepts
    Hinduism
    Islam
    Judaism
    Protestantism
    Religiosity
    Religious Affiliation
    Roman Catholicism
    Shamanism
    Sin
    Zen Buddhism
Related   Asceticism
    Attitudes/
    Bible
    Cultism
    Death Attitudes
    Ethics
    Existentialism
    Family Planning Attitudes
    Marriage Attitudes
    Morality
    Mysticism

Religious Beliefs — (Continued)
Related
        Religion/
        Religious Education
        Religious Literature
        Religious Practices
        Religious Prejudices
        Superstitions

Religious Buildings
Used For   Buildings (Religious)
Related   Architecture
        Community Facilities
        Religion/

Religious Education
Related   Education/
        Religion/
        Religious Beliefs
        Religious Personnel

Religious Literature
Used For   Literature (Religion)
Narrower   Bible
Related   Religion/
        Religious Beliefs

Religious Occupations
Use   Religious Personnel

Religious Personnel
Used For   Religious Occupations
Narrower   Chaplains
        Clergy
        Evangelists
        Lay Religious Personnel
        Ministers (Religion)
        Missionaries
        Monks
        Nuns
        Priests
        Rabbis
        Seminarians
Related   Personnel/
        Religion/
        Religious Education
        Volunteer Personnel

Religious Practices
Used For   Rites (Religion)
        Rituals (Religion)
        Worship
Narrower   Asceticism
        Confession (Religion)
        Faith Healing
        Glossolalia
        Meditation
        Prayer
Related   Mysticism
        Religion/
        Religious Affiliation
        Religious Beliefs

Religious Prejudices
Broader   Prejudice
        Social Influences
Related   Religion/
        Religious Beliefs

REM
Use   Rapid Eye Movement

REM Dream Deprivation
Broader   Deprivation
Related   Rapid Eye Movement

REM Dreams
Used For   Rapid Eye Movement Dreams
Broader   Dreaming
Related   Eye Movements
        Rapid Eye Movement
        REM Sleep

REM Sleep
Used For   Paradoxical Sleep
        Rapid Eye Movement Sleep
Broader   Sleep
Related   Eye Movements
        Rapid Eye Movement
        REM Dreams

Remedial Reading
Broader   Reading
Related   Reading Education

Remembering
Use   Retention

Remission (Disorders)
Narrower   Spontaneous Remission
        Symptom Remission
Related   Disorders/
        Mental Disorders/
        Recovery (Disorders)

Remote Associates Test
(See)   Intelligence Measures

Repairmen
Use   Technical Service Personnel

Repetition (Compulsive)
Use   Compulsive Repetition

Reply (To Professional Criticism)
Identifier   Professional Criticism Reply

Repression (Defense Mechanism)
Broader   Defense Mechanisms
Related   Suppression (Defense Mecha-
        nism)

Repression Sensitization
Used For   Sensitization Repression
Broader   Personality Traits

Repression Sensitization Scale
(See)   Nonprojective Personality Meas-
        ures
        Personality Measures

Reptiles
- Broader   Vertebrates
- Narrower   Crocodilians
  - Lizards
  - Snakes
  - Turtles

Republican Party
- Use   Political Parties

Research
- Use   Experimentation/

Research Design
- Use   Experimental Design

Research Methods
- Use   Methodology/

Resentment
- Use   Hostility

Reserpine
- Used For   Serpasil
- Broader   Alkaloids
  - Antihypertensive Drugs
  - Antipsychotic Drugs
  - Neuroleptic Drugs
  - Sedatives
  - Sympatholytic Drugs
  - Tranquilizing Drugs
- Related   Rauwolfia

Residence Halls
- Use   Dormitories

Residency (Medical)
- Use   Medical Residency

Residential Care Attendants
- Use   Attendants (Institutions)

Residential Care Institutions
- Used For   Institutions (Residential Care)
- Narrower   Halfway Houses
  - Hospitals
  - Nursing Homes
  - Orphanages
  - Psychiatric Hospitals
  - Sanatoriums
- Related   Institution Visitation
  - Institutionalized Mentally Retarded
  - Treatment Facilities

Resistance (Psychotherapeutic)
- Use   Psychotherapeutic Resistance

Resistance (Skin)
- Use   Skin Resistance

Resocialization (Psychosocial)
- Use   Psychosocial Resocialization

Resonance
- Use   Vibration

Resource Teachers
- Broader   Educational Personnel
  - Teachers

Respiration
- Used For   Breathing
  - Exhalation
  - Inhalation
- Related   Artificial Respiration
  - Carbon Dioxide
  - Carbon Monoxide
  - Respiration Stimulating Drugs
  - Respiratory Distress
  - Respiratory System
  - Respiratory Tract Disorders

Respiration (Artificial)
- Use   Artificial Respiration

Respiration Stimulating Drugs
- Narrower   Caffeine
- Related   Drugs/
  - Respiration

Respiratory Distress
- Broader   Symptoms
- Narrower   Apnea
  - Dyspnea
  - Hyperventilation
- Related   Anoxia
  - Respiration

Respiratory System
- Narrower   Bronchi
  - Diaphragm (Anatomy)
  - Larynx
  - Lung
  - Nasal Mucosa
  - Nose
  - Olfactory Mucosa
  - Paranasal Sinuses
  - Pharynx
  - Pulmonary Alveoli
  - Thorax
  - Trachea
  - Vocal Cords
- Related   Anatomical Systems/
  - Artificial Respiration
  - Respiration

Respiratory Tract Disorders
- Narrower   Apnea
  - Asthma
  - Bronchial Disorders
  - Common Colds
  - Dyspnea
  - Hay Fever
  - Hyperventilation
  - Laryngeal Disorders
  - Lung Disorders
  - Pharyngeal Disorders
  - Pneumonia

Respiratory Tract Disorders — (Continued)
Narrower
      Pulmonary Emphysema
      Pulmonary Tuberculosis
      Tracheal Disorders
Related   Artificial Respiration
      Disorders/
      Influenza
      Poliomyelitis
      Respiration

Respondent Conditioning
Use   Classical Conditioning

Response Amplitude
Used For   Amplitude (Response)
Broader   Response Parameters

Response Bias
Used For   Bias (Response)
Related   Cultural Test Bias
      Measurement/
      Predisposition

Response Duration
Used For   Duration (Response)
Broader   Response Parameters

Response Frequency
Used For   Frequency (Response)
Broader   Response Parameters

Response Generalization
Used For   Generalization (Response)
Broader   Response Parameters

Response Lag
Use   Reaction Time

Response Latency
Used For   Latency (Response)
Broader   Response Parameters

Response Parameters
Used For   Parameters (Response)
Narrower   Interresponse Time
      Reaction Time
      Response Amplitude
      Response Duration
      Response Frequency
      Response Generalization
      Response Latency
      Response Probability
      Response Set
      Response Variability
Related   Responses

Response Probability
Broader   Chance (Fortune)
      Probability
      Response Parameters

Response Set
Used For   Set (Response)
Broader   Response Parameters

Response Speed
Use   Reaction Time

Response Time
Use   Reaction Time

Response Variability
Used For   Variability (Response)
Broader   Response Parameters

Responses
Narrower   Conditioned Emotional Respon-
      ses
      Conditioned Responses
      Conditioned Suppression
      Emotional Responses
      Mediated Responses
      Orienting Responses
      Unconditioned Responses
Related   Response Parameters

Responsibility

Broader   Social Behavior

Restlessness
Used For   Dysphoria
Broader   Emotional States
      Symptoms
Related   Hyperkinesis

Retail Stores
Use   Shopping Centers

Retaliation
Use   Reciprocity

Retardation (Mental)
Use   Mental Retardation

Retarded (Mentally)
Use   Mentally Retarded

Retarded Speech Development
Broader   Speech Disorders
Related   Speech Handicapped

Retention
Used For   Remembering
Narrower   Recall (Learning)
      Recognition (Learning)
      Reconstruction (Learning)
Related   Forgetting
      Free Recall
      Interference (Learning)
      Learning/
      Memory
      Retention Measures

Retention Measures
Used For   Measures (Retention)
Narrower   Free Recall
      Recall (Learning)
      Recognition (Learning)
      Reconstruction (Learning)

Retention Measures — (Continued)
Related	Measurement/
	Retention

Reticular Formation
Broader	Brain
	Brain Stem
	Central Nervous System
	Nervous System

Retina
Broader	Eye (Anatomy)
	Sense Organs
Narrower	Cones (Eye)
	Rods (Eye)

Retinal Detachment
Used For	Detached Retina
Broader	Eye Disorders
	Sense Organ Disorders
Related	Scotoma

Retinal Image
Used For	Image (Retinal)
Related	Eye (Anatomy)

Retinal Vessels
Use	Arteries (Anatomy)

Retirement
Related	Personnel Termination
	Personnel/
	Unemployment

Retroactive Inhibition
Used For	Inhibition (Retroactive)
Broader	Interference (Learning)

Reversal Shift Learning
Broader	Concept Learning

Review (of Literature)
Identifier	Literature Review

Revolutions (Political)
Use	Political Revolution

Rewards
Broader	Reinforcement
Narrower	External Rewards
	Internal Rewards
	Monetary Rewards
	Preferred Rewards
Related	Incentives

Rh Incompatibility
Used For	Erythroblastis Fetalis
	Incompatibility (Rh)
Broader	Blood and Lymphatic Disorders
	Blood Group Incompatibility
	Genetic Disorders
	Immunologic Disorders
Related	Blood Coagulation Disorders
	Neonatal Disorders

Rheoencephalography
Broader	Diagnosis
	Electrophysiology
	Encephalography
	Medical Diagnosis
Related	Electroencephalography

Rheumatic Fever
Related	Bacterial Disorders
	Heart Disorders
	Rheumatoid Arthritis

Rheumatism
Use	Arthritis

Rheumatoid Arthritis
Broader	Arthritis
	Joint Disorders
	Musculoskeletal Disorders
Related	Rheumatic Fever

Rhythm Method
Broader	Family Planning
Related	Birth Control

Ribonuclease
Broader	Enzymes
	Esterases
Related	Ribonucleic Acid

Ribonucleic Acid
Used For	RNA (Ribonucleic Acid)
Broader	Acids
	Nucleic Acids
Related	Ribonuclease

Ribs
Broader	Musculoskeletal System
Related	Bones

Rigidity (Muscles)
Use	Muscle Contractions

Rigidity (Personality)
Broader	Personality Traits

Riley Day Syndrome
Use	Dysautonomia

Riots
Broader	Aggressive Behavior
	Collective Behavior
	Conflict
	Interpersonal Interaction
	Social Behavior
	Social Interaction

Risk Taking
Broader	Social Behavior
Narrower	Gambling

Ritalin
Use	Methylphenidate

Rites (Nonreligious)
Used For	Rituals (Nonreligious)
Related	Rites Of Passage

Rites (Religion)
Use	Religious Practices

Rites of Passage
Used For	Passage (Rites of)
Broader	Sociocultural Factors
Narrower	Birth Rites
	Death Rites
	Initiation Rites
	Marriage Rites
Related	Ethnic Groups
	Ethnography
	Rites (Nonreligious)
	Taboos

Rituals (Nonreligious)
Use	Rites (Nonreligious)

Rituals (Religion)
Use	Religious Practices

Rivalry
Broader	Interpersonal Interaction
	Social Behavior
	Social Interaction

RNA (Ribonucleic Acid)
Use	Ribonucleic Acid

Robbery
Use	Theft

Robins
Broader	Birds
	Vertebrates

Rocking (Body)
Use	Body Rocking

Rod And Frame Test
(See)	Nonprojective Personality Measures
	Perceptual Measures
	Personality Measures

Rodents
Broader	Mammals
	Vertebrates
Narrower	Beavers
	Chinchillas
	Gerbils
	Guinea Pigs
	Hamsters
	Mice
	Minks
	Norway Rats
	Rats
	Squirrels

Rods (Eye)
Broader	Cells (Biology)
	Eye (Anatomy)
	Nervous System
	Neurons
	Photoreceptors

Rods (Eye) — (Continued)
Broader	
	Retina
	Sense Organs
	Sensory Neurons

Roentgenography
Used For	X Ray Diagnosis
Broader	Diagnosis
	Medical Diagnosis
Narrower	Angiography
	Pneumoencephalography
Related	Encephalography
	Radiation

Rokeach Dogmatism Scale
(See)	Nonprojective Personality Measures
	Personality Measures

Role (Counselor)
Use	Counselor Role

Role Conflicts
Used For	Conflicts (Role)
Related	Roles

Role Expectations
Used For	Expectations (Role)
Related	Roles

Role Perception
Related	Perception/
	Roles

Role Playing
Related	Psychotherapeutic Techniques
	Roles

Roles
Narrower	Parental Role
	Sex Roles
Related	Role Conflicts
	Role Expectations
	Role Perception
	Role Playing

Roman Catholicism
Used For	Catholicism (Roman)
Broader	Christianity
	Religious Affiliation
	Religious Beliefs

Roommates
Broader	Students

Rorschach Test
(See)	Personality Measures
	Projective Personality Measures
	Projective Techniques

Rosenzweig Picture Frustration Study
(See)	Personality Measures
	Projective Personality Measures
	Projective Techniques

Rotary Pursuit
Used For	Pursuit (Rotary)
Broader	Perceptual Motor Processes
	Tracking
Related	Attention

Rotation Methods (Statistical)
Use	Statistical Rotation

ROTC Students
Broader	College Students
	Government Personnel
	Military Personnel
	Students
	Volunteer Military Personnel
	Volunteer Personnel

Rote Learning
Related	Learning/
	Memory

Rotter Incomplete Sentences Blank
(See)	Personality Measures
	Projective Personality Measures
	Projective Techniques

Rotter Intern Extern Locus Cont Scal
(See)	Nonprojective Personality Measures
	Personality Measures

Roughness
Related	Perceptual Stimulation
	Somesthetic Stimulation

RT (Response)
Use	Reaction Time

Rubella
Used For	German Measles
Broader	Infectious Disorders
	Viral Disorders
Related	Measles

Rulon Test
Broader	Nonparametric Statistical Tests
	Statistical Analysis
	Statistical Tests
Related	Statistical Reliability

Runaway Behavior
Broader	Antisocial Behavior

Running
Broader	Motor Performance
	Motor Processes

Runways (Maze)
Use	Maze Pathways

Rural Environments
Broader	Environment
	Social Environments

Saccharin
Related	Sugars

Sacral Spinal Cord
Broader	Central Nervous System
	Nervous System
	Spinal Cord

Sadism
Broader	Sadomasochism
Narrower	Sexual Sadism
Related	Masochism
	Sadistic Personality

Sadistic Personality
Broader	Personality Disorders
	Sadomasochistic Personality
Related	Sadism
	Sexual Sadism

Sadness
Used For	Melancholy
Related	Depression (Emotion)
	Emotions/

Sadomasochism
Narrower	Masochism
	Sadism
	Sexual Masochism
	Sexual Sadism
	Sexual Sadomasochism
Related	Mental Disorders/
	Sadomasochistic Personality

Sadomasochistic Personality
Broader	Personality Disorders
Narrower	Masochistic Personality
	Sadistic Personality
Related	Sadomasochism

Safety
Narrower	Air Traffic Control
	Aviation Safety
	Highway Safety
	Occupational Safety
	Water Safety
Related	Accident Prevention
	Accident Proneness
	Accidents
	Fire Prevention
	Hazards
	Injuries
	Prevention/
	Safety Devices

Safety Belts
Broader	Safety Devices
Related	Driving Behavior
	Transportation Accidents

Safety Devices
Used For	Devices (Safety)
Narrower	Safety Belts
Related	Hazards
	Safety

Salamanders
Broader   Amphibia
          Vertebrates

Salaries
Used For   Pay
          Wages
Broader   Employee Benefits
Related   Bonuses

Sales Personnel
Used For   Insurance Agents
          Salesmen
Broader   Business And Industrial Personnel
          White Collar Workers

Salesmen
Use   Sales Personnel

Salience (Stimulus)
Use   Stimulus Salience

Saliva
Broader   Body Fluids
Related   Salivation

Salivary Glands
Broader   Glands
Related   Digestive System
          Mouth (Anatomy)

Salivation
Broader   Secretion (Gland)
Related   Digestion
          Physiology/
          Saliva

Salmon
Broader   Fishes
          Vertebrates

Saltiness
Use   Taste Stimulation

Sampling (Experimental)
Narrower   Biased Sampling
          Random Sampling
Related   Experimental Design
          Experimentation/
          Population (Statistics)
          Statistical Analysis
          Statistical Reliability
          Statistical Variables

Sanatoriums
Broader   Hospitals
          Residential Care Institutions
          Treatment Facilities
Related   Nursing Homes
          Psychiatric Hospitals

Sarcomas
Use   Neoplasms

Satiation
Related   Appetite
          Motivation

Satisfaction
Used For   Fulfillment
Narrower   Job Satisfaction
          Need Satisfaction

Scales (Attitude)
Use   Attitude Measures

Scales (Intelligence)
Use   Intelligence Measures

Scales (Interest)
Use   Interest Inventories

Scales (Personality)
Use   Personality Measures

Scales (Preference)
Use   Preference Measures

Scales (Rating)
Use   Rating Scales

Scaling (Testing)
Broader   Testing
Related   Measurement/

Scalp (Anatomy)
Related   Anatomy/
          Hair
          Head (Anatomy)
          Skin (Anatomy)

Scalp Disorders
Use   Skin Disorders

SCAT (Test)
Identifier   School And College Ability Test

Schedules (Learning)
Use   Learning Schedules

Schedules (Reinforcement)
Use   Reinforcement Schedules

Scheduling (Work)
Use   Work Scheduling

Schizoid Personality
Broader   Personality Disorders
Related   Schizophrenia

Schizophrenia
Used For   Dementia Praecox
          Process Schizophrenia
          Reactive Schizophrenia
Broader   Psychosis
Narrower   Acute Schizophrenia
          Catatonic Schizophrenia
          Childhood Schizophrenia
          Chronic Schizophrenia
          Hebephrenic Schizophrenia
          Paranoid Schizophrenia
          Pseudoneurotic Schizophrenia

Schizophrenia — (Continued)
Narrower
             Pseudopsychopathic Schizophrenia
             Simple Schizophrenia
             Undifferentiated Schizophrenia
Related   Antischizophrenic Drugs
             Catalepsy
             Fragmentation (Schizophrenia)
             Schizoid Personality
             Word Salad

Schizophrenogenic Family
Broader   Family Structure
Related   Double Bind Interaction
             Mental Disorders/
             Schizophrenogenic Mothers

Schizophrenogenic Mothers
Broader   Family Members
             Mothers
             Parents
Related   Double Bind Interaction
             Mother Child Relations
             Schizophrenogenic Family

Scholarships
Use   Educational Financial Assistance

Scholastic Achievement
Use   Academic Achievement

Scholastic Aptitude
Use   Academic Aptitude

School Achievement
Use   Academic Achievement

School Adjustment
Related   Adjustment/
             Education/

School Administration
Use   Educational Administration

School Administrators
Broader   Educational Personnel
Narrower   School Principals
             School Superintendents
Related   Management Personnel

School Age Children
Broader   Children
             Developmental Age Groups
Related   Childhood Development
             Developmental Differences

School And College Ability Test
Used For   SCAT (Test)
(See)   Aptitude Measures

School Attendance
Used For   Attendance (School)
Broader   School Enrollment

School Club Membership
Broader   Extracurricular Activities

School Counselors
Broader   Counselors
             Educational Personnel
Related   School Psychologists
             Vocational Counselors

School Dropouts
Broader   Dropouts

School Enrollment
Used For   Enrollment (School)
             Matriculation
Narrower   School Attendance
             School Expulsion
             School Suspension
             School Truancy
Related   Dropouts
             Education/

School Environment
Broader   Academic Environment
             Environment
             Social Environments
Related   Classroom Environment
             School Facilities
             Schools

School Expulsion
Used For   Expulsion (School)
Broader   School Enrollment

School Facilities
Narrower   Campuses
             Classrooms
             Dormitories
             Educational Laboratories
             Gymnasiums
             Language Laboratories
             Learning Centers (Educational)
             School Libraries
Related   Education/
             Playgrounds
             School Environment
             Schools

School Federal Aid
Use   Educational Financial Assistance

School Financial Assistance
Use   Educational Financial Assistance

School Integration (Racial)
Used For   Racial Segregation (Schools)
Broader   Racial Integration
             Social Processes
Related   Activist Movements
             Education/

School Learning
Related   Academic Achievement
             Education/
             Learning/

School Libraries
Used For   Libraries (School)

School Libraries — (Continued)
    Broader   School Facilities

School Nurses
    Broader   Educational Personnel
                 Medical Personnel
                 Nurses

School Organization
    Use   Educational Administration

School Phobia
    Broader   Phobias
    Related   Separation Anxiety

School Principals
    Broader   Educational Personnel
                 School Administrators

School Psychologists
    Broader   Educational Personnel
                 Educational Psychologists
                 Mental Health Personnel
                 Psychologists
    Related   School Counselors

School Psychology
    Broader   Applied Psychology
                 Educational Psychology
                 Psychology
                 Sciences
                 Social Sciences

School Readiness
    Used For   Readiness (School)
    Related   Education/
                 Project Head Start

School Superintendents
    Broader   Educational Personnel
                 School Administrators

School Suspension
    Used For   Suspension (School)
    Broader   School Enrollment

School Truancy
    Broader   School Enrollment

Schools
    Narrower   Colleges
                 Elementary Schools
                 Graduate Schools
                 High Schools
                 Junior High Schools
                 Kindergartens
                 Military Schools
                 Nongraded Schools
                 Nursery Schools
                 Seminaries
                 Technical Schools
    Related   Community Facilities
                 Education/
                 School Environment
                 School Facilities

Sciatic Nerve
    Use   Spinal Nerves

Science (Social)
    Use   Social Sciences

Science Education
    Broader   Curriculum

Sciences
    Narrower   Adolescent Psychology
                 Anesthesiology
                 Anthropology
                 Applied Psychology
                 Biochemistry
                 Biology
                 Botany
                 Cardiology
                 Chemistry
                 Child Psychiatry
                 Child Psychology
                 Clinical Psychology
                 Community Psychiatry
                 Community Psychology
                 Comparative Psychology
                 Consumer Psychology
                 Counseling Psychology
                 Dentistry
                 Developmental Psychology
                 Educational Psychology
                 Endocrinology
                 Engineering Psychology
                 Epidemiology
                 Experimental Psychology
                 Forensic Psychiatry
                 Geography
                 Geriatrics
                 Gerontology
                 Immunology
                 Industrial Psychology
                 Mathematical Psychology
                 Medical Psychology
                 Medical Sciences
                 Military Psychology
                 Neuroanatomy
                 Neurobiology
                 Neurochemistry
                 Neurology
                 Neuropathology
                 Neurophysiology
                 Neuropsychiatry
                 Neuropsychology
                 Neurosciences
                 Obstetrics Gynecology
                 Opthalmology
                 Orthopsychiatry
                 Physics
                 Physiological Psychology
                 Psychiatry
                 Psychology

Sciences — (Continued)

Narrower
- Psychopathology
- Radiology
- School Psychology
- Social Psychiatry
- Social Psychology
- Social Sciences
- Sociology
- Surgery
- Transcultural Psychiatry
- Veterinary Sciences
- Zoology

Related   Technology

Scientific Communication

Used For
- Communication (Professional)
- Newsletters (Professional)
- Professional Communication
- Professional Newsletters

Narrower   Professional Meetings And Symposia
- Psychological Terminology

Related   Communication/
- Interpersonal Communication
- Verbal Communication

Scientific Methods

Use   Experimental Methods

Scientists/

Related
- Aerospace Personnel
- Anthropologists
- Business And Industrial Personnel
- Engineers
- Mathematicians
- Medical Personnel
- Personnel/
- Physicists
- Psychologists
- Sociologists

Sclera

Use   Eye (Anatomy)

Sclerosis (Nervous System)

Broader   Nervous System Disorders
Narrower   Multiple Sclerosis
Related   Neuromuscular Disorders
- Paralysis

Scopolamine

Used For
- Hyoscine
- Scopolamine Hydrobromide

Broader
- Alkaloids
- Amines
- Analgesic Drugs
- Cholinergic Blocking Drugs
- CNS Affecting Drugs
- CNS Depressant Drugs

Scopolamine — (Continued)

Broader
- Mydriatic Drugs
- Sedatives

Related   Bromides

Scopolamine Hydrobromide

Use   Scopolamine

Scores (Test)

Use   Test Scores

Scoring (Testing)

Broader   Testing
Related   Measurement/

Scotland

Scotoma

Broader
- Eye Disorders
- Sense Organ Disorders

Related
- Retinal Detachment
- Tunnel Vision

Scotopic Stimulation

Broader
- Illumination
- Visual Stimulation

Related   Photopic Stimulation

Scratching

Broader   Symptoms
Related   Pruritus

Screening (Job Applicants)

Use   Job Applicant Screening

Screening Tests

Use   Selection Tests

Sculpturing

Broader
- Art
- Arts

SD (Statistics)

Use   Standard Deviation

Sea Gulls

Used For   Gulls
Broader
- Birds
- Vertebrates

Seals (Animal)

Broader
- Mammals
- Vertebrates

Seasonal Variations

Used For   Variations (Seasonal)
Broader   Environmental Effects
Related
- Biological Rhythms
- Temperature Effects

Secobarbital

Used For   Seconal
Broader
- Barbiturates
- Hypnotic Drugs
- Sedatives

Seconal
  Use   Secobarbital

Secondary Education
  Related   Education/

Secondary Reinforcement
  Used For Token Reinforcement
  Broader   Reinforcement

Secretarial Personnel
  Broader   Business And Industrial Personnel
           White Collar Workers
  Related   Clerical Personnel

Secretarial Skills
  Use   Clerical Secretarial Skills

Secretion (Gland)
  Narrower Adrenal Gland Secretion
           Endocrine Gland Secretion
           Lactation
           Salivation
           Sweating
  Related   Endocrine Disorders
           Physiology/

Sectioning (Lesion)
  Use   Lesions

Security (Emotional)
  Use   Emotional Security

Sedatives
  Narrower Ammonium Bromide
           Amobarbital
           Atropine
           Barbital
           Calcium Bromide
           Chloral Hydrate
           Chlorpromazine
           Glutethimide
           Haloperidol
           Heroin
           Hexobarbital
           Hyoscyamine (L-)
           Lithium Bromide
           Meperidine
           Methaqualone
           Paraldehyde
           Pentobarbital
           Phenaglycodol
           Phenobarbital
           Potassium Bromide
           Promethazine
           Rauwolfia
           Reserpine
           Scopolamine
           Secobarbital
           Sodium Bromide
           Strontium Bromide
           Thalidomide
           Thiopental

Sedatives — (Continued)
  Related   Analgesic Drugs
           Anesthetic Drugs
           Anticonvulsive Drugs
           Antiemetic Drugs
           Antihistaminic Drugs
           Antihypertensive Drugs
           Barbiturates
           CNS Depressant Drugs
           Drugs/
           Hypnotic Drugs
           Tranquilizing Drugs

Segregation (Racial)
  Use   Racial Integration

Seizures
  Use   Convulsions

Selected Readings

Selection (Personnel)
  Use   Personnel Selection

Selection Tests
  Used For Screening Tests
  Related   Measurement/
  Identifier Psychological Screening Inventory

Selective Attention
  Broader   Attention
           Awareness
           Consciousness States
  Related   Divided Attention
           Monitoring
           Vigilance

Selective Breeding
  Broader   Animal Breeding
  Related   Eugenics

Self Actualization
  Used For Actualization (Self)
           Self Realization
  Related   Personality/

Self Analysis Form
  Used For Anxiety Scale Questionnaire
  (See)   Nonprojective Personality Measures
           Personality Measures

Self Assessment
  Use   Self Evaluation

Self Concept
  Used For Concept (Self)
           Identity (Personal)
           Self Image
  Narrower Self Esteem
  Related   Personality/
           Self Perception

Self Confidence
Use   Self Esteem

Self Control
Broader   Personality Traits

Self Disclosure
Related   Interpersonal Communication
           Personality/

Self Esteem
Used For   Esteem (Self)
           Self Confidence
           Self Respect
Broader   Self Concept
Related   Self Perception

Self Evaluation
Used For   Evaluation (Self)
           Self Assessment
Broader   Evaluation
Related   Personality/

Self Image
Use   Self Concept

Self Inflicted Wounds
Broader   Injuries
           Wounds

Self Mutilation
Used For   Mutilation (Self)
Broader   Behavior Disorders
Narrower   Head Banging

Self Perception
Used For   Perception (Self)
Related   Personality/
           Self Concept
           Self Esteem

Self Realization
Use   Self Actualization

Self Reinforcement
Broader   Reinforcement
Related   Self Stimulation

Self Respect
Use   Self Esteem

Self Stimulation
Broader   Stimulation
Related   Electrical Brain Stimulation
           Operant Conditioning
           Reinforcement
           Self Reinforcement

Selfishness
Broader   Personality Traits

Semantic Differential
Related   Measurement/

Semantic Generalization
Used For   Generalization (Semantic)
Broader   Cognitive Processes

Semantic Generalization — (Continued)
Related   Cognitive Generalization
           Connotations
           Semantics

Semantics
Broader   Language
           Linguistics
           Verbal Communication
Related   Semantic Generalization

Semicircular Canals
Broader   Ear (Anatomy)
           Labyrinth (Anatomy)
           Sense Organs

Seminarians
Broader   Religious Personnel
           Students

Seminaries
Broader   Schools

Senescence
Use   Aged

Senile Dementia
Used For   Dementia (Senile)
Broader   Brain Disorders
           Central Nervous System Disorders
           Nervous System Disorders
           Organic Brain Syndromes
           Syndromes
Narrower   Senile Psychosis
Related   Aged
           Cerebral Arteriosclerosis
           Mental Disorders/
           Physiological Aging
           Presenile Dementia

Senile Psychosis
Broader   Brain Disorders
           Central Nervous System Disorders
           Nervous System Disorders
           Organic Brain Syndromes
           Psychosis
           Senile Dementia
           Syndromes

Senior Citizens
Use   Aged

Sensation
Use   Perception/

Sensation Seeking Scale
(See)   Nonprojective Personality Measures
           Personality Measures

Sense Organ Disorders
Narrower   Amblyopia
           Anosmia

Sense Organ Disorders — (Continued)

Narrower
Cataracts
Color Blindness
Ear Disorders
Eye Disorders
Glaucoma
Hemianopia
Hyperopia
Hypotonia (Eye)
Labyrinth Disorders
Menieres Disease
Motion Sickness
Myopia
Nystagmus
Otosclerosis
Refraction Errors
Retinal Detachment
Scotoma
Strabismus
Tinnitus
Tunnel Vision

Related
Anesthesia (Feeling)
Disorders/
Sense Organs

Sense Organs

Narrower
Cochlea
Cones (Eye)
Cornea
Ear (Anatomy)
External Ear
Eye (Anatomy)
Iris (Eye)
Labyrinth (Anatomy)
Lens (Eye)
Middle Ear
Olfactory Mucosa
Pupil (Eye)
Retina
Rods (Eye)
Semicircular Canals
Taste Buds
Vestibular Apparatus

Related
Anatomy/
Sense Organ Disorders

Sensitivity (Drugs)

Use   Drug Sensitivity

Sensitivity (Personality)

Used For   Insensitivity (Personality)
Broader   Personality Traits

Sensitivity Training

Used For   Encounter Groups
Human Relations Training
T Groups
Related   Encounter Group Therapy
Group Dynamics

Sensitivity Training — (Continued)

Related
Marathon Group Therapy
Personnel Training

Sensitization (Protein)

Use   Anaphylactic Shock

Sensitization Repression

Use   Repression Sensitization

Sensorimotor Measures

Related   Measurement/
Identifier   Purdue Perceptual Motor Survey

Sensory Adaptation

Used For   Adaptation (Sensory)
Broader   Adaptation
Thresholds
Narrower   Dark Adaptation
Orienting Reflex
Orienting Responses

Sensory Deprivation

Broader   Deprivation
Stimulus Deprivation

Sensory Feedback

Broader   Feedback
Perceptual Stimulation
Narrower   Auditory Feedback
Delayed Auditory Feedback
Visual Feedback

Sensory Handicaps (Attit Toward)

Broader   Handicapped (Attitudes Toward)

Sensory Motor Processes

Use   Perceptual Motor Processes

Sensory Neurons

Broader   Cells (Biology)
Nervous System
Neurons
Narrower   Auditory Neurons
Cones (Eye)
Rods (Eye)

Sentence Comprehension

Broader   Comprehension

Sentence Structure

Broader   Grammar
Language
Linguistics
Syntax
Verbal Communication

Sentences

Broader   Language
Linguistics
Verbal Communication

Separation (Marital)

Use   Marital Separation

Separation Anxiety
Broader   Anxiety
Related   School Phobia

Sephardim
Use   Judaism

Septum (Brain) Lesions
Use   Brain Lesions

Sequential Learning
Related   Learning/

Serial Anticipation (Learning)
Used For   Anticipation (Serial Learning)
Broader   Serial Learning
            Verbal Learning
Related   Learning/

Serial Compulsions
Used For   Compulsions (Serial)
Broader   Compulsions

Serial Learning
Broader   Verbal Learning
Narrower   Serial Anticipation (Learning)
Related   Learning/

Seriousness
Broader   Personality Traits

Serotonin
Used For   Hydroxytryptamine (5-)
Broader   Amines
            Vasoconstrictor Drugs
Related   Adrenergic Drugs
            Serotonin Antagonists

Serotonin Antagonists
Narrower   Lysergic Acid Diethylamide
            Tetrabenazine
Related   Drugs/
            Serotonin

Serpasil
Use   Reserpine

Serum (Blood)
Use   Blood Serum

Serum Albumin
Broader   Albumins
            Blood Proteins
            Proteins

Servicemen
Use   Military Personnel

SES (Income)
Use   Socioeconomic Status

Set (Response)
Use   Response Set

Severely Mentally Retarded
Used For   Imbeciles
Broader   Handicapped
            Mentally Retarded

Sex Chromosome Disorders
Broader   Chromosome Disorders
            Genetic Disorders
Narrower   Klinefelters Syndrome
            Neonatal Sex Chromosome Dis-
            orders
            Turners Syndrome
Related   Sex Linked Hereditary Disorders

Sex Chromosomes
Broader   Chromosomes
Related   Sex/

Sex Differences (Animal)
Use   Animal Sex Differences

Sex Differences (Human)
Use   Human Sex Differences

Sex Differentiation Disorders
Use   Genital Disorders

Sex Drive
Broader   Motivation
Related   Sex/

Sex Education
Broader   Curriculum
            Health Education
Related   Sex/

Sex Hormones
Broader   Hormones
Narrower   Androgens
            Estradiol
            Estrogens
            Estrone
            Progesterone
            Testosterone
Related   Gonadotropic Hormones
            Sex/

Sex Identity
Use   Sex Roles

Sex Linked Developmental Differences
Broader   Developmental Differences
            Human Sex Differences
Related   Adolescent Development
            Heterosexuality
            Physical Development
            Psychogenesis
            Psychosexual Behavior
            Sex Roles
            Sexual Development

Sex Linked Hereditary Disorders
Broader   Genetic Disorders
Narrower   Hemophilia
            Testicular Feminization Syn-
            drome
Related   Sex Chromosome Disorders

Sex Roles
Used For   Sex Identity

Sex Roles — (Continued)
Broader	Psychosexual Behavior
	Roles
Related	Heterosexuality
	Homosexuality
	Sex Linked Developmental Differences
	Sexual Deviations
	Transsexualism
	Transvestism

Sex/
Related	Genital Disorders
	Human Sex Differences
	Psychosexual Behavior
	Sex Chromosomes
	Sex Drive
	Sex Education
	Sex Hormones
	Sexual Reproduction

Sexual Abstinence
Used For	Abstinence (Sexual)
	Celibacy
Broader	Psychosexual Behavior
Related	Birth Control

Sexual Arousal
Use	Psychosexual Behavior

Sexual Attitudes
Related	Attitudes/
	Psychosexual Behavior

Sexual Behavior
Use	Psychosexual Behavior

Sexual Delinquency
Use	Promiscuity

Sexual Development
Used For	Pubescence
Broader	Physical Development
Related	Adolescent Development
	Development/
	Heterosexuality
	Psychogenesis
	Psychosexual Behavior
	Sex Linked Developmental Differences

Sexual Deviations
Used For	Deviations (Sexual)
Broader	Psychosexual Behavior
Narrower	Exhibitionism
	Fetishism
	Incest
	Pedophilia
	Sexual Masochism
	Sexual Sadism
	Sexual Sadomasochism
	Transsexualism
	Transvestism
	Voyeurism

Sexual Deviations — (Continued)
Related	Mental Disorders/
	Pornography
	Sex Roles

Sexual Disorders (Physiological)
Use	Genital Disorders

Sexual Fetishism
Use	Fetishism

Sexual Function Disturbances
Broader	Psychosexual Behavior
Narrower	Dyspareunia
	Frigidity
	Impotence
	Premature Ejaculation
	Vaginismus
Related	Psychosomatic Disorders
	Urogenital Disorders

Sexual Intercourse (Human)
Used For	Coitus
	Copulation
	Intercourse (Sexual)
Broader	Psychosexual Behavior
Narrower	Dyspareunia
	Extramarital Intercourse
	Incest
	Premarital Intercourse
	Rape
Related	Female Orgasm
	Male Orgasm
	Petting
	Sexual Reproduction

Sexual Masochism
Broader	Masochism
	Psychosexual Behavior
	Sadomasochism
	Sexual Deviations
	Sexual Sadomasochism
Related	Fetishism
	Masochistic Personality
	Sexual Sadism

Sexual Receptivity (Animal)
Use	Animal Sexual Receptivity

Sexual Reproduction
Related	Animal Mating Behavior
	Birth
	Fertilization
	Genetics/
	Ovum
	Physiology/
	Pregnancy
	Sex/
	Sexual Intercourse (Human)
	Sperm

Sexual Sadism
Broader	Psychosexual Behavior
	Sadism

Sexual Sadism — (Continued)
Broader
      Sadomasochism
      Sexual Deviations
  Related   Fetishism
      Sadistic Personality
      Sexual Masochism

Sexual Sadomasochism
  Broader   Psychosexual Behavior
      Sadomasochism
      Sexual Deviations
  Narrower   Sexual Masochism
  Related   Fetishism

Sexuality
  Broader   Personality Traits

Shamanism
  Broader   Religious Affiliation
      Religious Beliefs
  Related   Cultism
      Ethnic Groups
      Ethnology/
      Faith Healing
      Folk Medicine
      Transcultural Psychiatry

Shame
  Use   Guilt

Shape Perception
  Use   Form And Shape Perception

Sheath (Myelin)
  Use   Myelin Sheath

Sheep
  Used For   Lambs
      Rams
  Broader   Mammals
      Vertebrates

Sheltered Workshops
  Used For   Workshops (Sheltered)
  Broader   Rehabilitation Centers
  Related   Community Facilities

Shifts (Workday)
  Use   Workday Shifts

Shock
  Broader   Symptoms
  Related   Anaphylactic Shock
      Culture Shock
      Electrical Injuries
      Electrical Stimulation
      Electroconvulsive Shock
      Injuries
      Shock Therapy
      Shock Units
      Syncope

Shock Therapy
  Broader   Organic Therapies

Shock Therapy — (Continued)
  Narrower   Electroconvulsive Shock Therapy
      Insulin Shock Therapy
  Related   Aversion Therapy
      Shock

Shock Units
  Used For   Units (Shock)
  Broader   Apparatus
      Stimulators (Apparatus)
  Related   Shock
      Shuttle Box Grids
      Volt Meters

Shoplifting
  Broader   Antisocial Behavior
      Behavior Disorders
      Crime
      Theft

Shopping
  Use   Consumer Behavior

Shopping Centers
  Used For   Retail Stores
  Broader   Community Facilities
  Related   Consumer Behavior

Short Term Memory
  Broader   Memory

Short Term Psychotherapy
  Use   Brief Psychotherapy

Shoshone Indians
  Use   American Indians

Shoulder (Anatomy)
  Broader   Musculoskeletal System
  Related   Arm (Anatomy)

Shuttle Box Grids
  Used For   Grid (Shuttle Box)
  Broader   Apparatus
      Shuttle Boxes
  Related   Shock Units

Shuttle Box Hurdles
  Used For   Hurdle (Shuttle Box)
  Broader   Apparatus
  Related   Shuttle Boxes

Shuttle Boxes
  Used For   Boxes (Shuttle)
  Broader   Apparatus
  Narrower   Shuttle Box Grids
  Related   Shuttle Box Hurdles

Shyness
  Use   Timidity

Siamese Twins
  Broader   Twins

Sibling Relations
  Broader   Family Relations

Siblings
Broader	Family Members
Narrower	Brothers
	Heterozygotic Twins
	Monozygotic Twins
	Multiple Births
	Quadruplets
	Sisters
	Triplets
	Twins

Sick Leave
Use	Employee Leave Benefits

Sickness (Motion)
Use	Motion Sickness

Side Effects (Drug)
Broader	Drug Effects
Narrower	Drug Addiction
	Drug Adverse Reactions
	Drug Allergies
	Drug Dependency
	Drug Sensitivity
	Heroin Addiction
Related	Drug Tolerance

Sight Vocabulary
Broader	Language
	Verbal Communication
	Vocabulary
Related	Reading

Sign Language
Broader	Language
	Verbal Communication
Related	Fingerspelling

Sign Rank Test
Use	Wilcoxon Sign Rank Test

Sign Test
Broader	Nonparametric Statistical Tests
	Statistical Analysis
	Statistical Tests
Related	Statistical Significance

Signal Detection (Perception)
Used For	Detection (Signal)
	Warning Signal
Related	Attention
	Perception/
	Threshold Determination

Signal Intensity
Use	Stimulus Intensity

Significance (Statistical)
Use	Statistical Significance

Silent Reading
Broader	Reading

Silicones
Related	Prostheses

Similarity (Stimulus)
Use	Stimulus Similarity

Simple Schizophrenia
Broader	Psychosis
	Schizophrenia

Simulation
Used For	Modeling
	Simulators
Narrower	Computer Simulation
	Flight Simulation
	Heuristic Modeling
	Markov Chains
	Mathematical Modeling
	Simulation Games
	Stochastic Modeling
Related	Game Theory

Simulation Games
Broader	Games
	Simulation
Related	Computer Simulation

Simulators
Use	Simulation

Sin
Broader	Religious Beliefs

Sincerity
Broader	Personality Traits

Single Persons
Related	Marital Status

Sisters
Broader	Family Members
	Siblings

Situational Attitude Scale
(See)	Attitude Measures

Sixteen Personality Factors Question
Used For	Sixteen PF Questionnaire
(See)	Nonprojective Personality Measures
	Personality Measures

Sixteen PF Questionnaire
Identifier	Sixteen Personality Factors Question

Size
Related	Perceptual Stimulation

Size (Apparent)
Use	Apparent Size

Size (Group)
Use	Group Size

Size Discrimination
Broader	Spatial Perception
Narrower	Apparent Size

Skeletal Muscle Relaxant Drugs
Use	Muscle Relaxing Drugs

Skeletomuscular Disorders
Use   Musculoskeletal Disorders

Skepticism
Broader   Philosophies

Skewed Distribution
Used For   Poisson Distribution
Broader   Frequency Distribution
      Statistical Analysis
      Statistical Measurement

Skill Learning
Narrower   Fine Motor Skill Learning
      Gross Motor Skill Learning
Related   Learning/
      Perceptual Motor Learning

Skilled Industrial Workers
Broader   Blue Collar Workers
      Business And Industrial Person-
      nel

Skills
Use   Ability/

Skin (Anatomy)
Used For   Epithelium
Broader   Tissues (Body)
Related   Absorption (Physiological)
      Epithelial Cells
      Hair
      Head (Anatomy)
      Scalp (Anatomy)

Skin Conduction
Use   Skin Resistance

Skin Disorders
Used For   Scalp Disorders
Narrower   Acne
      Allergic Skin Disorders
      Alopecia
      Dermatitis
      Eczema
      Herpes Simplex
      Lupus
      Neurodermatitis
      Pruritus
Related   Albinism
      Disorders/
      Psychosomatic Disorders
      Sweating
      Tuberculosis

Skin Electrical Properties
Used For   Electrical Properties (Skin)
Broader   Electrophysiology
Narrower   Basal Skin Resistance
      Skin Potential
      Skin Resistance

Skin Potential
Broader   Electrophysiology
      Skin Electrical Properties

Skin Potential — (Continued)
Related   Galvanic Skin Response
      Skin Resistance

Skin Resistance
Used For   Resistance (Skin)
      Skin Conduction
Broader   Electrophysiology
      Skin Electrical Properties
Narrower   Basal Skin Resistance
Related   Galvanic Skin Response
      Skin Potential

Skin Temperature
Used For   Temperature (Skin)
Broader   Body Temperature

Skinner Boxes
Used For   Boxes (Skinner)
Broader   Apparatus

Skull
Broader   Musculoskeletal System

Slang
Broader   Language
      Verbal Communication
      Vocabulary
Related   Nonstandard English

Sleep
Used For   Natural Sleep
Narrower   NREM Sleep
      REM Sleep
Related   Consciousness Disturbances
      Consciousness States
      Dream Content
      Dreaming
      Nocturnal Teeth Grinding
      Sleep Deprivation
      Sleep Disorders
      Sleep Onset
      Sleep Talking
      Sleep Treatment

Sleep Deprivation
Broader   Deprivation
Related   Sleep
      Sleep Disorders

Sleep Disorders
Broader   Consciousness Disturbances
Narrower   Insomnia
      Narcolepsy
      Sleepwalking
      Somnambulism
Related   Hypnagogic Hallucinations
      Sleep
      Sleep Deprivation

Sleep Inducing Drugs
Use   Hypnotic Drugs

Sleep Onset
Used For   Drowsiness

Sleep Onset — (Continued)
Related   Sleep

Sleep Talking
Broader   Consciousness Disturbances
Related   Sleep

Sleep Treatment
Broader   Drug Therapy
Narcoanalysis
Organic Therapies
Related   Sleep

Sleepwalking
Broader   Consciousness Disturbances
Sleep Disorders
Narrower   Somnambulism

Slosson Intelligence Test For Child
(See)   Intelligence Measures

Slow Learners
Used For   Borderline Mentally Retarded
Broader   Handicapped
Related   Educable Mentally Retarded
Mentally Retarded

Slow Wave Sleep
Use   NREM Sleep

Slums
Use   Poverty Areas

Smell Perception
Use   Olfactory Perception

Smiles
Broader   Facial Expressions
Nonverbal Communication

Smoking (Cigarettes)
Use   Tobacco Smoking

Smoking (Tobacco)
Use   Tobacco Smoking

Smooth Muscle Relaxant Drugs
Use   Muscle Relaxing Drugs

Snails
Broader   Invertebrates
Mollusca

Snake Phobia
Use   Ophidiophobia

Snakes
Broader   Reptiles
Vertebrates

Sniffing (Glue)
Use   Glue Sniffing

Sociability
Broader   Personality Traits
Related   Gregariousness

Social Acceptance
Used For   Acceptance (Social)
Broader   Social Behavior

Social Acceptance — (Continued)
Related   Social Approval

Social Adaptation
Use   Social Adjustment

Social Adjustment
Used For   Adaptation (Social)
Maladjustment (Social)
Social Adaptation
Social Maladjustment
Broader   Social Behavior
Related   Adjustment/

Social Approval
Used For   Approval (Social)
Popularity
Broader   Social Behavior
Social Influences
Related   Criticism
Social Acceptance
Social Reinforcement

Social Behavior
Narrower   Aggressive Behavior
Altruism
Animal Aggressive Behavior
Animal Communication
Animal Courtship Behavior
Animal Courtship Displays
Animal Distress Calls
Animal Division of Labor
Animal Dominance
Animal Maternal Behavior
Animal Mating Behavior
Animal Sexual Receptivity
Animal Social Behavior
Arguments
Assistance (Social Behavior)
Attack Behavior
Attribution
Bargaining
Charitable Behavior
Collective Behavior
Competition
Compliance
Conflict
Conformity (Personality)
Conversation
Cooperation
Criticism
Double Bind Interaction
Encouragement
Eye Contact
Friendship
Gambling
Group Discussion
Group Participation
Group Performance
Interpersonal Attraction
Interpersonal Communication

227

Social Behavior — (Continued)

Narrower
- Interpersonal Compatibility
- Interpersonal Influences
- Interpersonal Interaction
- Interviewing
- Interviews
- Involvement
- Job Applicant Interviews
- Leadership
- Leadership Style
- Militancy
- Negotiation
- Nonverbal Reinforcement
- Participation
- Peer Relations
- Persecution
- Praise
- Psychodiagnostic Interview
- Reciprocity
- Responsibility
- Riots
- Risk Taking
- Rivalry
- Social Acceptance
- Social Adjustment
- Social Approval
- Social Dating
- Social Demonstrations
- Social Drinking
- Social Facilitation
- Social Interaction
- Social Perception
- Social Reinforcement
- Threat Postures
- Trust (Social Behavior)
- Verbal Reinforcement
- Victimization
- Violence
- War

Related
- Dominance Hierarchy
- Personal Space
- Privacy
- Psychodynamics
- Social Change
- Social Influences

Social Casework
Used For   Social Work
Related   Family Therapy
         Treatment/

Social Caseworkers
Use   Social Workers

Social Change
Used For   Change (Social)
Related   Fads And Fashions
         Social Behavior
         Social Influences

Social Change — (Continued)
Related
- Social Movements
- Social Programs

Social Class
Broader   Social Structure
         Socioeconomic Status
Narrower   Lower Class
         Middle Class
         Upper Class
Related   Disadvantaged
         Income Level
         Socioeconomic Class Attitudes

Social Class Attitudes
Use   Socioeconomic Class Attitudes

Social Clubs (Therapeutic)
Use   Therapeutic Social Clubs

Social Dating
Used For   Dating (Social)
Broader   Human Courtship
         Interpersonal Interaction
         Social Behavior
         Social Interaction
Related   Friendship
         Petting
         Premarital Intercourse

Social Demonstrations
Used For   Demonstrations (Social)
         Picketing
Broader   Social Behavior
Related   Collective Behavior
         Social Movements
         Student Activism

Social Deprivation
Broader   Deprivation
         Social Processes
         Stimulus Deprivation
Narrower   Social Isolation

Social Desirability
Used For   Desirability (Social)
Broader   Social Influences

Social Drinking
Broader   Alcohol Drinking Patterns
         Social Behavior

Social Environments
Broader   Environment
Narrower   Academic Environment
         Animal Environments
         Classroom Environment
         College Environment
         Communes
         Communities
         Environmental Adaptation
         Ghettoes
         Home Environment

Social Environments — (Continued)
Narrower
- Kibbutz
- Neighborhoods
- Poverty Areas
- Rural Environments
- School Environment
- Suburban Environments
- Towns
- Urban Environments
- Working Conditions

Related   Cultural Deprivation

Social Equality
Used For   Equality (Social)
Related   Racial Integration

Social Facilitation
Used For   Facilitation (Social)
Broader   Social Behavior

Social Groups
Used For   Cadres
- Cliques
- Groups (Social)

Narrower   Dyads
- Minority Groups

Social Immobility
Use   Social Mobility

Social Influences
Used For   Influences (Social)
Narrower   Criticism
- Ethnic Values
- Power
- Prejudice
- Propaganda
- Religious Prejudices
- Social Approval
- Social Desirability
- Social Values
- Superstitions
- Taboos

Related   Ethics
- Interpersonal Influences
- Social Behavior
- Social Change
- Social Movements
- Social Reinforcement

Social Interaction
Used For   Interaction (Social)
Broader   Social Behavior
Narrower   Arguments
- Assistance (Social Behavior)
- Bargaining
- Charitable Behavior
- Collective Behavior
- Conflict
- Conversation
- Cooperation

Social Interaction — (Continued)
Narrower
- Double Bind Interaction
- Encouragement
- Eye Contact
- Friendship
- Group Discussion
- Group Participation
- Group Performance
- Interpersonal Attraction
- Interpersonal Communication
- Interpersonal Compatibility
- Interpersonal Influences
- Interpersonal Interaction
- Interviewing
- Interviews
- Job Applicant Interviews
- Negotiation
- Participation
- Peer Relations
- Persecution
- Psychodiagnostic Interview
- Riots
- Rivalry
- Social Dating
- Victimization
- Violence
- War

Related   Aggressive Behavior
- Psychodynamics

Social Isolation
Used For   Isolation (Social)
Broader   Deprivation
- Social Deprivation
- Social Processes
- Stimulus Deprivation

Social Learning
Narrower   Imitation (Learning)
- Imprinting
- Nonverbal Learning

Related   Learning/
- Social Reinforcement

Social Maladjustment
Use   Social Adjustment

Social Mobility
Used For   Mobility (Social)
- Social Immobility

Broader   Social Processes

Social Movements
Used For   Movements (Social)
Narrower   Activist Movements
- Black Power Movement
- Civil Rights Movement
- Homosexual Liberation Movement
- Student Activism
- Womens Liberation Movement

Social Movements — (Continued)
Related	Radical Movements
	Social Change
	Social Demonstrations
	Social Influences
	Social Programs

Social Perception
Used For	Interpersonal Perception
Broader	Social Behavior
Narrower	Attribution
Related	Perception/

Social Processes
Used For	Processes (Social)
Narrower	Coalition Formation
	Human Migration
	Immigration
	Industrialization
	Racial Integration
	School Integration (Racial)
	Social Deprivation
	Social Isolation
	Social Mobility
	Socialization
	Urbanization
Related	Political Processes
	Sociocultural Factors

Social Programs
Related	Housing
	Social Change
	Social Movements

Social Psychiatry
Broader	Medical Sciences
	Psychiatry
	Sciences
Related	Social Psychology

Social Psychologists
Broader	Psychologists
Related	Industrial Psychologists
	Sociologists

Social Psychology
Broader	Applied Psychology
	Psychology
	Sciences
	Social Sciences
Related	Social Psychiatry

Social Reinforcement
Broader	Reinforcement
	Social Behavior
Narrower	Nonverbal Reinforcement
	Praise
	Verbal Reinforcement
Related	Encouragement
	Eye Contact
	Social Approval
	Social Influences
	Social Learning

Social Sciences
Used For	Behavioral Sciences
	Science (Social)
Broader	Sciences
Narrower	Adolescent Psychology
	Anthropology
	Applied Psychology
	Child Psychology
	Clinical Psychology
	Community Psychology
	Comparative Psychology
	Consumer Psychology
	Counseling Psychology
	Developmental Psychology
	Educational Psychology
	Engineering Psychology
	Experimental Psychology
	Gerontology
	Industrial Psychology
	Mathematical Psychology
	Medical Psychology
	Military Psychology
	Neuropsychology
	Physiological Psychology
	Psychology
	School Psychology
	Social Psychology
	Sociology

Social Stress
Broader	Stress

Social Structure
Narrower	Caste System
	Lower Class
	Middle Class
	Social Class
	Upper Class
Related	Dominance Hierarchy

Social Values
Broader	Ethics
	Social Influences
	Values
Related	Morality

Social Work
Use	Social Casework

Social Work Education
Related	Education/

Social Workers
Used For	Caseworkers
	Social Caseworkers
Narrower	Psychiatric Social Workers
Related	Counselors
	Law Enforcement Personnel
	Mental Health Personnel
	Personnel/
	Psychologists
	Sociologists

Social Workers — (Continued)
Related
        Visiting Homemakers
        Vocational Counselors

Socialism
  Broader   Political Economic Systems

Socialization
  Broader   Social Processes

Socially Disadvantaged
  Use   Disadvantaged

Society

Sociocultural Factors
  Used For   Factors (Sociocultural)
  Narrower   Acculturation
           Birth Rites
           Cross Cultural Differences
           Cultural Assimilation
           Cultural Deprivation
           Culture Change
           Death Rites
           Ethnic Identity
           Ethnic Values
           Initiation Rites
           Marriage Rites
           Rites of Passage
  Related   Childrearing Practices
           Cultism
           Culture (Anthropological)
           Ethnic Groups
           Ethnography
           Ethnolinguistics
           Ethnology/
           Family Structure
           Kinship Structure
           Race (Anthropological)
           Social Processes

Socioeconomic Class Attitudes
  Used For   Class Attitudes
           Social Class Attitudes
  Narrower   Lower Class Attitudes
           Middle Class Attitudes
           Upper Class Attitudes
  Related   Attitudes/
           Social Class
           Socioeconomic Status

Socioeconomic Status
  Used For   SES (Income)
  Narrower   Family Socioeconomic Level
           Income Level
           Lower Class
           Lower Income Level
           Middle Class
           Middle Income Level
           Social Class

Socioeconomic Status — (Continued)
Narrower
        Upper Class
        Upper Income Level
  Related   Disadvantaged
           Income (Economic)
           Poverty
           Socioeconomic Class Attitudes

Sociograms
  Related   Measurement/

Sociologists
  Related   Anthropologists
           Counselors
           Personnel/
           Scientists/
           Social Psychologists
           Social Workers

Sociology
  Broader   Sciences
           Social Sciences

Sociometric Tests
  Related   Measurement/

Sociopath
  Use   Antisocial Personality

Sociopathology
  Use   Antisocial Behavior

Sociotherapy
  Related   Mental Health Program Evaluation
           Treatment/

Sodium
  Broader   Chemical Elements
           Metallic Elements
  Narrower   Sodium Ions

Sodium Bromide
  Broader   Anticonvulsive Drugs
           Antiepileptic Drugs
           Bromides
           Hypnotic Drugs
           Sedatives

Sodium Ions
  Broader   Chemical Elements
           Electrolytes
           Metallic Elements
           Sodium

Sodium Pentobarbital
  Use   Pentobarbital

Somatosensory Cortex
  Used For   Cortex (Somatosensory)
  Broader   Brain
           Central Nervous System
           Cerebral Cortex
           Nervous System

Somatosensory Cortex — (Continued)
Broader
    Parietal Lobe
    Telencephalon

Somatosensory Evoked Potentials
Used For Motor Evoked Potentials
Broader   Electrical Activity
    Electrophysiology
    Evoked Potentials
Related   Cortical Evoked Potentials

Somatotropin
Broader   Hormones
    Pituitary Hormones

Somatotypes
Used For Body Types
Related   Personality/
    Physique

Somesthetic Perception
Narrower Cutaneous Sense
    Kinesthetic Perception
    Pain Perception
    Pain Thresholds
    Tactual Perception
    Temperature Perception
    Vibrotactile Thresholds
Related   Labyrinth Disorders
    Perception/
    Pressure Sensation

Somesthetic Stimulation
Used For Vestibular Stimulation
Broader   Perceptual Stimulation
    Stimulation
Narrower Tactual Stimulation
Related   Roughness
    Weightlessness

Somnambulism
Broader   Consciousness Disturbances
    Dissociative Patterns
    Sleep Disorders
    Sleepwalking

Sonar
Broader   Apparatus

Sons
Broader   Family Members

Sorority Membership
Broader   Extracurricular Activities

Sorting (Cognition)
Use   Classification (Cognitive Process)

Sound
Use   Auditory Stimulation

Sound Localization
Use   Auditory Localization

Sound Pressure Level
Use   Loudness

Sourness
Use   Taste Stimulation

South America

South Vietnam

Southeast Asia

Space (Personal)
Use   Personal Space

Spacecraft
Related   Air Transportation
    Astronauts

Spaceflight
Broader   Aviation
Related   Acceleration Effects
    Decompression Effects
    Gravitational Effects
    Weightlessness

Spain

Spasms
Broader   Symptoms
Related   Anticonvulsive Drugs
    Antispasmodic Drugs
    Convulsions
    Pain

Spatial Discrimination
Use   Spatial Perception

Spatial Distortion
Broader   Illusions (Perception)
    Spatial Perception

Spatial Organization
Used For Organization (Spatial)
Broader   Spatial Perception

Spatial Orientation (Perception)
Used For Orientation (Spatial)
Broader   Perceptual Orientation
    Spatial Perception

Spatial Perception
Used For Spatial Discrimination
Narrower Apparent Distance
    Apparent Movement
    Apparent Size
    Autokinetic Illusion
    Depth Perception
    Distance Perception
    Motion Perception
    Size Discrimination
    Spatial Distortion
    Spatial Organization
    Spatial Orientation (Perception)
    Stereoscopic Vision

Spatial Perception — (Continued)
Related   Discrimination/
           Figure Ground Discrimination
           Perception/

Spearman Brown Test
Broader   Statistical Analysis
           Statistical Tests
Related   Statistical Reliability

Spearman Rho
Use   Rank Difference Correlation

Special Education
Used For   Special Education (Aurally
             Handicap)
           Special Education (Emot Dis-
             turbed)
           Special Education (Gifted)
           Special Education (Learning
             Disabil)
           Special Education (Mentally Re-
             tard)
           Special Education (Phys Handi-
             caps)
           Special Education (Visual Hand-
             icap)
Related   Ability Grouping
           Education/

Special Education (Aurally Handicap)
Use   Aurally Handicapped
           Special Education

Special Education (Emot Disturbed)
Use   Emotionally Disturbed
           Special Education

Special Education (Gifted)
Use   Gifted
           Special Education

Special Education (Learning Disabil)
Use   Learning Disabilities
           Special Education

Special Education (Mentally Retard)
Use   Mentally Retarded
           Special Education

Special Education (Phys Handicaps)
Use   Physically Handicapped
           Special Education

Special Education (Visual Handicap)
Use   Special Education
           Visually Handicapped

Special Education Students
Broader   Students

Special Education Teachers
Broader   Educational Personnel
           Teachers

Specialization (Academic)
Use   Academic Specialization

Spectral Sensitivity
Use   Color Perception

Speech
Use   Verbal Communication

Speech And Hearing Measures
Used For   Hearing Measures
           Speech Measures
Related   Measurement/
Identifier TROCA (Computer Screening
             Battery)
           Wepman Test of Auditory Dis-
             crim

Speech Characteristics
Broader   Verbal Communication
Narrower   Articulation (Speech)
           Pronunciation
           Speech Pauses
           Speech Pitch
           Speech Rate
           Speech Rhythm
Related   Inflection

Speech Development
Broader   Motor Development
           Physical Development
           Psychogenesis
           Psychomotor Development
Related   Cognitive Development
           Language Development

Speech Disorders
Narrower   Articulation Disorders
           Dysarthria
           Dysphonia
           Echolalia
           Elective Mutism
           Mutism
           Retarded Speech Development
           Stammering
           Stuttering
Related   Aphasia
           Cleft Palate
           Disorders/

Speech Handicapped
Broader   Handicapped
Related   Aphasia
           Articulation Disorders
           Cleft Palate
           Dysphonia
           Echolalia
           Mutism
           Retarded Speech Development

Speech Measures
Use   Speech And Hearing Measures

Speech Pauses
Broader   Speech Characteristics
           Verbal Communication

Speech Perception
Broader	Auditory Perception
Related	Lipreading

Speech Pitch
Broader	Auditory Stimulation
	Perceptual Stimulation
	Pitch (Frequency)
	Speech Characteristics
	Verbal Communication

Speech Processing (Mechanical)
Broader	Verbal Communication
Narrower	Clipped Speech (Mechanical)
	Compressed Speech
	Filtered Speech
	Synthetic Speech
Related	Auditory Stimulation

Speech Rate
Used For	Accelerated Speech
Broader	Speech Characteristics
	Verbal Communication
Related	Verbal Fluency

Speech Rhythm
Broader	Speech Characteristics
	Verbal Communication

Speech Therapists
Related	Educational Personnel
	Personnel/
	Therapists/

Speech Therapy
Related	Treatment/

Speed
Use	Velocity

Speed (Response)
Use	Reaction Time

Spelling
Broader	Curriculum
	Language Arts Education
Related	Orthography

Sperm
Broader	Cells (Biology)
	Germ Cells
Related	Sexual Reproduction

Spiders
Use	Arachnida

Spinal Column
Broader	Musculoskeletal System
Related	Bones
	Spinal Cord

Spinal Cord
Broader	Central Nervous System
	Nervous System
Narrower	Cranial Spinal Cord
	Dorsal Roots
	Extrapyramidal Tracts

Spinal Cord — (Continued)
Narrower	Lumbar Spinal Cord
	Pyramidal Tracts
	Sacral Spinal Cord
	Spinothalamic Tracts
	Thoracic Spinal Cord
	Ventral Roots
Related	Spinal Column

Spinal Cord Injuries
Broader	Injuries
Related	Central Nervous System Disorders
	Neuromuscular Disorders
	Paralysis

Spinal Fluid
Use	Cerebrospinal Fluid

Spinal Ganglia
Broader	Ganglia
	Nervous System

Spinal Nerves
Used For	Brachial Plexus
	Cauda Equina
	Cervical Plexus
	Femoral Nerve
	Lumbrosacral Plexus
	Median Nerve
	Musculocutaneous Nerve
	Nerves (Spinal)
	Obturator Nerve
	Phrenic Nerve
	Radial Nerve
	Sciatic Nerve
	Thoracic Nerves
	Ulnar Nerve
Broader	Nervous System
	Peripheral Nerves

Spinothalamic Tracts
Broader	Central Nervous System
	Nervous System
	Spinal Cord

Spleen
Related	Cardiovascular System

Split Personality
Use	Multiple Personality

Spokane Indians
Use	American Indians

Spontaneous Abortion
Used For	Abortion (Spontaneous)
	Miscarriage
Related	Induced Abortion

Spontaneous Recovery (Learning)
Broader	Memory
Related	Conditioning
	Learning/

Spontaneous Remission
Broader	Remission (Disorders)
Related	Psychotherapy
	Treatment/

Sports
Broader	Recreation
Narrower	Badminton
	Baseball
	Basketball
	Football
	Judo
	Swimming
	Tennis
Related	Athletes
	Athletic Participation
	Gymnasiums

Spouses
Used For	Married Couples
	Mates (Humans)
Broader	Family Members
Narrower	Housewives
	Husbands
	Wives
Related	Parents

Spreading Depression
Used For	Depression (Spreading)
Broader	Brain Stimulation
	Stereotaxic Techniques
	Stimulation

Squirrels
Broader	Mammals
	Rodents
	Vertebrates

SRA Primary Mental Abilities Test
(See)	Aptitude Measures
	Intelligence Measures

Stability (Emotional)
Use	Emotional Stability

Stage Plays
Use	Theatre

Stammering
Broader	Articulation Disorders
	Dysarthria
	Speech Disorders
Related	Stuttering

Standard Deviation
Used For	SD (Statistics)
Broader	Statistical Analysis
	Statistical Measurement
	Variability Measurement
Related	Frequency Distribution

Standardization (Test)
Use	Test Standardization

Standards (Professional)
Use	Professional Standards

Stanford Achievement Test
(See)	Achievement Measures

Stanford Binet Intelligence Scale
(See)	Intelligence Measures

Starfish
Use	Echinodermata

Startle Reflex
Broader	Reflexes
Related	Alarm Responses

Starvation
Broader	Nutritional Deficiencies
Related	Food Deprivation
	Hunger

State Hospitals
Use	Psychiatric Hospitals

State Trait Anxiety Inventory
(See)	Nonprojective Personality Measures
	Personality Measures

Statistical Analysis
Narrower	Analysis of Covariance
	Analysis of Variance
	Binomial Distribution
	Central Tendency Measures
	Chi Square Test
	Cluster Analysis
	Cochran Q Test
	Confidence Limits (Statistics)
	Consistency (Measurement)
	Equimax Rotation
	F Test
	Factor Analysis
	Frequency Distribution
	Interaction Analysis (Statistics)
	Interaction Variance
	Item Analysis (Statistical)
	Kolmogarov Smirnov Test
	Kuder Richardson Test
	Latin Squares Test
	Mann Whitney U Test
	McNemar Test
	Mean
	Median
	Mode
	Nonparametric Statistical Tests
	Normal Distribution
	Oblique Rotation
	Orthogonal Rotation
	Parametric Statistical Tests
	Predictability (Measurement)
	Quartimax Rotation
	Rulon Test
	Sign Test
	Skewed Distribution

Statistical Analysis — (Continued)

Narrower
Spearman Brown Test
Standard Deviation
Statistical Measurement
Statistical Norms
Statistical Probability
Statistical Rotation
Statistical Significance
Statistical Tests
T Test
Variability Measurement
Varimax Rotation
Walsh Test
Wilcoxon Sign Rank Test
Yates Test

Related
Analysis/
Experimental Design
Experimentation/
Hypothesis Testing
Mathematics (Concepts)
Measurement/
Population (Statistics)
Prediction Errors
Sampling (Experimental)
Statistical Correlation
Statistical Reliability
Statistical Validity
Statistical Variables

Statistical Correlation

Used For
Correlation (Statistical)
Pearson Prod Moment Correl Coeff

Narrower
Linear Regression
Negative Correlation
Nonlinear Regression
Phi Coefficient
Point Biserial Correlation
Rank Difference Correlation
Rank Order Correlation
Tetrachoric Correlation

Related
Experimentation/
Factor Analysis
Measurement/
Statistical Analysis
Statistical Significance
Statistical Validity
Statistical Variables
Variability Measurement

Statistical Measurement

Broader
Statistical Analysis

Narrower
Analysis of Covariance
Analysis of Variance
Binomial Distribution
Central Tendency Measures
Cluster Analysis
Consistency (Measurement)
Equimax Rotation

Statistical Measurement — (Continued)

Narrower
Factor Analysis
Frequency Distribution
Interaction Analysis (Statistics)
Interaction Variance
Item Analysis (Statistical)
Mean
Median
Mode
Normal Distribution
Oblique Rotation
Orthogonal Rotation
Predictability (Measurement)
Quartimax Rotation
Skewed Distribution
Standard Deviation
Statistical Norms
Statistical Probability
Statistical Rotation
Variability Measurement
Varimax Rotation

Related
Confidence Limits (Statistics)
Measurement/
Statistical Significance
Statistical Tests

Statistical Norms

Used For
Norms (Statistical)

Broader
Statistical Analysis
Statistical Measurement

Statistical Probability

Used For
Bayes Theorem

Broader
Chance (Fortune)
Probability
Statistical Analysis
Statistical Measurement

Narrower
Binomial Distribution

Statistical Reliability

Used For
Reliability (Statistical)

Related
Consistency (Measurement)
Experimentation/
Kuder Richardson Test
Measurement/
Population (Statistics)
Prediction Errors
Rulon Test
Sampling (Experimental)
Spearman Brown Test
Statistical Analysis
Statistical Validity

Statistical Rotation

Used For
Rotation Methods (Statistical)

Broader
Factor Analysis
Statistical Analysis
Statistical Measurement

Narrower
Equimax Rotation
Oblique Rotation

Statistical Rotation — (Continued)
Narrower
> Orthogonal Rotation
> Quartimax Rotation
> Varimax Rotation

Statistical Sample Parameters
Broader   Population (Statistics)
> Statistical Samples

Statistical Samples
Broader   Population (Statistics)
Narrower   Statistical Sample Parameters

Statistical Significance
Used For   Significance (Statistical)
Broader   Statistical Analysis
Related   Chi Square Test
> Confidence Limits (Statistics)
> Experimentation/
> Factor Analysis
> Hypothesis Testing
> McNemar Test
> Measurement/
> Sign Test
> Statistical Correlation
> Statistical Measurement
> Statistical Tests
> T Test

Statistical Tests
Used For   Tests (Statistical)
Broader   Statistical Analysis
Narrower   Chi Square Test
> Cochran Q Test
> F Test
> Kolmogarov Smirnov Test
> Kuder Richardson Test
> Latin Squares Test
> Mann Whitney U Test
> McNemar Test
> Nonparametric Statistical Tests
> Parametric Statistical Tests
> Rulon Test
> Sign Test
> Spearman Brown Test
> T Test
> Walsh Test
> Wilcoxon Sign Rank Test
> Yates Test
Related   Confidence Limits (Statistics)
> Measurement/
> Statistical Measurement
> Statistical Significance

Statistical Validity
Used For   Validity (Statistical)
Narrower   Factorial Validity
> Predictive Validity
Related   Consistency (Measurement)
> Experimentation/
> Measurement/

Statistical Validity — (Continued)
Related
> Prediction Errors
> Statistical Analysis
> Statistical Correlation
> Statistical Reliability
> Statistical Variables

Statistical Variables
Used For   Variables (Statistical)
Narrower   Dependent Variables
> Independent Variables
Related   Experimental Design
> Experimentation/
> Measurement/
> Population (Statistics)
> Prediction Errors
> Sampling (Experimental)
> Statistical Analysis
> Statistical Correlation
> Statistical Validity

Status

Stealing
Use   Theft

Stein Leventhal Syndrome
Broader   Amenorrhea
> Endocrine Disorders
> Endocrine Sexual Disorders
> Genital Disorders
> Gynecological Disorders
> Menstrual Disorders
> Syndromes
> Urogenital Disorders
Related   Endocrine Neoplasms
> Sterility

Stelazine
Use   Trifluoperazine

Stellate Ganglion
Use   Autonomic Ganglia

Stepchildren
Broader   Family Members
Related   Children

Stepparents
Broader   Family Members
> Parents

Stereopsis
Use   Stereoscopic Vision

Stereoscopic Presentation
Broader   Perceptual Stimulation
> Stimulus Presentation Methods
> Visual Stimulation

Stereoscopic Vision
Used For   Stereopsis

Stereoscopic Vision — (Continued)
- Broader   Depth Perception
           Spatial Perception
           Vision
           Visual Perception

Stereotaxic Atlas
- Used For   Atlas (Stereotaxic)
           Brain Mapping
           Brain Maps
           Maps (Brain)
- Related   Stereotaxic Techniques

Stereotaxic Techniques
- Used For   Techniques (Stereotaxic)
- Broader   Surgery
- Narrower   Brain Stimulation
           Chemical Brain Stimulation
           Electrical Brain Stimulation
           Spreading Depression
- Related   Afferent Stimulation
           Nervous System
           Stereotaxic Atlas

Stereotyped Attitudes
- Related   Attitudes/
           Race Attitudes

Stereotyped Behavior
- Related   Animal Ethology
           Symptoms

Sterility
- Broader   Genital Disorders
           Infertility
           Urogenital Disorders
- Related   Gynecological Disorders
           Hermaphroditism
           Hypogonadism
           Male Genital Disorders
           Stein Leventhal Syndrome
           Testicular Feminization Syndrome
           Turners Syndrome
           Venereal Diseases

Sterilization (Sex)
- Narrower   Castration
           Hysterectomy
           Male Castration
           Ovariectomy
           Tubal Ligation
           Vasectomy
- Related   Birth Control
           Family Planning

Steroids
- Narrower   Aldosterone
           Cholesterol
           Corticosteroids
           Corticosterone
           Cortisone
           Deoxycorticosterone

Steroids — (Continued)
- Narrower   Hydrocortisone
           Prednisolone
- Related   Drugs/
           Hormones
           Lipids

Sticklebacks
- Broader   Fishes
           Vertebrates

Stimulation
- Narrower   Afferent Stimulation
           Auditory Stimulation
           Aversive Stimulation
           Brain Stimulation
           Chemical Brain Stimulation
           Electrical Brain Stimulation
           Perceptual Stimulation
           Prismatic Stimulation
           Self Stimulation
           Somesthetic Stimulation
           Spreading Depression
           Tactual Stimulation
           Taste Stimulation
           Visual Stimulation
- Related   Biofeedback
           Conditioned Stimulus
           Conditioning
           Feedback
           Stimulus Ambiguity
           Stimulus Change
           Stimulus Control
           Stimulus Deprivation
           Stimulus Discrimination
           Stimulus Generalization
           Stimulus Parameters
           Stimulus Presentation Methods
           Unconditioned Stimulus

Stimulators (Apparatus)
- Broader   Apparatus
- Narrower   Shock Units
- Related   Electrodes
           Vibrators (Apparatus)

Stimulus (Conditioned)
- Use   Conditioned Stimulus

Stimulus (Unconditioned)
- Use   Unconditioned Stimulus

Stimulus Ambiguity
- Used For   Ambiguity (Stimulus)
- Related   Stimulation
           Stimulus Generalization

Stimulus Attenuation
- Used For   Attenuation (Stimulus)
- Broader   Stimulus Parameters

Stimulus Change
- Used For   Change (Stimulus)

Stimulus Change — (Continued)
Related   Stimulation

Stimulus Complexity
Used For   Complexity (Stimulus)
Broader   Stimulus Parameters

Stimulus Control
Used For   Control (Stimulus)
Related   Stimulation
            Stimulus Presentation Methods

Stimulus Deprivation
Broader   Deprivation
Narrower   Food Deprivation
            Sensory Deprivation
            Social Deprivation
            Social Isolation
            Water Deprivation
Related   Stimulation

Stimulus Discrimination
Related   Discrimination/
            Stimulation

Stimulus Duration
Used For   Duration (Stimulus)
            Exposure Time (Stimulus)
            Stimulus Exposure Time
Broader   Stimulus Parameters

Stimulus Exposure Time
Use   Stimulus Duration

Stimulus Frequency
Used For   Frequency (Stimulus)
Broader   Stimulus Parameters

Stimulus Generalization
Used For   Generalization (Stimulus)
Related   Stimulation
            Stimulus Ambiguity

Stimulus Intensity
Used For   Intensity (Stimulus)
            Signal Intensity
Broader   Stimulus Parameters

Stimulus Intervals
Used For   Intervals (Stimulus)
Broader   Stimulus Parameters
Narrower   Interstimulus Interval
            Intertrial Interval

Stimulus Novelty
Used For   Novel Stimuli
Broader   Stimulus Parameters

Stimulus Parameters
Used For   Parameters (Stimulus)
Narrower   Interstimulus Interval
            Intertrial Interval
            Stimulus Attenuation
            Stimulus Complexity
            Stimulus Duration
            Stimulus Frequency

Stimulus Parameters — (Continued)
Narrower
            Stimulus Intensity
            Stimulus Intervals
            Stimulus Novelty
            Stimulus Salience
            Stimulus Similarity
            Stimulus Variability
Related   Stimulation

Stimulus Pattern
Use   Stimulus Variability

Stimulus Presentation Methods
Used For   Presentation Methods
            Presentation Modes
Narrower   Stereoscopic Presentation
            Tachistoscopic Presentation
Related   Stimulation
            Stimulus Control

Stimulus Salience
Used For   Salience (Stimulus)
Broader   Stimulus Parameters

Stimulus Similarity
Used For   Similarity (Stimulus)
Broader   Stimulus Parameters

Stimulus Variability
Used For   Pattern (Stimulus)
            Stimulus Pattern
            Variability (Stimulus)
Broader   Stimulus Parameters

Stipends
Use   Educational Financial Assistance

Stochastic Modeling
Broader   Simulation
Narrower   Markov Chains
Related   Information Theory
            Mathematical Modeling

Stock Options
Broader   Employee Benefits
Related   Bonuses

Stomach
Broader   Digestive System
            Gastrointestinal System

Storytelling Technique
Use   Mutual Storytelling Technique

Strabismus
Used For   Crossed Eyes
Broader   Eye Disorders
            Sense Organ Disorders
Related   Amblyopia

Strain Differences (Animal)
Use   Animal Breeding
            Genetics/

Strategies

Strength (Physical)
Use   Physical Strength

Stress
Narrower   Environmental Stress
            Occupational Stress
            Physiological Stress
            Psychological Stress
            Social Stress
            Stress Reactions
Related   Adrenal Cortex Hormones
            Anxiety
            Crises
            Deprivation
            Disasters
            Endurance
            Family Crises
            Identity Crisis
            Natural Disasters
            Organizational Crises

Stress Reactions
Used For   Crisis (Reactions To)
            Reactions To Crisis
Broader   Stress
Related   Deprivation
            Psychological Endurance
            Psychological Stress

Strikes
Related   Labor Management Relations

Stroboscopic Movement
Use   Apparent Movement

Stroke (Cerebrum)
Use   Cerebrovascular Accidents

Strong Vocational Interest Blank
Used For   SVIB (Test)
(See)   Occupational Interest Measures

Strontium
Broader   Chemical Elements
            Metallic Elements

Strontium Bromide
Broader   Antiepileptic Drugs
            Bromides
            Sedatives

Stroop Color Word Test
(See)   Perceptual Measures

Structuralism
Broader   History of Psychology

Strychnine
Broader   Alkaloids
            Analeptic Drugs
            CNS Affecting Drugs
            CNS Stimulating Drugs

Student Activism
Used For   Activism (Student)
            Protest (Student)
            Student Protest
Broader   Activist Movements
            Social Movements
Related   Social Demonstrations

Student Admission Criteria
Used For   Admission Criteria (Student)
Related   Academic Aptitude
            Education/
            Entrance Examinations

Student Attitudes
Related   Attitudes/
            Education/

Student Protest
Use   Student Activism

Student Teachers
Broader   Educational Personnel
            Teachers

Student Teaching
Used For   Teaching Internship
Broader   Teacher Education

Students
Narrower   Business Students
            Classmates
            College Students
            Community College Students
            Dental Students
            Elementary School Students
            Foreign Students
            Graduate Students
            High School Students
            Intermediate School Students
            Junior College Students
            Junior High School Students
            Kindergarten Students
            Medical Students
            Nursery School Students
            Nursing Students
            Postgraduate Students
            Primary School Students
            Roommates
            ROTC Students
            Seminarians
            Special Education Students
            Transfer Students
            Vocational School Students
Related   Education/

Students T Test
Use   T Test

Studies (Followup)
Use   Followup Studies

Studies (Longitudinal)
Use   Longitudinal Studies

Study Habits
  Related   Education/

Stuttering
  Broader   Articulation Disorders
             Dysarthria
             Speech Disorders
  Related   Stammering

Style (Leadership)
  Use   Leadership Style

Subconscious
  Broader   Psychoanalytic Personality Fac-
             tors

Subcortical Lesions
  Use   Brain Lesions

Subculture (Anthropological)
  Used For   Hippies
  Broader   Culture (Anthropological)

Subcutaneous Injections
  Broader   Injections

Subjectivity
  Use   Objectivity

Sublimation
  Broader   Defense Mechanisms

Subliminal Perception
  Related   Perception/

Submarines
  Broader   Transportation
             Water Transportation

Submissiveness
  Use   Obedience

Submucous Plexus
  Use   Autonomic Ganglia

Subnormality (Mental)
  Use   Mental Retardation

Subprofessional Personnel
  Use   Paraprofessional Personnel

Substantia Nigra
  Use   Mesencephalon

Subtests
  Related   Measurement/
             Testing Methods

Suburban Environments
  Broader   Environment
             Social Environments

Subvocalization
  Broader   Vocalization

Success
  Use   Achievement

Successive Contrast
  Use   Brightness Perception

Succinylcholine
  Broader   Muscle Relaxing Drugs
  Related   Choline

Suffering
  Broader   Emotional States
  Related   Distress
             Grief
             Pain

Sugars
  Broader   Carbohydrates
  Narrower   Blood Sugar
             Glucose
  Related   Saccharin

Suggestibility
  Broader   Consciousness Disturbances
             Personality Traits
  Related   Catalepsy
             Hysteria

Suicide
  Broader   Behavior Disorders
  Related   Attempted Suicide
             Mental Disorders/
             Suicide Prevention

Suicide (Attempted)
  Use   Attempted Suicide

Suicide Prevention
  Broader   Crisis Intervention
  Related   Attempted Suicide
             Prevention/
             Suicide
             Suicide Prevention Centers

Suicide Prevention Centers
  Broader   Community Facilities
             Crisis Intervention Services
             Mental Health Programs
  Related   Community Mental Health Cen-
             ters
             Hot Line Services
             Suicide Prevention

Sulpiride
  Broader   Antiemetic Drugs
             Neuroleptic Drugs

Summer Camps (Recreation)
  Used For   Day Camps (Recreation)
             Recreational Day Camps
  Broader   Recreation
  Related   Camping
             Vacationing

Superego
  Broader   Psychoanalytic Personality Fac-
             tors
  Narrower   Conscience

Superior Colliculus
Broader Brain
Central Nervous System
Corpora Quadrigemina
Mesencephalon
Nervous System

Superiority (Emotional)
Use Emotional Superiority

Superstitions
Broader Social Influences
Related Religious Beliefs
Taboos

Supervisors
Use Management Personnel

Support (For Theories)
Identifier Professional Contribution

Supportive Psychotherapy
Use Psychotherapy

Suppression (Conditioned)
Use Conditioned Suppression

Suppression (Defense Mechanism)
Broader Defense Mechanisms
Related Forgetting
Repression (Defense Mechanism)

Surgeons
Used For Neurosurgeons
Broader Medical Personnel
Physicians
Related Gynecologists
Neurologists
Pathologists

Surgery
Used For Circumcision
Operation (Surgery)
Broader Medical Sciences
Physical Treatment Methods
Sciences
Narrower Adrenalectomy
Amputation
Autopsy
Castration
Colostomy
Decerebration
Decortication (Brain)
Dental Surgery
Endocrine Gland Surgery
Heart Surgery
Hemispherectomy
Hypophysectomy
Hysterectomy
Induced Abortion
Male Castration
Mastectomy
Neurosurgery
Organ Transplantation

Surgery — (Continued)
Narrower
Ovariectomy
Pancreatectomy
Pinealectomy
Plastic Surgery
Psychosurgery
Pyramidotomy
Stereotaxic Techniques
Sympathectomy
Thalamotomy
Thymectomy
Thyroidectomy
Tractotomy
Vagotomy
Related Afferent Stimulation
Biopsy
Body Image Disturbances
Lesions
Postsurgical Complications
(Physical

Surgical Complications
Use Postsurgical Complications
(Physical

Surgical Patients
Broader Patients

Surrogate Parents (Humans)
Broader Family Members
Parents

Surveys
Narrower Consumer Surveys
Related Measurement/

Surveys (Interest)
Use Interest Inventories

Surveys (Opinion)
Use Attitude Measures

Surveys (Personality)
Use Personality Measures

Surveys (Preference)
Use Preference Measures

Susceptibility (Disorders)
Related Disorders/
Mental Disorders/

Susceptibility (Hypnotic)
Use Hypnotic Susceptibility

Suspension (School)
Use School Suspension

Suspicion
Used For Distrust
Related Doubt
Emotions/

SVIB (Test)
Identifier Strong Vocational Interest Blank

Sweat
Used For	Perspiration
Broader	Body Fluids
Related	Sweating

Sweating
Broader	Secretion (Gland)
Related	Skin Disorders
	Sweat

Sweden

Sweetness
Use	Taste Stimulation

Swimming
Broader	Recreation
	Sports

Switzerland

Syllables
Broader	Language
	Linguistics
	Phonetics
	Verbal Communication

Syllogistic Reasoning
Use	Inductive Deductive Reasoning

Symbiosis (Biological)
Use	Biological Symbiosis

Symbiotic Infantile Psychosis
Broader	Childhood Psychosis
	Psychosis
Related	Childhood Schizophrenia
	Early Infantile Autism
	Mother Child Relations

Symbolism
Related	Communication/
	Language

Sympathectomy
Broader	Neurosurgery
	Physical Treatment Methods
	Surgery
Related	Psychosurgery

Sympathetic Nervous System
Broader	Autonomic Nervous System
	Nervous System
Related	Adrenergic Blocking Drugs
	Adrenergic Drugs
	Adrenolytic Drugs
	Sympatholytic Drugs
	Sympathomimetic Drugs

Sympathetic Pain
Broader	Pain
	Psychosomatic Disorders
	Symptoms

Sympatholytic Drugs
Narrower	Hydralazine
	Reserpine
Related	Adrenergic Blocking Drugs
	Adrenolytic Drugs
	Drugs/
	Sympathetic Nervous System
	Sympathomimetic Drugs

Sympathomimetic Amines
Broader	Amines
	Sympathomimetic Drugs
Narrower	Amphetamine
	Catecholamines
	Dextroamphetamine
	Dopamine
	Ephedrine
	Epinephrine
	Methamphetamine
	Methoxamine
	Norepinephrine
	Phenmetrazine
	Tyramine

Sympathomimetic Drugs
Narrower	Amphetamine
	Catecholamines
	Dextroamphetamine
	Dopamine
	Ephedrine
	Epinephrine
	Fenfluramine
	Isoproterenol
	Methamphetamine
	Methoxamine
	Norepinephrine
	Phenmetrazine
	Sympathomimetic Amines
	Tyramine
Related	Adrenergic Drugs
	Drugs/
	Sympathetic Nervous System
	Sympatholytic Drugs

Sympathy
Related	Emotions/

Symposia
Use	Professional Meetings And Symposia

Symptom Remission
Broader	Remission (Disorders)

Symptoms
Narrower	Acting Out
	Anorexia Nervosa
	Anoxia
	Aphagia
	Apnea
	Appetite Disorders
	Apraxia

243

Symptoms — (Continued)
Narrower

Asthenia
Ataxia
Aura
Automatism
Body Rocking
Catalepsy
Catatonia
Coma
Convulsions
Delirium
Depersonalization
Distractibility
Dyskinesia
Dyspnea
Fatigue
Headache
Hematoma
Hemorrhage
Hyperglycemia
Hyperkinesis
Hyperphagia
Hyperthermia
Hyperventilation
Hypochondriasis
Hypoglycemia
Hypothermia
Insomnia
Migraine Headache
Muscle Contraction Headache
Myasthenia
Nausea
Obesity
Pain
Pruritus
Psychogenic Pain
Respiratory Distress
Restlessness
Scratching
Shock
Spasms
Sympathetic Pain
Syncope
Tics
Tremor
Underweight
Vertigo
Vomiting
Word Salad

Related
Behavior Disorders
Digestive System Disorders
Disorders/
Fecal Incontinence
Frigidity
Mental Disorders/
Nervous System Disorders
Physiological Correlates
Psychosomatic Disorders

Symptoms — (Continued)
Related

Stereotyped Behavior
Urinary Incontinence

Synapses
Broader
Nerve Endings
Nervous System

Syncope
Used For   Fainting
Broader   Blood Pressure Disorders
Cardiovascular Disorders
Symptoms
Related   Shock
Vertigo

Syndromes
Narrower
Addisons Disease
Alcoholic Hallucinosis
Alcoholic Psychosis
Alzheimers Disease
Battered Child Syndrome
Crying Cat Syndrome
Cushings Syndrome
Delirium Tremens
Downs Syndrome
Klinefelters Syndrome
Korsakoffs Psychosis
Menieres Disease
Organic Brain Syndromes
Picks Disease
Presenile Dementia
Senile Dementia
Senile Psychosis
Stein Leventhal Syndrome
Testicular Feminization Syn-
drome
Toxic Psychoses
Turners Syndrome
Wernickes Syndrome
Related   Disorders/

Synergism (Drugs)
Use   Drug Synergism

Synonyms
Broader   Language
Verbal Communication
Vocabulary

Synovial Bursa
Broader   Musculoskeletal System

Syntactic Structure
Use   Syntax

Syntax
Used For   Syntactic Structure
Broader   Grammar
Language
Linguistics
Verbal Communication
Narrower   Sentence Structure

Synthetic Speech
Broader	Speech Processing (Mechanical)
	Verbal Communication

Syphilis
Broader	Bacterial Disorders
	Infectious Disorders
	Venereal Diseases
Narrower	Neurosyphilis
Related	Congenital Disorders
	General Paresis

Systematic Desensitization Therapy
Used For	Desensitization (Systematic)
	Muscle Relaxation Therapy
	Relaxation Therapy
Broader	Behavior Modification
	Behavior Therapy
Related	Reciprocal Inhibition Therapy

Systems Analysis
Related	Analysis/
	Man Machine Systems
	Systems/
	Task Analysis

Systems/
Related	Anatomical Systems/
	Caste System
	Communication Systems
	Computer Software
	Computers
	Man Machine Systems
	Man Machine Systems Design
	Systems Analysis

Systolic Pressure
Used For	Pressure (Systolic)
Broader	Blood Pressure

Szondi Test
(See)	Personality Measures
	Projective Personality Measures
	Projective Techniques

T Groups
Use	Sensitivity Training

T Mazes
Used For	Mazes (T)
Broader	Apparatus
	Mazes

T Test
Used For	Students T Test
Broader	Parametric Statistical Tests
	Statistical Analysis
	Statistical Tests
Related	Central Tendency Measures
	Statistical Significance

Taboos
Broader	Social Influences
Related	Animism
	Ethnic Groups

Taboos — (Continued)
Related	
	Ethnology/
	Rites of Passage
	Superstitions
	Transcultural Psychiatry

Tachistoscopes
Broader	Apparatus

Tachistoscopic Presentation
Broader	Perceptual Stimulation
	Stimulus Presentation Methods
	Visual Stimulation

Tachycardia
Broader	Arrhythmias (Heart)
	Cardiovascular Disorders
	Heart Disorders
Related	Hyperthyroidism

Tactual Discrimination
Use	Tactual Perception

Tactual Displays
Broader	Displays

Tactual Perception
Used For	Tactual Discrimination
	Touch
Broader	Cutaneous Sense
	Somesthetic Perception
Narrower	Vibrotactile Thresholds
Related	Anesthesia (Feeling)
	Discrimination/
	Perception/

Tactual Stimulation
Broader	Perceptual Stimulation
	Somesthetic Stimulation
	Stimulation

Taiwan

Talent
Use	Ability/

Talented
Use	Gifted

Tantrums
Broader	Behavior Disorders

Tape Recorders
Used For	Recorders (Tape)
Broader	Apparatus
Narrower	Videotape Recorders

Taraxein
Broader	Blood Proteins
	Proteins
	Psychotomimetic Drugs

Task Analysis
Related	Analysis/
	Job Analysis

Task Analysis — (Continued)
Related
 Systems Analysis
 Task Complexity

Task Complexity
Used For Complexity (Task)
 Task Difficulty
Related Task Analysis

Task Difficulty
Use Task Complexity

Taste Buds
Broader Digestive System
 Sense Organs
 Tongue
Related Chemoreceptors

Taste Discrimination
Use Taste Perception

Taste Perception
Used For Gustatory Perception
 Taste Discrimination
Related Discrimination/
 Olfactory Perception
 Perception/

Taste Stimulation
Used For Bitterness
 Saltiness
 Sourness
 Sweetness
Broader Perceptual Stimulation
 Stimulation

TAT (Test)
Identifier Thematic Apperception Test

Taxonomies
Used For Classification Systems

Tay Sachs Disease
Use Amaurotic Familial Idiocy

Taylor Manifest Anxiety Scale
Used For MA Scale (Test)
(See) Nonprojective Personality Measures
 Personality Measures

Tea (Drug)
Use Caffeine

Teacher (Evaluation of)
Use Personnel Evaluation
 Teachers

Teacher Accreditation
Use Accreditation (Education Personnel)

Teacher Aides
Broader Educational Personnel
 Paraprofessional Personnel

Teacher Attitudes
Broader Teacher Characteristics
Related Attitudes/
 Education/
 Teacher Personality
 Teacher Student Interaction

Teacher Characteristics
Used For Teacher Effectiveness
Narrower Teacher Attitudes
 Teacher Personality
Related Teacher Student Interaction
 Teachers
 Teaching

Teacher Education
Used For Teacher Training
Narrower Inservice Teacher Education
 Student Teaching
Related Education/

Teacher Effectiveness
Use Teacher Characteristics

Teacher Personality
Broader Teacher Characteristics
Related Education/
 Personality/
 Teacher Attitudes
 Teacher Student Interaction

Teacher Recruitment
Used For Recruitment (Teachers)
Broader Personnel Management
 Personnel Recruitment

Teacher Student Interaction
Related Classroom Discipline
 Education/
 Teacher Attitudes
 Teacher Characteristics
 Teacher Personality

Teacher Supply
Broader Personnel Supply

Teacher Tenure
Used For Tenure (Teacher)
Broader Occupational Tenure
Related Education/

Teacher Training
Use Teacher Education

Teachers
Used For Classroom Teachers
 Coaches
 Instructors
 Teacher (Evaluation of)
 Tutors
Broader Educational Personnel
Narrower College Teachers
 Elementary School Teachers
 High School Teachers
 Junior High School Teachers

Teachers — (Continued)

Narrower
> Resource Teachers
> Special Education Teachers
> Student Teachers

Related   Teacher Characteristics

Teaching

Used For   Classroom Instruction
> Instruction

Narrower   Audiovisual Instruction
> Computer Assisted Instruction
> Departmentalized Teaching Method
> Directed Discussion Method
> Discovery Teaching Method
> Educational Audiovisual Aids
> Educational Field Trips
> Group Instruction
> Individualized Instruction
> Instructional Media
> Lecture Method
> Lesson Plans
> Montessori Method
> Motion Pictures (Educational)
> Nondirected Discussion Method
> Open Classroom Method
> Peer Tutoring
> Programed Instruction
> Programed Textbooks
> Reading Materials
> Teaching Machines
> Teaching Methods
> Team Teaching Method
> Televised Instruction
> Tutoring
> Videotape Instruction

Related   Education/
> Teacher Characteristics

Teaching (Programed)

Use   Programed Instruction

Teaching Internship

Use   Student Teaching

Teaching Machines

Broader   Instructional Media
> Teaching

Related   Computer Assisted Instruction
> Programed Instruction

Teaching Methods

Broader   Teaching

Narrower   Audiovisual Instruction
> Computer Assisted Instruction
> Departmentalized Teaching Method
> Directed Discussion Method
> Discovery Teaching Method
> Educational Field Trips
> Group Instruction

Teaching Methods — (Continued)

Narrower
> Individualized Instruction
> Lecture Method
> Lesson Plans
> Montessori Method
> Nondirected Discussion Method
> Open Classroom Method
> Peer Tutoring
> Programed Instruction
> Team Teaching Method
> Televised Instruction
> Tutoring
> Videotape Instruction

Related   Initial Teaching Alphabet

Team Teaching Method

Broader   Teaching
> Teaching Methods

Related   Open Classroom Method

Technical Schools

Used For   Vocational Schools

Broader   Schools

Technical Service Personnel

Used For   Repairmen

Related   Blue Collar Workers
> Business And Industrial Personnel
> Personnel/

Technique (Projective Testing)

Use   Projective Testing Technique

Technique (Q Sort Testing)

Use   Q Sort Testing Technique

Techniques (Stereotaxic)

Use   Stereotaxic Techniques

Technology

Related   Sciences

Teenagers

Use   Adolescents

Teeth (Anatomy)

Broader   Digestive System

Related   Mouth (Anatomy)

Teeth Grinding (Nocturnal)

Use   Nocturnal Teeth Grinding

Telecommunications Media

Broader   Communications Media

Narrower   Closed Circuit Television
> Educational Television
> Radio
> Telephone Systems
> Television
> Television Advertising

Related   Telemetry

Telekinesis

Use   Psychokinesis

Telemetry
- Related   Telecommunications Media

Telencephalon
- Broader   Brain
             Central Nervous System
             Nervous System
- Narrower   Amygdaloid Body
             Auditory Cortex
             Basal Ganglia
             Caudate Nucleus
             Cerebral Cortex
             Cerebral Ventricles
             Corpus Callosum
             Frontal Lobe
             Globus Pallidus
             Gyrus Cinguli
             Hippocampus
             Limbic System
             Motor Cortex
             Occipital Lobe
             Parietal Lobe
             Somatosensory Cortex
             Temporal Lobe
             Visual Cortex

Telepathy
- Broader   Parapsychological Phenomena
             Parapsychology
- Related   Extrasensory Perception

Telephone Hot Lines
- Use   Hot Line Services

Telephone Systems
- Broader   Communications Media
             Mass Media
             Telecommunications Media

Televised Instruction
- Broader   Audiovisual Instruction
             Teaching
             Teaching Methods
- Related   Educational Audiovisual Aids
             Educational Television

Television
- Broader   Audiovisual Communications
                Media
             Communications Media
             Mass Media
             Telecommunications Media
- Narrower   Closed Circuit Television
             Educational Television
             Television Advertising
- Related   Apparatus

Television Advertising
- Broader   Advertising
             Audiovisual Communications
                Media
             Communications Media
             Mass Media

Television Advertising — (Continued)
- Broader
             Telecommunications Media
             Television

Television Viewing
- Broader   Recreation

Tell A Story Kit (Taskit)
- (See)   Projective Techniques

Temperament
- Use   Personality/

Temperature (Body)
- Use   Body Temperature

Temperature (Skin)
- Use   Skin Temperature

Temperature Effects
- Broader   Environmental Effects
- Narrower   Cold Effects
             Heat Effects
- Related   Atmospheric Conditions
             Pollution
             Seasonal Variations
             Thermal Acclimatization

Temperature Perception
- Broader   Somesthetic Perception

Temporal Lobe
- Broader   Brain
             Central Nervous System
             Cerebral Cortex
             Nervous System
             Telencephalon
- Narrower   Auditory Cortex

Temporal Spatial Concept Scale
- (See)   Intelligence Measures

Temptation
- Broader   Motivation
- Related   Incentives

Tendency Measures (Central)
- Use   Central Tendency Measures

Tendons
- Broader   Musculoskeletal System

Tennessee Self Concept Scale
- (See)   Nonprojective Personality Meas-
                ures
             Personality Measures

Tennis
- Broader   Recreation
             Sports

Tension (Premenstrual)
- Use   Premenstrual Tension

Tenure (Occupational)
- Use   Occupational Tenure

Tenure (Teacher)
Use   Teacher Tenure

Terminal Cancer
Broader   Neoplasms
Related   Death And Dying
             Terminally Ill Patients

Terminally Ill Patients
Used For   Dying Patients
Broader   Patients
Related   Death And Dying
             Terminal Cancer

Terminology (Psychological)
Use   Psychological Terminology

Territoriality
Used For   Habitat Selection
Broader   Animal Ethology
Related   Animal Aggressive Behavior
             Animal Courtship Displays
             Animal Dominance
             Animal Innate Behavior
             Animal Instinctive Behavior

Test (Achievement)
Use   Achievement Measures

Test (Aptitude)
Use   Aptitude Measures

Test (Intelligence)
Use   Intelligence Measures

Test Administration
Used For   Administration (Test)
Broader   Testing
Related   Group Testing
             Individual Testing
             Measurement/
             Testing Methods

Test Anxiety
Related   Anxiety

Test Bias (Cultural)
Use   Cultural Test Bias

Test Construction
Used For   Construction (Test)
Narrower   Content Analysis (Test)
             Cultural Test Bias
             Difficulty Level (Test)
             Item Analysis (Test)
             Item Content (Test)
             Test Items
             Test Reliability
             Test Standardization
             Test Validity
Related   Experimental Design
             Measurement/

Test Items
Broader   Test Construction
             Testing

Test Items — (Continued)
Related   Measurement/

Test Normalization
Use   Test Standardization

Test Norms
Used For   Norms (Test)
Related   Measurement/

Test Reliability
Used For   Reliability (Test)
Broader   Test Construction
             Testing
Related   Measurement/
             Test Standardization

Test Scores
Used For   Scores (Test)
Related   Measurement/

Test Standardization
Used For   Normalization (Test)
             Standardization (Test)
             Test Normalization
Broader   Test Construction
             Testing
Related   Measurement/
             Test Reliability
             Test Validity

Test Validity
Used For   Validity (Test)
Broader   Test Construction
             Testing
Related   Measurement/
             Test Standardization

Testes
Broader   Endocrine Glands
             Endocrine System
             Glands
             Gonads
             Male Genitalia
             Urogenital System

Testes Disorders
Use   Endocrine Sexual Disorders

Testicular Feminization Syndrome
Used For   Feminization Syndrome (Testicular)
Broader   Endocrine Disorders
             Endocrine Sexual Disorders
             Genetic Disorders
             Genital Disorders
             Male Genital Disorders
             Sex Linked Hereditary Disorders
             Syndromes
             Urogenital Disorders
Related   Hermaphroditism
             Sterility

Testimony (Expert)
Use   Expert Testimony

Testing
Narrower	Content Analysis (Test)
	Cultural Test Bias
	Difficulty Level (Test)
	Item Analysis (Test)
	Item Content (Test)
	Rating
	Scaling (Testing)
	Scoring (Testing)
	Test Administration
	Test Items
	Test Reliability
	Test Standardization
	Test Validity
Related	Measurement/
	Psychometrics

Testing (Hypothesis)
Use	Hypothesis Testing

Testing (Job Applicant)
Use	Job Applicant Screening

Testing (Reality)
Use	Reality Testing

Testing Methods
Narrower	Forced Choice (Testing Method)
	Multiple Choice (Testing Method)
	Q Sort Testing Technique
Related	Measurement/
	Posttesting
	Pretesting
	Subtests
	Test Administration

Testosterone
Broader	Androgens
	Hormones
	Sex Hormones

Tests
Use	Measurement/

Tests (Personality)
Use	Personality Measures

Tests (Statistical)
Use	Statistical Tests

Tetanus (Disease)
Broader	Bacterial Disorders
	Infectious Disorders
Related	Nervous System Disorders
	Toxic Disorders

Tetrabenazine
Broader	Antipsychotic Drugs
	Neuroleptic Drugs
	Serotonin Antagonists
	Tranquilizing Drugs

Tetracaine
Used For	Dicaine

Tetracaine — (Continued)
Broader	Anesthetic Drugs
	Local Anesthetics

Tetrachoric Correlation
Broader	Statistical Correlation

Tetracycline
Broader	Antibiotics

Tetrahydrocannabinol
Broader	Alcohols
Related	Cannabis
	Hallucinogenic Drugs
	Hashish
	Marihuana

Textbooks (Programed)
Use	Programed Textbooks

Thailand

Thalamic Nuclei
Broader	Brain
	Central Nervous System
	Diencephalon
	Nervous System
	Thalamus

Thalamotomy
Broader	Neurosurgery
	Physical Treatment Methods
	Psychosurgery
	Surgery

Thalamus
Broader	Brain
	Central Nervous System
	Diencephalon
	Nervous System
Narrower	Geniculate Bodies (Thalamus)
	Thalamic Nuclei

Thalidomide
Broader	Amines
	Hypnotic Drugs
	Sedatives
Related	Drug Induced Congenital Disorders

Theatre
Used For	Stage Plays
Broader	Arts
Narrower	Drama

Theft
Used For	Robbery
	Stealing
Broader	Antisocial Behavior
	Behavior Disorders
	Crime
Narrower	Shoplifting

Thematic Apperception Test
Used For	TAT (Test)

Thematic Apperception Test — (Continued)
- (See)   Personality Measures
          Projective Personality Measures
          Projective Techniques

Theology
- Use   Religion/

Theophylline
- Broader   Alkaloids
          Heart Rate Affecting Drugs
          Muscle Relaxing Drugs
- Related   Analeptic Drugs
          Vasodilation

Theories of Education
- Related   Education/
          Theories/

Theories/
- Related   Communication Theory
          Darwinism
          History of Psychology
          Information Theory
          Learning Theory
          Personality Theory
          Psychoanalytic Theory
          Theories of Education
          Theory of Evolution

Theory Formulation
- Related   Methodology/

Theory of Evolution
- Used For   Evolution (Theory of)
- Related   Darwinism
          Theories/

Theory Verification
- Used For   Verification (of Theories)

Therapeutic Abortion
- Use   Induced Abortion

Therapeutic Community
- Used For   Milieu Therapy
- Broader   Group Psychotherapy
          Psychiatric Hospital Programs
          Psychotherapy

Therapeutic Devices (Medical)
- Use   Medical Therapeutic Devices

Therapeutic Social Clubs
- Used For   Social Clubs (Therapeutic)
- Broader   Psychosocial Rehabilitation

Therapeutic Techniques (Psychother)
- Use   Psychotherapeutic Techniques

Therapist Attitudes
- Use   Therapist Characteristics

Therapist Characteristics
- Used For   Therapist Attitudes
          Therapist Effectiveness

Therapist Characteristics — (Continued)
- Used For
          Therapist Experience
          Therapist Personality
- Related   Therapists/

Therapist Effectiveness
- Use   Therapist Characteristics

Therapist Experience
- Use   Therapist Characteristics

Therapist Patient Interaction
- Use   Psychotherapeutic Processes

Therapist Personality
- Use   Therapist Characteristics

Therapist Trainees
- Used For   Psychotherapist Trainees
- Related   Therapists/

Therapists/
- Related   Occupational Therapists
          Physical Therapists
          Psychotherapists
          Speech Therapists
          Therapist Characteristics
          Therapist Trainees

Therapy
- Use   Treatment/

Therapy (Drug)
- Use   Drug Therapy

Therapy (Encounter Group)
- Use   Encounter Group Therapy

Therapy (Individual)
- Use   Individual Psychotherapy

Therapy (Insulin Shock)
- Use   Insulin Shock Therapy

Therapy (Music)
- Use   Music Therapy

Thermal Acclimatization
- Used For   Acclimatization (Thermal)
- Related   Atmospheric Conditions
          Environmental Stress
          Physiological Stress
          Temperature Effects

Thermoreceptors
- Broader   Nerve Endings
          Nervous System
          Neural Receptors

Thermoregulation (Body)
- Broader   Body Temperature

Theta Rhythm
- Broader   Electrical Activity
          Electrophysiology
- Related   Electroencephalography

Thigh
- Related — Anatomy/
- Leg (Anatomy)

Thinking
- Broader — Cognitive Processes
- Narrower — Abstraction
- Autistic Thinking
- Divergent Thinking
- Inductive Deductive Reasoning
- Inference
- Logical Thinking
- Magical Thinking
- Reasoning

Thiopental
- Used For — Pentothal
- Broader — Anesthetic Drugs
- Barbiturates
- General Anesthetics
- Hypnotic Drugs
- Narcoanalytic Drugs
- Sedatives

Thioridazine
- Used For — Mellaril
- Broader — Phenothiazine Derivatives
- Tranquilizing Drugs

Thiothixene
- Broader — Tranquilizing Drugs

Thirst
- Broader — Motivation
- Related — Animal Drinking Behavior
- Water Deprivation

Thoracic Duct
- Used For — Duct (Thoracic)
- Broader — Lymphatic System

Thoracic Nerves
- Use — Spinal Nerves

Thoracic Spinal Cord
- Broader — Central Nervous System
- Nervous System
- Spinal Cord

Thorax
- Used For — Chest
- Broader — Musculoskeletal System
- Respiratory System
- Related — Diaphragm (Anatomy)

Thorazine
- Use — Chlorpromazine

Thought Disturbances
- Narrower — Amnesia
- Autistic Thinking
- Confabulation
- Delusions
- Fantasies (Thought Disturbances)

Thought Disturbances — (Continued)
- Narrower — Fragmentation (Schizophrenia)
- Fugue Reaction
- Judgment Disturbances
- Magical Thinking
- Megalomania
- Memory Disorders
- Obsessions
- Perseveration
- Word Salad
- Related — Mental Confusion
- Mental Disorders/

Threat
- Related — Punishment
- Threat Postures

Threat Postures
- Broader — Aggressive Behavior
- Animal Aggressive Behavior
- Animal Ethology
- Animal Social Behavior
- Social Behavior
- Related — Threat

Threshold Determination
- Related — Signal Detection (Perception)
- Thresholds

Thresholds
- Used For — Differential Limen
- Limen
- Narrower — Auditory Thresholds
- Critical Flicker Fusion Threshold
- Dark Adaptation
- Olfactory Thresholds
- Pain Thresholds
- Sensory Adaptation
- Vibrotactile Thresholds
- Visual Thresholds
- Related — Perceptual Measures
- Threshold Determination

Thrombophlebitis
- Broader — Cardiovascular Disorders

Thromboses
- Broader — Cardiovascular Disorders
- Narrower — Cerebral Thromboses
- Coronary Thromboses
- Related — Embolisms

Thumb
- Broader — Fingers (Anatomy)
- Musculoskeletal System

Thumbsucking
- Broader — Habits
- Related — Behavior Disorders

Thymectomy
Broader	Endocrine Gland Surgery
	Physical Treatment Methods
	Surgery

Thyroid Disorders
Broader	Endocrine Disorders
Narrower	Cretinism
	Goiters
	Hyperthyroidism
	Hypothyroidism
	Thyrotoxicosis
Related	Endocrine Sexual Disorders
	Pituitary Disorders

Thyroid Extract
Related	Drugs/
	Hypothyroidism
	Thyroid Hormones

Thyroid Gland
Broader	Endocrine Glands
	Endocrine System
	Glands

Thyroid Hormones
Broader	Hormones
Narrower	Thyroxine
	Triiodothyronine
Related	Thyroid Extract

Thyroid Stimulating Hormone
Use	Thyrotropin

Thyroidectomy
Broader	Endocrine Gland Surgery
	Physical Treatment Methods
	Surgery

Thyrotoxicosis
Broader	Endocrine Disorders
	Thyroid Disorders
	Toxic Disorders
Related	Hyperthyroidism
	Toxic Psychoses

Thyrotropic Hormone
Use	Thyrotropin

Thyrotropin
Used For	Thyroid Stimulating Hormone
	Thyrotropic Hormone
Broader	Hormones
	Pituitary Hormones
Related	Hypothyroidism

Thyroxine
Broader	Hormones
	Thyroid Hormones
Related	Hypothyroidism

Tic Doloureux
Use	Trigeminal Neuralgia

Tics
Broader	Symptoms

Time
Narrower	Interresponse Time

Time (Interresponse)
Use	Interresponse Time

Time Disorientation
Used For	Disorientation (Time)
Broader	Consciousness Disturbances

Time Estimation
Used For	Estimation (Time)
Broader	Estimation
	Time Perception

Time Perception
Narrower	Time Estimation
Related	Perception/

Timers (Apparatus)
Broader	Apparatus

Timidity
Used For	Shyness
Broader	Personality Traits

Tinnitus
Broader	Ear Disorders
	Sense Organ Disorders

Tiredness
Use	Fatigue

Tissues (Body)
Narrower	Bone Marrow
	Bones
	Cartilage
	Connective Tissues
	Membranes
	Meninges
	Myelin Sheath
	Nasal Mucosa
	Nerve Tissues
	Nictitating Membrane
	Olfactory Mucosa
	Skin (Anatomy)
Related	Anatomy/
	Histology
	Muscles
	Physiology/

Title V Projects
Broader	Educational Programs
	Government Programs
Related	Government

Toads
Broader	Amphibia
	Vertebrates

Tobacco (Drug)
Use	Nicotine

Tobacco Smoking
Used For	Cigarette Smoking
	Smoking (Cigarettes)
	Smoking (Tobacco)

Tobacco Smoking — (Continued)
Broader	Habits
Related	Carcinogens
	Nicotine

Tobago

Tocopherols
Broader	Vitamins

Toenails
Use	Nails (Anatomy)

Toes (Anatomy)
Use	Feet (Anatomy)

Tofranil
Use	Imipramine

Toilet Training
Broader	Childrearing Practices

Token Economy Programs
Broader	Behavior Modification
	Contingency Management
Related	Correctional Institutions
	Psychiatric Hospital Programs

Token Reinforcement
Use	Secondary Reinforcement

Tolbutamide
Broader	Hypoglycemic Agents

Tolerance
Broader	Personality Traits
Related	Tolerance For Ambiguity

Tolerance (Drug)
Use	Drug Tolerance

Tolerance For Ambiguity
Used For	Ambiguity (Tolerance)
Related	Personality/
	Tolerance

Tone (Frequency)
Use	Pitch (Frequency)

Tongue
Broader	Digestive System
Narrower	Taste Buds
Related	Mouth (Anatomy)

Top Level Managers
Used For	Executives
Broader	Business And Industrial Personnel
	Management Personnel
	White Collar Workers
Related	Middle Level Managers

Topography
Used For	Landscapes
Broader	Ecological Factors

Torticollis
Used For	Neck (Wry)
	Wryneck
Broader	Muscular Disorders
	Musculoskeletal Disorders

Tortoises
Use	Turtles

Totalitarianism
Broader	Political Economic Systems

Touch
Use	Tactual Perception

Towns
Broader	Environment
	Social Environments

Toxic Disorders
Used For	Intoxication
	Poisoning
Narrower	Acute Alcoholic Intoxication
	Alcohol Intoxication
	Barbiturate Poisoning
	Botulism
	Carbon Monoxide Poisoning
	Chronic Alcoholic Intoxication
	Drug Induced Congenital Disorders
	Lead Poisoning
	Mercury Poisoning
	Metal Poisoning
	Narcosis
	Thyrotoxicosis
	Toxic Encephalopathies
	Toxic Hepatitis
	Toxic Psychoses
Related	Alcoholism
	Dermatitis
	Digestive System Disorders
	Disorders/
	Gastrointestinal Disorders
	Liver Disorders
	Tetanus (Disease)
	Toxicity
	Toxicomania

Toxic Encephalopathies
Used For	Encephalopathies (Toxic)
Broader	Brain Disorders
	Toxic Disorders
Narrower	Acute Alcoholic Intoxication
	Alcohol Intoxication
	Chronic Alcoholic Intoxication
Related	Toxic Psychoses

Toxic Hepatitis
Broader	Digestive System Disorders
	Hepatitis
	Liver Disorders
	Toxic Disorders

Toxic Psychoses
Broader	Brain Disorders
	Central Nervous System Disorders
	Nervous System Disorders
	Organic Brain Syndromes
	Psychosis
	Syndromes
	Toxic Disorders
Related	Alcohol Intoxication
	Alcoholic Psychosis
	Metal Poisoning
	Thyrotoxicosis
	Toxic Encephalopathies

Toxicity
Related	Drugs/
	Toxic Disorders

Toxicomania
Broader	Mania
Related	Pica
	Toxic Disorders

Toxins
Use	Poisons

Toxoplasmosis
Broader	Blood and Lymphatic Disorders
	Infectious Disorders
	Parasitic Disorders

Toy Selection
Related	Toys

Toys
Narrower	Educational Toys
Related	Childrens Recreational Games
	Games
	Recreation
	Toy Selection

Trace (Memory)
Use	Memory Trace

Trachea
Broader	Respiratory System

Tracheal Disorders
Broader	Respiratory Tract Disorders

Tracking
Broader	Perceptual Motor Processes
Narrower	Rotary Pursuit
	Visual Tracking
Related	Attention
	Monitoring
	Motor Skills
	Perceptual Motor Learning

Tractotomy
Broader	Neurosurgery
	Physical Treatment Methods
	Surgery

Tractotomy — (Continued)
Related	Psychosurgery
	Pyramidotomy

Traditionalism
Use	Political Conservatism

Traffic Accidents (Air)
Use	Air Traffic Accidents

Traffic Accidents (Motor)
Use	Motor Traffic Accidents

Traffic Control (Air)
Use	Air Traffic Control

Trainable Mentally Retarded
Used For	Imbeciles
	Moderately Mentally Retarded
Broader	Handicapped
	Mentally Retarded
Related	Downs Syndrome

Training
Use	Education/

Training (Autogenic)
Use	Autogenic Training

Training (Clinical Methods)
Use	Clinical Methods Training

Training (Clinical Psychology Grad)
Use	Clinical Psychology Grad Training

Training (Community Mental Health)
Use	Community Mental Health Training

Training (Graduate Psychology)
Use	Graduate Psychology Education

Training (Mental Health Inservice)
Use	Mental Health Inservice Training

Training (Motivation)
Use	Motivation Training

Training (Personnel)
Use	Personnel Training

Training (Psychiatric)
Use	Psychiatric Training

Training (Psychoanalytic)
Use	Psychoanalytic Training

Training (Psychotherapy)
Use	Psychotherapy Training

Trains (Railroad)
Use	Railroad Trains

Tranquilizing Drugs
Used For	Anxiety Reducing Drugs
	Ataractic Drugs
	Ataraxic Drugs

Tranquilizing Drugs — (Continued)
 Narrower Amitriptyline
    Benactyzine
    Butyrylperazine
    Carphenazine
    Chlordiazepoxide
    Chlorpromazine
    Chlorprothixene
    Chorazepate Dipotassium
    Diazepam
    Fluphenazine
    Haloperidol
    Hydroxyzine
    Meprobamate
    Mesoridazine
    Minor Tranquilizers
    Neuroleptic Drugs
    Perphenazine
    Phenothiazine Derivatives
    Pimozide
    Prochlorperazine
    Promazine
    Reserpine
    Tetrabenazine
    Thioridazine
    Thiothixene
    Trifluoperazine
    Triflupromazine
 Related Anticonvulsive Drugs
    Antiemetic Drugs
    Antihypertensive Drugs
    Drugs/
    Muscle Relaxing Drugs
    Narcotic Drugs
    Sedatives

Transactional Analysis
 Broader Psychotherapy

Transaminases
 Used For Aminotransferases
 Broader Enzymes
    Transferases

Transcultural Psychiatry
 Broader Medical Sciences
    Psychiatry
    Sciences
 Related Ethnology/
    Ethnospecific Disorders
    Folk Medicine
    Myths
    Shamanism
    Taboos

Transducers
 Broader Apparatus

Transfer (Learning)
 Narrower Negative Transfer
    Positive Transfer
 Related Learning/

Transfer Students
 Broader Students

Transferases
 Broader Enzymes
 Narrower Transaminases

Transference (Psychotherapeutic)
 Use Psychotherapeutic Transference

Transformational Generative Grammar
 Broader Grammar
    Language
    Linguistics
    Verbal Communication

Transformers (Apparatus)
 Broader Apparatus

Transfusion (Blood)
 Use Blood Transfusion

Transistors (Apparatus)
 Broader Apparatus

Translocation (Chromosome)
 Broader Chromosome Disorders
    Genetic Disorders

Transplants (Organ)
 Use Organ Transplantation

Transportation
 Narrower Air Transportation
    Automobiles
    Ground Transportation
    Public Transportation
    Railroad Trains
    Submarines
    Water Transportation
 Related Transportation Accidents

Transportation Accidents
 Broader Accidents
 Narrower Air Traffic Accidents
    Highway Hypnosis Accidents
    Motor Traffic Accidents
 Related Accident Prevention
    Air Traffic Control
    Aviation Safety
    Highway Safety
    Safety Belts
    Transportation

Transposition (Cognition)
 Broader Cognitive Processes

Transsexualism
 Broader Psychosexual Behavior
    Sexual Deviations
 Related Bisexuality
    Homosexuality
    Lesbianism
    Male Homosexuality
    Sex Roles
    Transvestism

Transvestism
Broader   Psychosexual Behavior
         Sexual Deviations
Related   Bisexuality
         Fetishism
         Homosexuality
         Lesbianism
         Male Homosexuality
         Sex Roles
         Transsexualism

Tranylcypromine
Broader   Antidepressant Drugs
         Monoamine Oxidase Inhibitors

Trauma (Emotional)
Use   Emotional Trauma

Trauma (Physical)
Use   Injuries

Traumatic Amputations
Broader   Injuries
Related   Amputation

Traumatic Neurosis
Broader   Neurosis

Traumatic Psychosis
Use   Reactive Psychosis

Traveling
Broader   Recreation
Related   Vacationing

Treatment Effectiveness Evaluation
Used For   Evaluation (Treatment Effectiveness)
Related   Mental Health Program Evaluation
         Psychotherapeutic Outcomes
         Treatment/

Treatment Facilities
Narrower   Child Guidance Clinics
         Clinics
         Community Mental Health Centers
         Halfway Houses
         Hospitals
         Nursing Homes
         Psychiatric Clinics
         Psychiatric Hospitals
         Sanatoriums
         Walk In Clinics
Related   Crisis Intervention Services
         Residential Care Institutions

Treatment Methods (Physical)
Use   Physical Treatment Methods

Treatment/
Used For   Therapy
Related   Aftercare
         Behavior Modification

Treatment/ — (Continued)
Related
         Bibliotherapy
         Crisis Intervention
         Detoxification
         Drug Rehabilitation
         Interdisciplinary Treatment Approach
         Mental Health Program Evaluation
         Occupational Therapy
         Organic Therapies
         Outpatient Treatment
         Patient History
         Physical Therapy
         Physical Treatment Methods
         Posttreatment Followup
         Psychosocial Readjustment
         Psychosocial Rehabilitation
         Psychosocial Resocialization
         Psychotherapeutic Outcomes
         Psychotherapeutic Processes
         Psychotherapeutic Techniques
         Psychotherapy
         Recreation Therapy
         Social Casework
         Sociotherapy
         Speech Therapy
         Spontaneous Remission
         Treatment Effectiveness Evaluation

Tremor
Broader   Symptoms
Related   Antitremor Drugs
         Parkinsons Disease

Trial And Error Learning
Related   Learning/

Tribes
Broader   Ethnic Groups

Trifluoperazine
Used For   Stelazine
Broader   Antipsychotic Drugs
         Antischizophrenic Drugs
         Neuroleptic Drugs
         Phenothiazine Derivatives
         Tranquilizing Drugs

Triflupromazine
Broader   Antipsychotic Drugs
         Antischizophrenic Drugs
         Neuroleptic Drugs
         Phenothiazine Derivatives
         Tranquilizing Drugs

Trigeminal Nerve
Broader   Cranial Nerves
         Nervous System
         Peripheral Nerves

Trigeminal Neuralgia
- Used For   Tic Doloureux
- Broader   Nervous System Disorders
  - Neuralgia
  - Peripheral Nerve Disorders

Trihexyphenidyl
- Broader   Alcohols
  - Amines
  - Antispasmodic Drugs
  - Antitremor Drugs
  - Cholinergic Blocking Drugs

Triiodothyronine
- Broader   Hormones
  - Thyroid Hormones

Trinidad

Triplets
- Broader   Family Members
  - Multiple Births
  - Siblings

Trisomy
- Broader   Chromosome Disorders
  - Genetic Disorders
- Narrower   Trisomy 18
  - Trisomy 21
- Related   Nondisjunction (Chromosome)

Trisomy 18
- Broader   Autosome Disorders
  - Chromosome Disorders
  - Genetic Disorders
  - Trisomy
- Related   Mental Retardation

Trisomy 21
- Broader   Autosome Disorders
  - Chromosome Disorders
  - Genetic Disorders
  - Trisomy
- Related   Downs Syndrome

TROCA (Computer Screening Battery)
- (See)   Speech and Hearing Measures

Trochlear Nerve
- Use   Cranial Nerves

Truancy
- Broader   Behavior Disorders

Trust (Social Behavior)
- Broader   Social Behavior

Tryptamine
- Broader   Amines
  - Vasoconstrictor Drugs

Tryptophan
- Broader   Acids
  - Amino Acids

Tubal Ligation
- Broader   Birth Control
  - Family Planning
  - Sterilization (Sex)

Tuberculosis
- Broader   Bacterial Disorders
  - Infectious Disorders
- Narrower   Pulmonary Tuberculosis
- Related   Addisons Disease
  - Antitubercular Drugs
  - Lupus
  - Musculoskeletal Disorders
  - Nervous System Disorders
  - Skin Disorders

Tubocurarine
- Broader   Alkaloids
  - Muscle Relaxing Drugs
- Related   Antitubocurarine Drugs
  - Curare

Tumors
- Use   Neoplasms

Tunnel Vision
- Broader   Eye Disorders
  - Sense Organ Disorders
- Related   Scotoma
  - Vision

Turkey

Turners Syndrome
- Broader   Chromosome Disorders
  - Endocrine Disorders
  - Endocrine Sexual Disorders
  - Genetic Disorders
  - Genital Disorders
  - Hypogonadism
  - Neonatal Chromosome Disorders
  - Neonatal Disorders
  - Neonatal Genetic Disorders
  - Neonatal Sex Chromosome Disorders
  - Sex Chromosome Disorders
  - Syndromes
  - Urogenital Disorders
- Related   Sterility

Turnover
- Use   Employee Turnover

Turtles
- Used For   Tortoises
- Broader   Reptiles
  - Vertebrates

Tutoring
- Broader   Teaching
  - Teaching Methods
- Narrower   Peer Tutoring

Tutoring — (Continued)
Related   Individualized Instruction

Tutors
Use   Teachers

Twins
Broader   Family Members
               Multiple Births
               Siblings
Narrower   Heterozygotic Twins
               Monozygotic Twins
               Siamese Twins
Related   Genetics/

Tympanic Membrane
Use   Middle Ear

Type I Errors
Broader   Prediction Errors

Type II Errors
Broader   Prediction Errors

Typing
Use   Clerical Secretarial Skills

Typists
Use   Clerical Personnel

Typologies (Psychodiagnostic)
Use   Psychodiagnostic Typologies

Tyramine
Broader   Adrenergic Drugs
               Amines
               Oxytocic Drugs
               Sympathomimetic Amines
               Sympathomimetic Drugs
               Vasoconstrictor Drugs
Related   Ergot Derivatives

Tyrosine
Broader   Acids
               Amino Acids
Related   Melanin

UCR (Conditioning)
Use   Unconditioned Responses

UCS (Conditioning)
Use   Unconditioned Stimulus

Ulcerative Colitis
Broader   Colitis
               Colon Disorders
               Digestive System Disorders
               Gastrointestinal Disorders

Ulcers (Gastrointestinal)
Use   Gastrointestinal Ulcers

Ulnar Nerve
Use   Spinal Nerves

Ultrasound
Broader   Auditory Stimulation
               Perceptual Stimulation
               Pitch (Frequency)

Uncles
Broader   Family Members

Unconditioned Reflex
Use   Unconditioned Responses

Unconditioned Responses
Used For   Reflex (Unconditioned)
               UCR (Conditioning)
               Unconditioned Reflex
Broader   Classical Conditioning
               Conditioning
               Responses

Unconditioned Stimulus
Used For   Stimulus (Unconditioned)
               UCS (Conditioning)
Broader   Classical Conditioning
               Conditioning
Related   Stimulation

Unconscious (Personality Factor)
Broader   Psychoanalytic Personality Fac-
               tors
Related   Id

Underachievement (Academic)
Use   Academic Underachievement

Undergraduate Degrees
Use   Educational Degrees

Undergraduates
Use   College Students

Underprivileged
Use   Disadvantaged

Understanding
Use   Comprehension

Underwater Effects
Broader   Environmental Effects
Related   Decompression Effects
               Gravitational Effects

Underweight
Broader   Body Weight
               Physique
               Symptoms
Narrower   Anorexia Nervosa
Related   Appetite Disorders
               Hyperthyroidism
               Nutritional Deficiencies

Undifferentiated Schizophrenia
Broader   Psychosis
               Schizophrenia

Unemployment
   Related   Personnel Termination
              Personnel/
              Retirement

UNESCO Silent Reading Test
   (See)   Reading Measures

Union of South Africa

Union of Soviet Socialist Republics

United Arab Republic

United Kingdom

United States

Units (Shock)
   Use   Shock Units

Universities
   Use   Colleges

Unskilled Industrial Workers
   Broader   Blue Collar Workers
              Business And Industrial Person-
              nel

Unwed Mothers
   Broader   Family Members
              Mothers
              Parents

Upper Class
   Broader   Social Class
              Social Structure
              Socioeconomic Status

Upper Class Attitudes
   Broader   Socioeconomic Class Attitudes

Upper Income Level
   Broader   Income Level
              Socioeconomic Status

Upward Bound
   Broader   Educational Programs
              Government Programs
   Related   Government

Urban Environments
   Used For Cities
              Inner City
   Broader   Environment
              Social Environments
   Narrower Ghettoes
   Related   Urban Planning

Urban Ghettoes
   Use   Ghettoes

Urban Planning
   Related   Architecture
              Community Facilities
              Environment
              Recreation Areas
              Urban Environments

Urbanization
   Broader   Social Processes
   Related   Industrialization

Ureter
   Broader   Urinary Tract
              Urogenital System

Urethra
   Broader   Urinary Tract
              Urogenital System

Urges
   Use   Motivation

Uric Acid
   Broader   Acids

Urinalysis
   Used For Urinary Analysis
   Broader   Diagnosis
              Medical Diagnosis

Urinary Analysis
   Use   Urinalysis

Urinary Function Disorders
   Broader   Urogenital Disorders
   Narrower Urinary Incontinence
   Related   Psychosomatic Disorders

Urinary Incontinence
   Used For Enuresis
              Incontinence (Urinary)
   Broader   Urinary Function Disorders
              Urogenital Disorders
   Related   Behavior Disorders
              Symptoms

Urinary Tract
   Broader   Urogenital System
   Narrower Bladder
              Kidneys
              Ureter
              Urethra

Urination
   Used For Micturition
   Broader   Excretion
   Related   Diuretics

Urine
   Broader   Body Fluids

Urogenital Disorders
   Narrower Amenorrhea
              Dysmenorrhea
              Endocrine Sexual Disorders
              Genital Disorders
              Gynecological Disorders

Urogenital Disorders — (Continued)

Narrower
Hermaphroditism
Hypogonadism
Infertility
Klinefelters Syndrome
Male Genital Disorders
Menstrual Disorders
Premenstrual Tension
Pseudocyesis
Stein Leventhal Syndrome
Sterility
Testicular Feminization Syndrome
Turners Syndrome
Urinary Function Disorders
Urinary Incontinence

Related Disorders/
Psychosomatic Disorders
Sexual Function Disturbances
Urogenital System
Venereal Diseases

Urogenital System

Narrower Bladder
Cervix
Clitoris
Female Genitalia
Gonads
Kidneys
Male Genitalia
Ovaries
Penis
Prostate
Testes
Ureter
Urethra
Urinary Tract
Uterus
Vagina

Related Anatomical Systems/
Urogenital Disorders

Uterus

Broader Female Genitalia
Urogenital System
Narrower Cervix
Related Placenta

Vacation Benefits

Use Employee Leave Benefits

Vacationing

Broader Recreation
Related Camping
Summer Camps (Recreation)
Traveling

Vaccination

Use Immunization

Vagina

Broader Female Genitalia
Urogenital System

Vaginismus

Broader Psychosexual Behavior
Sexual Function Disturbances
Related Dyspareunia
Frigidity

Vagotomy

Broader Neurosurgery
Physical Treatment Methods
Surgery

Vagus Nerve

Broader Autonomic Nervous System
Cranial Nerves
Nervous System
Parasympathetic Nervous System
Peripheral Nerves
Related Heart

Validity (Statistical)

Use Statistical Validity

Validity (Test)

Use Test Validity

Valium

Use Diazepam

Values

Used For Mores
Broader Ethics
Narrower Ethnic Values
Personal Values
Social Values
Related Morality

Valves (Heart)

Use Heart Valves

Vane Kindergarten Test

(See) Intelligence Measures

Variability (Response)

Use Response Variability

Variability (Stimulus)

Use Stimulus Variability

Variability Measurement

Used For Variance
Broader Statistical Analysis
Statistical Measurement
Narrower Analysis of Covariance
Analysis of Variance
Interaction Variance
Standard Deviation
Related Central Tendency Measures
F Test
Statistical Correlation

Variable Interval Reinforcement

Used For Interval Reinforcement

Variable Interval Reinforcement — (Continued)
- Broader   Reinforcement
  - Reinforcement Schedules

Variable Ratio Reinforcement
- Used For   Ratio Reinforcement
- Broader   Reinforcement
  - Reinforcement Schedules

Variables (Statistical)
- Use   Statistical Variables

Variance
- Use   Variability Measurement

Variations (Seasonal)
- Use   Seasonal Variations

Varimax Rotation
- Broader   Factor Analysis
  - Orthogonal Rotation
  - Statistical Analysis
  - Statistical Measurement
  - Statistical Rotation

Vascular Disorders
- Use   Cardiovascular Disorders

Vasectomy
- Broader   Birth Control
  - Family Planning
  - Sterilization (Sex)

Vasoconstriction
- Related   Blood Pressure Disorders
  - Epinephrine

Vasoconstrictor Drugs
- Used For   Pressors (Drugs)
  - Vasopressor Drugs
- Narrower   Amphetamine
  - Angiotensin
  - Bufotenine
  - Dihydroergotamine
  - Ephedrine
  - Methamphetamine
  - Methoxamine
  - Norepinephrine
  - Serotonin
  - Tryptamine
  - Tyramine
- Related   Blood Pressure
  - Drugs/
  - Heart Rate Affecting Drugs
  - Vasodilator Drugs
  - Vasopressin

Vasodilation
- Related   Blood Pressure Disorders
  - Epinephrine
  - Muscle Relaxing Drugs
  - Theophylline

Vasodilator Drugs
- Narrower   Nicotinic Acid
  - Nitroglycerin
- Related   Antihypertensive Drugs
  - Blood Pressure
  - Drugs/
  - Heart Rate Affecting Drugs
  - Vasoconstrictor Drugs

Vasopressin
- Broader   Hormones
  - Pituitary Hormones
  - Posterior Pituitary Hormones
- Related   Vasoconstrictor Drugs

Vasopressor Drugs
- Use   Vasoconstrictor Drugs

Veins (Anatomy)
- Broader   Blood Vessels
  - Cardiovascular System

Velocity
- Used For   Speed
- Related   Vibration

Venereal Diseases
- Used For   Diseases (Venereal)
- Broader   Infectious Disorders
- Narrower   Gonorrhea
  - Syphilis
- Related   Infertility
  - Sterility
  - Urogenital Disorders

Venezuela

Ventral Roots
- Broader   Central Nervous System
  - Nervous System
  - Spinal Cord

Ventricles (Cerebral)
- Use   Cerebral Ventricles

Ventricles (Heart)
- Use   Heart Ventricles

Ventricular Fibrillation
- Use   Fibrillation (Heart)

Verbal Ability
- Related   Ability/
  - Academic Aptitude

Verbal Communication
- Used For   Oral Communication
  - Speech
  - Verbalization
- Narrower   Adjectives
  - Adverbs
  - Alphabets
  - Anagrams
  - Antonyms
  - Articulation (Speech)

Verbal Communication — (Continued)

Narrower

Bilingualism
Clipped Speech (Mechanical)
Compressed Speech
Consonants
Conversation
Cursive Writing
Dialect
Ethnolinguistics
Etymology
Filtered Speech
Fingerspelling
Foreign Languages
Form Classes (Language)
Grammar
Handwriting
Handwriting Legibility
Homographs
Homonyms
Inflection
Initial Teaching Alphabet
Language
Language Development
Letters (Alphabet)
Linguistics
Literacy
Monolingualism
Morphemes
Morphology (Language)
Multilingualism
Neologisms
Nonstandard English
Nouns
Numbers (Numerals)
Orthography
Paragraphs
Phonemes
Phonetics
Phonology
Phrases
Printing (Handwriting)
Pronouns
Pronunciation
Psycholinguistics
Public Speaking
Semantics
Sentence Structure
Sentences
Sight Vocabulary
Sign Language
Slang
Speech Characteristics
Speech Pauses
Speech Pitch
Speech Processing (Mechanical)
Speech Rate
Speech Rhythm
Syllables

Verbal Communication — (Continued)

Narrower

Synonyms
Syntax
Synthetic Speech
Transformational Generative
    Grammar
Verbal Fluency
Verbs
Vocabulary
Vowels
Words (Phonetic Units)
Written Language

Related   Communication/
Scientific Communication
Vocalization

Verbal Conditioning

Use   Verbal Learning

Verbal Fluency

Used For Fluency
Broader   Verbal Communication
Related   Speech Rate

Verbal Learning

Used For Conditioning (Verbal)
Verbal Conditioning
Narrower Nonsense Syllable Learning
Paired Associate Learning
Serial Anticipation (Learning)
Serial Learning
Related   Learning/

Verbal Meaning

Broader   Meaning

Verbal Reinforcement

Broader   Reinforcement
Social Behavior
Social Reinforcement
Narrower Praise

Verbal Tests

Related   Measurement/

Verbalization

Use   Verbal Communication

Verbs

Broader   Form Classes (Language)
Grammar
Language
Linguistics
Verbal Communication

Verification (of Theories)

Use   Theory verification

Vertebrates

Narrower Amphibia
Baboons
Bass (Fish)
Bats

Vertebrates — (Continued)
Narrower

Beavers
Birds
Blackbirds
Budgerigars
Canaries
Carp
Cats
Cattle
Chickens
Chimpanzees
Chinchillas
Cichlids
Crocodilians
Deer
Dogs
Dolphins
Doves
Ducks
Electric Fishes
Elephants
Fishes
Foxes
Frogs
Geese
Gerbils
Goats
Goldfish
Gorillas
Guinea Pigs
Hamsters
Horses
Kangaroos
Lemurs
Lizards
Mammals
Marsupials
Mice
Minks
Monkeys
Norway Rats
Opossums
Penguins
Pigeons
Pigs
Porpoises
Primates (Nonhuman)
Quails
Rabbits
Rats
Reptiles
Robins
Rodents
Salamanders
Salmon
Sea Gulls
Seals (Animal)
Sheep

Vertebrates — (Continued)
Narrower

Snakes
Squirrels
Sticklebacks
Toads
Turtles
Wolves
Related   Animals/
           Invertebrates

Vertigo
Used For   Dizziness
Broader   Symptoms
Related   Labyrinth Disorders
            Menieres Disease
            Syncope

Vessels (Blood)
Use   Blood Vessels

Vessels (Lymph)
Use   Lymph Vessels

Vestibular Apparatus
Broader   Ear (Anatomy)
            Labyrinth (Anatomy)
            Sense Organs

Vestibular Stimulation
Use   Somesthetic Stimulation

Veterans (Military)
Use   Military Veterans

Veterinary Medicine
Broader   Medical Sciences
            Sciences

Vibration
Used For   Resonance
Related   Velocity

Vibrators (Apparatus)
Broader   Apparatus
Related   Stimulators (Apparatus)

Vibrotactile Thresholds
Broader   Cutaneous Sense
            Somesthetic Perception
            Tactual Perception
            Thresholds
Related   Perceptual Measures

Vicarious Experiences
Used For   Reinforcement (Vicarious)
            Vicarious Reinforcement
Broader   Experiences (Events)
Related   Imagination
            Reinforcement

Vicarious Reinforcement
Use   Vicarious Experiences

Victimization
Broader   Social Behavior
            Social Interaction

264

Videotape Instruction
Broader	Audiovisual Instruction
	Teaching
	Teaching Methods
Related	Educational Audiovisual Aids

Videotape Recorders
Broader	Apparatus
	Tape Recorders

Videotapes
Broader	Audiovisual Communications
	Media
	Communications Media

Vigilance
Broader	Attention
	Awareness
	Consciousness States
	Monitoring
Related	Attention Span
	Selective Attention

Vineland Social Maturity Scale
(See)	Nonprojective Personality Measures
	Personality Measures

Violence
Broader	Aggressive Behavior
	Conflict
	Interpersonal Interaction
	Social Behavior
	Social Interaction

Viral Disorders
Broader	Infectious Disorders
Narrower	Common Colds
	Encephalitis
	Herpes Simplex
	Influenza
	Measles
	Poliomyelitis
	Rubella
	Viral Meningitis
Related	Pneumonia

Viral Meningitis
Broader	Central Nervous System Disorders
	Infectious Disorders
	Infectious Meningitis
	Meningitis
	Nervous System Disorders
	Viral Disorders

Virgin Islands

Virginity
Broader	Psychosexual Behavior
Related	Premarital Intercourse

Vision
Narrower	Autokinetic Illusion
	Binocular Vision
	Brightness Perception
	Color Perception
	Critical Flicker Fusion Threshold
	Dark Adaptation
	Monocular Vision
	Stereoscopic Vision
	Visual Discrimination
	Visual Field
	Visual Perception
	Visual Thresholds
Related	Tunnel Vision
	Visual Cortex
	Visual Evoked Potentials
	Visual Hallucinations
	Visual Tracking
	Visually Handicapped

Vision Disturbances (Hysterical)
Use	Hysterical Vision Disturbances

Visions (Mysticism)
Use	Mysticism

Visitation (Hospital)
Use	Institution Visitation

Visitation (Institution)
Use	Institution Visitation

Visitation (Psychiatric Hospital)
Use	Institution Visitation

Visiting Homemakers
Broader	Paraprofessional Personnel
Related	Social Workers

VISTA Volunteers
Use	Volunteers In Service To America

Visual Cortex
Used For	Cortex (Visual)
Broader	Brain
	Central Nervous System
	Cerebral Cortex
	Nervous System
	Occipital Lobe
	Telencephalon
Related	Vision

Visual Discrimination
Broader	Vision
	Visual Perception
Related	Visual Tracking

Visual Displays
Broader	Displays

265

Visual Evoked Potentials
Broader   Electrical Activity
     Electrophysiology
     Evoked Potentials
Related   Cortical Evoked Potentials
     Vision

Visual Feedback
Broader   Feedback
     Perceptual Stimulation
     Sensory Feedback
     Visual Stimulation

Visual Field
Used For   Field (Visual)
Broader   Vision
     Visual Perception

Visual Hallucinations
Broader   Hallucinations
     Perceptual Disturbances
Related   Vision

Visual Masking
Broader   Masking
Related   Visual Stimulation

Visual Perception
Broader   Vision
Narrower   Autokinetic Illusion
     Binocular Vision
     Brightness Perception
     Color Perception
     Critical Flicker Fusion Threshold
     Dark Adaptation
     Monocular Vision
     Stereoscopic Vision
     Visual Discrimination
     Visual Field
     Visual Thresholds
Related   Eye (Anatomy)
     Eye Disorders
     Lipreading
     Perception/
     Visual Tracking

Visual Stimulation
Used For   Noise (Visual)
Broader   Perceptual Stimulation
     Stimulation
Narrower   Illumination
     Photopic Stimulation
     Prismatic Stimulation
     Scotopic Stimulation
     Stereoscopic Presentation
     Tachistoscopic Presentation
     Visual Feedback
Related   Color
     Visual Masking

Visual Thresholds
Used For   Luminance Threshold
     Photic Threshold
Broader   Thresholds
     Vision
     Visual Perception
Narrower   Critical Flicker Fusion Threshold
     Dark Adaptation
Related   Perceptual Measures

Visual Tracking
Broader   Perceptual Motor Processes
     Tracking
Related   Vision
     Visual Discrimination
     Visual Perception

Visually Handicapped
Used For   Special Education (Visual Handicap)
Broader   Handicapped
Narrower   Blind
     Partially Sighted
Related   Braille Instruction
     Eye Disorders
     Vision

Vitamin C
Use   Ascorbic Acid

Vitamin Deficiency Disorders
Broader   Nutritional Deficiencies
Narrower   Pellagra
     Wernickes Syndrome
Related   Vitamins

Vitamins
Narrower   Ascorbic Acid
     Choline
     Nicotinamide
     Nicotinic Acid
     Tocopherols
Related   Drugs/
     Vitamin Deficiency Disorders

Vocabulary
Used For   Words (Vocabulary)
Broader   Language
     Verbal Communication
Narrower   Anagrams
     Antonyms
     Homographs
     Homonyms
     Neologisms
     Sight Vocabulary
     Slang
     Synonyms

Vocal Cords
Broader   Larynx
     Respiratory System

Vocalization
Narrower	Animal Distress Calls
	Animal Vocalizations
	Crying
	Infant Vocalization
	Subvocalization
	Voice
Related	Animal Communication
	Communication/
	Verbal Communication

Vocalization (Infant)
Use	Infant Vocalization

Vocalizations (Animal)
Use	Animal Vocalizations

Vocational Adjustment
Use	Occupational Adjustment

Vocational Aspirations
Use	Occupational Aspirations

Vocational Choice
Use	Occupational Choice

Vocational Counseling
Use	Occupational Guidance

Vocational Counselors
Broader	Counselors
Related	School Counselors
	Social Workers

Vocational Education
Broader	Curriculum
Related	Education/

Vocational Guidance
Use	Occupational Guidance

Vocational Interests
Use	Occupational Interests

Vocational Mobility
Use	Occupational Mobility

Vocational Neurosis
Use	Occupational Neurosis

Vocational Preference
Use	Occupational Preference

Vocational Rehabilitation
Used For	Rehabilitation (Vocational)
Broader	Psychosocial Rehabilitation
	Rehabilitation

Vocational School Students
Broader	Students

Vocational Schools
Use	Technical Schools

Vocations
Use	Occupations/

Voice
Broader	Vocalization

Voice — (Continued)
Narrower	Crying
	Infant Vocalization
Related	Communication/

Volt Meters
Used For	Meters (Volt)
Broader	Apparatus
Related	Shock Units

Volume (Blood)
Use	Blood Volume

Volunteer Civilian Personnel
Broader	Volunteer Personnel
Related	Paraprofessional Personnel

Volunteer Military Personnel
Used For	Enlistees
Broader	Government Personnel
	Military Personnel
	Volunteer Personnel
Narrower	National Guardsmen
	ROTC Students

Volunteer Personnel
Narrower	National Guardsmen
	ROTC Students
	Volunteer Civilian Personnel
	Volunteer Military Personnel
Related	Educational Personnel
	Paraprofessional Personnel
	Personnel/
	Religious Personnel

Volunteers (Experiment)
Use	Experiment Volunteers

Volunteers In Service To America
Used For	VISTA Volunteers
Broader	Government Programs
Related	Government

Vomit Inducing Drugs
Use	Emetic Drugs

Vomiting
Broader	Digestive System Disorders
	Gastrointestinal Disorders
	Symptoms
Related	Antiemetic Drugs
	Nausea

Voting Behavior
Broader	Political Processes
	Politics
Related	Political Attitudes
	Political Elections
	Political Issues

Vowels
Broader	Language
	Linguistics
	Phonemes

Vowels — (Continued)
Broader
        Phonetics
        Verbal Communication

Voyeurism
Broader   Psychosexual Behavior
        Sexual Deviations
Related   Exhibitionism

Wages
Use   Salaries

WAIS (Test)
Identifier   Wechsler Adult Intelligence
        Scale

Wakefield Self Assessment Depression
(See)   Nonprojective Personality Measures
        Personality Measures

Wakefulness
Broader   Consciousness States

Wales

Walk In Clinics
Broader   Clinics
        Treatment Facilities
Related   Crisis Intervention Services
        Psychiatric Clinics

Walking
Broader   Motor Performance
        Motor Processes

Walsh Test
Broader   Nonparametric Statistical Tests
        Statistical Analysis
        Statistical Tests

War
Broader   Aggressive Behavior
        Conflict
        Interpersonal Interaction
        Social Behavior
        Social Interaction
Related   Foreign Policy Making
        Government
        Government Policy Making

Warning Signal
Use   Signal Detection (Perception)

Water Deprivation
Broader   Deprivation
        Stimulus Deprivation
Related   Thirst

Water Intake
Related   Animal Drinking Behavior

Water Safety
Broader   Safety

Water Transportation
Broader   Transportation
Narrower   Submarines

Weaning
Broader   Childrearing Practices
        Feeding Practices
Related   Breast Feeding

Wechsler Adult Intelligence Scale
Used For   WAIS (Test)
(See)   Intelligence Measures

Wechsler Bellevue Intelligence Scale
(See)   Intelligence Measures

Wechsler Intelligence Scale Children
Used For   WISC (Test)
(See)   Intelligence Measures

Weight (Body)
Use   Body Weight

Weight Perception
Related   Perception/

Weightlessness
Broader   Environmental Effects
        Gravitational Effects
Related   Somesthetic Stimulation
        Spaceflight

Welfare
Use   Welfare Services (Government)

Welfare Services (Government)
Used For   Welfare
Broader   Government Programs
Related   Community Welfare Services
        Government

Welsh Figure Preference Test
(See)   Nonprojective Personality Measures
        Personality Measures

Wepman Test of Auditory Discrim
(See)   Speech And Hearing Measures

Wernickes Syndrome
Broader   Alcoholism
        Behavior Disorders
        Nutritional Deficiencies
        Syndromes
        Vitamin Deficiency Disorders

West German Federal Republic

West Indies

West Pakistan

White Betz A B Scale
(See)   Nonprojective Personality Measures
        Personality Measures

White Blood Cells
Use   Leucocytes

White Collar Workers
Broader   Business And Industrial Personnel
Narrower   Accountants
     Clerical Personnel
     Management Personnel
     Middle Level Managers
     Sales Personnel
     Secretarial Personnel
     Top Level Managers

White Noise
Broader   Auditory Stimulation
     Perceptual Stimulation

White Rats
Use   Rats

Whites
Use   Caucasians

Wide Range Achievement Test
(See)   Achievement Measures

Widowers
Related   Family/
     Marital Status
     Parental Absence

Widows
Related   Family/
     Marital Status
     Parental Absence

Wilcoxon Sign Rank Test
Used For   Sign Rank Test
Broader   Nonparametric Statistical Tests
     Statistical Analysis
     Statistical Tests

Wilson Patterson Conservatism Scale
(See)   Attitude Measures

Windigo Psychosis
Used For   Witigo Psychosis
Broader   Psychosis

Windward Islands

Wine
Broader   Alcoholic Beverages

WISC (Test)
Identifier   Wechsler Intelligence Scale Children

Wishes
Use   Motivation

Witchcraft
Related   Ethnology/
     Faith Healing
     Parapsychology

Withdrawal (Coitus Interruptus)
Use   Coitus Interruptus

Withdrawal (Defense Mechanism)
Broader   Defense Mechanisms

Withdrawal (Drug)
Use   Drug Withdrawal

Withdrawal Effects (Drug)
Use   Drug Withdrawal Effects

Witigo Psychosis
Use   Windigo Psychosis

Wives
Broader   Family Members
     Spouses
Narrower   Housewives

Wolves
Broader   Mammals
     Vertebrates

Womens Liberation Movement
Broader   Social Movements
Related   Activist Movements

Word Associations
Used For   Associations (Word)
Related   Associative Processes
     Cognitive Processes
     Paired Associate Learning

Word Blindness (Aphasia)
Use   Aphasia

Word Blindness (Dyslexia)
Use   Dyslexia

Word Deafness
Use   Aphasia

Word Frequency
Related   Contextual Associations

Word Meaning
Broader   Meaning
Related   Contextual Associations

Word Salad
Broader   Symptoms
     Thought Disturbances
Related   Neologisms
     Schizophrenia

Words (Form Classes)
Use   Form Classes (Language)

Words (Origin)
Use   Etymology

Words (Phonetic Units)
Broader   Language
     Linguistics
     Phonetics
     Verbal Communication
Related   Morphology (Language)

Words (Vocabulary)
Use   Vocabulary

Work (Attitudes Toward)
Related   Attitudes/
             Employee Attitudes
             Employer Attitudes
             Occupational Attitudes

Work Attitude Scale
(See)   Attitude Measures

Work Environments
Use   Working Conditions

Work Rest Cycles
Used For   Cycles (Work Rest)
Broader   Working Conditions
Related   Work Scheduling

Work Scheduling
Used For   Scheduling (Work)
Related   Management Methods
             Work Rest Cycles

Work Study Programs
Use   Educational Programs

Work Week Length
Broader   Working Conditions

Workday Shifts
Used For   Shifts (Workday)
Broader   Working Conditions

Workers
Use   Personnel/

Workers (Agricultural Extension)
Use   Agricultural Extension Workers

Working Conditions
Used For   Factory Environments
             Work Environments
Broader   Environment
             Social Environments
Narrower   Job Enrichment
             Noise Levels (Work Areas)
             Occupational Safety
             Work Rest Cycles
             Work Week Length
             Workday Shifts
             Working Space
Related   Human Factors Engineering
             Organizational Climate
             Personnel/

Working Space
Broader   Working Conditions

Workmens Compensation Insurance
Broader   Employee Benefits
             Employee Health Insurance
             Health Insurance
             Insurance

Workshops (Sheltered)
Use   Sheltered Workshops

Worms
Broader   Invertebrates
Narrower   Earthworms
             Planarians

Worship
Use   Religious Practices

Wounds
Broader   Injuries
Narrower   Self Inflicted Wounds
Related   Burns
             Electrical Injuries
             Head Injuries

Wrist
Broader   Musculoskeletal System
Related   Arm (Anatomy)
             Hand (Anatomy)

Writing (Creative)
Use   Literature

Writing (Cursive)
Use   Cursive Writing

Writing (Handwriting)
Use   Handwriting

Written Language
Broader   Language
             Verbal Communication
Narrower   Alphabets
             Cursive Writing
             Handwriting
             Handwriting Legibility
             Initial Teaching Alphabet
             Letters (Alphabet)
             Literacy
             Numbers (Numerals)
             Paragraphs
             Printing (Handwriting)

Wryneck
Use   Torticollis

X Ray Diagnosis
Use   Roentgenography

X Ray Equipment
Broader   Apparatus

X Ray Therapy
Use   Radiation Therapy

Xylocaine
Use   Lidocaine

Yates Test
Broader   Nonparametric Statistical Tests
             Statistical Analysis
             Statistical Tests

Yerkes Boxes
Used For   Boxes (Yerkes)

Yerkes Boxes — (Continued)
  Broader   Apparatus

Yoga

Young Adults
  Used For   Youth (Adults)
  Broader   Adults
               Developmental Age Groups
  Related   Adolescents

Youth (Adolescents)
  Use   Adolescents

Youth (Adults)
  Use   Young Adults

Youth (Children)
  Use   Children

Yugoslavia

Zen Buddhism
  Broader   Buddhism
               Religious Affiliation
               Religious Beliefs

Zoology
  Broader   Biology
               Sciences

Zulliger Z Test
  (See)   Personality Measures
            Projective Personality Measures
            Projective Techniques

Zungs Self Rating Depression Scale
  (See)   Nonprojective Personality Measures
            Personality Measures

Zygote
  Broader   Developmental Stages
               Nonprojective Personality Measures
               Prenatal Development
               Prenatal Developmental Stages

Users Guide to the Alphabetic Section

Each thesaurus term used for indexing is listed in alphabetical order to facilitate rapid selection of search terms and verification of spelling. This section includes all of the terms listed in the Relationship Section with the exception of nonpreferred synonymous terms.

Abdomen
Abdominal Wall
Abducens Nerve
Ability Grouping
Ability/
Abortion Laws
Absorption (Physiological)
Abstraction
Academic Achievement
Academic Achievement Motivation
Academic Achievement Prediction
Academic Aptitude
Academic Environment
Academic Overachievement
Academic Specialization
Academic Underachievement
Acalculia
Acceleration Effects
Accelerometers
Accident Prevention
Accident Proneness
Accidents
Accountants
Accreditation (Education Personnel)
Acculturation
Acetazolamide
Acetylcholine
Acetylcholinesterase
Achievement
Achievement Measures
Achievement Motivation
Achievement Potential
Achilles Tendon Reflex
Achromatic Color
Acid Phosphatases
Acids
Acne
Acoustic Nerve
Acoustic Reflex
Acrophobia
Acting Out
Activist Movements
Acupuncture
Acute Alcoholic Intoxication
Acute Psychosis
Acute Psychotic Episode
Acute Schizophrenia
Adaptability (Personality)
Adaptation

Addiction
Addisons Disease
Adenosine
Adjectives
Adjudication
Adjustment/
Adler (Alfred)
Adolescent Development
Adolescent Psychology
Adolescents
Adopted Children
Adoption (Child)
Adoptive Parents
Adrenal Cortex Hormones
Adrenal Gland Disorders
Adrenal Gland Secretion
Adrenal Glands
Adrenal Medulla Hormones
Adrenalectomy
Adrenergic Blocking Drugs
Adrenergic Drugs
Adrenergic Nerves
Adrenochrome
Adrenolytic Drugs
Adult Education
Adults
Adventitiously Handicapped
Adverbs
Advertising
Aerospace Personnel
Aesthetic Preferences
Aesthetics
Affection
Affective Disturbances
Affective Psychosis
Afferent Stimulation
Affiliation Motivation
Africa
Aftercare
Afterimage
Age Differences
Aged
Aggressive Behavior
Aggressiveness
Agnosia
Agnosticism
Agoraphobia
Agraphia
Agricultural Extension Workers

Agricultural Workers
Air Force Personnel
Air Traffic Accidents
Air Traffic Control
Air Transportation
Aircraft
Aircraft Pilots
Alanines
Alarm Responses
Alaska
Albinism
Albumins
Alcohol Dehydrogenases
Alcohol Drinking Attitudes
Alcohol Drinking Patterns
Alcohol Intoxication
Alcoholic Beverages
Alcoholic Hallucinosis
Alcoholic Psychosis
Alcoholics Anonymous
Alcoholism
Alcohols
Aldolases
Aldosterone
Algorithms
Alienation
Alkaloids
Allergic Disorders
Allergic Skin Disorders
Allport Vernon Lindzey Study Values
Alopecia
Alpha Rhythm
Alphabets
Altitude Effects
Altruism
Alzheimers Disease
Amaurotic Familial Idiocy
Ambivalence
Amblyopia
Amenorrhea
American Indians
Amine Oxidase Inhibitors
Amine Oxidases
Amines
Amino Acids
Amitriptyline
Ammonium Bromide
Ammons Full Range Picture Vocab Test
Amnesia

Amniotic Fluid
Amobarbital
Amphetamine
Amphibia
Amplifiers (Apparatus)
Amputation
Amputees
Amygdaloid Body
Amylases
Anabolism
Anaclitic Depression
Anagram Problem Solving
Anagrams
Analeptic Drugs
Analgesic Drugs
Analog Computers
Analysis of Covariance
Analysis of Variance
Analysis/
Analytical Psychotherapy
Anaphylactic Shock
Anatomical Systems/
Anatomy/
Ancestors
Androgens
Anemia
Anencephaly
Anesthesia (Feeling)
Anesthesiology
Anesthetic Drugs
Aneurysms
Anger
Angina Pectoris
Angiography
Angiotensin
Animal Aggressive Behavior
Animal Biological Rhythms
Animal Breeding
Animal Circadian Rhythms
Animal Communication
Animal Courtship Behavior
Animal Courtship Displays
Animal Distress Calls
Animal Division of Labor
Animal Dominance
Animal Drinking Behavior
Animal Environments
Animal Escape Behavior
Animal Ethology

Animal Exploratory Behavior
Animal Feeding Behavior
Animal Hoarding Behavior
Animal Innate Behavior
Animal Instinctive Behavior
Animal Maternal Behavior
Animal Mating Behavior
Animal Motivation
Animal Nocturnal Behavior
Animal Open Field Behavior
Animal Play
Animal Sex Differences
Animal Sexual Receptivity
Animal Social Behavior
Animal Vocalizations
Animals/
Animism
Ankle
Annual Report
Anonymity
Anorexia Nervosa
Anosmia
Anoxia
Antarctica
Anthropologists
Anthropology
Antibiotics
Antibodies
Anticoagulant Drugs
Anticonvulsive Drugs
Antidepressant Drugs
Antiemetic Drugs
Antiepileptic Drugs
Antihistaminic Drugs
Antihypertensive Drugs
Antipsychotic Drugs
Antischizophrenic Drugs
Antisemitism
Antisocial Behavior
Antisocial Personality
Antispasmodic Drugs
Antitremor Drugs
Antitubercular Drugs
Antitubocurarine Drugs
Antonyms
Ants
Anxiety
Anxiety Neurosis

Aorta
Apathy
Aphagia
Aphasia
Aphrodisiacs
Apnea
Apomorphine
Appalachia
Apparatus
Apparent Distance
Apparent Movement
Apparent Size
Apperception
Appetite
Appetite Depressing Drugs
Appetite Disorders
Applied Psychology
Apprenticeship
Apraxia
Aptitude Measures
Arachnida
Arachnoiditis
Architects
Architecture
Arecoline
Arguments
Arm (Anatomy)
Army General Classification Test
Army Personnel
Arrhythmias (Heart)
Art
Art Education
Art Therapy
Arterial Pulse
Arteries (Anatomy)
Arteriosclerosis
Arthritis
Arthropoda
Articulation (Speech)
Articulation Disorders
Artificial Pacemakers
Artificial Respiration
Artistic Ability
Artists
Arts
Asceticism
Ascorbic Acid
Asia
Aspartic Acid

275

Aspiration Level
Aspirations
Aspirin
Assertiveness
Assistance (Social Behavior)
Associationism
Associative Processes
Asthenia
Asthenic Personality
Asthma
Astrology
Astronauts
Ataxia
Atheism
Atherosclerosis
Athetosis
Athletes
Athletic Participation
Atmospheric Conditions
Atropine
Attack Behavior
Attempted Suicide
Attendants (Institutions)
Attention
Attention Span
Attitude Change
Attitude Formation
Attitude Measurement
Attitude Measures
Attitude Similarity
Attitudes/
Attorneys
Attribution
Audiences
Audiology
Audiometers
Audiometry
Audiotapes
Audiovisual Communications Media
Audiovisual Instruction
Auditory Cortex
Auditory Discrimination
Auditory Displays
Auditory Evoked Potentials
Auditory Feedback
Auditory Hallucinations
Auditory Localization
Auditory Masking
Auditory Neurons

Auditory Perception
Auditory Stimulation
Auditory Thresholds
Aunts
Aura
Aurally Handicapped
Australia
Austria
Authoritarianism
Authoritarianism Rebellion Scale
Authority
Autism
Autistic Children
Autistic Thinking
Autobiography
Autogenic Training
Autohypnosis
Autokinetic Illusion
Automated Information Coding
Automated Information Processing
Automated Information Retrieval
Automated Information Storage
Automation
Automatism
Automobiles
Autonomic Ganglia
Autonomic Nervous System
Autonomic Nervous System Disorders
Autonomy (Government)
Autopsy
Autosome Disorders
Autosomes
Aversion
Aversion Therapy
Aversive Stimulation
Aviation
Aviation Safety
Avoidance
Avoidance Conditioning
Awareness
Axons
Babinski Reflex
Baboons
Back (Anatomy)
Bacterial Disorders
Bacterial Meningitis
Badminton
Bahama Islands
Bannister Repertory Grid

Barbados
Barbital
Barbiturate Poisoning
Barbiturates
Bargaining
Barium
Baroreceptors
Barrett Lennard Relationship Invent
Barron Welsh Art Scale
Basal Ganglia
Basal Metabolism
Basal Skin Resistance
Baseball
Basketball
Bass (Fish)
Bass Famous Sayings Test
Bats
Battered Child Syndrome
Beavers
Beer
Bees
Beetles
Behavior Change
Behavior Disorders
Behavior Modification
Behavior Problems
Behavior Therapy
Behavior/
Behaviorism
Belgium
Bemegride
Benactyzine
Bender Gestalt Test
Bene Anthony Family Relations Test
Benign Neoplasms
Benton Revised Visual Retention Test
Biased Sampling
Bible
Bibliography
Bibliotherapy
Bile
Bilingualism
Binocular Vision
Binomial Distribution
Biochemistry
Biofeedback
Biographical Inventories
Biography
Biological Rhythms

Biological Symbiosis
Biology
Biopsy
Biosynthesis
Birds
Birth
Birth Control
Birth Injuries
Birth Order
Birth Rites
Birth Trauma
Bisexuality
Black Power Movement
Blackbirds
Blacky Pictures Test
Bladder
Blind
Blood
Blood and Lymphatic Disorders
Blood Cells
Blood Circulation
Blood Coagulation
Blood Coagulation Disorders
Blood Flow
Blood Group Incompatibility
Blood Groups
Blood Plasma
Blood Platelets
Blood Pressure
Blood Pressure Disorders
Blood Proteins
Blood Serum
Blood Sugar
Blood Transfusion
Blood Vessels
Blood Volume
Blue Collar Workers
Body Fluids
Body Height
Body Image
Body Image Disturbances
Body Language
Body Rocking
Body Sway Testing
Body Temperature
Body Weight
Bone Conduction Audiometry
Bone Disorders
Bone Marrow

277

Bone Marrow Cells
Bones
Bonuses
Book
Books
Borderline Mental Retardation
Boredom
Botany
Bottle Feeding
Botulism
Bradycardia
Braille Instruction
Brain
Brain Concussion
Brain Damage
Brain Damaged
Brain Disorders
Brain Lesions
Brain Neoplasms
Brain Size
Brain Stem
Brain Stimulation
Brain Weight
Brazil
Breast
Breast Feeding
Breast Neoplasms
Brief Psychotherapy
Brightness Perception
Bromides
Bronchi
Bronchial Disorders
Brothers
Buddhism
Budgerigars
Bufotenine
Burns
Business
Business And Industrial Personnel
Business Education
Business Management
Business Organizations
Business Students
Butterflies
Butyrylperazine
Caffeine
Cage Apparatus
Calcification
Calcium

Calcium Bromide
Calcium Ions
Calcium Metabolism Disorders
California F Scale
California Psychological Inventory
California Test of Mental Maturity
California Test of Personality
Calories
Cambodia
Cameras
Camping
Campuses
Canada
Canaries
Cannabis
Capillaries (Anatomy)
Capital Punishment
Capitalism
Carbachol
Carbohydrate Metabolism
Carbohydrate Metabolism Disorders
Carbohydrates
Carbon
Carbon Dioxide
Carbon Monoxide
Carbon Monoxide Poisoning
Carbonic Anhydrase
Carcinogens
Cardiography
Cardiology
Cardiovascular Disorders
Cardiovascular System
Carotid Arteries
Carotid Body
Carp
Carphenazine
Cartilage
Cartoons (Humor)
Case Report
Caste System
Castration
Castration Anxiety
Cat Learning
Catabolism
Catalepsy
Cataplexy
Cataracts
Catatonia
Catatonic Schizophrenia

Catecholamines
Catharsis
Catheterization
Cathexis
Cats
Cattle
Caucasians
Caudate Nucleus
Cell Nucleus
Cells (Biology)
Central America
Central Nervous System
Central Nervous System Disorders
Central Tendency Measures
Cerebellum
Cerebral Anoxia
Cerebral Arteriosclerosis
Cerebral Cortex
Cerebral Dominance
Cerebral Embolisms
Cerebral Hemorrhage
Cerebral Ischemia
Cerebral Palsy
Cerebral Thromboses
Cerebral Ventricles
Cerebrospinal Fluid
Cerebrovascular Accidents
Cerebrovascular Disorders
Cerebrum Affecting Drugs
Cervix
Chance (Fortune)
Chaplains
Charitable Behavior
Cheating
Chemical Brain Stimulation
Chemical Elements
Chemistry
Chemoreceptors
Chess
Chi Square Test
Chickens
Child Abuse
Child Behavior Diagnostic Inventory
Child Day Care
Child Discipline
Child Guidance Clinics
Child Psychiatry
Child Psychology

Child Psychotherapy
Childhood Development
Childhood Neurosis
Childhood Play Development
Childhood Psychosis
Childhood Schizophrenia
Childrearing Attitudes
Childrearing Practices
Children
Childrens Apperception Test
Childrens Manifest Anxiety Scale
Childrens Personality Questionnaire
Childrens Recreational Games
Chimpanzees
Chinchillas
Chloral Hydrate
Chloralose
Chlordiazepoxide
Chloride Ions
Chlorimipramine
Chlorisondamine
Chloroform
Chlorpheniramine
Chlorpromazine
Chlorprothixene
Choice Behavior
Cholesterol
Choline
Cholinergic Blocking Drugs
Cholinergic Drugs
Cholinergic Nerves
Cholinesterase
Cholinesterase Inhibitors
Cholinomimetic Drugs
Chorazepate Dipotassium
Chorea
Christianity
Chromosome Disorders
Chromosomes
Chronic Alcoholic Intoxication
Chronic Psychosis
Chronic Schizophrenia
Cichlids
Cirrhosis (Liver)
Citizenship
Civil Rights Movement
Clairvoyance
Classical Conditioning

Classification (Cognitive Process)
Classmates
Classroom Behavior
Classroom Behavior Modification
Classroom Discipline
Classroom Environment
Classrooms
Claustrophobia
Cleft Palate
Clergy
Clerical Personnel
Clerical Secretarial Skills
Client Centered Therapy
Client Characteristics
Clients
Clinical Judgment (Not Diagnosis)
Clinical Methods Training
Clinical Psychologists
Clinical Psychology
Clinical Psychology Grad Training
Clinical Psychology Internship
Clinicians
Clinics
Clipped Speech (Mechanical)
Clitoris
Clonidine
Closed Circuit Television
Clothing Fashions
Cloze Testing
Clubs (Social Organizations)
Cluster Analysis
CNS Affecting Drugs
CNS Depressant Drugs
CNS Stimulating Drugs
Coalition Formation
Cobalt
Cocaine
Cochlea
Cochran Q Test
Cockroaches
Codeine
Coeducation
Coenzymes
Cognition
Cognitive Ability
Cognitive Complexity
Cognitive Contiguity
Cognitive Development

Cognitive Discrimination
Cognitive Dissonance
Cognitive Generalization
Cognitive Mediation
Cognitive Processes
Cognitive Style
Cohabitation
Coitus Interruptus
Cold Effects
Colitis
Coll Ent Exam Bd Scholastic Apt Test
Collective Behavior
College Academic Achievement
College Dropouts
College Environment
College Students
College Teachers
Colleges
Colon
Colon Disorders
Color
Color Blindness
Color Perception
Color Pyramid Test
Colostomy
Columbia Mental Maturity Scale
Coma
Commissioned Officers
Commitment (Psychiatric)
Common Colds
Common Law Marriage
Communes
Communication Skills
Communication Systems
Communication Theory
Communication/
Communications Media
Communism
Communities
Community Attitudes
Community College Students
Community Facilities
Community Mental Health
Community Mental Health Centers
Community Mental Health Training
Community Psychiatry
Community Psychology
Community Services
Community Welfare Services

Comparative Psychology
Compensation (Defense Mechanism)
Compensatory Education
Competition
Compliance
Comprehension
Comprehension Tests
Compressed Speech
Compulsions
Compulsive Orderliness
Compulsive Repetition
Computer Applications
Computer Assisted Diagnosis
Computer Assisted Instruction
Computer Programing Languages
Computer Simulation
Computer Software
Computers
Concentration Camps
Concept Formation
Concept Learning
Concept Mastery Test
Concepts
Conceptual Imagery
Conditioned Emotional Responses
Conditioned Responses
Conditioned Stimulus
Conditioned Suppression
Conditioning
Cones (Eye)
Confabulation
Conference Proceedings
Confession (Religion)
Confidence Limits (Statistics)
Conflict
Conformity (Personality)
Congenital Disorders
Congenitally Handicapped
Conjoint Therapy
Connective Tissue Cells
Connective Tissues
Connotations
Consanguineous Marriage
Conscience
Conscious (Personality Factors)
Consciousness Disturbances
Consciousness States
Conservation (Concept)

Conservatism
Consistency (Measurement)
Consonants
Constipation
Consumer Attitudes
Consumer Behavior
Consumer Protection
Consumer Psychology
Consumer Research
Consumer Surveys
Contact Lenses
Content Analysis (Test)
Contextual Associations
Contingency Management
Contraceptive Devices
Contusions
Conversation
Conversion Neurosis
Convulsions
Cooperation
Coping Behavior
Copper
Cornea
Coronary Thromboses
Corpora Quadrigemina
Corpus Callosum
Correctional Institutions
Cortical Evoked Potentials
Corticosteroids
Corticosterone
Corticotropin
Cortisone
Costs And Cost Analysis
Counseling Psychology
Counseling/
Counselor Attitudes
Counselor Characteristics
Counselor Education
Counselor Role
Counselor Trainees
Counselors
Counterconditioning
Countertransference
Countries
Courage
Cousins
Crabs
Crafts

Cranial Nerves
Cranial Spinal Cord
Crayfish
Creativity
Creativity Measurement
Credibility
Cretinism
Crime
Criminal Conviction
Criminal Law
Criminals
Criminology
Crises
Crisis Intervention
Crisis Intervention Services
Critical Flicker Fusion Threshold
Criticism
Crocodilians
Cromwells Adult Locus of Cont Scale
Cross Cultural Differences
Cruelty
Crustacea
Crying
Crying Cat Syndrome
Cuba
Cues
Cultism
Cultural Assimilation
Cultural Deprivation
Cultural Test Bias
Culture (Anthropological)
Culture Change
Culture Fair Intelligence Test
Culture Shock
Curare
Curiosity
Curriculum
Curriculum Development
Cursive Writing
Cushings Syndrome
Cutaneous Sense
Cybernetics
Cycloheximide
Cyclothymic Personality
Cynicism
Cysteine
Cytochrome Oxidase
Cytology

Cytoplasm
Czechoslovakia
Dance
Dance Therapy
Dark Adaptation
Darwinism
Data Processing
Daughters
Day Care Centers
Daydreaming
DDT (Insecticide)
Deaf
Death And Dying
Death Attitudes
Death Rites
Decarboxylases
Deception
Decerebration
Decision Making
Decompression Effects
Decortication (Brain)
Deer
Defecation
Defense Mechanisms
Defensiveness
Dehydrogenases
Delayed Auditory Feedback
Delayed Development
Delayed Feedback
Deletion (Chromosome)
Delirium
Delirium Tremens
Delta Rhythm
Delusions
Democracy
Demographic Characteristics
Denatured Alcohol
Dendrites
Denial
Denmark
Dental Education
Dental Students
Dental Surgery
Dental Treatment
Dentistry
Dentists
Deoxycorticosterone
Deoxyribonucleic Acid

Departmentalized Teaching Method
Dependency (Personality)
Dependent Variables
Depersonalization
Depression (Emotion)
Deprivation
Depth Perception
Depth Psychology
Dermatitis
Describing Personality Test
Desipramine
Detoxification
Development/
Developmental Age Groups
Developmental Differences
Developmental Psychology
Developmental Stages
Dextroamphetamine
Diabetes
Diabetes Insipidus
Diabetes Mellitus
Diagnosis
Dialect
Dialectics
Dialysis
Diaphragm (Anatomy)
Diaphragms (Birth Control)
Diarrhea
Diastolic Pressure
Diazepam
Dictionary
Dieldrin
Diencephalon
Differential Aptitude Tests
Differential Diagnosis
Differential Personality Inventory
Differential Reinforcement
Difficulty Level (Test)
Digestion
Digestive System
Digestive System Disorders
Digit Span Testing
Digital Computers
Dihydroergotamine
Diphenhydramine
Diphenylhydantoin
Diplomacy (Foreign Policy)
Diptera
Directed Discussion Method

Disadvantaged
Disappointment
Disasters
Discovery Teaching Method
Discrimination/
Dishonesty
Disorders/
Displacement (Defense Mechanism)
Displays
Dissatisfaction
Dissociative Neurosis
Dissociative Patterns
Distance Perception
Distractibility
Distress
Distributed Practice
Diuresis
Diuretics
Divergent Thinking
Divided Attention
Divorce
Divorced Persons
Dogs
Doll Play
Dolphins
Domestic Service Personnel
Dominance Hierarchy
Dominance/
Dominican Republic
Dopa
Dopamine
Dormitories
Dorsal Roots
Double Bind Interaction
Doubt
Doves
Downs Syndrome
Draftees
Drama
Drawing
Dream Analysis
Dream Content
Dream Recall
Dreaming
Driver Education
Drivers
Driving Behavior
Dropouts
Drosophila

Drug Abuse
Drug Addiction
Drug Administration Methods
Drug Adverse Reactions
Drug Allergies
Drug Dependency
Drug Dosages
Drug Education
Drug Effects
Drug Induced Congenital Disorders
Drug Induced Hallucinations
Drug Laws
Drug Potentiation
Drug Rehabilitation
Drug Sensitivity
Drug Synergism
Drug Therapy
Drug Tolerance
Drug Usage
Drug Usage Attitudes
Drug Withdrawal
Drug Withdrawal Effects
Drugs/
Dualism
Ducks
Dyads
Dysarthria
Dysautonomia
Dyskinesia
Dyslexia
Dysmenorrhea
Dysmorphophobia
Dyspareunia
Dysphonia
Dyspnea
Ear (Anatomy)
Ear Disorders
Early Childhood Development
Early Experience
Early Infantile Autism
Earthworms
East German Democratic Republic
Eating
Eating Patterns
Echinodermata
Echoencephalography
Echoes
Echolalia
Echolocation

Ecological Factors
Ecology
Economy
Eczema
Educable Mentally Retarded
Education/
Educational Administration
Educational Aspirations
Educational Audiovisual Aids
Educational Background
Educational Counseling
Educational Degrees
Educational Field Trips
Educational Financial Assistance
Educational Incentives
Educational Laboratories
Educational Measurement
Educational Personnel
Educational Program Evaluation
Educational Program Planning
Educational Programs
Educational Psychologists
Educational Psychology
Educational Television
Educational Toys
Edwards Personal Preference Schedule
Edwards Personality Inventory
Edwards Social Desirability Scale
Ego
Egotism
Eidetic Imagery
Elbow (Anatomy)
Elective Mutism
Electra Complex
Electric Fishes
Electrical Activity
Electrical Brain Stimulation
Electrical Injuries
Electrical Stimulation
Electro Oculography
Electrocardiography
Electroconvulsive Shock
Electroconvulsive Shock Therapy
Electrodes
Electroencephalography
Electrolytes
Electromyography
Electronystagmography
Electrophysiology

Electroplethysmography
Electroretinography
Elementary Education
Elementary School Students
Elementary School Teachers
Elementary Schools
Elephants
Elopement (Marriage)
Embarrassment
Embedded Figures Testing
Embolisms
Embryo
Emergency Services
Emetic Drugs
Emotional Adjustment
Emotional Content
Emotional Control
Emotional Development
Emotional Immaturity
Emotional Inferiority
Emotional Instability
Emotional Maturity
Emotional Responses
Emotional Security
Emotional Stability
Emotional States
Emotional Superiority
Emotional Trauma
Emotionality (Personality)
Emotionally Disturbed
Emotions/
Empathy
Empirical Methods
Employability
Employee Absenteeism
Employee Attitudes
Employee Benefits
Employee Efficiency
Employee Health Insurance
Employee Leave Benefits
Employee Life Insurance
Employee Motivation
Employee Pension Plans
Employee Productivity
Employee Skills
Employee Turnover
Employer Attitudes
Employment Tests
Encephalitis

Encephalography
Encephalomyelitis
Encounter Group Therapy
Encouragement
Endocrine Disorders
Endocrine Gland Secretion
Endocrine Gland Surgery
Endocrine Glands
Endocrine Neoplasms
Endocrine Sexual Disorders
Endocrine System
Endocrinology
Endogamous Marriage
Endurance
Energy Expenditure
Engineering Psychology
Engineers
England
Enlisted Military Personnel
Enthusiasm
Entrance Examinations
Entrapment Games
Environment
Environmental Adaptation
Environmental Effects
Environmental Stress
Enzymes
Ephedrine
Epidemiology
Epilepsy
Epileptic Seizures
Epinephrine
Epistemology
Epithelial Cells
Equilibrium
Equimax Rotation
Erection (Penis)
Ergot Derivatives
Eroticism
Error Analysis
Errors
Erythrocytes
Escape Conditioning
Eskimos
Esophagus
Essay Testing
Essential Hypertension
Esterases

Estimation
Estradiol
Estrogens
Estrone
Estrus
Ethanol
Ether (Anesthetic)
Ethics
Ethnic Groups
Ethnic Identity
Ethnic Values
Ethnocentrism
Ethnography
Ethnolinguistics
Ethnology/
Ethnospecific Disorders
Etiology
Etymology
Eugenics
Eugenol
Euphoria
Europe
Euthanasia
Evaluation
Evangelists
Evoked Potentials
Excretion
Exercise
Exhibitionism
Existential Therapy
Existentialism
Exogamous Marriage
Expectations
Experiences (Events)
Experiential Psychotherapy
Experiment Controls
Experiment Volunteers
Experimental Design
Experimental Instructions
Experimental Laboratories
Experimental Methods
Experimental Neurosis
Experimental Psychologists
Experimental Psychology
Experimental Psychosis
Experimental Replication
Experimentation/
Experimenter Bias
Experimenter Expectations

Experimenters
Expert Testimony
Exploratory Behavior
Explosive Personality
Expressive Psychotherapy
Extended Family
External Ear
External Rewards
Externalization
Extinction (Learning)
Extracurricular Activities
Extramarital Intercourse
Extrapyramidal Tracts
Extrasensory Perception
Extraversion
Extrinsic Motivation
Eye (Anatomy)
Eye Contact
Eye Disorders
Eye Movements
Eyeblink Reflex
Eyelid Conditioning
Eysenck Personality Inventory
F Test
Face (Anatomy)
Facial Expressions
Facial Features
Facial Muscles
Facial Nerve
Facism
Factor Analysis
Factorial Validity
Fads And Fashions
Failure
Faith Healing
Faking
Familiarity
Family Background
Family Crises
Family Members
Family Physicians
Family Planning
Family Planning Attitudes
Family Relations
Family Size
Family Socioeconomic Level
Family Structure
Family Therapy
Family/

Fantasies (Thought Disturbances)
Fantasy (Defense Mechanism)
Fascia
Fatalism
Father Absence
Father Child Relations
Fathers
Fatigue
Fatty Acids
Fear
Fear Survey Schedule
Fecal Incontinence
Feedback
Feeding Practices
Feet (Anatomy)
Female Animals
Female Criminals
Female Delinquents
Female Genitalia
Female Orgasm
Femininity
Fenfluramine
Fertility Enhancement
Fertilization
Fetishism
Fetus
Fibrillation (Heart)
Field Dependence
Figure Ground Discrimination
Film Strips
Filtered Noise
Filtered Speech
Fine Motor Skill Learning
Finger Tapping
Fingers (Anatomy)
Fingerspelling
Finland
Fire Prevention
Fishes
Fixed Interval Reinforcement
Fixed Ratio Reinforcement
Flexion Reflex
Flight Instrumentation
Flight Simulation
Fluphenazine
Folic Acid
Folie A Deux
Folk Medicine

Followup Studies
Food Allergies
Food Deprivation
Food Intake
Food Preferences
Football
Forced Choice (Testing Method)
Foreign Language Education
Foreign Language Learning
Foreign Language Translation
Foreign Languages
Foreign Organizations
Foreign Policy Making
Foreign Students
Foreign Study
Forensic Psychiatry
Forgetting
Form And Shape Perception
Form Classes (Language)
Foster Children
Foster Parents
Foxes
Fragmentation (Schizophrenia)
France
Franck Drawing Completion Test
Fraternity Membership
Free Recall
Frequency Distribution
Freud (Sigmund)
Freudian Psychoanalytic School
Friendship
Frigidity
Frogs
Frontal Lobe
Frostig Development Test Vis Percept
Frustration
Fugue Reaction
Functionalism
Fund Interper Rela Orientat Beh Ques
Fundamentalism
Galanthamine
Gall Bladder
Galvanic Skin Response
Gambling
Game Theory
Games
Gamma Globulin
Ganglia
Ganglion Blocking Drugs

Gastrointestinal Disorders
Gastrointestinal System
Gastrointestinal Ulcers
Gates MacGinitie Reading Test
Geese
General Anesthetics
General Aptitude Test Battery
General Paresis
General Practitioners
Generation Gap
Generators (Apparatus)
Genes
Genetic Disorders
Genetic Dominance
Genetic Recessiveness
Genetics/
Geniculate Bodies (Thalamus)
Genital Disorders
Genotypes
Geography
Gerbils
Geriatric Patients
Geriatric Psychotherapy
Geriatrics
Germ Cells
Gerontology
Gestalt Psychology
Gestalt Therapy
Gestures
Ghettoes
Gifted
Gilles De La Tourette Disorder
Glands
Glaucoma
Globulins
Globus Pallidus
Glossary
Glossolalia
Glucagon
Glucose
Glue Sniffing
Glutamic Acid
Glutamine
Glutathione
Glutethimide
Glycine
Glycogen

Goals
Goats
God Concepts
Goiters
Goldfish
Goldstein Scheerer Object Sort Test
Gonadotropic Hormones
Gonads
Gonorrhea
Goodenough Harris Draw A Person Test
Gorillas
Gough Adjective Check List
Government
Government Agencies
Government Personnel
Government Policy Making
Government Programs
Grading (Educational)
Graduate Education
Graduate Psychology Education
Graduate Record Examination
Graduate Schools
Graduate Students
Grammar
Grand Mal Epilepsy
Grandchildren
Grandparents
Grasshoppers
Gravitational Effects
Great Britain
Greater Antilles
Greece
Gregariousness
Grief
Grimaces
Gross Motor Skill Learning
Ground Transportation
Group Cohesion
Group Counseling
Group Discussion
Group Dynamics
Group Instruction
Group Participation
Group Performance
Group Problem Solving
Group Psychotherapy
Group Size
Group Structure

Group Testing
Guanethidine
Guessing
Guilford Zimmerman Temperament Surv
Guilt
Guinea Pigs
Gun Control Laws
Gymnasiums
Gynecological Disorders
Gynecologists
Gypsies
Gyrus Cinguli
Habits
Habituation
Hair
Hair Pulling
Haiti
Halfway Houses
Hallucinations
Hallucinogenic Drugs
Hallucinosis
Haloperidol
Hamsters
Hand (Anatomy)
Handicapped
Handicapped (Attitudes Toward)
Handwriting
Handwriting Legibility
Happiness
Hashish
Hate
Hawaii
Hay Fever
Hazards
Head (Anatomy)
Head Banging
Head Injuries
Headache
Health
Health Education
Health Impaired
Health Insurance
Hearing Aids
Heart
Heart Auricles
Heart Disorders
Heart Rate
Heart Rate Affecting Drugs
Heart Surgery

Heart Valves
Heart Ventricles
Heat Effects
Hebephrenic Schizophrenia
Hedonism
Helicopters
Helium
Hematoma
Hemianopia
Hemispherectomy
Hemodialysis
Hemoglobin
Hemophilia
Hemorrhage
Henman Nelson Tests Mental Ability
Heparin
Hepatitis
Hermaphroditism
Heroin
Heroin Addiction
Herpes Simplex
Heterosexuality
Heterozygotic Twins
Heuristic Modeling
Hexamethonium
Hexobarbital
Hibernation
Hidden Figures Test
High Sch Personality Questionnaire
High School Students
High School Teachers
High Schools
Higher Education
Highway Hypnosis Accidents
Highway Safety
Hinduism
Hippocampus
Hips
Hispaniola
Histamine
Histidine
Histology
History
History of Psychology
Hoffmanns Reflex
Holtzman Inkblot Technique
Homatropine
Home Accidents
Home Environment

Home Reared Mentally Retarded
Home Visiting Programs
Homeostasis
Homicide
Homographs
Homonyms
Homosexual Liberation Movement
Homosexuality
Honesty
Hormones
Horses
Hospital Accreditation
Hospital Admission
Hospital Discharge
Hospitalization
Hospitalized Patients
Hospitals
Hostility
Hot Line Services
Housewives
Housing
Hue
Human Biological Rhythms
Human Channel Capacity
Human Courtship
Human Development/
Human Factors Engineering
Human Females
Human Figures Drawing
Human Information Storage
Human Males
Human Migration
Human Sex Differences
Humanism
Humiliation
Humor
Hungary
Hunger
Huntingtons Chorea
Husbands
Hybrids (Biology)
Hydantoins
Hydralazine
Hydrocephaly
Hydrocortisone
Hydrogen
Hydroxylamine
Hydroxylases
Hydroxyzine

Hyoscyamine (L-)
Hyperglycemia
Hyperkinesis
Hypermania
Hyperopia
Hyperphagia
Hypersexuality
Hypertension
Hyperthermia
Hyperthyroidism
Hyperventilation
Hypnagogic Hallucinations
Hypnosis
Hypnotherapists
Hypnotherapy
Hypnotic Drugs
Hypnotic Susceptibility
Hypnotists
Hypochondriasis
Hypoglycemia
Hypoglycemic Agents
Hypogonadism
Hypomania
Hypophysectomy
Hypopituitarism
Hypotension
Hypothalamo Hypophyseal System
Hypothalamus
Hypothalamus Lesions
Hypothermia
Hypothesis Testing
Hypothyroidism
Hypotonia (Eye)
Hysterectomy
Hysteria
Hysterical Anesthesia
Hysterical Paralysis
Hysterical Personality
Hysterical Vision Disturbances
Id
Idealism
Ideation
Identification (Defense Mechanism)
Identity Crisis
Idiot Savants
Illegitimate Children
Illinois Test Psycholinguist Abil
Illumination
Illusions (Perception)

Imagery
Imagination
Imipramine
Imitation (Learning)
Immigration
Immunization
Immunoglobulins
Immunologic Disorders
Immunology
Implosive Therapy
Impotence
Imprinting
Impulsiveness
Inadequate Personality
Incarceration
Incentives
Incest
Incidental Learning
Income (Economic)
Income Level
Incomplete Man Test
Incubators (Apparatus)
Independence (Personality)
Independent Variables
India
Individual Differences
Individual Psychology
Individual Psychotherapy
Individual Testing
Individuality
Individualized Instruction
Induced Abortion
Inductive Deductive Reasoning
Industrial Accidents
Industrial Foremen
Industrial Psychologists
Industrial Psychology
Industrialization
Infant Development
Infant Intelligence Scale
Infant Vocalization
Infantilism
Infants
Infectious Disorders
Infectious Meningitis
Inference
Inferior Colliculus
Infertility
Inflection

Influenza
Information Exchange
Information Seeking
Information Theory
Information/
Inhibition (Personality)
Initial Teaching Alphabet
Initiation Rites
Initiative
Injections
Injuries
Insecticides
Insects
Inservice Teacher Education
Insight
Insight (Psychotherapeutic Process)
Insight Therapy
Insomnia
Institution Visitation
Institutional Functioning Inventory
Institutionalization
Institutionalized Mentally Retarded
Instructional Media
Insulin
Insulin Shock Therapy
Insurance
Intellectual Development
Intellectualism
Intellectualization
Intelligence
Intelligence Measures
Intelligence Quotient
Intentional Learning
Interaction Analysis (Statistics)
Interaction Variance
Intercostal Muscles
Interdisciplinary Treatment Approach
Interest Inventories
Interest Patterns
Interests
Interfaith Marriage
Interference (Learning)
Intergroup Dynamics
Intermediate School Students
Internal External Locus of Control
Internal Rewards
International Organizations
International Relations
Internists

Interpersonal Attraction
Interpersonal Communication
Interpersonal Compatibility
Interpersonal Influences
Interpersonal Interaction
Interracial Marriage
Interresponse Time
Interstimulus Interval
Intertrial Interval
Interviewing
Interviews
Intestines
Intimacy
Intramuscular Injections
Intraperitoneal Injections
Intrauterine Devices
Intravenous Injections
Intrinsic Motivation
Introjection
Introspection
Introversion
Intuition
Inventories
Inventory of College Activities
Invertebrates
Involutional Depression
Involutional Paranoid Psychosis
Involvement
Iowa Tests of Basic Skills
Iproniazid
Iran
Ireland
Iris (Eye)
Iron
Ischemia
Islam
Isocarboxazid
Isolation (Defense Mechanism)
Isolation Effect
Isoniazid
Isoproterenol
Isozymes
Israel
Italy
Item Analysis (Statistical)
Item Analysis (Test)
Item Content (Test)
Jamaica

Japan
Jaundice
Jaw
Jealousy
Job Analysis
Job Applicant Attitudes
Job Applicant Interviews
Job Applicant Screening
Job Corps
Job Enrichment
Job Experience Level
Job Performance
Job Satisfaction
Joint Disorders
Joints (Anatomy)
Jokes
Journalists
Jr Sr High School Personality Quest
Judaism
Judgment
Judgment Disturbances
Judo
Jumping
Jung (Carl)
Jungian Psychology
Junior College Students
Junior High School Students
Junior High School Teachers
Junior High Schools
Justice
Juvenile Delinquency
Juvenile Delinquents
Juvenile Gangs
Kangaroos
Kibbutz
Kidneys
Kindergarten Students
Kindergartens
Kinesthetic Perception
Kinship Structure
Kleptomania
Klinefelters Syndrome
Knee
Knowledge of Results
Kohs Block Design Test
Kolmogarov Smirnov Test
Korea
Korsakoffs Psychosis
Kuder Occupational Interest Survey

Kuder Preference Record
Kuder Richardson Test
Kupfer Detre Self Rating Scale
Kwashiorkor
Labor (Childbirth)
Labor Management Relations
Labor Union Members
Labor Unions
Labyrinth (Anatomy)
Labyrinth Disorders
Lactate Dehydrogenase
Lactation
Language
Language Arts Education
Language Development
Language Laboratories
Larvae
Laryngeal Disorders
Larynx
Laser Irradiation
Latent Learning
Lateral Dominance
Latin Squares Test
Law (Government)
Law Enforcement Personnel
Laws
Lay Religious Personnel
Lead (Metal)
Lead Poisoning
Leadership
Leadership Style
Learning Ability
Learning Centers (Educational)
Learning Disabilities
Learning Disorders
Learning Rate
Learning Schedules
Learning Theory
Learning/
Leary Interpersonal Check List
Least Preferred Coworker Scale
Lecture Method
Leeward Islands
Leg (Anatomy)
Legal Arrest
Legal Detention
Legal Processes
Legislative Processes
Leisure Time

Leiter Adult Intelligence Scale
Lemurs
Lens (Eye)
Lesbianism
Lesions
Lesser Antilles
Lesson Plans
Letters (Alphabet)
Leucine
Leucocytes
Leukemias
Levodopa
Liberalism
Libido
Lidocaine
Life Experiences
Life Insurance
Ligaments
Limbic System
Linear Regression
Linguistics
Lipid Metabolism
Lipid Metabolism Disorders
Lipids
Lipoproteins
Lipreading
Lips (Face)
Liquor
Listening Comprehension
Literacy
Literature
Literature Review
Lithium
Lithium Bromide
Lithium Carbonate
Liver
Liver Disorders
Lizards
Local Anesthetics
Logic (Philosophy)
Logical Thinking
Logotherapy
Loneliness
Long Term Memory
Longitudinal Studies
Lorge Thorndike Intelligence Test
Loudness
Loudness Discrimination
Loudness Perception

Love
Lowenfeld Mosaic Test
Lower Class
Lower Class Attitudes
Lower Income Level
Loyalty
Lumbar Spinal Cord
Lumbosacral Region
Lunar Synodic Cycle
Lung
Lung Disorders
Lupus
Lymph
Lymph Nodes
Lymph Vessels
Lymphatic System
Lymphocytes
Lysergic Acid Diethylamide
Machiavellianism
Magazines
Magical Thinking
Magnesium
Magnesium Ions
Magnetic Test
Malaria
Male Animals
Male Castration
Male Criminals
Male Delinquents
Male Genital Disorders
Male Genitalia
Male Homosexuality
Male Orgasm
Malingering
Mammals
Mammary Glands
Man Machine Systems
Man Machine Systems Design
Management Decision Making
Management Methods
Management Personnel
Management Planning
Management Training
Management/
Mania
Manic Depression
Manic Depressive Psychosis
Mann Whitney U Test

Mantis
Maple Syrup Urine Disease
Marathon Group Therapy
Marihuana
Marihuana Laws
Marihuana Legalization
Marihuana Usage
Marine Personnel
Marital Conflict
Marital Relations
Marital Separation
Marital Status
Marketing
Markov Chains
Marlowe Crowne Soc Desirabil Scale
Marriage
Marriage Attitudes
Marriage Counseling
Marriage Rites
Marsupials
Masculinity
Masking
Masochism
Masochistic Personality
Mass Hysteria
Mass Media
Massed Practice
Mastectomy
Masticatory Muscles
Masturbation
Materialism
Mathematical Ability
Mathematical Modeling
Mathematical Psychology
Mathematicians
Mathematics (Concepts)
Mathematics Achievement
Mathematics Education
Matriarchy
Maudsley Personality Inventory
Maze Learning
Maze Pathways
Mazes
McNemar Test
Mean
Meaning
Meaningfulness
Measles

Measurement/
Mecamylamine
Mechanical Aptitude
Mechanoreceptors
Median
Mediated Responses
Medical Diagnosis
Medical Education
Medical Internship
Medical Patients
Medical Personnel
Medical Personnel Supply
Medical Psychology
Medical Residency
Medical Sciences
Medical Students
Medical Therapeutic Devices
Medical Treatment (General)
Medics
Meditation
Medulla Oblongata
Megalomania
Melanin
Melatonin
Membranes
Memory
Memory Decay
Memory Disorders
Memory Drums
Memory For Designs Test
Memory Trace
Menarche
Menieres Disease
Meninges
Meningitis
Menopause
Menstrual Cycle
Menstrual Disorders
Menstruation
Mental Age
Mental Confusion
Mental Disorders/
Mental Health
Mental Health Consultation
Mental Health Inservice Training
Mental Health Personnel
Mental Health Personnel Supply
Mental Health Program Evaluation
Mental Health Programs

Mental Illness (Attitudes Toward)
Mental Retardation
Mental Retardation (Attit Toward)
Mentally Retarded
Meperidine
Mephenesin
Meprobamate
Mercury (Metal)
Mercury Poisoning
Mescaline
Mesencephalon
Mesoridazine
Messages
Metabolic Rates
Metabolism
Metabolism Disorders
Metabolites
Metal Poisoning
Metallic Elements
Metaphysics
Methadone
Methamphetamine
Methanol
Methaqualone
Methionine
Methodology/
Methohexital
Methoxamine
Methyldopa
Methylphenidate
Metronomes
Metropolitan Reading Readiness Test
Mexican Americans
Mexico
Mice
Microcephaly
Microscopes
Middle Aged
Middle Class
Middle Class Attitudes
Middle Ear
Middle Income Level
Middle Level Managers
Migraine Headache
Migrant Farm Workers
Migratory Behavior (Animal)
Militancy
Military Enlistment
Military Medical Personnel

Military Personnel
Military Psychology
Military Recruitment
Military Schools
Military Training
Military Veterans
Miller Analogies Test
Mineral Deficiency Disorders
Minimal Brain Disorders
Minimally Brain Damaged
Ministers (Religion)
Minks
Minn Multiphasic Personality Inven
Minnesota Teacher Attitude Inventory
Minor Tranquilizers
Minority Groups
Misanthropy
Missionaries
Mnemonic Learning
Mode
Models
Modern Language Aptitude Test
Mollusca
Monetary Incentives
Monetary Rewards
Money
Monitoring
Monkeys
Monks
Monoamine Oxidase Inhibitors
Monoamine Oxidases
Monocular Vision
Monolingualism
Monozygotic Twins
Montessori Method
Moodiness
Mooney Problem Check List
Moral Development
Morality
Morals
Morphemes
Morphine
Morphology
Morphology (Language)
Mortality Rate
Mother Absence
Mother Child Relations
Mothers

Moths
Motion Perception
Motion Pictures
Motion Pictures (Educational)
Motion Pictures (Entertainment)
Motion Sickness
Motivation
Motivation Training
Motor Coordination
Motor Cortex
Motor Development
Motor End Plates
Motor Neurons
Motor Performance
Motor Processes
Motor Skills
Motor Traffic Accidents
Mouth (Anatomy)
Mucus
Multilingualism
Multiple Births
Multiple Choice (Testing Method)
Multiple Personality
Multiple Sclerosis
Multiply Handicapped
Muscle Contraction Headache
Muscle Contractions
Muscle Relaxation
Muscle Relaxing Drugs
Muscle Spasms
Muscles
Muscular Atrophy
Muscular Disorders
Muscular Dystrophy
Musculoskeletal Disorders
Musculoskeletal System
Music
Music Education
Music Therapy
Musical Ability
Musical Instruments
Mutations
Mutism
Mutual Storytelling Technique
Myasthenia
Myasthenia Gravis
Mydriatic Drugs
Myelin Sheath

Myelitis
Myers Briggs Type Indicator
Myocardial Infarctions
Myocardium
Myoclonia
Myopia
Myotonia
Mysticism
Myths
Nail Biting
Nails (Anatomy)
Nalorphine
Narcissism
Narcissistic Personality
Narcoanalysis
Narcoanalytic Drugs
Narcolepsy
Narcosis
Narcotic Antagonists
Narcotic Drugs
Nasal Mucosa
National Guardsmen
Nationalism
Natural Disasters
Nausea
Navy Personnel
Neck (Anatomy)
Need Satisfaction
Needs
Negative Correlation
Negative Reinforcement
Negative Transfer
Negativism
Negotiation
Negroes
Neighborhoods
Neologisms
Neonatal Autosome Disorders
Neonatal Chromosome Disorders
Neonatal Development
Neonatal Disorders
Neonatal Genetic Disorders
Neonatal Sex Chromosome Disorders
Neonates
Neoplasms
Neopsychoanalytic School
Neostigmine
Nerve Endings
Nerve Tissues

Nervous System
Nervous System Disorders
Nervous System Neoplasms
Nervousness
Nest Building
Netherlands
Netherlands West Indies
Neural Analyzers
Neural Lesions
Neural Receptors
Neuralgia
Neurasthenic Neurosis
Neuritis
Neuroanatomy
Neurobiology
Neurochemistry
Neurodermatitis
Neuroleptic Drugs
Neurologists
Neurology
Neuromuscular Disorders
Neurons
Neuropathology
Neurophysiology
Neuropsychiatry
Neuropsychology
Neurosciences
Neurosis
Neurosurgery
Neurosyphilis
Neurotic Depressive Reaction
Neuroticism
Neuroticism Scale Questionnaire
New Guinea
New Zealand
Newspapers
Nialamide
Nicotinamide
Nicotine
Nicotinic Acid
Nictitating Membrane
Nightmares
Nihilism
Nitrogen
Nitroglycerin
Nocturnal Emission
Nocturnal Teeth Grinding
Noise Effects
Noise Levels (Work Areas)

297

Non Zero Sum Games
Nonchromaffin Paraganglia
Noncommissioned Officers
Nonconformity (Personality)
Nondirected Discussion Method
Nondisjunction (Chromosome)
Nongraded Schools
Nonlinear Regression
Nonmetallic Elements
Nonparametric Statistical Tests
Nonprofit Organizations
Nonprojective Personality Measures
Nonreversal Shift Learning
Nonsense Syllable Learning
Nonstandard English
Nonverbal Communication
Nonverbal Learning
Nonverbal Meaning
Nonverbal Reinforcement
Norepinephrine
Normal Distribution
North America
North Vietnam
Northern Ireland
Norway
Norway Rats
Nose
Nouns
Novocaine
NREM Sleep
Nuclear Family
Nucleic Acids
Nudity
Null Hypothesis Testing
Number Comprehension
Number Systems
Numbers (Numerals)
Numerosity Perception
Nuns
Nursery School Students
Nursery Schools
Nurses
Nursing
Nursing Education
Nursing Homes
Nursing Students
Nutrition
Nutritional Deficiencies
Nystagmus

Obedience
Obesity
Obituary
Objectivity
Oblique Rotation
Observation Methods
Observational Learning
Observers
Obsessions
Obsessive Compulsive Neurosis
Obsessive Compulsive Personality
Obstetrics Gynecology
Occipital Lobe
Occupational Adjustment
Occupational Aspirations
Occupational Attitudes
Occupational Choice
Occupational Guidance
Occupational Interest Measures
Occupational Interests
Occupational Mobility
Occupational Neurosis
Occupational Preference
Occupational Safety
Occupational Stress
Occupational Success Prediction
Occupational Tenure
Occupational Therapists
Occupational Therapy
Occupations/
Octopus
Ocular Dominance
Oculomotor Muscles
Odor Discrimination
Oedipal Complex
Olfactory Bulb
Olfactory Evoked Potentials
Olfactory Mucosa
Olfactory Nerve
Olfactory Perception
Olfactory Thresholds
Omnibus Personality Inventory
On The Job Training
Onomatopoeia And Images Test
Onset (Disorders)
Open Classroom Method
Operant Conditioning
Ophidiophobia
Ophthalmologic Examination

Ophthalmology
Opiates
Opinion Attitude And Interest Survey
Opossums
Optic Chiasm
Optic Lobe
Optic Nerve
Optical Aids
Optimism
Optometrists
Optometry
Oral Contraceptives
Oral Reading
Organ Transplantation
Organic Brain Syndromes
Organic Therapies
Organizational Change
Organizational Climate
Organizational Crises
Organizational Development
Organizational Merger
Organizational Objectives
Organizational Structure
Organizations
Orgasm
Orienting Reflex
Orienting Responses
Orphanages
Orphans
Orphenadrine
Orthogonal Rotation
Orthography
Orthopsychiatry
Oscilloscopes
Osteochondritis
Otosclerosis
Outpatient Treatment
Outpatients
Ovariectomy
Ovaries
Overlearning
Overpopulation
Ovulation
Ovum
Oxidases
Oxygen
Oxygenation
Oxytocic Drugs
Oxytocin

Pacifism
Pain
Pain Perception
Pain Thresholds
Painting (Art)
Paired Associate Learning
Palm (Anatomy)
Pancreas
Pancreatectomy
Panic
Papaverine
Paragraphs
Paralydehyde
Paralysis
Paramedical Personnel
Paramedical Sciences
Parametric Statistical Tests
Paranasal Sinuses
Paranoia (Psychosis)
Paranoid Personality
Paranoid Schizophrenia
Paraprofessional Education
Paraprofessional Personnel
Parapsychological Phenomena
Parapsychology
Parasitic Disorders
Parasympathetic Nervous System
Parathion
Parathyroid Disorders
Parathyroid Glands
Parathyroid Hormone
Parent Attitude Research Instrument
Parent Child Communication
Parent Child Relations
Parent Educational Background
Parental Absence
Parental Attitudes
Parental Occupation
Parental Permissiveness
Parental Role
Parents
Pargyline
Parietal Lobe
Parkinsons Disease
Parole
Parole Officers
Partially Hearing Impaired
Partially Sighted
Participation

Passive Aggressive Personality
Passiveness
Pastoral Counseling
Pathological Lying
Pathologists
Pathology
Patient History
Patients
Patriarchy
Pattern Discrimination
Peabody Picture Vocabulary Test
Peace Corps
Pectoralis Muscles
Pedestrian Accidents
Pedestrians
Pediatricians
Pediatrics
Pedophilia
Peer Relations
Peer Tutoring
Pellagra
Pelvis
Penguins
Penicillins
Penis
Penis Envy
Penology
Pentobarbital
Pentylenetetrazol
Peoples Republic of China
Pepsin
Pepsinogen
Peptides
Perception/
Perceptiveness (Personality)
Perceptual Aftereffect
Perceptual Closure
Perceptual Development
Perceptual Discrimination
Perceptual Disturbances
Perceptual Localization
Perceptual Measures
Perceptual Motor Coordination
Perceptual Motor Learning
Perceptual Motor Processes
Perceptual Orientation
Perceptual Stimulation
Perceptual Style
Performance

Performance Tests
Pericardium
Peripheral Nerve Disorders
Peripheral Nerves
Peritoneum
Perphenazine
Persecution
Perseveration
Persistence
Personal Orientation Inventory
Personal Space
Personal Values
Personality Change
Personality Correlates
Personality Development
Personality Disorders
Personality Measures
Personality Processes/
Personality Theory
Personality Traits
Personality/
Personnel Evaluation
Personnel Management
Personnel Placement
Personnel Recruitment
Personnel Selection
Personnel Supply
Personnel Termination
Personnel Training
Personnel/
Persuasion Therapy
Persuasive Communication
Pessimism
Petit Mal Epilepsy
Petting
Peyote
Phantom Limbs
Pharmacology
Pharyngeal Disorders
Pharynx
Phenacetin
Phenaglycodol
Phenelzine
Pheniprazine
Phenmetrazine
Phenobarbital
Phenomenology
Phenothiazine Derivatives
Phenotypes

Phenoxybenzamine
Phenylalanine
Phenylketonuria
Pheromones
Phi Coefficient
Philippines
Philosophies
Phobias
Phobic Neurosis
Phonemes
Phonetics
Phonics
Phonology
Phosphatases
Phosphatides
Phosphorus
Phosphorylases
Photographic Art
Photographs
Photopic Stimulation
Photoreceptors
Phrases
Phylogenesis
Physical Agility
Physical Attractiveness
Physical Development
Physical Dexterity
Physical Education
Physical Endurance
Physical Fitness
Physical Geography
Physical Handicaps (Attit Toward)
Physical Maturity
Physical Strength
Physical Therapists
Physical Therapy
Physical Treatment Methods
Physically Handicapped
Physicians
Physicists
Physics
Physiological Aging
Physiological Arousal
Physiological Correlates
Physiological Psychology
Physiological Stress
Physiology/
Physique
Physostigmine

Piaget (Jean)
Piagetian Tasks
Pica
Picks Disease
Picrotoxin
Pigeons
Pigments
Pigs
Pilocarpine
Pimozide
Pineal Body
Pinealectomy
Pipradrol
Pitch (Frequency)
Pitch Discrimination
Pitch Perception
Pituitary Disorders
Pituitary Gland
Pituitary Hormones
Place Disorientation
Placebo
Placenta
Placental Hormones
Planarians
Plastic Surgery
Play Therapy
Playgrounds
Pleasure
Plethysmography
Pneumoencephalography
Pneumonia
Poetry
Point Biserial Correlation
Poisons
Poland
Police Personnel
Poliomyelitis
Political Anarchy
Political Assassination
Political Attitudes
Political Campaigns
Political Candidates
Political Conservatism
Political Economic Systems
Political Elections
Political Issues
Political Liberalism
Political Parties
Political Processes

Political Radicalism
Political Revolution
Politics
Pollution
Polygamy
Polygraphs
Polyneuritis
Pons
Population
Population (Statistics)
Population Genetics
Pornography
Porphyria
Porpoises
Porteus Maze Test
Positive Reinforcement
Positive Transfer
Positivism
Posterior Pituitary Hormones
Postgraduate Students
Postgraduate Training
Postnatal Period
Postpartum Depression
Postsurgical Complications (Physical
Posttesting
Posttreatment Followup
Posture
Potassium
Potassium Bromide
Potassium Ions
Potential Dropouts
Poverty
Poverty Areas
Power
Practice
Practice Effects
Pragmatism
Praise
Prayer
Precocious Development
Precognition
Predictability (Measurement)
Prediction
Prediction Errors
Predictive Validity
Predisposition
Prednisolone
Preference Measures
Preferences

Preferred Rewards
Pregnancy
Prejudice
Premarital Counseling
Premarital Intercourse
Premature Birth
Premature Ejaculation
Premenstrual Tension
Prenatal Development
Prenatal Developmental Stages
Preschool Age Children
Preschool Education
Presenile Dementia
Pressure Sensation
Pretesting
Prevention/
Preventive Medicine
Pride
Priests
Primacy Effect
Primary Mental Health Prevention
Primary Reinforcement
Primary School Students
Primates (Nonhuman)
Primidone
Printed Communications Media
Printing (Handwriting)
Prismatic Stimulation
Prison Personnel
Prisoners
Prisoners Dilemma Game
Prisoners of War
Prisons
Privacy
Private School Education
Privileged Communication
Proactive Inhibition
Probability
Probability Learning
Probation
Probation Officers
Problem Drinking
Problem Solving
Process Psychosis
Prochlorperazine
Professional Certification
Professional Consultation
Professional Contribution

Professional Criticism
Professional Criticism Reply
Professional Ethics
Professional Licensing
Professional Meetings And Symposia
Professional Organizations
Professional Referral
Professional Standards
Profiles (Measurement)
Profoundly Mentally Retarded
Progesterone
Prognosis
Programed Instruction
Programed Textbooks
Project Follow Through
Project Head Start
Projection (Defense Mechanism)
Projective Personality Measures
Projective Techniques
Projective Testing Technique
Prolactin
Promazine
Promethazine
Promiscuity
Pronouns
Pronunciation
Propaganda
Propranolol
Proprioceptors
Prose
Prostate
Prostheses
Prostitution
Proteases
Protein Deficiency Disorders
Protein Metabolism
Proteinases
Proteins
Protestantism
Protozoa
Pruritus
Pseudocyesis
Pseudoneurotic Schizophrenia
Pseudopsychopathic Schizophrenia
Psilocybin
Psychedelic Drugs
Psychedelic Experiences
Psychiatric Aides
Psychiatric Clinics

Psychiatric Hospital Admission
Psychiatric Hospital Programs
Psychiatric Hospital Readmission
Psychiatric Hospital Staff
Psychiatric Hospitalization
Psychiatric Hospitals
Psychiatric Nurses
Psychiatric Patients
Psychiatric Social Workers
Psychiatric Training
Psychiatrists
Psychiatry
Psychic Energizers
Psychoanalysis
Psychoanalysts
Psychoanalytic Interpretation
Psychoanalytic Personality Factors
Psychoanalytic Theory
Psychoanalytic Training
Psychodiagnosis
Psychodiagnostic Interview
Psychodiagnostic Typologies
Psychodrama
Psychodynamics
Psychogenesis
Psychogenic Pain
Psychokinesis
Psycholinguistics
Psychological Endurance
Psychological Screening Inventory
Psychological Stress
Psychological Terminology
Psychologists
Psychology
Psychometrics
Psychomotor Development
Psychopathology
Psychopathy
Psychopharmacology
Psychophysical Measurement
Psychophysics
Psychophysiology
Psychosexual Behavior
Psychosis
Psychosocial Development
Psychosocial Mental Retardation
Psychosocial Readjustment
Psychosocial Rehabilitation
Psychosocial Resocialization

Psychosomatic Disorders
Psychosurgery
Psychotherapeutic Breakthrough
Psychotherapeutic Counseling
Psychotherapeutic Outcomes
Psychotherapeutic Processes
Psychotherapeutic Resistance
Psychotherapeutic Techniques
Psychotherapeutic Transference
Psychotherapist Attitudes
Psychotherapists
Psychotherapy
Psychotherapy Training
Psychotic Depressive Reaction
Psychotomimetic Drugs
Puberty
Public Health Service Nurses
Public Health Services
Public Opinion
Public Relations
Public School Education
Public Speaking
Public Transportation
Puerto Rico
Pulmonary Alveoli
Pulmonary Emphysema
Pulmonary Tuberculosis
Punishment
Pupil (Eye)
Pupil Dilation
Purdue Perceptual Motor Survey
Puromycin
Pyramidal Tracts
Pyramidotomy
Pyromania
Q Sort Testing Technique
Quadruplets
Quails
Quartimax Rotation
Questionnaires
Quinidine
Quinine
Rabbis
Rabbits
Race (Anthropological)
Race Attitudes
Racial Differences
Racial Discrimination
Racial Integration

Racism
Radiation
Radiation Therapy
Radical Movements
Radiculitis
Radio
Radiology
Railroad Trains
Random Sampling
Rank Difference Correlation
Rank Order Correlation
Rape
Rapid Eye Movement
Rat Learning
Rating
Rating Scales
Rationalization
Rats
Rauwolfia
Raven Coloured Progressive Matrices
Ravens Progressive Matrices
Reaction Formation
Reaction Time
Reactive Depression
Reactive Psychosis
Reading
Reading Ability
Reading Achievement
Reading Comprehension
Reading Disabilities
Reading Education
Reading Materials
Reading Measures
Reading Readiness
Reading Skills
Reading Speed
Realism (Philosophy)
Reality
Reality Testing
Reality Therapy
Reasoning
Recall (Learning)
Recency Effect
Recidivism
Reciprocal Inhibition Therapy
Reciprocity
Recognition (Learning)
Reconstruction (Learning)
Recovery (Disorders)

Recreation
Recreation Areas
Recreation Therapy
Reductionism
Reflexes
Reformatories
Refraction Errors
Regression (Defense Mechanism)
Rehab Counselor Judgement Scale
Rehabilitation
Rehabilitation Centers
Reinforcement
Reinforcement Amounts
Reinforcement Schedules
Relapse (Disorders)
Relationship Therapy
Relaxation
Relearning
Religion/
Religiosity
Religious Affiliation
Religious Beliefs
Religious Buildings
Religious Education
Religious Literature
Religious Personnel
Religious Practices
Religious Prejudices
REM Dream Deprivation
REM Dreams
REM Sleep
Remedial Reading
Remission (Disorders)
Remote Associates Test
Repression (Defense Mechanism)
Repression Sensitization
Repression Sensitization Scale
Reptiles
Reserpine
Residential Care Institutions
Resource Teachers
Respiration
Respiration Stimulating Drugs
Respiratory Distress
Respiratory System
Respiratory Tract Disorders
Response Amplitude
Response Bias
Response Duration

Response Frequency
Response Generalization
Response Latency
Response Parameters
Response Probability
Response Set
Response Variability
Responses
Responsibility
Restlessness
Retarded Speech Development
Retention
Retention Measures
Reticular Formation
Retina
Retinal Detachment
Retinal Image
Retirement
Retroactive Inhibition
Reversal Shift Learning
Rewards
Rh Incompatibility
Rheoencephalography
Rheumatic Fever
Rheumatoid Arthritis
Rhythm Method
Ribonuclease
Ribonucleic Acid
Ribs
Rigidity (Personality)
Riots
Risk Taking
Rites (Nonreligious)
Rites of Passage
Rivalry
Robins
Rod And Frame Test
Rodents
Rods (Eye)
Roentgenography
Rokeach Dogmatism Scale
Role Conflicts
Role Expectations
Role Perception
Role Playing
Roles
Roman Catholicism
Roommates
Rorschach Test

Rosenzweig Picture Frustration Study
Rotary Pursuit
ROTC Students
Rote Learning
Rotter Incomplete Sentences Blank
Rotter Intern Extern Locus Cont Scal
Roughness
Rubella
Rulon Test
Runaway Behavior
Running
Rural Environments
Saccharin
Sacral Spinal Cord
Sadism
Sadistic Personality
Sadness
Sadomasochism
Sadomasochistic Personality
Safety
Safety Belts
Safety Devices
Salamanders
Salaries
Sales Personnel
Saliva
Salivary Glands
Salivation
Salmon
Sampling (Experimental)
Sanatoriums
Satiation
Satisfaction
Scaling (Testing)
Scalp (Anatomy)
Schizoid Personality
Schizophrenia
Schizophrenogenic Family
Schizophrenogenic Mothers
School Adjustment
School Administrators
School Age Children
School And College Ability Test
School Attendance
School Club Membership
School Counselors
School Dropouts
School Enrollment
School Environment

School Expulsion
School Facilities
School Integration (Racial)
School Learning
School Libraries
School Nurses
School Phobia
School Principals
School Psychologists
School Psychology
School Readiness
School Superintendents
School Suspension
School Truancy
Schools
Science Education
Sciences
Scientific Communication
Scientists/
Sclerosis (Nervous System)
Scopolamine
Scoring (Testing)
Scotland
Scotoma
Scotopic Stimulation
Scratching
Sculpturing
Sea Gulls
Seals (Animal)
Seasonal Variations
Secobarbital
Secondary Education
Secondary Reinforcement
Secretarial Personnel
Secretion (Gland)
Sedatives
Selected Readings
Selection Tests
Selective Attention
Selective Breeding
Self Actualization
Self Analysis Form
Self Concept
Self Control
Self Disclosure
Self Esteem
Self Evaluation
Self Inflicted Wounds
Self Mutilation

Self Perception
Self Reinforcement
Self Stimulation
Selfishness
Semantic Differential
Semantic Generalization
Semantics
Semicircular Canals
Seminarians
Seminaries
Senile Dementia
Senile Psychosis
Sensation Seeking Scale
Sense Organ Disorders
Sense Organs
Sensitivity (Personality)
Sensitivity Training
Sensorimotor Measures
Sensory Adaptation
Sensory Deprivation
Sensory Feedback
Sensory Handicaps (Attit Toward)
Sensory Neurons
Sentence Comprehension
Sentence Structure
Sentences
Separation Anxiety
Sequential Learning
Serial Anticipation (Learning)
Serial Compulsions
Serial Learning
Seriousness
Serotonin
Serotonin Antagonists
Serum Albumin
Severely Mentally Retarded
Sex Chromosome Disorders
Sex Chromosomes
Sex Drive
Sex Education
Sex Hormones
Sex Linked Developmental Differences
Sex Linked Hereditary Disorders
Sex Roles
Sex/
Sexual Abstinence
Sexual Attitudes
Sexual Development
Sexual Deviations

Sexual Function Disturbances
Sexual Intercourse (Human)
Sexual Masochism
Sexual Reproduction
Sexual Sadism
Sexual Sadomasochism
Sexuality
Shamanism
Sheep
Sheltered Workshops
Shock
Shock Therapy
Shock Units
Shoplifting
Shopping Centers
Short Term Memory
Shoulder (Anatomy)
Shuttle Box Grids
Shuttle Box Hurdles
Shuttle Boxes
Siamese Twins
Sibling Relations
Siblings
Side Effects (Drug)
Sight Vocabulary
Sign Language
Sign Test
Signal Detection (Perception)
Silent Reading
Silicones
Simple Schizophrenia
Simulation
Simulation Games
Sin
Sincerity
Single Persons
Sisters
Situational Attitude Scale
Sixteen Personality Factors Question
Size
Size Discrimination
Skepticism
Skewed Distribution
Skill Learning
Skilled Industrial Workers
Skin (Anatomy)
Skin Disorders
Skin Electrical Properties

Skin Potential
Skin Resistance
Skin Temperature
Skinner Boxes
Skull
Slang
Sleep
Sleep Deprivation
Sleep Disorders
Sleep Onset
Sleep Talking
Sleep Treatment
Sleepwalking
Slosson Intelligence Test For Child
Slow Learners
Smiles
Snails
Snakes
Sociability
Social Acceptance
Social Adjustment
Social Approval
Social Behavior
Social Casework
Social Change
Social Class
Social Dating
Social Demonstrations
Social Deprivation
Social Desirability
Social Drinking
Social Environments
Social Equality
Social Facilitation
Social Groups
Social Influences
Social Interaction
Social Isolation
Social Learning
Social Mobility
Social Movements
Social Perception
Social Processes
Social Programs
Social Psychiatry
Social Psychologists
Social Psychology
Social Reinforcement
Social Sciences

Social Stress
Social Structure
Social Values
Social Work Education
Social Workers
Socialism
Socialization
Society
Sociocultural Factors
Socioeconomic Class Attitudes
Socioeconomic Status
Sociograms
Sociologists
Sociology
Sociometric Tests
Sociotherapy
Sodium
Sodium Bromide
Sodium Ions
Somatosensory Cortex
Somatosensory Evoked Potentials
Somatotropin
Somatotypes
Somesthetic Perception
Somesthetic Stimulation
Somnambulism
Sonar
Sons
Sorority Membership
South America
South Vietnam
Southeast Asia
Spacecraft
Spaceflight
Spain
Spasms
Spatial Distortion
Spatial Organization
Spatial Orientation (Perception)
Spatial Perception
Spearman Brown Test
Special Education
Special Education Students
Special Education Teachers
Speech And Hearing Measures
Speech Characteristics
Speech Development
Speech Disorders
Speech Handicapped

Speech Pauses
Speech Perception
Speech Pitch
Speech Processing (Mechanical)
Speech Rate
Speech Rhythm
Speech Therapists
Speech Therapy
Spelling
Sperm
Spinal Column
Spinal Cord
Spinal Cord Injuries
Spinal Ganglia
Spinal Nerves
Spinothalamic Tracts
Spleen
Spontaneous Abortion
Spontaneous Recovery (Learning)
Spontaneous Remission
Sports
Spouses
Spreading Depression
Squirrels
SRA Primary Mental Abilities Test
Stammering
Standard Deviation
Stanford Achievement Test
Stanford Binet Intelligence Scale
Startle Reflex
Starvation
State Trait Anxiety Inventory
Statistical Analysis
Statistical Correlation
Statistical Measurement
Statistical Norms
Statistical Probability
Statistical Reliability
Statistical Rotation
Statistical Sample Parameters
Statistical Samples
Statistical Significance
Statistical Tests
Statistical Validity
Statistical Variables
Status
Stein Leventhal Syndrome
Stepchildren
Stepparents

Stereoscopic Presentation
Stereoscopic Vision
Stereotaxic Atlas
Stereotaxic Techniques
Stereotyped Attitudes
Stereotyped Behavior
Sterility
Sterilization (Sex)
Steroids
Sticklebacks
Stimulation
Stimulators (Apparatus)
Stimulus Ambiguity
Stimulus Attenuation
Stimulus Change
Stimulus Complexity
Stimulus Control
Stimulus Deprivation
Stimulus Discrimination
Stimulus Duration
Stimulus Frequency
Stimulus Generalization
Stimulus Intensity
Stimulus Intervals
Stimulus Novelty
Stimulus Parameters
Stimulus Presentation Methods
Stimulus Salience
Stimulus Similarity
Stimulus Variability
Stochastic Modeling
Stock Options
Stomach
Strabismus
Strategies
Stress
Stress Reactions
Strikes
Strong Vocational Interest Blank
Strontium
Strontium Bromide
Stroop Color Word Test
Structuralism
Strychnine
Student Activism
Student Admission Criteria
Student Attitudes
Student Teachers
Student Teaching

Students
Study Habits
Stuttering
Subconscious
Subculture (Anthropological)
Subcutaneous Injections
Sublimation
Subliminal Perception
Submarines
Subtests
Suburban Environments
Subvocalization
Succinylcholine
Suffering
Sugars
Suggestibility
Suicide
Suicide Prevention
Suicide Prevention Centers
Sulpiride
Summer Camps (Recreation)
Superego
Superior Colliculus
Superstitions
Suppression (Defense Mechanism)
Surgeons
Surgery
Surgical Patients
Surrogate Parents (Humans)
Surveys
Susceptibility (Disorders)
Suspicion
Sweat
Sweating
Sweden
Swimming
Switzerland
Syllables
Symbiotic Infantile Psychosis
Symbolism
Sympathectomy
Sympathetic Nervous System
Sympathetic Pain
Sympatholytic Drugs
Sympathomimetic Amines
Sympathomimetic Drugs
Sympathy
Symptom Remission

Symptoms
Synapses
Syncope
Syndromes
Synonyms
Synovial Bursa
Syntax
Synthetic Speech
Syphilis
Systematic Desensitization Therapy
Systems Analysis
Systems/
Systolic Pressure
Szondi Test
T Mazes
T Test
Taboos
Tachistoscopes
Tachistoscopic Presentation
Tachycardia
Tactual Displays
Tactual Perception
Tactual Stimulation
Taiwan
Tantrums
Tape Recorders
Taraxein
Task Analysis
Task Complexity
Taste Buds
Taste Perception
Taste Stimulation
Taxonomies
Taylor Manifest Anxiety Scale
Teacher Aides
Teacher Attitudes
Teacher Characteristics
Teacher Education
Teacher Personality
Teacher Recruitment
Teacher Student Interaction
Teacher Supply
Teacher Tenure
Teachers
Teaching
Teaching Machines
Teaching Methods
Team Teaching Method

Technical Schools
Technical Service Personnel
Technology
Teeth (Anatomy)
Telecommunications Media
Telemetry
Telencephalon
Telepathy
Telephone Systems
Televised Instruction
Television
Television Advertising
Television Viewing
Tell A Story Kit (Taskit)
Temperature Effects
Temperature Perception
Temporal Lobe
Temporal Spatial Concept Scale
Temptation
Tendons
Tennessee Self Concept Scale
Tennis
Terminal Cancer
Terminally Ill Patients
Territoriality
Test Administration
Test Anxiety
Test Construction
Test Items
Test Norms
Test Reliability
Test Scores
Test Standardization
Test Validity
Testes
Testicular Feminization Syndrome
Testing
Testing Methods
Testosterone
Tetanus (Disease)
Tetrabenazine
Tetracaine
Tetrachoric Correlation
Tetracycline
Tetrahydrocannabinol
Thailand
Thalamic Nuclei
Thalamotomy
Thalamus

Thalidomide
Theatre
Theft
Thematic Apperception Test
Theophylline
Theories of Education
Theories/
Theory Formulation
Theory of Evolution
Theory Verification
Therapeutic Community
Therapeutic Social Clubs
Therapist Characteristics
Therapist Trainees
Therapists/
Thermal Acclimatization
Thermoreceptors
Thermoregulation (Body)
Theta Rhythm
Thigh
Thinking
Thiopental
Thioridazine
Thiothixene
Thirst
Thoracic Duct
Thoracic Spinal Cord
Thorax
Thought Disturbances
Threat
Threat Postures
Threshold Determination
Thresholds
Thrombophlebitis
Thromboses
Thumb
Thumbsucking
Thymectomy
Thyroid Disorders
Thyroid Extract
Thyroid Gland
Thyroid Hormones
Thyroidectomy
Thyrotoxicosis
Thyrotropin
Thyroxine
Tics
Time
Time Disorientation

Time Estimation
Time Perception
Timers (Apparatus)
Timidity
Tinnitus
Tissues (Body)
Title V Projects
Toads
Tobacco Smoking
Tobago
Tocopherols
Toilet Training
Token Economy Programs
Tolbutamide
Tolerance
Tolerance For Ambiguity
Tongue
Top Level Managers
Topography
Torticollis
Totalitarianism
Towns
Toxic Disorders
Toxic Encephalopathies
Toxic Hepatitis
Toxic Psychoses
Toxicity
Toxicomania
Toxoplasmosis
Toy Selection
Toys
Trachea
Tracheal Disorders
Tracking
Tractotomy
Trainable Mentally Retarded
Tranquilizing Drugs
Transactional Analysis
Transaminases
Transcultural Psychiatry
Transducers
Transfer (Learning)
Transfer Students
Transferases
Transformational Generative Grammar
Transformers (Apparatus)
Transistors (Apparatus)
Translocation (Chromosome)
Transportation

Transportation Accidents
Transposition (Cognition)
Transsexualism
Transvestism
Tranylcypromine
Traumatic Amputations
Traumatic Neurosis
Traveling
Treatment Effectiveness Evaluation
Treatment Facilities
Treatment/
Tremor
Trial And Error Learning
Tribes
Trifluoperazine
Triflupromazine
Trigeminal Nerve
Trigeminal Neuralgia
Trihexyphenidyl
Triiodothyronine
Trinidad
Triplets
Trisomy
Trisomy 18
Trisomy 21
TROCA (Computer Screening Battery)
Truancy
Trust (Social Behavior)
Tryptamine
Tryptophan
Tubal Ligation
Tuberculosis
Tubocurarine
Tunnel Vision
Turkey
Turners Syndrome
Turtles
Tutoring
Twins
Type I Errors
Type II Errors
Tyramine
Tyrosine
Ulcerative Colitis
Ultrasound
Uncles
Unconditioned Responses
Unconditioned Stimulus
Unconscious (Personality Factor)

Underwater Effects
Underweight
Undifferentiated Schizophrenia
Unemployment
UNESCO Silent Reading Test
Union of South Africa
Union of Soviet Socialist Republics
United Arab Republic
United Kingdom
United States
Unskilled Industrial Workers
Unwed Mothers
Upper Class
Upper Class Attitudes
Upper Income Level
Upward Bound
Urban Environments
Urban Planning
Urbanization
Ureter
Urethra
Uric Acid
Urinalysis
Urinary Function Disorders
Urinary Incontinence
Urinary Tract
Urination
Urine
Urogenital Disorders
Urogenital System
Uterus
Vacationing
Vagina
Vaginismus
Vagotomy
Vagus Nerve
Values
Vane Kindergarten Test
Variability Measurement
Variable Interval Reinforcement
Variable Ratio Reinforcement
Varimax Rotation
Vasectomy
Vasoconstriction
Vasoconstrictor Drugs
Vasodilation
Vasodilator Drugs
Vasopressin
Veins (Anatomy)

Velocity
Venereal Diseases
Venezuela
Ventral Roots
Verbal Ability
Verbal Communication
Verbal Fluency
Verbal Learning
Verbal Meaning
Verbal Reinforcement
Verbal Tests
Verbs
Verification (of Theories)
Vertebrates
Vertigo
Vestibular Apparatus
Veterinary Medicine
Vibration
Vibrators (Apparatus)
Vibrotactile Thresholds
Vicarious Experiences
Victimization
Videotape Instruction
Videotape Recorders
Videotapes
Vigilance
Vineland Social Maturity Scale
Violence
Viral Disorders
Viral Meningitis
Virgin Islands
Virginity
Vision
Visiting Homemakers
Visual Cortex
Visual Discrimination
Visual Displays
Visual Evoked Potentials
Visual Feedback
Visual Field
Visual Hallucinations
Visual Masking
Visual Perception
Visual Stimulation
Visual Thresholds
Visual Tracking
Visually Handicapped
Vitamin Deficiency Disorders
Vitamins

Vocabulary
Vocal Cords
Vocalization
Vocational Counselors
Vocational Education
Vocational Rehabilitation
Vocational School Students
Voice
Volt Meters
Volunteer Civilian Personnel
Volunteer Military Personnel
Volunteer Personnel
Volunteers In Service To America
Vomiting
Voting Behavior
Vowels
Voyeurism
Wakefield Self Assessment Depression
Wakefulness
Wales
Walk In Clinics
Walking
Walsh Test
War
Water Deprivation
Water Intake
Water Safety
Water Transportation
Weaning
Wechsler Adult Intelligence Scale
Wechsler Bellevue Intelligence Scale
Wechsler Intelligence Scale Children
Weight Perception
Weightlessness
Welfare Services (Government)
Welsh Figure Preference Test
Wepman Test of Auditory Discrim
Wernickes Syndrome
West German Federal Republic
West Indies
West Pakistan
White Betz A B Scale
White Collar Workers

White Noise
Wide Range Achievement Test
Widowers
Widows
Wilcoxon Sign Rank Test
Wilson Patterson Conservatism Scale
Windigo Psychosis
Windward Islands
Wine
Witchcraft
Withdrawal (Defense Mechanism)
Wives
Wolves
Womens Liberation Movement
Word Associations
Word Frequency
Word Meaning
Word Salad
Words (Phonetic Units)
Work (Attitudes Toward)
Work Attitude Scale
Work Rest Cycles
Work Scheduling
Work Week Length
Workday Shifts
Working Conditions
Working Space
Workmens Compensation Insurance
Worms
Wounds
Wrist
Written Language
X Ray Equipment
Yates Test
Yerkes Boxes
Yoga
Young Adults
Yugoslavia
Zen Buddhism
Zoology
Zulliger Z Test
Zungs Self Rating Depression Scale
Zygote

Users Guide to the Hierarchical Section

Terms used to represent each of the 17 major classification categories in *PA* are placed at the primary level in this listing with terms representing subcategories being placed at the secondary level. All other terms representing concepts related to these very broad areas are listed in descending order according to breadth of concept represented. Families of concepts, represented by the *PA* classification categories, were defined empirically on the basis of patterns of reported subject matter competence within the psychological community. The hierarchical structuring of terms under each family heading was created by computer, using the broader and narrower term designations provided in the Relationship Section. The thesaurus user who wishes to see how a particular term or concept is hierarchically related to all other concepts in a content area or to examine the content associated with a broad area of psychology should use this listing.

The descriptors representing families of concepts in psychology are listed below along with the page number where the hierarchical structure of terms related to each family is displayed.

The order in which the content areas are presented follow that indicated above. Terms conceptually related to each of these content areas are listed alphabetically within each hierarchical level. Discounting the two hierarchical levels used to indicate broad content areas, up to 6 levels have been used to show the relative breadth of concepts represented by different terms. For example: *Ear (Anatomy)* and *Eye (Anatomy)* represent equivalent conceptual levels but *External Ear, Middle Ear,* and *Labyrinth (Anatomy)* represent narrower concepts that are related to *Ear (Anatomy)* and *Lens (Eye), Pupil (Eye)* and *Retina* represent narrower concepts that are related to *Eye (Anatomy)*. In turn, *Cochlea* and *Semicircular Canals* represent narrower conceptual levels to *Labyrinth (Anatomy)*.

To determine the relative specificity of a concept represented by a term, determine which major content area it is most associated with, and scan the terms hierarchically listed within that content area for the specific term. The listing will show the relative hierarchical level of the term with narrower and broader terms that are related to it.

GENERAL

Apparatus
  Accelerometers
  Amplifiers (Apparatus)
  Audiometers
  Cage Apparatus
  Cameras
  Computers
  Electrodes
  Generators (Apparatus)
  Incubators (Apparatus)
  Mazes
    Maze Pathways
    T Mazes
  Memory Drums
  Metronomes
  Microscopes
  Oscilloscopes
  Polygraphs
  Shuttle Box Hurdles
  Shuttle Boxes
    Shuttle Box Grids
  Skinner Boxes
  Sonar
  Stimulators (Apparatus)
    Shock Units
  Tachistoscopes
  Tape Recorders
    Videotape Recorders
  Timers (Apparatus)
  Transducers
  Transformers (Apparatus)
  Transistors (Apparatus)
  Vibrators (Apparatus)
  Volt Meters
  X Ray Equipment
  Yerkes Boxes
Computer Applications
  Computer Simulation
Empirical Methods
  Observation Methods
Sampling (Experimental)
  Biased Sampling
  Random Sampling
Sciences
  Biology
    Botany
    Neurobiology
    Zoology
  Chemistry
    Biochemistry
      Neurochemistry
  Geography
  Medical Sciences
    Anesthesiology
    Cardiology
    Dentistry

Endocrinology
Epidemiology
Geriatrics
Immunology
Neurology
Neuropathology
Obstetrics Gynecology
Ophthalmology
Psychiatry
  Child Psychiatry
  Community Psychiatry
  Forensic Psychiatry
  Neuropsychiatry
  Orthopsychiatry
  Social Psychiatry
  Transcultural Psychiatry
Radiology
Surgery
Veterinary Medicine
Neurosciences
  Neuroanatomy
  Neurobiology
  Neurochemistry
  Neurology
  Neuropathology
  Neurophysiology
  Neuropsychiatry
  Neuropsychology
Physics
Social Sciences
  Anthropology
  Psychology
    Applied Psychology
      Clinical Psychology
      Community Psychology
      Consumer Psychology
      Counseling Psychology
      Educational Psychology
        School Psychology
      Engineering Psychology
      Industrial Psychology
      Medical Psychology
      Military Psychology
      Social Psychology
    Comparative Psychology
    Developmental Psychology
      Adolescent Psychology
      Child Psychology
      Gerontology
    Experimental Psychology
    Mathematical Psychology
    Physiological Psychology
      Neuropsychology
  Sociology
Scientific Communication
  Professional Meetings And Symposia
  Psychological Terminology

PSYCHOMETRICS AND STATISTICS

Test Construction And Validation
Achievement Measures

PSYCHOMETRICS AND STATISTICS

Test Construction And Validation (Continued)
Iowa Tests Of Basic Skills
Stanford Achievement Test
Wide Range Achievement Test
Aptitude Measures
Army General Classification Test
Coll Ent Exam Bd Scholastic Apt Test
Differential Aptitude Tests
General Aptitude Test Battery
Graduate Record Examination
Modern Language Aptitude Test
School And College Ability Test
SRA Primary Mental Abilities
Attitude Measures
Allport Vernon Lindzey Study Values
Minnesota Teacher Attitude Inventory
Opinion Attitude And Interest Survey
Parent Attitude Research Instrument
Rehab Counselor Judgement Scale
Situational Attitude Scale
Wilson Patterson Conservatism Scale
Work Attitude Scale
Educational Measurement
Entrance Examinations
Intelligence Measures
Ammons Full Range Picture Vocab Test
Benton Revised Visual Retention Test
California Test Of Mental Maturity
Columbia Mental Maturity Scale
Concept Mastery Test
Culture Fair Intelligence Test
Frostig Development Test Vis Percept
Goodenough Harris Draw A Person Test
Henman Nelson Tests Mental Ability
Hidden Figures Test
Illinois Test Psycholinguist Abil
Infant Intelligence Scale
Kohs Block Design Test
Leiter Adult Intelligence Scale
Lorge Thorndike Intelligence Test
Lowenfeld Mosaic Test
Miller Analogies Test
Peabody Picture Vocabulary Test
Porteus Maze Test
Raven Coloured Progressive Matrices
Ravens Progressive Matrices
Remote Associates Test
Slosson Intelligence Test For Child
SRA Primary Mental Abilities
Stanford Binet Intellingence Scale
Temporal Spatial Concept Scale
Vane Kindergarten Test
Wechsler Adult Intelligence Scale
Wechsler Bellevue Intelligence Scale
Wechsler Intelligence Scale Children
Occupational Interest Measures
Kuder Occupational Interest Survey
Strong Vocational Interest Blank
Perceptual Measures

Test Construction And Validation (Continued)
Rod And Frame Test
Stroop Color Word Test
Personality Measures
Nonprojective Personality Measures
Authoritarianism Rebellion Scale
Bannister Repertory Grid
Barrett Lennard Relationship Invent
Barron Welsh Art Scale
Bass Famous Sayings Test
Bene Anthony Family Relations Test
California F Scale
California Psychological Inventory
California Test of Personality
Child Behavior Diagnostic Inventory
Childrens Manifest Anxiety Scale
Childrens Personality Questionnaire
Cromwells Adult Locus of Cont Scale
Describing Personality Test
Differential Personality Inventory
Edwards Personal Preference Schedule
Edwards Social Desirability Scale
Embedded Figures Testing
Eysenck Personality Inventory
Fear Survey Schedule
Fund Interper Rela Orientat Beh Ques
Goldstein Scheerer Object Sort Test
Gough Adjective Check List
Guilford Zimmerman Temperament Surv
High Sch Personality Questionnaire
Jr Sr High School Personality Quest
Kupfer Detre Self Rating Scale
Leary Interpersonal Check List
Magnetic Test
Marlowe Crowne Soc Desirabil Scale
Maudsley Personality Inventory
Memory for Designs Test
Minn Multiphasic Personality Inven
Mooney Problem Check List
Myers Briggs Type Indicator
Neuroticism Scale Questionnaire
Omnibus Personality Inventory
Personal Orientation Inventory
Psychological Screening Inventory
Repression Sensitization Scale
Rod and Frame Test
Rokeach Dogmatism Scale
Rotter Intern Extern Locus Cont Scal
Self Analysis Form
Sensation Seeking Scale
Sixteen Personality Factors Question
State Trait Anxiety Inventory
Taylor Manifest Anxiety Scale
Tennessee Self Concept Scale
Vineland Social Maturity Scale
Wakefield Self Assessment Depression
Welsh Figure Preference Test
White Betz A B Scale
Zungs Self Rating Depression Scale
Projective Personality Measures
Bender Gestalt Test
Blacky Pictures Test
Childrens Apperception Test
Color Pyramid Test
Franck Drawing Completion Test

Test Construction And Validation (Continued)
    Holtzman Inkblot Technique
    Human Figures Drawing
    Onomatopoeia and Images Test
    Rorschach Test
    Rosenzweig Picture Frustration Study
    Rotter Incomplete Sentences Blank
    Szondi Test
    Thematic Apperception Test
    Zulliger Z Test
Preference Measures
    Kuder Preference Record
    Least Preferred Coworker Scale
Reading Measures
    Gates MacGinitie Reading Test
    Metropolitan Reading Readiness Test
    UNESCO Silent Reading Test
Retention Measures
    Recall (Learning)
        Free Recall
    Recognition (Learning)
    Reconstruction (Learning)
Sensorimotor Measures
    Purdue Perceptual Motor Survey
Speech And Hearing Measures
    TROCA (Computer Screening Battery)
    Wepman Test Of Auditory Discrim
Surveys
    Consumer Surveys

Mathematical Models And Statistics
Statistical Analysis
    Confidence Limits (Statistics)
    Statistical Measurement
        Central Tendency Measures
            Mean
            Median
            Mode
        Consistency (Measurement)
        Factor Analysis
            Cluster Analysis
            Interaction Analysis (Statistics)
            Item Analysis (Statistical)
            Statistical Rotation
                Oblique Rotation
                Orthogonal Rotation
                    Equimax Rotation
                    Quartimax Rotation
                    Varimax Rotation
        Frequency Distribution
            Normal Distribution
            Skewed Distribution
        Predictability (Measurement)
        Statistical Norms
        Statistical Probability
            Binomial Distribution
        Statistical Significance
        Statistical Tests
            Latin Squares Test
            Nonparametric Statistical Tests
                Chi Square Test
                Cochran Q Test
                Kolmogarov Smirnov Test

Mathematical Models And Statistics (Continued)
                Kuder Richardson Test
                Mann Whitney U Test
                McNemar Test
                Rulon Test
                Sign Test
                Walsh Test
                Wilcoxon Sign Rank Test
                Yates Test
            Parametric Statistical Tests
                F Test
                T Test
            Spearman Brown Test
        Variability Measurement
            Analysis Of Covariance
            Analysis Of Variance
            Interaction Variance
            Standard Deviation
Statistical Correlation
    Linear Regression
    Negative Correlation
    Nonlinear Regression
    Phi Coefficient
    Point Biserial Correlation
    Rank Difference Correlation
    Rank Order Correlation
    Tetrachoric Correlation
Statistical Validity
    Factorial Validity
    Predictive Validity
Statistical Variables
    Dependent Variables
    Independent Variables

PERCEPTION AND MOTOR
PERFORMANCE

Perceptual Motor Learning
    Fine Motor Skill Learning
    Gross Motor Skill Learning
Practice
    Distributed Practice
    Massed Practice
Sensorimotor Measures
    Purdue Perceptual Motor Survey
Thresholds
    Auditory Thresholds
    Olfactory Thresholds
    Pain Thresholds
    Sensory Adaptation
        Dark Adaptation
        Orienting Reflex
        Orienting Responses
    Vibrotactile Thresholds
    Visual Thresholds
        Critical Flicker Fusion Threshold
        Dark Adaptation

Perceptual Processes
Extrasensory Perception

Perceptual Processes (Continued)
Illusions (Perception)
  Perceptual Aftereffect
    Afterimage
  Spatial Distortion
Masking
  Auditory Masking
  Visual Masking
Monitoring
  Vigilance
Olfactory Perception
  Odor Discrimination
  Olfactory Thresholds
Perceptual Discrimination
  Figure Ground Discrimination
  Odor Discrimination
  Pattern Discrimination
Perceptual Measures
  Rod And Frame Test
  Stroop Color Word Test
Somesthetic Perception
  Cutaneous Sense
    Tactual Perception
      Vibrotactile Thresholds
  Kinesthetic Perception
  Pain Perception
    Pain Thresholds
  Temperature Perception
Spatial Perception
  Depth Perception
    Stereoscopic Vision
  Distance Perception
    Apparent Distance
  Motion Perception
    Apparent Movement
      Autokinetic Illusion
  Size Discrimination
    Apparent Size
  Spatial Distortion
  Spatial Organization
  Spatial Orientation (Perception)
Stimulus Discrimination

Auditory Perception
Audiometry
  Bone Conduction Audiometry
Auditory Perception
  Auditory Discrimination
    Loudness Discrimination
    Pitch Discrimination
  Auditory Localization
  Loudness Perception
    Loudness Discrimination
  Pitch Perception
    Pitch Discrimination
  Speech Perception

Visual Perception
Visual Perception
  Autokinetic Illusion
  Binocular Vision

Visual Perception (Continued)
  Brightness Perception
  Color Perception
  Monocular Vision
  Stereoscopic Vision
  Visual Discrimination
  Visual Field
  Visual Thresholds
    Critical Flicker Fusion Threshold
    Dark Adaptation

Motor Processes And Performance
Motor Processes
  Exercise
  Motor Coordination
  Motor Performance
    Finger Tapping
    Jumping
    Running
    Walking
  Motor Skills
  Physical Agility
    Physical Dexterity

COGNITIVE PROCESSES AND MOTIVATION

Cognitive Processes
  Associative Processes
    Cognitive Contiguity
    Connotations
    Contextual Associations
  Classification (Cognitive Process)
  Cognitive Discrimination
  Cognitive Generalization
  Cognitive Mediation
  Concept Formation
  Decision Making
    Choice Behavior
  Ideation
    Imagination
  Problem Solving
    Anagram Problem Solving
    Group Problem Solving
  Semantic Generalization
  Thinking
    Abstraction
    Divergent Thinking
    Logical Thinking
    Reasoning
      Inductive Deductive Reasoning
      Inference
  Transposition (Cognition)
Cognitive Style
  Cognitive Complexity
Empirical Methods
  Observation Methods
Experiences (Events)
  Early Experience
  Life Experiences

NEUROLOGY AND PHYSIOLOGY

Blood Vessels
  Arteries (Anatomy)
    Aorta
    Carotid Arteries
  Capillaries (Anatomy)
  Veins (Anatomy)
Heart
  Heart Auricles
  Heart Valves
  Heart Ventricles
  Myocardium
  Pericardium
Lymph Vessels
Cells (Biology)
  Blood Cells
    Erythrocytes
    Leucocytes
      Lymphocytes
  Bone Marrow Cells
  Chromosomes
  Connective Tissue Cells
  Epithelial Cells
  Germ Cells
    Ovum
    Sperm
  Neurons
    Axons
    Dendrites
    Motor Neurons
    Sensory Neurons
      Auditory Neurons
      Cones (Eye)
      Rods (Eye)
Digestive System
  Esophagus
  Gastrointestinal System
    Gall Bladder
    Intestines
      Colon
    Liver
    Stomach
  Lips (Face)
  Mouth (Anatomy)
  Peritoneum
  Pharynx
  Teeth (Anatomy)
  Tongue
    Taste Buds
Endocrine System
  Endocrine Glands
    Adrenal Glands
    Gonads
      Ovaries
      Testes
    Parathyroid Glands
    Pineal Body
    Pituitary Gland
      Hypothalamo Hypophyseal System
    Thyroid Gland
Enzymes
  Aldolases
  Amylases
  Carbonic Anhydrase

Decarboxylases
Dehydrogenases
  Alcohol Dehydrogenases
  Lactate Dehydrogenase
Esterases
  Acetylcholinesterase
  Cholinesterase
  Ribonuclease
Glutathione
Hydroxylases
Isozymes
Oxidases
  Amine Oxidases
    Monoamine Oxidases
  Cytochrome Oxidase
Pepsin
Phosphatases
  Acid Phosphatases
Phosphorylases
Proteases
  Proteinases
Transferases
  Transaminases
Ergot Derivatives
  Dihydroergotamine
Glands
  Endocrine Glands
    Adrenal Glands
    Gonads
      Ovaries
      Testes
    Parathyroid Glands
    Pineal Body
    Pituitary Gland
      Hypothalamo Hypophyseal System
    Thyroid Gland
  Mammary Glands
  Pancreas
  Salivary Glands
Hormones
  Adrenal Cortex Hormones
    Aldosterone
    Corticosterone
    Cortisone
    Deoxycorticosterone
    Hydrocortisone
    Prednisolone
  Adrenal Medulla Hormones
    Norepinephrine
  Epinephrine
  Glucagon
  Gonadotropic Hormones
    Prolactin
  Insulin
  Melatonin
  Parathyroid Hormone
  Pituitary Hormones
    Corticotropin
    Posterior Pituitary Hormones
      Oxytocin
      Vasopressin
    Somatotropin

Thyrotropin
Placental Hormones
Sex Hormones
  Androgens
    Testosterone
  Estrogens
    Estradiol
    Estrone
  Progesterone
Thyroid Hormones
  Thyroxine
  Triiodothyronine
Lipids
  Fatty Acids
    Phosphatides
Lipoproteins
Lymphatic System
  Lymph Nodes
  Lymph Vessels
  Thoracic Duct
Musculoskeletal System
  Ankle
  Arm (Anatomy)
  Bones
  Elbow (Anatomy)
  Fascia
  Feet (Anatomy)
  Fingers (Anatomy)
    Thumb
  Hand (Anatomy)
  Hips
  Jaw
  Joints (Anatomy)
  Knee
  Leg (Anatomy)
  Ligaments
  Muscles
    Abdominal Wall
    Diaphragm (Anatomy)
    Facial Muscles
    Intercostal Muscles
    Masticatory Muscles
    Oculomotor Muscles
    Pectoralis Muscles
  Ribs
  Shoulder (Anatomy)
  Skull
  Spinal Column
  Synovial Bursa
  Tendons
  Thorax
  Wrist
Peptides
  Glutathione
Physique
  Body Height
  Body Weight
    Obesity
    Underweight
Pigments
  Hemoglobin

Melanin
Proteins
  Albumins
    Serum Albumin
  Blood Proteins
    Hemoglobin
    Immunoglobulins
      Gamma Globulin
    Serum Albumin
    Taraxein
  Globulins
    Antibodies
    Immunoglobulins
      Gamma Globulin
Respiratory System
  Bronchi
  Diaphragm (Anatomy)
  Larynx
    Vocal Cords
  Lung
    Pulmonary Alveoli
  Nose
    Nasal Mucosa
      Olfactory Mucosa
  Paranasal Sinuses
  Pharynx
  Thorax
  Trachea
Sense Organs
  Ear (Anatomy)
    External Ear
    Labyrinth (Anatomy)
      Cochlea
      Semicircular Canals
      Vestibular Apparatus
    Middle Ear
  Eye (Anatomy)
    Cornea
    Iris (Eye)
    Lens (Eye)
    Pupil (Eye)
    Retina
      Cones (Eye)
      Rods (Eye)
  Olfactory Mucosa
  Taste Buds
Steroids
  Cholesterol
  Corticosteroids
    Aldosterone
    Corticosterone
    Cortisone
    Deoxycorticosterone
    Hydrocortisone
    Prednisolone
Urogenital System
  Female Genitalia
    Clitoris
    Ovaries
    Uterus
      Cervix
    Vagina
  Gonads

Ovaries
Testes
Male Genitalia
Penis
Prostate
Testes
Urinary Tract
Bladder
Kidneys
Ureter
Urethra
Vertebrates
Amphibia
Frogs
Salamanders
Toads
Birds
Blackbirds
Budgerigars
Canaries
Chickens
Doves
Ducks
Geese
Penguins
Pigeons
Quails
Robins
Sea Gulls
Fishes
Bass (Fish)
Carp
Goldfish
Cichlids
Electric Fishes
Salmon
Sticklebacks
Mammals
Bats
Cats
Cattle
Deer
Dogs
Dolphins
Elephants
Foxes
Goats
Horses
Lemurs
Marsupials
Kangaroos
Opossums
Pigs
Porpoises
Primates (Nonhuman)
Baboons
Chimpanzees
Gorillas
Monkeys
Rabbits
Rodents
Beavers
Chinchillas
Gerbils
Guinea Pigs

Hamsters
Mice
Minks
Rats
Norway Rats
Squirrels
Seals (Animal)
Sheep
Wolves
Reptiles
Crocodilians
Lizards
Snakes
Turtles
Vitamins
Ascorbic Acid
Choline
Nicotinamide
Nicotinic Acid
Tocopherols

Neuroanatomy And Electrophysiology
Cerebral Dominance
Lateral Dominance
Electrolytes
Calcium Ions
Chloride Ions
Magnesium Ions
Potassium Ions
Sodium Ions
Electrophysiology
Electrical Activity
Alpha Rhythm
Delta Rhythm
Evoked Potentials
Auditory Evoked Potentials
Cortical Evoked Potentials
Olfactory Evoked Potentials
Somatosensory Evoked Potentials
Visual Evoked Potentials
Theta Rhythm
Electrical Brain Stimulation
Electro Oculography
Electrocardiography
Electroencephalography
Electromyography
Electronystagmography
Electroplethysmography
Electroretinography
Galvanic Skin Response
Rheoencephalography
Skin Electrical Properties
Skin Potential
Skin Resistance
Basal Skin Resistance

Physiological Processes
Anesthesia (Feeling)
Appetite
Hunger
Biological Rhythms
Animal Biological Rhythms
Animal Circadian Rhythms

326

Physiological Processes (Continued)
Human Biological Rhythms
Birth
Premature Birth
Blood Pressure
Diastolic Pressure
Systolic Pressure
Deprivation
REM Dream Deprivation
Sleep Deprivation
Stimulus Deprivation
Food Deprivation
Sensory Deprivation
Social Deprivation
Social Isolation
Water Deprivation
Dreaming
Nightmares
REM Dreams
Environmental Effects
Altitude Effects
Atmospheric Conditions
Gravitational Effects
Weightlessness
Noise Effects
Seasonal Variations
Temperature Effects
Cold Effects
Heat Effects
Underwater Effects
Excretion
Defecation
Urination
Menstrual Cycle
Menstruation
Menarche
Ovulation
Metabolism
Anabolism
Basal Metabolism
Carbohydrate Metabolism
Catabolism
Lipid Metabolism
Metabolites
Protein Metabolism
Nutritional Deficiencies
Mineral Deficiency Disorders
Protein Deficiency Disorders
Kwashiorkor
Starvation
Vitamin Deficiency Disorders
Pellagra
Wernickes Syndrome
Secretion (Gland)
Endocrine Gland Secretion
Adrenal Gland Secretion
Lactation
Salivation
Sweating
Sleep

Physiological Processes (Continued)
NREM Sleep
REM Sleep
Stress
Environmental Stress
Occupational Stress
Physiological Stress
Psychological Stress
Social Stress
Stress Reactions
Thresholds
Auditory Thresholds
Olfactory Thresholds
Pain Thresholds
Sensory Adaptation
Dark Adaptation
Orienting Reflex
Orienting Responses
Vibrotactile Thresholds
Visual Thresholds
Critical Flicker Fusion Threshold
Dark Adaptation

Genetics
Chromosomes
Autosomes
Sex Chromosomes

PSYCHOPHARMACOLOGY AND PHYSIOLOGICAL INTERVENTION

Medical Therapeutic Devices
Artificial Pacemakers
Hearing Aids
Optical Aids
Contact Lenses
Prostheses
Physical Treatment Methods
Acupuncture
Artificial Respiration
Blood Transfusion
Catheterization
Dental Treatment
Dental Surgery
Dialysis
Hemodialysis
Immunization
Medical Treatment (General)
Diuresis
Radiation Therapy
Surgery
Amputation
Mastectomy
Autopsy
Colostomy
Dental Surgery
Endocrine Gland Surgery
Adrenalectomy
Castration
Male Castration

Ovariectomy
Hypophysectomy
Pancreatectomy
Pinealectomy
Thymectomy
Thyroidectomy
Heart Surgery
Hysterectomy
Induced Abortion
Neurosurgery
Decerebration
Decortication (Brain)
Hemispherectomy
Psychosurgery
Thalamotomy
Pyramidotomy
Sympathectomy
Tractotomy
Vagotomy
Organ Transplantation
Plastic Surgery
Sterilization (Sex)
Castration
Male Castration
Ovariectomy
Hysterectomy
Tubal Ligation
Vasectomy

Brain And Electrical Stimulation And Lesions
Lesions
Brain Lesions
Hypothalamus Lesions
Neural Lesions

Drug Effects
Cannabis
Hashish
Marihuana
Chemical Elements
Metallic Elements
Barium
Calcium
Calcium Ions
Cobalt
Copper
Iron
Lead (Metal)
Lithium
Magnesium
Magnesium Ions
Mercury (Metal)
Potassium
Potassium Ions
Sodium
Sodium Ions
Strontium
Nonmetallic Elements
Carbon
Chloride Ions
Helium
Hydrogen
Nitrogen
Oxygen
Phosphorus

Drug Effects (Continued)
Cholinergic Blocking Drugs
Atropine
Benactyzine
Carphenazine
Homatropine
Hyoscyamine (L-)
Nicotine
Orphenadrine
Scopolamine
Trihexyphenidyl
Cholinergic Drugs
Physostigmine
Pilocarpine
Cholinesterase Inhibitors
Galanthamine
Neostigmine
Physostigmine
Cholinomimetic Drugs
Acetylcholine
Arecoline
Carbachol
Neostigmine
Physostigmine
Pilocarpine
CNS Affecting Drugs
Cerebrum Affecting Drugs
Chlorpromazine
CNS Depressant Drugs
Amobarbital
Barbital
Calcium Bromide
Chlorpromazine
Glutethimide
Haloperidol
Lithium Bromide
Scopolamine
CNS Stimulating Drugs
Amphetamine
Analeptic Drugs
Bemegride
Picrotoxin
Strychnine
Caffeine
Clonidine
Dextroamphetamine
Ephedrine
Methamphetamine
Methylphenidate
Pentylenetetrazol
Pipradrol
Hydantoins
Diuretics
Acetazolamide
Caffeine
Drug Effects
Side Effects (Drug)
Drug Adverse Reactions
Drug Allergies
Drug Dependency
Drug Addiction

Drug Effects (Continued)
Ammonium Bromide
Amobarbital
Atropine
Barbital
Calcium Bromide
Chloral Hydrate
Chlorpromazine
Glutethimide
Haloperidol
Heroin
Hexobarbital
Hyoscyamine (L-)
Lithium Bromide
Meperidine
Methaqualone
Paralydehyde
Pentobarbital
Phenaglycodol
Phenobarbital
Potassium Bromide
Promethazine
Rauwolfia
Reserpine
Scopolamine
Secobarbital
Sodium Bromide
Strontium Bromide
Thalidomide
Thiopental
Serotonin Antagonists
Lysergic Acid Diethylamide
Tetrabenazine
Steroids
Cholesterol
Corticosteroids
Aldosterone
Corticosterone
Cortisone
Deoxycorticosterone
Hydrocortisone
Prednisolone
Sympatholytic Drugs
Hydralazine
Reserpine
Sympathomimetic Drugs
Fenfluramine
Isoproterenol
Sympathomimetic Amines
Amphetamine
Catecholamines
Dopamine
Epinephrine
Norepinephrine
Dextroamphetamine
Ephedrine
Methamphetamine
Methoxamine
Phenmetrazine
Tyramine

Drug Effects (Continued)
Vasoconstrictor Drugs
Amphetamine
Angiotensin
Bufotenine
Dihydroergotamine
Ephedrine
Methamphetamine
Methoxamine
Norepinephrine
Serotonin
Tryptamine
Tyramine
Vasodilator Drugs
Nicotinic Acid
Nitroglycerin

ANIMAL PSYCHOLOGY

Animal Breeding
Selective Breeding
Animal Ethology
Animal Biological Rhythms
Animal Circadian Rhythms
Animal Drinking Behavior
Animal Escape Behavior
Animal Exploratory Behavior
Animal Feeding Behavior
Animal Hoarding Behavior
Animal Innate Behavior
Animal Instinctive Behavior
Animal Nocturnal Behavior
Animal Open Field Behavior
Animal Play
Animal Sex Differences
Animal Social Behavior
Animal Aggressive Behavior
Attack Behavior
Threat Postures
Animal Communication
Animal Distress Calls
Animal Courtship Behavior
Animal Courtship Displays
Animal Division Of Labor
Animal Dominance
Animal Maternal Behavior
Animal Mating Behavior
Animal Sexual Receptivity
Animal Vocalizations
Animal Distress Calls
Hibernation
Imprinting
Migratory Behavior (Animal)
Nest Building
Territoriality
Apparatus
Accelerometers
Amplifiers (Apparatus)
Audiometers

ANIMAL PSYCHOLOGY

Cage Apparatus
Computers
Electrodes
Generators (Apparatus)
Incubators (Apparatus)
Mazes
  Maze Pathways
  T Mazes
Memory Drums
Microscopes
Oscilloscopes
Polygraphs
Shuttle Box Hurdles
Shuttle Boxes
  Shuttle Box Grids
Skinner Boxes
Sonar
Stimulators (Apparatus)
  Shock Units
Tachistoscopes
Tape Recorders
  Videotape Recorders
Timers (Apparatus)
Transducers
Transformers (Apparatus)
Transistors (Apparatus)
Vibrators (Apparatus)
Volt Meters
X Ray Equipment
Yerkes Boxes
Developmental Differences
  Age Differences
  Delayed Development
  Precocious Development
  Sex Linked Developmental Differences
Developmental Stages
  Prenatal Developmental Stages
    Embryo
    Fetus
    Zygote
Environment
  Social Environments
    Animal Environments
Environmental Effects
  Altitude Effects
  Atmospheric Conditions
  Gravitational Effects
    Weightlessness
  Noise Effects
  Seasonal Variations
  Temperature Effects
    Cold Effects
    Heat Effects
  Underwater Effects
Excretion
  Defecation
  Urination
Experimental Design
  Followup Studies
  Hypothesis Testing

Null Hypothesis Testing
  Longitudinal Studies
Feeding Practices
  Weaning
Food Intake
  Eating
Invertebrates
  Arthropoda
    Arachnida
    Crustacea
      Crabs
      Crayfish
    Insects
      Ants
      Bees
      Beetles
      Butterflies
      Cockroaches
      Diptera
        Drosophila
      Grasshoppers
      Larvae
      Mantis
      Moths
  Echinodermata
  Mollusca
    Octopus
    Snails
  Protozoa
  Worms
    Earthworms
    Planarians
Vertebrates
  Amphibia
    Frogs
    Salamanders
    Toads
  Birds
    Blackbirds
    Budgerigars
    Canaries
    Chickens
    Doves
    Ducks
    Geese
    Penguins
    Pigeons
    Quails
    Robins
    Sea Gulls
  Fishes
    Bass (Fish)
    Carp
      Goldfish
    Cichlids
    Electric Fishes
    Salmon
    Sticklebacks
  Mammals
    Bats
    Cats
    Cattle
    Deer
    Dogs

Dolphins
Elephants
Foxes
Goats
Horses
Lemurs
Marsupials
  Kangaroos
  Opossums
Pigs
Porpoises
Primates (Nonhuman)
  Baboons
  Chimpanzees
  Gorillas
  Monkeys
Rabbits
Rodents
  Beavers
  Chinchillas
  Gerbils
  Guinea Pigs
  Hamsters
  Mice
  Minks
  Rats
    Norway Rats
  Squirrels
Seals (Animal)
Sheep
Wolves
Reptiles
  Crocodilians
  Lizards
  Snakes
  Turtles

Learning And Motivation
Appetite
  Hunger
Classical Conditioning
  Conditioned Responses
    Conditioned Emotional Responses
    Conditioned Suppression
  Conditioned Stimulus
  Unconditioned Responses
  Unconditioned Stimulus
Deprivation
  Sleep Deprivation
  Stimulus Deprivation
    Food Deprivation
    Sensory Deprivation
    Social Deprivation
      Social Isolation
    Water Deprivation
Exploratory Behavior
  Animal Exploratory Behavior
Feedback
  Delayed Feedback
    Delayed Auditory Feedback
  Sensory Feedback
    Auditory Feedback
      Delayed Auditory Feedback
    Visual Feedback

Learning And Motivation (Continued)
Incidental Learning
  Latent Learning
Interference (Learning)
  Proactive Inhibition
  Retroactive Inhibition
Learning Schedules
  Distributed Practice
  Massed Practice
Masking
  Auditory Masking
  Visual Masking
Memory
  Long Term Memory
  Memory Decay
  Memory Trace
  Short Term Memory
Motivation
  Animal Motivation
  Hunger
  Incentives
  Thirst
Operant Conditioning
  Avoidance Conditioning
  Conditioned Emotional Responses
  Escape Conditioning
  Eyelid Conditioning
Perceptual Motor Learning
  Fine Motor Skill Learning
  Gross Motor Skill Learning
Reinforcement
  Differential Reinforcement
  Negative Reinforcement
  Positive Reinforcement
  Primary Reinforcement
  Punishment
  Reinforcement Amounts
  Reinforcement Schedules
    Fixed Interval Reinforcement
    Fixed Ratio Reinforcement
    Variable Interval Reinforcement
    Variable Ratio Reinforcement
  Rewards
    External Rewards
    Internal Rewards
    Preferred Rewards
  Secondary Reinforcement
  Self Reinforcement
Retention
  Recall (Learning)
  Recognition (Learning)
  Reconstruction (Learning)
Stimulation
  Afferent Stimulation
  Aversive Stimulation
  Brain Stimulation
  Perceptual Stimulation
    Auditory Stimulation
    Somesthetic Stimulation
    Tactual Stimulation

Learning And Motivation (Continued)

Taste Stimulation
   Visual Stimulation
     Prismatic Stimulation
Self Stimulation
Stimulus Discrimination
Stress
   Environmental Stress
   Physiological Stress
   Psychological Stress
   Social Stress
   Stress Reactions
Transfer (Learning)
   Negative Transfer
   Positive Transfer

Social And Sexual Behavior

Animal Social Behavior
   Animal Aggressive Behavior
     Attack Behavior
     Threat Postures
   Animal Communication
     Animal Distress Calls
   Animal Courtship Behavior
     Animal Courtship Displays
   Animal Division Of Labor
   Animal Dominance
   Animal Maternal Behavior
   Animal Mating Behavior
     Animal Sexual Receptivity

Sensory Processes

Auditory Perception
   Auditory Discrimination
     Loudness Discrimination
     Pitch Discrimination
   Auditory Localization
   Loudness Perception
     Loudness Discrimination
   Pitch Perception
     Pitch Discrimination
Olfactory Perception
   Odor Discrimination
   Olfactory Thresholds
Perceptual Discrimination
   Figure Ground Discrimination
   Odor Discrimination
   Pattern Discrimination
Somesthetic Perception
   Cutaneous Sense
     Tactual Perception
       Vibrotactile Thresholds
   Kinesthetic Perception
   Pain Perception
     Pain Thresholds
   Temperature Perception
Spatial Perception
   Depth Perception
     Stereoscopic Vision
   Distance Perception
     Apparent Distance
   Motion Perception

Sensory Processes (Continued)

Size Discrimination
   Apparent Size
Spatial Distortion
Spatial Organization
Spatial Orientation (Perception)
Thresholds
   Auditory Thresholds
   Olfactory Thresholds
   Pain Thresholds
   Sensory Adaptation
     Dark Adaptation
     Orienting Reflex
     Orienting Responses
   Vibrotactile Thresholds
   Visual Thresholds
     Critical Flicker Fusion Threshold
     Dark Adaptation
Visual Perception
   Binocular Vision
   Brightness Perception
   Color Perception
   Monocular Vision
   Stereoscopic Vision
   Visual Discrimination
   Visual Field
   Visual Thresholds
     Critical Flicker Fusion Threshold
     Dark Adaptation

DEVELOPMENTAL PSYCHOLOGY

Birth
   Premature Birth
Childhood Development
   Early Childhood Development
   Infant Development
     Neonatal Development
Developmental Age Groups
   Adolescents
   Adults
     Aged
     Middle Aged
     Young Adults
   Children
     Infants
       Neonates
     Preschool Age Children
     School Age Children
Developmental Differences
   Age Differences
   Delayed Development
   Precocious Development
   Sex Linked Developmental Differences
Developmental Stages
   Menopause
   Prenatal Developmental Stages
     Embryo
     Fetus
     Zygote

Puberty
Feeding Practices
  Bottle Feeding
  Breast Feeding
  Weaning
Psychogenesis
  Cognitive Development
    Intellectual Development
      Language Development
    Perceptual Development
  Emotional Development
  Moral Development
  Psychomotor Development
    Speech Development
  Psychosocial Development
    Childhood Play Development
    Personality Development
Students
  Business Students
  Classmates
  College Students
    Community College Students
    Dental Students
    Graduate Students
    Junior College Students
    Medical Students
    Postgraduate Students
    ROTC Students
  Elementary School Students
    Intermediate School Students
    Primary School Students
  Foreign Students
  High School Students
  Junior High School Students
  Kindergarten Students
  Nursery School Students
  Nursing Students
  Roommates
  Seminarians
  Special Education Students
  Transfer Students
  Vocational School Students

Cognitive And Physical Development
Artistic Ability
  Musical Ability
Cognitive Processes
  Associative Processes
    Cognitive Contiguity
    Connotations
    Contextual Associations
  Classification (Cognitive Process)
  Cognitive Discrimination
  Cognitive Generalization
  Cognitive Mediation
  Concept Formation
  Decision Making
    Choice Behavior
  Ideation
    Imagination
  Problem Solving
    Anagram Problem Solving

Cognitive And Physical Development (Continued)
  Group Problem Solving
  Semantic Generalization
  Thinking
    Abstraction
    Divergent Thinking
    Logical Thinking
    Reasoning
      Inductive Deductive Reasoning
      Inference
  Transposition (Cognition)
Cognitive Style
  Cognitive Complexity
Concept Learning
  Nonreversal Shift Learning
  Reversal Shift Learning
Incidental Learning
  Latent Learning
Mathematics (Concepts)
  Algorithms
  Number Systems
  Numbers (Numerals)
Motor Processes
  Exercise
  Motor Coordination
  Motor Performance
    Finger Tapping
    Jumping
    Running
    Walking
  Motor Skills
  Physical Agility
    Physical Dexterity
Perceptual Motor Learning
  Fine Motor Skill Learning
  Gross Motor Skill Learning
Physical Development
  Motor Development
    Psychomotor Development
      Speech Development
  Prenatal Development
  Sexual Development
Physique
  Body Height
  Body Weight
    Obesity
    Underweight
Skill Learning
  Fine Motor Skill Learning
  Gross Motor Skill Learning
Transfer (Learning)
  Negative Transfer
  Positive Transfer
Verbal Learning
  Nonsense Syllable Learning
  Paired Associate Learning
  Serial Learning
    Serial Anticipation (Learning)

Emotional And Personality Development
Emotional Adjustment

DEVELOPMENTAL PSYCHOLOGY

Emotional And Personality Development (Continued)
- Emotional Control
  - Coping Behavior
- Identity Crisis
- Emotional States
  - Alienation
  - Ambivalence
  - Boredom
  - Depression (Emotion)
  - Distress
  - Emotional Trauma
  - Euphoria
  - Fear
    - Panic
  - Loneliness
  - Mental Confusion
    - Doubt
  - Optimism
  - Pessimism
  - Pleasure
  - Restlessness
  - Suffering
- Self Concept
  - Self Esteem

Social Behavior And Family Relations
- Family Background
  - Family Socioeconomic Level
  - Parent Educational Background
  - Parental Occupation
- Family Members
  - Adopted Children
  - Ancestors
    - Grandparents
    - Parents
      - Adoptive Parents
      - Fathers
      - Foster Parents
      - Mothers
        - Schizophrenogenic Mothers
        - Unwed Mothers
      - Stepparents
      - Surrogate Parents (Humans)
  - Aunts
  - Cousins
  - Daughters
  - Foster Children
  - Grandchildren
  - Illegitimate Children
  - Orphans
  - Siblings
    - Brothers
    - Multiple Births
      - Quadruplets
      - Triplets
      - Twins
        - Heterozygotic Twins
        - Monozygotic Twins
    - Sisters
  - Sons
  - Spouses
    - Husbands

Social Behavior And Family Relations (Continued)
- Wives
  - Housewives
- Stepchildren
- Uncles
- Family Relations
  - Childrearing Practices
    - Child Discipline
      - Parental Permissiveness
  - Marital Relations
    - Marital Conflict
  - Parent Child Relations
    - Father Child Relations
    - Mother Child Relations
    - Parental Attitudes
    - Parental Permissiveness
  - Parental Role
  - Sibling Relations
- Family Structure
  - Birth Order
  - Extended Family
  - Family Size
  - Matriarchy
  - Nuclear Family
  - Parental Absence
    - Father Absence
    - Mother Absence
  - Patriarchy
  - Schizophrenogenic Family
- Games
  - Chess
  - Childrens Recreational Games
  - Entrapment Games
  - Non Zero Sum Games
  - Prisoners Dilemma Game
  - Simulation Games
- Marriage
  - Common Law Marriage
  - Elopement (Marriage)
  - Endogamous Marriage
    - Consanguineous Marriage
  - Exogamous Marriage
    - Interfaith Marriage
    - Interracial Marriage
  - Polygamy
- Psychosexual Behavior
  - Erection (Penis)
  - Eroticism
  - Heterosexuality
  - Homosexuality
    - Bisexuality
    - Lesbianism
    - Male Homosexuality
  - Human Courtship
  - Hypersexuality
  - Masturbation
  - Orgasm
    - Female Orgasm
    - Male Orgasm
      - Nocturnal Emission
      - Premature Ejaculation

Social Behavior And Family Relations (Continued)
Petting
Promiscuity
  Prostitution
Sex Roles
Sexual Abstinence
Sexual Deviations
  Incest
Recreation
  Athletic Participation
  Camping
  Childrens Recreational Games
  Clubs (Social Organizations)
  Dance
  Doll Play
  Gambling
  Sports
    Badminton
    Baseball
    Basketball
    Football
    Judo
    Swimming
    Tennis
  Summer Camps (Recreation)
  Television Viewing
  Traveling
  Vacationing
Recreation Areas
  Playgrounds
Social Behavior
  Aggressive Behavior
    Conflict
      Arguments
      Violence
  Altruism
  Attribution
  Competition
  Compliance
  Conformity (Personality)
  Criticism
  Involvement
  Leadership
    Leadership Style
  Reciprocity
  Responsibility
  Risk Taking
    Gambling
  Social Acceptance
  Social Adjustment
  Social Approval
  Social Demonstrations
  Social Facilitation
  Social Interaction
    Encouragement
    Interpersonal Interaction
      Assistance (Social Behavior)
      Charitable Behavior
      Collective Behavior
      Conflict
        Arguments

Social Behavior And Family Relations (Continued)
    Violence
    Cooperation
    Friendship
    Group Performance
    Interpersonal Attraction
    Interpersonal Communication
      Arguments
      Conversation
      Double Bind Interaction
      Eye Contact
      Group Discussion
      Negotiation
        Bargaining
    Interpersonal Compatibility
    Interpersonal Influences
    Participation
      Group Participation
    Peer Relations
    Persecution
    Rivalry
    Social Dating
    Victimization
  Social Perception
    Attribution
  Social Reinforcement
    Nonverbal Reinforcement
    Verbal Reinforcement
    Praise
  Trust (Social Behavior)
Social Groups
  Dyads
  Minority Groups
Social Influences
  Criticism
  Ethnic Values
  Power
  Prejudice
    Religious Prejudices
  Propaganda
  Social Approval
  Social Desirability
  Social Values
  Superstitions
  Taboos
Social Learning
  Imitation (Learning)
  Imprinting
  Nonverbal Learning
Social Processes
  Coalition Formation
  Racial Integration
    School Integration (Racial)
  Social Deprivation
    Social Isolation
  Social Mobility
  Socialization
Socioeconomic Status
  Family Socioeconomic Level
  Income Level
    Lower Income Level
    Middle Income Level

Social Behavior And Family Relations (Continued)

Upper Income Level
Social Class
  Lower Class
  Middle Class
  Upper Class
Toys
  Educational Toys
Verbal Communication
  Fingerspelling
  Language
    Conversation
    Dialect
      Nonstandard English
    Foreign Languages
    Language Development
    Linguistics
      Alphabets
        Initial Teaching Alphabet
        Letters (Alphabet)
      Antonyms
      Ethnolinguistics
      Etymology
      Grammar
        Form Classes (Language)
          Adjectives
          Adverbs
          Nouns
          Pronouns
          Verbs
        Inflection
        Morphology (Language)
        Orthography
        Phonology
        Syntax
          Sentence Structure
          Transformational Generative Grammar
      Homographs
      Paragraphs
      Phonetics
        Morphemes
        Phonemes
          Consonants
          Vowels
        Syllables
        Words (Phonetic Units)
      Phrases
      Psycholinguistics
      Semantics
      Sentences
    Monolingualism
    Multilingualism
      Bilingualism
    Public Speaking
    Sign Language
    Vocabulary
      Anagrams
      Antonyms
      Homographs
      Homonyms
      Neologisms
      Sight Vocabulary
      Slang
      Synonyms
    Written Language

Social Behavior And Family Relations (Continued)

Alphabets
  Initial Teaching Alphabet
  Letters (Alphabet)
Handwriting
  Cursive Writing
  Handwriting Legibility
  Printing (Handwriting)
Literacy
Numbers (Numerals)
Paragraphs
Speech Characteristics
  Articulation (Speech)
  Pronunciation
  Speech Pauses
  Speech Pitch
  Speech Rate
  Speech Rhythm
Speech Processing (Mechanical)
  Clipped Speech (Mechanical)
  Compressed Speech
  Filtered Speech
  Synthetic Speech
Verbal Fluency

Adult Development And Aging

CULTURAL INFLUENCES AND SOCIAL ISSUES

Culture And Ethnology And Race Relations And Religion

Culture (Anthropological)
  Subculture (Anthropological)
Ethnic Groups
  American Indians
  Eskimos
  Gypsies
  Mexican Americans
  Tribes
Race (Anthropological)
  Caucasians
  Negroes
Race Attitudes
  Antisemitism
  Ethnocentrism
  Racism
Religious Beliefs
  Agnosticism
  Atheism
  God Concepts
  Religiosity
  Religious Affiliation
    Buddhism
      Zen Buddhism
    Christianity
      Protestantism
        Fundamentalism
      Roman Catholicism
    Hinduism
    Islam
    Judaism
    Shamanism

Culture And Ethnology And Race Relations And Religion (Continued)

Sin
Religious Literature
  Bible
Religious Practices
  Asceticism
  Confession (Religion)
  Faith Healing
  Glossolalia
  Meditation
  Prayer
Sociocultural Factors
  Acculturation
  Cross Cultural Differences
  Cultural Assimilation
  Cultural Deprivation
  Culture Change
  Ethnic Identity
  Ethnic Values
  Rites Of Passage
    Birth Rites
    Death Rites
    Initiation Rites
    Marriage Rites

Social Issues And Social Processes

Alcoholic Beverages
  Beer
  Liquor
  Wine
Chance
  Probability
    Response Probability
    Statistical Probability
      Binomial Distribution
Community Facilities
  Community Mental Health Centers
  Housing
  Public Transportation
  Shopping Centers
  Suicide Prevention Centers
Disasters
  Natural Disasters
Ecological Factors
  Pollution
  Topography
Environment
  Social Environments
    Academic Environment
      College Environment
      School Environment
    Communities
      Communes
        Kibbutz
      Neighborhoods
    Home Environment
    Poverty Areas
    Rural Environments
    Suburban Environments
    Towns

Social Issues And Social Processes (Continued)

    Urban Environments
      Ghettoes
    Working Conditions
Environmental Effects
  Altitude Effects
  Atmospheric Conditions
  Gravitational Effects
    Weightlessness
  Noise Effects
  Seasonal Variations
  Temperature Effects
    Cold Effects
    Heat Effects
  Underwater Effects
Ethics
  Professional Ethics
  Values
    Personal Values
    Social Values
Experiences (Events)
  Early Experience
  Life Experiences
  Vicarious Experiences
Fads And Fashions
  Clothing Fashions
Family Planning
  Birth Control
    Coitus Interruptus
    Contraceptive Devices
      Diaphragms (Birth Control)
      Intrauterine Devices
      Oral Contraceptives
    Tubal Ligation
    Vasectomy
  Rhythm Method
Family Relations
  Childrearing Practices
    Child Discipline
      Parental Permissiveness
  Marital Relations
    Marital Conflict
  Parent Child Relations
    Father Child Relations
    Mother Child Relations
    Parental Attitudes
    Parental Permissiveness
    Parental Role
    Sibling Relations
Government Policy Making
  Foreign Policy Making
    Diplomacy (Foreign Policy)
  Laws
    Abortion Laws
    Drug Laws
      Marihuana Laws
        Marihuana Legalization
    Gun Control Laws
  Legislative Processes
Government Programs

338

Social Issues And Social Processes (Continued)
- Job Corps
- Peace Corps
- Project Follow Through
- Project Head Start
- Title V Projects
- Upward Bound
- Volunteers In Service To America
- Welfare Services (Government)
- Handicapped (Attitudes Toward)
  - Mental Illness (Attitudes Toward)
  - Mental Retardation (Attit Toward)
  - Physical Handicaps (Attit Toward)
  - Sensory Handicaps (Attit Toward)
- Insurance
  - Health Insurance
    - Employee Health Insurance
      - Workmens Compensation Insurance
  - Life Insurance
    - Employee Life Insurance
- Interests
  - Occupational Interests
- Law (Government)
  - Criminal Law
- Legal Processes
  - Adjudication
  - Adoption (Child)
  - Committment (Psychiatric)
  - Expert Testimony
  - Incarceration
  - Legal Arrest
  - Legal Detention
  - Legislative Processes
  - Parole
  - Probation
- Marital Separation
  - Divorce
- Political Economic Systems
  - Capitalism
  - Communism
  - Democracy
  - Facism
  - Socialism
  - Totalitarianism
- Politics
  - Political Attitudes
  - Political Candidates
  - Political Issues
  - Political Parties
  - Political Processes
    - Political Campaigns
    - Political Elections
    - Voting Behavior
- Population
  - Overpopulation
  - Population (Statistics)
- Psychosexual Behavior
  - Erection (Penis)
  - Eroticism

Social Issues And Social Processes (Continued)
- Heterosexuality
- Homosexuality
  - Bisexuality
  - Lesbianism
  - Male Homosexuality
- Human Courtship
- Hypersexuality
- Masturbation
- Orgasm
  - Female Orgasm
  - Male Orgasm
    - Nocturnal Emission
    - Premature Ejaculation
- Petting
- Promiscuity
  - Prostitution
- Sex Roles
- Sexual Abstinence
- Sexual Deviations
  - Exhibitionism
  - Fetishism
  - Incest
  - Pedophilia
  - Sexual Sadism
  - Sexual Sadomasochism
    - Sexual Masochism
  - Transsexualism
  - Transvestism
  - Voyeurism
- Sexual Function Disturbances
  - Dyspareunia
  - Frigidity
  - Impotence
  - Premature Ejaculation
  - Vaginismus
- Sexual Intercourse (Human)
  - Dyspareunia
  - Extramarital Intercourse
  - Incest
  - Premarital Intercourse
  - Rape
- Virginity
- Radical Movements
  - Political Anarchy
  - Political Revolution
- Recreation
  - Athletic Participation
  - Camping
  - Childrens Recreational Games
  - Clubs (Social Organizations)
  - Dance
  - Doll Play
  - Gambling
  - Sports
    - Badminton
    - Baseball
    - Basketball
    - Football
    - Judo
    - Swimming
    - Tennis

Social Issues And Social Processes (Continued)
  Summer Camps (Recreation)
  Television Viewing
  Traveling
  Vacationing
Safety
  Aviation Safety
    Air Traffic Control
  Highway Safety
  Occupational Safety
  Water Safety
Safety Devices
  Safety Belts
Social Behavior
  Aggressive Behavior
    Conflict
      Arguments
      Riots
      Violence
      War
  Altruism
  Attribution
  Competition
  Compliance
  Conformity (Personality)
  Criticism
  Involvement
  Leadership
    Leadership Style
  Militancy
  Reciprocity
  Responsibility
  Risk Taking
    Gambling
  Social Acceptance
  Social Adjustment
  Social Approval
  Social Demonstrations
  Social Drinking
  Social Facilitation
  Social Interaction
    Encouragement
    Interpersonal Interaction
      Assistance (Social Behavior)
      Charitable Behavior
      Collective Behavior
        Riots
      Conflict
        Arguments
        Riots
        Violence
        War
      Cooperation
      Friendship
      Group Performance
      Interpersonal Attraction
      Interpersonal Communication
        Arguments
        Conversation
        Double Bind Interaction
        Eye Contact
        Group Discussion

Social Issues And Social Processes (Continued)
      Interviewing
      Interviews
        Job Applicant Interviews
      Negotiation
        Bargaining
      Interpersonal Compatibility
      Interpersonal Influences
      Participation
        Group Participation
      Peer Relations
      Persecution
      Rivalry
      Social Dating
      Victimization
  Social Perception
    Attribution
  Social Reinforcement
    Nonverbal Reinforcement
    Verbal Reinforcement
    Praise
  Trust (Social Behavior)
Social Groups
  Dyads
  Minority Groups
Social Influences
  Criticism
  Ethnic Values
  Power
  Prejudice
    Religious Prejudices
  Propaganda
  Social Approval
  Social Desirability
  Social Values
  Superstitions
  Taboos
Social Movements
  Activist Movements
    Student Activism
  Black Power Movement
  Civil Rights Movement
  Homosexual Liberation Movement
  Womens Liberation Movement
Social Processes
  Coalition Formation
  Human Migration
  Immigration
  Industrialization
  Racial Integration
    School Integration
  Social Deprivation
    Social Isolation
  Social Mobility
  Socialization
  Urbanization
Social Structure
  Caste System
  Social Class
    Lower Class
    Middle Class

SOCIAL BEHAVIOR AND INTERPERSONAL PROCESSES

Social Issues And Social Processes (Continued)
Upper Class
Socioeconomic Class Attitudes
Lower Class Attitudes
Middle Class Attitudes
Upper Class Attitudes
Socioeconomic Status
Family Socioeconomic Level
Income Level
Lower Income Level
Middle Income Level
Upper Income Level
Social Class
Lower Class
Middle Class
Upper Class
Sterilization (Sex)
Castration
Male Castration
Ovariectomy
Hysterectomy
Tubal Ligation
Vasectomy

SOCIAL BEHAVIOR AND INTER-PERSONAL PROCESSES

Social Behavior
Aggressive Behavior
Conflict
Arguments
Altruism
Competition
Compliance
Conformity (Personality)
Criticism
Involvement
Leadership
Leadership Style
Reciprocity
Responsibility
Risk Taking
Gambling
Social Acceptance
Social Adjustment
Social Approval
Social Facilitation
Social Interaction
Encouragement
Interpersonal Interaction
Assistance (Social Behavior)
Charitable Behavior
Collective Behavior
Conflict
Arguments
Violence
Cooperation
Friendship
Group Performance
Interpersonal Attraction

Interpersonal Communication
Arguments
Conversation
Double Bind Interaction
Eye Contact
Group Discussion
Interviewing
Interviews
Negotiation
Bargaining
Interpersonal Compatibility
Interpersonal Influences
Participation
Group Participation
Peer Relations
Persecution
Rivalry
Social Dating
Victimization
Social Perception
Attribution
Social Reinforcement
Nonverbal Reinforcement
Verbal Reinforcement
Praise
Trust (Social Behavior)
Social Influences
Criticism
Ethnic Values
Power
Prejudice
Religious Prejudices
Propaganda
Social Approval
Social Desirability
Social Values
Superstitions
Taboos
Social Processes
Coalition Formation
Social Deprivation
Social Isolation
Socialization
Vocalization
Subvocalization
Voice
Crying
Infant Vocalization

Group Dynamics And Interpersonal Processes
Humor
Cartoons (Humor)
Jokes
Nonverbal Communication
Body Language
Eye Contact
Facial Expressions
Grimaces
Smiles
Gestures
Roles

Group Dynamics And Interpersonal Processes (Continued)
  Parental Role
  Sex Roles
Social Groups
  Dyads
  Minority Groups
Verbal Communication
  Fingerspelling
  Language
    Conversation
    Dialect
      Nonstandard English
    Foreign Languages
    Linguistics
      Ethnolinguistics
      Grammar
        Inflection
        Syntax
          Sentence Structure
      Psycholinguistics
      Semantics
    Monolingualism
    Multilingualism
      Bilingualism
    Public Speaking
    Sign Language
    Vocabulary
      Neologisms
      Slang
  Speech Characteristics
    Articulation (Speech)
    Pronunciation
    Speech Pauses
    Speech Pitch
    Speech Rate
    Speech Rhythm
  Speech Processing (Mechanical)
    Clipped Speech (Mechanical)
    Compressed Speech
    Filtered Speech
    Synthetic Speech
  Verbal Fluency

Social Perception And Motivation And Attitudes
Games
  Chess
  Childrens Recreational Games
  Entrapment Games
  Non Zero Sum Games
  Prisoners Dilemma Game
  Simulation Games
Motivation
  Achievement Motivation
    Academic Achievement Motivation
  Affiliation Motivation
  Extrinsic Motivation
  Incentives
    Educational Incentives
    Monetary Incentives
  Intrinsic Motivation
  Sex Drive
  Temptation

Social Perception And Motivation And Attitudes (Continued)
Satisfaction
  Job Satisfaction
  Need Satisfaction

COMMUNICATION AND LANGUAGE

Advertising
  Television Advertising
Artistic Ability
  Musical Ability
Arts
  Architecture
  Art
    Crafts
    Drawing
    Painting (Art)
    Photographic Art
    Sculpturing
  Dance
  Literature
    Poetry
    Prose
      Biography
        Autobiography
  Motion Pictures (Entertainment)
  Music
    Musical Instruments
  Theatre
    Drama
Automated Information Processing
  Automated Information Coding
  Automated Information Retrieval
  Automated Information Storage
Consumer Surveys
Fads And Fashions
  Clothing Fashions
Humor
  Cartoons (Humor)
  Jokes
Meaning
  Nonverbal Meaning
  Verbal Meaning
  Word Meaning
Meaningfulness
Nonverbal Communication
  Body Language
  Eye Contact
  Facial Expressions
    Grimaces
    Smiles
  Gestures
Philosophies
  Animism
  Asceticism
  Dualism
  Epistemology
  Existentialism
  Fatalism
  Humanism

Idealism
Intellectualism
Logic (Philosophy)
Materialism
Metaphysics
Mysticism
Nihilism
Pacifism
Pragmatism
Realism (Philosophy)
Reductionism
Skepticism
Religious Literature
  Bible
Religious Practices
  Asceticism
  Confession (Religion)
  Faith Healing
  Glossolalia
  Meditation
  Prayer
Scientific Communication
  Professional Meetings And Symposia
  Psychological Terminology
Surveys
  Consumer Surveys
Verbal Communication
  Fingerspelling
  Language
    Conversation
    Dialect
      Nonstandard English
    Foreign Languages
    Language Development
    Linguistics
      Alphabets
        Initial Teaching Alphabet
        Letters (Alphabet)
      Antonyms
      Ethnolinguistics
      Etymology
      Grammar
        Form Classes (Language)
          Adjectives
          Adverbs
          Nouns
          Pronouns
          Verbs
        Inflection
        Morphology (Language)
        Orthography
        Phonology
        Syntax
          Sentence Structure
        Transformational Generative Grammar
      Homographs
      Paragraphs
      Phonetics
        Morphemes
        Phonemes
          Consonants
          Vowels

Syllables
  Words (Phonetic Units)
Phrases
Psycholinguistics
Semantics
Sentences
Monolingualism
Multilingualism
  Bilingualism
Public Speaking
Sign Language
Vocabulary
  Anagrams
  Antonyms
  Homographs
  Homonyms
  Neologisms
  Sight Vocabulary
  Slang
  Synonyms
Written Language
  Alphabets
    Initial Teaching Alphabet
    Letters (Alphabet)
  Handwriting
    Cursive Writing
    Handwriting Legibility
    Printing (Handwriting)
  Literacy
  Numbers (Numerals)
  Paragraphs
Speech Characteristics
  Articulation (Speech)
  Pronunciation
  Speech Pauses
  Speech Pitch
  Speech Rate
  Speech Rhythm
Speech Processing (Mechanical)
  Clipped Speech (Mechanical)
  Compressed Speech
  Filtered Speech
  Synthetic Speech
Verbal Fluency
Vocalization
  Animal Vocalizations
    Animal Distress Calls
  Subvocalization
  Voice
    Crying
    Infant Vocalization

PERSONALITY

Anger
  Hostility
Anxiety
  Anxiety Neurosis
  Castration Anxiety
  Separation Anxiety
Aspirations
  Educational Aspirations

PERSONALITY

Jr Sr High School Personality Quest
Kupfer Detre Self Rating Scale
Leary Interpersonal Check List
Magnetic Test
Marlowe Crowne Soc Desirabil Scale
Maudsley Personality Inventory
Memory for Designs Test
Minn Multiphasic Personality Inven
Mooney Problem Check List
Myers Briggs Type Indicator
Neuroticism Scale Questionnaire
Omnibus Personality Inventory
Personal Orientation Inventory
Psychological Screening Inventory
Repression Sensitization Scale
Rod and Frame Test
Rokeach Dogmatism Scale
Rotter Intern Extern Locus Cont Scal
Self Analysis Form
Sensation Seeking Scale
Sixteen Personality Factors Question
State Trait Anxiety Inventory
Taylor Manifest Anxiety Scale
Tennessee Self Concept Scale
Vineland Social Maturity Scale
Wakefield Self Assessment Depression
Welsh Figure Preference Test
White Betz A B Scale
Zungs Self Rating Depression Scale
Projective Personality Measures
  Bender Gestalt Test
  Blacky Pictures Test
  Childrens Apperception Test
  Color Pyramid Test
  Franck Drawing Completion Test
  Holtzman Inkblot Technique
  Human Figures Drawing
  Onomatopoeia and Images Test
  Rorschach Test
  Rosenzweig Picture Frustration Study
  Rotter Incomplete Sentences Blank
  Szondi Test
  Thematic Apperception Test
  Zulliger Z Test
Personality Traits
  Adaptability (Personality)
  Aggressiveness
  Assertiveness
  Authoritarianism
  Conformity (Personality)
  Conservatism
  Courage
  Creativity
  Cruelty
  Curiosity
  Cynicism
  Defensiveness
  Dependency (Personality)
  Dishonesty
  Egotism
  Emotional Immaturity
  Emotional Inferiority
  Emotional Instability

  Emotional Maturity
  Emotional Security
  Emotional Stability
  Emotional Superiority
  Emotionality (Personality)
  Empathy
  Extraversion
  Femininity
  Gregariousness
  Honesty
  Hypnotic Susceptibility
  Idealism
  Impulsiveness
  Independence (Personality)
  Individuality
  Initiative
  Insight
  Internal External Locus Of Control
  Introversion
  Liberalism
  Loyalty
  Machiavellianism
  Masculinity
  Misanthropy
  Moodiness
  Negativism
  Nervousness
  Neuroticism
  Nonconformity (Personality)
  Obedience
  Objectivity
  Optimism
  Passiveness
  Perceptiveness (Personality)
  Persistence
  Pessimism
  Positivism
  Repression Sensitization
  Rigidity (Personality)
  Self Control
  Selfishness
  Sensitivity (Personality)
  Seriousness
  Sexuality
  Sincerity
  Sociability
  Suggestibility
  Timidity
  Tolerance
Phobias
  Acrophobia
  Agoraphobia
  Claustrophobia
  Dysmorphophobia
  Ophidiophobia
  School Phobia
Psychoanalytic Personality Factors
  Conscious (Personality Factors)
  Ego

Electra Complex
Id
Libido
Oedipal Complex
Subconscious
Superego
  Conscience
Unconscious (Personality Factor)
Psychogenesis
  Cognitive Development
    Intellectual Development
      Language Development
    Perceptual Development
  Emotional Development
  Moral Development
  Psychomotor Development
    Speech Development
  Psychosocial Development
    Childhood Play Development
    Personality Development
Self Concept
  Self Esteem

PROFESSIONAL PERSONNEL

Clinical Methods Training
  Clinical Psychology Grad Training
  Clinical Psychology Internship
  Community Mental Health Training
    Mental Health Inservice Training
  Counselor Education
  Psychiatric Training
  Psychoanalytic Training
  Psychotherapy Training
Community Services
  Community Welfare Services
  Crisis Intervention Services
    Hot Line Services
  Home Visiting Programs
  Public Health Services
Counselors
  School Counselors
  Vocational Counselors
Sciences
  Biology
    Neurobiology
  Chemistry
    Biochemistry
      Neurochemistry
  Geography
  Medical Sciences
    Anesthesiology
    Cardiology
    Dentistry
    Endocrinology
    Epidemiology
    Geriatrics
    Immunology
    Neurology

Neuropathology
Obstetrics Gynecology
Ophthalmology
Psychiatry
  Child Psychiatry
  Community Psychiatry
  Forensic Psychiatry
  Neuropsychiatry
  Orthopsychiatry
  Social Psychiatry
  Transcultural Psychiatry
Radiology
Surgery
Veterinary Medicine
Neurosciences
  Neuroanatomy
  Neurobiology
  Neurochemistry
  Neurology
  Neuropathology
  Neurophysiology
  Neuropsychiatry
  Neuropsychology
Social Sciences
  Psychology
    Applied Psychology
      Clinical Psychology
      Community Psychology
      Consumer Psychology
      Counseling Psychology
      Educational Psychology
        School Psychology
      Engineering Psychology
      Industrial Psychology
      Medical Psychology
      Military Psychology
      Social Psychology
    Comparative Psychology
    Developmental Psychology
      Adolescent Psychology
      Child Psychology
      Gerontology
    Experimental Psychology
    Mathematical Psychology
    Physiological Psychology
      Neuropsychology
  Sociology
Ethics
  Professional Ethics
  Values
    Personal Values
    Social Values
Insurance
  Health Insurance
    Employee Health Insurance
      Workmens Compensation Insurance
  Life Insurance
    Employee Life Insurance
Medical Personnel
  Dentists
  Military Medical Personnel
  Nurses
    Psychiatric Nurses
    Public Health Service Nurses

PHYSICAL AND PSYCHOLOGICAL DISORDERS

School Nurses
Optometrists
Paramedical Personnel
  Attendants (Institutions)
  Medics
  Physical Therapists
  Psychiatric Aides
Physicians
  General Practitioners
    Family Physicians
  Gynecologists
  Internists
  Neurologists
  Pathologists
  Pediatricians
  Psychiatrists
  Surgeons
Psychiatric Hospital Staff
  Psychiatric Aides
Mental Health Personnel
  Clinical Psychologists
  Psychiatric Hospital Staff
    Psychiatric Aides
  Psychiatric Nurses
  Psychiatric Social Workers
  Psychiatrists
  Psychotherapists
    Hypnotherapists
    Psychoanalysts
  School Psychologists
Paramedical Sciences
  Audiology
  Nursing
  Optometry
  Pharmacology
    Psychopharmacology
  Physical Therapy
Paraprofessional Personnel
  Paramedical Personnel
    Attendants (Institutions)
    Medics
    Physical Therapists
    Psychiatric Aides
Personnel Training
  Apprenticeship
  On The Job Training
Professional Consultation
  Mental Health Consultation
Psychologists
  Clinical Psychologists
  Educational Psychologists
    School Psychologists
  Experimental Psychologists
  Industrial Psychologists
  Social Psychologists
Scientific Communication
  Professional Meetings And Symposia
  Psychological Terminology
Social Workers
  Psychiatric Social Workers
Students

College Students
  Community College Students
  Graduate Students
  Junior College Students
  Medical Students
  Postgraduate Students
Nursing Students
Seminarians
Volunteer Personnel
  Volunteer Civilian Personnel

PHYSICAL AND PSYCHOLOGICAL DISORDERS

Patients
  Geriatric Patients
  Hospitalized Patients
  Medical Patients
  Outpatients
  Psychiatric Patients
  Surgical Patients
  Terminally Ill Patients
Psychosomatic Disorders
  Anorexia Nervosa
  Hypochondriasis
  Neurodermatitis
  Pseudocyesis
  Psychogenic Pain
  Sympathetic Pain
Remission (Disorders)
  Spontaneous Remission
  Symptom Remission
Symptoms
  Acting Out
  Anoxia
  Appetite Disorders
    Anorexia Nervosa
    Hyperphagia
    Obesity
  Apraxia
  Asthenia
    Myasthenia
  Ataxia
  Aura
  Automatism
  Body Rocking
  Catalepsy
  Catatonia
  Coma
  Convulsions
  Delirium
  Depersonalization
  Distractibility
  Dyskinesia
  Fatigue
  Hemorrhage
    Hematoma
  Hyperglycemia
  Hyperkinesis

Hyperthermia
Hypochondriasis
Hypoglycemia
Hypothermia
Insomnia
Nausea
Pain
  Aphagia
  Headache
    Migraine Headache
    Muscle Contraction Headache
  Psychogenic Pain
  Sympathetic Pain
Pruritus
Respiratory Distress
  Apnea
  Dyspnea
  Hyperventilation
Restlessness
Scratching
Shock
Spasms
Syncope
Tics
Tremor
Underweight
  Anorexia Nervosa
Vertigo
Vomiting
Word Salad
Syndromes
  Addisons Disease
  Battered Child Syndrome
  Crying Cat Syndrome
  Cushings Syndrome
  Downs Syndrome
  Klinefelters Syndrome
  Menieres Disease
  Organic Brain Syndromes
    Alcoholic Psychosis
      Alcoholic Hallucinosis
        Delirium Tremens
        Korsakoffs Psychosis
    Presenile Dementia
      Alzheimers Disease
      Picks Disease
    Senile Dementia
      Senile Psychosis
    Toxic Psychoses
  Stein Leventhal Syndrome
  Testicular Feminization Syndrome
  Turners Syndrome
  Wernickes Syndrome

Mental Disorders
Affective Disturbances
  Anaclitic Depression
  Involutional Depression
  Neurotic Depressive Reaction
  Psychotic Depressive Reaction
  Reactive Depression
Anesthesia (Feeling)

Mental Disorders (Continued)
  Hysterical Anesthesia
Anxiety
  Anxiety Neurosis
  Castration Anxiety
  Separation Anxiety
Autism
  Early Infantile Autism
Compulsions
  Compulsive Orderliness
  Compulsive Repetition
  Serial Compulsions
Defense Mechanisms
  Compensation (Defense Mechanism)
  Denial
  Displacement (Defense Mechanism)
  Fantasy (Defense Mechanism)
  Identification (Defense Mechanism)
  Intellectualization
  Introjection
  Isolation (Defense Mechanism)
  Projection (Defense Mechanism)
  Rationalization
  Reaction Formation
  Regression (Defense Mechanism)
  Repression (Defense Mechanism)
  Sublimation
  Suppression (Defense Mechanism)
  Withdrawal (Defense Mechanism)
Dissociative Patterns
  Amnesia
    Fugue Reaction
  Multiple Personality
  Somnambulism
Emotional Adjustment
  Emotional Control
    Coping Behavior
  Identity Crisis
Emotional States
  Alienation
  Ambivalence
  Boredom
  Depression (Emotion)
    Anaclitic Depression
    Involutional Depression
    Manic Depression
    Neurotic Depressive Reaction
    Psychotic Depressive Reaction
    Reactive Depression
  Distress
  Emotional Trauma
  Euphoria
  Fear
    Panic
  Loneliness
  Mental Confusion
    Doubt
  Optimism
  Pessimism
  Pleasure

348

PHYSICAL AND PSYCHOLOGICAL DISORDERS

Mental Disorders (Continued)
- Restlessness
- Suffering
- Hysteria
  - Mass Hysteria
- Mania
  - Hypermania
  - Hypomania
  - Kleptomania
  - Megalomania
  - Pica
  - Pyromania
  - Toxicomania
- Neurosis
  - Anxiety Neurosis
  - Childhood Neurosis
  - Conversion Neurosis
    - Hysterical Anesthesia
    - Hysterical Paralysis
    - Hysterical Vision Disturbances
  - Dissociative Neurosis
  - Experimental Neurosis
  - Neurasthenic Neurosis
  - Neurotic Depressive Reaction
  - Obsessive Compulsive Neurosis
  - Occupational Neurosis
  - Phobic Neurosis
  - Traumatic Neurosis
- Perceptual Disturbances
  - Agnosia
  - Hallucinations
    - Auditory Hallucinations
    - Drug Induced Hallucinations
    - Hypnagogic Hallucinations
    - Visual Hallucinations
- Personality Disorders
  - Antisocial Personality
  - Asthenic Personality
  - Cyclothymic Personality
  - Explosive Personality
  - Hysterical Personality
  - Inadequate Personality
  - Narcissistic Personality
  - Obsessive Compulsive Personality
  - Paranoid Personality
  - Passive Aggressive Personality
  - Sadomasochistic Personality
    - Masochistic Personality
    - Sadistic Personality
  - Schizoid Personality
- Phobias
  - Acrophobia
  - Agoraphobia
  - Claustrophobia
  - Dysmorphophobia
  - Ophidiophobia
  - School Phobia
- Psychoanalytic Personality Factors
  - Conscious (Personality Factors)
  - Ego

Mental Disorders (Continued)
- Electra Complex
- Id
- Libido
- Oedipal Complex
- Subconscious
- Superego
  - Conscience
- Unconscious (Personality Factor)
- Psychosis
  - Acute Psychosis
    - Acute Psychotic Episode
    - Acute Schizophrenia
  - Affective Psychosis
    - Involutional Depression
    - Manic Depressive Psychosis
    - Psychotic Depressive Reaction
  - Alcoholic Psychosis
    - Alcoholic Hallucinosis
      - Delirium Tremens
      - Korsakoffs Psychosis
  - Childhood Psychosis
    - Childhood Schizophrenia
    - Early Infantile Autism
    - Symbiotic Infantile Psychosis
  - Chronic Psychosis
    - Chronic Schizophrenia
  - Experimental Psychosis
  - Folie A Deux
  - Hallucinosis
    - Alcoholic Hallucinosis
      - Delirium Tremens
      - Korsakoffs Psychosis
  - Involutional Paranoid Psychosis
  - Paranoia (Psychosis)
  - Process Psychosis
  - Reactive Psychosis
  - Schizophrenia
    - Acute Schizophrenia
    - Catatonic Schizophrenia
    - Childhood Schizophrenia
    - Chronic Schizophrenia
    - Hebephrenic Schizophrenia
    - Paranoid Schizophrenia
    - Pseudoneurotic Schizophrenia
    - Pseudopsychopathic Schizophrenia
    - Simple Schizophrenia
    - Undifferentiated Schizophrenia
  - Senile Psychosis
  - Toxic Psychoses
  - Windigo Psychosis
- Sadomasochism
  - Masochism
    - Sexual Masochism
  - Sadism
    - Sexual Sadism
  - Sexual Sadomasochism
    - Sexual Masochism

Behavior Disorders
- Behavior Disorders
  - Addiction

349

Behavior Disorders (Continued)
  Alcoholism
    Korsakoffs Psychosis
    Wernickes Syndrome
  Drug Addiction
    Heroin Addiction
  Antisocial Behavior
    Child Abuse
      Battered Child Syndrome
    Crime
      Homicide
      Rape
      Theft
        Shoplifting
    Juvenile Delinquency
    Recidivism
    Runaway Behavior
  Attempted Suicide
  Deception
    Cheating
    Confabulation
    Malingering
    Pathological Lying
  Drug Abuse
    Drug Addiction
      Heroin Addiction
  Nail Biting
  Self Mutilation
    Head Banging
  Suicide
  Tantrums
  Truancy
Criminals
  Female Criminals
  Male Criminals
Juvenile Delinquents
  Female Delinquents
  Male Delinquents

Learning Disorders And Mental Retardation
Handicapped
  Mentally Retarded
    Educable Mentally Retarded
    Home Reared Mentally Retarded
    Idiot Savants
    Institutionalized Mentally Retarded
    Profoundly Mentally Retarded
    Severely Mentally Retarded
    Trainable Mentally Retarded
  Slow Learners
Learning Disorders
  Learning Disabilities
    Dyslexia
  Reading Disabilities
    Dyslexia

Speech Disorders
Speech Handicapped
Speech Disorders
  Articulation Disorders
    Dysarthria
      Stammering
      Stuttering

Speech Disorders (Continued)
  Dysphonia
  Echolalia
  Mutism
    Elective Mutism
  Retarded Speech Development

Physical And Toxic Disorders
Blood And Lymphatic Disorders
  Anemia
  Blood Coagulation Disorders
    Hemophilia
  Blood Group Incompatibility
    Rh Incompatibility
  Leukemias
  Malaria
  Porphyria
  Toxoplasmosis
Cardiovascular Disorders
  Aneurysms
  Arteriosclerosis
    Atherosclerosis
    Cerebral Arteriosclerosis
  Blood Pressure Disorders
    Hypertension
      Essential Hypertension
    Hypotension
    Syncope
  Cerebrovascular Disorders
    Cerebral Anoxia
    Cerebral Arteriosclerosis
    Cerebral Embolisms
    Cerebral Hemorrhage
    Cerebral Ischemia
    Cerebral Thromboses
    Cerebrovascular Accidents
  Embolisms
    Cerebral Embolisms
  Heart Disorders
    Angina Pectoris
    Arrhythmias (Heart)
      Bradycardia
      Fibrillation (Heart)
      Tachycardia
    Coronary Thromboses
    Myocardial Infarctions
  Hemorrhage
    Cerebral Hemorrhage
  Ischemia
    Cerebral Ischemia
  Thrombophlebitis
  Thromboses
    Cerebral Thromboses
    Coronary Thromboses
Congenital Disorders
  Cleft Palate
  Drug Induced Congenital Disorders
  Hermaphroditism
Digestive System Disorders
  Gastrointestinal Disorders
    Colon Disorders
      Colitis

Physical And Toxic Disorders (Continued)
  Ulcerative Colitis
  Constipation
  Diarrhea
  Fecal Incontinence
  Gastrointestinal Ulcers
  Vomiting
 Liver Disorders
  Cirrhosis (Liver)
  Hepatitis
   Toxic Hepatitis
  Jaundice
Endocrine Disorders
 Adrenal Gland Disorders
  Addisons Disease
  Cushings Syndrome
 Diabetes
  Diabetes Insipidus
  Diabetes Mellitus
 Endocrine Neoplasms
 Endocrine Sexual Disorders
  Hypogonadism
   Klinefelters Syndrome
   Turners Syndrome
  Premenstrual Tension
  Stein Leventhal Syndrome
  Testicular Feminization Syndrome
 Parathyroid Disorders
 Pituitary Disorders
  Hypopituitarism
 Thyroid Disorders
  Goiters
  Hyperthyroidism
  Hypothyroidism
   Cretinism
  Thyrotoxicosis
Genetic Disorders
 Albinism
 Chromosome Disorders
  Autosome Disorders
   Neonatal Autosome Disorders
    Crying Cat Syndrome
    Downs Syndrome
   Trisomy 18
   Trisomy 21
  Deletion (Chromosome)
  Neonatal Chromosome Disorders
   Neonatal Autosome Disorders
    Crying Cat Syndrome
    Downs Syndrome
   Neonatal Sex Chromosome Disorders
    Klinefelters Syndrome
    Turners Syndrome
  Nondisjunction (Chromosome)
  Sex Chromosome Disorders
   Neonatal Sex Chromosome Disorders
    Klinefelters Syndrome
    Turners Syndrome
  Translocation (Chromosome)
  Trisomy
   Trisomy 18
   Trisomy 21
 Neonatal Genetic Disorders
  Amaurotic Familial Idiocy

Physical And Toxic Disorders (Continued)
  Maple Syrup Urine Disease
  Neonatal Chromosome Disorders
   Neonatal Autosome Disorders
    Crying Cat Syndrome
    Downs Syndrome
   Neonatal Sex Chromosome Disorders
    Klinefelters Syndrome
    Turners Syndrome
  Phenylketonuria
 Porphyria
 Rh Incompatibility
 Sex Linked Hereditary Disorders
  Hemophilia
  Testicular Feminization Syndrome
Handicapped
 Adventitiously Handicapped
 Aurally Handicapped
  Deaf
  Partially Hearing Impaired
 Brain Damaged
  Minimally Brain Damaged
 Congenitally Handicapped
 Multiply Handicapped
 Physically Handicapped
  Amputees
  Health Impaired
 Visually Handicapped
  Blind
  Partially Sighted
Immunologic Disorders
 Allergic Disorders
  Allergic Skin Disorders
  Drug Allergies
  Food Allergies
  Hay Fever
 Anaphylactic Shock
 Blood Group Incompatibility
  Rh Incompatibility
Lesions
 Brain Lesions
  Hypothalamus Lesions
 Neural Lesions
Metabolism Disorders
 Calcium Metabolism Disorders
 Carbohydrate Metabolism Disorders
  Cushings Syndrome
  Diabetes
   Diabetes Insipidus
   Diabetes Mellitus
 Lipid Metabolism Disorders
  Amaurotic Familial Idiocy
 Maple Syrup Urine Disease
 Phenylketonuria
 Porphyria
Musculoskeletal Disorders
 Bone Disorders
  Osteochondritis
 Joint Disorders
  Arthritis
   Rheumatoid Arthritis
 Muscular Disorders

Physical And Toxic Disorders (Continued)
- Cataplexy
- Muscle Contraction Headache
- Muscular Atrophy
- Muscular Dystrophy
- Myasthenia Gravis
- Myoclonia
- Myotonia
- Torticollis

Neonatal Disorders
- Anencephaly
- Cleft Palate
- Neonatal Genetic Disorders
  - Amaurotic Familial Idiocy
  - Maple Syrup Urine Disease
  - Neonatal Chromosome Disorders
    - Neonatal Autosome Disorders
      - Crying Cat Syndrome
      - Downs Syndrome
    - Neonatal Sex Chromosome Disorders
      - Klinefelters Syndrome
      - Turners Syndrome
  - Phenylketonuria

Neoplasms
- Benign Neoplasms
- Breast Neoplasms
- Endocrine Neoplasms
- Leukemias
- Nervous System Neoplasms
  - Brain Neoplasms
- Terminal Cancer

Nervous System Disorders
- Autonomic Nervous System Disorders
  - Dysautonomia
- Central Nervous System Disorders
  - Ataxia
  - Brain Disorders
    - Anencephaly
    - Aphasia
      - Acalculia
      - Agraphia
    - Athetosis
    - Brain Damage
      - Brain Concussion
      - Brain Lesions
        - Hypothalamus Lesions
    - Brain Neoplasms
    - Cerebral Palsy
    - Cerebrovascular Accidents
    - Encephalitis
    - Epilepsy
      - Epileptic Seizures
      - Grand Mal Epilepsy
      - Petit Mal Epilepsy
    - Hydrocephaly
    - Microcephaly
    - Minimal Brain Disorders
    - Organic Brain Syndromes
      - Alcoholic Psychosis
        - Alcoholic Hallucinosis
        - Delirium Tremens
        - Korsakoffs Psychosis
      - Presenile Dementia
        - Alzheimers Disease

Physical And Toxic Disorders (Continued)
- Picks Disease
- Senile Dementia
  - Senile Psychosis
  - Toxic Psychoses
- Parkinsons Disease
- Chorea
  - Huntingtons Chorea
- Dysautonomia
- Meningitis
  - Arachnoiditis
  - Infectious Meningitis
    - Bacterial Meningitis
    - Viral Meningitis
- Myelitis
  - Encephalomyelitis
  - Poliomyelitis
- Neurosyphilis
- Convulsions
- Dyskinesia
- Hyperkinesis
- Nervous System Neoplasms
  - Brain Neoplasms
- Neuromuscular Disorders
  - Cataplexy
  - Gilles De La Tourette Disorder
  - Muscular Dystrophy
  - Myasthenia Gravis
  - Paralysis
    - Cerebral Palsy
    - General Paresis
    - Parkinsons Disease
- Peripheral Nerve Disorders
  - Myasthenia Gravis
  - Neuralgia
    - Trigeminal Neuralgia
  - Neuritis
    - Polyneuritis
    - Radiculitis
- Sclerosis (Nervous System)
  - Multiple Sclerosis

Nutritional Deficiencies
- Mineral Deficiency Disorders
- Protein Deficiency Disorders
  - Kwashiorkor
- Starvation
- Vitamin Deficiency Disorders
  - Pellagra
  - Wernickes Syndrome

Respiratory Tract Disorders
- Apnea
- Bronchial Disorders
- Common Colds
- Dyspnea
  - Asthma
- Hay Fever
- Hyperventilation
- Laryngeal Disorders
- Lung Disorders
  - Pneumonia
  - Pulmonary Emphysema
  - Pulmonary Tuberculosis
- Pharyngeal Disorders

TREATMENT AND PREVENTION

Ataxia
Aura
Automatism
Body Rocking
Catalepsy
Catatonia
Coma
Convulsions
Delirium
Depersonalization
Distractibility
Dyskinesia
Fatigue
Hemorrhage
  Hematoma
Hyperglycemia
Hyperkinesis
Hypochondriasis
Hypoglycemia
Hypothermia
Insomnia
Nausea
Pain
  Aphagia
  Headache
    Migraine Headache
    Muscle Contraction Headache
  Psychogenic Pain
  Sympathetic Pain
Pruritus
Respiratory Distress
  Apnea
  Dyspnea
  Hyperventilation
Restlessness
Scratching
Shock
Spasms
Syncope
Tics
Tremor
Underweight
  Anorexia Nervosa
Vertigo
Vomiting
Word Salad
Syndromes
  Addisons Disease
  Battered Child Syndrome
  Crying Cat Syndrome
  Cushings Syndrome
  Downs Syndrome
  Klinefelters Syndrome
  Menieres Disease
  Organic Brain Syndromes
    Alcoholic Psychosis
      Alcoholic Hallucinosis
        Delirium Tremens
        Korsakoffs Psychosis
      Presenile Dementia
        Alzheimers Disease

      Picks Disease
      Senile Dementia
        Senile Psychosis
      Toxic Psychoses
  Stein Leventhal Syndrome
  Testicular Feminization Syndrome
  Turners Syndrome
  Wernickes Syndrome
Treatment Facilities
  Clinics
    Child Guidance Clinics
    Psychiatric Clinics
    Walk In Clinics
  Community Mental Health Centers
  Halfway Houses
  Hospitals
    Psychiatric Hospitals
    Sanatoriums
  Nursing Homes

Psychotherapy And Psychotherapeutic Processes
Organic Therapies
  Drug Therapy
    Narcoanalysis
      Sleep Treatment
  Psychosurgery
  Shock Therapy
    Electroconvulsive Shock Therapy
    Insulin Shock Therapy
Psychotherapeutic Processes
  Countertransference
  Insight (Psychotherapeutic Process)
  Psychotherapeutic Breakthrough
  Psychotherapeutic Resistance
  Psychotherapeutic Transference
Psychotherapeutic Techniques
  Autogenic Training
  Dream Analysis
  Mutual Storytelling Technique
  Psychodrama
Psychotherapy
  Analytical Psychotherapy
  Brief Psychotherapy
  Child Psychotherapy
    Play Therapy
  Client Centered Therapy
  Existential Therapy
  Experiential Psychotherapy
  Expressive Psychotherapy
  Geriatric Psychotherapy
  Gestalt Therapy
  Group Psychotherapy
    Encounter Group Therapy
      Marathon Group Therapy
    Therapeutic Community
  Hypnotherapy
  Individual Psychotherapy
  Insight Therapy
  Logotherapy
  Persuasion Therapy
  Psychoanalysis

Psychotherapy And Psychotherapeutic Processes (Continued)

Dream Analysis
Psychodrama
Psychotherapeutic Counseling
  Conjoint Therapy
  Family Therapy
Reality Therapy
Relationship Therapy
Transactional Analysis
Recreation Therapy
  Art Therapy
  Dance Therapy
  Music Therapy

Drug Therapy And Drug Rehabilitation

Behavior And Group Therapy

Behavior Modification
  Behavior Therapy
    Aversion Therapy
    Implosive Therapy
    Reciprocal Inhibition Therapy
    Systematic Desensitization Therapy
  Classroom Behavior Modification
  Contingency Management
    Token Economy Programs

Psychoanalysis

Counseling And Community Mental Health And Crisis Intervention

Community Services
  Community Welfare Services
  Crisis Intervention Services
    Hot Line Services
  Home Visiting Programs
  Public Health Services
Crisis Intervention
  Suicide Prevention

Physical Treatment

Physical Treatment Methods
  Acupuncture
  Artificial Respiration
  Blood Transfusion
  Catheterization
  Dental Treatment
    Dental Surgery
  Dialysis
    Hemodialysis
  Immunization
  Medical Treatment (General)
    Diuresis
  Radiation Therapy
  Surgery
    Amputation
      Mastectomy
    Autopsy
    Colostomy
    Dental Surgery
    Endocrine Gland Surgery
      Adrenalectomy

Physical Treatment (Continued)

    Castration
      Male Castration
      Ovariectomy
    Hypophysectomy
    Pancreatectomy
    Pinealectomy
    Thymectomy
    Thyroidectomy
  Heart Surgery
  Hysterectomy
  Induced Abortion
  Neurosurgery
    Decerebration
    Decortication (Brain)
    Hemispherectomy
    Psychosurgery
      Thalamotomy
    Pyramidotomy
    Sympathectomy
    Tractotomy
    Vagotomy
  Organ Transplantation
  Plastic Surgery
Sterilization
  Castration
    Male Castration
    Ovariectomy
  Hysterectomy
  Tubal Ligation
  Vasectomy

Social Casework And Rehabilitation

Psychosocial Rehabilitation
  Therapeutic Social Clubs
  Vocational Rehabilitation
Rehabilitation Centers
  Sheltered Workshops

Hospital Programs And Hospitalization And Institutionalization

Correctional Institutions
  Prisons
  Reformatories
Psychiatric Hospital Programs
  Therapeutic Community
Residential Care Institutions
  Halfway Houses
  Hospitals
    Psychiatric Hospitals
    Sanatoriums
  Nursing Homes
  Orphanages

EDUCATIONAL PSYCHOLOGY

Sciences
  Biology
    Botany
    Neurobiology
    Zoology
  Chemistry

EDUCATIONAL PSYCHOLOGY

Biochemistry
  Neurochemistry
Geography
Medical Sciences
  Anesthesiology
  Cardiology
  Dentistry
  Endocrinology
  Epidemiology
  Geriatrics
  Immunology
  Neurology
  Neuropathology
  Obstetrics Gynecology
  Ophthalmology
  Psychiatry
    Child Psychiatry
    Community Psychiatry
    Forensic Psychiatry
    Neuropsychiatry
    Orthopsychiatry
    Social Psychiatry
    Transcultural Psychiatry
  Radiology
  Surgery
  Veterinary Medicine
Neurosciences
  Neuroanatomy
  Neurobiology
  Neurochemistry
  Neurology
  Neuropathology
  Neurophysiology
  Neuropsychiatry
  Neuropsychology
Physics
Social Sciences
  Anthropology
  Psychology
    Applied Psychology
      Clinical Psychology
      Community Psychology
      Consumer Psychology
      Counseling Psychology
      Educational Psychology
        School Psychology
      Engineering Psychology
      Industrial Psychology
      Medical Psychology
      Military Psychology
      Social Psychology
    Comparative Psychology
    Developmental Psychology
      Adolescent Psychology
      Child Psychology
      Gerontology
    Experimental Psychology
    Mathematical Psychology
    Physiological Psychology
      Neuropsychology
  Sociology
Extracurricular Activities
  Fraternity Membership
  School Club Membership

Sorority Membership
School Enrollment
  School Attendance
  School Expulsion
  School Suspension
  School Truancy
School Facilities
  Campuses
  Classrooms
  Dormitories
  Educational Laboratories
    Language Laboratories
  Gymnasiums
  Learning Centers (Educational)
  School Libraries
Schools
  Colleges
  Elementary Schools
  Graduate Schools
  High Schools
  Junior High Schools
  Kindergartens
  Military Schools
  Nongraded Schools
  Nursery Schools
  Seminaries
  Technical Schools
Students
  Business Students
  Classmates
  College Students
    Community College Students
    Dental Students
    Graduate Students
    Junior College Students
    Medical Students
    Postgraduate Students
    ROTC Students
  Elementary School Students
    Intermediate School Students
    Primary School Students
  Foreign Students
  High School Students
  Junior High School Students
  Kindergarten Students
  Nursing Students
  Roommates
  Seminarians
  Special Education Students
  Transfer Students
  Vocational School Students
Verbal Communication
  Fingerspelling
  Language
    Conversation
    Dialect
      Nonstandard English
    Foreign Languages
    Language Development
    Linguistics
      Alphabets

Initial Teaching Alphabet
Letters (Alphabet)
Antonyms
Ethnolinguistics
Etymology
Grammar
    Form Classes (Language)
        Adjectives
        Adverbs
        Nouns
        Pronouns
        Verbs
    Inflection
    Morphology (Language)
    Orthography
    Phonology
    Syntax
        Sentence Structure
    Transformational Generative Grammar
    Homographs
    Paragraphs
    Phonetics
        Morphemes
        Phonemes
            Consonants
            Vowels
        Syllables
        Words (Phonetic Units)
    Phrases
    Psycholinguistics
    Semantics
    Sentences
Monolingualism
Multilingualism
    Bilingualism
Public Speaking
Sign Language
Vocabulary
    Anagrams
    Antonyms
    Homographs
    Homonyms
    Neologisms
    Sight Vocabulary
    Slang
    Synonyms
Written Language
    Alphabets
        Initial Teaching Alphabet
        Letters (Alphabet)
    Handwriting
        Cursive Writing
        Handwriting Legibility
        Printing (Handwriting)
    Literacy
    Numbers (Numerals)
    Paragraphs
Speech Characteristics
    Articulation (Speech)
    Pronunciation
    Speech Pauses
    Speech Pitch
    Speech Rate
    Speech Rhythm
Speech Processing (Mechanical)

    Clipped Speech (Mechanical)
    Compressed Speech
    Filtered Speech
    Synthetic Speech
Verbal Fluency

School Administration And Educational Processes

Community Facilities
    Community Mental Health Centers
Educational Personnel
    School Administrators
        School Principals
        School Superintendents
    School Counselors
    School Nurses
    School Psychologists
    Teacher Aides
    Teachers
        College Teachers
        Elementary School Teachers
        High School Teachers
        Junior High School Teachers
        Resource Teachers
        Special Education Teachers
        Student Teachers
Paraprofessional Personnel
    Paramedical Personnel
        Attendants (Institutions)
        Medics
        Physical Therapists
        Psychiatric Aides
    Teacher Aides
Personnel Training
    Apprenticeship
    Inservice Teacher Education
    On The Job Training
Professional Consultation
    Mental Health Consultation
Teacher Education
    Inservice Teacher Education
    Student Teaching
Volunteer Personnel
    Volunteer Civilian Personnel

Curriculum Development And Teaching Methods

Behavior Modification
    Classroom Behavior Modification
    Contingency Management
        Token Economy Programs
Classical Conditioning
    Conditioned Responses
        Conditioned Emotional Responses
        Conditioned Suppression
    Conditioned Stimulus
    Unconditioned Responses
    Unconditioned Stimulus
Computer Applications
    Computer Assisted Diagnosis
    Computer Assisted Instruction
    Computer Simulation
Curriculum

**Curriculum Development And Teaching
Methods** (Continued)

Art Education
Braille Instruction
Business Education
Compensatory Education
Driver Training
Foreign Language Education
Health Education
   Drug Education
   Sex Education
Language Arts Education
   Phonics
   Reading Education
   Spelling
Mathematics Education
Music Education
Physical Education
Science Education
Vocational Education
Educational Programs
   Foreign Study
   Project Follow Through
   Project Head Start
   Title V Projects
   Upward Bound
Feedback
   Biofeedback
   Delayed Feedback
      Delayed Auditory Feedback
   Knowledge Of Results
   Sensory Feedback
      Auditory Feedback
         Delayed Auditory Feedback
      Visual Feedback
Games
   Chess
   Childrens Recreational Games
   Entrapment Games
   Non Zero Sum Games
   Prisoners Dilemma Game
   Simulation Games
Government Programs
   Job Corps
   Peace Corps
   Project Follow Through
   Project Head Start
   Title V Projects
   Upward Bound
   Volunteers In Service To America
   Welfare Services (Government)
Learning Schedules
   Distributed Practice
   Massed Practice
Operant Conditioning
Practice
   Distributed Practice
   Massed Practice
Recreation

**Curriculum Development And Teaching
Methods** (Continued)

Athletic Participation
Camping
Childrens Recreational Games
Clubs (Social Organizations)
Dance
Doll Play
Sports
   Badminton
   Baseball
   Basketball
   Football
   Judo
   Swimming
   Tennis
Summer Camps (Recreation)
Television Viewing
Recreation Areas
Playgrounds
Reinforcement
   Differential Reinforcement
   Negative Reinforcement
   Positive Reinforcement
      Praise
   Primary Reinforcement
Punishment
Reinforcement Amounts
Reinforcement Schedules
   Fixed Interval Reinforcement
   Fixed Ratio Reinforcement
   Variable Interval Reinforcement
   Variable Ratio Reinforcement
Rewards
   External Rewards
   Internal Rewards
   Monetary Rewards
   Preferred Rewards
Secondary Reinforcement
Self Reinforcement
Social Reinforcement
   Nonverbal Reinforcement
   Verbal Reinforcement
      Praise
Teaching
   Instructional Media
      Educational Audiovisual Aids
         Motion Pictures (Educational)
      Programed Textbooks
      Reading Materials
      Teaching Machines
   Teaching Methods
      Audiovisual Instruction
         Televised Instruction
         Videotape Instruction
      Computer Assisted Instruction
      Departmentalized Teaching Method
      Directed Discussion Method
      Discovery Teaching Method
      Educational Field Trips
      Group Instruction
      Individualized Instruction

Curriculum Development And Teaching Methods (Continued)
- Lecture Method
- Lesson Plans
- Montessori Method
- Nondirected Discussion Method
- Open Classroom Method
- Programed Instruction
- Team Teaching Method
- Tutoring
  - Peer Tutoring

Academic Learning And Adjustment And Achievement

Achievement
- Academic Achievement
  - Academic Overachievement
  - Academic Underachievement
  - College Academic Achievement
  - Mathematics Achievement
  - Reading Achievement
Artistic Ability
- Musical Ability
Comprehension
- Listening Comprehension
- Number Comprehension
- Reading Comprehension
- Sentence Comprehension
Concept Learning
- Nonreversal Shift Learning
- Reversal Shift Learning
Dropouts
- College Dropouts
- Potential Dropouts
- School Dropouts
Mathematics (Concepts)
- Algorithms
- Number Systems
- Numbers (Numerals)
Meaning
- Nonverbal Meaning
- Verbal Meaning
- Word Meaning
Meaningfulness
Memory
- Eidetic Imagery
- Long Term Memory
- Memory Decay
- Memory Trace
- Short Term Memory
Motivation
- Achievement Motivation
  - Academic Achievement Motivation
- Affiliation Motivation
- Employee Motivation
- Extrinsic Motivation
- Incentives
  - Educational Incentives
  - Monetary Incentives
- Intrinsic Motivation
- Temptation

Academic Learning And Adjustment And Achievement (Continued)

Nonverbal Communication
- Body Language
- Eye Contact
- Facial Expressions
  - Grimaces
  - Smiles
- Gestures
Perceptual Motor Learning
- Fine Motor Skill Learning
- Gross Motor Skill Learning
Radical Movements
- Political Anarchy
- Political Revolution
Reading
- Oral Reading
- Remedial Reading
- Silent Reading
Retention
- Recall (Learning)
- Recognition (Learning)
- Reconstruction (Learning)
Skill Learning
- Fine Motor Skill Learning
- Gross Motor Skill Learning
Transfer (Learning)
- Negative Transfer
- Positive Transfer
Verbal Learning
- Nonsense Syllable Learning
- Paired Associate Learning
- Serial Learning
  - Serial Anticipation (Learning)

Special Education
Correctional Institutions
- Reformatories
Institutionalization
- Hospitalization
  - Hospital Admission
    - Psychiatric Hospital Admission
      - Psychiatric Hospital Readmission
  - Hospital Discharge
  - Psychiatric Hospitalization
    - Committment (Psychiatric)
    - Psychiatric Hospital Admission
      - Psychiatric Hospital Readmission
- Incarceration
Learning Disorders
- Learning Disabilities
  - Dyslexia
- Reading Disabilities
  - Dyslexia
Mental Retardation
- Amaurotic Familial Idiocy
- Anencephaly
- Borderline Mental Retardation
- Cretinism
- Crying Cat Syndrome

Special Education (Continued)

Downs Syndrome
Microcephaly
Psychosocial Mental Retardation
Residential Care Institutions
  Halfway Houses
  Hospitals
    Psychiatric Hospitals
    Sanatoriums
  Orphanages

Counseling And Measurement

Achievement Measures
  Iowa Tests Of Basic Skills
  Stanford Achievement Test
  Wide Range Achievement Test
Aptitude Measures
  Army General Classification Test
  Coll Ent Exam Bd Scholastic Apt Test
  Differential Aptitude Tests
  General Aptitude Test Battery
  Graduate Record Examination
  Modern Language Aptitude Test
  School And College Ability Test
  SRA Primary Mental Abilities Test
Aspirations
  Educational Aspirations
  Occupational Aspirations
Educational Measurement
  Entrance Examinations
  Grading (Educational)
Errors
  Prediction Errors
Intelligence Measures
  Ammons Full Range Picture Vocab Test
  Benton Revised Visual Retention Test
  California Test Of Mental Maturity
  Columbia Mental Maturity Scale
  Concept Mastery Test
  Culture Fair Intelligence Test
  Frostig Development Test Vis Percept
  Goodenough Harris Draw A Person Test
  Henman Nelson Tests Mental Ability
  Hidden Figures Test
  Illinois Test Psycholinguist Abil
  Infant Intelligence Scale
  Kohs Block Design Test
  Leiter Adult Intelligence Scale
  Lorge Thorndike Intelligence Test
  Lowenfeld Mosaic Test
  Miller Analogies Test
  Peabody Picture Vocabulary Test
  Porteus Maze Test
  Raven Coloured Progressive Matrices
  Ravens Progressive Matrices
  Remote Associates Test
  Slosson Intelligence Test For Child
  SRA Primary Mental Abilities Test

Counseling And Measurement (Continued)

Stanford Binet Intelligence Scale
Temporal Spatial Concept Scale
Vane Kindergarten Test
Wechsler Adult Intelligence Scale
Wechsler Bellevue Intelligence Scale
Wechsler Intelligence Scale Children
Interests
  Occupational Interests
Occupational Interest Measures
  Kuder Occupational Interest Survey
  Strong Vocational Interest Blank
Preference Measures
  Kuder Preference Record
Reading Measures
  Gates MacGinitie Reading Test
  Metropolitan Reading Readiness Test
  UNESCO Silent Reading Test
Retention Measures
  Recall (Learning)
    Free Recall
  Recognition (Learning)
  Reconstruction (Learning)
Speech And Hearing Measures
  TROCA (Computer Screening Battery)
  Wepman Test Of Auditory Discrim

APPLIED PSYCHOLOGY

Aerospace Personnel
  Aircraft Pilots
  Astronauts
Agricultural Workers
  Migrant Farm Workers
Aircraft
  Helicopters
Apparatus
  Accelerometers
  Amplifiers (Apparatus)
  Audiometers
  Cage Apparatus
  Cameras
  Computers
  Electrodes
  Generators (Apparatus)
  Incubators (Apparatus)
  Mazes
    Maze Pathways
    T Mazes
  Memory Drums
  Metronomes
  Microscopes
  Oscilloscopes
  Polygraphs
  Shuttle Box Hurdles
  Shuttle Boxes
    Shuttle Box Grids

Skinner Boxes
Sonar
Stimulators (Apparatus)
  Shock Units
Tachistoscopes
Tape Recorders
  Videotape Recorders
Timers (Apparatus)
Transducers
Transformers (Apparatus)
Transistors (Apparatus)
Vibrators (Apparatus)
Volt Meters
X Ray Equipment
Yerkes Boxes
Automated Information Processing
  Automated Information Coding
  Automated Information Retrieval
  Automated Information Storage
Aviation
  Flight Instrumentation
  Spaceflight
Business And Industrial Personnel
  Architects
  Blue Collar Workers
    Industrial Foremen
    Skilled Industrial Workers
    Unskilled Industrial Workers
  Industrial Psychologists
  White Collar Workers
    Accountants
    Clerical Personnel
    Management Personnel
      Middle Level Managers
      Top Level Managers
    Sales Personnel
    Secretarial Personnel
Computer Applications
  Computer Assisted Instruction
  Computer Simulation
Ecological Factors
  Pollution
  Topography
Ethics
  Professional Ethics
  Values
    Personal Values
    Social Values
Government Personnel
  Agricultural Extension Workers
  Law Enforcement Personnel
    Parole Officers
    Police Personnel
    Prison Personnel
    Probation Officers
  Military Personnel
    Air Force Personnel
    Army Personnel
    Commissioned Officers
    Enlisted Military Personnel
    Marine Personnel

Military Medical Personnel
Navy Personnel
Noncommissioned Officers
Volunteer Military Personnel
  National Guardsmen
  ROTC Students
Public Health Service Nurses
Government Programs
  Job Corps
  Peace Corps
  Volunteers In Service To America
  Welfare Services (Government)
Insurance
  Health Insurance
    Employee Health Insurance
      Workmens Compensation Insurance
  Life Insurance
    Employee Life Insurance
Organizations
  Business Organizations
  Foreign Organizations
  Government Agencies
  International Organizations
  Labor Unions
  Nonprofit Organizations
  Professional Organizations
Paraprofessional Personnel
  Paramedical Personnel
    Attendants (Institutions)
    Medics
    Physical Therapists
    Psychiatric Aides
Personnel Supply
  Medical Personnel Supply
  Mental Health Personnel Supply
  Teacher Supply
Rehabilitation Centers
  Sheltered Workshops
Scientific Communication
  Professional Meetings And Symposia
  Psychological Terminology
Simulation
  Computer Simulation
  Flight Simulation
  Heuristic Modeling
  Mathematical Modeling
  Stochastic Modeling
Volunteer Personnel
  Volunteer Civilian Personnel
  Volunteer Military Personnel
    National Guardsmen

Occupation Guidance And Personnel Selection And Training

Educational Programs
  Foreign Study
Occupational Interest Measures
  Kuder Occupational Interest Survey
  Strong Vocational Interest Blank
Personnel Management

APPLIED PSYCHOLOGY

Occupation Guidance And Personnel Selection And Training (Continued)
    Job Analysis
    Labor Management Relations
  Personnel Evaluation
    Job Applicant Interviews
    Job Applicant Screening
    Occupational Success Prediction
  Personnel Placement
  Personnel Recruitment
    Military Recruitment
    Teacher Recruitment
  Personnel Selection
  Personnel Termination
Personnel Training
  Apprenticeship
  Management Training
  Military Training
  On The Job Training

Job Performance And Satisfaction
Employee Attitudes
  Job Satisfaction
Employee Benefits
  Bonuses
  Employee Health Insurance
    Workmens Compensation Insurance
  Employee Leave Benefits
  Employee Life Insurance
  Employee Pension Plans
  Salaries
  Stock Options
Employee Skills
  Clerical Secretarial Skills
Job Performance
  Employee Efficiency
  Employee Productivity
Motivation
  Achievement Motivation

Job Performance And Satisfaction
(Continued)
  Affiliation Motivation
  Employee Motivation
  Extrinsic Motivation
  Incentives
    Educational Incentives
    Monetary Incentives
  Intrinsic Motivation

Management And Leadership

Organizational Structure And Climate
Organizational Change
  Organizational Merger

Human Factors Engineering And Safety
Accidents
  Home Accidents
  Industrial Accidents
  Pedestrian Accidents
  Transportation Accidents
    Air Traffic Accidents
    Motor Traffic Accidents
      Highway Hypnosis Accidents
Displays
  Auditory Displays
  Tactual Displays
  Visual Displays
Monitoring
  Vigilance
Safety
  Aviation Safety
    Air Traffic Control
  Highway Safety
  Occupational Safety
  Water Safety
Safety Devices
  Safety Belts